The History of Building Trades and Professionalism

The Proceedings of the Eighth Annual Conference of the
Construction History Society

Queens' College, University of Cambridge, 27-28th August 2021

Edited by

James W P Campbell
Nina Baker
Michael Driver
Michael Heaton
Natcha Ruamsanitwong
Michael Tutton
Christine Wall
David Yeomans

Published by The Construction History Society
1 Scroope Terrace
Cambridge
CB2 1PX

www.construction.co.uk

© 2021, First Edition
ISBN 978-0-9928751-7-6

Cover images from the Wellcome Collection Image Library

Copyright © by the Construction History Society
All rights reserved. These proceedings may not be reproduced. In whole or in part, in any form without permission from the Construction History Society

Formatting and layout by Natcha Ruamsanitwong
First printed by Lulu print on demand for the Construction History Society

Proceedings of the Seventh Construction History Society Conference
edited by James W P Campbell, Nina Baker, Karey Draper, Michael Driver,
Michael Heaton, Yiting Pan, Natcha Ruamsanitwong, David Yeomans

The Eighth Annual Construction History Society Conference

Organised by:

The Construction History Society
in association with Queens' College, Cambridge

Held by:

Queens' College, University of Cambridge &
The Department of Architecture, University of Cambridge

Organising Committee

Chair: James W P Campbell
Secretary: Natcha Ruamsanitwong
Treasurer: Jonathan Lee

Scientific Committee

Chair: David Yeomans
Secretary: Natcha Ruamsanitwong
James Campbell
Nina Baker
Michael Driver
Mike Heaton
Will Mclean
Michael Tutton
Christine Wall

Editorial Committee

Chair: James W P Campbell
Secretary: Natcha Ruamsanitwong
Nina Baker
Michael Driver
Michael Heaton
Michael Tutton
Christine Wall
David Yeomans

In memory of Thelma Seear

Acknowledgements

The preparation of any conference takes an enormous amount of time and effort on behalf of a large number of people. I am hugely grateful to all those who have assisted in the planning of this, Eighth Annual Construction History Society Conference in the second year of this global pandemic. In particular I would like to thank Natcha Ruamsanitwong who started as secretary of the conference last year whose gathered all the abstracts, sent them out for review and worked so hard to put these proceedings together, coordinating the formatting on her own. David Yeomans as chair of the Scientific Committee again took on the unenviable task again of managing the scientific committee. I am as always grateful for his sage advice and I would like to thank him and all the other members of that committee for their efforts in reviewing all these proposals. Once the papers were in the editorial committee took over and went painstakingly through every paper. Any errors remaining are my fault not theirs.

I would like to thank all those staff of the Architecture Department and Queens' College, in the University of Cambridge who agreed to host this conference, without whose aid none of this would be possible. I would like to thank all those members of the Committee of the Construction History Society who give their time so generously to the society without any form of remuneration. They are Michael Driver, Michael Heaton, Will Mclean, Nicholas von Behr, Michael Tutton, Nina Baker, Andrew Jackson, Jonathan Lee, and the journal editors Christine Wall, Hermann Schlimme, Inge Bertels and Will Mclean, ably assisted by Angharad Hart (Editorial Secretary) and Karey Draper (Book Reviews). Without their support the Society would not function.

This year we have a session on water supply in memory of Thelma Seear. Thelma was founder of the Fountain Society and left a substantial legacy to Queens' for the study of Architecture and History of Art and for the promotion of the study of fountains. We are seeking to start that process by including various papers in this conference looking at the broader topic of water supply. The conference was entirely paid for by a generous donation from the Seear Fund. We hope Thelma would have approved. The idea for the main theme of the conference, Professionalism and the Trades came from Robert Carvais and Inge Bertels. Most of all I would like to thank the contributors to this book without whose papers none of this would be possible.

James W P Campbell
2021

Contents

Preliminaries

Campbell, James WP.	Introduction	i

Keynote Lecture

Stephenson, Judy	Day Work, Task Work and Watch Work: Labourers at St Paul's Cathedral 1672-1748	3

Ancient World (pre-1000AD)

Gelder, John	The Documentation of Stonework in the Ancient World	15
Gelder, John	Professional Roles in Greek Construction Contracts	23
Campbell, James WP.	The Development of Water Pipes: a Brief Introduction from Ancient Times until the Industrial Revolution	33
Rosado-Torres, Ana Laura & Gilabert-Sansalvador, Laura & Montuori, Riccardo	Stonecutting in Maya Architecture: The Palace of the Governor at Uxmal (Yucatan, Mexico)	47

Medieval World (1000 CE – 1400 CE)

Gutiérrez-Hernández, Alexandra M.	The Art du Trait in the Monastery of La Vid in Burgos (Spain)	63
Mazzone, Giuseppe	Through the Layers of Time – The Evolution of Interlaced Ribbed Domes from Islamic Spain to the Italian Baroque	73

Contents

Mazzanti, Claudio & Bulfone Gransinigh, Federico	Medieval watchtowers of the mountainous areas of the Abruzzi Region: typologies, construction techniques and territorial landscape	85
Maira-Vidal, Rocío	Two Masters, Two Methods. First Steps Towards English Standardisation in The Construction of The Sexpartite Vaults in Canterbury Cathedral	97
Vandenabeele, Louis	Medieval formwork imprints in the Basilica of St Anthony in Padua	111

Renaissance and Late Gothic World (1400-1600)

Celli, Sofia & Ottoni, Federica	From construction to maintenance. The history of the wooden chain encircling the dome of Santa Maria del Fiore	121
Maissen, Manuel	Late Gothic Vaulting in the Canton of Grisons, Switzerland	133
Knobling, Clemens	Vaults Without Buttresses: A Survey of Swiss Roodscreens	147
Carocci, Caterina F & Finocchiaro, Renata & Macca, Valentina	The so-called 'Palazzetto' in the Palazzo di Venezia Complex: A small construction history among the huge transformation events of the Rome centre in the early twentieth century	157
Diaz, Martina	Contextualisation of the timber trade between the sixteenth and nineteenth centuries in the Basilica of St Anthony, Padua	169
Bentz, Bruno	On The Origins of Hydro-Technics: The Gardens of Noisy (1570)	183

The Seventeenth and Eighteenth Centuries (1600-1800)

Holzer, Stefan M.	How to Build a Dome	197
Pirlet, Gabriel & Schumacher, Guido & Vanden Eynde, Jean-Louis	Ornamental Hydraulics in the Arenberg Park of Enghien in the 17th Century: a possible link to Salomon de Caus	207
O'Dwyer, Dermot	William Colles (1702-1770) Kilkenny Mayor, Entrepreneur, and Marble Necromancer	229
Lluis-Teruel, Cinta & Ugalde-Blázquez, Iñigo & Lluis i Ginovart, Josep & Hadji, Zahra	The Behaviour of Tile Vaulted Structures in Spanish Military Engineering	243
Bill, Nicholas A.	Pioneering Education for a Unique Engineering Profession – British Military Engineers	257
Carvais, Robert	The social status of Parisian building contractors in the 18th century. A hierarchical and ambitious professional "body" : between nobility and destitution	269

Long Nineteenth Century (1800-1914)

Buchenau, Geraldine & Kuban, Sabine	Time to Re-Evaluate? – New Findings on the Application of the Hennebique System in Germany	289
Ellis, Clifton	Agrarian Capitalism and The Cost of Building in Antebellum Virginia	303
Prisco, Gian Marco	The Madrid-Delicias Railway Station: between formal and technological innovation in the 19th century Iberian Peninsula	313

Contents

Burgos Núñez, Antonio & Kite, Maxwell Adrian	Plate Girder Bridges in Andalusia, 1850-1910. The Spread of an Unusual Genre of Iron Bridges	327
Yagci Ergun, Saniye Feyza and Schuller, Manfred	Timber frame system after the western influence on the houses of Istanbul	339
Spencer, Chelsea	Faulty Figures and Paper Technologies: Cost Estimating in Late Nineteenth-Century America	347
von Behr, Nick	The Influence of Standards and Regulations for Steel and Reinforced Concrete on the Development of Modern Architecture in Pre-WW1 Paris and Brussels	355
Campolongo, Alessandro & Guagliardi, Valentina	Architecture and building traditions in the territory of Cosenza: the 1910 Colonia Silana	365

The Twentieth Century (1900-2000)

Baker, Nina	Development of the UK Government's support for Construction-related Research in the 20th Century: the role of the Department of Scientific and Industrial Research	379
Yeomans, David	Not Just the Dirty Work: engineers' contributions to architecture	389
Mestre-Martí, Maria & Jiménez-Vicario, Pedro M. & Ródenas-López, Manuel A.	The History of the Construction of the Cuban National Capitol	401
Baker, Nina	Women engineers in UK construction research establishments in the mid-20th century. A preliminary survey	415

Greco, Laura	Construction Standardisation in Italian Service Stations (1930s-1950s). Projects by Luigi Piccinato and Mario Bacciocchi	425
Ladinski, Vladimir	A Century of Professionalism in Construction in North Macedonia (1920-2020)	437
Rusak, Maryia	From 'Workers' to 'Operators': Labour of Moelven Brug	451
Yeomans, David	Frank Newby's Star Beams	463
Spada, Francesco	Società Generale Immobiliare (SGI) Prefabrication Methods for Italian School Buildings in 1960s	473
Nozawa, Shuntaro & Komiyama, Yosuke	High Tech Attitude as a Corrective of Japanese Industrialised Housing: The Work and Discourses of Kohko Takahashi	483
Giannetti, Ilaria	Experimental structures and reinforced concrete in church building in Italy: design and construction of three hyperbolic paraboloids (1961-68)	497

James W.P. Campbell

Introduction

This is a eighth volume in the series of books published by the Construction History Society containing the proceedings of the international conferences held at Queens' College, Cambridge in April each year. This year, 2021, is the second year that has been disrupted by the global pandemic (called at the time COVID-19). Learning from a year of working online, this year's conference was been held in hybrid format, with a small audience in Queens' and most people forced to attend and present online. The last volume contained a series of chapters on Iron and Steel in Construction History. This conference carried the theme of the Trades and Professionalism, although this was loosely interpreted and the papers cover a wide range of topics in Construction History. One session was also devoted to water supply in memory of Thelma Seear (see acknowledgments above). The papers have been arranged chronologically as far as possible, although obviously many papers span ranges of dates and longer periods. In total there are 41 papers of the 43 delivered at the conference (the text of Professor Sir Robert Floud keynote lecture not appearing here). Together they provide a snapshot of the very wide range of interests in the discipline today.

Keynote Lectures

Judy Stephenson delivered one of the keynote lectures this year. The proceedings do not always contain the texts of keynote lecturers, which are sometimes published later in the Construction History, the Journal of the Construction History Society, although often the speaker chooses not to submit a text at all and just to deliver from the podium. We are thus pleased to be able to publish the text of this keynote here. The topic was the payment of labourers in the rebuilding of St Paul's Cathedral after the Great Fire. Dr Stephenson is an economic historian. The building accounts for St Paul's are a particularly rich source. There are over 100 volumes surviving. The accounts were particularly detailed to try to avoid fraud. They include entries for each month or quarter listing how many days labourers were employed, naming the individuals, the number of days they worked that month/quarter and providing an overall description of the work carried out by the labourers collectively that month. Dr Stephenson and her team have transcribed the accounts for the complete period from 1672-1748. The paper details their findings not just for our understanding of what building labourers did in this period but also the important wider implications of the survey to the history of prices and wages in this period, the ramifications of which are wide ranging and controversial. The second keynote lecturer, Professor Sir Robert Floud, gave a brilliant lecturer based on his book *An Economic History of the English Garden,* outlining how hugely expensive these were and the extraordinary technical innovations they included. Those interested in learning more are directed to the book.

Conference Papers

Just as in previous volumes in this series, the papers cover a very board range of subjects ranged under the umbrella of "Construction History". The papers are more evenly distributed that in previous years although there continue to be more paper for the 19th and 20th centuries than for the earlier periods. The overall distribution is roughly as follows:

Introduction

Time Period	Papers Covering this Period	
	Number	**Percentage**
Ancient World	4 papers*	(9%)
Medieval World	6 papers*	(14%)
15-16th century	7 papers*	(16%)
17th Century	4 papers*	(9%)
18th Century	6 papers*	(14%)
Nineteenth Century	8 Papers	(19%)
Twentieth century	12 papers	(28%)

Number of Papers in Volume = 41

Table. 1 Table showing distribution of papers in this volume by period (those marked with an asterisk note that some papers are counted twice as they cover two periods)

While it is a more balanced volume than previous years, geographically it is narrower, with most papers concentrating on Western Europe and a welcome few from the Cuba and the Americas but none from China or Asia or Australia, areas which have all featured in previous volumes. This may be because this year coincided with the Seventh International Congress on Construction History held which was held online thanks to the pandemic but was meant to have been in Lisbon, Portugal. This had papers from around the world, some of which might otherwise have been presented here.

The Ancient World

Construction History and archaeology most clearly overlap in the study of the development of building construction in the ancient world. Despite this, disappointingly few archaeological papers are submitted each year both to the annual conference and to the Journal. The first two papers in this section are based on documentary sources. The third, by the author of this introduction, is a survey work, while the last is archaeological in nature.

The first two papers, both by John Gelder deal with similar problems: exactly how the building site worked in the West in ancient times. The first covers Egypt, Greece and Rome and looks at documents used to specify stonework, including drawings, models and contracts and their survival. The second paper looks specifically at the Greek world. Here contracts were inscribed on stone tablets (stele), which have ensured their survival. The paper provides a careful dissection of the terms used in the contracts for the various documents to be supplied by the stone mason/architect, giving us a clear description of the design process and how much it differed from modern practice, and thus our understanding of what the term "architect" meant in ancient Greece. My own paper, that follows, provides a description of the development of the water pipe from ancient times until the 19th century, providing an introduction to the subject and areas where research seems still to be lacking.

The last paper in this section looks at Mayan Architecture, providing a very detail analysis of the stonecutting used in the Palace of the Governor at Uxmal. The stonework in this building is exceptional and is all the more remarkable because it was, as far as we know, cut without metal tools. Blocks are laid in courses of varying depths, but are cut into perfect rectangles, the ashlars being laid in walls with rubble cores. The quality of decoration is astonishing and it is interesting to see pattern like Greek key appearing without any influence from Europe, indocating how univesal these paterns are.

James W.P. Campbell

Medieval World (1000-1400)

The last volume of this series lacked papers on the Middle Ages so it is gratifying to see a return to papers on this period in the current volume. One of the problems that continues those studying Construction History is the methods used to create Gothic vaults in all their intricacy. Alexandra Gutiérrez-Hernandez's paper explores the issue of surviving tracing floors and drawings, including some interesting drawings on church walls. While the use of drawings on tracing floors is well-understood and obvious, the purpose and exact use of those found on church walls is still something of a mystery and one that deserves to be explore din more detail. This paper relates well with those by Giuseppe Mazzone and Rocío Maira-Vidal in this section that explore the issue of vaulting, an obvious area of flamboyant building construction that challenged Medieval craftsmen. Claudio Mazzanti and Federico Bulfone Gransinigh's paper looks at the construction of stone towers in the Abruzzi region of Italy and their constructional and formal similarities. Lastly, Louis Vandenabeele's paper looks at timber formwork for making medieval vaults, a subject which links with Stefan Holzer's excellent paper in the seventeenth century chapter (see below) on the centering and formwork for Late Renaissance and Medieval domes.

Renaissance and Late Gothic World (1400-1600)

The term Renaissance, while convenient in conveying the changing outlook of the 1400s in Western Europe, particularly in Italy, is misleading. For much of Northern Europe a Gothic spirit and style in architecture persisted well into the 1500 and even 1600s and as the outward stylistic form of a building inevitably determines the techniques and methods used to construct it, so Medieval practices persisted in some parts of Europe and were replaced in others in their period. The mixture of papers in this section richly demonstrates that. There can hardly be a building that more completely marks the beginning of Renaissance architecture than Bruneslleschi's dome for Florence Cathedral. Its structure has been the subject of many papers in construction history conferences over the last few decades and indeed remains the subject of heated debate. It is thus exiting to see that the parts of its construction are now coming under detailed examination. Here Sofia Celli and Federica Ottoni's excellent paper examines the wooden chain and its iron fixings in minute detail, providing a brilliant case study in building recording and observation. Similarly in this section, Martina Diaz's paper manages to trace with stunning detail the marks and origins of the timbers used in the building of St Anthony, Padua, providing a beautiful example of what can be done with painstaking forensic examination of timbers combined with dendrochonology and documentary research, producing some of the most exciting discoveries in this conference.

The continuation of Gothic forms is evident in the papers on vaulting. Manuel Maisson produces a tantalising insight into the vaulting employed in an extraordinary number of churches built in a single Swiss Canton in one period, while Clemens Knobling continued the Swiss theme but looked at how iron rods contributed to the structures of stone vaults in screens, a form that clearly related to similar unbuttressed Italian Renaissance vaults of the same period. Caterina F. Carocci, Renata Finocchiaro and Valentina Macca's paper looks at the vexed problem of what happens when a building gets in the way of future development and how parts of a Renaissance courtyard building were moved and reconstructed in central Rome in the early Twentieth while other parts of the same structure were simply discarded, providing an insight into both the original building and attitudes to conservation and reconstruction in late period. This paper thus belongs both here and in the Twentieth century section.

Lastly in this section, Bruno Bentz's paper presents the archaeological work being done of the fountains and waterworks and Noisy, presenting his proposal that *jet de l'eau* fountain here was possibly one of the first directly driven pumped fountains in the world. Sadly only the foundations of the pump house remain so the finding

Introduction

remain conjectural, but if true, this is an important discovery and changes our understanding of the history of fountains in Europe. All known fountains from this period are fed from tanks because pumps in this period flowed intermittently and thus the tanks smoothed out the flow, providing a continuous pressure.

The Seventeenth and Eighteenth Centuries (1600-1800)

This section begins with Stefan Holzer's wonderful paper on the construction of masonry domes in the 18th and 19th century. What he reveals is that many domes in this period had timber formwork supported from the floor by brickwork columns which were subsequently dismantled. These lost brick structures are revealed in drawings and accounts. The paper by Cinta Lluis-Tureuel, Iñigo Ugalde-Blázquez, Josep Lluis i Gionovart, and Zahra Hadji, by contrast looks at how thin tile vaults, which need minimal formwork, were widely adopted in the Spanish military in the 18th century.

Gabriel Pirlet, Guido Schumacher and Jean-Louis Vanden Eynde's paper was presented in the session on water. It discusses the remarkable waterworks built to power automata and fountains in this extraordinary lost garden and discusses how on the back of the research done they hope to create a school for fountain restoration which will bring together people working on these wonderful fountains in the hope of training future generations to maintain and restore them.

Dermot O'Dwyer returned to the theme of the conference — professionalism — looking at the life of William Coles (1702-1770), a remarkable 18th century entrepreneur and engineer working in Kilkenny in Ireland. Nicholas Bill returned to the subject of military engineers, in this case their training in the 18th and 19th century in Britain. While the French schools for training for military engineers are well known and their importance has long been documented, the English ones have not received as much attention. It was particularly interesting to note the amount of mathematics being taught in these courses in contrast to the amount that appeared to be used in the early 19th century engineers in practice. Robert Carvais's paper looks at the status of 18th century masons in Paris and reveals the extraordinary hierarchies that persisted within the trade at the time.

The Long Nineteenth Century (1800-1914)

The papers in this section all relate from the period between 1900 and 1914 (the beginning of the First World War). The section starts with a paper by Geraldine Buchenau and Sabine Kuban that examines a particularly early use of the Hennebique system of concrete reinforcement in Germany, thought to be the earliest yet discovered. Clifton Ellis paper could not be on a more different subject. In a chilling reminder of the callousness of mankind, he examines the extent of the use of slaves for building construction on a particular plantation in Virginia before the American Civil War, revealing that while few slaves were employed in the construction of the slave-owner's grand house they were subsequently employed in building stone slave quarters and with the experience gained did go on to be used for construction elsewhere.

The third papers that follow look at structures, the first two in iron and the third in timber. Marco Prisco examines the use of iron in the construction of the Madrid-Delicias Railway Station, while Antonio Burgos Núñez and Adrian Maxwell Kite look at Plate Girder Bridges in Adaluscia and Saniye Feyza Yagci Ergun and Manfred Schuller show detailed analyses of timber framed buildings in Istanbul, the latter showing the influence of Western techniques.

Books are key way of transmitting ideas. In England in the 17th and 18th century there were many books on estimating costs designed for the builder. However differences in currency and in the costs of building materials mean that such books could not easily to used elsewhere. Chelsea Spencer's paper looks at how books designed for estimating first appeared in the nineteenth century in America. Nick von Behr's interests are not in costs but in regulation. Specifically he outlines how he is seeking to explore regulations for steel and concrete in Paris and Brussels before World War I. The last paper in this section by Alessandro Campolongo and Valentina Guagliardi also looks at the first decades of the twentieth century, focusing on the buildings of the Colonia Silana, a sanatorium complex built after the earthquake in 1908 for children suffering from malaria. The camp is being restored and the original construction of the original and later buildings is described in detail.

Twentieth Century

As usual the twentieth century attracted more papers than any other. Nina Baker contributed two papers. The first looked at the general increase in support in the UK for research, while the second looked at how many women in these establishments made valuable and often overlooked contributions. David Yeomans discussed the role of engineers, whose rarely publicized while architects tend to steal the limelight. He went on later in the same section to demonstrate this with a paper on Frank Newby, a prominent engineer and his concrete "star-beams". Vladimir Ladinski's paper traces the appearance and profesionalisation of architecture and engineering in the newly formed Macedonia (now Northern Macedonia) both before and after its final independence.

Italy particularly valued architects and engineers in the twentieth century and it produced some remarkable concrete and steel structures in the twentieth century and the papers here continue the series of papers that have appeared in pervious volumes. Laura Greco provides drawings for early serviced stations showing how their designs were standardized and repeated to create recognizable brands. Francesco Spada described the various methods used for prefabricating school buildings in the 1960s and Ilaria Giannetti introduced the extraordinary brutalist concrete churches in Bergamo which resulted from a design collaboration between the architect Vito Sonzogni (1924-2017) and the engineer Enzo Lauletta (1927-71) and deserve to be better known.

Lastly, Maryia Rusak produced an elegant paper on the Norwegian Construction firm of Moelven Brug as it moved from skilled craftsmen to increasing mechanisation; Maria Mestre-Martí, Pedro M. Jiménez-Vicario and Manuel A. Ródenas-López described the construction of the concrete domes for the neoclassical Capitol Building in Cuba and Shuntaro Nozawa and Yosuke Komiyama introduced us to the incredible Hi Tech architecture of the Japanese architect Kohko Takahashi.

Concluding Remarks

As this description has hopefully shown, these 41 papers that make up this the eighth volume in the series cover the whole field of construction history from the study of the profession and legal and contractual problems to archaeology and the history of engineering. There are a number of trends that can be observed.

Subject	Number	Percentage
Stone construction	6 papers	14%
Iron or steel	5 papers	12%
Domes and Vaults	5 papers	12%
Concrete	5 papers	12%

Introduction

Engineers	4 papers	10%
Wages and Labour	3 papers	7%
Training and Research	3 papers	7%
Cost Estimation	3 papers	7%
Timber structures/supply	3 papers	7%
Fountains/Water supply	3 papers	7%
Contractors	3 papers	7%
Contracts and accounts	3 papers	7%
Professional/Trade Bodies	2 papers	5%
Prefabrication	2 papers	5%
Formwork and scaffolding	2 papers	5%
Bridges	1 paper	2%
Regulations	1 paper	2%
Thin concrete shells	1 papers	2%
Women in Construction	1 paper	2%
Thin tile vaults	1 paper	2%
Drawing and design	1 paper	2%
Construction and Slavery	1 paper	2%

Table. 2 Table showing distribution of papers in this volume by subject (many papers are on several of these topics)

In a year when the theme was professionalism and the trades, 14 of the papers were on these subjects. However the range of topics is diverse and many papers touched on many different areas of construction history. Many archives have been closed for most or indeed all of the last 18 months so more of the papers than usual were reliant on observation and recording. However the range of topics remains diverse and bodes well for the future of the discipline. The Ninth Annual Conference is already being planned.

James W.P. Campbell
Conference Chairman
Construction History Society
August 2021

Keynote Lecture

Day Work, Task Work and Watch Work: Labourers at St Paul's Cathedral 1672-1748

Judy Z. Stephenson[1], Meredith Paker[2], Patrick Wallis[3]

1: The Bartlett School of Sustainable Construction, University College London
2: Oxford University
3: London School of Economics and Political Science

Introduction

Construction and architectural historians have thoroughly researched many aspects of the design and draughtsmanship, management, organisation, and construction of Wren's St Paul's, particularly in relation to some of the better-known craftsmen and draughtsmen. There is still emerging research, and plenty remains to be done on those and on the matters of contracting, finance, and supply chains. However, as Campbell notes, very little is known about those who worked on the ground on site, particularly the 'unskilled' labourers the Commissioners relied on throughout the 35-year main construction period [1].

Construction history does not often focus on labour and labourers. Economic and social historians have long been interested in building craftsmen and labourers, however, viewing them as epitomising the premodern skilled and unskilled workforce, especially in urban environments. Since the mid nineteenth century they have utilised labourers' day wages as indicators of the average unskilled wage and interpolated various series extracted from building records to construct long run average real wage series and welfare ratios [2]. It is rare for information other than wage rates to permeate the narratives of living standards, industrialisation and development which these wages usually accompany [3].

Mostly, economic and social historians accept, explicitly or otherwise, three facts about labourers that are slightly contradictory: firstly, that labourers assisted skilled craftsmen; secondly that labouring was *casual* work and that hiring happened in some sort of spot market; and thirdly that the unskilled workforce was just that – a workforce, homogenous for purposes of analysis, and, indeed any further enquiry into the experience of work or the attributes of workers is usually prohibited by the limitation of sources which rarely list men's names or even full details of work done.

The exception amongst studies is Donald Woodward's 'Men at Work', a study of craftsmen and labourers in the Northern Towns of England 1450-1750 [4]. Woodward highlighted that labourers were in a market for general labouring and haulage, and portering (in other words transport and distribution, and public services) not just building trades. At most of the sites he studied, which tended to be long run institutions, or vital investment in infrastructure or local mega-projects (such as Church and bridge building) he also showed there was a distinction between small number of retained regular employees who had regular work in any place, up to c. 200 days a year or more, alongside casual labourers who were hired on a project basis and had less than 149 days a year work on average. By contrast, there is very little dedicated research on labourers in London through the early modern period. Beier and Findlay asserted that labourers made up over 5% of the London workforce (although they did not clarify whether in building or haulage) [5], and Boulton found wage rates 1700 - 1721 of 24d. per day [6]. Schwarz reiterated transport workers as predominant in groups of labourers for the later eighteenth century [7].

Day Work, Task Work and Watch Work: Labourers at St Paul's Cathedral 1672-1748

A recent research project into work and wages in London in the seventeenth and eighteenth centuries between Dr Judy Stephenson (UCL) and Prof. Patrick Wallis (LSE), and Dr Meredith Paker (Oxford) has (with the help of Dr Kate Osborne) digitised the employment records of all labourers on site at St Paul's 1672 – 1748 for the first time. The result – a database of just over 22,000 observations of over 1,000 men, offers economic, social and construction historians the opportunity for a rare insight into the identity, work, income and organisation of one of the most cited but least researched groups in economic, social, or construction history. By coincidence there have recently begun similar studies of labouring groups at St Peters in Rome, [8] and the Grand Palace Madrid [9] in similar periods to compare to. This keynote lecture attempts to bring construction historians up to date with what we have found so far.

The big questions about the characteristics of the workforce at Pauls are the big questions about early modern labour generally. How skilled were they? How much were they paid? Were they coerced or free? What did they contribute? How did they live? In many ways what we have discovered through acquiring such a big dataset (as historians of early modern London will expect) is frustratingly little. But overall, there are three insights. Firstly, that labourers were far from a homogenous group – their employment, income and the fragments we can see of their experience at the Cathedral – all suggest a heterogenous group of age, ability and various brawn, petty entrepreneurship, semi-skilled trades, and human and social capital. By implication it's far from obvious that we should be treating them as unskilled. Secondly, their working lives and income were precarious and variable. The most obvious observation is how fleeting most employment relations at the cathedral were. Thirdly, there is enough in the analysis of working practice so far to suggest that the late seventeenth and early eighteenth century may have been a period of profound change in the contracting and organisation of labouring work.

The paper is organised as follows. In section two we describe the project to digitise and database the records and the original hypothesis. In section three we describe the labourers human capital or skill and their work. In section four we discuss how this translated into income, and in section five we use matches with other records from the period to contextualise the lives and identities of the men. In section six we summarise and consider the implications for what we know about construction labour organisation in the long run before concluding and highlighting what remains to be done.

The source and resulting data set

As Woodward described, the term 'labourers' is used to represent several groups in the building trades: semi-skilled men assisting craftsmen; more general hard labourers, and handymen; regularly employed unskilled hauliers and labourers and maintenance officials: casually hired men; hauliers and porters [10]. In long run organisations in England with large buildings or fixed assets (usually those of the church, boroughs, corporations and colleges) there are often descriptions of their all of their activities in annual abstracts and accounts.

The rebuilding of St Paul's Cathedral after the Great Fire of London, funded by a coal tax levied by Parliament, and administered by a Commission of both Crown and Corporation representatives necessitated and produced a set of accounts and abstracts of exceptional detail and persistence. In each accounting period day work for craftsmen and contractors directly supervised by the clerk-of- the works was detailed, with the names, and the number of days worked by every labourer. Task and measured work with contractors were separately detailed, salaries, allowances and provisions, were recorded, and, during the late 1680s and 1690s creditors and the cost of their loans and finance were also added to the accounts.

The records of the construction of the Cathedral are exceptionally well kept. Housed for many years in the Guildhall they were moved to the London Metropolitan Archives by 2015 [11]. The series runs from book 10 starting in October 1672 and contains 33 volumes of material. There is a a gap from June 1710 to June 1714 (between volumes 41 and 42 of the series); there is another shorter gap from April 1674 to October 1675 (from the end of vol. 10 to the start of vol. 11). The accounts do not fall neatly into yearly runs. From 1672-5, there is no consistent pattern. From 1676-1710, all years have an account in January. From 1714, all years start in June.

Data input of the labourers' names and days worked form each of these periods gave us 22,039 entries in 402 accounting periods from 1 Oct 1672 to the 24 Jun 1748, about work by 1,011 uniquely identified men, for whom we have names. Since the account books are so well entered, and so well maintained, only 1% of entries gave us a problem where the identification of the labourer was uncertain (2 people with the same name, no 'senior' or 'junior' appellation); 69 of the men in the accounts were described as 'disabled'.

Immediately on creation of the data set, expertly input by Dr Kate Osborne, we could see that the group of labourers were heterogenous in important ways. Labourers appear between one and 547 times in accounts. Only 45 men (under 5%) appear more than 100 times. The modal labourer appears *once* (as do another 174 of his colleagues). 518 labourers appear one to five times.

Our initial hypothesis, on eyeballing the records rested of three related observations. Firstly, some men (there are no women) seemed to persist in the records, working at the Cathedral for a very long time. Secondly, even if men had long 'careers' at the Cathedral their pay was nominally almost absolutely rigid (with seasonal variation) over the more than seven decades of records: 16d. per day during 5 months of the year - on average – at the winter rate, and 18d. per day for the other 7 months of the year – on average – at the summer rate. Boys, disabled men, and messengers got from 6d. to 12.d, and again these rates did not change. Thirdly, we noted that many of those that were present over years seemed to appear in the list of watchmen too. It seemed then that these labourers were not just casual labour, but perhaps a stable (and therefore significant?) team. It looked like there might be an internal labour market for extra work.

The size of the data set has allowed us to test this econometrically and we have a produced a Working Paper on tenure where some of this data can be found, which is discussed below [12].

In beginning to analyse the dataset we have found out more about the important questions of skill, working experience, pay, freedom to contract and their contribution to the rebuilding. We also have fragments to report of the men themselves.

What did labourers do? Skills.

At St Paul's labourers were – as they had been since at least the time of Inigo Jones and before - directly employed by the clerk-of-the-works but there were also many labourers directly employed by mason contractors on site, and bills from carter John Slyford make clear he directly employed them too. Those directly employed by the clerk-of-the-works seem to have fulfilled all of these roles described by Woodward above, for instance, men "employed in making mortar wheeling rubble to the several hoysting places unloading stone marbles timber & boards burning and beating of plaister cleaning the leads scaffolds making lead and running cramps", but also "watching the dores and counting the loads" [13].

Assisting the masons seems to have been a large, if not the significant part of the year-round work of labourers. Labourers mixed a lot of mortar. They moved things for masons. There are various implications of this. We know there were various experiments with mortars at St Paul's, and their involvement implies that at least some labourers were well monitored - or trusted. Secondly, the provision of labourers as a pretty much permanent onsite resource means that the mason contractors were 'supported', or had resources ready for them when tendering or estimating for labour costs on site. One question must be then whether there was crossover between cathedral and mason contractor teams, and whether the cathedral offered unskilled men the opportunity to work with and gain skills from craftsmen and skilled contractors. The only route to check this is to see if there are any names which also appear in the known records of masons on site – which are severely limited. The wage books of William Kempster, who worked on and completed the Southwest Tower, including the library and staircase, and became master mason of the cathedral in 1714 (Stephenson 2018, 2020), run from

Day Work, Task Work and Watch Work: Labourers at St Paul's Cathedral 1672-1748

1700 – 1703 and 1706-1709. There are 11 men in the cathedral's labourers lists who also worked for Kempster. What is surprising is that these men seemed to have also worked for the cathedral after commencing their work with Kempster. Of course, without earlier records we cannot be sure of this. But the direction of movement could easily be either way. If it were from Kempster to the cathedral, this would be surprising as the cathedral paid a marginally lower rate per day.

Labourers also, as Campbell highlighted, did a lot of heavy ground work, and demolition. The records for day work are meticulous, but between 1672 and 1696 the Commissioners signed ninety-three contracts of between £1 and £140 for labouring task work on the site with men who were also employed and paid as day labourers. By signing these contracts, which priced demolition and groundwork by the foot or ton, the labourers accepted risk for managing and completing heavy construction work (subcontracting labour), at profit more than their own day rate.

Examples of task work undertaken by labourers range from measured demolition by the foot to flat rate contracts for specific undertakings. "For taking up onehundren and ninety foot of foundation walls and butterises belonging to the same on the southside of vaults at 6s 8d running measure?" precedes "for taking up the bottom of the staircase and two butterises on southside £2.0.0.". Later "taking down the walls of the same gable and load the cornish stones with the scrolls etc. £16.0.0" (in 1686).

In 1690 "5 tasks, 1071 yds of east gabledown at 6d yd, £26 15s 6d; 40 yds of foundationwall 16d yd, £2 13s4d, 31yds ditto £2 1s 4d, ditto 72 yds £416s0d, digging and throwing 697 yds of earth from Mr Fulkes and Mr Thompson foundation £23 4s 8d. paid in December 1690".

In all about 49 men undertook task work. They were all labouring by the day also, although only some of them worked a high number of days. This sort of task work involved some considerable sums and about 30% of the contacts had at least one signatory who was a labourer who actually signed his name – not just marked. It would not be expected that common labourers would be literate enough to sign at the time so this, alongside the undertaking of financial risk suggests significant human capital. Supporting this conclusion is the fact that, of the names of eleven contracting labourers who took on contracts on the City Churches, (Wren Society Vol. XIII) -William Cooke, James Hurst , John Jay (slater), Thomas Paise, Bartholomew Scott, James Trahern, Edward Hide, John Hoy, John Pledge , Henry Russell, John Simpson- the last five are found in the St Paul's accounts also.

Finally, labourers acted as watchmen in addition to their regular labouring shifts. The St Paul's watch was drawn exclusively from the pool of labourers. This additional duty was potentially a lucrative perk for labourers—a night's watch paid 8d. until 1700 and 12d. thereafter, equivalent to half to two-thirds of a daily wage. Longer term workers were more likely to be given watch work. The number of shifts a labourer could take was capped at two per week or ten per month, increasing their monthly income by c. 15%. That they had watch work, and indeed that they were the sole labour source for the role suggest that longstanding St Paul's labourers were a trusted group in the eyes of the Cathedral, again reiterating the point that they would have had social and human capital.

After 1711 the cathedral moved into a maintenance phase of construction. This phase has yet to be fully analysed, but the work relied less on brawn and more on organisational tasks. The workforce was steadier in the long run with a higher average number of days worked per year.

What were they paid?

The brief answer to this is not as much as has been previously assumed. Stephenson covers this from an economic historian's perspective in some detail [15]. As noted above the rates of 16d. and 18d. per day held until the late 1740s. How these day rates translated into men's income is not a simple matter, however. With such set rates a labourer's income was a function of the number of days he worked. This was influenced by two things: Firstly, seasonality, of which there will be a forthcoming paper which looks at the question across Europe. The average January had only 51% of the number of days worked than one would expect from its length. July to September all had 17-20% more work than one would expect if seasonality did not matter. In short, most men did not have a lot of work in January and February.

The second determinant of income was how many days in each accounting period a man was hired for. This seems to have been the decision of the clerk, who we have shown, favoured longer term workers. The longer a labourer had been working on the site the more days work he got [16].

That tenure or length of employment mattered is illustrated by describing the extreme polarisation of the employment records (Figure 1). Today, construction is a high turnover industry, with worker flows three times higher than manufacturing firms [17]. The monthly worker and job flows for seventeenth and early eighteenth century St Paul's are roughly twice the level seen in modern US data [18], where hires and separations run at around 5.5 per cent of the workforce. The quarterly hiring and separation rates at St Paul's are around 17 per cent of the workforce, compared to around 14 per cent in modern US data. In other words, while construction is always relatively precarious, early modern construction, on the most stable site in the city, was even more so.

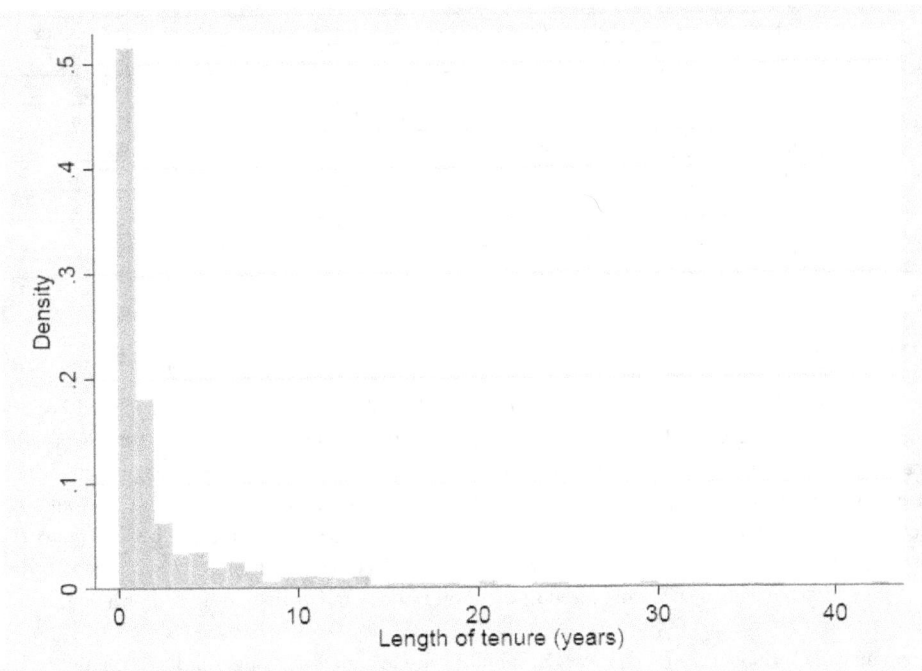

Figure 1: Histogram of employment tenure of cathedral labourers at St Paul's 1672-1748

Of all the labourers in our data set, a fifth were employed at the cathedral for up to a month only, a third were employed for up to two months, and just shy of half were employed for up to three months or less. Yet, at the top of the distribution a small share of labourers worked for long periods: Labourers in the 75th percentile of duration of employment worked for 432 days (over two or more years), and the top decile worked for ten years or more. Twelve men appear in the accounts for a period of thirty or more years, with one, Simon Satchell, who took on task work, and worked the watch, active for 43 years in total.

Day Work, Task Work and Watch Work: Labourers at St Paul's Cathedral 1672-1748

The system can be described as an internal labour market for work, in an efficiency-wage turnover-management model. Once a man had worked at the cathedral for over a year his employment was likely to stabilise and on average, he worked c.200 days a year. He also experienced less seasonal volatility in employment, giving him a steadier working pattern and income. This, established, steady work is significantly fewer days per year than economic historians have traditionally assumed, but of course, and as the task work contracts indicate, many men were working at other places too or had 'outside options. Stephenson calculates that with 200 days a year at these rates a man would not have been able to support a wife and children but would have had a good standard of living [19]. (Table 1.) It should be noted that hierarchy or differentiation in day wage was virtually non-existent at St Paul's. Opportunities to get paid more per day through joining a more productive or more senior group were virtually nil. There was little opportunity for progression at St Paul's. Therefore, to increase income men had to increase their number of days worked or take financial risk. Becoming regular at the Cathedral was one way to do this.

Table 1. Pay for day labouring in £ per year based on the mean, median and top and bottom quartile of number of days worked

decade	£mean	£ lowest 25%	£median	£ highest 25%
1670	11.1	4.3	12.6	16.8
1680	13	9.5	14	16.5
1690	16.8	14.7	17.6	19.6
1700	19.7	17.6	20	21.9
1710	18.9	15.2	20.9	22.1
1720	19	19.6	21.7	22.4
1730	19	22.1	22.4	22.4
1740	18.2	22.3	22.4	22.4

Freedom to contract:

It is apparent that St Paul's labourers were free to contract. And the fact many of them signed contracts, suggests heterogeneity, human and social capital. Tests looking at the pattern of hiring and departure from the site in our work on tenure demonstrate that there were not fixed gangs who were hired in. A very small number of men, however, do seem to have progressed to positions of responsibility or 'foreman', but surprisingly few. There are only 11 men in the labourer's accounts who received day rates above 18d. at any time during the construction period (up to 1710). None of them, apart from clerk-of-the-works are identified or named in the accounts as monitor or foreman, and the pattern of records suggest they may have been specialist hired in for short periods rather than more senior labourers. They include:

Lawrence Spencer called 'Labourer of Trust' by Campbell [20]. He appears throughout the accounts and acceded to be clerk-of-the-works, on John Tillison's death, at the end of 1685. Spencer received 24d.(2s) per day. He signed for labourers pay with John Crismas until December 1685.

Lawrence Spencer Jnr latter period. His name speaks for itself.

John Crismas described by Campbell as the foreman in 1666 [21]. Crismas signed for all labourer's accounts until 1685 with John Tillison.

Henry Wiggins 2 observations at 22d in 1672. Not seen again.

Edward Stretton 5 observations only at 2s 6d in 1675/ 6. This is brief enough to not be 'progression'.

William Ireland paid 2d above everyone else once Spencer appears. Listed with Spencer at the end of accounts in 1685. This looks like Ireland may have progressed to be a 'foreman'. He worked the watch.

John Norrice who is listed alongside Stretton until for 21 days in January 1676 and 25 days in Feb 1676. Not seen again.

John Normand worked 14 days only in January 1683 at 20d. After March 1683 not seen again.

Thomas Cooke paired with Dickinson at the end of accounts once Dickinson appears throughout 1700s. It seems that Cooke 'progressed', however he worked only one shift on the watch.

John Widdows from summer 1703 paid 2s per day, and listed at end of the accounts, but he did not work watch.

William Dickenson first observation was at 2s., so began on at higher rate. Worked one watch.

Men who did not get paid any higher rates but who are notable for other reasons were:

William White who signed or witnessed watchman's wages until September '85; **Adam Northam** who took over such witnessing or signing until September 1686 (when these stop being signed). And, as mentioned above **Simon Satchell** who worked at the cathedral for 43 years, also signed for the watchmen until 1687.

The fact that only two men seem to have progressed to foreman, and that Dickinson came from outside reinforce the lack of progression or formal career development opportunities at St Paul's. This is notably different to what we know of the other large European projects studied recently. At St Peter's, Rome in the sixteenth century there is clear evidence of variable pay rates and hierarchy for labourers [22]. At the Grand Palace, Madrid in the mid eighteenth century there is similar evidence of hierarchy, seniority pay, and variable pay [23]. Gary shows clearly that workers on large city projects in Malmo returned regularly to the site alongside other seasonal employments [24].

The situation is however, similar in many ways to that found at other London sites - Greenwich, Westminster Abbey, Bridge House and those managed by the Office of the Kings's Works. However, at those sites, there are far fewer numbers of workers, there are not records of labourers paid directly and there are rarely named records, and there is no year-round employment. At Westminster Abbey from 1712 the acting Clerk Ralph Sims billed labourers at 20d. per day [25], but there was an average of only 5 men on site per week in 1712 and 1713, so the chance of being able to stay on site for a long time with regular work like at St Paul's was limited. St Paul's was the largest and most consistently active site in London.

Who were they?

With 22,000 observations and over 1,000 labourers we had hoped that we would be able to match our men's names with the records of data sets like the marriage duty assessment, the poll-tax, or the hearth tax or baptismal and other parish records. Frustratingly, matches with all these were almost insignificant – and the matches that were made were usually indeterminate matches because they were for names that were far too common. (For our 1,000 labourers, a cross match on a database of London Middlesex, Surrey, Kent, Essex parish records 1630 – 1730 provided by Dr Neil Cummins (LSE) produced over 12,000 matches) [26]. Work on this continues, but further analysis gives 121 good matches with 71 'perfect' matches; 16 matches based on names and 'average' ages, and 33 matches based on marriage with this database.

Of this group of 121 the average age of commencing employment at the Cathedral was 33, the youngest was 14, the oldest was 60. About 25% were in their teens and about another quarter in their forties. Ten percent of them were in their fifties or older. These varied ages suggests a workforce not chosen for physical characteristics, but rather one made up of heterogeneous skill, brawn and social capital. On such a large project over such a long period we should not make too much of this, but alongside the precarity and polarization of the employment records, one is struck by the heterogeneity of the men themselves, as well as that of their working experience. Of this matched set the average tenure is two and a half years however – longer than that of our total data set.

The implications of our work so far are that labourers at St Paul's were a heterogeneous bunch of men from London (and outlying areas). Their working lives involved a lot of time searching for work. Their average age may have been between 30 and 40 on their arrival at the cathedral, and, many brought considerable experience, with a mix of teenagers and hardy men in their forties mingling in teams. They were not organized as gang labour. On entrance into the cathedral's workforce, most worked at the cathedral for just a few months, but if they were not immediately dismissed and began to work out there, the longer they stayed the more stable career they had the opportunity to build. A stable career at the cathedral offered work most of the year and in times of downturn or seasonal slump these long-term workers were more likely to be rehired than new men. They had various general construction and haulage skills and were trustworthy. Some of them were petty entrepreneurs. However, even the most entrepreneurial would have only supported a family if their wives worked.

References

[1] J. Campbell, *Building St Paul's*, London: Thames & Hudson. 2007.

[2] J. Rogers, *Six centuries of Work and Wages: The history of English labour,* London: W.S. Sonnenschein, 1886; R. Allen, 'The Great Divergence in European Wages and Prices from the Middle Ages to the First World War', *Explorations in Economic History*, Vol. 38, no.4, 2001, pp.411-447; G. Clark, 'The Condition of the Working Class in England, 1209–2004', *Journal of Political Economy 1307-1340,* Vol.113, No.6, 2005, pp.1307-1340.

[3] P.H. Wallis, 'Labour markets and Training', *Cambridge Economic History of Modern Britain*, Cambridge: Cambridge University Press, 2014; J. Boulton, 'The 'Meaner Sort': Labouring People and the Poor', *A Social History of England, 1500–1750*, Cambridge: Cambridge University Press, 2017, pp. 310-329.

[4] D. Woodward, *Men at Work: Labourers and Building Craftsmen in the Towns of Northern England, 1450–1750* Cambridge: Cambridge University Press, 1995.

[5] A. L. Beier, 'Engine of Manufacture: The Trades of London, 141-167', A. L. Beier A. L and R. Finlay, *The Making of the Metropolis*, London: Longman, 1986.

[6] J. Boulton, 'Food Prices and the Standard of Living in London in the 'Century of Revolution', 1580-1700', *The Economic History Review*, Vol.53, No.3, 2000, pp. 455-492.

[7] L.D. Schwarz, *London in the Age of Industrialisation,* Cambridge: Cambridge University Press, 1992.

[8] M. Rota and J. Weisdorf, 'Why was the First Industrial Revolution English?' https://warwick.ac.uk/fac/soc/economics/research/centres/cage/publications/workingpapers/2019/why_was_the_first_industrial_reolution_english_roman_real_wages_and_the_little_divergence_within_europe_reconsidered/, 2019.

[9] M. García-Zúñiga, 'Builders' Working Time in Eighteenth Century Madrid', *EHES Working Paper*, No. 195, 2020.

[10] Woodward, *Men at Work,* (Note 4).

[11] The London Metropolitan Archives, LMA CLC/313/I/B/003/25473 10-43.

[12] M. Paker, J. Z. Stephenson, and P. Wallis, 'Unskilled labour before the Industrial Revolution', *LSE Economic History Working paper*, No. 322, January 2021, https://www.lse.ac.uk/Economic-History/Assets/Documents/WorkingPapers/Economic-History/2020/WP-322.pdf

[13] The London Metropolitan Archives, LMA CLC/313/I/B/003/25473 -14, f12.

[14] J. Z. Stephenson, "'Real' wages? Contractors, workers, and pay in London building trades, 1650–1800', *Economic History Review*, Vol. 71, No. 1, 2018, pp. 106-132; J. Z. Stephenson, *Contracts and Pay: Work in London Construction 1650-1785*, London: Palgrave, 2020; J. Z. Stephenson, 'Working Days in a London Construction Team in the Eighteenth Century: Evidence from St Paul's Cathedral', *The Economic History Review*, Vol. 73, No. 2, 2020, pp. 409-30.

[15] ibid. also see Campbell, J. W. P., (2005) 'The Finances of the Carpenter in England 1660-1710: A Case Study on the Implications of the Change from Craft to Designer-Based Construction,' in L'edilizia Prima Della Rivoluzione Industriale. Secc.Xiii-Xviii, ed. S. Cavaciocchi (Prato: Instituto Internazionale di Storia Economica), pp. 313-346.

[16] Paker, Stephenson and Wallis, 'Unskilled labour before the Industrial Revolution', (Note 12).

[17] S. J. Davis, R. J. Faberman, and J. C. Haltiwanger, 'The flow approach to labor markets: new data sources and micro-macro links', *Journal of Economic Perspectives*, Vol. 20m No.3, 2006, pp.3–26.

[18] US Bureau of Labor Statistics, 'Job Openings and Labor Turnover, Monthly economic news release', 2020, https://www.bls.gov/news.release/pdf/jolts.pdf

[19] Stephenson, 'Working Days in a London Construction Team', (Note 14).

[20] Campbell, *Building St Paul's*, (Note 1) p. 42.

[21] ibid.

[22] Rota and Weisdorf, 'Why was the First Industrial Revolution English?', (Note 8).

[23] García-Zúñiga, "Builders' Working Time in Eighteenth Century Madrid', (Note 9).

[24] K. Gary, 'The distinct seasonality of early modern casual labor and the short durations of individual working years: Sweden 1500-1800', *Lund Papers in Economic History*. Education and the Labour Market, No. 2019, Vol. 189, 2019.

[25] Stephenson, *Contracts and Pay*, (Note 14).

[26] N. Cummins, 'Living standards and plague data set', neilcummins.com, 2021.

Ancient World (pre-1000AD)

The Documentation of Stonework in the Ancient World

John Gelder
University of South Australia

Introduction

Stone has been used as a construction material since humanity first started to build. Its properties have not changed – granite quarried today is the same material as granite quarried in the ancient world. Indeed some ancient quarries are still in use, such as the marble quarries of the Apuan Alps in Italy, and the Greek rosso antico quarries [1]. On the other hand, the way stonework is designed and documented has changed somewhat over the centuries, an example being the development of stereotomy from the 13th century [2]. But there are some continuities, such as the preparation of full-scale drawings of stonework. This has been the norm since antiquity, from drawings inscribed on unfinished in situ stonework for the Greek temple of Apollo at Didyma (below), to those inscribed on medieval tracing floors (as at York Minster and Wells Cathedral), [3] to rolls of full-scale details provided for a stonework elevation in London in the 1980s, [4] to contemporary 1:1 BIM documentation.

Most of the extant construction documents from ancient Egypt, Greece and Rome concern stonework for monumental buildings. The documents include written descriptions (notably the Greek syggraphai), full-scale in situ drawings, and small-scale stone models. On a given project, all three will have been read together, but unfortunately, we do not have a 'set' of this kind. This paper outlines the nature of this documentation using some examples – it is not comprehensive.

Pharaonic to Greco-Roman Egypt

Construction stone was readily available in ancient Egypt. Harrell & Storemyr list 39 miscellaneous hardstone quarries (basalt, granite, diorite, porphyry etc), nine travertine quarries, 99 limestone quarries, and 38 sandstone quarries in Egypt, used from the prehistoric to Islamic periods. Hardstone was sourced from quarries mostly in the Red Sea Hills, requiring land transport, but travertines and limestones were extracted along the Lower Nile and sandstone along the Upper Nile, enabling river transport. Preference varied with time. For example, most of the hardstone quarries were used primarily in the Greco-Roman period (with the stone often exported?), whereas travertine usage was mostly Pharaonic [5].

Two written descriptions of stonework from ancient Egypt are in the form of annotations on a drawing and a model. One is below-ground, one is above-ground. From the floor plan on an ostrakon of the Tomb for Ramesses IV, KV 2, Valley of the Kings (1155-1149 BCE) is a description of the stonework that is repeated four times, describing the execution of the relief murals (unfinished in many tombs): '[The room] … being drawn with outlines, graven with the chisel, filled with colours, and completed [6].' From the stone base of a model for the temple gateway at Heliopolis, Seti I (1323-1279 BCE), made after the temple was completed:

> The good god is making foundations for his father, Ra Horakhty. He made in the temple, which is of good quartzite, two pylon towers of white crystalline limestone, doors of bronze, a pair of flagstaffs of msdt stone, a pair of obelisks of bkhn stone established in Iunu, the horizon of heaven. The souls of Iunu exult at seeing them [7].

Many construction drawings of stonework survive from ancient Egypt [8]. Small-scale drawings for below-ground projects include sketches for the tomb of Ramesses IV, KV2 in the Valley of the Kings (Turin Papyrus 1885 recto), and the tomb of Ramesses IX, KV6 (Cairo CG 25184) on an ostrakon, [9] a pillared chapel (London BM 41228), and ceiling patterns (Cairo CG 66260, 66261, 66263, 66265), all on ostraka [10]. For above-ground projects, the oldest drawing is a vault section on an ostrakon (Imhotep Museum, Saqqara, JE 50036) [11]. Otherwise above-ground project drawings all concern columns and include small-scale column sketches (Paris Louvre 3043 & E25334, New York Metropolitan Museum of Art MMA 23.3.34 & 35), on ostraka, and later (perhaps following Greek practice – below) full-scale in situ inscribed drawings of columns, capitals and cornices at the temple of Horus, Edfu, the temple of Isis, Philae, the temple of Mandulis, Kalabsha, and the quarry at Gebel Abu Fodah.

Small-scale models of stone columns and capitals from Egypt were common, with examples held in the Ägyptisches Museum und Papyrussammlung, Staatlichen Museen, Berlin (Saqqara, ÄM 1627 & 1629; Tuna el-Gebel, ÄM 20351 & 20351), the Metropolitan Museum of Art, New York (MMA 12.182.6), the Petrie Museum, London (UC69263, UC33425, UC28720, UC28721), Strasbourg (Philae, 1388), and Cairo (33.395, 33.396, 33.397) for example. Some are ceramic and crude and some are stone and precise. These models range in date from Pharaonic to Roman Egypt and indicate a consistent tradition in Egypt down the timeline. The Greek tradition of full-scale paradeigma (below) does not seem to have been adopted in the Hellenic and Roman periods.

Small-scale stone construction models from Egypt of buildings or parts of buildings were less common (unlike votive models) and include an underground tomb at the pyramid of Hawara, Dahshur [12] and another small tomb (Petrie UC57155). Above ground we have two pyramids from Memphis and Dahshur (Petrie UC16519 & UC14793), the floor of a columned hall at Tod near Luxor (Louvre E 14762), a multi-part model of the contra-temple of Soknopaiou Nesos, Dime es-Seba, Fayyum [13], a water tank (Petrie UC14530), a hydreuma (Petrie UC75646), and altar steps (Cairo 33.401).

Greece

Construction stone was widely available and widely used across Greece, from the red marble used at Minos (Crete) onwards. In the Greek period, construction projects used local stone as much as possible, given difficulties of transport. While the white marbles of Penteleikon (at least 30 quarries active in antiquity) and Hymettos are perhaps best known, and convenient to Athens (an ancient road linking them was found in 2009), white marble was also available on Naxos, Paros and Thasos. Polychromic (grey, green, pink and so on) stones were available, but their use peaked for export in the Roman Imperial period as more exotic materials were sought by architects. However, the most widely used construction stones were the less glamorous limestone – 'the bread and butter of construction activities through Antiquity' – and sandstone [14].

At least 40 written Greek construction contracts survive, in whole or in part, in the form of inscribed texts (syggraphai) on stone steles, describing the required work in some detail [15]. They included contractual material (the parties, payments, penalties and so on), quantities, layout, and specifications. Five specified the stone quarries to be used most in Attica (Table 1). These were IG II2 1666 A&B for the Prostoon at Eleusis, IG II2 1685 for the sanctuary of Asclepius at Athens, IG II2 1668 for the naval tackle store at Zeia, IG II2 1665 for tripod plinths at Kynosarges, a suburb of Athens, and IG II2 1680 for the Prostoon at Eleusis. The marble from the Penteleikon quarries was favoured for column capitals, which entailed intricate carving.

One of these, IG II2 1666 A&B, is complete but was never let, being replaced by a series of subsequent contracts. Nevertheless, the inscription is very informative about the prescriptive nature of Greek stone specifications (Table 2). This inscription covered separately the quarrying, rough cutting, storage, transport to site, carving, hoisting and laying of 19 different stone units: kanonides, triglyphs, metopes, cornices, plinths, capitals, thresholds, gable blocks, roof tiles, foundation stones, paving, and stylobates. As Table 2 indicates, common requirements were that stones be sound, white, stainless and unbroken. Workmanship is repeatedly specified in terms of tight, unbroken and flush joints and straight level tops, with the stones generally clamped, dowelled, and lead poured around. The apergon referred to was a temporary protective skin of stone. For some units cutting and carving relied on an anagraphe provided by the architect. Excavation for the foundations was also included. For this project, the city was to provide the lead, iron clamps and hoists. Some quantities and sizes were left unresolved (for larger foundation stones), but generally quantities and sizes were given throughout. The repetitive nature of the inscriptions resulted in some internal conflict, in terms of the quantities given and the work to be done. For example, two capitals are to be quarried but three were to be carved and installed, 42 stylobates are quarried and 44 are carved and installed, two corner stones are transported, carved and installed but not quarried, and four capitals are quarried and transported but not carved or installed. No doubt these errors would have been resolved during execution.

Table 1: Stone types specified in 5 syggraphai

	Location, date BCE	Penteleikon	Hymettos	Eleusis	Megaris	Aktitēs	Agryleikon	Aegina, Saronic Gulf
IG II2 1665	Athens, 400-350	Capitals	-	Orthostats, 'grasping stones'			Foundations	-
IG II2 1666 A&B	Eleusis, 356	Capitals, metopes, cornices, pilasters, gables, roof tiles	-	Stylobates, corners	-	Foundations, euthynteria	-	Kanonides, triglyphs
IG II2 1668	Piraeus, 347-6	Capitals, lintels, pilasters, columns	Pilasters, thresholds	-	-	-	-	-
IG II2 1680	Eleusis, 350-300	Capitals	-	-	-	-	-	-
IG II2 1685	Athens, c.300	Capitals	Columns, pilasters	-	-	-	-	-

This prescriptive approach to stonework quality was the norm. But another syggraphai, IG II2 3073, for a temple at Lebadeia (no later than 220 BCE), specified the stonework for the steles and foundations both prescriptively and in terms of processes – the specific tools and ephemerals to be used. It may have only been describing normal practice, but no other syggraphai did this. The first part of the inscription described the inscription of the syggraphai themselves, and related processes such as cleaning the steles with nitron (also used as flux in glass production, according to Pliny the Elder [16]) and painting and washing out the letters. Other syggraphai mention the preparation of inscriptions (e.g. IG XII, 9 191, for draining a swamp at Ptechai), but rightly left the processes to the contractor. The second part described the processes of levelling and smoothing stonework in detail, specifying chisels of several kinds, and olive oil and the mineral miltos, or red lead, for levelling. Again, other contracts left these matters to the contractor. The specification of processes is deprecated today and was not usual then [17]. This technique may have been used here as skill sets had been lost due to long-running wars in the region, between Rome and Macedonia, and so could not be assumed for the contracting teams as they are in conventional prescriptive specifications.

Stonework did not comprise just stone. A contract for bronze empolia and tenons, IG II2 1675, described them in some detail:

> For the sanctuary at Eleusis, for the column-drums of the columns of the Prostoon, for the joints provide bronze tenons and empolia, two empolia for each joint and, inside, (a) tenon. The lower ones, the first (i.e. the empolia): six dactyl each way, square, then the uppermost five dactyl each way, the remainder changing equally from the biggest to the smallest. The latter, tenons: cylindrical, the lower ones length five daktyl, but thickness two daktyl, the upper ones length on one hand (a) palastai, thickness on the other hand daktyl and half daktyl, the remainder changing, for length and for thickness, equally from the biggest to the smallest. Then work of copper from Marion, mixing twelve parts, eleven of copper, but the twelfth of tin. And deliver the former, empolia, straight and immovable and equal-angled. The latter, tenons, turn with a lathe, cylindrical to match the paradeigma, and fit into the empolia tightly and straight and turned with a lathe each way such that it can be rotated. (author's translation)

Full-scale drawings of stonework were prepared during the construction process and inscribed in situ. Some that survive are plan views of columns – two for the temple of Aphaia at Aegina, [18] and two for the temple of Apollo at Didyma. Others are vertical drawings of columns – a column base, a drawing showing column entasis (vertical scale is 1:16), and a full section, for the temple of Apollo at Didyma. The setout of a volute is inscribed onto a column base at the Prytaneion at Ephesos [19], and the plan of a ceiling panel on the walls at the temple of Apollo at Didyma. The Didyma drawings were inscribed into the apergon which, as the temple was never finished, was never removed as specified for the Prostoon at Eleusis, above.

Table 2: Requirements for the 19 stone units, by frequency, in IG II2 1666 A&B

Requirement	Frequency (units, of 19)
Dimensions & quantities	
• Item identification	19
• Length x width x thickness (palaste)	19
• Number	19
Quarrying	
• Quarry	19
• With *apergon* all over	18
• Straight in every direction	16
• Square in every direction	13
• According to the *anagraphe* provided by the architect	11
Transport and delivery	
• Transport from quarry or storage to Eleusis sanctuary	19
• Deliver sound and unbroken	15
• Deliver to storage sound	5
• Deliver to storage white and stainless	4
Carving	
• According to the *anagraphe* provided by the architect	4
• Match existing	2

• Doric or Ionic	■
• Remove *apergon*	■
• Straight and square in every direction	■
• Trim smooth	■
• Carve the lion heads	■
• At the corners also dress the sides, along all the walls	■
Installation	
• Fit together with joints tight-fitting in every direction	■■■■■■■■■■■
• Level the tops [straight]	■■■■■■■■■■
• Clamp and pour lead around	■■■■■■■■■
• Hoist	■■■■■■■■
• Lay unbroken	■■■■■■■
• Dowel	■■■■■■
• Fit flush	■■■■■
• Joints 1 palastai wide	■■■■
• Level each course throughout, lengthwise and crosswise	■■■
• Level according to the *periteneian* provided by the architect	■■
• Under the columns, dowel and pour lead around	■
• Tight-fitting joints [unqualified]	■
• Remove *apergon* to 3 palastai high where visible	■
• Erect on foundations	■
• Erect upon beds in the rock on solid ground	■
• Trim edges to 2 palastai high	■
• Smooth at the required height and dress upper surface leaving raised panels	■
• Lay and bed overlapping 0.5 palastai	■
• Square in every direction	■
• Fix *as directed* by the architect	■
• Hoist at the proper place	■
• Width of 3 pilasters according to the *measurements* provided by the architect	■
• Erect on pilasters	■
• Erect on thresholds	■
• Use as many as necessary where needed	■

Just a few construction models survive from ancient Greece. One reason is that, for complex objects such as capitals, full-size paradeigma were prepared and, after being copied, were incorporated into the works. These 'models' are not distinguishable from the copies [20]. Tile standards were prepared at full-scale in stone, but not incorporated into the works. Three are extant, for Messene, Athens and Assos [21]. Small-scale models that might have been used for construction include an Argive roof at the Acropolis, Athens, [22] and triglyphs and metopes for the temple of Aphaia at Aegina [23].

Rome

In the early period, Rome sourced its stone locally, [24] but as the Empire grew, so did the range of quarries used. Stone was imported by sea from Egypt, for example, even at the risk of losing a cargo of 50-foot (14.8 m) columns for the Pantheon in Rome [25]. The online Stone Quarries Database lists 792 quarries across the Empire but notes that 'there must have been hundreds if not thousands of other quarries that have yet to be documented in any way [26]'. Stone types listed include marble, limestone, sandstone, granite, gypsum, travertine, alabaster, schist, basalt, porphyry, volcanic tuff, quartzite, conglomerate and lava.

Only one construction specification survives from Rome. For a porch in an existing wall at Puteoli, 105 BCE, this describes prescriptively a range of materials and work, including stones and stonework, albeit briefly. The relevant extracts are as follows [CIL 12.698 (author's translation)]:

… Make the width p 6, height p 7. From this wall, project two antae towards the sea forwards, length p 2, thickness p 1 ¼. … For the same, make the furthest garden-wall, the existing wall, (and) the (new) wall with coping of height p 10.

For the same, the existing entrance-door entering into the site and the windows which (are) in the wall near that site are (now) wall, (and) must be filled in.

And place upon the existing wall near the road an uninterrupted coping. And all the walls and copings which (are) not (coated) with beach-sand will be rendered with lime (plaster). … No heavier rough quarry stones may be laid than rough quarry stones (of) dry weight p 15, nor make corner stones higher (than) [4.5 unciae]. …

As for Greece, full-scale drawings of stonework were prepared during the construction process. Likewise, most were inscribed into the architectural fabric, in situ. Examples include a drawing of entasis and another of a column profile at the theatre of Aphrodisias in Asia Minor; a pediment elevation, an arc elevation, a plan of the orchestra and cavea, a courtyard plan and an arch elevation at the temple of Jupiter at Baalbek, Lebanon; [27] details of the Pantheon at Rome, inscribed in the paving near the Mausoleum of Augustus; an elevation of an arch and a rosette and other patterns now at Santa Maria di Capua Vetere; elevations of a pediment and entablature at Bziza, Lebanon; elevations of entablature and a column at Pergamon; and elevations of a roof crown and arch and pediment at the temple of Bacchus, Baalbek. We also have a portable inscribed drawing of a volute, from Thysdrus, Tunisia [28].

Stone construction models from around the Roman Empire dealt with whole buildings, and so were small-scale. They include a model of the temple of Luna at Ostia (Museo d'Ostica Antica 189), a thermal bath at Taormina (Akademischen Kunstmuseums der Universität Bonn, B 298), the adyton for Temple A at Niha, Lebanon, [29] the stairs of the Great Altar at Baalbek, Lebanon, [30] the stadium at Villa Adriana, Tivoli (Museo Didattico di Villa Adriana, Tivoli, 4714/A&B), and the open-air theatre at Baalbek [31]. It can be assumed that the Romans followed the Greek practice of built-in full-scale paradeigma for column capitals and the like.

Conclusion

The documentation of stonework for prestige buildings in the ancient world came in the form of written descriptions, drawings and models. All could have been prepared for a project and will have been read together. The initial contractual document was typically a written description, for Greece at least. They will have been prepared on portable but ephemeral materials such as papyrus but, from Greece, copies of the syggraphai inscribed in stone for public display survive (along with many other kinds of inscriptions).

Some of the drawings were small-scale and some were full-size. Small-scale drawings were not to scale, often in the form of sketches, and were drawn on ostraka, which have survived, and on ephemeral materials, which generally have not. Full-size drawings were inscribed in stone on or near the site, during the construction process. Those on site were often inscribed on the walls in a temporary protective layer of stone which was removed in the finished project – those that survive do so only because some projects were unfinished.

Some of the models were small-scale and some were full-size. In the Egyptian tradition, small-scale models of capitals were also often 'sketches', roughly made, often in clay, but some were very precise, to scale, and durable being carved in stone. Sculptors could have enlarged them using callipers or grids without too much difficulty. In the Greek tradition, full-size models of stone capitals and the like were prepared by the architect or master carver, and subsequently copied and then incorporated into the works.

Today stone masonry is one product in thousands used in the construction of a modern building, but the element of prestige remains. Recently it has rarely been used structurally, being largely reserved for non-loadbearing lining, flooring, cladding and benchtops. Fixings are phosphor bronze or stainless steel, rather than brass, iron and lead, and the design and specification of stone and stonework is scientific, referencing international standards such as EN 771-6 and Eurocode 6 [32]. But interestingly, loadbearing stonework might be making a comeback [33].

References

[1] P. Warren, 'The rediscovery of Greek rosso antico marble and its use in Britain in the nineteenth and twentieth centuries', Annual of the British School at Athens 107, 2012; 341-386.
[2] J. Calvo-Lopéz, Stereotomy: Stone construction and geometry in Western Europe 1200-1900, Basel: Birkhäuser, 2020.
[3] A.B. Holton, 'The working space of the medieval master mason: The tracing houses of York Minster and Wells Cathedral', in Proceedings of the Second International Congress on Construction History, Volume II, 2006; 1579-1597.
[4] At 1 St Paul's Churchyard, London. The stone was from Portland, Dorset. The author was the site architect for this project over 1986.
[5] J.A. Harrell & P. Storenyr, 'Ancient Egyptian quarries – an illustrated overview', in N. Abu-Jaber, E.G. Bloxam, P. Degryse & T. Heldal (eds.) QuarryScapes: ancient stone quarry landscapes in the eastern Mediterranean, Geological Survey of Norway, 2009; 7-50.
[6] H. Carter & A.H. Gardiner, 'The tomb of Ramesses IV and the Turin plan of a royal tomb', Journal of Egyptian Archaeology 4, 1917; 134, 136-37.
[7] A. Badawy, A monumental gateway for a temple of King Sety I: An ancient model restored, Miscellanea Wilbouriana 1, New York: Brooklyn Museum, 1972; 15.
[8] Many of the construction drawings listed in this paper are collected in J.P. Heisel, Antike Bauzeichnungen, Darmstadt: Wissenschaftliche Buchgesellschaft, 1993.
[9] For the accuracy of this and other documents for three tombs, see J. Gelder, 'Comparing 'as documented' with 'as constructed' in Ancient Egypt', in J.W.P. Campbell et al (eds.), Building histories: The proceedings of the fourth conference of the Construction History Society, Queen's College Cambridge, 7-9 April 2017, Cambridge: Construction History Society, 2017; 55-66.
[10] W.C. Hayes, Ostraka and name stones from the tomb of Sen-Mūt (No. 71) at Thebes, Publications of the Metropolitan Museum of Art Egyptian Expedition 15, New York: Metropolitan Museum of Art, 1942.
[11] For the set-out and accuracy of this and another vault curve, see J. Gelder, 'Two Egyptian curves revisited', in J.W.P. Campbell et al (eds.), Proceedings of the First Conference of the Construction History Society, Queens' College, Cambridge, April 2014, Cambridge: Construction History Society, 2014; 145-156.
[12] D. Arnold, 'Der Pyramidenbezirk des Königs Amenemhet III in Dahschur: Band 1: Die Pyramide', Archäologische Veröffentlichungen 53, 1987; 86-88, taf 35, 66-68.

[13] P. Davoli, 'The contra-temple of Soknopaios and its architectural model', Egyptian Archaeology 55, 2019; 40-43.
[14] B.J. Russell, 'Stone quarrying in Greece: ten years of research', Archaeological Reports 63, 2017; 77-78.
[15] For an analysis of 36 syggraphai see J. Gelder, 'Professional roles in Greek construction contracts', in this volume. The article explores the nature and roles of syggraphai, paradeigma, anagraphe, periteneian, measurements and site directions by the architect.
[16] Pliny the Elder, Natural history, Book 36.65; I. Despina et al, 'Nitrum Chalestricum: The natron of Macedonia', Annales du 16e Congrès de l'Association Internationale pour l'Histoire du Verre, AIHV, 2008; 64-67.
[17] J. Gelder, 'Specifying construction processes', NBS Journal 01, November 2002; 3-4; J. Gelder, 'Process clarification', NBS Journal 02, May 2003; 3.
[18] E-L. Schwandner, 'Zu Entwurf, Zeichnung und Maszsystem des Älteren Aphaiatempels von Aegina', in J. Frézouls, C. Margueron, G. Siebert & J.M. Spieser (eds.), Le dessin d'architecture dans les sociétés antiques, Actes du Colloque de Strasbourg, 26-28 January 1984, Leiden: EJ Brill, 1985; 277-281; 80-81, Abb 3&4.
[19] M. Steskal, 'Konstruktionszeichnungen zweier Voluten aus dem Prytaneion in Ephesos', Jahreshefte des Österreichischen Archäologischen Institutes in Wien 76, 2007; 374, 378.
[20] J. Gelder, 'Professional roles in Greek construction contracts', in this volume.
[21] J.T. Clarke, F.H. Bacon & R. Koldewey, Investigations at Assos, Cambridge MA: Archaeological Institute of America, 1902; 71, fig.2; G.P. Stevens, 'A tile standard in the Agora of ancient Athens', Hesperia 19/3, 1949; 174-188, plate 82/1; P. Themelis, 'Hellenistic architectural terracottas from Messene', Hesperia Supplements 27, 1994, 141-169, 390-398, plate 48d.
[22] N. Winter, Greek architectural terracottas, Oxford: Oxford University Press, 1993; 155-157, figs 16-17, plates 60-2.
[23] L. Haselberger, 'Architectural likenesses: models and plans of architecture in classical antiquity', Journal of Roman Archaeology 10, 1997; 80, fig 16.
[24] M. Jackson & F. Marra, 'Roman stone masonry: Volcanic foundations of the ancient city', American Journal of Archaeology 110/3; 403-436.
[25] T.A. Marder & M. Wilson-Jones (eds.), The Pantheon: From antiquity to the present, Cambridge: Cambridge University Press, 2015; 214ff.
[26] B.J. Russell, Gazetteer of stone quarries in the Roman world, Version 1.0, 2013, online at: www.romaneconomy.ox.ac.uk/databases/stone_quarries_database/ (accessed 2 June 2021).
[27] D. Lohmann, 'Drafting and design: Roman architectural drawings and their meaning for the construction of Heliopolis/Baalbek, Lebanon', in K-E. Kurrer, W. Lorenz & V. Wetzk (eds.) Proceedings of the third international congress on construction history, BUT, Cottbus, Germany, 20-24 May 2009, volume 2, Berlin: Neunplus 1, 2009; 959-966.
[28] T. Loertscher, 'Voluta constructa: Zu einem kaiserzeitlichen Volutenkonstruktionsmodell aus Nordafrika', Antike Kunst 32, 1989; 82-103.
[29] E. Will, 'La maquette de l'adyton du Temple A de Niha (Beqa)', in Frézouls et al, Le dessin d'architecture; 277-281; figs 1, 3, 4, plate 4. [Note 18]
[30] R. Taylor, Roman builders: A study in architectural process, Cambridge: Cambridge University Press, 2003; 33 fig 8
[31] A. Ghadban, 'Maqueta d'un teatre procedent d'Heliopolis-Baalbek', in P. Azara (ed.), Les cases de l'ànima: Maquetes arquitectòniques de l'antiguitat (5500 AC/300 DC), Barcelona: Centre de Cultura Contemporania de Barcelona & Institut d'Edicions de la Disputacio de Barcelona, 1997; 239-40. Several of the Roman construction models listed here are included in this catalogue.
[32] EN 771-6:2011 Specification for masonry units. Natural stone masonry units; EN 1996-2:2006 Eurocode 6. Design of masonry structures, Design considerations, selection of materials and execution of masonry.
[33] T. Ravenscroft, 'Groupwork designs 30-storey stone skyscraper', Dezeen, 10 March 2020; online at: www.dezeen.com/2020/03/10/stone-skyscraper-groupwork-amin-taha/ (accessed 2 June 2021).

Professional Roles in Greek Construction Contracts

John Gelder
University of South Australia

Introduction

The classical Greek architect did not have quite the same function as the modern architect. The role was more akin to that of the medieval master builder. To some extent it was defined in contractual documents of the time. For example, they often referred to other documents that the architect would provide.

Inscribed on stone steles for public display and durability, many written construction contracts – syggraphai – survive, in whole or in part, for a range of projects. Table 1 lists 36 syggraphai, for 13 religious, 4 military and one civil project. The discrepancy arises because, for most large projects, multiple contracts were let in sequence as for Eleusis, e.g. for the foundations (IG II2 1671), then for the column fittings (IG II2 1675), and then for the capitals (IG II2 1680). Many are available online in Greek and English [1]. To avoid confusion the Greek term is used for these documents. Whilst they included contractual material (such as date, cost, delivery dates, payment regime, penalties and parties), they also included material now located outside the conditions of contract, such as construction quality (in the specification), quantities of items (in the bills of quantities), and location of items (on the floor plans). Written integrated documents of this kind continued to be used through to the medieval period in Europe [2].

Table 1: 36 surviving Greek syggraphai, in approximate chronological order

Project	Date BCE	Inscription
Wooden coffered ceiling, Erechtheum, Athens	409-8	Erechtheum VII
Repair of walls, Piraeus	394-3	IG II2 1657
Tripod plinths, Kynosarges, Athens	400-350	IG II2 1665
Temple of Apollo, Delphi	c.370	FD III 5 88
Stonework, Prostoon, Eleusis	356	IG II2 1666 A
Stonework, Prostoon, Eleusis	356	IG II2 1666 B
Middle wall, Prostoon, Eleusis	354-3	IG II2 1682
Naval tackle store, Zeia	347-6	IG II2 1668
Dowels, Eleusis	341-0	IG II2 1681
Repair of walls, Piraeus	337	IG II3 1 429
Foundations, Prostoon, Eleusis	350-300	IG II2 1671
Empolia and tenons, Prostoon, Eleusis	340-320	IG II2 1675
Stylobates, Prostoon, Eleusis	350-300	IG II2 1670
Capitals, Prostoon, Eleusis	350-300	IG II2 1680
Capitals, Prostoon, Eleusis	350-300	IG II2 1679
Drainage channel, Amphiaraos, Oropos	335-22	IG VII 4255
Swamp drainage, Ptechai	320-15	IG XII, 9 191
Portico, Taurinum, Delos	Before 315	IG II2 1678
Orthostats, Asklepion, Mytilene	330-300	IG VII XII 2 10

Project	Date BCE	Inscription
Long walls, Athens	307-6	IG II2 463
Tower & stair, Kyzikos	400-200	GIBM IV Supp 1005
Columns, Asklepion, Athens	c. 300	IG II2 1685
Temple of Apollo?, Delos	c.300	ID 503
Asklepion, Delos	297	ID 500
Paving, Temple of Apollo, Delos	297	ID 502
Steps, Eleusis	289-8	IG II2 1684
Portico, Mytilene	300-275	IG VII XII suppl. 14
Temple of Apollo?, Delos	300-266	ID 505
Temple of Apollo?, Delos	c.280	ID 504
Delos	277-6	ID 506
Temple of Herakles?, Thasos	3rd century	IG XII 8 266
Asklepion, Delos	c.250	ID 507
Delos	c.248	ID 507B
Delos	c.230	ID 508
Delos	c.230-20	ID 509
Inscriptions & flagstones, Temple of Zeus Basileos, Lebadeia	Before 220	IG VII 3073

The content of each syggraphai with respect to the various professional roles involved in the project – architect, contractor and guarantor – is summarised in Table 2 [3]. Eight mention all three. Seven mention none. While some of the inscriptions are complete or nearly so (notably IG II2 1668), many are fragmentary, with the start and/or end of the inscription often lost. Given that the client and the architect are usually identified at the start of the syggraphai, and the contractors and guarantors at the end, their omission in this table does not always mean that they were omitted originally. But in some cases, it can be said with confidence that they were. For example, though complete, IG II2 1668 did not include the names of contractors and guarantors, or any information concerning costs, penalties and the like. This then raises the question of what this inscription was for. It has been shown to contain enough information to recreate the building with some confidence – any ambiguity could have been resolved at the time by the architect [4]. One possibility is that this inscription was the celebrated monograph by Philo on the 'arsenal' at Piraeus referred to by Vitruvius – the text could have been transcribed to papyrus for circulation, as an epitome of such a description [5].

Architects

Of the syggraphai listed here, 18 mention the architect (architektōn), and four name him. Architects had multiple roles. The most important was the design of the building and the preparation of the syggraphai that described it for construction (and other) purposes, sometimes with assistance [6]. For the Athenian temple of Athena Nike, the inscription IG I3 35 (c.450 or 438 BCE) recorded that 'the sanctuary be provided with gates in whatever way Kallikrates may specify', that 'that a temple be built in whatever way Kallikrates may specify', and then (perhaps upon careful reflection of the free hand given to him) that 'three men be selected from the Council, and they shall make the syggraphai with Kallikrates [7]'.

IG II2 1668 acknowledged the authorship of the syggraphai in the first sentence: 'Syggraphai for a stone tackle-store for hanging tackle, by Euthydomos (son) of Deimeitrios from Melite and Philonos (son) of Exeikestidos from Eleusis'. Others were not so explicit. Though it named the architect, IG II2 1665 merely mentioned this authoring role: 'as the architect writes below'. IG II2 1685 had 'as written below pending that the architect gives', inferring that the inscription was not the complete description – more was to come. For the repair of the walls at Piraeus the authorship of the specifications was open to anyone. IG II3 1 429 stated 'that the architects [contracted to the city and anyone else who wishes shall bring forward] specifications, having drawn them up for each of the works', and later 'the architects contracted to the city and anyone else who wishes may [draft] specifications [and bring them forward] [8]'. Architects did not enjoy 'protection of function'.

Table 2: Professional roles mentioned in 36 surviving Greek syggraphai

Inscription	Architect	Contractor	Guarantor
IG II2 1657	-	7 (named)	-
IG II2 1665	02 (named), 04	-	-
IG II2 1666A	07 (named), 23, 34, 48, 56, 75, 82, 90	-	-
IG II2 1666B	10, 24, 30, 35, 67	-	-
IG II2 1682	-	16 (named), 19 (named), 32 (named)	17 (named), 32 (named)
IG II2 1668	3 (named), 94, 96	94, 96	-
IG II2 1681	-	28 (named)	29 (named)
IG II3 1 429	5, 39	44 (named), 47, 54, 57, 60, 75, 97	34
IG II2 1671	-	52-54 (named)	-
IG II2 1675	18	22 (named)	23 (named)
IG II2 1670	16	11, 17, 21, 23 (named), 25 (named), 26 (named)	24 (named), 25 (named), 26 (named)
IG II2 1680	15	20 (named)	21 (named)
IG VII 4255	-	36 (named)	36 (named)
IG XII, 9 191	-	44 mentions (by name)	33, 40
IG II2 1678	02, 06, 11, 16 Over-architect: 08, 13	09, 10, 11, 12, 13, 17, 21, 25, 27 (named), 29 (named), 57	17, 20, 21, 22, 30-32 (named)
IG VII XII 2 10	-	1	-
GIBM IV Supp 1005	-	8 (named)	11 (named)
IG II2 1685	02	-	-
ID 503	-	-	17 mentions
ID 500	10, 22, 42, 44, 45, 47	-	A19, B14
ID 502	20	-	9, 25
IG II2 1684	25	26	26
ID 504	-	6, 9	8, 10, 12
ID 506	4	-	9
ID 507	24, 27, 34	16	21, 38
ID 507B	2 (named), 11	-	-
ID 508	15	-	7, 8
ID 509	-	21, 23, 43	-
IG VII 3073	53, 131, 160, 161 (sub-architect)	24 mentions	4, 25, 27, 28, 40, 47

Several syggraphai mention the need for the agreed contractual text to be inscribed and displayed (i.e. the text was agreed and written down, perhaps on papyrus or timber boards, before it was inscribed). IG XII, 9 191 is one example [9]. The inscribed steles were often erected so they could be seen from the construction site, [10] but this was not always the case. For example, IG XII, 9 191 required copies of the stele to be located at a couple of temples remote from the site, and if a stele described quarrying as well as assembly (as did IG II2 1666 A and B – inscribed on both sides of the same stele), then its building location will have been remote from the quarry. One stele describes its own inscription process in some detail. This is the first half of IG VII 3073, for the late unfinished temple of Zeus Basileos in Lebadeia (central Greece). It might be asked why such a detailed inscription was thought to be necessary since the process had been followed for centuries by this time. Perhaps the requisite skills had been lost during the wars between Rome and Macedonia, which ran from 214 to 148 BCE.

The inscriptions sometimes named the architects. IG II2 1668 has been noted above. IG II2 1665 named the architect as 'Architect, Xenophon (son) of Perithoide from Kynosarge'. IG II2 1666A, for the Prostoon at Eleusis, had 'Architect Philargos (son) of A[... from ...] [11]'. Given that the names will have been known before the inscription was made (they probably authored it, as noted), and given their ongoing roles during the project, it is surprising that more did not name them. Knowing who you were going to be dealing with would have been important to the tenderers and knowing the identity of the author would have been important to the community for accountability (another reason that the syggraphai were displayed).

Referenced documents

As well as the syggraphai, architects also prepared other referenced documents, including those termed paradeigma, anagraphe and periteneian. To some extent, the nature of these can be determined from the context of their citation in the syggraphai. However, there is no real consensus on what they were. Architects also provided measurements (metra) and promised to provide other information during the contract (Table 3) [12].

Fourteen mentioned syggraphai, often a self-reference at the start of the document (presumably so it was clear to the readers what the nature of the document they were about to read was), but they also sometimes referred to others. For example, IG II2 1678, which dealt with columns, capitals and stylobates, stated: 'Finish the work as contracted for the fourth of silver just as for the contractor of the orthostats in the syggraphai written'.

Paradeigma were mentioned in five of the documents. IG II2 1675 had 'The latter, tenons, turn with a lathe, cylindrical to match the paradeigma'. IG II2 1668 stated: 'Make [the chests] to the paradeigma and place them at every column and centred in the space opposite', and as a general requirement: 'In this way everywhere shall work be carried out by the contractors conforming to the syggraphai and to the measurements and to the paradeigma as directed by the architect'. ID 504 stated: '... contractor Phaneas working to the syggraphai everywhere against the paradeigma, three flights of steps and a manger, for drachma three-hundred'. ID II2 1678 had 'And then contract for lead to the paradeigma around the capitals ...', and 'And then to the paradeigma of the capital for Delos, the works contractor will complete'. ID II2 1685, for pilasters, had '... declare how against the paradeigma'.

Paradeigma seem to have been used for complex objects such as column capitals. It is thought that the Greeks used full-scale models of capitals. These models will have been incorporated into the works, [13] though one example of a purported paradeigma was not. This Corinthian capital for the Tholos of Polykleitos at Epidauros was an experimental piece produced as a part of the design process rather than a piece to be copied or replicated in construction, so does not qualify as a paradeigma at all [14]. However, it does support the idea that such objects were made by the architect himself, at least in some cases. In support of the idea that paradeigma were full-scale and incorporated into the works, one object labelled in situ as a 'paradegma' survives. This 5 m section of tunnel was an example of acceptable construction or workmanship that was built into the works, for the tunnel of Eupalinos at Samos (mid-6th century BCE) [15].

Anagraphe were mentioned in 11 of the documents – roughly twice as often as paradeigma. IG II2 1680 had: 'And then the width [and the length], upper and lower, [to match the anagraphe], larger than (the) twelve'. IG II2 1670, stated: 'And show [the stylobates] having completed as contracted and the anagraphe …'. IG II3 1 429, for cutting blocks of stone, had: '… and against the anagraphe to which each is contracted …', and 'And provide for themselves and the stone cutters anagraphes and everything else …'. IG II2 1685, for walls, stated: '… against the anagraphe given by the architect'. The Delian contracts cited them as follows: ID 500 'and then for steles the syggraphai and anagraphe …; ID 508 '… anagraphe and syggraphai for the steles …'; and ID 509 'and anagraphe for the doors'. IG II2 1666A and IG II2 1666B mention the anagraphe ('given by the architect') eleven times, for quarrying (metopes, cornices x 2, capitals, gable blocks and roof tiles) and carving (cornices x 2, capitals, gable blocks and roof tiles).

Table 3: Architectural communications referred to in 36 surviving Greek syggraphai

Inscription	Syggraphai	Paradeigma	Anagraphe	Periteneian	Metra	As directed
IG II2 1665	2	-	-	-	-	-
IG II2 1666A	-	-	34, 48, 55, 82, 90	-	75	23
IG II2 1666B	-	-	4, 10, 17. 23, 30, 34	67	-	-
IG II2 1668	2	87, 95	-	-	21, 28, 95	94
IG II2 1681	27	-	-	-	-	-
IG II3 1 429	6, 40, 41, 46	-	53, 105	-	52, 74	55, 57, 61
IG II2 1671	-	-	-	1, 43	2, 48	-
IG II2 1675	-	15	-	-	-	-
IG II2 1670	-	-	23	17	-	-
IG II2 1680	-	-	13	-	4, 20	15
IG II2 1678	15	10, 11	-	-	32	6
IG II2 463	35	-	-	-	-	-
IG II2 1685	3.9, 5.9	5.5	5.6	-	2.9, 2.13, 5.4, 5.6	5.8
ID 503	30	-	-	-	-	-
ID 500	B7	-	B7	-	-	-
ID 502	6, 15	-	-	-	-	-
ID 505	-	-	-	-	-	-
ID 504	B7	B7	-	-	-	-
ID 507	23	-	-	-	-	-
ID 508	5, 12	-	12	-	-	-
ID 509	-	-	29	-	-	-
IG VII 3073	16, 18, 52, 88, 176	-	-	69, 187	23, 97, 101, 181	24, 69, 87, 124, 182

The topics in IG II2 1666 includes roof tiles, and interestingly three full-scale stone 'tile standards' survive from across the Greek diaspora – Messene, Assos and Athens [16]. These, then, may be examples of a type of anagraphe. They were full-scale models but could not be incorporated into the works. An example of another type might be the full-scale drawings for columns that were inscribed into the apergon (a protective stone skin) on the walls of the temple of Apollo at Didyma [17]. The syggraphai suggests that some anagraphe were provided by the architect, and some by the contractor, which fits in with this example of 'shop drawings'.

'Outlines' (periteneian) were mentioned in four syggraphai. IG II2 1666B stated for laying the corners, 'And level the tops [straight] and according to the periteneian given by the architect'. IG II2 1671 mentioned them twice: '… according to the periteneian for the course', and 'Then cut down to each course straight and flush according to the original periteneian'. IG II2 1670 stated: '… according to the periteneian provided'. IG VII 3073 had 'according to the periteneian provided', for trimming the steles, and 'using the original periteneian of the paving blocks', for the new paving blocks. In all cases this concerned the horizontal level – perhaps for new construction the periteneian was simply a stretched string, set to the required level, running around (peri-) the building. For alterations to an existing building, it would have been the original level.

Measurements (metra) are mentioned in nine of the documents, sometimes provided by the architect. IG II2 1666A stated for the installation of the plinths, 'Width then is from [the pilasters and] according to the measurement given by the architect'. IG II2 1680 had: '… cutting stone to the measurements provided'. IG II2 1685 stated: '… and as given in the measurements and the anagraphe'. Most, though, are given in the syggraphai themselves, or determined on site.

A type of document mentioned only in one syggraphai (IG II2 1684, for steps) is a syggegrammena [18]. A handful of small-scale stone models incorporating steps survive from the ancient world, so perhaps this refers to something of this kind [19]. Using a model will have helped convey their 3D geometry.

Architects also gave direction on site. Seven syggraphai include this term (keleyē). For the kanonides IG II2 1666A stated 'And clamp and do[wel and pour lead around] as directed by the architect'. IG II2 1680, on the transport of capitals to Eleusis, stated 'Then [unload all into the] sanctuary boundary as directed [(by) the architect]'. IG II2 1668 stated 'So that there may be fresh air in the tackle-store, when building the walls of the tackle-store leave gaps in the masonry at the joints or as directed by the architect'. IG II3 1 429 used the term in three consecutive sentences: '… and to the anagraphe, as directed for the contracted works. And carry to the work site the type as first directed for the contracted works. And demolish to the work every stone as directed for the contracted works.' IG II2 1678 had: 'And then for the empolia set in lead as directed by the architect'. IG II2 1685 stated, 'Then do as needed for the work and all as directed by the architect'.

IG VII 3073 had several examples, indicative of close supervision: 'Then if during the work any written measurement is to be lengthened or cut short, make it as directed' (twice), 'And then upon the existing steles place eleven coping stones, after trimming the steles, taking as much as directed, according to the periteneian provided', 'Then cleanse with nitron the steles and show the letters clean and washed out, until when directed', and '… polish with approved red-lead all to the standard, as often as directed, against the approved original stone standard in the sanctuary'.

The authors of the syggraphai were essentially acknowledging that certain key information was missing or possibly inaccurate, and would be provided or corrected later, presumably verbally (though today verbal instructions on site must be recorded in writing to carry any weight). The examples given here are qualitative and (mostly) not the sort of thing for which a model, drawing or specification would be appropriate.

Clients, contractors, guarantors and others

Client bodies provided project management for the works, engaging and paying the architects and the contractors. But they also sometimes provided tools and materials, such as metals. ID 502 had 'Then bronze for the work the city-state provides', and IG II2 1666B had: 'Lead, then, and iron for fastening stones the city-state provides, and complete hoisting-equipment.' Though supervision of the works was usually left to the architect, sometimes the client took on this role. The Lebadeia temple project was not completed (it seems to have ground to a halt several times), perhaps because of the wars mentioned earlier [20]. The main surviving inscription (IG II2 3073) suggests another reason – an obsession with close supervision and detail. The document included process specifications for the inscriptions and for stonework. The specification of processes is deprecated today and was not usual then [21]. Enforcement of process specifications requires close supervision. A competent contractor would not have welcomed or needed this and so may have been unwilling to tender. Or, having won the work, this close supervision may have stifled progress and led to disputes over delays, ultimately stopping the project. Or incompetency may have been the case, in which case the contractor may simply have been unable to execute the works competently, despite the instructions, and after disputes on quality, and consequent delays, the work was abandoned.

Nineteen syggraphai mention the contractors (misthōn) or workers (ergōnēs), and 12 named them. Where named, we can be sure that the syggraphai was a contract document, intended for construction. Contractors were often given rights relevant to the works, beyond their payment. IG XII, 9 191 gives several such rights. For example, the contractor was given tax immunity for the materials, was exempt from a 'deposit' to Eretria provided that items he produced in the drained swamp were sold at a reasonable price, was to be compensated for losses due to battle, and with his co-workers was immune from 'harm' during the contract. Contractors may also have had obligations above the normal business of construction. For example, an account (IG II2 1673) describes work done to build a cart to transport stone from the quarry at Penteleikon to the construction site at Eleusis (327-326 BCE) [22].

Guarantors or sureties (eggyos) are mentioned in nineteen syggraphai and named in eight. They were typically wealthy citizens (whereas contractors could be foreign) with a sense of civic responsibility, as this could be a risky business. IG II2 1678 stipulated that each guarantor had to be capable of meeting a debt of 1000 drachmas, with enough guarantors assembled to cover the total cost of the contract. IG VII 3073 required, where a part of the contract was resold due to non-performance for whatever reason, the original guarantors (and contractor) to remain liable until the contractor taking on the resold portion had in turn found sufficient guarantors. As mentioned, this project was never finished.

The community itself was brought into the agreement recorded in IG XII, 9 191, which stipulated oath-taking by the local citizenry and required their names to be inscribed, as over 300 were on faces B and C of the stele. This would have been because the contractor needed to be sure that he could use the drained swamp for the agreed 10 years, without challenge.

Conclusion

The study could be extended by considering syggraphai not listed here, such as those for Tegea, Epidauros, and other fragments for Lebadeia. It could also consider more fully the roles stated or implied in the syggraphai for clients, contractors and guarantors [23].

Nevertheless, the 36 Greek syggraphai examined here shed some light on the roles of architects in the construction of monumental Greek architecture. Architects wrote the syggraphai themselves. They provided, and perhaps made, full-scale models of stonework and other objects to be incorporated into the works (paradeigma). They provided reference standards and shop drawings (anagraphe) and set out the levels for foundations and the like (periteneian). They provided measurements (metra) for the use of the contractors and gave directions on site. On the other hand, though they enforced quality on site using these various techniques, they did not administer the various construction contracts – this was done by the client bodies.

All these roles are found in construction projects today, but the architect only provides some of them, being supported now by the range of specialist disciplines that appeared after the Industrial Revolution [24].

References

[1] Many (but not all) of these inscriptions can be found online, at sites including the following: Greek transcriptions at Searchable Greek Inscriptions, https://inscriptions.packhum.org; English translations at Attic Inscriptions Online, www.atticinscriptions.com. For a general survey of Greek architectural inscriptions, see R.L. Scranton, 'Greek architectural inscriptions as documents', Harvard Library Bulletin 14/2, Spring 1960; 159-182.
[2] J. Gelder, 'Integrated. Dis-integrated. Coordinated. Re-integrated', Architectural Research Quarterly 16/3, 2012; 253-260.
[3] Client bodies such as epistatai and naopoioi are not listed as these were non-professional, elected, often specifically for the project, in which they could nevertheless be technically involved, as for IG VII 3073. R.K. Pitt, 'Just as it has been written: Inscribing building contracts at Lebadeia', in N. Papazarkadas, The epigraphy and history of Boeotia: New finds, new prospects, Leiden: Brill, 2014; 373-394. Syggraphai mentioning none of these parties are omitted from the table.
[4] Reconstructions can be found in the following: E. Fabricius, 'Die Skeuothek des Philon, das Zeughaus der Attischen Morine in zea', Hermes 17/4, 1882; 551-594; A. Choisy, L'arsenal du Pirée: d'après le devis original des travaux, Paris: Librairie de la Societe Anonyme de Publications Periodiques, 1883; V. Marstrand, Arsenalet i Piraeus og oldtidens byggeregler, Copenhagen: Egmont H. Petersens KGL, 1922; K. Jeppesen, Paradeigmata: Three mid-fourth century main works of Hellenic architecture reconsidered, Aarhus: Aarhus University Press, 1958; E. Lorenzen, The Arsenal at Piraeus, Copenhagen: Gads, 1964; W. Meyer-Christian, Das Arsenal des architekten Philon in Zea/Piräus, rekonstruktion, PhD Thesis: Universität Karlsruhe, 1983. Most also include translations. The footings for the building were finally found in 1988.
[5] Holloway suggested this equivalence in 1969: R.R. Holloway, 'Architect and engineer in Archaic Greece', Harvard Studies in Classical Philology 73, 1969; 281-290. Vitruvius, (transl. M. H. Morgan), The Ten Books on Architecture, Cambridge: Harvard University Press, 1914: Book VII, Introduction, 12. The building was destroyed by Sulla in 96 BCE. For a more recent example of such an epitome, see T. Donaldson, Handbook of specifications, Parts I & II, London: Lockwood & Co., 1859/60.
[6] Vitruvius described the role of the Roman architect in some detail, often citing Greek practices. Several anecdotes about the role of the architect can be found in Roman literature but, though Roman architects were often Greek, their relevance to practice in classical Greece is doubtful. Some are collected in A.N. Sherwood, M. Nikolic, J.W. Humphrey & J.P. Oleson, Greek and Roman technology: A sourcebook of translated Greek and Roman texts, London: Routledge, 2019.
[7] S. Lambert, J. Blok & R. Osborne (transl.), 'Decree about priestess and temple of Athena Nike', Attic Inscriptions Online, online at: www.atticinscriptions.com/inscription/Fornara/93 (accessed 25 May 2021). As well as this temple, Kallikrates was the architect of the Parthenon (with Iktinus), the circuit wall of the Acropolis, and one of the Long Walls protecting the route from Athens to Piraeus, all under Pericles (c.495-429 BCE), the Athenian statesman.
[8] S. Lambert (transl.) 'Law on repair of walls in the Piraeus, with appended specifications', Attic Inscriptions Online, online at: https://www.atticinscriptions.com/inscription/IGII31/429 (accessed 28 May 2021).
[9] For a translation and discussion, see J. Gelder, 'Ptechai and Oropos: Two ancient Greek drainage contracts compared', in J.W.P. Campbell et al (eds.) Water, doors and buildings: Studies in the history of construction, Cambridge: Construction History Society, 2019; 3-18.
[10] R.K. Pitt, 'Inscribing construction: The financing and administration of public building in Greek sanctuaries', in M.M. Miles (ed.) A companion to Greek architecture, Hoboken NJ: Wiley Blackwell, 2016; 194-205.

[11] Vitruvius named both the architects of the tackle-store and the Prostoon as 'Philo', which was incorrect and has led to some confusion (Book VII, Introduction, 12 & 17).

[12] Syggraphai mentioning none of these communications are omitted from the table.

[13] As suggested in J.J. Coulton, 'Greek architects and the transmission of design', in Actes du Colloque international organisé par le Centre national de la recherche scientifique et l'École française de Rome (Rome, 2-4 December 1980), 1983; 455-6. The preparation by a master carver of a paradigmatic stone capital (Corinthian), copied by the other carvers and then incorporated into the works, was the process followed for 1 St Pauls Churchyard, London, in 1986. The author was the site architect for the project.

[14] L. Haselberger, 'Architectural likenesses: models and plans of architecture in classical antiquity', Journal of Roman Archaeology 10, 1997; 90, fig 17.

[15] L. Haselberger, 'Architectural likenesses'; 90, figs 18a-b [Note 14].

[16] J.T. Clarke, F.H. Bacon & R. Koldewey, Investigations at Assos, Cambridge MA: Archaeological Institute of America, 1902; 71, fig.2; G.P. Stevens, 'A tile standard in the Agora of ancient Athens', Hesperia 19/3, 1949; 174-188; plate 82/1; P. Themelis, 'Hellenistic architectural terracottas from Messene', Hesperia Supplements 27, 1994, 141-169, 390-398; plate 48d.

[17] L. Haselberger, 'The construction plans for the Temple of Apollo at Didyma', Scientific American, December 1985; 114-122. Because the temple was unfinished, the apergon on the walls was never removed, hence the survival of the drawings (not plans but full-scale sections). Other examples of inscribed (in situ) full-scale drawings for Greek stonework include those for the temple of Aphaia at Aegina, the temple of Athena at Priene, and volutes for the Prytaneion at Ephesos.

[18] The term is not included in H.G. Liddell and R. Scott, Greek-English lexicon, Oxford: Clarendon Press, 1996.

[19] Stone small-scale models of steps from the Roman period include the plinth for the temple of Luna at Ostia (Museo d'Ostica Antica 189), a thermal bath at Taormina (Akademischen Kunstmuseums der Universität Bonn, inv. B 298), the adyton of temple A at Niha, Lebanon (Museo de Beirut), the Great Altar at Baalbek (Museo de Beirut), a water tank from Egypt (Petrie Museum UC14530), and altar steps from Egypt (Cairo 33.401).

[20] Pitt, Inscribing building contracts at Lebadeia, 2014 [Note 3].

[21] J. Gelder, 'Specifying construction processes', NBS Journal 01, November 2002; 3-4; J. Gelder, 'Process clarification', NBS Journal 02, May 2003; 3.

[22] A partial English translation is in A. Burford, The Greek temple builders at Epidauros, Liverpool: Liverpool University Press, 1969; Appendix IV. A full French translation is in G. Raepsaet, 'Transport de tambours de colonnes du Pentélique à Éleusis au IVe siècle avant notre ère', L'antiquité classique 53, 1984; 101-136. The construction of wagons for transporting stone was also described by Diodorus of Sicily (Library of history 4.80.5-6), and Vitruvius (De architectura, Book X 2.11-14). For more on the rights and obligations of Greek contractors see Table 1 in Burford (93-95).

[23] A broad study of this kind is P.H. Davis, 'The Delian building contracts', Bulletin de Correspondance Hellénique 61, 1937; 109-135.

[24] J. Gelder, 'Integrated. Dis-integrated. Coordinated. Re-integrated' [Note 2].

The Development of Water Pipes: a Brief Introduction from Ancient Times until the Industrial Revolution

James WP Campbell
Department of Architecture, University of Cambridge, UK

Summary

For as long as humans have built cities they have been concerned with the supply of water, for drinking and irrigation, and its removal to prevent flooding. With the exception of plastics, all of the materials we use today for pipes for the conveyance of water have been in use for centuries. This paper seeks to explore exactly how long each material has been used and by doing so to bring together the diverse sources for the history of the water pipe into one single paper, which will hopefully act as a useful guide for any historian seeking to start out on a study of water supply and drainage.

Definition

There are many ways of conveying water. For the purposes of this paper a pipe is defined as a hollow tube that is designed to be completely filled with water. This distinguishes it from a tunnel or an open conduit. Of course the pipe may not always be full of water. If it is for drainage it will probably be empty for much of the time. However when operating at full capacity or when used for supply it will probably be full and the water may be stationery or moving through it. The problem of making pipes is thus how to create a long tube that keeps the water in and is strong enough to resist breaking from the ground pressure above and from the water itself. As such tubes are of a finite length, the problem of making pipes is also the problem of joining those pipes together to form a pipeline without the water leaking out at the joints, which are inevitably weaker than the pipe itself and in providing an airtight seal at those points. Pipes need valves and taps (faucets) but these are not the subject of the current paper. What is of interest here is purely the pipe and the pipeline it is used to make. Pipes are discussed (usually in passing) in books on water supply and drainage.

Introduction

The literature on water supply is very extensive and too large to give but the briefest of summaries here. A good reasonable introduction can be found in Steven Solomon's *Water* [1]. The *Evolution of Water Supply Through the Millennia* [2] provides a good overview through the ages, with papers written by experts in each field. It lacks an overall bibliography, but the key works can be found in the notes in each section. This provides a good survey of the archaeological evidence for the pre-Roman period. A.Trevor Hodge's *Roman Aqueducts and Water Supply* remains the best source book for Roman water supply [3]. David Yeomans elsewhere in this current volume of proceedings notes its occasional lapse in technical understanding of hydrodynamics, but in terms of history and archaeology it remains sound and by far the best introduction. More recent research on Roman topics can be found in *Evolution of Water Supply Through the Millennia* cited above. Roberta J.Magnusson, *Water Technology in the Middle Ages* remains the best introduction to medieval water supply [4]. It has an excellent bibliography and much of the key information is in the notes. See also K. Grewe (ed), *Die Wasserversorgung im Mittelalter* [5] in the series of books produced on water supply by the Frontinus Society in Germany, which is the most important society for the study of water supply [6].

Because each of these texts concentrates on a particular period, none of them provides a summary across periods, so this is what the current paper sets out to do. The aim is to provide a very basic summary of early pipe technology from the

The Development of Water Pipes: a Brief History from Ancient Times until 1800

first pipes to the eighteenth century- that is ending before the mechanisation of pipe manufacturing that would begin the extrusion of ceramic pipes in the nineteenth century and the later extension of extrusion technology to metal pipe mass production which is a different story deserving of a paper in its own right. Pipes before mass production were made in seven materials: stone, terracotta, copper, lead, timber, brass/bronze and iron. Each will be examined in turn, each section attempting to identify when the materials were first used, how the pipes were made and the various types found and their uses for dating. The paper is organised roughly chronologically, with the earliest material first, although all these materials had a long usage, so once invented they carried on being used in various regions throughout the period.

Stone Pipes and Conduits

As we know that the Neolithic age predates the invention of ceramics, it might be assumed that the first pipes were in stone not clay. In fact, while the earliest settlements often required drainage and irrigation and occasionally this involved cutting channels in stone, these are invariably conduits or tunnels, not pipes. A conduit is an open topped trough through which water flows. It can be covered by a flat slab to create a covered waterway, but this is not a pipe. Many aqueducts from ancient times used stone conduits. Tunnels through rock also date from remarkably early periods, being covered conduits carved from solid rock, large enough for a man to crawl through. Hezekiah's tunnel in Jerusalem [7], the qnats in Iran [8] and the Epauline tunnel in Samos [9] are all early examples. Pipes are not tunnels or conduits. They are made in sections. A pipe is usually tubular on the inside (the external shape is irrelevant).

Manufacture

It is extremely difficult to create pipes out of stone. It involves boring or carving a hole through a block. This was time-consuming before the invention of metal tools and powered drills. Even when it could be achieved the joints were difficult to make. While stone pipes are not as common as pipes in other materials, there are still a remarkable number of examples. While other types of pipe tend to be cylindrical on the outside, stone pipes were often square in section with a cylindrical hole drilled down the middle. Where they were cylindrical on the outside this was to reduce weight which was a significant problem. A continual problem with stone pipes was pore selection of stone which subsequently proved to be porous and thus led to water loss (see below).

Examples

Perhaps surprisingly most stone pipes date from the Roman period where they were used in aqueducts. Stone pipes have been found in Amathus in Cyprus [10]. The site dates back to the Classical Period (750-325BC) but the pipes are probably related to the Roman repairs and improvements carried out after the earthquake in 77/78. The pipes are carved by hand with an internal dimension of 240mm and an external dimension of 700mm. The walls of the pipe are thus comparatively thick (220mm+) so that the pipe remains structurally sound. The pipes have a projecting rim on the male side which connects with a recessed edge on the other, the joints being sealed with lime mortar. Occasion rectangular holes in the upper surface allow air pockets to be removed. These stone pipes were part of a much larger water system and aqueduct which also used terracotta pipes. The stone pipes were used in the last section closest to the fountain. The reason for their use here is unclear. Perhaps they were thought to offer greater resistance to tremors. Stone pipes were also sometimes found in Roman aqueduct siphons, built into the structure and the Roman also used them occasionally for 90 degree joints in terracotta pipelines and in very short lengths as outlets in fountains. The principle use of stone pipes in Roman times was in aqueducts, particularly for siphons. Hodge provides a great many examples with pictures [11]. Particularly worth noting are Cadiz in Spain; Aspendos and Patara in Turkey; Zadar in Croatia; and the Bethlehem Siphon in Israel (sections of which are preserved and on display in the Museum of Israel). The Cadiz blocks are typical- they 860 x 800 x 280-

500mm and similarly had projecting rims. The holes to create the pipe were drilled and were 220-250mm in diameter [12].

Fig.1 Roman stone pipe from Bethlehem (photo by Ian Scott, commons licence

https://commons.wikimedia.org/wiki/File:Roman_water_pipes_(3743430835).jpg)

The stone pipes are also occasionally found in later periods, although they are generally rare, no doubt due to the difficulty of their manufacture. For instance, in the Middle Ages stone pipes are recorded for wall of Mildenburg, in Miltenberg, dating from before the 14th century and possibly even re-used from much earlier [13]. The stone pipes specified for use in Renaissance Rome were notable failures. In June 1571, Guilielmo della Porta began constructing a new trunk line in a type of travertine made out of "stone from the Orta quarry" which he described as "a type of travertine" [14]. The pipes were in three sizes, 1.3m, 1.8,m and 2.7m in length and 350mm in bore [15]. Problems became immediately apparent when tests were carried out in October 1571 on the first 100m laid and the pipes were found to "leak like a sieve" [16]. Elsewhere in this volume Dermot O'Dwyer discusses the manufacture of stone pipes by William Colles (1702-1770) in Kilkenny in the 18th century and how these were also unsuccessful. Similarly Victorian stone pipes are also on display in the Manchester Museum from the ill-fated Stone Pipe Company that in 1812 won the contract to supply pipes for the Manchester Water Company that proved too porous to use [17]. All these, however, are rare examples. Stone was difficult to make into pipes and the resulting sections were heavy. Clay and terracotta was lighter, cheaper and easier to use.

The Development of Water Pipes: a Brief History from Ancient Times until 1800

Terracotta Water Pipes

Throughout the world, from the earliest periods, pipes were created out of fired clay and ceramic water pipes of stoneware or terracotta remain in use to this day. Whilst today ceramic water pipes tend to be used for drainage systems and sewers, in the earlier examples they were used for water supply as well as water removal. The earliest known fired clay pipes are found in the Bronze Age with well-recorded examples in Mesopotamia, Mohenjo-Daro in the Indus Valley, and in Minoan Crete. Such systems were also widely used in Mesopotamia and in Archaic and Classical Greece, in Egypt and in China. They seem to have been less common in early settlements in North and South America.

Manufacture

It is possible to make clay pipes by rolling clay flat and then winding it round a central wooden form but it is difficult to form the seam. A more practical method is to roll the clay by hand and bend the rolls into loops and put the loops on top of each other, smoothing out the ridges by hand. Such pipes are rough on the inside and irregular in shape. For this reason, although occasionally found, the method was rarely used and most clay pipes seem to have been generally made on a potter's wheel. The potter's wheel seems to have been in use in Sumeria and the Indus valley around 3500 BC which coincides with the earliest pipes.

Pipes are made in exactly the same way as pots or vases. The clay is spun and lifted into the tubular shape. When complete, the base is removed with a knife and the finished pipe lifted off. The use of a wheel puts a practical limit on the length of pipe that can be produced, which is roughly 300-500mm long. This meant that, before machine production, clay pipelines had to have many joints and the pipes had to be designed to fit together as tightly as possible to avoid leakage. The diameter is typically 100-150mm. Very occasionally clay pipes were made by re-using other vessels: for example, in Bibracte, in Burgundy in France, a Roman pipeline is made entirely from re-used amphorae with their tops and bottoms sawn off [18]. As they tapered they fit into each other. The typical bore is up to 110mm [19]. The clay was fired in pottery kilns. No evidence has been found that specific kilns were set up for pipes, the presumption being that pipes were made and fired alongside other types of pottery vessels, the technology being the same and the size (before mass production) comparable. Glazing seems to have been applied to interior surfaces from early periods but more study needs to be done on how this was carried out. Glazing is rarely mentioned in texts. The easiest method, salt-glazing, damaged kilns and thus salt-glazed pipes would have been made alongside other salt-glazed products, but I have not seen this mentioned in existing texts.

Jointing

The making of clay pipes on wheels menat that lengths tended to be short and there were many joints. The four basic forms of clay pipe are found. The simplest type are conical. In this form, each pipe is inserted in the next in the direction of flow. In the second type, a projecting flange on one end fits into a flared end at the other. In the third socket type the pipe is outer surface of the pipe slightly recessed at one end, fitting snugly into the normal end of the pipe at the other. Lastly there is the form found commonly today, called the bell and spigot where the end of the pipe flares out in bell shape, into which the other regular end of the tube fits. All types of joint will be caulked with mortar. The Romans used a mixture of lime putty and oil.

Some Early Examples

There is some discussion over the identification of the first clay water pipes. It is doubtful that there was a single source: it is more likely that the same idea rose to prominence at about the same time in a number of regions, not long after the invention of the potters wheel that made the manufacture of pipes a realistic possibility. Certainly there are surviving ceramic pipes found in a number of sites in ancient Mesopotamia [20]. At more or less the same time extensive terracotta pipe systems were employed at Mohenjo Daro in the Indus Valley, where the water system was so complex that it included large pools or baths [21]. Early Minoan Crete (3200-2300 BC) developed a sophisticated water system which included wells, cisterns, piped water and aqueducts [22]. Those in Knossos were conical in design, about 800mm long and 170mm at the widest end, tapering to 85mm at the narrow end. As Angelaskis et al. observe, this shape was inefficient in terms of water flow but made the pipes easier to make and seal [23]. The Ancient Greeks used conical pipes but they also used cylindrical ones. For instance, examples in the aqueduct at Naxos constructed in the late sixth century BC are jointed using sockets [24]. In China stoneware and terracotta pipes were used extensively from the time of the first Emperor onwards [25]. The earliest examples from the 3rd century BC from buildings near the tomb of the first emperor in Lintung are pentagonal in cross section (and thus made by hand by folding a flat sheet), but elsewhere conventional cylindrical pipes were normal. These had socket joints [26]. The Romans took and developed Greek water technology to a new level of sophistication. Roman terracotta pipes are made in variety of forms with the most sophisticated have bell and spigot joints sealed with lime mortar and sometimes with lead [27]. Earthenware pipes continued in use throughout the Middle Ages, particularly for drains, while lead or wood piping was more popular for supply [28].

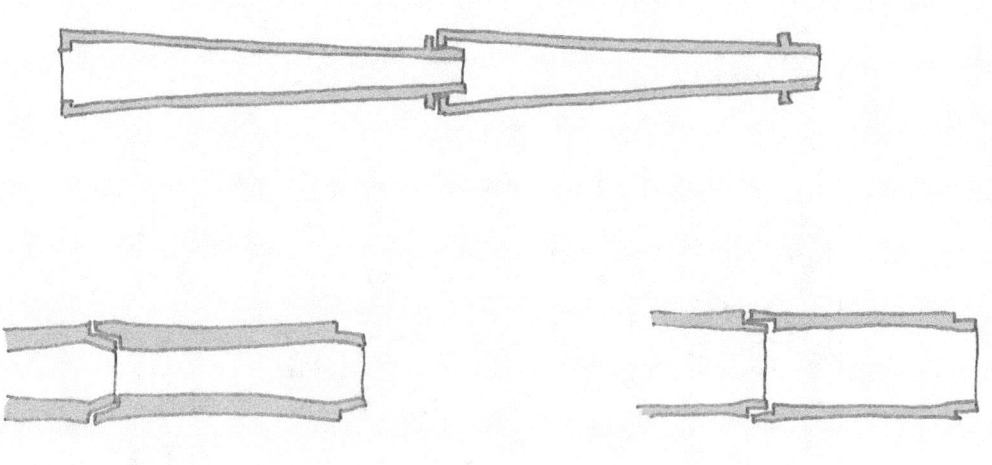

Fig. 2 Three sets of pipes from the ancient world showing the sophistication of jointing systems. Top: pipes from the palace of Knossos, Crete, which was constructed around 1600BC. Earlier pipes were often simply conical but these have complicated joints. The bottom two examples are from Athens and Corinth, possibly both Roman in period.

Industrialisation

Remarkably few innovations were made in the manufacture of ceramic pipes before the 19th century. The horse drawn pugmill, invented in the late 18th century, helped to improve the quality of clay. The horse driven pugmill led in the 1840s to the first patents for horse driven extruded pipe machinery which appeared at this time in the UK and US and would rapidly replace traditional handmade pipes [29].

Timber pipes

Today we find it difficult to understand how timber can ever have been considered suitable for making pipes but from Roman times timber pipes were routinely used. In the Medieval period timber pipelines were the most common and timber pipes were still being used in gardens for water and fountains well into the 18th century where they are frequently found in accounts and occasionally dug up. Examples can be seen in Museums all over the world [30]. Urban timber water supply systems included New York and London [31].

Manufacture

The manufacture of timber pipes is illustrated in Agricola [32] and this illustration is often featured in articles on the subject and reprinted here.

Fig. 3. Carpenter boring wooden pipes. Image from Agricola's De Re Metallica (1556)

Large trunks from trees are sawn down, the outer branches are removed but otherwise the outside can often be left relatively unfinished. Trunks are chosen that are particularly straight. The trunk is secured to keep it completely still and then an auger is used to bore out a hole through the centre. The two ends are more carefully worked to produce a projecting flange on one end and a corresponding rebate on the other. Joints in Roman times were often reinforced with iron collars (short iron pipes) fitted into the internal edges of the pipe between pipes. These are often the only surviving evidence of the wooden pipe [33]. Pliny notes that pipes are normally made of oak, but pitch pine and alder are also suitable [34]. Elm was also used in the Middle Ages [35]. Sizes varied accordingly to the trees available. Timber pipes could be used for larger bore pipes over 100mm diameter, whereas terracotta pipes were rarely over 100mm and lead ones generally about 40mm. In the 19th century in the US pipes were also manufactured using wooden staves bound together like barrels [36].

Examples

It is not clear when timber was first used. Timber does rot so evidence in archaeological remains is often difficult to find. It has been estimated that the typical useful lifespan of the Medieval pipe was 10-40 years [37]. The pipes last well if the wood can be completely saturated, but that requires quite high pressures [38]. In Roman times timber pipelines tended to be used outside major towns in rural areas and encampments, presumably where timber was plentiful [39]. In towns, the Romans generally preferred terracotta or lead [40]. The great advantage of timber pipelines was that the pieces of pipe could be as long as the tree trunk - lengths in Roman times were typically in the range 1.5-7metres - and this meant fewer joints [41]. What is remarkable is the continued use of timber pipes well into the 18th century. The pipes in many gardens driving fountains were timber, which implies that they could used under pressure, although generally lead would be used close to the fountain head and where areas needed to resist higher pressures. Timber pipes were used both at Sanssouci in Potsdam [42] and at Hellbrunn, Austria where they can be seen on display in the museum in the house.

In China, it was common to use bamboo [43]. Strictly speaking bamboo is a grass, not a timber. Its huge advantages were that it was hollow (although the dividing walls internally still need to be removed) and that it grows extremely fast, ensuring a ready supply. It is also light. However in tropical climates where it typically grows it tends to deteriorate quite fast so bamboo pipelines were typically supported on bamboo trestles above ground where the line could be continuously examined an maintained. Bamboo water systems were certainly in use in palaces and elsewhere from the Han Dynasty (202-220AD) [44].

Metal Pipes

Metal pipes have been used from ancient times. They are more expensive than timber or ceramic pipes but they can be made in greater lengths and can be made considerably stronger than other materials. Historically the chief materials used in water supply are: lead copper; brass or bronze; and iron.

Lead Pipes

Lead is a soft heavy metal which can be easily worked cold with a hammer and this made it perfect for the creation of complex pipes, connections, boxes and gutters. It was never a cheap metal and throughout the ages subject to theft or removal when buildings were abandoned. It was so common that we derive our word plumber from the Latin word for lead, *plumbum*.

Manufacture

Lead has a relatively low melting point and can thus be easily cast into thin sheets. These could then be bent by hand and using a soft mallet round a timber or brass mandrel while still warm. In fact the metal is so soft it could continue to be shaped at room temperature. The resulting tubular shape would have two edges that needed to be joined at a seam. This was sealed with molten lead. The usual Roman method was to make a prominent seam and then bore the lead on top using clay ridges to keep the molten material in place until it set. The resulting pipe was egg-shaped but the pressure of the water quickly re-shaped the interior to a perfect circle. Joints were formed by overlapping and similarly pouring molten lead round the joint to form a seal. By this relatively simple method a completely air-tight pipeline could be created which could create siphons, feed fountains and generally resist pressure [45]. There are some examples of cast lead piping [46]. The technology was not complicated but the folded sheet method remained by far the most common method up until the nineteenth century. In the Renaissance lead became common for rainwater drainpipes on the side of buildings. The seam was hidden at the back.

The Development of Water Pipes: a Brief History from Ancient Times until 1800

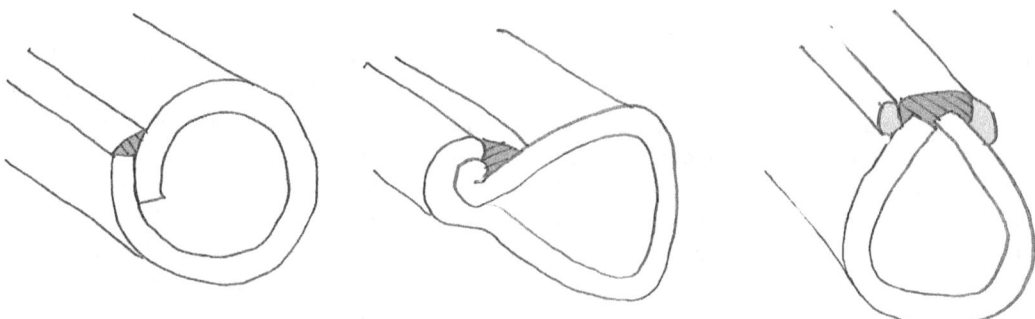

Fig. 4 Manufacture of lead pipes. The lead is folded round a mandrel (a wooden rod). The joint is formed either by pouring molten lead in the bare seam (left), folding the seam on itself and pouring the molten lean in the gap (centre) or in the manner favoured by the Romans, using two beads of clay to form a trough and pouring lead in to seal the two butt jointed ends (right). The irregular shape of the pipe corrects when water is passed through it under pressure to a round shape (author).

Examples

Lead was the material of choice for pipes in Roman times [47]. Frontinus even gives the standard sizes of pipes to be used in ancient Rome [48]. Lead continued to be used throughout the Middle Ages in Western Europe, where monasteries often contained surprisingly sophisticated water systems for which plans have survived [49]. Urban systems in the Middle Ages sometimes relied on timber but monastic systems, perhaps reflecting the greater wealth of the church, were generally in lead. The use of lead became widespread when domestic water supplies grew in the nineteenth century so that in most areas of North America and Western Europe had drinking water supplied through lead pipes until the end of the 1960s.

The issue of poisoning

No discussion of lead piping can avoid touching on the issue of lead poisoning. The subject has particularly exercised those looking at ancient Rome. The Romans were aware of the risks of lead poisoning and Vitruvius discusses it [50]. Although some scholars have made claims that lead poisoning from the water supply caused major health damage in Rome [51], the general consensus is that the build up of limescale would have prevented it being an issue in the water supply and various other sources have been pointed at to explain those cases recorded [52]. There is medical evidence however that the Romans did suffer from the effects of lead [53] so the jury is out on whether the source was lead piping or something else. A good summary of the discussions on both sides can be found in the paper by Monica Aneni [54]. The widespread use of lead piping in the 19th and 20th century in water supply installations continues to be a health concern in modern day America where many people are still drawing from theses supplies.

Copper

The earliest known example of copper piping was found in Ancient Egypt. Copper pipes are recorded in Mortuary Temple of King Sahura at Abusir dating from 2500BC. In this complex there was a system for draining off rainwater but there was also an elaborate system of water supply for five limestone basins each of which had a lead plug to stop the water flowing out attached to a brass ring pull. The drains for these basins consisted of copper pipes, the total system being over 1330ft (405m) long. Only one piece of pipe was fully intact. It was mortared into groove in the stonework. It was formed from a thin copper sheet 1.6mm thick that had been bent around a wooden mandrel to create a 48mm bore pipe, the seam being simply bent over and hammered flat without any soldering [55]. Copper bowls are well recorded in Egyptian work but this is a rare (possibly unique) surviving example of the use of copper for piping.

Despite this early occurrence, copper piping is not widely reported elsewhere in ancient times and indeed is not found in Roman work or in the Middle Ages. There is one account of it being used in China for water supply in the Ming Dynasty in Nanjing in the Wumiao Sluice which also had iron pipes [56]. There is however no mention of the use of copper pipes in Gwilt's Encyclopedia of Architecture (1872) which gives an extensive account of the use of lead piping and an account of copper for roofing [57]. Copper sheet was increasingly used for roofing from the 17th century onwards.

Despite its early use in Egypt at Abusir, copper piping seems to have only caught on again in the early twentieth century. It started being used in the UK for hot water systems in parts of the country with soft water which corroded lead pipes [58]. The reasons why it was not commonly used may lie in the problems associated with manufacturing satisfactory pipes in copper before mechanisation. A chapter in Sutcliffe's *Modern Plumber* describes how the pipes are cast but then need to be rolled while on a mandrel as otherwise the pipes are "spongy" and unsatisfactory [59]. By the early 20th century this could be done by machine. By the end of the twentieth century concerns about lead poisoning had led to the widespread adoption of copper piping for hot and cold drinking water supply in the UK and elsewhere.

Brass and Bronze

Neither brass nor bronze were used to make pipes but they were commonly used to make taps and valves in pipework systems. They were also used to create the spouts for fountains where a hard or decorative material was required. The bronze or brass was cast in a mould made for the purpose. Examples of bronze spouts can be found in many museums throughout the world from the Roman period onwards. It used to claim that the Madradag siphon built by Eumenes II (197-159 BC) at Pergamon was contructed using bronze pipes but testing of the soil in 1976 showed that the pipes were lead [60].

Iron Pipes

Short iron pipes had been used to join wooden pipes (collars) in Roman times (see above) and there is a suggestion of iron pipes in China in the Ming period (see above). However iron was not generally used in pipemaking in quantity in Europe before the Renaissance. Cast iron pipes were famously used in very large numbers to provide water for the fountains of Versailles. These pipes are well-recorded and indeed much of the system still survives in operation to this day. The pipes are in stone conduits. While this was a hugely expensive arrangement it was considered essential to allow regular maintenance and inspection. The chief problem was with the joints. The cast iron pipes used at Versailles were in short lengths (1m), bolted together with flanges, the joint being sealed with leather or lead gaskets [61]. It is often assumed in the literature that these were the first cast iron pipes used and this may indeed have been believed at the time, but iron founding began in the Middle Ages and it would perhaps not be surprising if earlier iron pipes appeared in areas known for iron making.

The Development of Water Pipes: a Brief History from Ancient Times until 1800

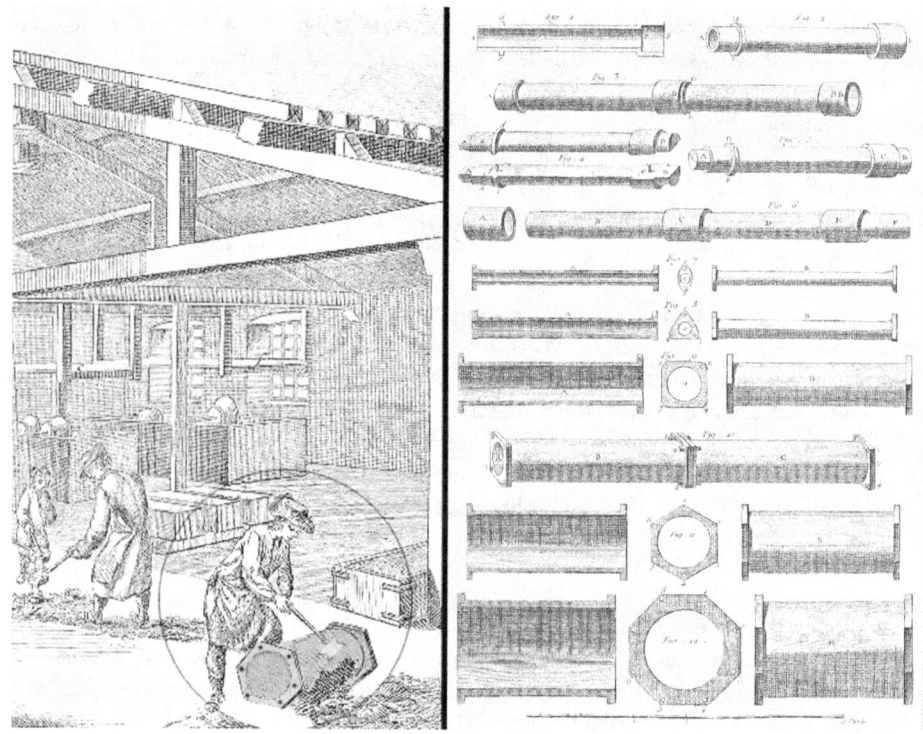

Fig. 5 Two pages from Diderot's Encyclodpedia (1777) showing (on the left) the finishing of an iron pipe which has just emerged from the mould. The pipe is similar to those used at Versailles. On the right is a page showing different forms of pipe joint and iron pipe used in the late 18th century.

There is considerable debate in the literature about when the first cast pipes were made and it is fair to say that there is currently no agreement. It terms of technology, it was certainly theoretically possible to cast pipes from the 15th century when the techniques were used to make cannons and shot, however it would seem unlikely that just because the technology was there it was immediately applied to pipes when other technologies were well-established. The earliest known example of an iron pipe dates from 1455 found in excavation of the Medieval remains of Dillenburg Castle [62]. These iron pipes were similar in form to clay examples in terms of jointing. There may be other isolated examples in iron-making areas but it seems likely that iron pipes were extremely rare before Versailles and that the production facilities set up to produce the very extensive pipework at Versailles led to the development of the technology and the continued us in 18th century France and its diffusion elsewhere. Certainly the manufacture of iron pipes was sufficiently widespread in the 18th century for Diderot and Alembert to include descriptions of the process in the Encyclopedia [63]. It was only in the 19th century that iron pipes started to be used in very large quantities for urban water supply, supplanting timber and lead pipes.

Manufacture

Pipes were cast from iron in wet sand held in boxes. The technology was familiar from canon manufacturing. Molten iron was pored into moulds. The whole process is illustrated in detail in the Encyclopedia which includes diagrams of how to make simple pipes and more complex junctions [64].

Conclusion

The development of pipes, as can be seen in this paper, was like so many areas, one of step changes, where many technologies are established early on and then remained in use continuously with minor improvements in manufacturing and form being introduced over time. Contrary to intuition, the earliest closed pipes were ceramic, rather than in stone. Stone pipes were used but were comparatively rare. Clay pipes were much more common. More work needs to be done on the types of clay pipes, their jointing and shapes, and whether they were glazed, and, if so, how. Timber and lead pipes were both used in Roman times but almost certainly were in use much earlier elsewhere. The lack of survival of timber pipes is a problem. Lead has survived better and was used more widely than one might expect, particularly in the Middle Ages. More work needs to be done on when the first complete pipes were cast from lead rather than the pipes being made from folded sheets. Copper, despite its common use today, was rarely used. There is one known instance in Ancient Egypt and some evidence that it may have been used in China. This may be a problem of survival, however, it seems likely that copper piping was rarely used at all in Europe before the 19th century. Similarly bronze piping was not used despite claims otherwise. Bronze was, however, used for spouts and valves. Iron pipes appear in the 15th and 16th century but only in very rare cases. They remain rare even after their well-publicised use at Versailles in the 17th century and really only become common in the 19th century when ductile cast iron allows for easier manufacture in greater lengths. Early cast iron was useful for its strength and thus typically appears in those areas where pressures were known to be very high. Nevertheless timber and lead piping predominated in the 17th and 18th century. This paper has touched on the changes that came about in the 19th century. This is an area that certainly warrants further research and one or more papers exploring how mass-production techniques changed the way pipes were made and thus used in the 19th and 20th century. These changes included the ability to extrude and roll pipes and the introduction of completely new materials (most notably steel, and plastics).

References

[1] S. Solomon, *Water: the Epic Struggle for Wealth, Power and Civilisation.* London: Harper Colins, 2010. See also Brain Fagan, *Elixir: a History of Water and Humankind.* London: Bloomsbury, 2011.

[2] A. Angelakis, L.Mays, D.Koutsoyiannis and N.Mamassis, *Evolution of Water Supply Through the Millennia.* London: IWA, 2012

[3] A. Trevor Hodge, *Roman Aqueducts and Water Supply.* Bristol: Bristol Classics Press, 2011, 2nd edn.

[4] R.J.Magnusson, *Cities, Monasteries and Waterworks after the Roman Empire* London and Baltimore: John Hopkins Press, 2001.

[5] P. von Zabern (ed), *Die Wasserversorgung im Mittelalter*, Mainz am Rhein: Verlag Philip von Zabern, 1991.

[6] For a full list of publications see https://www.frontinus.de. Their newsletter published a paper on pipes (K. A.Tietze, " Vom Blasrohr zur Kontinental-Pipeline" *Frontinus-Schriftenreihe*, Heft 3 (1980), 11-31) which unfortunately I have been unable to access in preparation of this paper. This is the only previous paper I have been able to find on the subject. The same volume contains two papers on wooden pipes, which likewise have not been accessed in preparation of this paper.

[7] A. Frumkin and A.Shimron, "Tunnel engineering in the Iron Age: Geoarchaeology of the Siloam Tunnel, Jerusalem", *Journal of Archaeological Science*, 33 no.2 (2006), 227–237. doi:10.1016/j.jas.2005.07.018

[8] For articles on qanats see J. Charbonnier, K.A.Hopper (eds), Special Issue: The Qanāt: Archaeology and Environment, *Water History*, Vol.10 No.1 (March 2018), *passim.*

[9] Angelakis, et al., (Note 2), pp. 85–87, 264, 355, 407.

[10] C.A. Kambanellas, "Historical Development of water supply in Cyprus" in Angelakis, et al., (Note 2), pp. 301-317, pp.306-308

[11] Hodge, (Note 3), pp.107-109.
[12] See http://www.romanaqueducts.info/aquasite/index.html: Cadiz for photographs and statistics. Accessed 1 July 2021.
[13] K.Grewe, "Wasserversorgung und-entsorgung im Mittelalter", in K.Grewe (ed.) *Die Wasserversorgung in Mittelalter*, Mainz: Verlag Philipp von Zabern, 1991, pp. 37-38.
[14] K.Rinne, *Water of Rome: Aqueducts, Fountains and the Birth of the Baroque City*, London: Yale, 2010, p.74.
[15] ibid.
[16] ibid.
[17] For a picture of the pipe see http://scienticity.net/efs/efsfetch.php?id=3660356086&s =025b459ce3&., accessed 1 July 2021. The exhibit is reviewed in Hamlin, Christopher. "'Underground Manchester' at the Greater Manchester Museum of Science and Industry." *Technology and Culture*, vol. 32, no. 1, 1991, pp. 97–101. JSTOR, www.jstor.org/stable/3106012. Accessed 10 Aug. 2021.
[18] Hodge, (Note 3), pp.114.
[19] Magnusson, (Note 4), p.77.
[20] A. Tamburrino, "Water Technology in Ancient Mesopotamia" in L.Mays (ed.) *Ancient Water Technologies*, London: Springer, 2010, 29-51, p.40-41; A.Neuburger, *The Technical Arts and Sciences of the Ancients*, London: Methuen, 1969, p.411
[21] M.Jansen, "Water Supply and Sewage Disposal at Mohenjo-Daro", *World Archaeology: the Archaeology of Public Health*, 21 (21), 177-192, p.190.
[22] A.Angelakis, et al., "Evolution of water supply technologies through the ages in Crete, Greece," in A.Angelakis, et al., (Note 2), pp.225-258, pp.234-235
[23] ibid.
[24] N.Zarkadoulas, D. Koutsoyiannis, N.Mamassis and A.Agrelakis, "A brief history of urban water management in ancient Greece", in A.Angelakis, et al., (Note 2), pp.259-270,-p.265
[25] J. Needham and W. Ling, *Science and Civilisation in China: Volume 4: Physics and Physical Technology Part II Mechanical Engineering*, Cambridge: CUP, 1965, 127-134, p.130.
[26] ibid.
[27] Hodge, (Note 3), pp.111-115.
[28] Magnusson, (Note 4), pp.72-76.
[29] The story of the introduction of extruded pipes is found in Kathleen Watt, 'Making drain tiles a "home manufacture", Agricultural Consumers and the Social Construction of Clayworking Technology in the 1840s', *Rural History*, 13 (2002), 39 - 60.
[30] For instance, Abbey Mills pumping station museum, London see http://www.sewerhistory.org/photosgraphics/pipes-wood/, accessed 13 July 2021. This site also has illustrations of stave pipes made from multiple pieces of timber held together with iron hoops.
[31] For London see J-C Shulman, *The Tale of Three Thirsty Cities*, Leiden: Brill, 2018, p.221; for New York see J.Goldman, *Bulding New York's Sewers*, West Layfayette: Purdue University Press, 1997, p.16.
[32] G.Agricola, *De Re Metallica*, Basel, 1556, trans. HC.Hoover and L.H.Hoover, New York: Dover, 1950, p.177.
[33] Illustrated in Agricola. For survival see Hodge, (Note 3), p.112.
[34] Pliny, *Natural History*, XVI, 81.
[35] Magnusson, (Note 4), p.76.
[36] For plans and photographs of stave pipes for sewers see http://www.sewerhistory.org/photosgraphics/pipes-wood/, accessed 13 July 2021.
[37] Magnusson, (Note 4), p.78.
[38] *ibid.*
[39] Hodge, (Note 3), pp.111.
[40] *ibid.* pp.315.
[41] *ibid.* pp.112

[42] R.Calinger, *Leonhard Euler*, Princeton: Princeton University Press, 2016, p.311
[43] J. Needham and W. Ling, (Note 24), pp.128-29.
[44] *ibid.*
[45] For a detailed explanation of the process of manufacturing and excellent diagrams see Hodge, (Note 3), pp.307-320.
[46] K.Grewe, (Note 12), p.41
[47] Hodge, (Note 3), p.307
[48] See J.Gelder, Roman Services and Architectural Manuals, in J.Campbell et. al., *Studies in the History Services and Construction History*, Cambridge: Construction History Society, 2018, 31-42, pp.33-35.
[49] See Magnusson, (Note 4), and Grewe, (Note 12), passim.
[50] Vitruvius, *De Architectura*, VIII.6.10-11
[51] J.O. Nriagu, "Occupational exposure to lead in ancient times", *Sci. Total Environ.* 32 (1983), 105-116.
[52] J. Scarborough, "The Myth of Lead Poisoning Among the Romans: An Essay Review", *Journal of the History of Medicine*, 39 (1984), 469-475.
[53] See J. Moore, *Death Metal: Characterising the effects of environmental lead pollution on mobility and childhood health within the Roman Empire*, PhD Thesis, Durham University 2019, available at http://etheses.dur.ac.uk/13292/1/Death_Metal_eThesis_.pdf?DDD6+, accessed 1 July 2021.
[54] M.Aneni, "Lead poisoning in Ancient Rome", *Nigeria and the Classics*, Vol 23, 2007, pp. 92-103, available at https://www.researchgate.net/publication/325023100_Lead_Poisoning_in_Ancient_Rome, accessed 1 July 2021.
[55] The description of the pipe is found in A.Neuberger, *The Technical Arts and Sciences of the Ancients,* Barnes and Noble, New York, trans. Henry L.Brose from orig. 1930, 1969, p.439-440 and references the original archaeological excavation by Borchardt.
[56] P.Du and A.Koenig, "A History of Water Supply in pre-modern China", in A. Angelakis, L.Mays, D.Koutsoyiannis and N.Mamassis, *Evolution of Water Supply Through the Millennia.* London: IWA, 2012, 169-226, p.179.
[57] J.Gwilt, *An Encylcopedia of Architecture..revised by Wyatt Papworth*, London: Longmans, 1872, Bk.II, pp.608-610.
[58] G.L. Sutcliffe, *The Modern Plumber and Sanitary Engineer,* Gresham: London, 1909, vol. 1, pp.20-23, 89.
[59] *Ibid.* pp.20-23.
[60] Hodge, (Note 3), p.43.
[61] M.Tournier, *Versailles: the fountains of the Sun King,* Les Loges-en-Joas: JDG, 2000, p.32. Tounrier claims these were the first iron pipes but this is no longer thought to be the case.
[62] Grewe, (Note 12), p.40.
[63] The relevant sections are reproduced in [D.Diderot and Alembert], *L'Encyclodpédie Dierdot et D'Alembert: Forges ou L'Art de Fer,* Paris: Inter-livres, 1988, Plates IX-XII
[64] ibid.

Stonecutting in Maya Architecture: The Palace of the Governor at Uxmal (Yucatan, Mexico)

Ana Laura Rosado-Torres, Laura Gilabert-Sansalvador and Riccardo Montuori
PEGASO Research Centre, Universitat Politècnica de València, Spain

Introduction

The ancient Maya civilisation developed in Mesoamerica between BC 1500 and AD 1500, the and reached an advanced understanding of various fields of knowledge, still visible today in its many architectural remains. Maya architecture has been studied from many disciplinary perspectives, including some architectural surveys, which have made it possible to identify regional differences in its architecture in terms of typological, aesthetic, and formal development. As a result, different architectural styles are currently associated with specific geographical areas, such as the Puuc architecture located in the Yucatan Peninsula, where a long building tradition has been revealed.

From the first Early Oxkintok architectural style to the last one, called Late Uxmal, the evolution of architecture in the Puuc region reveals the degree of sophistication achieved by Maya stonemasons, who developed great proficiency in stonecutting techniques, resulting in the skilful carving of the specialised pieces that make up the buildings erected during the Late Classic period (AD 750-1000).

Some of the most remarkable examples of stonemasonry can be seen in the later buildings of the ancient Maya city of Uxmal (Fig. 1), and yet there is still a lack of in-depth studies of their construction techniques and stereotomy. To address this issue, we have selected the Palace of the Governor, a Puuc palace in the Late Uxmal architectural style built around AD 900, for detailed study.

Figure 1: Geographic location of Uxmal within the Puuc Region of the Yucatan Peninsula, Mexico. Drawing: Laura Gilabert-Sansalvador and Riccardo Montuori, 2021

Stonecutting in Maya Architecture: The Palace of the Governor at Uxmal (Yucatan, Mexico)

Based on the chart of specialised stones necessary for the construction of a Classic Puuc type building drawn up by George F. Andrews [1], a similar one has been created for the south façade of the South Wing of the Palace of the Governor, with the aim of both assessing the degree of standardisation attained in its erection, and outlining and implementing a new methodology for the study of stonecutting techniques within Maya architecture.

The results presented in this paper are part of ongoing research, so that the data presented below represents preliminary results of an analysis of the stonemasonry of this unique edifice. This work is part of a thesis that aims to introduce a novel line of research which studies Maya architecture from the point of view of stereotomy.

Puuc Architecture

There are significant differences in the architecture of each geographical zone of the Maya area, particularly in terms of construction technology. The characteristics of the stone material, the systems used for its extraction, the development of the quality of the mortars and the advances in stonecutting techniques in each geographical area determined the particularities of the architecture of each region and its evolution over time, conditioning in many cases the architectural and stylistic features of the buildings, which were often determined more by constructive than aesthetic issues. [2]

The architecture of some geographical areas of the Maya area has been the subject of more specific studies. Such is the case of the architecture of the Puuc region, in which the study of its construction technology has been specifically dealt with, above all in terms of stylistic classification and dating.

Unlike other Maya architecture, the construction of the Puuc is the reflection of a long construction tradition in which there is clear evidence of the evolution of its construction systems, going from the construction systems of the corbelled to the veneer type, which are finely carved specialised pieces that function as lost, and at the same time permanent, formwork for the resistant fillings of this architecture, elaborated in limestone. With this technological development, the Puuc Maya achieved ever wider and higher interior spaces and ever more refined stone surfaces, which required only a thin layer of stucco facing. In addition, Puuc architecture is well known for its builders' mastery of carved stone mosaic decoration and its characteristic geometric iconographic motifs.

Puuc Architectural Styles

The 1930s saw the emergence of an interest in multidisciplinary studies in the field of Mesoamerican architecture. The first architectural studies in the Puuc region of the Maya area were conducted [3]. Pollock was the first one to propose a stylistic classification in temporal phases using the architectural characteristics of the buildings he surveyed in the 1940s. For each proposed phase or style (Early Oxkintok, Proto-Puuc, Early Puuc and Classic Puuc) he defined the formal and constructive characteristics of the different parts of the building [4].

Pollock's research was later extended by George F. Andrews and Geraldine Andrews . On the basis of a field study conducted for between 1965 and 1990 in the Maya area, Andrews characterised and classified the buildings surveyed, based on 13 architectural elements: Base, Lower Wall, Wall Construction, Doorways, Doorjambs, Medial Mouldings, Upper Wall Zones, Cornice Mouldings, Roof Combs, Vaults and Beams, Vault Construction, Cordholders & Rodholders, and Decoration.

In addition to narrowing the stylistic chronological dating previously proposed by Pollock, Andrews' studies added three sub-styles within Classic Puuc architecture (AD 770-1050). Thus, Andrews proposes the following classification of architectural styles: Early Oxkintok, Proto-Puuc, Early Puuc, Classic Puuc Junquillo, Classic Puuc Mosaic, and Late Uxmal [5].

The Palace of the Governor: A Masterpiece of Puuc Architecture

While Early Puuc architecture features rather crude stonework and simple ornamentation, the architecture of the Late Uxmal architectural style (AD 1000-1050) is the most advanced form of Puuc architecture, with finely-carved stonework and previously unseen architectural features: oversized medial and cornice mouldings; recessed jambs and lintels in all exterior doorways; and as higher vaults and upper wall zones, creating an increase in the monumentality of buildings. [6]

This is the case in the Palace of the Governor, a masterpiece of Puuc Architecture located in the ancient city of Uxmal. This building stands out from the rest because of the technical quality of the stonework of its ashlars, vault stones, and mosaic-type decorative pieces, which demonstrate exceptional advances in stonecutting techniques (Fig. 2). This fact is especially relevant, given that Maya stonemasons only had polished or carved stone tools made of lint, obsidian, and other hard stones to make chisels, axes and other tools [7] for carving all the blocks used in the construction of their buildings. The formal solutions of the House of the Governor have also been said to represent a final development in step-fret design in Puuc architecture [8]. The last construction stage of the Palace was built around AD 900, during the Late Classic Period (AD 750-1000) [9]. The quality of the limestone, the care and delicacy of its carving and the modular composition of its mosaic frieze make this building a striking example of the Puuc style in its final phase [10].

Figure 2: Northeast View of the Palace of the Governor at Uxmal, Mexico. Photo: Laura Gilabert Sansalvador, 2015

Floor Plan and Elevation of the Palace

Within the Palace of the Governor, many separate architectural forms are skilfully combined and adjusted by the architects of Uxmal [11]. The palace is a free-standing edifice of 98 m long, 12 m wide and 8.5 m high (Fig. 3). It consists of a central building and two side wings, unified by the two highest corbel-vaulted arches in Maya architecture. This structure stands on four platforms that contribute to its monumentality.

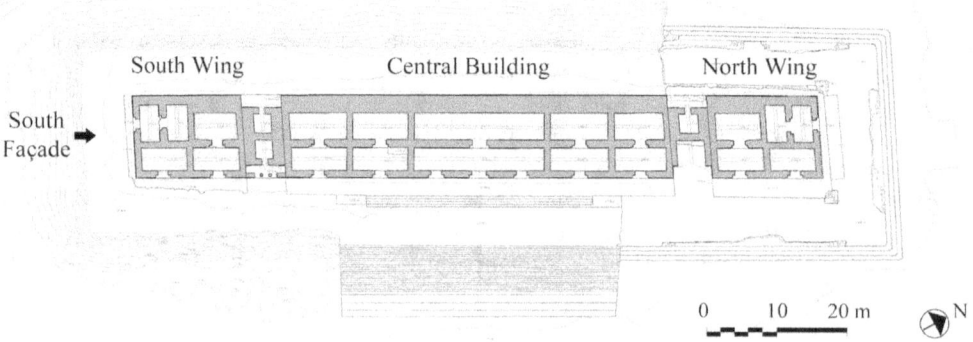

Figure 3: Floor plan of the Palace of the Governor at Uxmal, Mexico. Source: Modified from Muñoz Cosme & Vidal Lorenzo, 2020: Figure 9.

The South Wing is 16 m long, and has five rooms, two of them accessed by two doorways located on the eastern façade, while the other two are reached by a doorway on the south façade (Figs. 3-4). All its entrances have recessed jambs and lintels which are typical of the Late Uxmal architectural style.

Figure 4: South Façade of the Palace of the Governor. Photo: Ana Laura Rosado-Torres, 2013.

Methodology

In order to study in depth the Palace of the Governor, we took as a starting point the classification of pieces required for the construction of a typical Classic Puuc building, according to the proposal made by George F. Andrews. In this list, he identifies 24 specialised type pieces, both interior and exterior, for the following architectural elements: Basal Moulding (A), Perimeter Wall (B), Middle Moulding (C), Upper Walls, Exterior (D), Cornice (E), Upper Walls, Interior (F), and Vaults (G) [12].

Then, by means of the data surveyed in the field in April 2018 [13], the graphic restitution of the south façade of the South Wing of the Palace was carried out, distinguishing the following architectural elements on its façade: Basal Moulding (A), Lower Wall (B), Medial Moulding (C), Frieze (D), and Cornice (E). Subsequently, the study of the frieze was discarded since, in order to study the stone mosaic pieces located in this element, it would be necessary to address the architectural sculpture of the Palace as a whole, and not only in this façade. Thus, we have focused on the architectural elements in which carved pieces with a mainly constructive function are concentrated.

Hence, 18 of the 24 specialised pieces identified by Andrews were found on the façade, in addition to five new pieces, making a total of 23 specialised constructive pieces for the south façade of the South Wing of the Palace of the Governor. (Fig. 5)

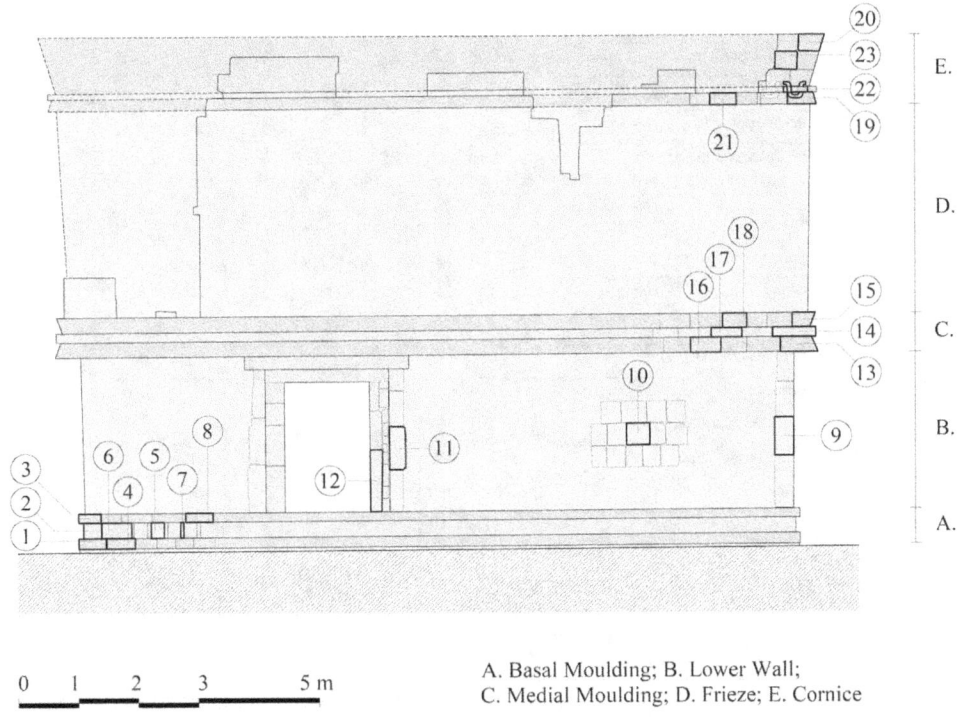

A. Basal Moulding; B. Lower Wall;
C. Medial Moulding; D. Frieze; E. Cornice

Figure 5: Schema of the South Façade of the Palace of the Governor: architectural elements and identification of specialised constructive pieces. Drawing: Riccardo Montuori, 2021

The South Façade of the Palace of the Governor: specialised stonemasonry pieces

The following table (Table 01) shows the 23 types of specialised constructive pieces identified on the south façade of the South Wing of the Palace of the Governor (1 to 23), organised according to the architectural element to which they belong (A, B, C, E). The table also includes the following data: number of pieces per type and their average dimensions in Width (W), Height (H) and Depth (D), as well as the carved surfaces identified (Visible or Partially Visible, Hidden, Total). The analysis of the total of 518 pieces identified allows us to present the results below.

Table 1: Specialised constructive pieces required for the construction of south façade of the Palace of the Governor.

	Specialised Constructive Pieces	Pieces per type	Average dimensions (cm)			Carved surfaces		
			W	H	D	Visible / Partially Visible	Hidden	Total
A. BASAL MOULDING		**120**						
1	Corner piece, lower member	2	42	17	36	3	3	6
2	Corner piece, central member	2	34	25	42	2	4	6
3	Corner piece, upper member	2	44	15	59	4	2	6
4	Typical lower member	30	35	17	(45)	1	4	5
5	*Typical central member: colonnette*	20	22	25	(25)	1	-	1*
6	*Typical central member: squared*	14	38	25	(25)	1	4	5
7	*Intermediate piece*	25	6	25	(10)	1	-	1
8	Typical upper member	25	52	15	(45)	3	2	5
B. LOWER WALLS		**256**						
9	Outside corner block	10	32	54	34	2	2	4
10	Typical wall facing block	232	29	32	(15)	1	-	1
11	*Outer Doorjamb*	7	25	65	30	2	2	4
12	*Inner Doorjamb*	7	33	63	60	3	2	5
C. MEDIAL MOULDING		**81**						
13	Corner block, lower member	2	65	25	86	3	3	6
14	Corner block, central member	2	50	18	(40)	3	2	5
15	Corner block, upper member	2	38	24	37	3	1	4
16	Typical lower member	24	46	25	(80)	2	3	5
17	Typical central member	24	46	18	(40)	3	2	5
18	Typical upper member	27	43	24	(45)	2	3	5
E. CORNICE		**61**						
19	Corner block, lower member	1	47	19	(40)	3	3	6
20	Corner block, upper member	3	35	29	(25)	2	1	3
21	Typical lower member	20	41	19	(40)	2	4	6
22	*Typical guilloche member*	13	38	26	35	1	4	5
23	Typical upper member	24	29	29	(25)	1	1	2
		518	**TOTAL NUMBER OF COMPONENTS**					

*Stonemasonry piece with a semi-cylindrical outer surface.
(x) Source: Kowalski, 1987, Fig. 64 (p. 101).

Basal Moulding (A)

The basal moulding of the south façade is composed of 120 pieces. Eight types of specialised construction stones that have been identified within this architectural element. These are: Corner piece, lower member (1); Corner piece, central member (2); Corner piece, upper member (3); Typical lower member (4); Typical central member: colonnette (5); Typical central member: squared (6); Intermediate piece, central member (7); and Typical upper member (8) (Table 02). Two of these types (6 & 7) are additional to the list of specialised stones in the basal moulding of a Classic Puuc building type previously proposed by Andrews.

Having carefully studied each type of stone block that makes up this architectural element, some interesting data can be extracted regarding the work required to achieve its final form. While in the typical intermediate pieces (4, 6-8) only one of their faces is completely visible on the façade, two of the surfaces that make up the corner pieces (1-3) are on the façade, requiring much more refined carving work than in the case of the former. In addition to the surfaces that make up the façade, it should be noted that there are other surfaces that are partially visible, either on their front or back side, so that the refined carving work is not limited to the visible side only. Thus, the pieces that make up the basal moulding have up to four carved surfaces that are visible or partially visible, while the rest remain embedded in the solid core of the wall.

The typical lower (4) and upper (8) intermediate pieces are in both cases quadrangular in their front elevation, with well-defined corners, with a constant average height —17 cm for the former and 15 cm for the latter—although their width varies. In the case of the lower intermediate piece (4), it ranges from 26 to 52 cm wide, although it is usually between 30 and 40 cm wide (the arithmetic mode is 35 cm). With regard to the upper intermediate piece (8), there are cases ranging from 19 to 58 cm wide, although they are usually 52 cm wide.

From the above it can be deduced that, although each piece of stonework was in principle designed to be executed according to standardised measurements that would allow them to be integrated into the architectural element for which they were conceived, with regard to the width of each piece there is great flexibility to adjust to the dimensions of the blocks extracted from the quarry. The width of the piece was not really relevant in achieving the final result as, after all, these intermediate elements were not intended to stand out.

Another interesting observation is that, for the harmonious decorative conformation of certain architectural elements, it was not so important that all the pieces had the same length, but that all of them conformed to the required module according to the design of the compositional rhythms on the façade. That is the case of the typical central members of the basal moulding (5-7), as seen in the following figure. (Fig. 6)

Lower Wall (B)

There are 256 pieces that make up this architectural element, in which we find four types of specialised stones: Outside corner block (9), Typical wall facing block (10), Outer doorjamb (11), and Inner doorjamb (12) (Table 02). The latter two had not been included in Andrews' list, as these architectural features only appear in buildings of the Late Uxmal architectural style. Lintels previously included in Andrew's list have been removed from ours, as they would have been made of wood rather than stone at the Palace of the Governor [14].

Thus, on the south façade there are a total of 10 outside corner blocks: four on the east side and six on the west side. These pieces have two finely carved faces, one facing the south façade and the other facing the east or west façade, respectively. It is observed that the number of pieces and their height is variable, although there are some cases where the corner pieces correspond or conform to the courses of facing stones. To give some general numbers, their width ranges from 26 to 38 cm, while their height ranges from 21 to 87 cm. Their average depth is around 34 cm.

The wall facing blocks (10) are by far the most numerous elements of the lower walls of the Palace of the Governor: there are 232 of them in total. These specialised stones are well squared, pecked and ground smooth. This type of masonry has been referred to as a veneer, given its appearance, but technically it is formwork masonry, as the facing stones must be set in place before the concrete core can set [15]. All the pieces are arranged very tightly, so that the joint between them is only a few millimetres. Because of the even surface, little stucco was required to cover the façades.

The lower wall of the south façade measures a total of 2.60 m in height and is composed of a total of 8 courses of facing stones, ranging in size from 36 cm high for the first course just above the basal moulding to 23 cm high for the eighth course below the medial moulding. The width of the facing stones also varies, ranging from 12 to 49 cm wide, although the standard piece is normally 29 cm wide (Fig. 7a). In terms of depth, these blocks are usually only half the size of their height and width, so that the back is usually about 15 cm deep.

In this standardised piece, however, there are some peculiarities: in some cases, the facing stones have a special geometry because they have been adapted to their relative position in the wall. Two examples are provided here to illustrate this: a piece that has been adapted to fit the dimensions of the corner piece (Fig. 7b), and another that has been adapted to form a constructive hole in the eighth course of the wall. (Fig. 7c).

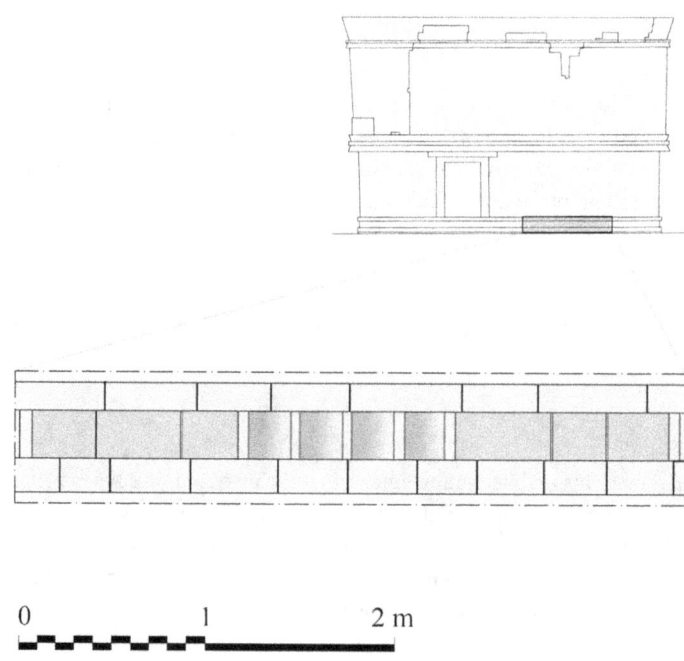

Figure 6: Scheme of Basal moulding showing different measures of specialised stones within Typical central member: squared. Drawing: Riccardo Montuori, 2021

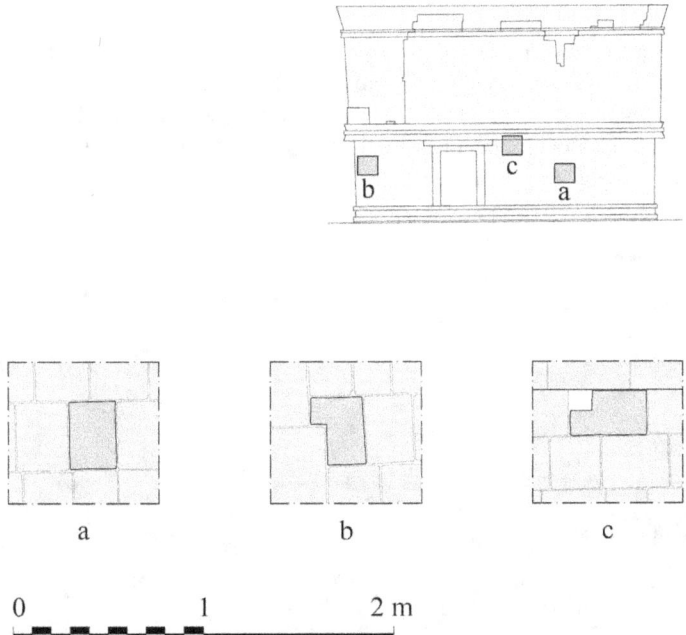

Figure 7: (a) Typical wall facing stone; (b) Modified wall facing stone to fit with corner block; (c) Facing stone modified to form a constructive hole. Drawing: Riccardo Montuori, 2021

This shows that although there were premeditated processes of carving that allowed the facing stones to be made of the same height to fit in their courses, in some cases it was also necessary to make adjustments according to the specific position they would occupy.

Lastly, we will briefly describe the pieces that make up the recessed entrances, which, as mentioned above, are a constructive novelty of this architectural style. On the south façade there are a total of 7 pieces of Outer doorjamb (11) and 7 pieces of Inner Doorjamb (12).

As seen in the façade diagram (Fig. 5), there are four outer doorjambs on the east (right) and three on the west (left) side of the entrance. They range size from 22 to 32 cm wide and from 32 to 80 cm high. Their depth constant. It is 30 cm, which is one third of the thickness of the wall. These pieces have two finely carved faces, one facing the south façade and the other facing the interior of the entrance.

As for the inner doorjambs, these are also seven in total: three on the east (right) side and four on the west (left) side. Unfortunately, their state of preservation is rather poor, as the pieces are fragmented and joined together with concrete. Nevertheless, it was possible to take the general measurements of the pieces. Their width varies between 19 and 32 cm, while their height ranges from 34 cm to 104 cm. These pieces are generally narrower in comparison with the outer jambs, but considerably wider: 60 cm in total, which corresponds to two thirds of the total thickness of the wall. These pieces have three finely-carved faces: one facing the south façade, one facing the entrance and one facing the interior of the room.

Medial Moulding (C)

This architectural element consists of two bevelled members separated by a rectangular course, which is also known as *atadura* or binder moulding. In the south façade of the Palace of the Governor, we have identified a total of 81 pieces within the same six types of specialised pieces referred to by Andrews, namely: Corner block, lower member (13); Corner block, central member (14); Corner block, upper member (15); Typical lower member (16); Typical central member (17); and Typical upper member (18). (Fig. 8)

Figure 8: Typical lower member on Medial moulding, finely carved and protruded from Lower wall. Photo: Riccardo Montuori, 2018

As for the lower members, both the corner and the typical ones (13 & 16) protrude some 40 to 42 cm from the inferior wall, which protects the typical wall facing blocks from deterioration caused by rain runoff (Fig. 8). The typical lower member (16) has only one bevel, with an angle of 64-65°, and has two finely carved and visible faces. Its average dimensions are 46 cm wide (with a minimum value of 34 cm and a maximum of 75 cm), 25 cm high and about 80 cm deep.

The Corner block, lower member (13), has three visible carved faces and two bevels (about 60-65° on both sides). It is 65 cm wide, 25 cm high and 86 cm deep. This piece is the largest of the lower pieces of the Medial moulding.

With respect to the Typical central member (17), it is a rectangular block with a finely carved face entirely visible, as well as two other carved faces, the upper and lower ones, which are only partially visible (7-8 cm), given that the rest of the piece is inserted into the core. There are 24 pieces in total, whose average dimensions are 46 cm wide (with values ranging from 22 to 59 cm), 18 cm high and 40 cm deep.

Finally, the upper members, like the lower ones, have two finely carved faces on their typical members (18) and three in the case of the corner members (15). In this case, the angle of the bevel is somewhat more obtuse: around 70° on both sides.

The upper typical member is on average 43 cm wide, 24 cm high and 40 cm deep, while the corner pieces have the same height, but are 38 cm wide and 37 cm deep. In other words, they all seem to come from roughly equilateral quadrangular quarry blocks.

Cornice (E)

With regard to the cornice, this architectural element is made up of 61 elements belonging to five types of specialised constructive pieces: Corner block, lower member (19); Corner block, upper member (20); Typical lower member (21); Typical guilloche member (22); and Typical upper member (23).

With a total height of 1.15 m, the cornice of the Governor's Palace presents three new pieces to be added to those in Andrews' classification. While the lower piece (21) is quite similar to the corresponding piece in the middle moulding (lower height and a less acute bevel angle), the central piece is a completely different element: the guilloche piece (22) (Fig. 9). This specialised stone, which as well as being a constructive element also serves as a decorative element, has a novel design not found so far in any other building in the Puuc region, making it a distinctive feature of this building. Although only 13 guilloches remain *in situ* on the south façade, the rest of the building's façades are surrounded by this rhythmic element. A detailed analysis of this element is beyond the scope of this paper, but we think it is worthy of in-depth analysis in order hypotheses can be developed about the process of tracing and cutting that would be necessary to achieve the standardised final result of this carved piece.

Figure 9: Cornice of the South Façade on the PG, with five specialised constructive pieces. Photo: Riccardo Montuori, 2018

Conclusions

The study of Maya architecture from a perspective of its construction techniques has been scarcely addressed so far, despite the importance of this subject for historical and constructive knowledge and for the preservation of these buildings.

Based on the identification and analysis of the different stone blocks that make up the south façade of the Palace of the Governor, it has been possible to classify and distinguish the different types of specialised pieces that make up the south façade of the South Wing of this building. These pieces have been characterised individually, analysing their measurements and final geometry, with special emphasis on the quality of the carved work required for their formal definition, which was designed in each case to fulfil a specific constructive function.

From the analysis of the above data, it has been possible to study the geometric and cutting solutions achieved, finding some examples of pieces that reflect very precise carving work, which leads us to believe that measuring, aligning and cutting tools would undoubtedly have been used in their manufacture.

It should be noted that, although specialised types of pieces have been detected, not all of them have been made with the exact same dimensions. One of the observations that can be drawn from this analysis is that the carving work conducted by the Puuc Maya stonemasons left a wide margin of flexibility for the execution of each of their stonework pieces, sometimes adjusting them to the dimensions of the exact position in which they were to be finally placed.

Another interesting observation is that, given that the building would have been covered with a thin layer of stucco, it is clear that the various pieces of specialised stonework that make up the building were not actually carved to be visible. For Maya stonemasons and architects, the most important thing was the overall view of the building and not the geometric precision of each individual piece.

Future research will address the characterisation of the stonemasonry pieces corresponding to the rest of the buildings that make up the whole palace: the three buildings and the two corbel-vaulted arches that join them together. From the total number of carved stones to be analysed, those of greatest interest in terms of their stereotomy will be selected and subsequently examined in detail, with the aim of developing hypotheses on the processes of tracing and carving necessary to achieve their final geometric shape.

Acknowledgments

This work has been carried out in the framework of the research project "Arquitectura maya. Sistemas constructivos, estética formal, simbolismo y nuevas tecnologías" (ref. PGC2018-098904-B-C21; Principal Investigator: Gaspar Muñoz Cosme), funded by the Spanish Ministry of Science, Innovation and Universities. Financial support from the Generalitat Valenciana (ref. GRISOLIAP/2018/139, ref. APOSTD/2020/004); and the Universitat Politècnica de València (ref. PAID-01-17) has been fundamental for conducting this research. The authors are especially grateful to the Project MAYATECH (http://mayatech.artemaya.es/) for facilitating access to the data analysed in this research.

References

[1] G. F. Andrews, Pyramids and Palaces, Monsters and Masks, *The Golden Age of Maya Architecture*, vol. I, Lancaster, California: Labyrinthos, 1995. p. 126.
[2] L. Gilabert Sansalvador, "La bóveda en la arquitectura maya," *Universitat Politècnica de València*, 2018. p. 244.
[3] H. E. D. Pollock, *The Puuc: An architectural survey of the Hill Country of Yucatan ans Northern Campeche,* Mexico. Cambridge (Massachusetts) : (USA): Peabody Museum of Archaeology and Ethnology, 1980.

[4] ibid., p. 584-590; Gilabert Sansalvador, (Note 2), p. 71.
[5] Andrews, (Note 1) p. 127.
[6] ibid., p. 81.
[7] Gilabert Sansalvador, (Note 2) p. 161.
[8] J. K. Kowalski, *The House of the Governor. A Maya Palace at Uxmal*, Yucatan, Mexico. Norman, Oklahoma: University of Oklahoma Press, 1987. p. 215.
[9] J. K. Kowalski, "Uxmal y la zona Puuc: arquitectura monumental, fachadas esculpidas y poder político en el periodo Clásico Terminal," in Los Mayas, P. Schmidt, M. De la Garza, and E. Nalda, Eds. *Ciudad de México: CONACULTA-INAH*, 1999, pp. 401–426. p. 401-402.
[10] G. Muñoz Cosme, and C. Vidal Lorenzo, (2020). New technologies for the documentation and preservation of the maya cultural heritage. The palace of the governor at Uxmal (Yucatán, Mexico). International Archives of the Ph," Int. Arch. Photogramm. Remote Sens. Spat. Inf. Sci. - ISPRS Arch., vol. 54, no. M–1, pp. 397–403, 2020, doi: 10.5194/isprs-archives-XLIV-M-1-2020-397-2020. p. 401.
[11] Kowalski, (Note 8), p. 113.
[12] Andrews, (Note 1), p. 126.
[13] Muñoz Cosme, (Note 10) p. 400.
[14] This modification is a constructive evolution, given that stone lintels have a limited length, both because of the weight of the material and the size of the entrances they allow.
[15] Kowalski, (Note 8), p. 103.

Medieval World (1000CE – 1400CE)

The Art du Trait in the Monastery of La Vid in Burgos (Spain)

Alexandra M. Gutiérrez-Hernández
University of Salamanca, Spain

Introduction

Stone construction has always been influenced by the *Art du Trait*, wich is, in turn, closely linked to the Art of Stonemasonry. It is not possible to understand one without the other.

The *Art du Trait* is an essential discipline to learn the secrets of stone construction. It is the best way to discover how to turn an inert, lifeless block of stone into an arch, vault, or staircase; in other words, it helps us understand the construction processes carried out by the stonemasons during the construction of a great stone monument. It allows us to decipher the absolute or partial volumetrics of a building, as the physiognomy of a construction may be controlled through a series of geometric exercises [1]. This Art belongs to the architectural praxis, and since practice is the mother of theory, "las distintas operaciones realizadas en la producción de una obra son una fuente de conocimientos [the various operations carried out in the production of a work are a source of knowledge]" [2]. The *Art du Trait* was one of the necessary skills that architects had to master [3], and its execution was already of an exceptional quality in Spain as early as in the fifteenth century [4].

This discipline developed in the stonemasonry workshops, known as 'tracing houses', which were common in Spain, England, and other countries. They were generally located in the buildings themselves, where an area was set aside for this purpose; however, they could also be established in other spaces within the factories, such as the tribunes, terraces, choirs or under the staircases [5]. The master stonemason would make the necessary full-scale tracings, architectural drawings, and templates in this 'mobile' or 'itinerant' workshop [6]. Tracing houses in Spain are known to have existed in El Escorial [7] and in the cathedrals of Granada [8], Salamanca [9] and Seville [10]. On the other hand, the cathedrals of York and Wells stand out as English examples [11]. In the case of York, this room: "provided accommodation for the Minster masons to work in comfort, having a large fireplace in the south wall of the eastern arm, and a garderobe entered by a passage form the east side of the southern arm. The plaster floor now extends over the whole of the southern arm and may originally have reached to the north wall, providing an area more than 40 feet long by over 16 feet wide. Such a space was needed in order to set out accurately the shapes of large windows, the curves of vaults, and other major details of the building" [12].

Within these workshops, the masters would make the tracings through a series of simple geometrical formulae [13], primarily following the *geometry fabrorum*, "la aprendida, usada y desarrollada por los artesanos [the one learnt, used and developed by craftsmen]" [14]. The tracings are the result of this *geometry fabrorum* and are considered one of the three means of graphic control in architectural practice [15].

These tracings helped the stonemasons to have precise control over the element that was being built [16] and were carried out using straight lines and curves [17], with an accurate principle of economy that allowed the use of minimum resources. This system of 'economy of means', whereby the master "solo dibuja aquello necesario para definir el elemento a construir [draws only what is necessary to define the element that needs to be built]" [18], also implied an 'economy of space' that allowed the reuse of the supports on which the different tracings were superimposed on top of each other [19]. The use of full-scale tracings proves that "medios sencillos utilizados con oficio, bastaban para resolver problemas arquitectónicos complejos de generación y control ... sin necesidad de recurrir a teorías sofisticadas que han alimentado la historia de la arquitectura hasta fechas recientes y de las que aún quedan seguidores pertinaces [simple means, when used with skill, were sufficient to solve complex architectural problems of generation and control ... without the need to resort to sophisticated theories that have nourished the history of architecture until recently and that still today have stubborn followers]" [20].

This paper will focus on the tracings of the monastery of La Vid in Burgos (Spain). However, some examples from other countries are worth highlighting, as they do reinforce the importance of this discipline. The tracings of the Temple of Apollo at Didyma, dated around 250 B.C. [21], stand out for their antiquity, as do the tracings found in the Mausoleum of Augustus for Hadrian's Pantheon in Rome [22]. In the aforementioned tracing house of the York Minster, numerous full-scale tracings have been preserved, including, among others, the tracing for the window tracery of the Lady Chapel, built around 1365 A.D. [23]. A similar example can be found in the Wells Cathedral's tracing house [24] and in the Cistercian abbeys of Byland (Yorkshire) and Jervaulx (East Witton), where some vestiges of tracings have been discovered [25]. In France, which holds an important stone building tradition, architectural drawings have been found in the cathedrals of Soissons [26], Clermont-Ferrand [27], and Chartres [28], but also in the temples of Bourges, Troyes, Trogir, and Orléans [29] and in the basilica of Saint-Quentin [30]. Some interesting drawings have also been found in the Anatolia region [31], ad-Dayr (Petra) [32], and Marrakesh [33]. All of them help us grasp the importance of the *Art du Trait*.

The *Art du Trait* in Spain: theory and practice

The theoretical aspects of the *Art du Trait* in Spain were reflected in the notebooks, manuals, and treatises where the master architects recorded their stonemasonry knowledge. These treatises on full-scale tracings detail how a construction is built [34] and the necessary techniques to carve up any type of architectural element (arches, vaults, staircases, etc.) [35]. These manuals, gathered by and for architects themselves, comprised both the theoretical explanation for diverse construction models and engravings defining such elements [36]. Most of these texts are in the form of manuscripts, as there was a certain secrecy surrounding the trade of stonemasonry, a sense of discretion inherited from the medieval guilds [37]. Few of them ever got printed, due to the high cost of printing such a large number of engravings and to the limited scope that this type of work could have beyond the professional stonemasons [38]. The oldest surviving text that contains some notions on stonemasonry techniques is the *Llivre de portraiture*, compiled by the Picard master Villard de Honnecourt in the thirteenth century.

The stonemasonry literature preserved in Spain is much later, although very rich. The first manuscript is dated around 1540 A.D., and similar texts were written until the end of the eighteenth century, with a total of 20 treatises of extraordinary importance. The writings of Alonso de Vandelvira (ca. 1585), Ginés Martínez de Aranda (ca. 1600), Fray Lorenzo de San Nicolás (1637 and 1663) and Tomás Vicente Tosca (1707-15), among others, stand out. Fray Lorenzo wrote *Arte y vso de Architectvra* in 1637, but also the continuation *Segunda parte del Arte y vso de Architectvra* in 1663, due to the objections that master mason Pedro de la Peña presented before the Royal Council. That second part served as a response to these objections [39].

Many of these manuals included designs of church plans, façades and architectural decorative elements, and drawings of the foundations necessary for the construction, in addition to practical instructions on the cutting of the stones. These texts help us identify, in most cases, the possible layouts of the stone monuments, but also allow us to understand the technical processes carried out by the stonemasons for the execution of the different architectural elements that make up a stone building.

As for the practice of the *Art du Trait* in Spain, there are progressively more discoveries of architectural drawings in some of the most significant buildings of the Spanish monumental corpus. The most significant examples are the texts found in the cities of Santiago de Compostela [40], Madrid [41], Seville [42], Jaén [43], Cuenca [44], and Salamanca [45], among others (Fig. 1).

Figure 1: Full-scale tracings in Spain. 1a Jaén Cathedral. 1b Cuenca Cathedral. 1c New Cathedral of Salamanca. Photographed by the author.

The full-scale tracings found in the monastery of La Vid

The monastery of Santa María de La Vid in Burgos (Spain) was one of the most powerful abbeys of the Premonstratensian order in Castile [46] (Fig. 2). In the sixteenth century, the main chapel, among other parts of the group, underwent a thorough architectural transformation, promoted by the Zúñiga family, which replaced the old Romanesque chapel [47]. We will not dive into the construction history of the monastic group, as important studies on the subject have already been made [48], but only focus on the architectural drawings found inside the workshops.

Figure 2: Monastery of Santa María de La Vid (Burgos, Spain). Photographed by the author.

The Art du Trait in the Monastery of La Vid in Burgos (Spain)

A number of tracings belonging to the different periods of intervention carried out on the ensemble are kept inside the walls of this magnificent building. The type of stone used for the construction, a very white sandstone from the Ciruelos de Cervera quarry (in Burgos, Spain), has hindered the research. Moreover, some rather aggressive interventions were carried out on the stone, possibly at some point in the recent history of the monastery, further complicating the work of locating and identifying the tracings. The incisions of the tracings can hardly be distinguished, so we had to mark these lines with white chalk. The tracings can be seen from a certain distance with the help of a camera. We have selected four of the 38 locations with tracings in La Vid, which are scattered throughout the different rooms of the monastery ensemble. The selected tracings are found inside the monastery church (Fig. 3).

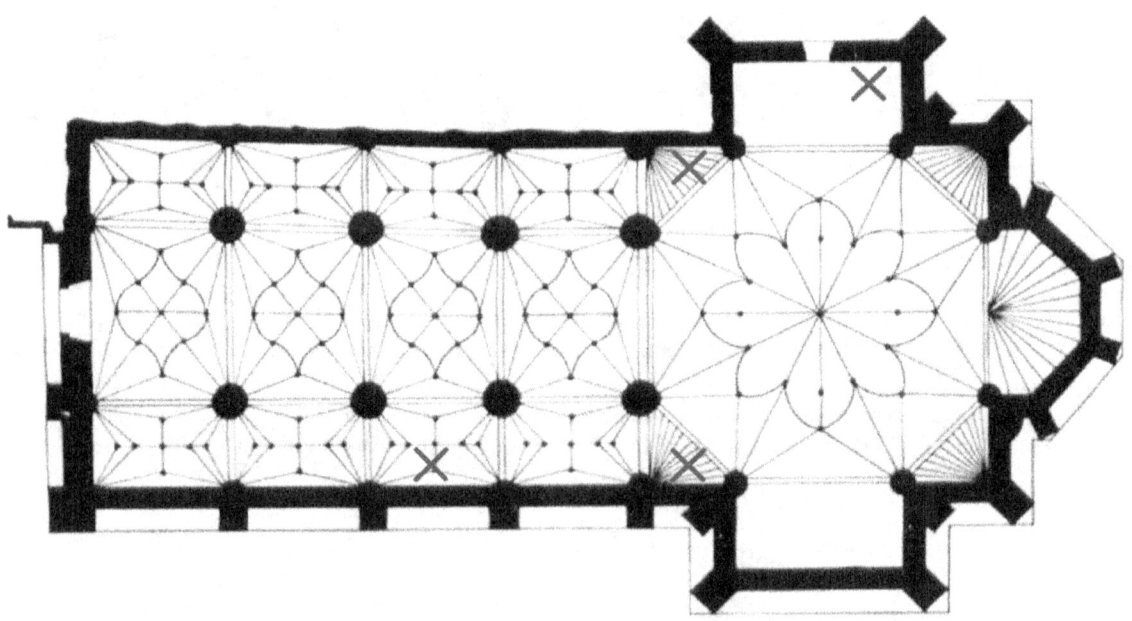

Figure 3: Location of the tracings on the ground plan of the church of Santa María de La Vid, drafted by J. D. Hoag.

In the first place, on the north wall of the transept we can find a series of tracings that seem to refer to the church access door from the interior of the ensemble, located in the transept (Fig. 4). They show a clear predominance of straight lines (mainly vertical and horizontal, but also a few diagonal ones), and a line that delimits the back of the lintelled arch at the top (1.46 metres long) can be observed. On the right side, several parallel lines run down from the back of the lintel, marking the molding of the jambs (1.21 metres long), while the diagonal line marks the junction between the lintel and the jambs on the left. In addition, another series of smaller incisions can be seen on the lower left side. The tracing is incomplete, which makes it difficult to ascertain the exact architectural element that it refers to. However, the proximity and similarity to the aforementioned door has led us to formulate this hypothesis.

Figure 4: 4a Tracings. 4b Church entrance door. Photographed by the author.

On the wall of the Gospel side, in the part of the transept before the grille that marks the division between the main chapel and the naves of the church, there is an interesting set of tracings which were probably made during the second stage of the construction, after 1542 [49], possibly under the direction of master Pedro de Rasines [50]. These large layouts (approximately 3.12 metres wide and about 2.85 metres high) are clearly superimposed and allow us to distinguish several architectural elements (Fig. 5). In the central right-hand side, we can see the cornice of an entablature, where the cymatium and the eaves can be distinguished. Right below this element, there is a geometric exercise known as 'The Seed of Life' as part of the 'Flower of Life', within the so-called 'Sacred Geometry'. On the left side, we can observe three concentric curved lines which, although incomplete, seem to represent a quarter of a sphere and correspond to the tracing for the construction of the squinches in the shape of scallop shells that serve as a transition from the square space of the transept to the octagonal vault, just above the tracings, so we can assume that the layout was probably made in different plans. This can be observed, for example, in the central part of the tracing, where the semicircles would refer to the *venera* (the scallop shell), although they are not found in the arch of the squinch. At the lower left side, we can find two triangular figures that seem to refer to the base of the squinch. Two incomplete circles can also be seen in the lower central part.

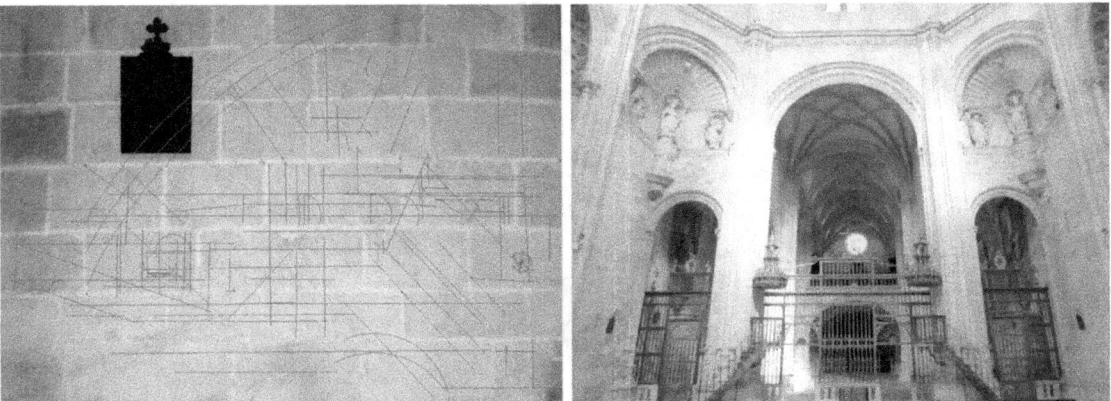

Figure 5: 5a Tracings digitally processed by J. Santos. 5b Interior of the church main chapel of the monastery of La Vid. Photographed by the author.

The manuscript of Alonso de Vandelvira (ca. 1585) includes the description and model for the construction of a 'pechina abenerada' [51] (a pendentive in the shape of a scallop shell) which, despite obvious differences and considering the overlapping of the tracings, shares some characteristics with the drawing found (Fig. 6). Unlike other squinch models in the manuscript, Vandelvira only focuses on the decorative aspect of this model but not on its architectural construction, since a shell shape could be carved in almost any type of squinch. In fact, the stonemason had to build this element following the instructions given for the 'peçhina quadrada' [52], so only the master would proceed with the shell-shaped decoration of this other model. To this aim, the fluting, known by the author as 'çerçha cabada' [53], was carved in the intrados plans of each voussoir. This truss was obtained by drawing the section of a standard voussoir, on which the stonemasons would then trace "la silueta de los traineles o juntas entre dovelas desde la imposta … hasta la clave [the silhouette of the traineles or joints between voussoirs from the impost ... to the keystone] [54]".

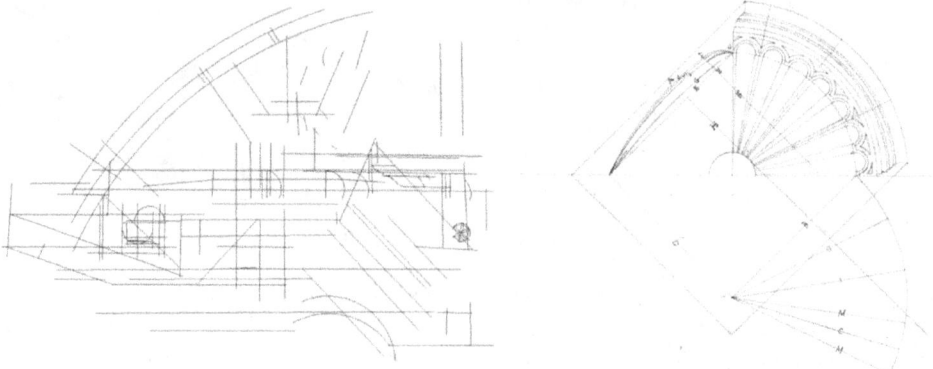

Figure 6: 6a Tracing vectorised by J. Santos. 6b 'Pechina abenerada' by Alonso de Vandelvira.

Just opposite to the previous one, on the Epistle side, the incomplete design of a semicircular arch is preserved (Fig. 7). The voussoirs are 20 centimetres in width and are located about 3.6 metres above the ground, so the use of a scaffold was needed to examine the tracing. In this case, the tracing seems to refer to the arches that give access to the side aisles of the church and link the chapel to the aisles (Fig. 5b). Despite stonemasonry literature addresses the construction of arches, semicircular arches are generally not detailed, as they are considered the simplest model. Vandelvira does include the semicircular arch in his manuscript as part of the 'Roman' arches, although he does not develop its parts or geometry for that same reason [55].

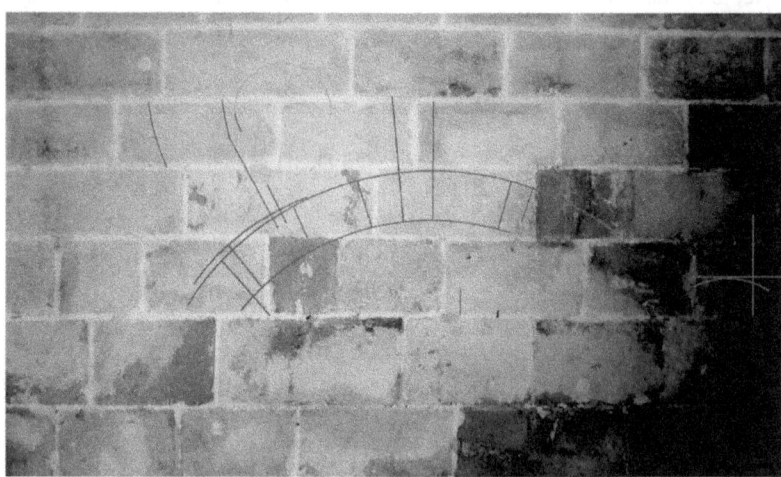

Fig. 7. Tracing of semicircular arch. Photographed by the author.

In the first third of the eighteenth century, the church of the monastery underwent a major renovation. The medieval body of the church was replaced by the one that remains today [56]. In the third section of the Epistle aisle we can observe the outline of a ribbed vault (Fig. 8). This drawing, which is not incised but drawn on the stone, represents nine keystones on a small square plan (30.5 x 29 centimetres) with tiercerons and liernes, and it is very similar to the vaults that cover the sections of the church naves, although these were built based on a rectangular plan. This drawing was not meant to serve as a template for the carving of the voussoirs in the construction of a ribbed vault. Furthermore, the irregularities in its execution indicate that it is a freehand sketch, which could mean that it is in fact an advice or instruction by the master so that his stonemasons could get an idea of what they were to execute.

Fig. 8. Tracing of a ribbed vault. Photographed by the author.

Conclusions

The Art du Trait is a fundamental discipline for understanding our stone building past. It is essential to understand the construction processes carried out by master masons to build the great stone monuments that surround us. It is also a key part of the architectural heritage, especially in countries where monumental stone construction is predominant. In the case of Spain, it is particularly important to be acquainted with this discipline, as a large part of its monumental landscape is built in stone.

Full-scale tracings are the essence of the Art du Trait, as they provide valuable information regarding the building where they are located, hence the importance of its study, dissemination, and conservation. However, locating this type of heritage is not easy. The location of the drawings and the characteristics of the material where they were made affect their condition. Natural erosion through time and human intervention, often unconscious when they are on the ground (due to footsteps), as well as the general lack of knowledge surrounding these architectural drawings, can lead to the loss of this extraordinary information. Human action can be decisive in their conservation or their disappearance.

The dissemination of these tracings is not only important to the scientific community. It is necessary to disseminate the drawings to the general public to promote their protection, especially considering that most of them are located in monuments that can be visited. An initiative that could be mimicked is the strategy carried out in the Seville Cathedral, where the important tracings located on the rooftops have been incorporated into the guided tour of the temple, so that anyone who visits it will have the opportunity to learn what a tracing is and see them in situ. This way, the public will begin to appreciate the importance of these drawings and, as a result, their disappearance will be prevented in the future. There are cases of incomplete or mutilated tracings, or with later elements placed on top. On some occasions, some treatments were applied to the walls for the conservation of the monument which however have led to the total or partial elimination of the tracings originally made by the masters who built it.

The tracings found in the monastery of La Vid are a further testimony to the importance of the Art du Trait. Despite the large number of tracings found within its walls, it is striking that they have not been noticed until now. This may be due to several factors: the general lack of knowledge around this discipline, which has caused that it has not been given the care it deserves; but also because of the building material of the monastery. Even so, they are part of its construction history and deserve our full attention. Since "El Arte de la Montea nos permitirá entender mejor los orígenes de la Construcción y de la Arquitectura [The Art du Trait will allow us to better understand the origins of Construction and Architecture]" [57], we must continue to try to 'understand', as history still awaits us.

Acknowledgments

I would like to thank the Augustinian Community of the monastery of Santa María de La Vid for their kind help during my research stay there.

I would also like to thank Juan Escorial for notifying me of the existence of some tracings in this magnificent location.

References

[1] V. Tovar, 'La cantería en la época de Rodrigo Gil de Hontañón' pp. 77-89 in *El Arte de la Cantería. Actas del congreso: V Centenario del nacimiento de Rodrigo Gil de Hontañón*, Santander 2000, Santander: Centro de Estudios Montañeses, 2000, p. 78.
[2] F. Gómez, *Manual de cantería*, Aguilar de Campoo (Palencia): Fundación Santa María la Real, Centro de Estudios del Románico, 2008, p. 19. Translated by author.
[3] J. Calvo, 'Estereotomía de la piedra' pp. 115-151 in *Máster de Restauración del Patrimonio Histórico: Murcia 2003/2004*, Murcia: Colegio Oficial de Aparejadores y Arquitectos Técnicos de la Región de Murcia, 2004, p. 116.
[4] M. Á. Aramburu-Zabala; C. Losada & A. Cagigas, *Los canteros de Cantabria*, Santander: COAATCAN, 2005, p. 75.
[5] J. Calvo (note 3), p. 117.
[6] J. A. Ruiz, 'El arquitecto en la Edad Media' pp. 151-174 in A. Graciani (Ed.), *La técnica de la arquitectura medieval*, Sevilla: Universidad de Sevilla, 2001, p. 168.
[7] A. Bustamante, *La octava maravilla del mundo. Estudio histórico sobre El Escorial de Felipe II*, Madrid: Alpuerto, 1994, p. 228.
[8] M. Gómez-Moreno, *Diego Siloe. Homenaje en el IV centenario de su muerte*, Granada: Universidad de Granada, 1963, p. 90.
[9] A. Castro, 'La organización económica y administrativa de la fábrica de la Catedral de Salamanca en los inicios de su construcción' pp. 85-110 in B. Alonso & F. Villaseñor (Eds.), *Arquitectura tardogótica en la Corona de Castilla: trayectorias e intercambios*, Sevilla: Universidad de Sevilla; Santander: Universidad de Cantabria, 2014, p. 97.
[10] J. C. Rodríguez, 'Los constructores de la catedral' pp. 147-207 in A. Jiménez et al, *La catedral gótica de Sevilla. Fundación y fábrica de la "obra nueva"*, Sevilla: Universidad de Sevilla, 2007, p. 187.
[11] A. Holton, 'The working space of the Medieval Master Mason: the Tracing Houses of York Minster and Wells Cathedral' pp. 1579-1597 in M. Dunkeld et al, *Proceedings of the Second International Congress on Construction History*, Queens' College Cambridge University, Cambridge: Construction History Society, 2006.

[12] J. H. Harvey, 'The tracing floor of York Minster' pp. 81-86 in L. T. Courtenay (Ed.), *The engineering of medieval cathedrals*, Aldershot (Hampshire): Ashgate Variorum, 1997, p. 81.

[13] J. Fernández, 'Geometría y función estructural en cantería. La cantería y la estereotomía de la piedra en el aprendizaje del arte de construir y otras consideraciones' pp. 189-196 in S. Huerta & E. Rabasa (Eds.), *Actas del Primer Congreso Nacional de Historia de la Construcción, Madrid 1996*, Madrid: Instituto Juan de Herrera, 1996, p. 191.

[14] J. A. Ruiz, 'Fuentes para el estudio de la *geometría fabrorum*. Análisis de documentos' pp. 1001-1008 in S. Huerta (Ed.), *Actas del Cuarto Congreso Nacional de Historia de la Construcción, Cádiz 2005*, Madrid: Instituto Juan de Herrera, 2005, p. 1001. Translated by the author.

[15] J. Calvo, 'Traza, montea y molde. Seis cuestiones abiertas sobre el dibujo de arquitectura medieval' pp. 163-175 in E. Rabasa, A. López & M. A. Alonso (Eds.). *Obra Congrua. Estudios sobre la construcción gótica peninsular y europea*, Madrid: Instituto Juan de Herrera, 2017, pp. 164-165.

[16] J. Calvo et al 'El uso de monteas en los talleres catedralicios: el caso murciano', *Semata. Ciencias Sociais e Humanidades*, no. 22, 2010, p. 520.

[17] J. A. Ruiz & J. C. Rodríguez, 'Monteas en las azoteas de la Catedral de Sevilla. Análisis de testimonios gráficos de su construcción' pp. 965-978 in A. Graciani et al (Eds.), *Actas del Tercer Congreso Nacional de Historia de la Construcción, Sevilla 2000*, Madrid: Instituto Juan de Herrera, 2000, p. 971.

[18] B. Alonso, 'Una montea gótica en la Capilla Saldaña de Santa Clara de Tordesillas" pp. 35-43 in S. Huerta & F. López (Eds.), *Actas del Octavo Congreso Nacional de Historia de la Construcción, Madrid 2013*, Madrid: Instituto Juan de Herrera, 2013, p. 38. Translated by the author.

[19] J. Calvo (note 15), p. 169.

[20] J. A. Ruiz & J. C. Rodríguez (note 17), p. 976. Translated by the author.

[21] L. Haselberger, 'Die Bauzeichnungen des Apollontempels von Dydima', Architectura, Vol. 13, no. 1, 1983, pp. 13-26; 'Aspekte der Bauzeichnungen von Didyma', *Revue Archéologique*, no. 1, pp. 99-113.

[22] L. Haselberger, 'The Hadrianic Pantheon-a working drawing discovered', *American Journal of Archaeology*, Vol. 98, no. 2, 1994, p. 327.

[23] J. Harvey (note 12), p. 83.

[24] L. S. Colchester & J. H. Harvey, 'Wells Cathedral', *Archaeological Journal*, Vol. 131, no. 1, 1974, pp. 200-214.

[25] P. J. Fergusson, 'Notes on two cistercians engraved designs', *Speculum. A Journal of Medieval Studies*, Vol. 54, no. 1, 1979, pp. 1-17.

[26] C. F. Jr Barnes, 'The Gothic Architectural Engravings in the Cathedral of Soissons', *Speculum. A Journal of Medieval Studies*, Vol. 47, no. 1, 1972, pp. 60-64; F. Bucher, 'A rediscovered tracing by Villard de Honnecourt', *Art Bulletin*, Vol. 59, no. 3, 1977, pp. 315-318.

[27] R. Branner, 'Villard de Honnecourt, Reims, and the origin of Gothic architectural drawing' pp. 63-80 in L. T. Courtenay (Ed.), *The engineering of medieval cathedrals*, Aldershot (Hampshire): Ashgate Variorum, 1997, p. 68.

[28] R. Branner, 'Villard de Honnecourt, Archimedes and Chartres', *Journal of the Society of Architectural Historians*, Vol. 19, no. 3, 1960, pp. 91-96.

[29] F. Bucher (note 26), p. 315.

[30] R. Branner, 'An Unknown Gothic (?) Drawing from Saint-Quentin', *Gesta*, Vol. 26, no. 2, 1987, pp. 151-152; E. M. Shortell, 'Beyond Villard: Architectural Drawings at Saint-Quentin and Gothic Design', *AVISTA Forum Journal*, no. 15, 2005, pp. 18-29.

[31] O. Bakirer, 'The story of three graffiti', *Muqarnas*, no. 16, 1999, pp. 42-69.

[32] A. Jiménez, 'Un dibujo de Petra (Jordania)' pp. 557-560 in A. Graciani et al (Eds.) (note 17).

[33] A. Jiménez, 'Unos dibujos de Marrakech', *EGA. Revista de Expresión Gráfica Arquitectónica*, no. 4, 1996, pp. 88-93.

[34] J. Gómez, 'La bóveda de crucería en la arquitectura española de la Edad Moderna' (Ph.D. thesis, University of Valladolid, 1994), p. 36.

[35] B. Alonso, 'Las trazas de montea en la construcción gótica: el caso de la montea de la Capilla Saldaña' pp. 329-344 in B. Alonso & F. Villaseñor (note 9), p. 333.

[36] A. Bonet, *Figuras, modelos e imágenes en los tratadistas españoles*, Madrid: Alianza, 1993, p. 108.
[37] Ibid., p. 108.
[38] Ibid., p. 119.
[39] Ibid., p. 98.
[40] M. Taín, 'Las monteas en Galicia: propuesta de una tipología', *Goya*, no. 297, 2003, pp. 339-355.
[41] A. López, 'Tres monteas escurialenses', *EGA. Revista de Expresión Gráfica Arquitectónica*, no. 13, 2008, pp. 190-197.
[42] J. A. Ruiz & J. C. Rodríguez (note 17).
[43] A. M. Gutiérrez-Hernández, 'Monteas en Jaén', *Boletín del Instituto de Estudios Giennenses*, no. 215, 2017, pp. 193-221.
[44] A. M. Gutiérrez-Hernández, 'Huellas en piedra: monteas en el claustro de la Catedral de Cuenca', *Atrio*, no. 23, 2017, pp. 24-39.
[45] A. M. Gutiérrez-Hernández, 'En construcción: monteas en la arquitectura de la Portada Rica de la Universidad de Salamanca' pp. 277-291 in E. Azofra & A. M. Gutiérrez-Hernández (Eds.), *Ex Vetere Novum. Rehabilitar el patrimonio arquitectónico*, Salamanca: Ediciones Universidad de Salamanca, 2018; 'Cuadernos de taller: de la teoría a la práctica en la cantería del siglo XVI' pp. 136-186 in P. M. Cátedra & J. M. Valero (Dirs.); J. Jiménez & C. Sánchez (Eds.), *Patrimonio textual y humanidades digitales. II, Libros, bibliotecas y cultura visual en la Edad Media*, Salamanca: IEMYRhd &laSEMYR, 2020.
[46] J. Escorial, 'Los III Condes de Miranda y sus fundaciones religiosas: entre el recuerdo familiar y la exaltación del linaje', *Ars Longa*, no. 28, 2019, p. 114.
[47] Ibid., p. 115.
[48] Entre otros: I. Cadiñanos, 'Proceso constructivo del monasterio de La Vid (Burgos)', *Archivo Español de Arte*, no. 61, 1988, pp. 21-36; M. J. Zaparaín, *El monasterio de Santa María de La Vid. Del medievo a las transformaciones arquitectónicas de los siglos XVII y XVIII*, Madrid: Religión y Cultura, 1994; B. Alonso, 'De la capilla gótica a la renacentista: Juan Gil de Hontañón y Diego de Siloé en La Vid', *Anuario del Departamento de Historia y Teoría del Arte*, no. 15, 2003, pp. 45-57; J. Escorial (note 46).
[49] I. Cadiñanos (note 48), p. 24.
[50] B. Alonso (note 48), p. 51.
[51] A. de Vandelvira, *Libro de traças de cortes de piedras*, Biblioteca Nacional de España, MSS/12719, ca. 1585, p. 15.
[52] Ibid., p. 2.
[53] Ibid., p. 15.
[54] J. C. Palacios, *Trazas y cortes de cantería en el Renacimiento español*, Madrid: Munilla-Lería, 2003, p. 51. Translated by author.
[55] A. de Vandelvira (note 51), p. 26.
[56] M. J. Zaparaín, 'El monasterio de la Vid en el arte de la Ribera' pp. 33-98 in L. Marín (Coord.), *El Monasterio de Santa María de la Vid: 850 años*, Madrid: Religión y cultura, 2004, p. 77.
[57] J. Fernández, 'Geometría y función estructural en cantería. La cantería y la estereotomía de la piedra en el aprendizaje del arte de construir y otras consideraciones' pp. 189-196 in A. de las Casas, S. Huerta y E. Rabasa (Eds.) (note 13), p. 189. Translated by author.

Through the Layers of Time – The Evolution of Interlaced Ribbed Domes from Islamic Spain to the Italian Baroque

Giuseppe Mazzone
Assistant Professor, University of Notre Dame – School of Architecture (Indiana, USA)

Introduction

The Mediterranean Sea, the cradle of western civilization, witnessed countless cultural interactions in its wine dark waters. Egyptian, Greek, and Roman civilizations are the main players in this historical drama, with Islamic civilization joining in 700 CE with its spread to the Iberian Peninsula. The Architectural heritage registers traces of this past in the interlaced ribbed domes found throughout the area. The typology is composed of intersecting arches transforming the mass of traditional domes into lattice structures. Interlaced ribbed domes appeared first in Andalusia, known at the time as the kingdom of al-Andalus. Outside the Iberian Peninsula the typology registers a limited spread reappearing in the works of Guarino Guarini almost one thousand years after its first introduction. A priest and mathematician from the seventeenth century, Guarini designed several iterations of interlaced ribbed domes, adapting its compositional and structural principles to Baroque sensibility. Most of these designs were never realized and survive in the present day in graphic form only. Guarini never mentioned the Islamic origin of the typology indicating instead Gothic architecture as precedent inspiring these compositions. Indeed, the Spanish chapter of Gothic architecture retains several influences rooted in Islamic principles. Starting in the sixteenth century, France and Spain would refine their construction techniques giving birth to Stereotomy (the art of stone cutting) by looking at Gothic architecture for inspiration. However, where France applies Gothic principles to compositions in line with Roman architecture, Spain embraces Gothic aesthetics building Stereotomy upon its own cultural heritage.

Therefore, the presence of Islamic themes in Guarini's architecture should not come as a surprise. The visual similarities between Guarini's dome for the Church of San Lorenzo (Turin, 1668-1687) and the vaults in Cordoba's mosque (711 CE) highlight a temporal link overriding cultural and religious differences while celebrating the artistic achievements of the human mind on a global level.

Genesis and evolution of interlaced ribbed domes in Spain and Italy

The first appearance of interlaced ribbed domes on the European stage can be traced back to the Islamic kingdom of *al-Andalus*. This satellite centre of Islamic civilization established its main city in Cordoba [1], whose foundation predated the arrival of the Muslims in 711 CE [2]. When the Umayyad Dynasty reached the city, Cordoba already had experienced a mingling between its Roman foundation and the traces of the following Visigoth domination. The arrival of a new civilization celebrated these traditions, promoting a peaceful coexistence. The roots for this cultural freedom were settled in a schism with the MiddleEastern homeland. Al-Andalus reclaimed its independence when its founding Umayyad Dynasty was replaced in the homeland by the Abbasid caliphate [3]. The new established culture embraced previous traditions and religious beliefs. In fact, the first congregational mosque in Cordoba was hosted in the original Visigoth cathedral of Saint Vincent – a building shared with the local Christian population [4]. With the building passing entirely into Muslim hands in 785 [5], the original cathedral was replaced by a new Islamic sanctuary [6] whose features combined Roman elements such as double-tiered arcades (which scholars link to the Roman aqueducts in Merida) [7]. The use of double-tiered arcades was not a novelty for mosques, having already appeared in the Great Mosque in Damascus [8] and in the Dome of the Rock in Jerusalem [9]. However, in these precedents the peripheral walls established a strong sense

Through the Layers of Time – The Evolution of Interlaced Ribbed Domes from Islamic Spain to the Italian Baroque

of enclosure which in Cordoba is virtually erased by a countless repetition of vertical supports. The arcades themselves are also open to re-interpretation. Their composition uses a chromatic alternation of bricks and stone while the arches are arranged in two tiers with different layouts: a semicircular profile in the upper tiers and a horseshoe setting in the lower ones [10]. These two features may constitute a visual device aimed to direct an observer's attention away from the irregular columns in the mosque. The vertical supports were acquired from various Roman ruins in the area, therefore displaying variable proportions. The re-use of architectural elements was a common practice which, in the specific case of Cordoba, may reflect the cultural mingling on site [11]. The disadvantage, however, was a necessity to introduce several bases and *pulvini* [12] to fit these elements into the existing composition.

Cordoba's mosque received several alterations and additions through time. Among them, the most relevant intervention for this research appears in 916 under *al-Hakam II* when a *maqsura* [13] was added to the building. A *maqsura* is composed of screen walls (usually in wood or metal) separating its occupants from other worshippers [14]. The typology is generally associated with Umayyad palaces, where it precedes the throne room [15]. Compositionally, a *maqsura* towers the rest of the building by raised gables (on the outside) and domes (in the inside) [16]. The inclusion of such as typology into a mosque is unusual but not unprecedented (the Great Mosque in Damascus had a *maqsura*). Here the complex separates the devotional space from the *mirhab* (which indicates the direction of the Kaaba in Mecca) [17]. In Cordoba the typology acquires a dynastic meaning – a celebration of the Umayyad resilience [18]. In line with the innovations in the mosque, the *maqsura* transforms – its carved screens disappear, leaving space to five-foiled interlaced arches overlapping to the double-tier arcades repeated in the building [19]. This new layer aims to strengthen the overall peripheral structure of the *maqsura*, counterbalancing the thrusts of its domes [20]. Composed of three bays, the *maqsura* presents two typologies of interlaced ribbed domes [21]: one type in its central bay and a second one for the two side bays.

Figure 1: Central bay (left) and side bay (right) of the maqsura in Cordoba's mosque (Spain, 916). Sketch and watercolour by Giuseppe Mazzone (central bay) and Katarzyna Baczynska (side bay.

In the maqsura's central bay (Fig. 01a), a drum sits on top of the arcades, transitioning the squared profile of the bay into an octagon. The transition is not perfect as the diagonal sides of the polygon cantilever above the bay's corners. On each side of the drum a five-foiled arch hosts a window open along the maqsura's peripheral walls. At the corners, squinches are decorated with muqarnas [22]. From each vertex of the drum paired columns sustain the ribs framing the dome. The bases for these supports protrude from the bay's profile while the transition between the columns and ribs (which are bigger in size than the columns) uses a pulvinus. The resulting dome is composed by eight intersecting ribs concentrating the main thrusts at the ribs' intersection. As a result, a traditional heavy dome is transformed into a light shell with a chance to open windows in the filling areas between ribs. The ribs, however, highlight the linearity of Cordoba's composition. In each of the structural nodes folding lines result by the angling of each rib towards its receiving supports – a solution later solved by Guarini in the seventeenth century by describing the ribs upon a sphere. Yet, the regularity of folding lines in Cordoba's central bay is remarkable.

In the side bays, the maqsura uses a different setting for its dome (Fig. 01b). The drum is still set upon an octagon although this time a single column occupies each vertex of the polygon. The columns still cantilever from their supporting structure while their pulvini grow in size to accommodate two adjacent ribs springing from each support. The ribs span across an area corresponding to three sides of the octagon instead of two as in the previous example. The number of structural nodes is therefore doubled and organized on two levels, each one hosting eight nodes. In the lower nodes, the ribs intersect at 90 degrees while in the upper ones the intersection's angle register 120 degrees. Once more, folding lines appear in each intersection. The overall setting appears less refined than the solution in the maqsura's central bay. Even the decorative apparatus reduces in details, with floral carvings in each filling area between ribs.

Interlaced ribbed domes will continue appearing in Spanish architecture until the late Renaissance and early Baroque although their original Islamic inspirations will slowly transition towards Romanesque and Gothic aesthetics which show an increase of the structural mass [23]. Conversely, similar architectural examples in Northern Africa will transforming interlaced domes into thin lattice structures hiding the actual roofing system. The difference indicates a diverging approach to domes, separating Islamic and European architecture. The latter presents a strong link between structural devices and decorative elements [24] with domes conceived as ornamental details executed through a carpentry framing covered with stucco or mastic [25]. In European architecture, instead, domes reflect a heritage tied to Roman construction techniques – masonry structures constituting the actual roof for a building. The Spanish-Arabic iteration sits in between these two opposites offering special attention to decorative details more than technical executions [26].

The dome from the Great Mosque in Tlemcen (Algeria, mid-thirteenth century) identifies the Islamic use of interlaced ribbed domes. (Fig. 02) In this example a squared bay transitions to a dodecagon although only four of the polygon's sides cantilever. Each vertex of the dodecagon hosts two ribs separated by a small pilaster – each rib spanning five sides of the polygon. The increased number of nodal intersections is organized on four levels, each one containing twelve nodes. The intersections still present folding lines although their visibility is reduced by slandering the ribs (acquiring a "T" profile in section). Additionally, the whole surface of the dome is removed of its weight by delicate carvings hiding the structural walls along the bay's perimeter and the windows open into them.

On opposition of this example, the Church of the Holy Sepulchre in Torres del Rio (twelfth century) displays a Romanesque approach. (Fig. 03) The octagonal setting of the dome is composed of paired ribs spanning along three sides of the polygon individuating a second smaller octagon on top of which a hemispherical dome rest. However, this time the ribs do not spring from the vertexes of the octagon but from the middle point of its sides. An additional set of ribs starting from the vertexes of the octagon interrupts upon reaching the intersection nodes of the main structure. The resulting 3-ribbed node is intentionally not solved: the two ribs from the main frame intersect with a folding line while the singular rib from the polygon's vertex joins the intersection on a receding plane. The effect promotes the illusion of two overlapping systems: the main interlaced ribbed dome, disconnected from the building's main orientation, and a second ribbed structure hidden behind the previous one and anchored to the building corners. The device appears as an attempt to suggest volumetric complexity in a setting where the composition is stripped by decorative patterns and windows.

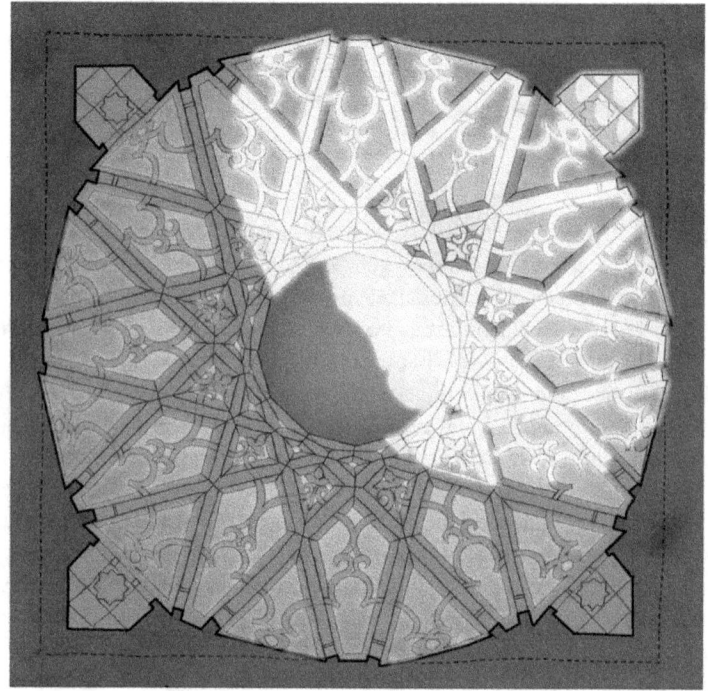

Figure 2: Plan of the dome in the Great Mosque in Tlemcen (Algeria, mid thirteenth century). Sketch and watercolour by Giuseppe Mazzone

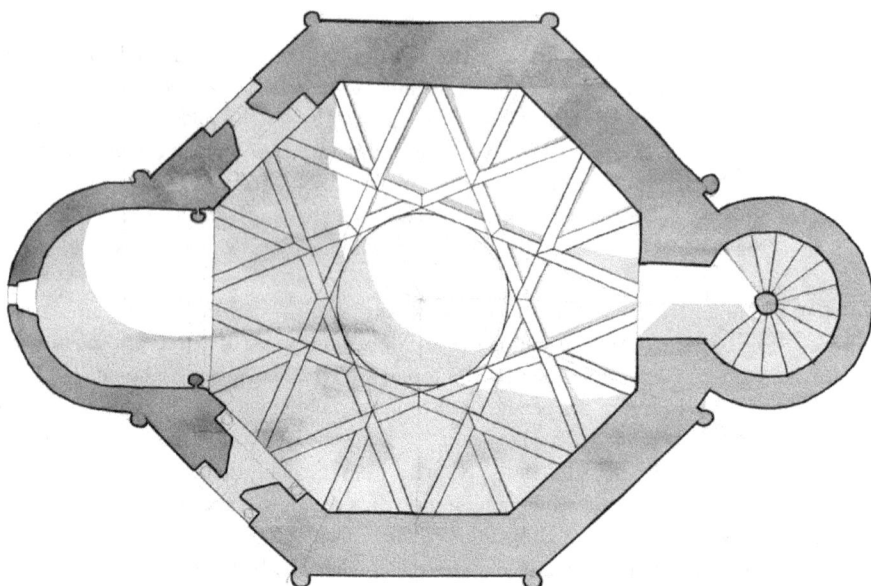

Figure 3: Plan of dome in the Church of the Holy Sepulchre in Torres del Rios (Spain, twelfth century). Sketch and watercolour by Giuseppe Mazzone

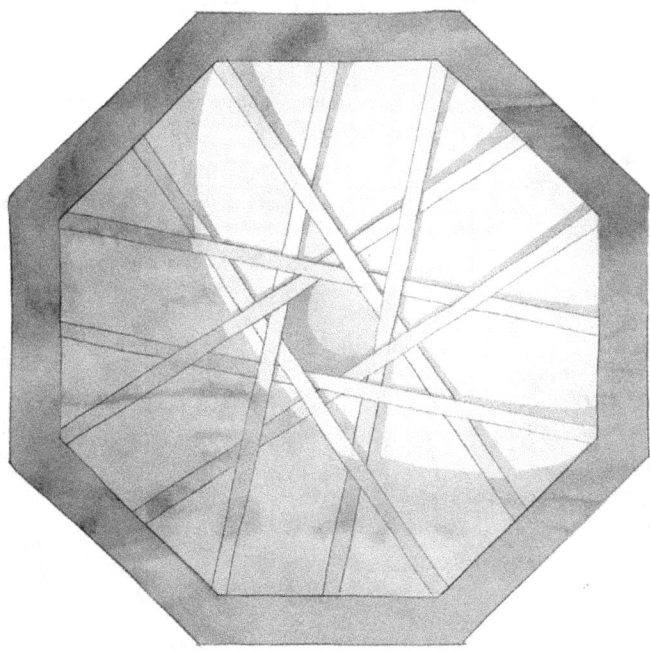

Figure 4: Plan of the dome for the Salamanca's Chapter House (Spain, twelfth-fourteenth century). Sketch and watercolour by Giuseppe Mazzone

A similar approach appears in Salamanca's Chapter House (included in the Old Cathedral's complex built between the twelfth and the fourteenth century). (Fig. 04) The dome is set up once again upon an octagon although its ribs span across the room following a skewed path. After springing from one of the octagon's vertexes as in previous examples, each rib skips three and a half vertexes ending in the middle point of the octagon's side instead of in one of its vertexes. The solution increases the number of overall ribs from eight to sixteen. The effects suggest the illusion of a dome subjected to helicoidal torsion. The solution still lacks refinement – an effect even more visible because of the decorative patterns carved on each rib. These very same elements appear excessively slender to perform a structural role which is now supplied by the dome's filling areas.

The progressive reduction in size of the ribs will, over time, direct Spanish interlaced ribbed domes towards Gothic structures. Ribs will still be present in these compositions moving along curvilinear patterns – their structural role now combined with filling areas. The exponential complexity in these configurations will refine structural nodes, becoming a major focus in Spanish Stereotomy.

An example of this bridge between Gothic and Islamic heritage is Burgos Cathedral. The building was started during the thirteenth century with further work executed between the fifteenth and sixteenth century. Among these later additions, interlaced structures appear in the Chapel of the Constable and in the church's central bay. The Chapel of the Constable (Fig. 05a) adopts an octagonal shape with two ribs per vertex – each rib connected to the vertex opposite to its springing point. However, upon reaching their first structural node, the ribs interrupt generating a new framework which repeats the previous pattern. Once again, this second pattern interrupts upon the rib's first intersection. From these last nodes the ribs reach the centre of the dome, thus closing the composition. As in Romanesque examples, the ribs are now extremely slender, highlighting the thrusting lines in the dome without performing a direct structural role. The filling areas indicate a clear advancement in construction techniques – their arched surfaces describe a hemispherical shell carved into irregular

Through the Layers of Time – The Evolution of Interlaced Ribbed Domes from Islamic Spain to the Italian Baroque

lozenges. Likewise, at the core of the composition the dome releases its mass by presenting screens punctured in geometric patterns.

In the central bay of the same cathedral (Fig. 05b), the dome follows a similar configuration although this time the screened surfaces further expand, engulfing the entire structure.

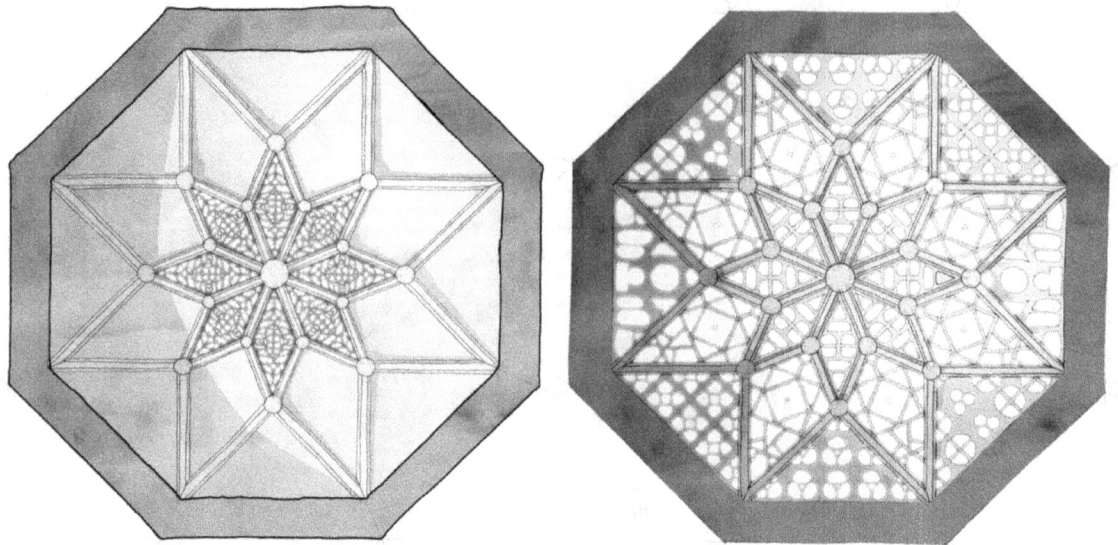

Figure 5: Dome in the Chapel of the Constable (at the left) and above the crossing bay (at the right) in Burgos Cathedral (Spain, fifteenth-sixteenth century). Sketch and watercolour by Giuseppe Mazzone

Figure 6: Plan of the dome in the Cathedral of Santa Maria de Mediavilla in Teruel (Spain, 1537). Sketch and watercolour by Giuseppe Mazzone

In later examples light sources will gradually disappear from the dome's surface while the overall setting will transition towards Renaissance forms. The ribs themselves cement their structural role according to Gothic principles gracefully moving along the vaults and domes. The lantern tower from the Cathedral of Santa Maria de Mediavilla in Teruel offers an interesting example for this new iteration of interlaced ribbed domes. (Fig. 06) Designed in 1537 by Juan Lucas Botero, the lantern's dome links the keystone of the window in the dome's lower tier to the oculus above where a second interlaced structure rest. The framing for this second structure appears in line with Renaissance structures presenting ribs directed towards the dome's centre. Compositional challenges in the structure are increased by the presence of curved ribs although their intersections are conveniently hidden from view by decorative elements. As in Romanesque examples, light no longer filters through the dome itself but radiates from windows open along the dome's spring plane.

Figure 7: Altar's vault in the church of San Nicholas in Priego, Cuenca (Spain, sixteenth century). Sketch and watercolour by Katarzyna Baczynska

The shift towards Renaissance aesthetics can be traced in the composition of Spanish vaults. The sixteenth century church of San Nicholas in Priego (Cuenca, Spain) presents a wonderful example in its altar vault, where interlaced ribs describe a flowery pattern (Fig. 07). The ribs are strategically located to hide folding lines along the ridges of the cross vault (whose profile is close to acquiring the spherical profile of a web vault). Intersection nodes are still partially hidden behind joints while the composition is stripped of any decorative element following the principle of structural decoration pursued by Stereotomy. It is during this time (mid-sixteenth century) that Spanish treatises on the topic start appearing. Their main focus will approach the geometric rigour of its applications, rejecting empirical methods based on the manipulation of geometric forms learned by rote in the shops [27]. Alonso de Vandelvira represents one of the major contributors on these applications. Most of his applications, still rooted in Gothic architecture, are based on examples from the works of Andres de Vandelvira [28], Alonso's father. His most representative works are the vaults for the Assumption of the Virgin Cathedral in Jaen (Andalusia, Spain), which mark the final transition of Spanish interlaced structures from Gothic forms to pure Renaissance themes. Ribs disappear, becoming embedded directly in the vault's structure as chromatic decorations dictating the structural composition of the vaults. (Fig. 08) Fusing decorative and structural patterns, Andres de Vandelvira creates in Jaen a variety of intricate patterns perfectly adherent to Stereortomic principles.

Figure 8: Transept vault in Jaen's Cathedral (Spain, sixteenth century) by Andres de Vandelvira. Sketch and watercolour by Katarzyna Baczynska

With the rise of the sixteenth century interlaced ribbed domes abandon the Iberian Peninsula to resurface once more during the late seventeenth century in the works of the Italian architect Guarino Guarini. It is not clear how Guarini became acquainted with this typology as his life accounts do not mention any direct link to Spain. However, as a teacher for the Theatine order – a monastic group working in direct contact with the papacy – Guarini spent most of his life in Messina (Sicily). At that time the southern territories of the Italian peninsula were under Spanish rule with Messina hosting the summer residence for the Spanish Royal family. Therefore, the city engaged in a constant dialogue with the Iberian Peninsula and, eventually, with its architectural heritage. The theme of interlaced ribbed domes pervades Guarini's designs where Spanish precedents have been critically approached and re-interpreted. The dome for San Lorenzo in Turin presents an astonishing resemblance to the maqsura's domes in Cordoba's mosque.

The major innovation found in San Lorenzo (and in most of the other designs by Guarini) consists in the substitution of a polygonal setting for a circular one. (Fig. 09f) Thanks to this new configuration, the ribs are now radially distributed around the dome's springer plane, removing their protrusion from the bay's profile. While spanning across the bay, the ribs move along a spherical surface witnessing a co-planar intersection when merging into structural joints. In consequence, the folding lines plaguing Spanish examples disappear. The updated configurations also experience a structural revision: each rib is now executed according to Roman traditions with Stereotomic applications concentrated into structural nodes only. This causes a lessening in the compositional refinements both French and Spanish Stereotomy aimed to introduce. Windows open again directly in the dome following the profile of the interlaced structure. At the top of the composition, a polygonal oculus becomes the setting for a second structure sustaining its own interlaced ribbed dome (reminiscent of the central bay from Cordoba's *maqsura*) on top of which the church lantern rests.

The innovations performed by Guarini on the typology appear throughout his designs with multiple iterations. (Fig. 09) The classical octagonal is substituted by new profiles such as triangles (as in the pendentive for the Chapel of the Holy Shroud in Turin, 1668-1694) (Fig. 09a), pentagons (San Gaetano in Nice, 1670) (Fig. 09b), and hexagons (Church of the Somaschi Fathers in Messina, 1660-1662 [Fig. 09c] and the presbytery from San Lorenzo in Turin, 1668-1687 [Fig. 09d]). Even when maintaining an octagonal setting, the typology always displays innovations with ribs skipping one vertex (as in the lantern from San Lorenzo in Turin) (Fig. 09e), two vertexes (main dome in San Lorenzo) (Fig. 09f), or even creating a double tier structure (Sainte-Anne-la-Royale in Paris, 1662) (Fig. 09g). Additional transformations also re-invent the typology turning the dome into a conical structure composed by overlapping tiers of arches, each tier springing from the keystone of the arches in the tier below (Chapel of the Holy Shroud in Turin, 1668-1694). (Fig. 09h)

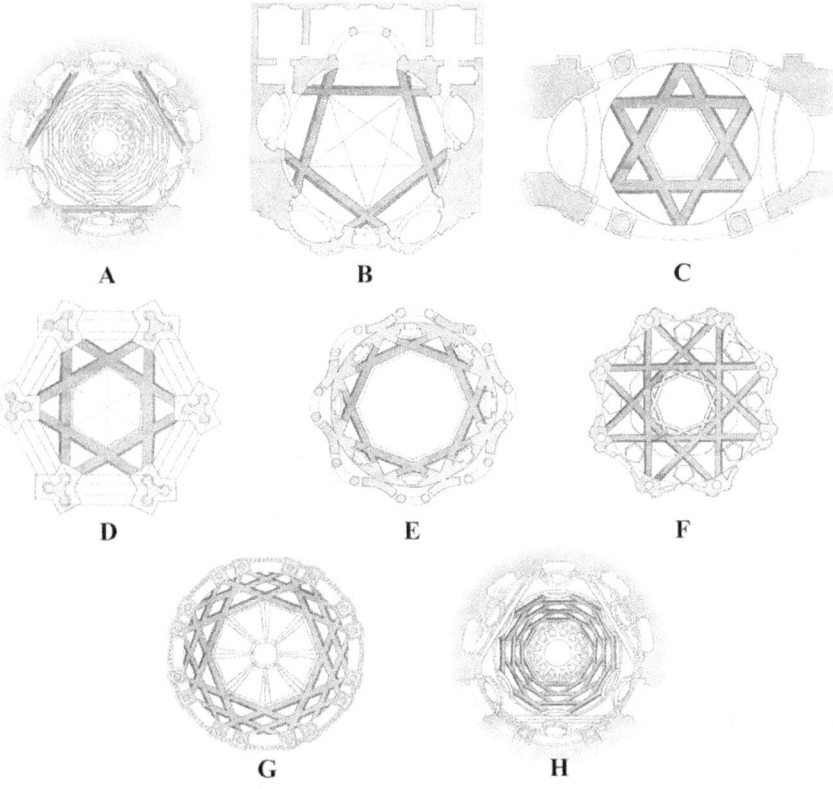

Figure 9: Guarini's variations on interlaced ribbed domes: A) Pendentive in the Chapel of the Holy Shroud, Turin; B) Dome in San Gaetano, Nice; C) Dome in the Church of Somaschi's Fathers, Messina; D) Presbytery, E) Lantern, F) main dome in San Lorenzo, Turin; G) Dome in Sainte-Anne-la-Royale, Paris; H) Main dome in the Chapel of the Holy Shroud, Turin. Sketch and watercolour by Giuseppe Mazzone

Through the Layers of Time – The Evolution of Interlaced Ribbed Domes from Islamic Spain to the Italian Baroque

Interlaced ribbed domes will make sporadic appearances before abandoning the Italian architectural stage in the mid-eighteenth century. The main reasons for this departure relate to their structural complexity and their Gothic-Islamic roots. Italian architecture did not fully embrace Stereotomy, opting instead to expand Roman construction principles. Likewise, Italy had limited exposure to Gothic architecture with sporadic appearances such as the Duomo in Milan.

After Guarini the typology appears once more in the works of Bernardo Vittone (1704-1770). An admirer of Guarini's work, Vittone will continue to experiment on interlaced domes designing the Visitation Sanctuary in Vallinotto (Carignano, 1738). (Fig. 10) The composition develops upon a hexagonal setting in a structure composed by three superimposed layers. Paired ribs spring from the hexagonal corners skipping one vertex in their spanning the bay (first layer). The polygonal oculus identified by the intersecting ribs opens into a hemispherical dome (second layer) whose circular oculus reveals a raised arch dome (third layer) – the sanctuary's roofing system. Windows hidden between the second and third layer of the composition filter the light coming in the sanctuary creates the illusion of shells levitating above the building.

Figure 10: Plan and section of the dome in the Visitation Sanctuary in Vallinotto (Carignano, 1738) by Bernardo Vittone. Sketch and watercolour by Giuseppe Mazzone.

Vittone's multi-layered composition further expands the typology by introducing structural devices responding to the Baroque's scenography demands. The surfaces of the dome are covered by *frescos* with the only exception being the ribs. The resulting effect enhances the lattice structure by covering its filling areas with colours and imagery while leaving the ribs unadorned – an inversion from the Baroque tendency to hide structural elements in the building mass or through a lavish decorative layer.

Conclusions

With Vittone the architectural chapter of interlaced ribbed domes reaches its conclusion. Hints of their spatial properties can still be perceived in Baroque advanced configurations involving intersected vaults. Here ribs may appear once more curving along the vaults surfaces or highlighting their structural joints. While the typology might have reached its final destination, the memory of it evokes a moment in time where cultures were able to set aside their differences to establish an architectural language based on cultural freedom and coexistence. The unique results reached in Spain are among the most interesting examples of this phenomenon. The resurfacing of interlaced ribbed domes in Italy during the seventeenth century certainly improved on its executions and final results. The attempt, however, clashed against a culture deeply rooted in an architectural heritage from which the Renaissance bloomed. Guarini's work, while remarkable, was not able to ignite the same spark lighted in Cordoba almost a thousand years before. Nonetheless, the message promoted was still the same: a boundless flow of human creativity through geographical areas, cultures, and time.

References

[1] Ali Wijdan, *The Arab contribution to Islamic art.* Cairo: The American University in Cairo Press, 1999, p. 175.
[2] Josef W. Meri, Jere L Cacharach, *Medieval Islamic Civilization.* New York: Routledge, 2006, p. 175.
[3] Amelia Helena Silowski, *Islamic ideology and ritual: architectural and spatial manifestations.* New York: UMI, 2007, p. 35.
[4] Janina M. Safran, *The second Umayyad Caliphate: the articulation of caliphal legitimacy in al-Andalus.* Cambridga, MA: Harvard University Press, 2000, p. 61, 182; Ali Wijdan, *The Arab contribution to Islamic art.* Cairo: The American University in Cairo Press, 1999, p. 96; see also Alejandro Lapunzina, *Architecture of Spain.* Westport: Greenwood Press, 2005, p. 81.
[5] Josef W. Meri, Jere L. Cacharach, *Medieval Islamic Civilization.* New York: Routledge, 2006, p.175; Spencer Baynes, *Encyclopædia Britannica*, XVI. Edinburgh: Adam and Charles Black, 1878, p. 864.
[6] Gurlu Necipogulu, *Muquarnas, an annual on the visual culture of the Islamic world: 1996.* Leiben: E. J. Brill, 1996, p. 84.
[7] Amelia Helena Silowski, *Islamic ideology and ritual: architectural and spatial manifestations.* New York: UMI, 2007, p. 35.
[8] Gurlu Necipogulu, *Muquarnas, an annual on the visual culture of the Islamic world: 1996.* Leiben: E. J. Brill, 1996, p. 80.
[9] Amelia Helena Silowski, *Islamic ideology and ritual: architectural and spatial manifestations.* New York: UMI, 2007, p. 35.
[10] The presence of horseshoe arches in Spanish architecture pre-dates the Arabic conquest. (Deborah K. Dietsch, *Architecture for dummies.* Hoboken, Wiley Publishing, Inc., 2002).
[11] Richard Ettinghauser, Oleg Grabar, *Islamic art and architecture 650-1250.* New Haven and London: Yale University Press, 1987, p. 132.
[12] A *pulvinus* is an impost-block between a column's capital and an arch.
[13] Amelia Helena Silowski, *Islamic ideology and ritual: architectural and spatial manifestations.* New York: UMI, 2007, p. 39; Alejandro Lapunzina, *Architecture of Spain.* Westport: Greenwood Press, 2005, p. 83.
[14] Robert Hillenbrand, *Islamic architecture: form, function, and meaning.* New York: Columbia University Press, 1994, p. 49.
[15] *Ibid.*, p. 49.
[16] *Ibid.*
[17] Richard Ettinghauser, Oleg Grabar, *Islamic art and architecture 650-1250.* New Haven and London: Yale University Press, 1987, p. 83.

[18] Janina M. Safran, *The second Umayyad Caliphate: the articulation of caliphal legitimacy in al-Andalus.* Cambridge, MA: Harvard University Press, 2000, p. 61.

[19] Lapunzina Alejandro, *Architecture of Spain* (Westport: Greenwood Press, 2005), p. 83.

[20] *Ibid.*, p. 83; Ali Wijdan, *The Arab contribution to Islamic art.* Cairo: The American University in Cairo Press, 1999, p. 96.

[21] Ali Wijdan, *The Arab contribution to Islamic art.* Cairo: The American University in Cairo Press, 1999, p. 96.

[22] A *muqarna* is a three-dimensional decoration composed by niche-like triangular elements arranged in tiers. Yvonne Dold-Asmplonius, Silvia Harmsen, "Muqarnas, Construction and Reconstruction", *Nexus V: Architecture and Mathematics*, ed. Kim Williams and Francisco Delgado Cepeda, Fucecchio (Florence): Kim Williams Books, 2004, pp. 60-77.

[23] Richard Ettinghauser, Oleg Grabar, *Islamic art and architecture 650-1250.* New Haven and London: Yale University Press, 1987, p. 137.

[24] *Ibid.*, p. 137.

[25] James Fergusson, *A history of architecture in all countries*, II. London: John Murray, 1987, p. 402.

[26] *Ibid.*, p. 402.

[27] S. L. Sanabria, 'From Gothic to Renaissance Stereotomy: The Design Methods of Philibert de l'Orme and Alonso de Vandelvira,' *Technology and Culture*, Vol. 30, 2, April 1989, Special Issue: Essays in Honor of Carl W. Condit, Apr. 1989, p. 268, 276; L. Shelby, 'The Geometric Knowledge of the Medieval Master Masons', Speculum 47, 1972, pp.395-421.

[28] S. L. Sanabria, 'From Gothic to Renaissance Stereotomy: The Design Methods of Philibert de l'Orme and Alonso de Vandelvira,' *Technology and Culture*, Vol. 30, 2, April 1989, Special Issue: Essays in Honor of Carl W. Condit, Apr. 1989, p. 276.

Medieval watchtowers of the mountainous areas of the Abruzzi Region: typologies, construction techniques and territorial landscape

Claudio Mazzanti and Federico Bulfone Gransinigh
Department of Architecture, University "G. d'Annunzio" of Chieti-Pescara, Italy

Introduction

The Abruzzi region is a border area with many building typologies of fortifications. These structures show the construction methods in the various eras. These buildings were widespread on the territory, on the coast and in the hinterland to ensure the security of the state. In order to know the transformations of the fortified settlements in the region, it is essential to analyze the historical-political and social events.

This territory is the northern limit of the kingdom of Naples; it has been dominated over the centuries by the Lombards, Normans, Swabians, Angevins and Aragonese. These situations make different architectural kinds. The small ancient urban centers were formed in close relationship with agricultural and rural development, as a result of economic and social relationships that have created a continuous landscape [1].

The geographic characteristics and the elevation of the mountain massifs affect the types and use of materials. The river valleys delimit a system of fortified structures. Along these valleys there are the historical access routes to the internal areas and the crossing roads coming from other territories: the *Salaria*, the *Caecilia*, the *Claudia Valeria*, the *Raussa*. The presence of the watchtowers along the coast integrates with the fortified structures of the hilly urban centers overlooking the Adriatic coast.

A greater number of defensive buildings are to the north, towards the Tronto river border with the Marche region; between the cities of Civitella del Tronto, Teramo, Montorio al Vomano and the sources of the Aterno. A high concentration of these architectures is present around L'Aquila and on the hills above Avezzano. The latter are also strategic because they were built on the border with Lazio. Another group of fortifications rises between Celano, Pescina and Sulmona and is opposed to the fortified system of the first valley of the Pescara river.

These two areas, separated by Morrone Mount, are in the territory controlled by the castle of Popoli, which dominates the homonymous Gorges. This passage, so called *la chiave degli Abruzzi* (the key of the different districts of the Abruzzi region), allowed communication between the coastal-hilly area and the Apennine mountainous area and, in general, between the Tyrrhenian and the Adriatic coast. In the southern part of the region, however, there is a lot of isolated fortresses. The only actual grouping of castles and watchtowers can be found along the Sangro river, especially around the Lake of Bomba. The analysis of these types allows to define some specific criteria necessary for the study of the single building and of the set of fortified works in the territory.

All these architectures are part of a system of intervisibility, control and defense of the state, in some cases based on a material mimicry. The first type found along the coast and within the river valleys is that of the watchtowers. The landscape is strongly characterized by these structures. The medieval watchtowers in the hinterland, and the Renaissance defense structures along the coast, had three main functions: control, sighting and signaling. The coastal towers, after the modern era reform, have rectangular or square plans, with a recognizable typology. The isolated towers placed along the river valleys or in the highlands of the inland areas, maintain a typically medieval shape. The towers have a square,

*Medieval watchtowers of the mountainous areas of the Abruzzi Region:
typologies, construction techniques and territorial landscape*

rectangular or, in some cases, round and polygonal plan, such as the tower of Goriano Valli and that of the castle of Beffi, both in the Aterno valley.

In the L'Aquila area, during the Middle Ages, the watchtowers had a mainly square and round plan. Polygonal plans, or those derived from the combination of a square and a triangular shape, are exceptions that broaden the typology, but they do not constitute a rule (Fig. 1).

Figure 1: Abruzzi region, Province of Aquila. Square towers: 1) Montereale; 2) San Vittorino; 3) L'Aquila; 4) Civitaretenga; 5) Molina Aterno; 6) Gagliano Aterno; 7) Casteld di Ieri; 8) Cocullo; 9) Introdacqua; 10) Bisegna; 11) Scanno; 12) Civita d'Antino; 13) Corcumello. Circular towers: 14) Santo Stegano di Sessanio; 15) Santa Iona; 16) Aielli; 17) Collarmele; 18) Trasacco; 19) Sperone; 20) Villalago.

The triangular towers can be identified in the literature with the term "strut"; an example of this is the tower of the Beffi castle, in the Aterno valley (Fig. 2). In the area of analysis, the latter are always near to other fortified architectures, even if presumably at one time there must have been isolated struts, or at least implemented as the first element destined to later play the role of a keep [2].

Figure 2: Triangular tower of Beffi, Acciano. View, plans, elevations and section taken from the survey. [Lab. of History, Department of Architecture, Unich]

The evolution of these fortified structures, of the L'Aquila area, is part of the broader phenomenon of fortification [3]. Many scholars identify the cause of the beginning of the fortification in the defense needs widespread after the Saracen raids and the Hungarian invasions. Wickham [4], on the other hand, proposes a theory based on the evolution of functions and settlement needs that determine, over the centuries, a transformation of the military settlements and castles. He proposes the birth of the castle from the transformation of the farmhouses into *villae* and, therefore, from the processes of centralization and subsequent fortification of the rural villages. More recent studies try to provide a reading that takes both aspects into account, focusing on the variety of reasons through which, between the ninth and thirteenth centuries, the Abruzzi settlement structures and their defensive architecture evolved.

Historical construction site, building types and techniques

During the Middle Ages, there were numerous construction sites involving local workers and those from beyond the Alps. These construction sites are started both in the religious buildings and in the isolated towers and castles. The professionals involved often used stone as a building material. The stones used, as confirmed by the inspections, come from quarries, erratic boulders and ancient monuments, stripped of their ashlars. Finally, the watchtowers placed near the waterways were built with materials from the river beds. From these sites come the river pebbles of various sizes and the more or less fine gravels for the mortars [5].

Medieval watchtowers of the mountainous areas of the Abruzzi Region: typologies, construction techniques and territorial landscape

The reasons for the use of these materials are to be found in the geo-morphological structure of the L'Aquila area and in the abundance of stones obtained from rivers or from quarries present, above all, in the northern part of the province [6]. The *spolio* technique is used, especially in the northern territories of the province, in an indistinct way both in religious architecture and in fortifications [7]. The square towers were built already in Roman era. This typology increased from 1059 when the Normans, settled in Puglia, began to make raids in the Abruzzi's territories [8]. Furthermore, around the city of L'Aquila, the territorial organization was based on a fortifications in any place.

These architectures were not organized in a real network, because the various feudal lords enjoyed a lot of autonomy in the management of the fiefdoms.

With the advent of the Normans, Abruzzi region returned to be part of the southern control orbit and this led to the creation of new communication routes. The axis of this road network became the *Via degli Abruzzi*. It, in eleven stages, connected Florence to Naples [9]. This route crossed inland Abruzzo, from the Sella di Corno pass to the Cinquemiglia plain, along the Aterno valley and the Peligna valley [10].

The revival of trade and the desire for control led *Ruggero* II of Sicily (1095-1154), to the decision to reform the borders. The King mainly fortified the territories bordering the Church's State [11]. In this period, the defensive system of the Abruzzi region was also reorganized. The impulse to build new fortifications and to restore the existing ones [12] allowed the establishment of a control network that had grown over the subsequent centuries.

However, the Norman interventions were limited, for the most part, to the restoration and modernization of the existing towers. This decision was made both to save resources and because there was a desire to strengthen crucial points within the network of routes and roads already identified in the Lombard era.

Many of the works created by the Normans were destroyed by the seismic events that followed one another in these territories. The surviving fortified architectures were profoundly altered by the interventions of the following centuries. Between the 10th and 11th centuries, Pietro da Celano (second half of the 13th century-1212) also fortified the territory within the fiefs of Celano and Albe. It is assumed that Peter also built numerous watchtowers to support the existing fortified system. The fortified architectures were built along the road that, from the Ovindoli pass, headed north and on the routes that crossed the upper valley of the Liri and Sangro rivers [13].

In the years of transition between Norman and Swabian domination, the *da Celano* family managed to bond with the new Lords. In fact, in the political changes that characterized this period, Pietro da Celano laid the Emperor Henry VI of Swabia (1165-1197), facilitating the domination of the Swabians in the Abruzzi territories. This support was very important for the strategic position of the county ensured a smoother passage to the south for the troops.

The Abruzzi region, hindered the Norman domination, promoting the Swabians and then divided into factions, decades later, in the struggles between Frederick II of Swabia (1194-1250) and the Church. As soon as Frederick II came to power he decided to set up a protectionist policy and control of the borders and of the whole L'Aquila and Abruzzi territory. The Emperor created a well-organized network of equipped architectures, towers and castles, directly dependent on the state. Frederick of Swabia promoted the construction of new fortified architectures (towers and castles). The new and pre-existing defensive works were integrated into an uninterrupted line of control that spanned the whole kingdom [14]. The cost of maintaining the fortified structures fell on the state coffers.

For this reason, the Emperor used, as in Norman times, the local workforce as required by the law that imposed the working hours owed to the feudal lord by the people. However, the death of the Emperor interrupted the implementation of his ambitious military program [15]. Frederick II had managed, however, to fortify the territory more carefully. Its system was based on the planning of interventions and on the adaptation of existing structures involving, at various levels, state officials, feudal lords, planners and the population.

Although the interventions carried out during this period are difficult to recognize, the documentation allows us to understand how there had been a renewal of the design methodology consisting in the preventive analysis of the existing and in the production of projects for the newly built structures [16]. The most significant buildings, for example, are found in the towns of Introdacqua, Castel di Ieri, Pescina and Tione.

The watchtowers in Goriano Sicoli (remains in the parish church), Collelongo and Civita d'Antino (towers with reduced height) are relevant. The Introdacqua tower (Fig. 3), built on Mount Plaia, is an example of a particular walled tower. The watchtower is composed of a vertical square-plan element, enhanced by a polygonal wall perimeter with an inclined base that surrounds the tower itself, built at a later date. This typology is halfway between the isolated watchtower and the dungeon. Simone I di Sangro [17] probably built this tower. In 1173 Simone I extended his dominion over this fief as well [18]. The watchtower stands on the highest site in the country. The surrounding wall, with a hexagonal plan of seven and a half meters on each side, has an entrance facing south which, raised from the road level by about three meters, is surmounted by a lowered arch.

Figure 3: Introdacqua tower. On the left view of the south-west front; on the right drawing of the northern elevation. [Lab. of History, Department of Architecture, Unich]

Medieval watchtowers of the mountainous areas of the Abruzzi Region: typologies, construction techniques and territorial landscape

The central tower, with a square plan of five meters and twenty on the side, has the entrance facing in the same direction as that of the enclosure, raised from the floor of the courtyard by about six meters. The loopholes have thresholds, edges and architraves in squared stone. The masonry, on the other hand, is made up of stone pebbles just roughly hewn and joined with mortar beds of varying thickness from about two to five centimeters (0.79-1.97 inches) [19].

Among the watchtowers in this area, the Civita d'Antino tower (Fig.4), founded in the 12th century, is also interesting. The analysis of the typology allows it to be dated to the Norman period. The watchtower was subsequently modified, together with the village. From 1463 the tower and the village were given to Antonio Piccolomini, who obtained the entire barony of Balsorano as a gift. The tower suffered a lot of damage during the Marsica earthquake (1915). This event ruin and unused.

Figure 4: Square tower of Civita d'Antino.

The plan of the tower is almost square (about 6.50 by 6.70 meters: 21.33-21.98 ft). The top part of the tower is compromised by the repeated collapses caused by the centuries-old abandonment and by the earthquakes that hit this area. The outer wall is inclined at the base; this modification was made by the Piccolomini family (15th century). The sloping wall at the base is about five meters high. It is assumed that the watchtower was equipped with a structure for the swooping shooting. The external walls have few openings, with the exception of some slits to which are added two arched entrances obtained in the north elevation. Of these two openings, the oldest is the one placed higher, about ten meters from the original floor, six meters if you consider the current one. The lower opening, on the other hand, is attributed to the restoration of the Renaissance period. The walls are rubble masonry. The external curtain is composed of stone blocks of compact limestone finished only on the outside. The structural and typological choices implemented in this watchtower are found in almost all the other towers analyzed both from the point of view of the masonry equipment and as regards the architectural proportions.

Even Frederick II and his feudal lords, as happened for some religious orders, relied on workers with experience from the eastern territories.

These architects took into consideration the languages and construction techniques of the territories where the crusades took place. The linearity of the laying of the stones and the shapes of the ashlars are a direct reference to the Arab and Byzantine defense structures that strongly influenced the models of these watchtowers [20].

Four years after the death of Emperor Frederick II, in 1254, the importance of the watchtowers and castles of the upper Aterno valley decreased due to the foundation of the city of L'Aquila. Towards the end of the thirteenth century, within the reform of the border fortifications, also in the province of L'Aquila, we witness the settlement of feudal lords of French origin [21].

The presence of French feudal lords determined influences on the types of watchtowers and castles; languages and forms that today can still be read in various fortified architectures. From the fourteenth to the fifteenth century the feudal struggles compromised the state of conservation of the towers and castles causing the destruction of those placed in more accessible places [22].

In the Angevin period there are some interventions characterized by two different phases. The first phase includes the restoration and modernization of the towers located on the coast. The second phase involved the defensive systems present in the hinterland [23]. In recent years, the approach to fortifying remains very similar to that of the Swabian era [24]. In the Angevin period, the watchtowers that controlled the landscape became the most interesting architectures from the point of view of updating techniques and features [25].

There is also a strong influence of the French workers [26] who slowly replace the Apulian masters of Swabian training. Interesting information about the professionals present in these construction sites can be drawn from the documents of the Angevin era. There is a lot of information especially about the French architects of the time of Charles I of Anjou (1226-1285): Thibaud de Seaumur, Jean de Toul [27], Paumier d'Arras, Pierre de Chaule, Baucelin de Linais [28] and Pierre d'Angicourt [29], a name among the best known also because he held the position of protomagister operum curie, that is, superintendent of all works financed by the Crown.

Thus, we are witnessing interventions carried out by architects and engineers employed by the State who created works with their own characteristics, different from the previous types. There was a deep link with French architecture which, mixing with local characteristics, perfected the construction method of the Frederick and Cistercian tradition [30].

In the Angevin era, the architectural culture of the Kingdom of Naples appears independent from the other influences of the period, but sometimes it is little manifest in the Abruzzi area. Some examples of round towers were built even before the Angevin domination, but this architectural typology was mostly used especially with Charles I of Anjou. Strong links existed between the "Leonessa" tower erected in the Angevin citadel of Lucera and some sighting towers in the L'Aquila area (in Aielli, Trasacco, Collarmele and others). In the inhabited area of Aielli, the tower can be traced back, typologically, to the models of the fourteenth century (Fig. 5). The site on which the tower stands was already occupied by a 13th-century sighting structure with a square plan. In later times two defensive walls were also erected, one more internal with three doors and one from a later period that exploited the conformation of the land set on natural steps. This outpost was very important within the Marsican territory, in fact, it was part of a wider control system including the localities of Collarmele, Cerchio, Pescina, Venere, Ortucchio and perhaps Celano.

The structure suffered damage from both the 1915 and 2009 earthquakes. On the stone lintel of a window, on the first level, in addition to the noble coat of arms, the date of construction and the name of the feudal lord who commissioned

*Medieval watchtowers of the mountainous areas of the Abruzzi Region:
typologies, construction techniques and territorial landscape*

the erection have been preserved. In the 16th century the tower belonged to the Piccolomini family; this building was improved with the construction of the vault on the lower floor and the Renaissance windows on the upper part.

Figure 5: Circular plan tower of Aielli

The height of the tower, measured from the ground level, is 17.30 meters (56.76 ft). Its overall diameter measures 9.30 meters, with a wall thickness, in the basement, of about 1.5 meters (4.92 ft). The thickness of the wall tapers slightly as it rises upwards. The internal diameter of the first and second level rooms is 6.60 meters (21.65 ft). The base cylinder is connected by a simple stone frame and a plinth which, shaped in an annular shape, has the function of reinforcement. The octagonal room on the ground floor is partly embedded in the rock. It is entirely probable that the octagonal room, contrary to what generally happened in contemporary isolated towers, did not serve as a deposit. A similar deduction has been reached by noting that the room in question is not directly communicating with the upper floors. This room, covered by an umbrella vault made of stones, has a maximum height of 8.15 meters (26.74 ft). The structure is divided into eight segments by polygonal section ribs that rest on corbels and converge on a keystone decorated with a floral motif. The communication with the outside is ensured by an arched portal open in the elevation facing south-east. A few meters above the main portal there is another entrance for the access to the rooms on the upper floors. This opening is surmounted by a straight architrave and has two shelves at its base. The second floor room is 4.70 meters high (15.42 ft). In the past there were perhaps some wooden floors, in the floors and even on the roof, resting on the recess corresponding to the reduction in the thickness of the wall structure.

Another interesting round watchtower is in Collarmele (Fig. 6); it was founded before the the Swabians domain, but with a wall system similar to the towers of the Angevin era [31].

Figure 6: Circular plan tower of Collarmele

This watchtower, like others, built far from the inhabited centers, with the passage of time has been partially incorporated into the first nucleus of the town. There was no particular military defense apparatus; probably the main function was the control of the territory and the warning of possible dangers signaled by the other sighting towers of the military network.

The Collarmele structure is also a round tower and with straight walls inside to form an octagonal plan. The outer diameter is 8 meters (26.25 ft), while the internal dimension is 2.20 meters (7.22 ft), with a height of about 16.5 meters (54.14). It is open only to the south, with a raised entrance; the portal, without architectural details and with a flat architrave, is high 1.80 meters (5.90 ft). Below its threshold there are two protruding shelves with double projection, the one on the left partially collapsed, which served to support a wooden plank which was supported by a ladder, also wooden, which could be retracted inside the building if necessary.

In this way the tower became completely inaccessible from the outside. Above the entrance there is a stone coat of arms depicting the heraldic symbol of the Berardi, lords of Celano since the 9th century and probable patrons of the watchtower. Unfortunately, due to the continuous seismic events and abandonment, which most of these structures have encountered, the height of the tower is not the original one. The walls, on the other hand, made up of square and regular ashlars recall the southern area walls of the Angevin era.

Medieval watchtowers of the mountainous areas of the Abruzzi Region:
typologies, construction techniques and territorial landscape

Conclusions

The kind of watchtowers have structural and formal features derived from the technical construction matters. The masonry is classified according to the conformation and with the size and position of the building elements.

These characteristics clarify the construction techniques related to the location of the towers and their dating. The watchtowers, moreover, placed in a system with the castles and fortified villages of the area, are part of a territorial organization project, for the control of the routes, structured since the Normans and already in the Lombard era. With the Swabians and the Angevins this defensive system became a real network for the control of the borders of the kingdom.

From the fifteenth century, with the advent of modern siege techniques and the systematic use of firearms, the now obsolete system decreased its defensive and sighting effectiveness.

The feudal lords and the population preferred to settle in urban centers, resulting in the abandonment of these specific elements in the landscape.

The only preserved watchtowers are those that changed their original use, such as the tower incorporated within Palazzo Piccolomini in Molina Aterno, the one inside the Dragonetti de Torres castle in Pizzoli and, finally, the building that stands out in the center of the main square of Montereale, north of the city of L'Aquila.

References

[1] G. Galasso, Il paesaggio disegnato dalla storia, in Il paesaggio italiano, idee contributi immagini, Milano: Touring Club, 2000, pp. 37-52.
[2] C. Perogalli, Castelli dell'Abruzzo e Molise, Milano: Görlich, 1975, p. 17.
[3] G. Chiarizia, C. Santoro, 'L'incastellamento', in U. Russo, E. Tiboni, (Eds), L'Abruzzo nel Medioevo, Pescara: EDIARS, 2003, pp. 305-326.
[4] C. Wickham, 'Castelli e incastellamento nell'Italia centrale: la problematica storica' pp. 137-148, in R. Comba, A. A. Settia, (Eds), Atti del colloquio Castelli. Storia e archeologia, Cuneo dicembre 1981, Torino: Regione Piemonte-Assessorato alla cultura, 1984; A. Augenti, P. Galetti, (Eds), L'incastellamento: storia e archeologia, Spoleto: Fondazione Centro Italiano di Studi sull'Alto Medioevo, 2018.
[5] Perogalli, (Note 2), p. 8.
[6] C.A. Cacciavillani, C. Mazzanti et al., 'La tecnica costruttiva nell'edilizia storica minore delle Comunità Montane in Abruzzo' pp. 1385-1394, in G. Mochi, (Ed.), Atti del Seminario Internazionale Teoria e pratica del costruire: saperi, strumenti, modelli. Esperienze didattiche e di ricerca a confronto, Ravenna 27-29 October 2005, Ravenna: Edizioni Moderna, 2005.
[7] M. C. Forlani, Tecnologie locali e costruzione della casa in Abruzzo, Pescara:Sigraf 2000, p. 10.
[8] L. Santoro, 'I castelli d'Abruzzo nell'evoluzione dell'architettura difensiva', in G. Chiarizia, (Eds), Abruzzo dei Castelli, Pescara: Carsa edizioni, 1988, p. 96.
[9] P. Gasparinetti, 'La via degli Abruzzi e l'attività commerciale di Aquila e Sulmona nei sec. XIII-XV', Bullettino della Deputazione abruzzese di storia patria, LIV-LVI, 1964, pp. 5-7; E. Paratore, 'La viabilità nell'alto medioevo', in U. Russo, E. Tiboni, (Eds), L'Abruzzo nel Medioevo, Pescara: EDIARS, 2003, pp. 63-68.
[10] P. Properzi, 'Terre, castelli e borghi fortificati nell'evoluzione delle strutture territoriali abruzzesi', in G. Chiarizia, (Eds), Abruzzo dei Castelli, Pescara: Carsa edizioni, 1988, p. 64.
[11] Santoro, (Note 8), p. 98.
[12] *Ibid.*, p. 103.

[13] *Ibid.*, (Note 8), p. 104.
[14] *Ibid.*, (Note 8), p. 110.
[15] M. Di Sano, 'Architettura fortificata medioevale nella provincia dell'Aquila: le torri isolate di avvistamento' (Master's degree thesis, University "G. d'Annunzio" of Chieti-Pescara, 2000).
[16] Ibid.
[17] F. Campanile, L'historia dell'illustrissima famiglia di Sangro scritta dal signor Filiberto Campanile, Napoli:Tarquinio Longo, 1615.
[18] B. Apollonj Ghetti, Castelli e fortificazioni nella provincia de L'Aquila, L'Aquila: Ente provinciale per il turismo, 1985.
[19] A. C. Cacciavillani, C. Mazzanti, 'The sighting medieval towers in the Abruzzo Region (italy): study and conservation' pp. 73-84, in R. Amoeda, S. Lira, C. Pinheiro, (Eds), REHAB 2014, Proceedings of the International Conference on Preservation, Maintenance and Rehabilitation of Historical Buildings and Structures, Tomar, Portugal 19-21 March, v. I, Spain: Green Line Institute, 2014.
[20] Santoro, (Note 8), p. 110.
[21] *Ibid.*, (Note 8), p. 122.
[22] R. Colapietra, 'Stato feudale e territorio in Abruzzo nel tardo Medioevo e in età moderna', in G. Chiarizia, (Eds), Abruzzo dei Castelli, Carsa edizioni, Pescara 1988, pp. 222-227.
[23] Santoro, (Note 8), p. 120.
[24] Di Sano, (Note 15).
[25] Perogalli, (Note 2), p.5.
[26] F. Redi, M. Pantaleo, 'Castello di Ocre (AQ). Ricerche archeologiche. Relazione preliminare', Archeologia Medievale, XXXIII, 2000-2004, pp. 325-342; A. Forgione, 'I castelli di Ocre, Ariscola e San Vittorino (L'Aquila)', in S. Patitucci Uggeri, (Ed.), Archeologia castellana nell'Italia meridionale. Bilanci e aggiornamenti: IV Conferenza italiana di archeologia medievale, Roma: CNR, 2010, pp. 27-48.
[27] A. Haseloff, Architettura sveva nell'Italia meridionale, Badi: Adda, 1992, pp. 167-168.
[28] E. Bertaux, 'Les artistes français au service des rois angevines de Naples', Gazette des Beaux-Arts, XXXIV, 1905, pp. 89-114, 313-325; L. Santoro, Castelli angioini e aragonesi nel Regno di Napoli, Milano: Rusconi, 1982, pp. 64, 74.
[29] P. Pistilli, 'Architetti oltremontani al servizio di Carlo I d'Angiò nel Regno di Sicilia', in V. Franchetti Pardo, (Ed.), Arnolfo di Cambio e la sua epoca, costruire scolpire, dipingere, decorare, Atti del Convegno Internazionale di Studi, Firenze-Colle di Val d'Elsa, 7-10 marzo 2006, p. 263.
[30] Santoro, (Note 8), p. 126.
[31] A. Melchiorre, Storia d'Abruzzo tra fatti e memoria, Penne: F. Ambrosini editore, 1989; G. Grossi, Aielli: storia, arte, tradizione, 1998.

Two Masters, Two Methods. First Steps Towards English Standardisation in The Construction of The Sexpartite Vaults in Canterbury Cathedral

Rocío Maira-Vidal
Institute of History. Spanish National Research Council (IH-CSIC)

Introduction

One of the most interesting documents for the history of construction is the well-known manuscript written by Gervase the monk, which describes the works carried out after the fire that destroyed the Norman cathedral of Canterbury in 1174. Gervase (1141-1210) witnessed the works directly and his account provides important information that serves to understand the complicated organisation of the work and the considerable mobilisation of resources for a construction of this type. His detailed description also allows us to attribute the vaults over the choir to a French master, presumably from Sens, and those over the east transept and the high altar to a master from England. I analysed the construction and geometry of these vaults on the basis of photogrammetric measurement, which has enabled me to corroborate this change of master. Comparing these results with an analysis carried out in Sens Cathedral (1138-75) enables us to confirm the origin of the first master mentioned, William of Sens, who used the geometric and construction resources of the French vaults. His English successor, on the other hand, replaced the geometry and the standardisation system with a completely new method, which had not been used in France, but which was later developed in the neighbouring Rochester Cathedral (1180-1240). This is known as English standardisation, where the particular use of geometry differs from that used in continental Gothic and was to give rise to one of the most refined and beautiful styles in Europe, the Perpendicular Gothic. The construction of the sexpartite vaults in Canterbury Cathedral (1174-80) is one of the first steps towards the development of this distinctively English system.

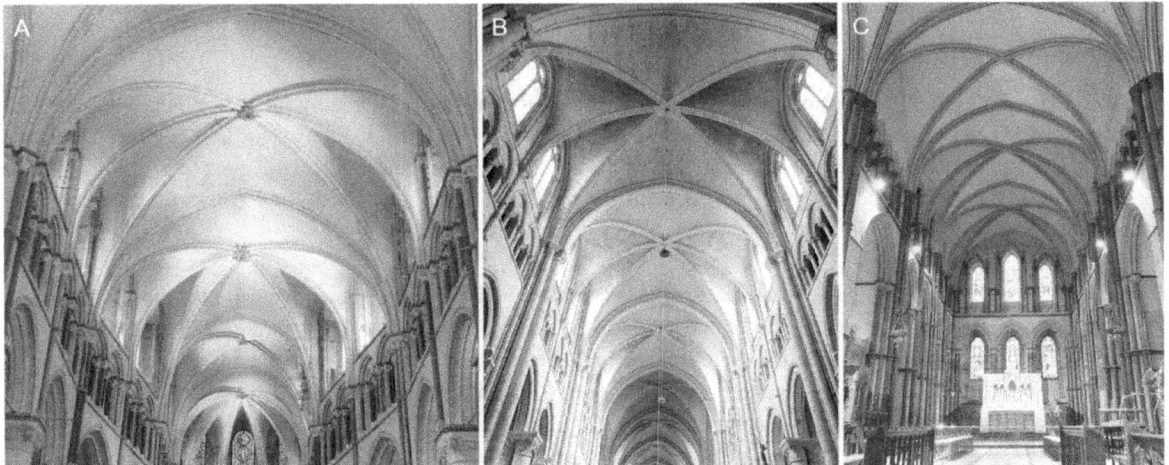

Figure 1: Cathedrals of Canterbury (A), Sens (B) and Rochester (C). Author's photographs.

Two Masters, Two Methods. First Steps Towards English Standardisation in The Construction of The Sexpartite Vaults in Canterbury Cathedral

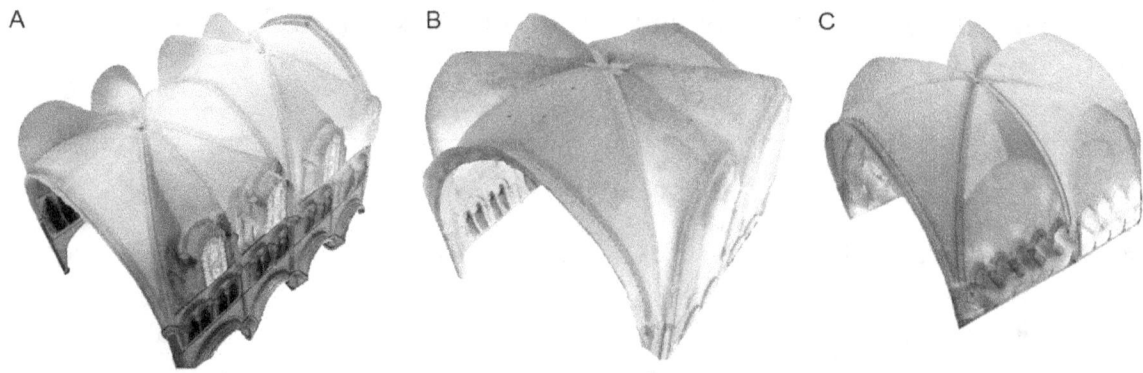

Figure 2: Photogrammetric models of Canterbury Cathedral (A), Sens (B) and Rochester (C). Author's drawings.

Sexpartite vaults. Method of study

Sexpartite vaults are one of the main early Gothic typologies. These structures had an ephemeral life [1]; they were used fundamentally between the second half of the twelfth and the first half of the thirteenth centuries and can be found in the most important buildings of the time. They have six ribs that divide their severy surfaces into six sections (Fig. 1). In order to carry out the comparative analysis of the cathedrals of Canterbury, Sens and Rochester, models were generated using photogrammetry (Fig. 2), which allowed their rib geometry and stereotomy to be studied in detail.

The importation of French geometries. The vaults of William of Sens

The manuscript written by Gervase the monk (1141-1210) is of exceptional interest [2]. In addition to describing the tasks carried out during the twelfth century reconstruction of the cathedral, where he specifies the exact date, it provides interesting details that help to understand how a construction of this type was organised in the Middle Ages. It is particularly interesting to note that the author mentions the name and provenance of the master masons who oversaw the works, uncommon in medieval sources.

Between 1174 and 1175, after the Norman Cathedral of Canterbury had been ravaged by fire, the monks hired William of Sens for the reconstruction work. The initial intention was to consolidate the remaining structures and reconstruct the building, a task that the French master considered feasible, or at least that is the idea he conveyed to the monks before the work began. However, once the works started, he suggested that a new building should be constructed, demolishing the previous one which he did not consider safe.

It is worth highlighting the qualities that the monks valued when hiring the master mason according to Gervase: "However, amongst the workmen there had come a certain William of Sens, a man active and ready, and as a workman most skilful both in wood and stone. Him, therefore, they retained, on account of his lively genius and good reputation, and dismissed the others. And to him, and to the providence of God was the execution of the work committed." [3]. The master had to be skilled in stonecutting but also in working with wood, which confirms the importance of the temporary works needed to build the stone structures. Assembly of the vaults required large wooden formwork that could support the thrusts of the structure as the work progressed. These temporary works had to be resistant and robust, and designed to ensure the stability of the assembly. As ephemeral structures, which were removed after completion of the building, they had to be designed to make the most of the materials, in an effort to keep the costs of the work down [4].

According to Gervase, the master was also responsible for designing the machines needed to load and transport the material, which again proves a knowledge of the wood he had to handle: " ... And now he addressed himself to the procuring of stone from beyond the sea. He constructed ingenious machines for loading and unloading ships, and for drawing mortar and stones. He delivered templates for shaping the stones to the sculptors who were assembled and diligently prepared other of the same kind. The choir thus condemned to destruction was pulled down, and nothing else was done in this year..." [5]. He also designed the templates that the stonecutters used to cut the ashlars and voussoirs, in addition to preparing the drawings for the vaults, the so-called monteas, the full-scale working drawings that provided the geometry defining the shape of the arches and stone surfaces.

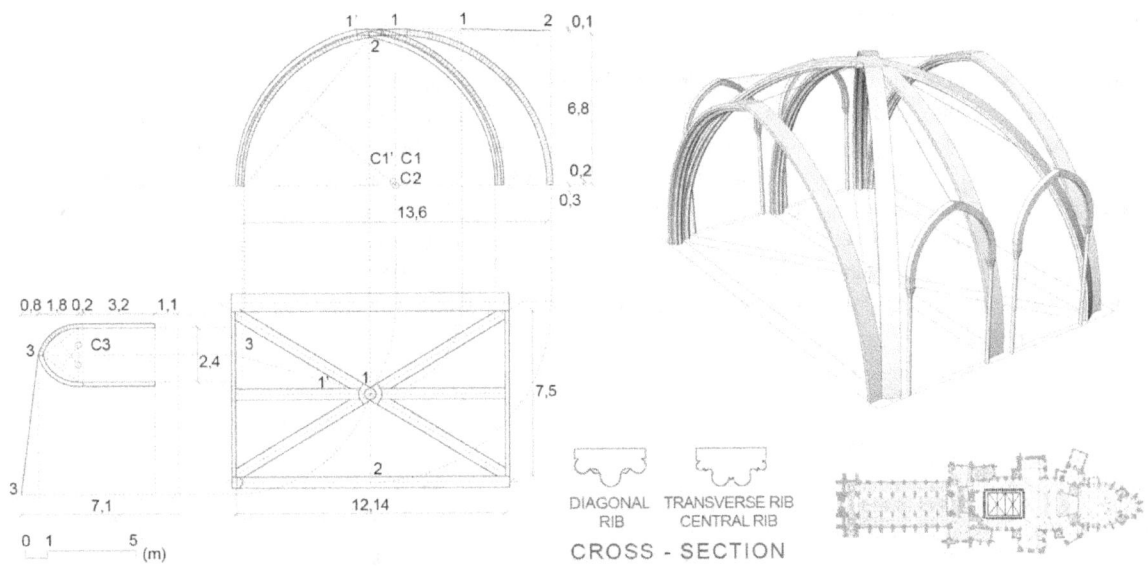

Figure 3: Geometric design of the two vaults over the choir of Canterbury Cathedral, by William of Sens. 3D Model based on the montea (full-size working drawing). Author's drawings.

Between 1176 and 1177, the French master worked on the construction of the three vaults of the choir, two of them sexpartite vaults (Fig. 3), and in the following year, between 1177 and 1178 prepared the temporary works necessary to build the remaining sexpartite vaults of the transept and the sanctuary. During the year 1178, the fourth year after the works began, William of Sens suffered a terrible accident that confined him to his bed and finally led to a change of master in the following year. The Frenchman fell to the ground from the wooden transept vault scaffolding, set up at the height of the vault springing at more than 14 metres above the church floor (50 feet).

> "... Upon these ten he placed arches and vaults. But after the two triforia and upper Windows on both sides were completed and he had prepared the machines for forming the great vault, suddenly the beams broke under his feet, and he fell to the ground, stones and timbers accompanying his fall, from the height of the [springing] capitals of the upper vault, that is to say, of fifty feet. ... The master, thus hurt, remained in his bed for some time under medical care in expectation of recovering, but was deceived in this hope, for his health amended not. ... And the master, perceiving that he derived no benefit from the physicians, gave up the work, and crossing the sea, returned to his home in France. And another succeeded him in the charge of the works." [6].

Two Masters, Two Methods. First Steps Towards English Standardisation in The Construction of The Sexpartite Vaults in Canterbury Cathedral

According to the manuscript, William of Sens built only two of the cathedral's sexpartite vaults. The analysis of their geometry reveals important differences in comparison to the remaining sexpartite vaults, those that were built by the second master mason (Figs 3-7).

Construction of the vaults over the choir of the Cathedral (1138-75) at Sens, the place where the master was originally from [7], began more than thirty years before the sexpartite vaults at Canterbury Cathedral, however the vaults over the nave were constructed from 1158 onwards. The last section at Sens was completed between 1175 and 1180, therefore overlapping with the works in the English cathedral [8]. Master William of Sens may have participated in both works. The similarity between the vaults of the two buildings is not only evident in the details of the keystones, the cross section of the ribs and the springers used for the supports but can also be seen in the use of the same geometry (Table 1) (Figs 3-5). A detailed comparison of the two vaults shows that the rib geometry is the same: the diagonals are semi-circular, and the transverse ribs are pointed, and the centres of both are on the impost line. The central ribs are pointed and slightly stilted above the impost line. In both cathedrals this slight stilt, 35 centimetres in Sens (Fig 4) and 20 centimetres in Canterbury (Fig 3), allowed the master to use the curvature of the diagonal ribs to create the central rib, making it possible to use just one type of formwork for the vault assembly. In Sens Cathedral, the transverse ribs are not standardised, their curvature is different from the others and therefore two kinds of formwork were needed for their execution (Fig 4). This change introduced an improvement in the English Cathedral, where all the ribs were built with one type of formwork (Fig 3). In Sens Cathedral, the transverse ribs seem to have been built before the vaults, as if they were an independent system. The application of standardisation indicates a thorough knowledge of construction, and the use of the same type of formwork for the execution of the different ribs of the vault made it possible to facilitate and simplify assembly [9] and reduce its cost.

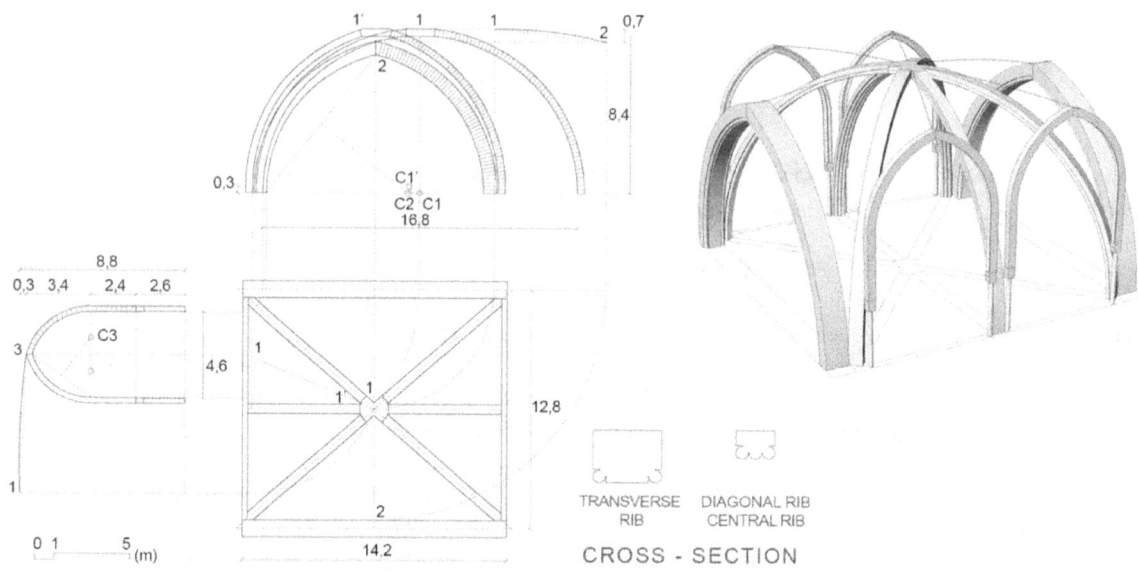

Figure 4: Geometric design of the vaults of Sens Cathedral. 3D Model based on the montea (full-size working drawing). Author's drawings.

Table 1: Comparison of the overall dimensions and of the voussoir dimensions of the vaults at the cathedrals of Canterbury, Sens and Rochester

	Construction date	Mean *voussoir* length (metres)	Plan (width x length) (metres)	Height of the keystone (metres)
Sens Cathedral	1138-80	18-22 (straight *voussoirs*)	12.78 x 14.19	24.25
Canterbury Cathedral (choir)	1176-77	16 (straight *voussoirs*)	12.14 x 9.70 (west choir) 12.14 x 7.50 (east choir)	21.61
Canterbury Cathedral (transept)	1179-80	16 (straight *voussoirs*)	10.23 x 9.51	20.82
Canterbury Cathedral (west sanctuary vault)	1179-80	17 (straight *voussoirs*)	12.09 x 10.14	20.82
Canterbury Cathedral (east sanctuary vault)	1179-80	16 (straight *voussoirs*)	12.13 (west side) x 10.26 (lenth) x 7.60 (east side)	20.82
Rochester Cathedral (sanctuary)	1180	21 (straight *voussoirs*)	8.67 x 6.42	14.88
Rochester Cathedral (east transept)	1240	14 (straight *voussoirs*)	8.63 x 9.11	15.47
Rochester Cathedral (choir)	1240	20 (straight *voussoirs*)	8.61 x 8.46	15.72
Rochester Cathedral (west transept)	1340	35- 54 (curved *voussoirs*)	9.43 x 6.25	16.68

Similarities in the stereotomy of the sexpartite vaults in the Cathedrals of Sens and Canterbury

The analysis of the stonecutting techniques used for the *voussoirs*, severies and keystones reveals remarkable similarities between the vaults as well as some differences (Fig. 5). In Sens Cathedral, the cross section of the transverse ribs is much larger than that of the other ribs and the shape of their *voussoirs* is also different. This feature highlights the fact that the nave was conceived as a series of different vaulted bays. In Canterbury, on the other hand, the interior of the building is composed as one space, where the transverse ribs are the same size as the other ribs and the *voussoirs* of the transverse and central ribs share the same cross-section design. This last feature seems to be intended to blur the function of the transverse ribs as a separation between the vaulted bays. Here the cross-section of the diagonal ribs differs from that of the other ribs, although they are all the same size.

Two Masters, Two Methods. First Steps Towards English Standardisation in The Construction of The Sexpartite Vaults in Canterbury Cathedral

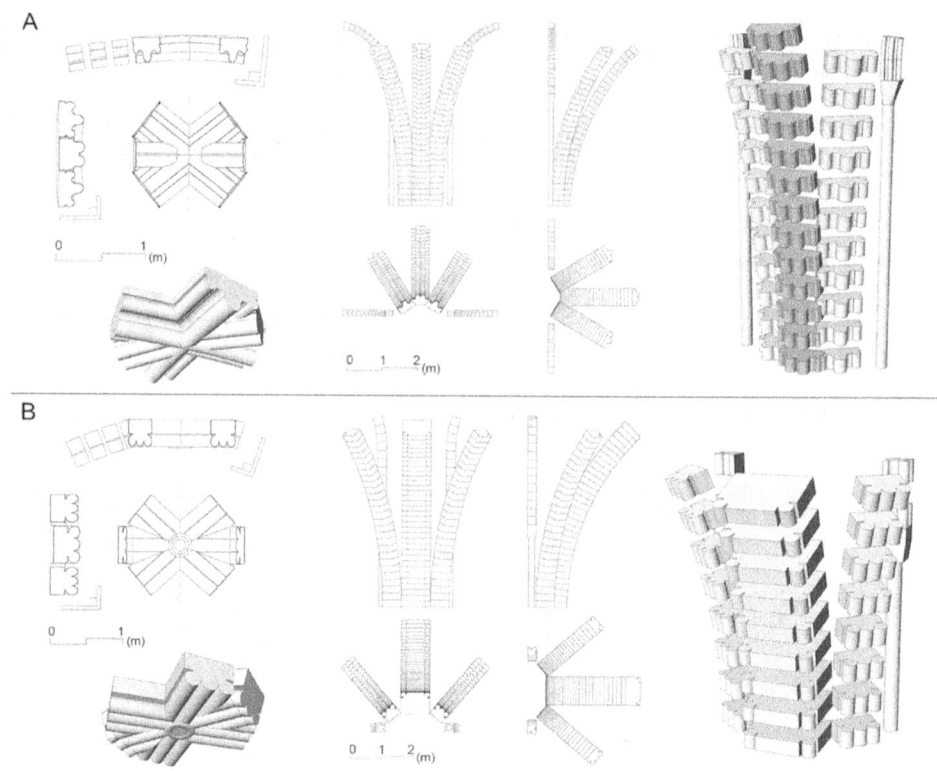

Figure 5: Comparison of rib cross-sections and construction of the springers and keystones in the cathedrals of Canterbury (A) and Sens (B). Author's drawings.

In both cathedrals the *voussoirs* are exceptionally short [10]. So short that they resemble brick *voussoirs* (Table 1). This proportion is very unconventional, to the point that within my extensive analysis of sexpartite vaults in Europe [11], these are the only two cases where the *voussoirs* were cut to this proportion. They have a very similar cross-section, although in the case of Sens the ribs have three shafts and in Canterbury, they have only two (Figs 3-4). The use of short *voussoirs* implies the use of the same type of tool to cut them, the square [12], which allowed them to be cut straight without a curve, unlike the vaults built with curved *voussoirs* where the bevel was the tool used.

In both buildings, the vault supports have no *tas-de-charges* (Fig. 5). The ribs rise up from the springer: the different *voussoirs* of each rib are trimmed to fit the available space on the support and are separate from each other. The absence of *tas-de-charges* is a very significant characteristic. Their beds are horizontal and so form part of the walls, not of the ribs, where the beds of the *voussoirs* lean toward the geometric centre of the arches. The *tas-de-charges* made it possible to reduce the size of the ribs and thus their thrust and the formwork used in their assembly. They also reinforced the structure on their supports by joining the different ribs of the vault in one piece of stone, avoiding misalignments and movements between them during the work. The absence of this type of solution indicates that the master's knowledge of this construction system was still rudimentary [13], which would again indicate the presence of William of Sens in both works.

The way the keystones are cut is peculiar to Sens and Canterbury, so this similarity also demonstrates the relationship between the two buildings. In both cases they have six very long arms dominated by the shape of the shafts. The outer faces were cut with a slant to receive the ribs. The dominant presence of the arms over the sculpted central boss highlights the unusual shape of these keystones, which differ from those that normally crown this type of vault (Fig. 5).

In both vaults, the severy stones are small ashlars, which must have been easy to cut in spite of the large quantity needed to close the stone surfaces at the ribs.

The consistent use of the same type of tools to cut the stones and of the same construction techniques for the rib connections, indicate the master's degree of knowledge. The latter decades of the twelfth century and the early decades of the thirteenth century marked a moment of great change for the medieval architecture of Europe, where some structures of this type can be seen to have evolved much more than others. Therefore, a comparison of the techniques used is very useful in assessing the knowledge of the master who created them and makes it possible to establish authorship relationships between different buildings.

A style of his own. The work of William the Englishman

Shortly after his accident, William of Sens was temporarily replaced by a monk qualified in the arts of construction: "Nevertheless, as the winter approached, and it was necessary to finish the upper vault he gave charge of the work to a certain ingenious and industrious monk, who was the overseer of masons,... But the master reclining in bed commanded that all things should be done in order. ... Two quadripartite vault-bays were also constructed on each side before winter [1178]. Heavy downpours did not permit of more work." [14].

In the fifth year after the works had begun, the master returned to his native land and was replaced by William the Englishman, who was also highly skilled and very knowledgeable in various tasks, an essential characteristic for this work: "...And another succeeded him in the charge of the works; William by name, English by nation, small in body, but in workmanship of many kinds acute and honest. He in the summer of the fifth year [1179] finished the transept on each end, that is, the north and the south, and closed the vault over the great Altar, ..." [15]. Geometry was one of these essential areas of knowledge since it was necessary to rethink and design the building and the more complex structures, such as the vaults. As Foyle says, William the Englishman had to review his predecessor's design, which apparently was conceived on the basis of one large geometric scheme [16]. Perhaps he did not have the same experience as William of Sens, as there are important differences in the design of the two masters' vaults.

William the Englishman constructed the two sexpartite vaults of the transept (Fig. 6) and the two over the sanctuary (Fig. 7) and continued with the foundations for the construction of the chapel of St Thomas, at the east end of the cathedral (Table 1). The vaults built by William the Englishman did not use the same geometry as the vaults of his predecessor. The geometry of the vaults on the transept arms is similar to that of the vaults of the Cathedral of Paris, in turn different from the vaults at the Cathedral of Sens since the central ribs are not pointed but semi-circular. However, contrary to the case of the French vaults based on the Parisian model, standardisation was employed for the transverse and the central rib rather than the diagonal and transverse ribs [17]. Perhaps the master initially tried to continue the vaults following the typical French designs, but rather it seems more likely that the formwork was already prepared for these vaults, preventing significant changes to be made to these structures. At the time of the accident, the transept's central vault was ready for assembly, and the temporary works had already been built for it, as Gervase mentioned. The master fell from the platform that supported the formwork of this vault, which would then be built by the abovementioned monk under the orders of William of Sens. The formwork and voussoirs of the vaults on the transept arms would probably already have been prepared.

Two Masters, Two Methods. First Steps Towards English Standardisation in The Construction of The Sexpartite Vaults in Canterbury Cathedral

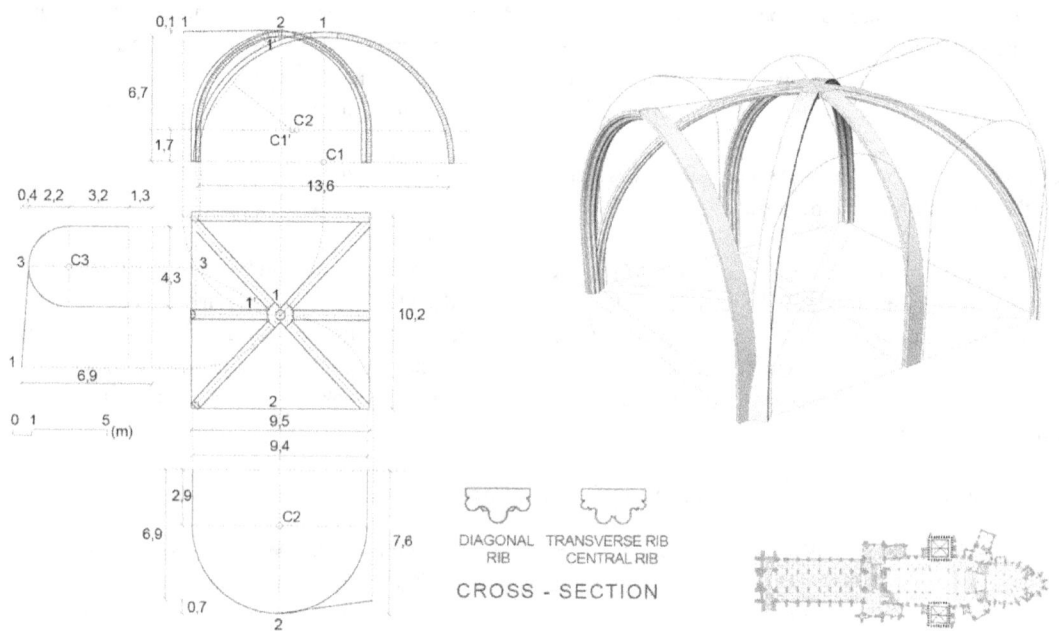

Figure 6: Geometric design of the two vaults over the transept arms of Canterbury Cathedral, by William the Englishman. 3D Model based on the montea (full-size working drawing). Author's drawings.

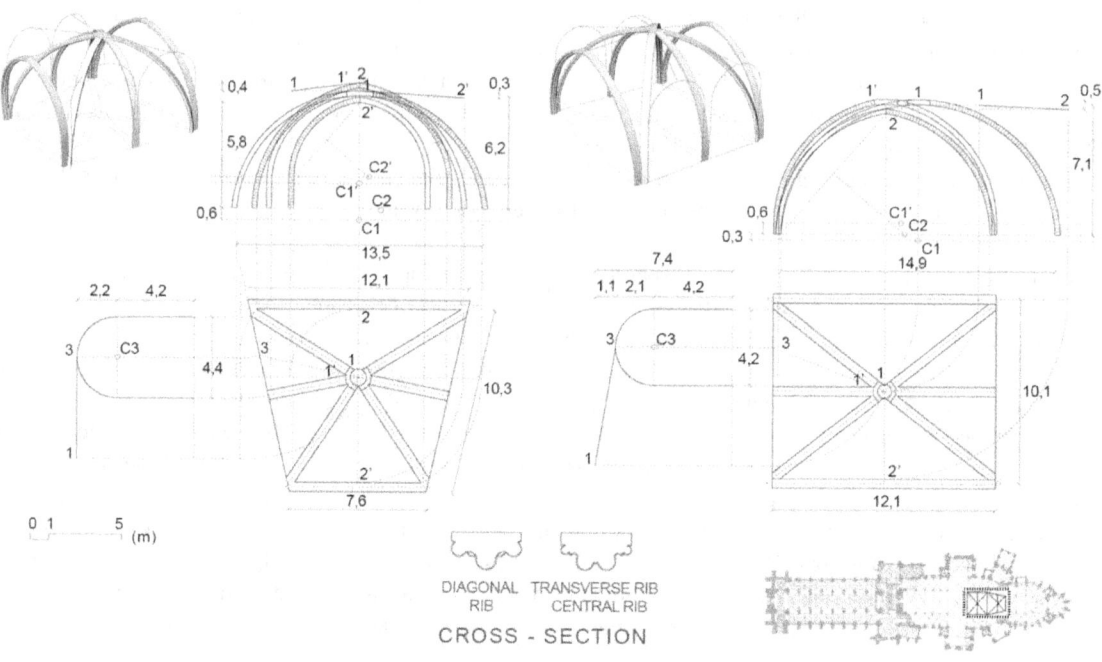

Figure 7: Geometric design of the two vaults over the sanctuary of Canterbury Cathedral, by William the Englishman. 3D Model based on the montea (full-size working drawing). Author's drawings.

Once the transept was completed, William the Englishman seemed to give free rein to his creativity, designing the two remaining sexpartite vaults based using completely different geometries. The vaults above the sanctuary had depressed diagonal ribs (Fig. 7). The transverse ribs and the central ribs were pointed arches with their centres level with, or above, the impost. In both these vaults, the ribs are partially standardised as in the others. In the western vault of the sanctuary only the transverse and the central ribs share the same curvature, while in the eastern vault only the diagonals and the western transverse rib have the same curve.

In the vault over the western section of the sanctuary the master could have standardised all the ribs easily, he would simply have had to lower the stilt of the central rib by half to be able to construct the rib with the curvature as the diagonal ribs. The transverse ribs could also have been constructed with these curves and would have been 27 centimetres higher at the keystone than they actually are. Both changes would have slightly varied the volume of the vault, but these modifications would not have been visible to the naked eye. In turn, one type of formwork could have been used instead of two. In addition, these vaults require the formwork to be placed at different heights for each rib, making different platforms necessary to lift each set of formwork into place above the previous one, again complicating construction. Perhaps this is the result of a lack of technical skill or simply the search for new designs using other geometric resources that would later culminate in the English medieval Late Gothic. What we can say is that these designs are distinctive and unique, especially the eastern vault of the sanctuary. Some of the ribs in this vault rise at a tangent to the impost line while others lean forward because they are depressed. In the Perpendicular Gothic, this same idea was used but was developed further: the ribs were tangential to their support or leaned forward or backward, with their centres on or above the impost [18]. In this way, the masters would have used the same arc to construct all the ribs, inclining them appropriately depending on the height they needed to reach. William the Englishman used different arcs without making use of the advantages offered by this methodology.

The stereotomy used in the vaults erected by the English master is the same as in the vaults of William of Sens (Table 1) (Figs 3-7). According to Gervase, the French master arrived from his native land with a group of stonecutters, who perhaps remained after his departure. In any case, continuing the cutting based on the templates defined by the first master would not have been a complicated matter.

First steps towards English standardisation. The vaults of Rochester Cathedral

A devastating fire broke out in Rochester Cathedral in 1179 that seriously affected the eastern end of the building. Sexpartite vaults were used for the reconstruction over the sanctuary (1180), the eastern transept (1240), the choir (1240) and the northern arm of the western transept (1340) (Table 1) (Figs 8-9) [19]. These vaults share a common feature whereby most of their ribs are depressed. The vaults covering the sanctuary, the eastern transept and the choir are similar to each other (Figs 8-9). Their diagonal ribs are semi-circular with their centres below the impost line. The centres of the transverse and central ribs, which are pointed arches, are located on or below the impost line. The vaults over the sanctuary, the first to be built, were the only ones where the ribs were completely standardised. The diagonal ribs and the central rib of the vaults over the eastern transept and over the choir show partial standardisation. Despite the use of similar geometries, this characteristic could indicate a different master mason in the sanctuary, which would not be surprising given that its vaults were built sixty years before those erected over the eastern transept and the choir.

The sexpartite vaults of the western transept are different due to their typical fourteenth century geometry (Fig. 9). The diagonal ribs form basket-handle arches and the transverse and central ribs are either pointed and depressed, or semi-circular with their centres on the impost line. In this case, standardisation was also partial, where the shapes of the diagonal, central and wall ribs was based on the same segment of a circle.

The methodology used by William the Englishman in Canterbury continued to be applied for the standardisation of the vaults at Rochester. The same arc leans to a greater or lesser extent from its springing on the impost line. A more complex

Two Masters, Two Methods. First Steps Towards English Standardisation in The Construction of The Sexpartite Vaults in Canterbury Cathedral

and developed version of this method was to be used later in the Perpendicular Gothic. In France, the methodology used by the master masons to standardise the ribs of vaults in the High Middle Ages was different. There, they were slightly stilted on the impost to reach the required height with the same curvature [20]. Depressed ribs were not used, and mainly the transverse and central ribs were stilted. The Cathedrals of Canterbury and Rochester could be the first examples that used English standardisation, although it would be necessary to study other buildings with other types of vaults of the same chronology in England.

The stereotomy of the vaults of Rochester Cathedral (sanctuary, western transept and choir) shares similarities with Canterbury (Fig. 10). Neither vaulting systems had *tas-de-charges* at the base and their *voussoirs* were cut with a square (Table 1). Their transverse and central ribs share the same cross-section, while the diagonals are different. The stereotomy of Rochester's western transept is different and more developed with *tas-de-charges* and curved *voussoirs* cut applying a bevel (Table 1).

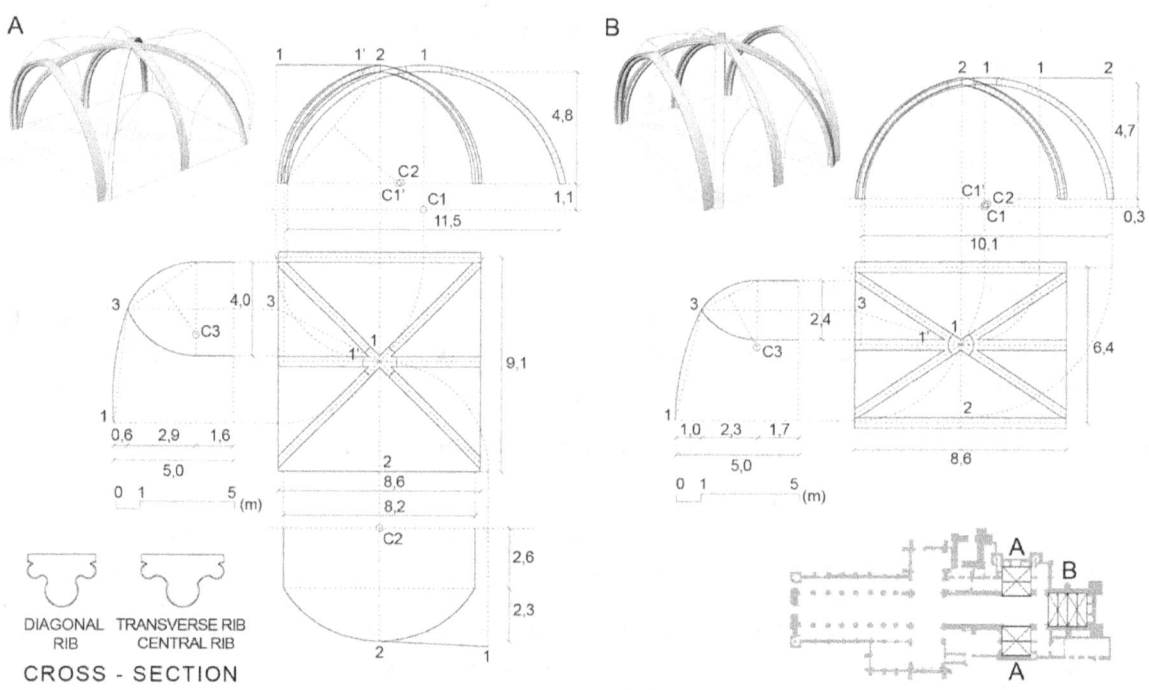

Figure 8: Geometric design of the two vaults over the sanctuary (B) and the east transept (A) of Rochester Cathedral. 3D Model based on the montea (full-size working drawing). Author's drawings.

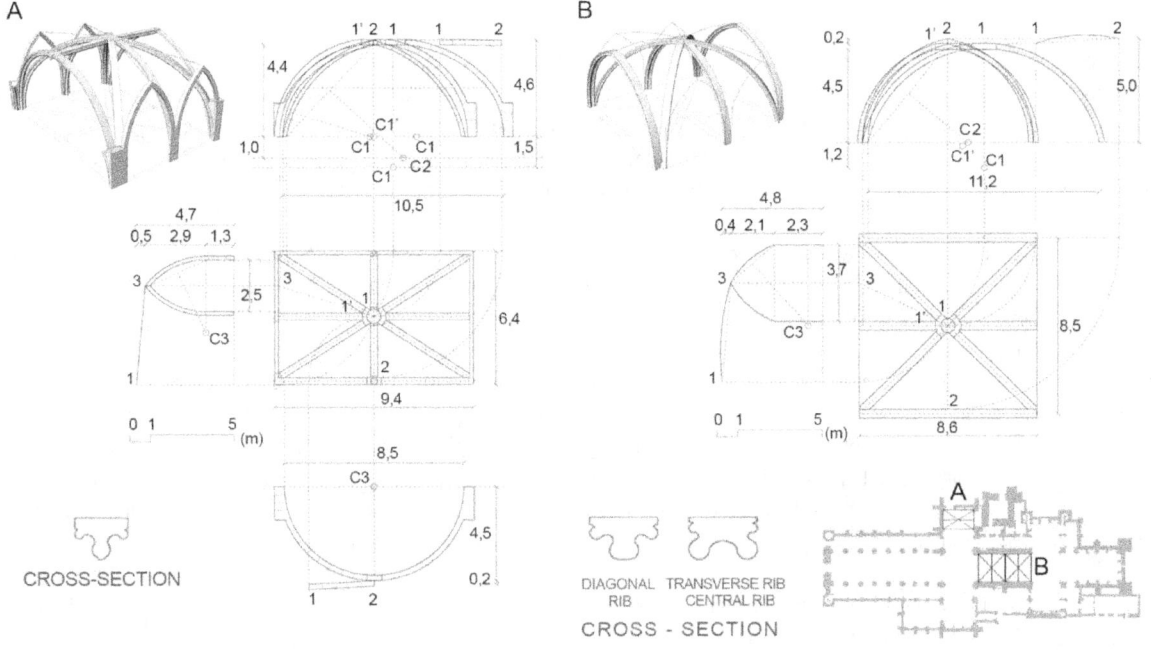

Figure 9: Geometric design of the two vaults over the choir (B) and the west transept (A) of Rochester Cathedral. 3D Model based on the montea (full-size working drawing). Author's drawings.

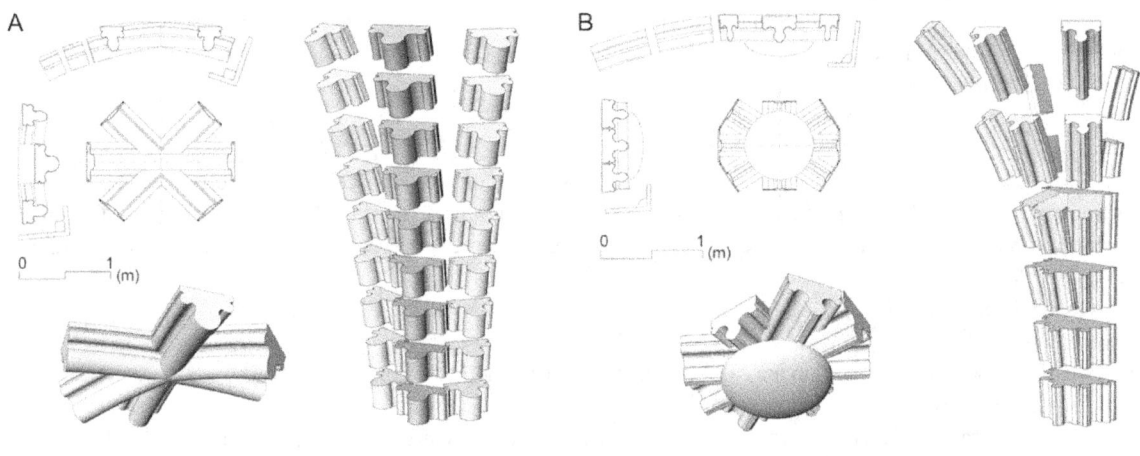

Figure 10: Construction details of the ribs, springers and keystones in Rochester Cathedral (A sanctuary, B west transept). Author's drawings.

Two Masters, Two Methods. First Steps Towards English Standardisation in The Construction of The Sexpartite Vaults in Canterbury Cathedral

Conclusions

This research aims to show new ways of analysing the authorship of buildings and of providing new data on their construction dates. By comparing the knowledge applied by the masters, different buildings can be related to each other based on the geometric and structural resources used. The end of the High Middle Ages was a fruitful period for architecture when some structural improvements began to be implemented and new tools started to be used. This development was not uniform, which is an advantage when studying authorship.

We can confirm that the vaults which according to Gervase are the work of William of Sens follow the geometric model of the Cathedral of Sens, the master's place of origin. In addition, their stereotomy and the technical solutions used are similar. However, the design of these structures changed with the change of master. The templates that William the Englishman employed for the geometry were different from those used by the Frenchman and showed a particular personality. These resources remind us of those used later in the Perpendicular Gothic, when all the ribs of the vault were built based on the same segment of a circle and leaned inwards from the springing to a greater or lesser degree. Canterbury and Rochester Cathedrals are evidence of the first attempts at using this technique, where the arches lean from their supports, but the curve is not always the same. These are the first examples to have been detected of this type of standardisation, which when further developed was to result in one of the most beautiful Gothic architectures in Europe, the Perpendicular Gothic.

The east end of Canterbury Cathedral is considered the first Gothic edifice in England to import the construction techniques being used in the Île de France. The vaults over the choir and the east transept are the only example of sexpartite vaults built in England following French models of geometry, since the geometries used in the neighbouring cathedrals of Rochester and Lincoln, also studied by the author of this text, have little in common with the designs imported to England by William of Sens.

References

[1] R. Maira Vidal, 'Abandonment of the sexpartite vault: difficulties associated with its construction and how it evolved prior to its disappearance ' pp. 879-886 in I. Wouters, S. Van de Voorde, I. Bertels ,(Eds), Building Knowledge, Construction Histories. Proceedings of the 6th International Congress on Construction History Vol.2 , Brussels 2018, Brussels: CRC Press. Taylor&Francis Group, 2018.
[2] J. Foyle, Architecture of Canterbury Cathedral, London: Scala Publishers, 2013. pp.76-95.
[3] ibid, p.77.
[4] R. Bechmann, 'Comment standardisation et préfabrication, développées aux XIIe-XIIIe siècles dans le système de construction, ont permis l'extraordinaire floraison des cathédrales "gothiques"' pp. 771-780 in V. Nègre, R. Carvais, A. Guillerme, J. Sakarovitch ,(Eds), Edifice & Artifice. Histoires Constructives. Actes du Premier Congrès Francophone d'Histoire de la Construction, París 2008, París: Picard, 2010.
[5] Foyle, Architecture, (Note 2), p.78.
[6] ibid, p.76-95.
[7] Y. Kusaba, 'Some observations on the early flying buttress and choir triforium of Canterbury Cathedral', Gesta, vol. 28, no 2, 1989, pp.175-189.
[8] J. Henriet, 'La cathédrale Saint Ettienne de Sens: le parti du premier maître et les campagnes du XIIe siècle', Bulletin monumental, tome 140, no 2, 1982, pp. 81-174; F. Salet, La cathédrale de sens et sa place en l'histoire de l'architecture médiévale, Comptes rendus des séances de l'Académie des Inscriptions et Belles-Lettres, 99 année, no 2, 1955, pp. 182-187.
[9] R. Bechmann, Les racines des cathédrales, París: Payot, 2011.
[10] R. Willis, The architectural history of Canterbury Cathedral, Richmond: Tiger of the stripe, 2006; R. Willis, On The Construction Of The Vaults Of The Middle Ages, London: The Royal Institute of British Architects, 1910.

[11] R. Maira Vidal, 'Bóvedas sexpartitas. Los orígenes del gótico' (Ph.D. thesis, Universidad Politécnica de Madrid, 2015).

[12] L. R. Shelby, 'Medieval mason's tools. II. Compass and square', Technology and Culture, vol. 6, no 2, 1965, pp. 236-248.

[13] R. Maira Vidal, 'Evolution of construction techniques in the Early Gothic: comparative study of the stereotomy of European sexpartite vaults using new measurement systems', Journal of Cultural Heritage, vol. 28, 2017, pp. 99-108.

[14] Foyle, Architecture, (Note 2), p.85.

[15] ibid, p.85.

[16] ibid, p.88.

[17] R. Maira Vidal, 'Expansion et développement des voûtes sexpartites en France: différences typologiques selon les régions' pp. 1101-1111 in G. Bienvenu, M. Monteil, H. Rousteau-Chambon ,(Eds), Construire! entre Antiquité et Époque contemporaine. Actes du 3e congrès francophone d'histoire de la construction, Nantes 2017, Paris: Picard, 2019.

[18] J. C. Palacios Gonzalo, La Cantería Medieval. La construcción de la bóveda gótica española, Madrid: Editorial Munilla-Lería, 2009. pp. 61-64.

[19] J. Meyrick, Rochester Cathedral, Rochester: St Ives Westerham Press, 2014.

[20] R. Maira Vidal, 'The evolution of the knowledge of geometry in Early Gothic construction: the development of the sexpartite vault in Europe', International Journal of Architectural Heritage, vol. 11, no 7, 2017, pp. 1005-1025.

Medieval formwork imprints in the Basilica of St Anthony in Padua

Louis Vandenabeele
Institute of Construction History and Preservation (IDB), ETH Zurich, Switzerland

Introduction

The construction of the Basilica of St Anthony started outside the walls of Padua shortly after the death of the Portuguese-born Franciscan friar in 1231 (Fig. 1). Already largely completed around 1310, the brick church and its timber domes were remodelled in the following centuries with the reconstruction of the bell towers and choir dome (fifteenth century), the addition of an eastern chapel or the replacement of five timber domes after a fire (eighteenth century). In the absence of medieval building archives and despite decades of art historical research, the understanding of the construction sequences remained subject to conflicting theories until recently [1].

Figure 1: North-eastern view of the Basilica of St Anthony in Padua (picture: Davide Boggian and Giacomo Ravenna)

Since 2019, the Basilica has been investigated from a building archaeology and construction history perspective by researchers of the Institute of Construction History and Preservation (ETH Zurich), under the direction of Prof. Stefan M. Holzer and in collaboration with the *Delegazione Pontificia per la Basilica di Sant'Antonio in Padova*. After a thorough analysis of the original brickwork supported by digital surveys and the absolute dating of its timber domes using dendrochronology, a scientifically-sound image of the early history of the pilgrimage landmark has started to emerge [2].

Medieval formwork imprints in the Basilica of St Anthony in Padua

The present paper on formwork imprints sheds light on subtle details recorded in the intricate network of passages and rooms hidden in the brick walls of the massive church. From the survey of traces of temporary timber structures – enriched by the discovery of intact elements – the construction techniques of short-span barrel vaults and medium-span pointed arches can be described with high precision. The missing portions of temporary works dismantled without leaving traces are hypothetically reconstructed based on well-documented examples gathered in a recent monograph [3]. Furthermore, the findings are supported by preliminary results from absolute dating (dendrochronology and radiocarbon) and wood species analyses. Finally, the paper introduces ongoing investigation using similar methods to reveal the erection process of the eight large-span masonry domes.

Short-span barrel vaults

The masonry of the western half of the church, likely built between the 1230s and 1260s, is partly hollowed out by more than 300 metres of narrow corridors leading to each roof and attic. This network, the length of which has to our knowledge no equivalent in medieval religious architecture, was certainly designed to facilitate construction, ease maintenance and provide a fast access to each part of the edifice in the event of a fire. Unlike exposed structures, most of these galleries underwent no modifications whatsoever since the thirteenth century, making it a privileged access to the Basilica's original state.

The width of these corridors varies between 55 and 80 cm and their inclination can reach up to 50°. The highest corridors are to be found in the front facade (3.65 m), likely explaining why some components of the original formwork which do not hinder the passage were left in place (Fig. 2). These transversal elements consist of 3.5-cm thick boards inserted after completion of the vertical bricklaying and before the start of the barrel vault (Fig. 3). As revealed by imprints in the abundant mortar binding the bricks, each board was topped by a semi-circular element (likely made of two or three pieces) supporting about ten longitudinal boards, the positions of which are still perfectly discernible on the mortar or at the ends of the corridors where corresponding notches can be observed. Some of these longitudinal elements, albeit absent in the front façade, have been recovered intact in other corridors above the crossing and at the base of the northern bell tower.

Figure 2: Boards used for vaulting the corridors of the front façade in the thirteenth century (picture: author)

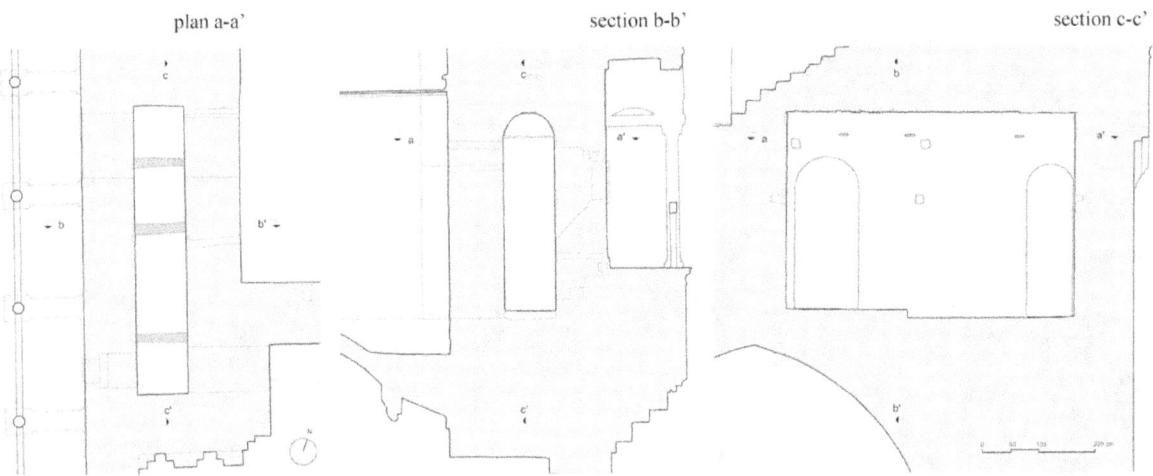

Figure 3: Three out of four original boards survived in this north-western corridor of the façade (drawing: author)

Wood species analyses have indicated that the transversal boards consist of spruce, unlike the original roof structures for which fine-grained larch were felled in the last quarter of the thirteenth century [4]. Some boards are also drilled multiple times, indicating that they could have been part of a previous structure, likely a scaffolding fastened with ropes. Thus, as one might have expected, medieval builders did not use timbers of similar qualities for temporary formwork and permanent roof structures.

The relatively large sections of preserved timber have raised hopes of dating the surrounding masonry using dendrochronology, but such attempts have not yet been successful due to the lack of reference curves for thirteenth-century spruce in the region. Samples of these boards were thus extracted for further radiocarbon analyses at the Laboratory for Ion Beam Physics (ETH Zurich).

Although rare, similar imprints of boards on intradoses of barrel vaults (showing a striking resemblance to modern concrete structures) enable the tracing of such formwork back to second-century Italy [5]. As a first step in the wide range of vaulting techniques applied in the Basilica of St Anthony, the exceptional preservation of some original boards offers a more precise understanding of an ancestral vaulting technique as well as a unique opportunity to date varied parts of the building.

Medium-span arches

The second example of formwork imprints relates to traces recorded in two hidden rooms formed by pointed arches at the base of each bell tower, connecting the spiral staircases of the buttresses to the attics of the ambulatory (Fig. 4). The sole presence of such arched rooms led previous scholars to surmise that these are the remains of an open upper gallery in a former variant of the ambulatory [6]. Yet it seems more likely that the primary role of these rooms was to lighten the masonry and help spread vertical loads to two distinct supports. Moreover, their surfaces were never intended to be visible, or they would still bear traces of plaster.

Medieval formwork imprints in the Basilica of St Anthony in Padua

Figure 4: Traces of wooden boards on the intrados of a pointed arch under the northern tower (picture: author)

Based on a photogrammetric survey and detailed onsite observations, the traces of formwork on the intrados of the northern arch have been precisely mapped. Similar imprints can be observed on the twin room under the southern tower, but the presence of the clock mechanism complicates their recording. Aligned with the edge of the arches, two non-structural brick walls were raised subsequently to close the rooms towards the transept and the roof of the ambulatory. Regarding the construction of the 5.5-m long arches, three main steps can be identified from the changing textures of the mortar (Fig. 5).

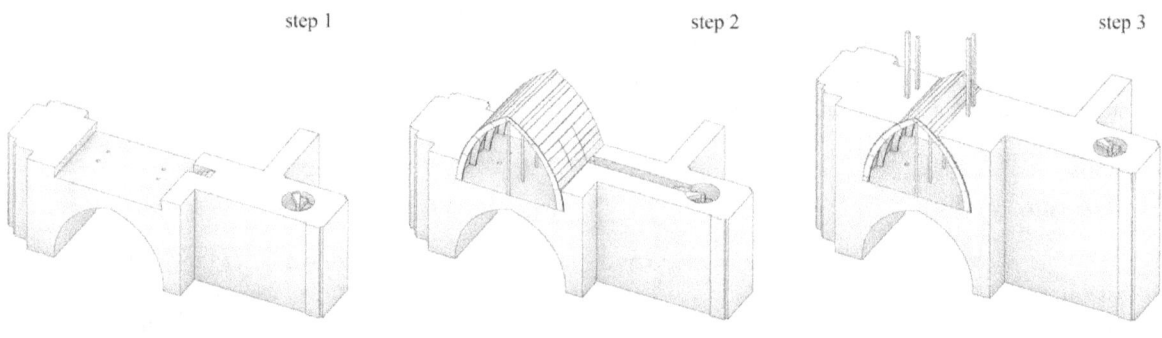

Figure 5: Construction sequence of the pointed arch under the northern tower (model: author)

Firstly, the landing of the arch was erected with the surrounding walls without any formwork until a height of 85 cm. In this lower section of the arch, the mortar joints are flush with the surface and were thus systematically smoothed by the masons who could freely access the intrados under construction (step1).

Then, a temporary timber structure was installed between the pre-existing layers of bricks acting as abutments (step 2). The main supporting elements consisted of four curved arches, each composed of two layers of 4-cm thick boards. The precise position and composition of these laminated arches can be obtained from their imprints left on the second type of mortar finishing. Indeed, between a height of 85 and 125 cm, the four timber arches were directly in contact with the masonry during the laying of the bricks. As masons could not reach the intrados anymore, the mortar joints are extruded in this cruder section of the arch.

Finally, above 125 cm and until the top of the room, the bricks were placed against a series of boards nailed to the underlying timber arches (step 3). The width of these boards varied between 14 and 50 cm and their length between 120 (in the lower part) and 410 cm (in the upper part). In cross section, the arch is 55 cm thick and randomly composed of two stretchers or one stretchers and two headers. Before reaching the top of the formwork, builders wisely inserted four timber posts among the bricks to prepare as many holes for the ropes operating the bells. Beyond a careful execution of this arch, the holes indicate that the position of the original towers did not largely differ from their fifteenth-century reconstruction.

Once the mortar had perfectly cured, the temporary structure was removed from beneath, not without leaving on the surface a few wood splinters ripped from the longitudinal boards. At this stage of the investigation, a fragment of wood extracted from the intrados has been imprecisely dated with radiocarbon to the twelfth century, decades before the start of the construction. This first result confirms that temporary structures were often composed of (very) old timbers. It also stresses that one should be critical when dating historical structures based on such fragments, or at least that such analyses should not be based on just a few samples. In the present case, a new set of samples collected over the entire height of the bell towers is currently under investigation to clarify their construction sequences.

Large-span domes

A last example of traces left by temporary structures can be observed on the intradoses of the masonry domes of the Basilica, the diameter of which varies from 14.3 to 14.46 m and the thickness from 32 to 43 cm. Although direct formwork imprints are masked by plaster and paint (Fig. 6), geometrical deformations introduced by the centring clearly appear on the laser scan survey, as the horizontal deviations from ideal circles can reach up to 8 cm. (Fig. 7). The first traces start about 120 cm above the windows, indicating that the lower halves of the drums were likely raised without formwork. In the upper parts, the traces show the arrangement of 16 equally spaced centres converging at the highest point of the slightly ogival dome. How the centring was assembled and supported is currently under investigation. By systematically comparing the position of the centres to those of the putlog holes visible on the exterior of the drums (using drone photogrammetry) or under the plaster of the intrados (thermal imagery), one should be able to determine whether the hemispherical formwork was "flying" or supported by a 30-m high scaffolding (examples of both systems can be found in [7]).

Compared to Gothic vaults which have been the subject of many studies supported by detailed onsite investigations, there is so far little research on the erection process of brick domes in Europe. Hence, the ongoing research on the domes of St Anthony will help fill this gap in medieval construction history, thanks mostly to the precise documentation of traces left by scaffolds, centring and formwork.

Medieval formwork imprints in the Basilica of St Anthony in Padua

Figure 6: Wide-angle view of the intrados of the façade dome (picture: author)

Figure 7: The meshed model of the intrados of the domes reveals traces of centring (model: author)

Conclusions

In the scope of an ongoing research project on the Basilica of St Anthony in Padua, the building techniques of short-span corridors, medium-span arches and large-span domes have been investigated based on detailed onsite surveys. The erection process of the first two examples has been depicted with high accuracy thanks to their formwork imprints and some intact elements, paving the way for a similar analysis of the domes.

The investigations on temporary works reveal that the large volumes of timber used during the construction of a basilica left not only imprints, but also fragments of wood embedded in the mortar. The knowledge of building techniques can thus significantly accelerate the discovery of such samples as one can concentrate research efforts on surfaces where the two materials were in contact. Applied in the present project, this method has already proven effective to recover more than 20 intact fragments of wood, also in parts of the building where all carpentry burnt in the eighteenth century. This fruitful combination of construction history and building archaeology enables a finer understanding of medieval building techniques in Northern Italy and in fine the absolute dating of the transformations of the Basilica of St Anthony.

Acknowledgements

This project is financed by the Swiss National Science Foundation (SNSF). The author wishes to thank the *Delegazione Pontificia per la Basilica di Sant'Antonio in Padova* and the *Veneranda Arca di S. Antonio* for the rewarding collaboration.

References

[1] B. Lucca, L. Bertazzo (Eds), Padova 1310. Percorsi nei cantieri architettonici e pittorici della Basilica di Sant'Antonio in Padova. Padua: Centro Studi Antoniani, 2012.
[2] L. Vandenabeele, 'The Medieval Transformations of the Basilica of St Anthony in Padua based on an Analysis of the Original Brickwork', Proceedings of the 7th International Congress on Construction History, in press; M. Diaz, L. Vandenabeele, S.M. Holzer, 'The Construction of the Medieval Domes of the Basilica of St Anthony in Padua', Proceedings of the 7th International Congress on Construction History, in press.
[3] S.M. Holzer, Gerüste und Hilfskonstruktionen im historischen Baubetrieb. Berlin: Ernst & Sohn, 2021.
[4] O. Pignatelli, 2020. Indagini dendrocronologiche sulle strutture lignee delle cupole della Basilica del Santo a Padova. Verona: unpublished report.
[5] S.M. Holzer, Gerüste, (Note 3) pp.92-93.
[6] H. Dellwing, 1975. 'Der Santo in Padua. Eine baugeschichtliche Untersuchung', Mitteilungen des Kunsthistorischen Institutes in Florenz, no.19, pp.197–240.
[7] S.M. Holzer, Gerüste, (Note 3) pp.167-261; M. Wilson Jones, 'Building on Adversity: The Pantheon and Problems with its Construction' in T.A. Marder, M. Wilson Jones (Eds), The Pantheon. From Antiquity to the Present, Cambridge: Cambridge University Press, 2015, pp.193–230.

Renaissance and Late Gothic World (1400-1600)

From construction to maintenance. The history of the wooden chain encircling the dome of Santa Maria del Fiore

Sofia Celli and Federica Ottoni
Department of Engineering and Architecture, Università di Parma, Italy

Introduction

While most features of the dome of Santa Maria del Fiore have been thoroughly analyzed over the centuries, little attention has so far been paid to the wooden ring encircling it, hidden between the two masonry shells. Indeed, the so called "chestnut chain" was never quite considered, if not as a collateral topic in the long-lasting debate concerning the dome's stability [1]. The present research thus had the aim to increase the knowledge of this device by retracing its construction history.

Figure 1: The structural arrangement of Brunelleschi's dome with the one built wooden ring in Joseph Durm's representation (1887) [2].

The wooden chain was already included in the 1420 cupola programme [3], as a part of the elaborate encircling system that was supposedly studied by the designers to contrast the (empirically acknowledged) outward thrusts of the masonry dome, thus preventing its typical collapse mechanism. Such system comprised several typologies of tie-rods, including

From construction to maintenance.
The history of the wooden chain encircling the dome of Santa Maria del Fiore

stone, iron and wooden rings. In particular, the wooden chains were initially meant to be four (one every 12 braccia, or 7 metres in height), but in the end, due to subsequent changes to the original plan [4], only one of them was actually realised (Fig. 1).

The resulting chain was built between 1423 and 1424, according to Brunelleschi's design, as confirmed by several archival documents [5].

Since its construction, the wooden ring has undergone several transformations owed to maintenance interventions and, most likely, repairs following periods of neglect or traumatic events (e.g. earthquakes and lightening). In particular, the archival documents indicate water as the main cause of damage, highlighting a strict correlation between filtrations from the dome's cracks and wooden rotting [6].

Through this process, the artefact slowly came to acquire its current configuration and, most importantly, was preserved and kept "intact" until current days, which was far from predictable, especially given the intrinsic perishability of wood. Moreover, the slim number of similar devices to be found nowadays increases its value and importance as a nearly unique evidence of a specific technology and its evolution in time. As a matter of fact, the substituted and added metallic joints that can be seen on the wooden ring testify to the progress of craftsmanship, with particular reference to ironmongery and timber joints.

For these (and yet other) reasons, it seemed opportune to begin the study herein summarised.

The state of the art

As aforementioned, literature focusing specifically on the wooden chain is rather scarce. The few scholars who addressed this topic mostly dwelled on its structural role (or lack thereof) [7]. Such assessments were largely made based on general considerations, such as the features of the building material, the position of the device, the ease of maintenance and so forth, without ever truly providing a systematic analysis of the artefact. Historically, the most relevant study of the wooden chain can be attributed to Giovan Battista Nelli, who, in 1695, performed a thorough survey of the wooden ring in order to verify its state of repair and functioning.

At the time, due to a quick worsening of the cracks of the cathedral's dome – possibly caused by an earthquake that occurred in the September of the same year [8] – the Florentine community was deeply concerned about the future of the structure. A committee, which included Nelli, was nominated to examine the situation and establish whether it was advisable to add a set of four hooping iron tie-rods to prevent the collapse of the building [9]. To that end, the committee gathered information on the wooden chain, both directly investigating the device and seeking suggestions from other fabric surveyors, such as those of the St. Peter's Basilica in Rome [10]. However, since the latter had never had any wooden rings, the most knowledge came from on-site observations. Nelli provides us with relevant data concerning both the state of repair of the chain – which, at the time, was rather poor [11] –, and with an approximate representation of the joints connecting the 24 beams [12] (Fig. 2).

Although not completely consistent with the reality, Nelli's drawing became the most reliable source for most of the scholars who later dealt with the topic. While adding a few details, Rondelet [13], Durm [14], Prager and Scaglia [15], and Ricci [16] all portrayed the wooden chain basing on Nelli's work, without ever rectifying its inaccuracies. As a matter of fact, given that a part of the joints is hidden within the spurs' thickness, their true arrangement is still unclear, although definitely different from the suggested hypothesis. Moreover, the existing illustrations of the wooden chain only focus on one type of joint (seemingly the original one), and miss taking into account all the subsequent solutions resulted from maintenance and repairs.

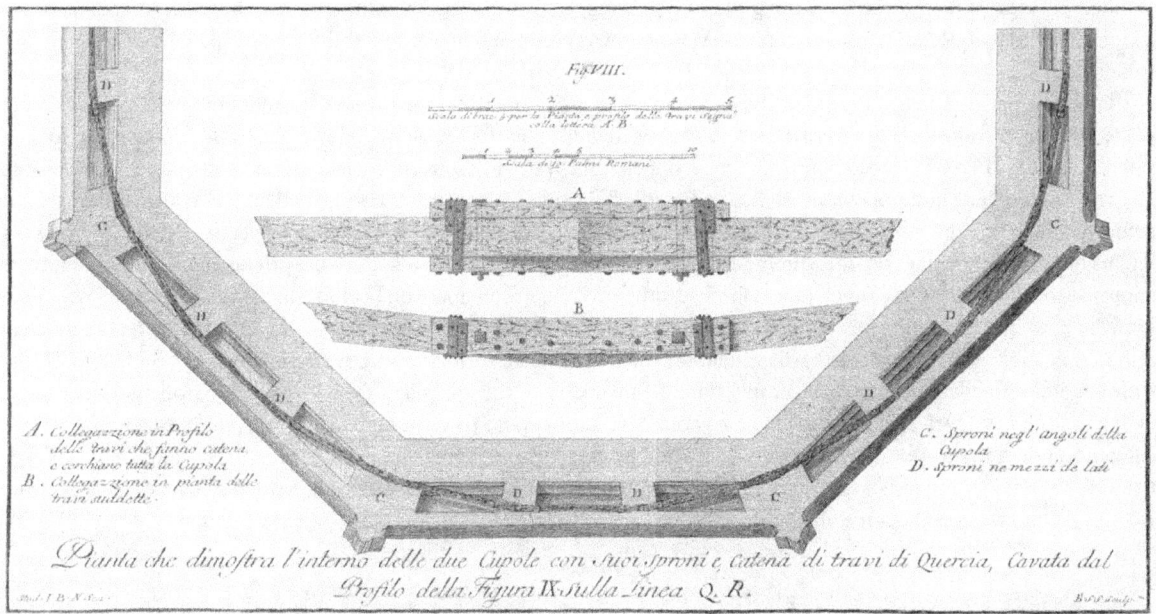

Figure 2: The joints of the chestnut chain according to Nelli's survey (1733) [17].

Beside the drawings of the chestnut ring produced over time, in the last fifty years there have been a few studies aiming at analysing the construction of this peculiar device [18]. While successfully discovering archival papers from the Fifteenth Century, the above studies did not make any attempt to correlate the historical data with the physical artefact in its current state. Later additions and maintenance interventions were not considered at that time either.

Renewed interest in the chestnut chain arose on the occasion of the celebrations for the six hundred years from the beginning of the dome construction (1420-2020). In view of the event the Opera di Santa Maria del Fiore fostered new studies, among which an archival research to investigate the history of the wooden ring and a laser scanner survey [19] to finally obtain a highly detailed representation of its geometry and dimensions. These two tools, in addition to the on-site observations, laid the basis for the integrated process that led to the dating of most of the metallic joints of the chain in question.

Method

As usual, the research started from the literature analysis, with particular reference to the collection of documents published by Cesare Guasti [15], and the digital archive of the sources of the Opera edited by Margaret Haines [20]. After isolating some significant dates - mostly related to catastrophic events such as earthquakes and lightening - the study resorted to the historical documents stored in the Opera's archive, shedding light on long-lost pieces of information spanning several centuries. A first reading of the documents allowed the acquisition of general knowledge about the way the wooden chain was perceived throughout time and how such a perception reflected on maintenance activities.

The complete understanding of the newly found data was however only achieved by comparing the historical information with the artefact in its present state, as well as with the accurate geometric survey that was recently performed. In fact, while rather detailed, the architects' annual reports, and the blacksmiths' and carpenters' expense records rarely offer spatial references. Thus, the mere analysis of archival documents would not have enabled the accurate location of the

From construction to maintenance.
The history of the wooden chain encircling the dome of Santa Maria del Fiore

maintenance interventions described along the wooden ring. By combining the information collected from the historical documents with that deduced from direct observation, it was possible to make up for the lack of spatial data.

Operationally, the first step was to identify, examine and classify the different kinds of metallic joints currently existing on the device. Overall, six types were detected, heterogeneously distributed along the wooden beams and tracing back to different epochs (Fig. 3). The comparison between the archival descriptions of the metallic components and the visible elements highlighted quite precise matches, allowing the establishment of a correspondence between the historical documents and the tangible artefact. The most plausible correspondences were subsequently verified through a dimensional crosschecking: the measurements indicated by the expense records, after opportune conversions [21], were compared to the dimensions obtained from laser scanning. While the comparison between linear measurements was quite immediate, weight measurements required a bit more effort. A geometrically regularized 3D model was created for each of the six metallic joints in order to easily obtain the rough volume, and, therefore, the possible weight. Undoubtedly, the approximations that were made – concerning both the geometry of the joints and the density of the iron alloys – entail a mediocre accuracy level. It should however be noted that the purpose of this comparison was not to ascertain a perfect coherence, but rather to verify whether the data could be considered compatible. In fact, even using the highest level of detail, the 3D model might not have provided overlapping results due to material decay, possible reductions in section, and lack of information about the alloy composition.

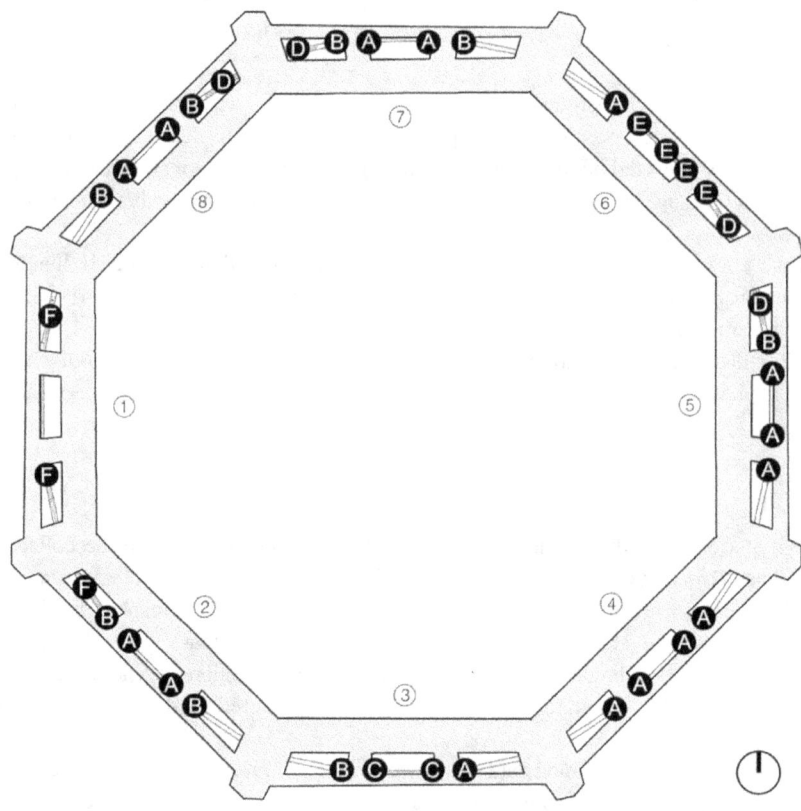

Figure 3: Spatial distribution of the different types of joints along the wooden chain.

Once attested the compatibility between the historical and current dimensions, the dating hypothesis were furtherly validated through the consultation of coeval architectural treaties. In several cases, the latter proved essential to dispel existing doubts regarding the technical systems adopted, as well as to better understand the archival papers' lexicon. Similarly, the close observation of similar case studies of known date offered useful hints to corroborate previous findings.

The metallic joints: an overview

The direct observation of the wooden chain, along with the possibility of accessing the dimensional data of the laser scan survey [22], allowed six different types of joints to be identified. Such joints differ from one another in terms of components, dimensions, workmanship and functioning (Fig. 4).

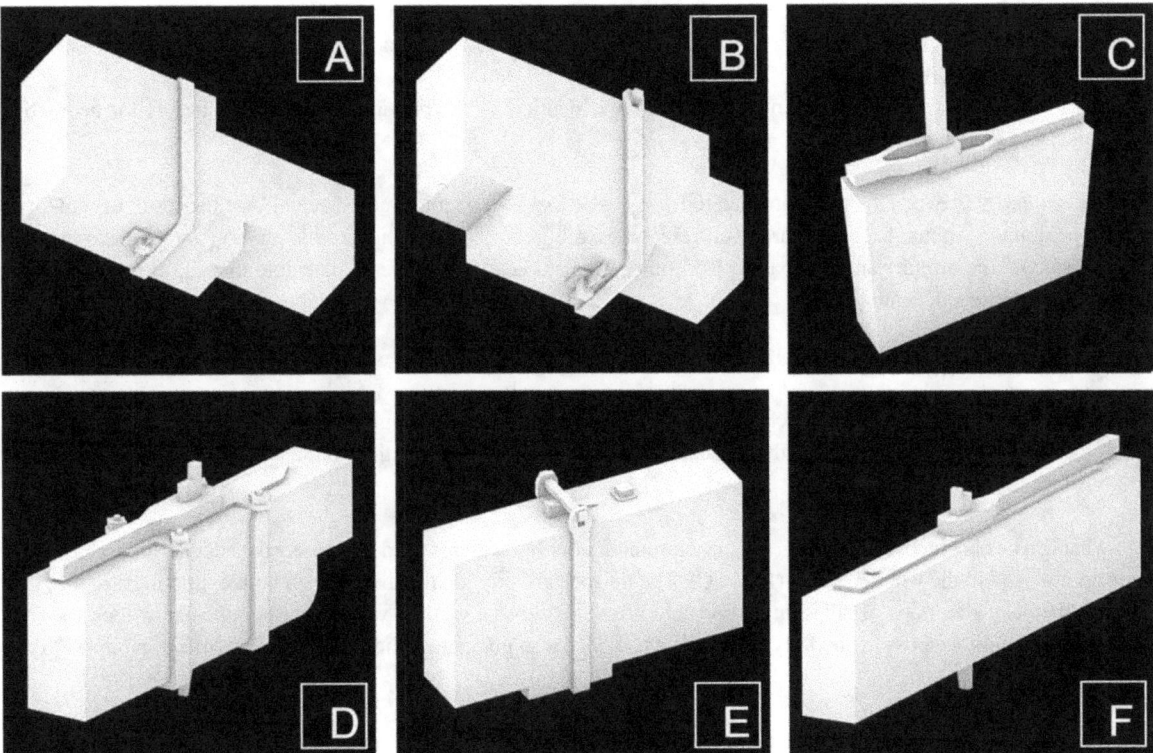

Figure 4: 3D representation of the six typologies of joints identified on the wooden chain.

Each of the six types was examined and catalogued before proceeding to the afore-described cross-checking process. In the end, four types out of six were dated based mostly on the information gathered from the archival research, while the remaining ones, given the lack of documental materials, were dated by comparison with similar case studies and architectural treaties. A brief overview of the joints' configuration is provided in the following subparagraphs.

Type A

The metallic joints named 'A', possibly the original ones (1423-1424), are by far the most common. They appear rather similar to the joints represented by Nelli in 1695 (Fig. 2), as they comprise an iron strap, an iron bolt and several nails (Fig. 4.A). The former is quite thin (1-1.5 cm thick) and is fastened to the beams through a variable number of irregularly disposed nails. The iron bolt has square section (average 3x3 cm) and is blocked on the lower end thanks to a hole and

From construction to maintenance.
The history of the wooden chain encircling the dome of Santa Maria del Fiore

key system. Finally, from two to six plain iron nails were added to further secure the vertical connection. All the metallic elements are visibly hand-crafted.

The components described were used to join together three overlapping wooden elements, namely the main chestnut beam (average section 30x30 cm) and the two *"panchoni di quercia"* [23], which are the oak boards positioned above and below the beam in close proximity to the dome's spurs.

Type B

The joints of the second type are almost completely analogous to those of the first type. The only slight difference can be found in the encircling element: while A-type joints present a simple iron strap wrapped all around the beams, B-type joints have a u-shaped iron strap which closes on the upper end by means of a transversal stake (Fig. 4.B). The latter crosses the thickness of the strap passing through eyelets and gets locked into place thanks to iron wedges.

Other than the iron strap, the components of the joint are identical to the previously described ones as for geometry, dimensions, and manufacturing.

The strict similarity between the two joints led to hypothesise that B-type joints could actually be the result of repairs to the A-type joints. Although further archival researches are required to validate this theory, by considering the craftsmanship of the artefact and comparing it to other case studies [24], it seems plausible that the iron straps were replaced in the Sixteenth century.

Type C

There are only two C-type joints on the chestnut chain, both located within the eighth sector of the dome, on the opposite ends of the beam. Unfortunately, due to the presence of a metallic sheet covering the wooden elements, the joints are only partly visible.

From what can be observed, the joint has a rather simple functioning and it is used to connect the added iron tie-rods both to one another and to the wooden beam (Fig. 4.C). The tie-rods are provided with a loop on both extremities; to join one arm with the next, the loops of adjacent tie-rods are aligned so that a vertical wedge can be inserted to lock them in position. By extending across the underlying beams, the wedge also guarantees the fastening of the metallic tie-rod to the wooden elements.

According to the historical analysis, type C joints can be attributed to the repairs coordinated by Gherardo Silvani in 1637 [25].

Type D

The metallic joints of type D are quite complex and comprise several elements (Fig. 4.D). On the one hand, there is a horizontal connection granted by an additional iron tie-rod located on top of the wooden beam; on the other a double u-shaped strap to vertically fasten the wooden and iron elements. Both the tie-rod and the straps are anchored to two iron plates nailed on the top and bottom surfaces of the beam. The former is blocked by a vertical wedge that passes through the tie-rod's loop and continues downward, transversally crossing the iron plates and the wooden elements. The u-shaped straps, also nailed to the wooden beams, are provided with threaded ends locked by square nuts on the upper part.

Since no archival records regarding this type were found, the installation period (Eighteenth Century) was hypothesized on the basis of architectural treaties and analogies with similar case studies.

Type E

Overall, five E-type joints can be found on the wooden chain, all of which are located in the sixth sector of the dome. Given the presence of one of the most severe cracks of the structure, in this portion the wooden chain has been doubled in section, adding a second wooden beam below the original one. The E-type joints have the role of joining together the two beams.

This kind of joint is composed of two main elements: a u-shaped strap and a bolt, both working vertically (Fig. 4.E). The former is closed on the upper end thanks to an eyelet-stake system, tightened using metallic wedges; the latter has circular section (average Ø 3 cm) and is locked with a square nut on bottom end.

Thanks to the rich archival documentation [26], it was possible to identify 1823 as the installation year. An in-depth description of the dating process will be provided in the next paragraph.

Type F

The last type of joint is the most recent one and dates back to the repairs coordinated by Gaetano Baccani between 1845 and 1848 [27]. It consists of a metallic tie-rod (fastened to the underlying beam thanks to a vertical wedge), and two bolts locked on the bottom end with square nuts (Fig. 4.F). As in type D, the system also includes two iron plates that are nailed to the upper and lower surfaces of the beam to improve the anchoring of the added tie-rod.

The comparative process: dating E-type joints

Once catalogued, each joint type was further analysed and assigned a plausible time of installation. To better explain the comparative process that led to that result, the case of E-type joints will be thoroughly illustrated, as a significant example.

As asserted before, E-type joints were placed on the wooden ring in 1823, at the request of the Opera surveyor Gaetano Baccani. Three very interesting archival documents describe this operation: the carpenter's and blacksmith's expense notes and a report by Architect Baccani [30]. The latter, even though written four years later (1827), provides an essential piece of information: the cause of the repairs. Baccani stated that the wooden ring was found broken at two different points because of the prolonged filtrations of rainwater. Although not univocal, this can be read as a hint to place the described repairs in one of the sectors that show the most severe cracks (four and six). Indeed, the dimensional cross-checking confirmed that the 1823 repairs occurred in sector six.

On the other hand, the expense notes offer detailed descriptions of the wooden and metallic pieces produced by the craftsmen. In particular, the attentive reading of the blacksmith's words allowed one to preliminary match the elements mentioned in the archival paper with those that can currently be observed within sector six. The artisan refers to u-shaped straps whose features resembles the ones in sector six: they have eyelets on the upper ends to insert the closing stake, iron wedges to tighten the straps and, as suggested in the document, they enclose not one, but two overlapping wooden beams (Fig. 5).

The bolts description is rather fitting as well: there are three of them, they are at least partially threaded so that they lock with nuts and have washers both under the head and above the nut. Moreover, the expense note mentions that a square wrench was used to tighten the bolts' nuts, which testifies to the fact that the nuts installed in 1823 were square, just like the existing ones (Fig. 6).

From construction to maintenance.
The history of the wooden chain encircling the dome of Santa Maria del Fiore

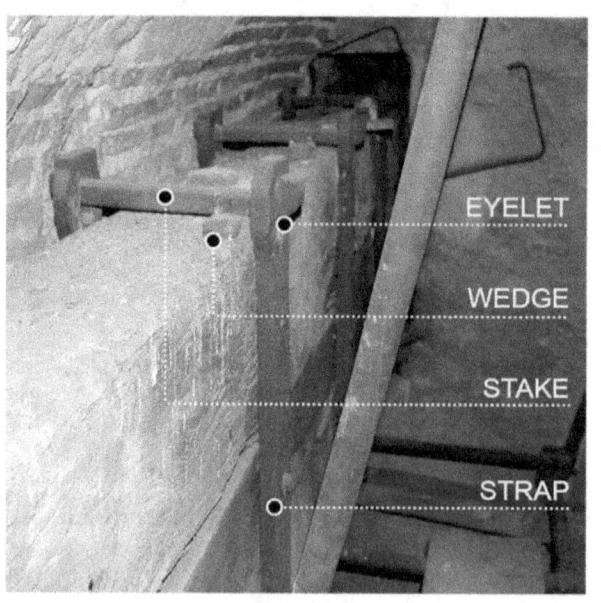
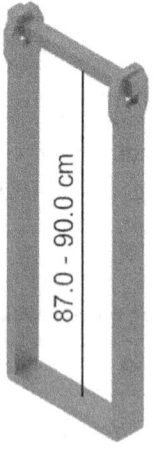

Figure 5: The iron straps of E-type joints and their components. Photo by the authors (2018)

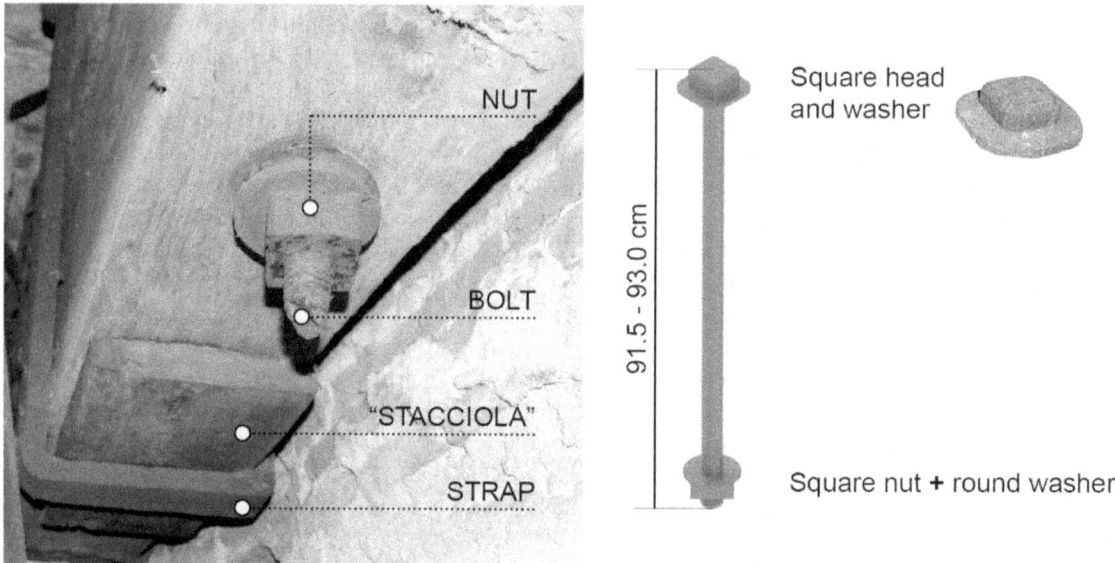

Figure 6: E-type joint seen from below. Notice the lower end of the bolt and the wooden "stacciola". Photo by the authors (2018)

Despite the good level of coherence between the historical document and the built artefact, the note also includes ambiguous information. First of all, the blacksmith affirms to have made 15 u-shaped straps, while today we only see five. We could however assume – as also suggested by a later document [28] – that the missing straps were subsequently removed. Another uncertainty regards the wording "*Colonnone di Legno della Cupola*" ("Big wooden column of the dome") which seems to refer to a vertical element, rather than a horizontal one. Nevertheless, given that the only relevant wooden device within the dome is the chestnut chain, it seemed reasonable to overlook this specific aspect and proceed to the dimensional crosschecking to definitively dispel any residual doubts.

The first dimension recorded by the blacksmith is the height of the u-shaped straps (87.5 cm) which is consistent with the present situation. According to the 2018 laser scan survey, the height range of the metallic straps is from 87 to 90 cm.

The second measure in the note regards an element referred to as "*stacciola*", which is not a very common term in literature and was not found in the main historical Italian vocabularies. It was however recorded by an Eighteenth-century Italian-French dictionary [29], were it is described as a straight edge or square, clearly suggesting the use of the "*stacciola*" as an aid to control orthogonality. Thanks to this new piece of information, it was possible to formulate the hypothesis that the term "*stacciola*" refers to the wooden plank positioned between the bottom surface of the beam and the iron strap (Fig. 6). Indeed, the blacksmith's expense note reports that the "*stacciole*" were 29 cm wide, which is very close to reality since the three existing wooden planks measure 26 to 28 cm. No dimensions are provided with regard to the thickness or length of the planks. The hypothesis was finally validated thanks to Giuseppe Valadier's architectural treatise [30]. When illustrating the possible ways to join two wooden beams together, he mentions the opportunity of positioning a wooden element between the beam and the strap to improve the adherence between them (Fig. 7).

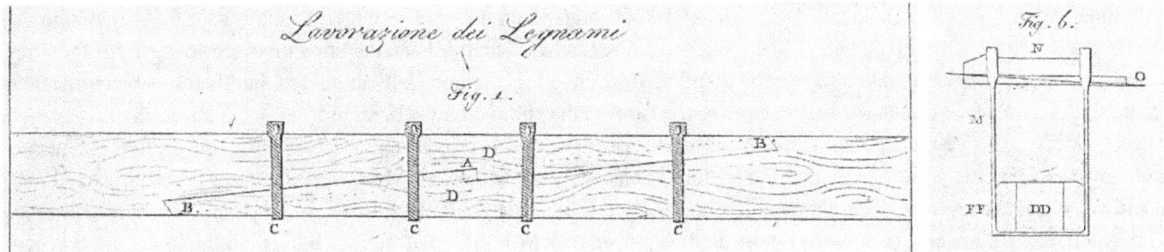

Figure 7: Possible use of U-shaped straps illustrated in Valadier's treatise.. On the right, the mentioned wooden element ("stacciola") to be inserted between the beam and the strap (DD)

After analysing the straps, the cross-checking moved to the bolts, which, according to the blacksmith were three in total. Although the expense note does not provide any dimensions, their description is rather precise and, as previously noted, perfectly fits the current configuration of E-type joints. Once again, architectural manuals offered useful confirmations: among the different types of bolts, Cavalieri San Bertolo (1832) [31] includes threaded bolts, such as the ones described in the archival document.

As usual, due to the fact that metals were priced based on weight, the expense note ends with the overall weight of the listed pieces, which, in the specific case, amounts to 465.311 Kg. In order to check the compatibility of this measurement with the present situation, a rough 3D model of both a u-shaped strap and a bolt was made, considering the average dimensions acquired through laser scanning. The volume of the models was automatically calculated by the software and then multiplied by the density (7.85 g/cm3) to obtain the mass of the analyzed elements. As a result, the average weight of the straps is 30 Kg; that of the bolts is 10 Kg. Finally, the unitary weight values were multiplied by the number of elements produced (that is 15 for the straps and three for the bolts) and finally summed to have the total weight. The

From construction to maintenance.
The history of the wooden chain encircling the dome of Santa Maria del Fiore

result of this calculation is 480 Kg which, given the substantial approximations that were made, can be considered compatible with the historical data.

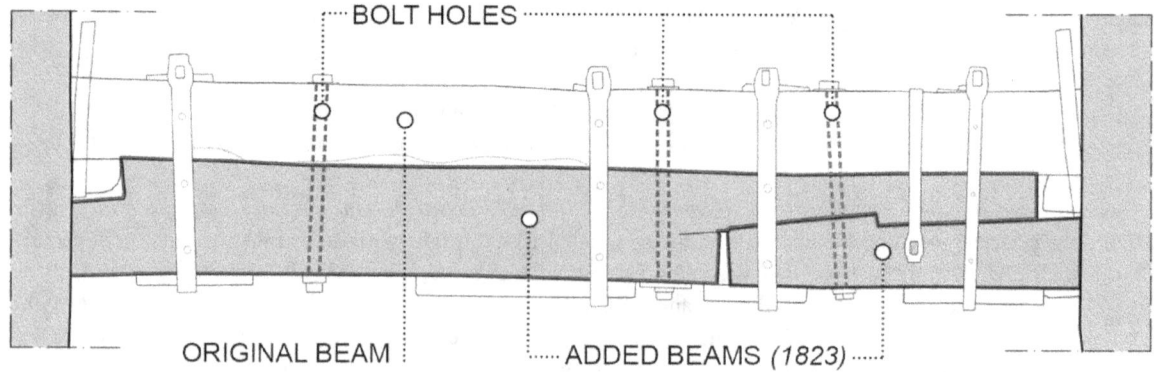

Figure 8: The wooden elements currently existing in the central room of sector six. The darkened beams were supposedly added in 1823.

A few considerations were finally made with regard to the carpenter's work (Fig. 8). In his brief expense note he explains installing two new wooden chains: the first one is 350 cm long, 35 cm tall and 29 cm wide and is said to "stay within the spur". The second one is 440 cm long, 48 cm high and 32 cm wide. The third and last item on the note concerns the three holes the wooden worker had to make in the mentioned beams to fit the iron bolts in. Given that the bolts were installed in the sixth sector of the dome, the best guess was to also find the "new" chains there. Indeed, when observing this portion of the wooden ring, we notice that the beam is actually composed of two overlapping beams: the one on the top appears to be the original one, while the one on the bottom is clearly a later addition. Moreover, the latter is a composed beam itself, as it comprises two different wooden elements connected by a stop-splayed scarf joint. The availability of dimensional data allowed a comparison to be made between the two wooden elements composing the lower, most recent beam and the chains supplied by the carpenter. It should be noted that, since it was not possible to survey the portion of the beams entering the spurs, the cross-checking was only made on the visible part.

Even in this case, the level of compatibility appears to be quite high, especially for the longer segment (Fig. 9 left). Some discrepancies emerged with regard to the smaller beam, which, given the fact that the thickness of the spur is only 150 cm, about 70 cm shorter than the length indicated in the expense note (Fig. 9 right). It is however plausible that the chain was cut during assembling to better fit the designated space.

In the end, considering the overall results of the critical analysis performed, it seems reasonable to assert that the wooden and iron elements added during the repairs occurred in 1823 are the ones located in sector six.

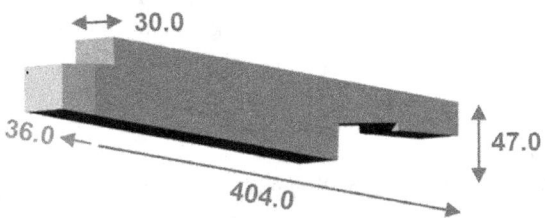
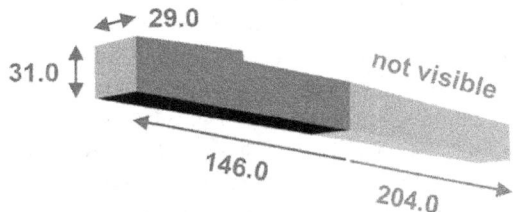
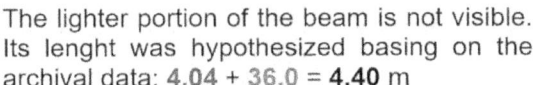

The lighter portion of the beam is not visible. Its lenght was hypothesized basing on the archival data: 4.04 + 36.0 = **4.40 m**

The length of the portion of beam that is not visible was hypothesized basing on the archival data: 1.46 + 2.04 = **3.50 m**

1823 expense note	2018 survey
Lenght *braccia* 7₁/₂ = **4.40 m**	4.04 m *(visibile)*
Height *braccia* 5/6 = **48** cm	47 cm
Width *soldi 11* = **32** cm	30 cm

1823 expense note	2018 survey
Length *braccia* 6 = **3.50 m**	1.46 m *(visible)*
Height *soldi 12* = **35** cm	31 cm
Width *soldi 10* = **29** cm	29 cm

Figure 9: 3D model of the two wooden pieces composing sector six's lower beam and comparison between historical and current dimensions.

Conclusions

The systematic application of the described method allowed a dating hypothesis to be formulated for each of the six types of metallic joints. The accuracy of the hypotheses is variable and largely depends on the availability (and nature) of the archival data. Further verifications could be obtained by using specific methods such as dendrochronology and radio-carbon dating. The archival research should also be continued, with particular reference to the least studied centuries (Sixteenth and Eighteenth).

Leaving aside the precision of the results, the study once again underlines the importance of achieving (or at least aiming at) a full integration between the pure historical data and built reality. By intertwining the information collected from the reading of the archival documents with those retrieved from the direct observation of the artefact it was finally possible to retrace the construction and maintenance history of the wooden chain encircling the dome of Santa Maria del Fiore.

Acknowledgments

The research has been possible thanks to the Opera del Duomo di Firenze who promoted the most recent studies concerning the wooden chain. A sincere thanks goes to the Opera's archivists who guided our steps through the archive collection, and to Studio Scaletti and Studio Comes (Prof. Carlo Blasi) who provided the laser scanning of the chain.

References

[1] F. Ottoni, E. Coïsson, C. Blasi, 'The crack pattern in Brunelleschi's dome in Florence. Damage evolution from historical to modern system analysis', Advanced Materials Research, Vols. 133-134, 2010, pp. 53-64.
[2] J. Durm, Die domkuppel in Florenz und die kuppel der Peterskirche in Rom, Berlin: Verlag Von Ernst & Korn, 1887, tav. 43.
[3] Archivio di Stato di Firenze (ASF), Arte della Lana 149, cc. 59v-60r.
[4] Archivio dell'Opera di Santa Maria del Fiore (AOSMF), II.1.80, c. 17v; AOSMF, II.2.1, c. 170v-171.
[5] AOSMF, II.4.9, c. 68; AOSMF, II.1.83, c. 68; AOSMF, II.4.9, c. 67; AOSMF, II.1.83, c. 67.
[6] AOSMF, V.3.19, f. 166; AOSMF, XI.2.5, fasc. 23; AOSMF, XI.8.9.

From construction to maintenance.
The history of the wooden chain encircling the dome of Santa Maria del Fiore

[7] *Relazione dell'ultima visita del cav. Francesco Fontana* - AOSMF, III.1.9, fasc. 305; C. Nelli, Discorsi di Architettura del senatore Giovan Batista Nelli, Florence: Per gli Eredi Paperini, 1753; L. Ximenes, Del vecchio e nuovo gnomone fiorentino e delle osservazioni astronomiche, fisiche e architettoniche, Florence: Nella Stamperia Imperiale, 1757; F. D. Prager, G. Scaglia, Brunelleschi. Studies of His Technology and Inventions, New York: Dover Publications Inc, 1970; R. J. Mainstone, 'Brunelleschi's Dome of Santa Maria del Fiore and some related structures', Transaction of the Newcomen Society, vol. 42, 1969, pp. 107-126; P. Sanpaolesi, La cupola di Santa Maria del Fiore. Il progetto - la costruzione, Florence: Editrice EDAM, 1977; P.A. Rossi, Le cupole del Brunelleschi, Bologna: Edizioni Calderini, 1982; C. Blasi, F. Ottoni, E. Coïsson, C. Tedeschi, 'Battistero di San Giovanni in Firenze. Note su dissesti, lesioni e catene', pp. 119-133, in F. Gurrieri (Ed.), Il Battistero di San Giovanni. Conoscenza, diagnostica, conservazione, Florence: Mandragora, 2017.

[8] C. Guasti, La Cupola di Santa Maria del Fiore illustrata con i documenti dell'Archivio dell'Opera secolare, Florence: Barbèra, Bianchi e Comp, 1857, pp. 177-183.

[9] F. Ottoni, C. Blasi, 'Hooping as an ancient remedy for conservation of large masonry domes', International Journal of Architectural Heritage, Vol. 10, no. 2-3, 2016, pp. 164-181.

[10] Biblioteca Nazionale Centrale di Firenze (BNCF), Ms.II.21, c. 31r.

[11] Ibid.

[12] B. S. Sgrilli, Descrizione e studi dell'insigne fabbrica di S. Maria del Fiore, Florence: Per Bernardo Paperini, 1733, tav. VII.

[13] G. Rondelet, Trattato teorico e pratico dell'arte di edificare, Mantua: a spese della società editrice coi tipi di L. Caranenti, 1831, tav. CLXXXIX.

[14] Durm, Die domkuppel in Florenz und die kuppel der Peterskirche in Rom, (Note 2).

[15] Prager, G. Scaglia, Brunelleschi. Studies of His Technology and Inventions, (Note 7).

[16] M. Ricci, 'La catena de' castagni della cupola di S. Maria del Fiore', pp. 89-93, in G. Tampone (Ed.), Legno e restauro. Ricerche e restauri su architetture e manufatti lignei, Florence: Messaggerie Toscane, 1989.

[17] Sgrilli, Descrizione e studi dell'insigne fabbrica di S. Maria del Fiore, (Note 12).

[18] Ricci, 'La catena de' castagni della cupola di S. Maria del Fiore', (Note 16); H. Saalman, Filippo Brunelleschi. The Cupola of Santa Maria del Fiore, London: A. Zwemmer Ltd, 1980; S. Di Pasquale, Brunelleschi. La costruzione della cupola di Santa Maria del Fiore, Venice: Marsilio Editore, 2002.

[19] Studio Scaletti and Studio Comes, May 2018.

[20] M. Haines (Ed.), The Years of the Cupola. Digital archive of the sources of the Opera di Santa Maria del Fiore, 1417-1436, Florence: Opera di Santa Maria del Fiore, 2015. http://duomo.mpiwg-berlin.mpg.de (consulted on 15th May 2021).

[21] Conversions were made according to the 'Tavole di riduzione delle misure e pesi toscani alle misure e pesi analoghi del nuovo sistema metrico dell'impero francese', Florence: Presso Molini, Landi e comp., 1809.

[22] Studio Scaletti and Studio Comes, (Note 19).

[23] AOSMF, II.4.9, n° 71v.

[24] P.P. Derinaldis, G. Tampone, 'The failure of the timber structures caused by incorrect design-execution of the joints. Two case study', in Proceedings of ICOMOS IWC – XVI International Symposium, Florence, Venice and Vicenza 2006.

[25] AOSMF, V.3.18 (II), f. 33; AOSMF, V.3.19, f. 166; AOSMF, V.3.42, f. 268.

[26] AOSMF, XI.3.3, fasc. 93 (Woodworker); AOSMF, XI.3.3, fasc. 84 (Blacksmith); AOSMF, XI.2.5, fasc. 23 (Baccani).

[27] AOSMF, XI.2.14, fasc. 1; AOSMF, XI.3.17, n°61; AOSMF, XI.3.20, n°90, 117; AOSMF, XI.2.16, fasc. 16.

[28] AOSMF, XI.3.20, f. 90.

[29] G. Veneroni, Dittionario italiano e francese, Venice: Appresso Lorenzo Basegio, 1703.

[34] G. Valadier, L'architettura pratica, Rome: Con permesso dei superiori, 1831, Tav. LXVIII.

[31] N. Cavalieri San Bertolo, Istituzioni di architettura statica e idraulica, Florence: A spese dell'ingegnere Vittorio Bellini, 1832.

Late Gothic Vaulting in the Canton of Grisons, Switzerland

Manuel Maissen
Institute of Construction History and Preservation (IDB), ETH Zurich, Switzerland

Introduction

The 15th century was a turbulent time for the region of what is today the canton of Grisons in south-eastern Switzerland, yet it was also a time of progress and change. With the establishment of new transit routes, such as the Via Mala as a connection to the Splügen and San Bernardino passes, the economy experienced a significant upswing, which also led to a considerable growth of population. However, the 15th century also saw the emergence of a sense of autonomy among the population, which subsequently led to the amalgamation of the judicial communes in the Free State of the Three Confederations, the predecessor of today's canton of Grisons.

Around the middle of the 15th century, ecclesiastical building also awoke from its almost two-century slumber and a growing number of churches were again built in the contemporary Late Gothic forms. This was not a local phenomenon, but can be observed throughout German-speaking Europe at this time. However, what is special for the region of today's Grisons is that due to the preceding stagnation in building, the Late Gothic architectural forms had not developed out of the local tradition itself, but were rather introduced from external influences. Furthermore, the building industry did not only change fundamentally in the capital Chur, but through the spread of this new construction knowledge – which can be traced amazingly well due to the alpine, mountainous location of this almost self-contained territory – the entire canton prospered within a few years.

In the course of a dissertation project [1], the intensive Late Gothic building period was scrutinised based on the executed vault constructions. The foundation of the thesis was always the building itself, which means that the conclusions and results of this study are not based on objective and aesthetic details, but can be verified by exact measurements with total station and laser scanner. In the present study, an overview of Late Gothic vaulting in Grisons will be given and the key results and major findings of the conducted research will be discussed.

A short history of vaulting in Grisons

The first church in Grisons to be completely vaulted in both the chancel and the nave was the Cathedral of St. Mary's Assumption in Chur (1150–1272). In retrospect, however, the vaults built in the early 13th century [2] in a Romanesque style seem outdated, since at that time the much finer and more precise Gothic ribbed vaults were already standard in most parts of Central Europe. After the completion of Chur Cathedral, vaulting developed hardly at all over the next two centuries, which is why the few churches from the 14th century and even the first Late Gothic churches around 1450 still have broad and heavy ribs with trapezoidal profiles (Fig. 1). The main reasons for the lack of a developing and evolving vaulting tradition in the High and Late Middle Ages were internal tensions in the diocese, which led to a complete standstill in ecclesiastical building after 1350, and missing connections to the western parts of Europe, which is why the Gothic architectural forms never even reached the canton of Grisons.

Late Gothic Vaulting in the Canton of Grisons, Switzerland

In the 15th century, profound changes took place in Grisons, sparked by the formation of the three leagues as well as their merger to form the Free State and the autonomous founding of new church parishes. The new parishes required their own churches, which led to the first slight increase in the potential building volume for churches after 1450 in the northern parts of the region. In the following years, however, only scattered churches were built. This was to change after a severe city fire occurred in Chur in 1464 [3], which destroyed many buildings below the bishop's court, including the parish church of St. Martin. At this time, Ortlieb von Brandis, a bishop who was particularly keen on building, was at the helm of the diocese, and so the rebuilding of St. Martin's was quickly pushed forward.

Figure 1: Vault in the Steigkirche on the St. Luzisteig Pass rebuilt around 1457 (M. Maissen)

For the reconstruction of St Martin's, the master stonemason Steffan Klain from Freistadt in Upper Austria was appointed by the city council. Master Steffan probably began his work in the early 1470s and completed the new chancel structure as early as 1473 [4]. Since the development of Late Gothic vault construction was already considerably more advanced in Upper Austria at this time, Master Steffan was able to establish a new architectural language practically overnight through the knowledge he had brought with him. The completion of the chancel vault of St. Martin's (Fig. 2) thus introduced a new standard of Late Gothic vault design that spread throughout Grisons within a short time. During his two decades of practice, Master Steffan passed on his construction knowledge and experience to young master stonemasons, among them Andreas Bühler from Carinthia and Bernhard von Puschlav. These young masters continuously improved the art of vaulting – however, such a significant technical advancement, as after the arrival of Master Steffan, was not to take place again.

Figure 2: Interior view of the Parish Church of St. Martin in Chur (M. Maissen)

The Late Gothic building stock

The Late Gothic period was an intensive age of church building in Grisons, the extent of which has not been equalled again in relation to the comparatively short time span of only 75 years. The vast majority of the completed building projects spanned an even shorter period of 55 years between 1470 and 1525. However, compiling a conclusive inventory of the Late Gothic period is a problematic endeavour, as no exact construction data or detailed studies of many of the smaller buildings exist. In addition, many churches were rebuilt again after the end of the Grisons turmoil, after destruction by town fires or for a variety of other reasons, which is why their Late Gothic features are no longer visible today, or at least only superficially.

The evaluation of the Late Gothic construction period has shown that between 1450 and 1525 at least 118 churches (Fig. 3) were either rebuilt from scratch or at least rebuilt or modified to a certain extent [5]. Additionally there were at least another eight built or modified within two independent construction phases, bringing the total number of completed projects to over 125. Of the 118 churches, 97 have a vault at least in the presbytery, corresponding to a share of 82%. From the available data, it can be assumed that at least 69 of the 118 buildings were entirely new buildings. This would correspond to a new-build share of 58.5%, which means that in slightly more than 40% of the existing Late Gothic building stock, at least one part of the predecessor building was included in the new construction. The intensity of the Late Gothic period in Grisons becomes even more apparent in relation to the total ecclesiastical building stock: today, there are 670 churches and chapels [6] in the territory of Grisons, which means that almost every fifth church was either built or at least fundamentally rebuilt in the Late Gothic period. Or to put it another way: the stock of churches in the middle of the 15th century probably doubled by 1525.

Late Gothic Vaulting in the Canton of Grisons, Switzerland

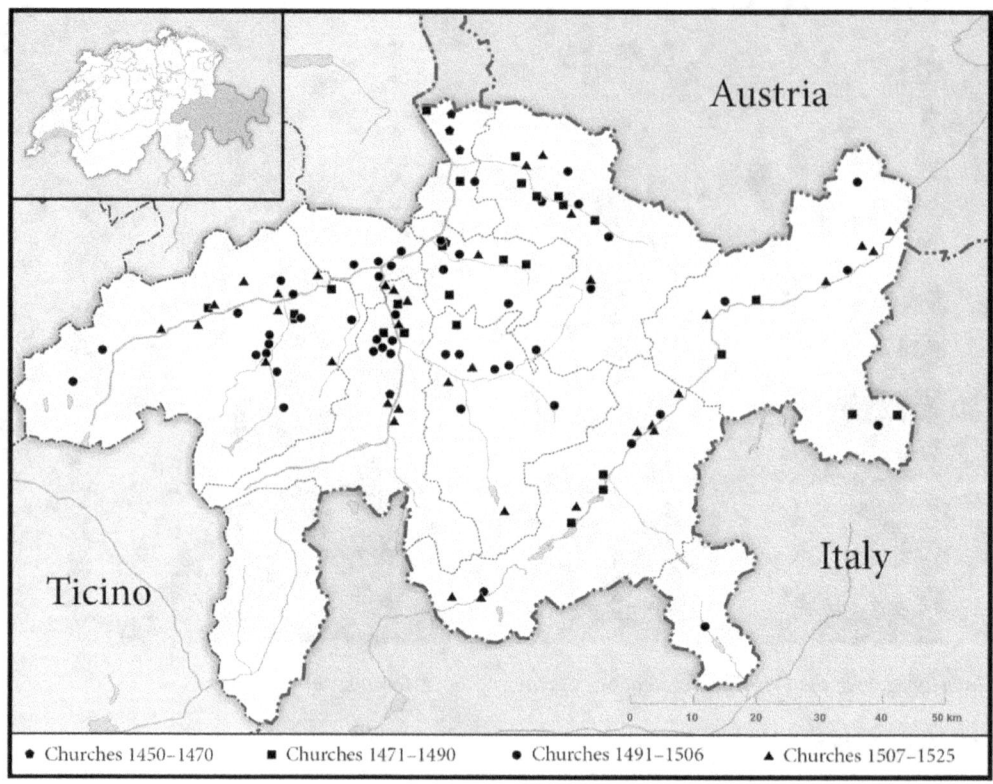

Figure 3: Spatial distribution of all 118 built or rebuilt Late Gothic churches (M. Maissen)

Design and construction of Late Gothic vaults in Grisons

With the arrival of Master Steffan in Chur, the comprehension of vaults and especially of ribs changed radically. Thus, geometrically accurately designed and precisely manufactured contemporary vaults promptly substituted the formerly rather rudimentary vaults with their ponderous-looking ribs. This new approach can already be observed in the chancel vault of St. Martin: The vault pattern derives directly from the proportions of the ground plan itself, which allows it to be designed solely with a compass and straightedge. This design process also works for more complicated vault patterns, such as the *'Haspelstern'* (roughly translates to a spinner's wheel) vault, which is widespread in Grisons and was also applied by Master Steffan in several churches [7]. To design such a pattern in the ground plan (Fig. 4), all bay dimensions AA must be sized equally. The same distance AA is then traced with a compass, which already defines all the needed intersection points and allows the pattern to be connected.

Another method, which can be verified for a range of vault patterns in Grisons, is the utilisation of auxiliary grids as the basis of the design. Once again, the bay dimensions were determined first, before the surfaces were proportioned in both longitudinal and transverse directions. The proportions were not random, but based on dimensions of the ground plan or on geometric principles, such as segment division with compasses. The application of auxiliary grids allowed for greater freedom in the design of vaulting patterns, thereby creating a greater variety of rib patterns and shapes. Even elaborate vault patterns, such as the chancel vault of the parish church of St. Maria Magdalena in Stierva, can be traced back to simple auxiliary grids (Fig. 5). In Stierva, the bays were quartered in the transverse direction and then divided longitudinally into five equal sections. The division of a reference line into *n* parts can be done with a compass by tracing *n* circles of arbitrary but constant radius on a second line, whose last intersection point is linked to the end of the reference line and shifted parallel to the other intersections (Fig. 5, No. 1). All the major intersection points of the rib pattern are already located on this auxiliary grid (Fig. 5, No. 4), while the remaining intersections can be defined by bisecting the zigzag path (Fig. 5, No. 5). To complete the design, the transition of the pattern into the apse is still missing, and this too could be resolved with only a compass in a few steps (Fig. 5, Nos. 6–8).

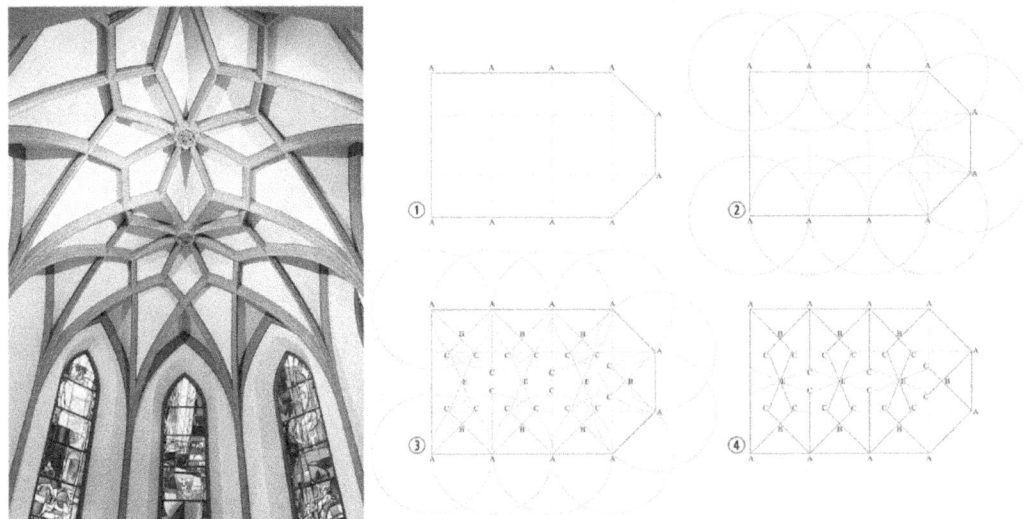

Figure 4: The chancel vault of the Church of St. Regula in Chur and a possible reconstruction of the design process of the rib pattern (M. Maissen)

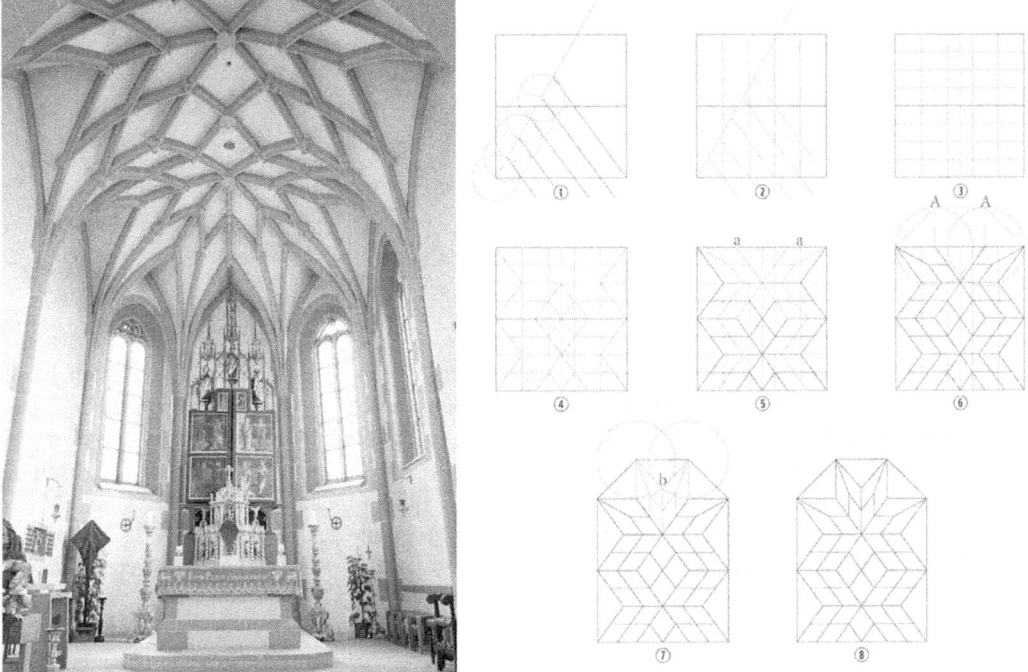

Figure 5: The chancel vault of the Church of St. Maria Magdalena in Stierva and a possible reconstruction of the design process of the rib pattern (M. Maissen)

Late Gothic Vaulting in the Canton of Grisons, Switzerland

The Late Gothic churches in Grisons reveal a diverse catalogue of vault patterns, most of which consist of a combination of simple geometric shapes – complex vault patterns, such as those in Stierva or Thusis (see Fig. 6), are an exception. As described in the few surviving contemporary German *'Werkmeisterbücher'* (master builder's books), the design often refers to the dimensions of the chancel [8], e.g. its clear width or the width of one bay. Nevertheless, as seen in the above case of Stierva, this reference can also be only indirect as a basis for the auxiliary grid. All vaults in Grisons, however, have in common that their rib patterns can easily be designed in the ground plan following basic geometric rules with compasses and straightedges.

Figure 6: Total station survey of the vault ribs in the Reformed Church of Thusis (M. Maissen)

Ribs, geometry and radii

It was not only the shape of the ribs and the design of the vault patterns that changed through Master Steffan, but also the function of the ribs: Henceforth, the ribs no longer followed the groins of the vault in order to conceal and strengthen them, but rather defined the shape of the vault itself through their geometric definition [9]. For a more accurate analysis of the radii of the vault ribs, precise surveys of a number of previously selected vaults were conducted using a total station. The ribs were metered centrally along their extrados at short intervals of 5 to 10 cm, which resulted in several thousand individual measurements for each object. Thus, for the analysis of the vault ribs of the Reformed Church of Thusis, altogether 2682 individual total station measurements (1149 in the chancel and 1533 in the nave) were conducted (Fig. 6).

Table 1: Analysis of the rib curvature in the chancel vault of the Ref. Church of Thusis

Rib Sequence	Radius [m]	Max. Distance [m]	Mean Distance [m]
Rib 01	3.5942	0.0247	0.0149
Rib 02	3.5919	0.0078	0.0025
Rib 03	3.5902	0.0261	0.0110
Rib 04	3.6141	0.0201	0.0096
Rib 05	3.6017	0.0181	0.0048
Rib 06	3.6013	0.0178	0.0800
Rib 07	3.6307	0.0052	0.0018
Rib 08	3.6129	0.0137	0.0057
Rib 09	3.6167	0.0135	0.0052
Rib 10	3.6291	0.0094	0.0044
Rib 11	3.6351	0.0056	0.0022
Rib 12	3.6157	0.0283	0.0104
Ø Radius: **3.6111 m**	Mean deviation: **0.0127 m**	Ø max. distance: **0.0159 m**	Ø mean distance: **0.0127 m**

In a second phase, the radii of the rib sequences were computed using a programme based on the method of least squares developed by Prof. Dr.-Ing. Stefan M. Holzer. As rib sequences, we sought contiguous rib paths between the springers and the keystone. In the case of a *'Haspelstern'* vault, this is quite simple, since all rib sequences ACE are identical and extend from any springer A via a crossing point C to the respective keystone E (see Fig. 4, No. 4). The chancel vault pattern of the Church of Thusis, on the other hand, seems rather heterogeneous at first glance, but all possible rib sequences from any springer to the respective keystone can be formed from one tierceron and two lierne ribs (Fig. 6). This results in different rib sequences that describe a divergent path but cover the same distance.

The computed and evaluated radii of the rib sequences of the chancel vault of the Church of Thusis yielded surprisingly uniform results (Table 1): From the twelve analysed rib sequences, the average radius is 3.6111m with a standard deviation of only 0.0127 m. However, the rib sequences are also very precise in themselves, which is indicated by the two other values in the table: The value "max. distance" indicates the furthest distance of a single measurement point to the computed radius, whereas the value "mean distance" states the average distance of all measurement points to the computed radius. Both values of 0.0159 m, respectively 0.0127 m are equally astonishing for a half-century-old vault structure.

All rib voussoirs in the chancel vault of the Church of Thusis could thus be planned and manufactured with the same radius, which not only simplified the production of the voussoirs but also the preparation of the falsework – the same is true for the *'Haspelstern'* vaults, which also consist of only one uniform radius. However, in the research project, the application of two or more different uniform radii in the same vault could be verified for several objects [10]. Yet, the different uniform radii were never randomly applied, but rather attributed to specific rib sections. For example, in the intricate chancel vault of the Church of St. Maria Magdalena in Stierva, the tierceron ribs were built with a radius of 3.1431 m, the lower lierne ribs stretching in transverse direction with a radius of 3.6081 m, and finally the liernes extending longitudinally along the flatter apex with a radius of 3.9053 m [11].

Late Gothic Vaulting in the Canton of Grisons, Switzerland

Uniform radii could be proven for all examined vaults. The results of the measurements can be verified not only by the small deviations, but also by the fact that the uniform radii can be converted to integer contemporary foot measures in nearly all cases. The original Late Gothic foot gauge is still attached to the town hall in Chur and has a size of almost exactly 30 cm [12]. Thus, the computed radius of 3.611 m for the ribs in the chancel vault of the church of Thusis corresponds to 12 foot. In a few rare cases, however, the computed uniform radius is not convertible to integer foot measures, but refers directly to ground plan dimensions, such as in the chancel vault of the Collegiate Church of San Vittore Mauro in Poschiavo [13].

Webs, shapes and compositions

Along with the new conception of the rib, the shape of the vaults and the design of the webs also changed. The vaults were directly dependent on the curvature of the ribs, which determined the shape and course of the webs. However, the constructional design or composition [14] of the vault webs was primarily a matter of the material used. In the Late Gothic period, it was conventional in Central Europe to construct vault webs from bricks. As there were only major clay deposits in the immediate vicinity of the capital Chur, brick vaults can only be found here in the two parish churches of St. Martin and St. Regula as well as in the Hieronymus Chapel in the episcopal cathedral deanery. The main advantage of using bricks was that the vault webs could be vaulted freehand and without a full-surface formwork. For the two vaults examined in the churches of St. Martin and St. Regula, however, the suspicion is that here too the vaults were built on a formwork. This is a suspicion resulting from the geometric shape of the vault webs, which show negative curvatures that may have been caused by compression settling after the stripping of the formwork (see the elevation plan of St. Regula in Fig. 7).

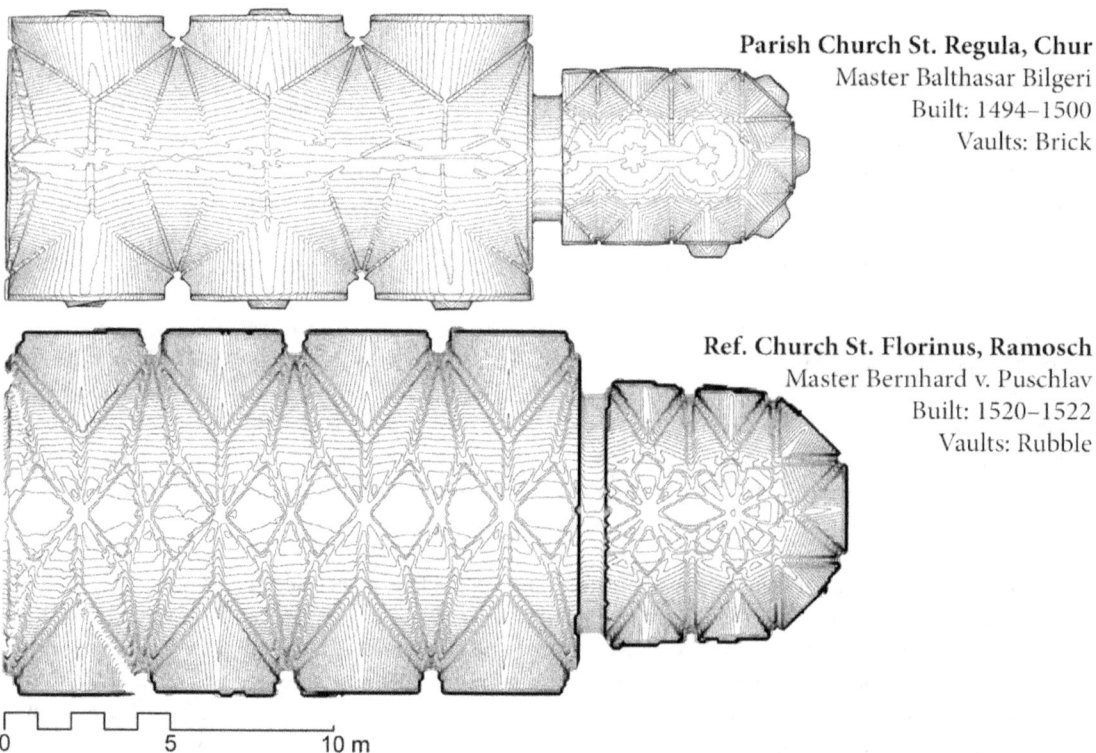

Figure 7: Elevation plans with intervals of 10 cm of the churches St. Regula in Chur and St. Florinus in Ramosch (M. Maissen)

Apart from the three vaults in Chur, all the other vaults were made of a compound of rubble stones and a high amount of mortar – similar to the Roman *'opus caementitium'*. The main disadvantage of this construction method was that a solid formwork was necessary, that was strong enough to support the massive load of the vault until it hardened. Furthermore, with a rubble stone vault, it was important to ensure that as many adjacent sections as possible, i.e. at least one full bay, were simultaneously vaulted, so that the scaffolding and the formwork were evenly loaded and the unfinished structure was always in equilibrium [15]. On the other hand, the advantage of vaulting with rubble stones and mortar was that the required raw materials could be quarried locally in vast quantities and did not have to be transported over far distances.

Since vault webs are larger surfaces, their shapes are better analysed with laser scans and the subsequent computed elevation plans (Fig. 7). The web, as already mentioned, is predetermined by the rib configuration, which means that not only continuously curved circular shapes are possible. The early vaults in particular reveal shapes that expand dome-like within the boundaries of each bay; around 1500, the shapes of the copings began to change, slowly converging towards barrel vaults with lunettes. If one compares the elevation plans of the churches of St. Regula (built 1494–1500) and St. Florinus in Ramosch (built 1520–22), this development becomes obvious in the nave (Fig. 7). Even more interesting, however, are the two chancel vaults, for they both show a *'Haspelstern'* rib pattern; though in Ramosch the ground plan was dimensioned wider, so that even here the webs approximate a barrel vault.

Not only the shape of the vault was decisive for its permanent safety, but also the strength or thickness of the webs, because in order to avoid dangerous cracks forming, the thrust forces must extend within the web masonry. In the studied objects, the cap thickness at the apex was between 20 and 30 cm, although this does not mean that this is a continuous cross-section throughout the web. Rather, it must be assumed that the thickness of the vaults webs was steadily increased from the apex downwards to the springers [16].

Subsequent vaulting

Crowning a liturgical interior with a Late Gothic vault was a challenging task requiring all the structural elements of a church to be tailored to the vault and the massive forces involved. With new constructions, the ground plans and the walls could be correctly dimensioned from the start, but as mentioned above, just over 40% of the churches were not built from scratch. In an existing structure, parameters such as wall thickness or ground plan proportions cannot be determined directly, which makes the subsequent vaulting of an already existing church even more complicated. So why were churches or some of their fabric reused at all?

The main reason for the continued use of the existing building fabric is obvious: by integrating existing architectural elements, material, time and thus costs could be saved. A central idea here was that if structures or elements, such as the exterior walls, were reused, the foundations did not have to be rebuilt either. The construction of foundations was certainly one of the more time-consuming and expensive sections of a new building. How elaborate the foundation of a church used to be is preserved in one of the rare *'Werkmeisterbücher'*, which bears the title "Unterweisungen" (English: Instructions) and was written around 1516 by the Heidelberg master builder Lorenz Lechler [17]. The basis of the foundation was a close-fitting pile foundation made of high-quality piles of oak, elm or alder timber. The spaces in between were then filled with crushed coal. Above this, a grate was erected from further timbers, which was stuffed with stones and poured over with hot mortar – only on top of this was the building's substructure constructed. This method remained practically unchanged until modern times, hence the treatise "Von wirklicher Baukunst" (1780) by Lukas Voch still contains some drawings of various pile foundation techniques on the first plate (Fig. 8).

Therefore, if the existing structure was large enough and did not need to be extended, integrating it into the intended new building was reasonable simply because no new foundations and substructures had to be built for it. In the objects studied in the thesis, it is striking that generally only the structure of the nave was reused, while the presbytery was built from scratch. This most likely relates to the ground plans and designs of the respective structures: The form of the nave on a rectangular ground plan hardly changed from the Early Middle Ages to the Late Gothic period and beyond, which is why the nave, unless it required enlargement, could simply be integrated into the new building.

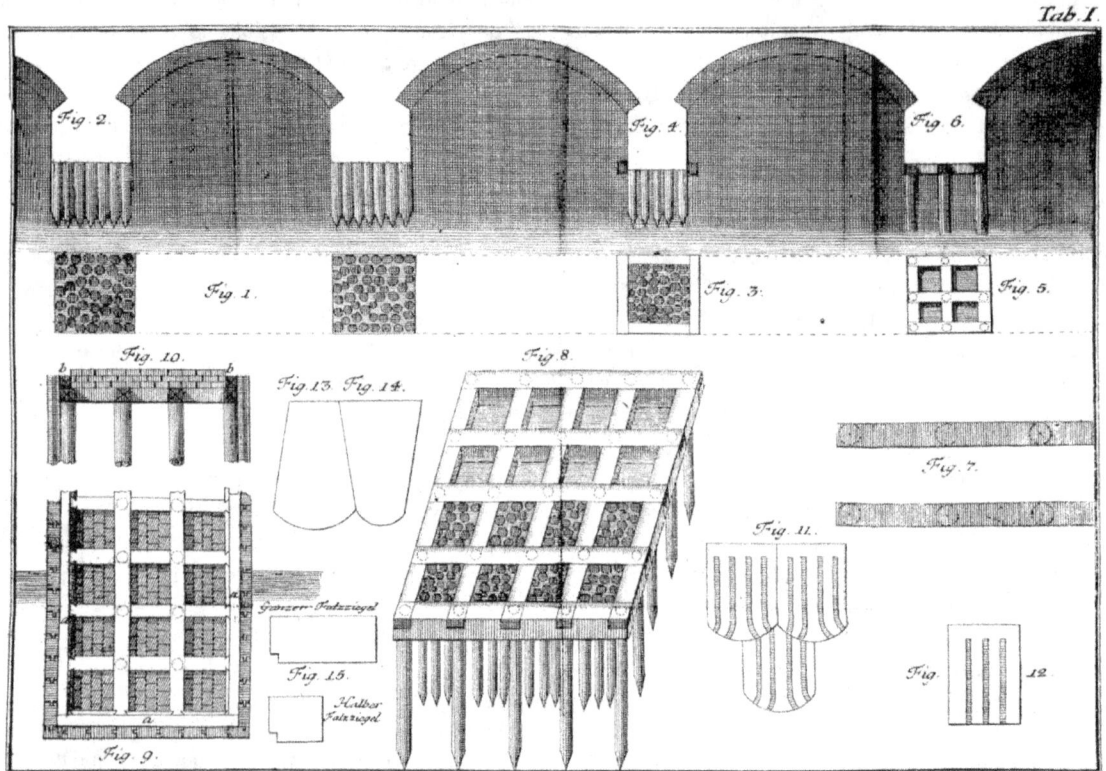

Figure 8: Different types of pile foundations (Lukas Voch, Wirkliche Baupraktik der bürgerlichen Baukunst. Augsburg: Matthäus Rieger, 1780, Plate 1)

If the conditions for a conversion were not met, the existing structures had to be adapted and modified to their new tasks. The addition of a vault primarily affected the walls through lateral shear forces, for which they were not intended. To counterbalance these forces, several solutions were possible, which could all be verified in multiple objects. For most objects, the addition of buttresses was sufficient to balance the forces emanating from the vault. Buttresses allowed the wall to be reinforced and extended at the points with the greatest forces – a principle that was obviously also applied to new vaulted buildings. However, due to adjacent buildings or lack of space, it was sometimes not possible to add external or internal buttresses. Another fundamental solution was therefore to deliberately position the vault springers very low on the wall so that the superimposed load on them would increase, which meant that some of the forces could already be counterbalanced [18]. This approach is best observed in the Collegiate Church of San Vittore Mauro in Poschiavo [19], but has been adopted in several churches in Grisons.

Beyond these two most commonly applied solutions, a third option was possible: converting the church into another architectural type. The most famous example of such a conversion is the Convent Church of St. John in Müstair. In Müstair, the adjacent convent buildings meant that buttresses could not be added and the 12 m wide interior could not be directly vaulted, as this would have disturbed the high apses (Fig. 9). The simplest solution was to inter-support the vault on columns, which resulted in the Carolingian hall church being converted into a three-aisled hall church from 1488–92. Since the middle nave and side nave vaults in Müstair are approximately the same height, part of the horizontal thrust forces are already equalised at the columns and the walls are less stressed. A similar solution can be found in the church of St. Maria and Michael of the former Premonstratensian monastery in Churwalden.

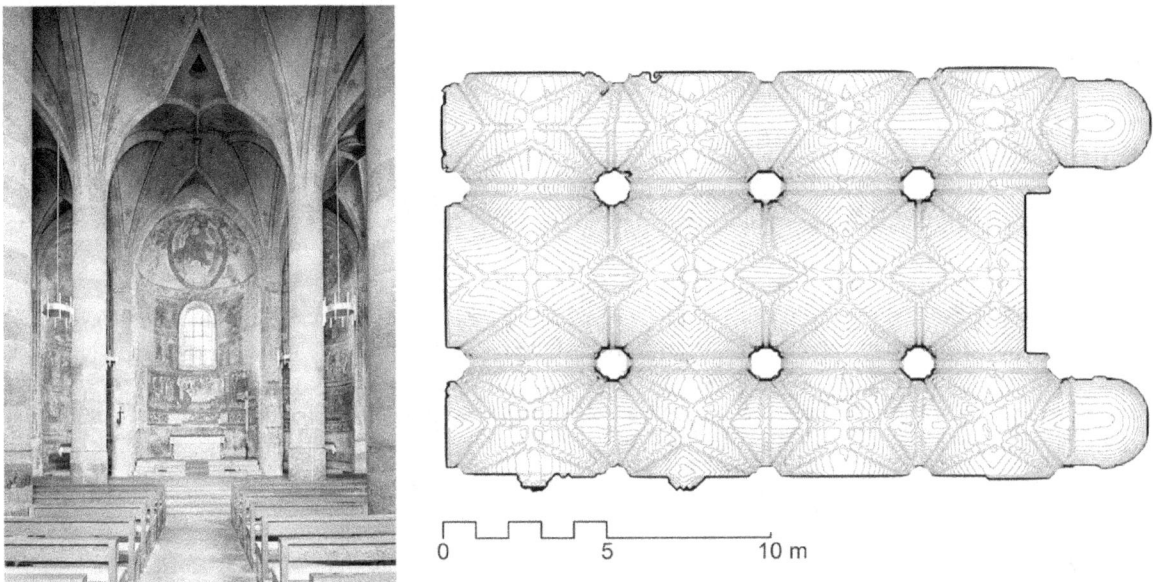

Figure 9: Interior of the Convent Church of St. John in Müstair and elevation plan with intervals of 10 cm (Photo: Foundation 'Stiftung Pro Kloster St. Johann' / Plan: M. Maissen)

After the existing structure had been optimised for the new tasks and for the acting forces, the further vaulting procedure no longer differed from a newly built structure. The use of uniform radii and an approximation of the vault webs towards a barrel shape can also be verified for all the subsequently vaulted objects.

Conclusion

The art of vaulting in Grisons did not evolve continuously from within itself, but was rather introduced from outside and thereby skipped several intermediate stages. Almost overnight, the fundamental understanding of ribs changed and a new level of aspiration for Late Gothic vault construction was established. The completion of the chancel vault of the Church of St. Martin in Chur not only served as a prototype, but above all as an impetus and incentive, after which the new architectural forms spread to all the valleys of Grisons within a very short time thanks to diligent master builders and their work crews. The steadily rising building volume demanded more efficient construction processes so that the churches could be built in the shortest possible time. Thus, building techniques imported from southern Germany or Austria were combined with local traditions, which subsequently created the basis for optimised construction practices.

A massive optimisation of the construction processes was possible by simplifying the procedures in the planning and execution of the vaults. When designing the vault patterns, the master builders used their profound knowledge of the Euclidean geometry, though all the patterns could still only be drawn with compasses, straightedges or an auxiliary grid. At the same time, a new standard in the production of the voussoirs and the construction of the vaults was established, which was adapted to the problem to be solved by a few parameters, such as the curvature radius and the selection of the material. However, these parameters were kept as simple as possible to ensure the most efficient construction workflow. When choosing the materials, locally available types of stone were used in order to reduce transport distances and to enable on-site processing. In addition, when applying the arch radii, a few uniform radii were used to simplify the fabrication of the ribs and the prefabrication of the falsework even further. The design and construction of a vault should therefore not be considered as a rigid method, but as an interconnected process [20] that could be adapted to the given circumstances.

After 1470, the approach to the design and construction of vaults in Grisons no longer differed from the Central European standard. In contrast, the subsequent vaulting of existing churches was rather specific to the Late Gothic construction period in Grisons. Whether the technique of subsequent vaulting also had a similar significance in Late Gothic construction outside Grison cannot be answered more precisely at this time due to the lack of data. The existing churches had to be adapted to the new forces, which in Grisons was mainly achieved by adding massive buttresses or low-lying springers to increase the superimposed load, and in a few rare cases, the church was even converted into a new building type.

An efficient and cost-effective construction industry caused and promoted the Late Gothic building boom in equal measure, without the interaction of which it would hardly have been possible to cope with the volume of building that occurred. The optimisation of costs and labour time by reducing transport routes, by simplifying the fabrication of voussoirs or of temporary auxiliary constructions, as well as building in existing fabric and the continued use of existing structures therefore are topics that were just as relevant 500 years ago as they still are today.

Acknowledgment

This present study is part of a doctoral thesis at ETH Zurich supervised by Prof. Dr.-Ing. Stefan M. Holzer. The research project was concluded in 2020 and the thesis is now publicly accessible via the Research Collection of ETH Zurich (www.research-collection.ethz.ch).

References

[1] M. Maissen, *'Gewölbebau der Spätgotik in Graubünden'* (Doctoral thesis, ETH Zurich, 2020).
[2] E. Poeschel, *Die Kunstdenkmäler des Kantons Graubünden: Vol. 7*. Basel: Birkhäuser, 1948, pp. 36–37 and pp. 97–98.
[3] U. Campbell, *Historia Raetica: Tomus 1*. Quellen zur Schweizer Geschichte, Vol. 8. Basel: F. Schneider, 1887, p. 545.
[4] T. Bruggmann, *Wachsendes Selbstbewusstsein und zunehmende Verschriftlichung. Churer Quellen des 15. Jahrhunderts*. Chur: Desertina, 2017, p. 193.
[5] Full list of all Late Gothic churches in Grisons: Maissen, thesis (Note 1), pp. 285–289.
[6] H. Batz, *Die Kirchen und Kapellen des Kantons Graubünden*. Vol. 1. Chur: Casanova, 2003, p. 8.
[7] Maissen, thesis (Note 1), pp. 45–50.
[8] U. Coenen, *Die spätgotischen Werkmeisterbücher in Deutschland: Untersuchung und Edition der Lehrschriften für Entwurf und Ausführung von Sakralbauten*. Munich: Scaneg, 1990, pp. 91–94.
[9] W. Müller, *Grundlagen gotischer Bautechnik*. Munich: Deutscher Kunstverlag, 1999. pp. 152–155.
[10] Maissen, thesis (Note 1), pp. 299–319.
[11] ibid. p. 316.
[12] ibid. p. 39.
[13] M. Maissen, 'On the Subsequent Vaulting of Churches in the Late Gothic Period: The Collegiate Church of San Vittore Mauro in Poschiavo, Switzerland' in J. Campbell et al. (Eds): *Iron, Steel and Building: Studies in the History of Construction. Proceedings of the Seventh Conference of the Construction History Society*. Cambridge: Construction History Society, 2020, p. 253.

[14] M. Trautz, *'Zur Entwicklung von Form und Struktur historischer Gewölbe aus der Sicht der Statik'* (Doctoral thesis, Univ. Stuttgart, 1998), pp. 16–17.

[15] G. Ungewitter, *Lehrbuch der gotischen Konstruktionen*. Third edition revised by Karl Mohrmann, Leipzig: T.O. Weigel Nachfolger, 1892, p. 119.

[16] S. M. Holzer, *Statische Beurteilung historischer Tragwerke. Vol. 1: Mauerwerks-konstruktionen*. Berlin: Ernst & Sohn, 2013, pp. 123–124.

[17] U. Coenen, *Die spätgotischen Werkmeisterbücher in Deutschland: Untersuchung und Edition der Lehrschriften für Entwurf und Ausführung von Sakralbauten*. Munich: Scaneg, 1990, pp. 95–99.

[18] J. Heyman, *The Stone Skeleton*. Cambridge: University Press, 1995, pp. 71–73.

[19] Maissen, Subsequent vaulting (Note 13), pp. 256–259.

[20] D. Wendland, *Steinerne Ranken, wunderbare Maschinen: Entwurf und Planung spätgotischer Gewölbe und ihrer Einzelteile*. Petersberg: Michael Imhof, 2019, pp. 24–29.

Vaults Without Buttresses: A Survey of Swiss Roodscreens

Clemens Knobling
Institute of Construction History and Preservation (IDB), ETH Zurich, Switzerland

Introduction

In the late Middle Ages, a new architectural motif prevailed: Vaults on very slender supports lacking a massive abutment.

The motif is well known to us from the Italian loggias south of the Alps, which became a ubiquitous part of cityscapes at the end of the 14th century. In the north, too, loggias were built on the Italian model, albeit more than 100 years later.

In fact, however, the same phenomenon has existed in the north for just as long, but in a different place: inside the churches, in the form of late Gothic rood screens. This refers primarily to the so-called "hall rood screens" [1], i.e. those that form a spatial structure in the form of rows of masonry canopies. According to J. Jung, they would be called "bridges" [2].

Even if rood screens and Italian loggias have little in common in terms of architectural history, they are very close in terms of construction history.

A new research project at the Institute of Construction History and Preservation at ETH Zurich will address the phenomenon of such filigree and delicate articulated vaults - *vaults without buttresses*. The aim is to look at and analyse the Italian loggia and the late Gothic hall rood screen as a comparable phenomenon in terms of construction history. Special interest will be given to the vaulting techniques as well as the extensive use of wrought-iron tie rods. The project itself is still in preparation. In the course of this, however, initial surveys (including 3D laser scans) have already taken place. In the following, three late medieval rood screens from Switzerland will be presented: the rood screens in the *Leonhardskirche* in Basel (1455/60, enlarged at the end of the 15th century) [3], in the parish church (Stadtkirche) of Aarau (before 1479) [4] and in the parish church (*Stadtkirche*) in Burgdorf, which was built in 1511 - 1512 and relocated to the east side of the nave in 1867 – 1868 [5].

The architectural history of the rood screen has been well researched, most recently in the works of M. Schmelzer [6] and J. Jung [7]. However, it is astonishing that they were not yet analysed from the perspective of construction history. The delicate appearance of the rood screen is, however, primarily due to its construction. The architecture of slender supports creates a filigree and yet spatially effective construct. Since the rood screens which have been examined have a massive vault, the construction challenge should not be underestimated for, despite their small size, the horizontal forces which were generated could not be resolved by massive abutments which would have run counter to the desired impression of the rood screen. In contrast to the majority of the loggias, the rood screen also lacks a superimposed load.

For this reason, iron tie rods were used extensively. Tie rods are a ubiquitous phenomenon in Italian vaults. Their use in medieval and early modern construction has recently been the subject of research [8]. North of the Alps, iron was also used on a large scale, for example as tie rods in the walls of Gothic cathedrals [9]. Visible tie rods in vaults were obviously avoided. In the case of slender rood screens, however, tie rods couldn't be hidden efficiently in the masonry. So far, the use of iron in the context of rood screens has not been discussed. The future research project should provide new insights here.

Vaults Without Buttresses: A Survey of Swiss Roodscreens

The structural demands of the rood screen and thus its relevance to construction history can be well illustrated by the following examples.

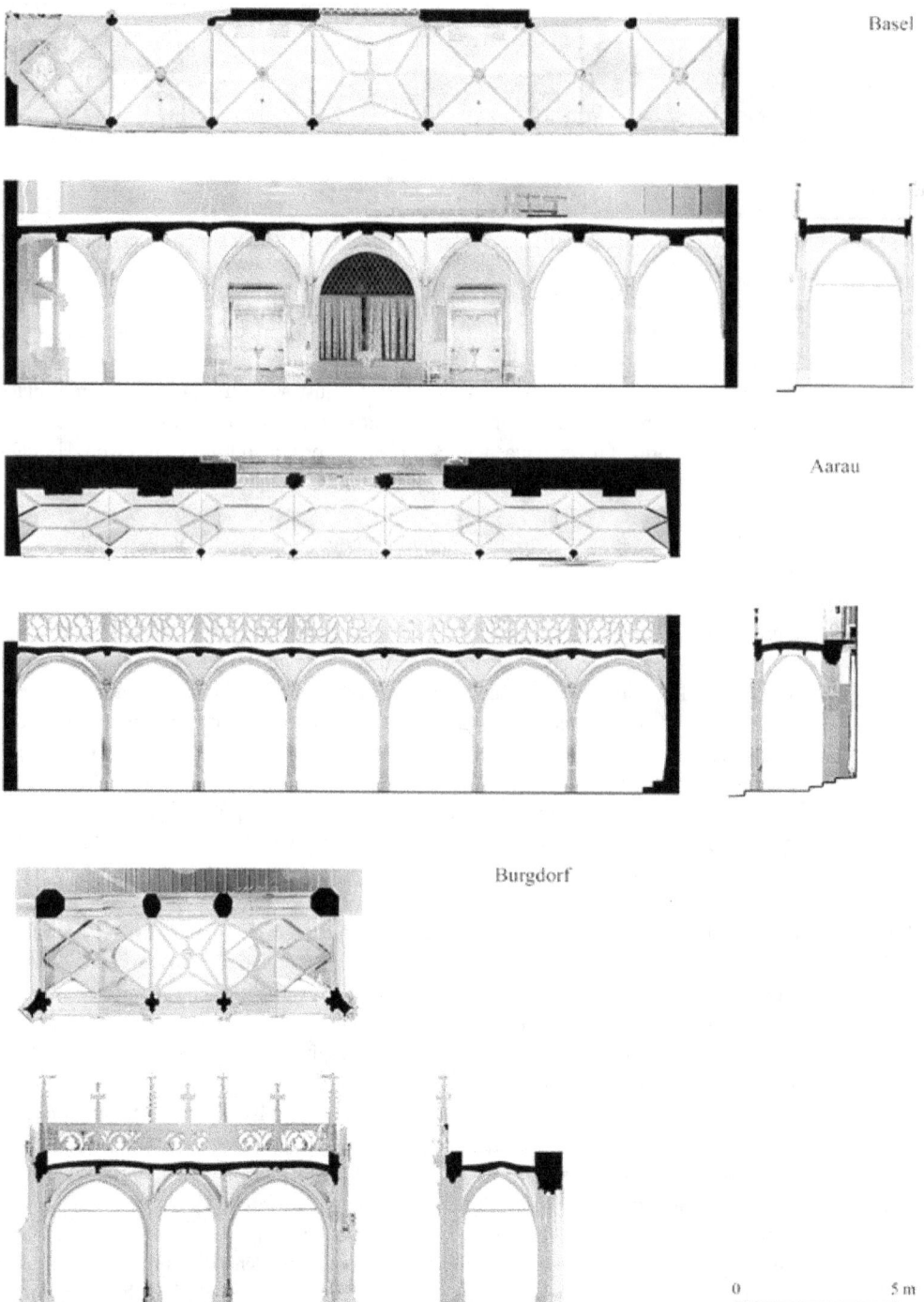

Fig. 1. Plans from the point clouds of the surveyed rood-screens. Drawings: Xijie Ma

Leonhard church in Basel

The rood screen in the Leonhard church *(Leonhardskirche)* in Basel was built between 1455 and 1460. (Fig. 1, Basel) In the course of a transformation of the church from 1489 onwards, the old basilica was demolished and the present hall church built (master builder Hans Niesenberger, Hans Nußdorfer). The rood screen, however, was taken over from the previous building. It was adapted to the wider new hall church in 1496 by extending it by one bay at each side [10]. After the Reformation in 1529, the rood screen remained in the church – not like the most rood screens in catholic churches, which were removed in the 16th century due to the reorganisations after the council of Trent [11].

The middle five bays represent the first construction phase of the rood screen. The central bay with a simple star-shaped rib vault is adjoined by two further square bays with ribbed vaults. (Fig. 2) The northern bay is irregular due to the connection to the new outer wall, its ribs form a rhomboid pattern. The front of the rood screen opens to the nave with wide-span pointed arches (2.80 m each, central arch 3.20 m).

The octagonal pillars have a diameter of only 36 cm. The transverse arches are not profiled more strongly than the cross ribs. The rood screen is 4.63 m high, measured from floor to key stone. The slender columns have a cross-section of 0.1 m² and are 2.33 m high, measured from floor to rein. This corresponds to a slenderness ratio of 25.9 [12]. The thickness of the vault could not be measured because the rood screen is covered with a floor. Since the other vaults of the church were made of brick, it is assumed that this material was also used for the rood screen, which would require a vault thickness, referring to other Swiss examples, of about 12.5 cm [13]. A plan showing the contour lines of the vault was generated from the measurements. This shows a slight rising of the vault caps to their middle axis, which could indicate freehand vaulting [14].

Fig. 2. Basel, Leonhard church, rood screen. Photo: author.

Vaults Without Buttresses: A Survey of Swiss Roodscreens

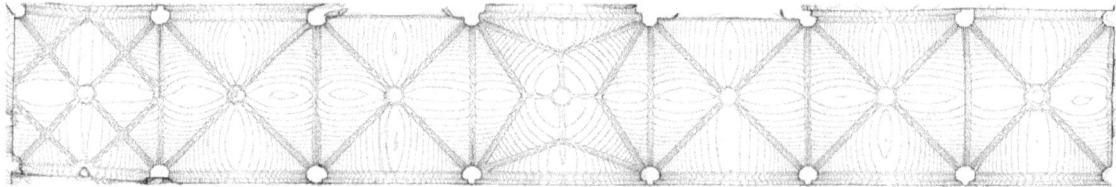

Fig. 3. Basel, Leonhard church, contour lines of the vaults of the rood screen. Drawing: Xijie Ma.

The second and fourth bays have a solid slender back wall. The adjoining bays merely rest on the filigree supports. In the middle bay, a door opens at the back, taking up almost its entire width. The outer walls of the church serve as lateral abutments.

The high structural demands of the rood screen become clear when taking a closer look at the proportions in one bay. A column has a cross-section of 0.10 m^2, the referring vault has a surface area of $10.70 \text{ m}^2 / 4 = 2.675 \text{ m}^2$ per quarter bay (projected on the ground). This corresponds to a ratio of 1: 26,75 (for simplification and for better comparability with the other rood screens, the cross-section is calculated with only one support and the area of a quarter bay).

The horizontal thrust is compensated by iron tie-rods. These have an average cross-section of 2.8×5 cm in the older parts of the rood screen, and a cross-section of 1.6×5.5 cm in the outer and thus younger bays. There are only transverse tie-rods which are anchored efficiently into the masonry just above the rein. A survey of the cloister of nearby Basel Cathedral, finished 1492 [15] (Fig. 4) suggests that in comparable contemporary buildings, tie rods were also attached in the longitudinal direction (perhaps as a reaction to the earthquake in Basel in 1356) and later removed - possibly due to the aesthetic concerns already mentioned above. There is no evidence of this in the rood screen of the Leonhard Church. The installation of tie rods in the longitudinal direction would indeed have been necessary if there had been no lateral abutments, e.g. to avoid a progressive collapse [16].

Fig. 4. Basel, cloister (Kleiner Kreuzgang) next to the Basel Minster. Photo: author.

Parish Church in Aarau

The parish church *(Stadtkirche)* in Aarau was rebuilt between 1471 and 1479 (master builder Sebastian Gisel) as a three-nave basilica with a flat ceiling. The rood screen (Fig. 1, Aarau) was completed together with the church. Here, too, the Reformation (1529) prevented it from being demolished. Its late medieval substance has been completely preserved. (Fig. 5) Minor changes were made in 1880 with the opening of two new doors next to the original gate to the presbytery. A new balustrade was contructed and finials on the front were added in 1939 [17]. Until 1818, the church's late Baroque organ was situated on top of the slender rood screen [18].

Fig. 5. Aarau, rood screen. Photo: author.

The rood screen uses the east wall of the church as back abutment. Below the quire arch, it is opened to the presbytery by three arches (only the central pointed arch being from the original building period, see above). The rood screen opens towards the nave with seven (almost round-shaped) arcades, each with a clearance of 2.66 m between the columns. Only the southern bay is somewhat wider (2.78 m) due to the irregular ground plan of the nave.

The dimensions of the rectangular bays are 2.17 × 2.96 m each. Thus, an area of 6.42 m² is vaulted per bay. The vaults have an almost round-arched cross-section, i.e. they are flatter than those in Basel. The ribs are figured as an elongated net without transversal arches. In Aarau, too, it was not possible to determine the thickness of the vault. However, it is assumed that here, too, vaulting was done with the common brick format of about 12.5 cm thickness. The contour lines of the vault show no superelevation of the caps, but very shallow apexes. The small dimensions of the vault do not allow a definite statement, but it can be assumed that vaulting was carried out on a formwork.

Vaults Without Buttresses: A Survey of Swiss Roodscreens

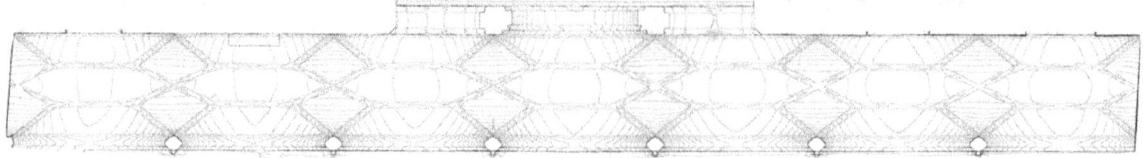

Fig. 6. Aarau, contour lines of the vault of the rood screen. Drawing: Xijie Ma.

The supports of the vaults are particularly filigree. Being 2.60 m high (measured from floor to rein), they have a diameter of only 29 cm, which corresponds to a slenderness ratio of 35.9. A column cross-section of 0.07 m² refers to a vaulted area per quarter bay of 6.42 m² / 4 = 1.605 m² (ratio 1:23).

Here too, transversal wrought-iron tie rods are attached just above the rein of the vault. These have a cross-section of 2.1 3×.8 cm. There is no evidence of tie-rods in the longitudinal direction.

Parish church in Burgdorf near Bern

A new church was built in the town of Burgdorf in the canton of Bern between 1471 and 1490. The building is designed as a three-nave basilica with flat ceilings in the nave and a vaulted choir. In 1511 – 1512, a three-bay rood screen (Fig. 1, Burgdorf) was erected in the eastern part of the nave, directly in front of the quire arch. As in the examples discussed before, the rood screen probably owes its survival to the Reformation, which found no further use for the presbytery behind it. Between 1867 and 1868, the interior of the church was redesigned, and the rood screen was moved to the west between the first pair of free pillars of the nave. It was rotated by 180° for the new installation. The remaining open space between the back of the rood screen and the east wall of the tower was covered with a wooden gallery, whose splendid prospectus was to become the late medieval rood screen [19].

The rood screen has an irregular bay sequence. The central arcade opens with a clearence of 1.76 m, the wider side arcades with a clearence of 2.96 m to the nave. The rood screen is open on all sides. The nave-side arches are strongly profiled, while the transversal arches are only slightly more profiled than the ribs. The vault is supported by six pillars. The outer piers, formerly on the east side and now on the west side, were once connected to the eastern wall of the church and are now connected to the western pair of pillars. The arcades of the small sides were each partly renewed so that they could be connected directly to the pier. The rich tracery of the front, consisting of interlocking ogee arches, pinnacles and finials, and the rich profiles of the arches results in an unusually elaborate decoration, which can otherwise only be found on a few preserved rood screens, cf. e.g. Breisach, Tübingen or Halberstadt [20].

The unusual rhythm of the bays can be traced back to the crucifix altar that once stood in the central narrow bay, the rear arcade of which was closed with a wooden grille [21]. The wider arcades were open on all sides and thus offered an unusually generous view into the presbytery.

The vaults in the outer bays are figured with rhomboid patterns. In the narrow inner bay, the ribs form a simple star. The contour lines suggest that vaulting was done partly freehand. (Fig. 8) The bays have dimensions of 3.80 × 3.60 m (lateral) and 2.30 × 3.60 m (central). According to sources, the wrought-iron tie rods with a cross-section of 2.5 × 5.5 cm were reused during the reconstruction [22]. However, the findings cast doubt on whether this also applies to their connection to the wall.

Fig. 7. Burgdorf, rood screen. Photo: author.

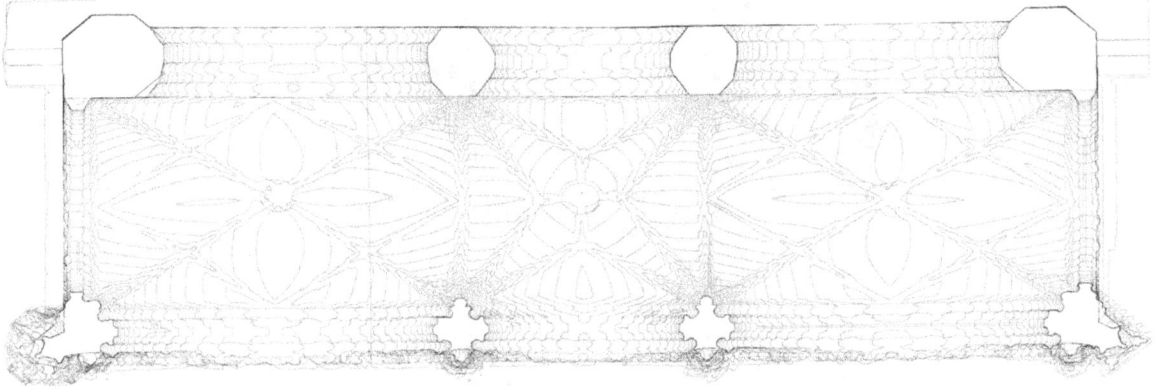

Fig. 8. Burgdorf, contour lines of the vault of the rood screen. Drawing: Xijie Ma.

Vaults Without Buttresses: A Survey of Swiss Roodscreens

Further research both on site and in the archives is required. However, it is certain that in the originally there were tie rods in both the transverse and longitudinal direction. This is necessary here, since on the small side - in contrast to the rood screens in Aarau and Basel - there was no abutment (e.g. the outer wall), and the rood screen was designed as a canopy open all around. The fact that the rear arcades manage without tie rods may be because the pillars of the church provided sufficient abutment, both in their original location and at the new site, thereby avoiding investment in expensive iron components

The pillars of the rood screen are, compared to the other rood screens, thicker. So, the ratio of column cross-section to vaulted area is not as ambitious as in the other rood screens. If we consider the more filigree central pillars, there is still a ratio of 0.20 m^2 to 3.4 m^2 (quarter bay) or 1:17. The slenderness ratio of the most slender pillars is 19.

Since the rood screen was relocated, it would first be necessary to reconstruct its original state. For this, the original components would have to be distinguished from the new components, which is partly possible by eye (Fig. 9), but partly can only be achieved with the help of archival documents and in-depth building archaeology. This is the task for an individual research campaign on this highly exciting object. For further research within the framework of the planned project, the rood screen is less suitable as it is no longer in situ. However, due to its importance in architectural history, it should not go unmentioned here. The relocation of rood screens was not uncommon in the 19th century, as the close example in Basel Minster shows [23].

Fig. 9. Burgdorf, connection of the rood screen to the western pillar of the nave. Photo: author.

The investigations outlined are only the beginning of a far-reaching research project, which will also be devoted to the material properties of the iron tie rods and their anchoring in the masonry by the aid of non-destructive testing methods. Further building archaeology will take each stone into account.

The aim of this article firstly is, however, to address the often-unmentioned constructional challenge of such filigree vaults - vaults without buttresses.

References

[1] M. Schmelzer, Der mittelalterliche Lettner im deutschsprachigen Raum. Typologie und Funktion. Petersberg: Imhof, 2004. pp. 64-118.
[2] Jung, The Gothic Screen. Cambridge: Cambridge University Press, 2012. pp. 45-70.
[3] F. Mauerer, Die Kunstdenkmäler des Kantons Basel-Stadt. Band IV: Die Kirchen, Klöster und Kapellen. Zweiter Teil: St. Katharina bis St. Niklaus, Basel: Birkhäuser, 1961. pp. 164-219.
[4] M. Stettler, Die Kunstdenkmäler des Kantons Aargau. Band I: Die Bezirke Aarau, Kulm, Zofingen, Basel: Birkhäuser, 1948. pp. 41-52.
[5] J. Schweizer, Die Kunstdenkmäler des Kantons Bern. Landband 1: Die Stadt Burgdorf, Basel: Birkhäuser 1985. pp. 186-234.
[6] M. Schmelzer, Der mittelalterliche Lettner im deutschsprachigen Raum, (Note 1).
[7] Jung, The Gothic Screen, (Note 2).
[8] M. L'Heritier, 'Le fer et le plomb dans la construction monumentale au Moyen Âge, de l'étude des sources écrites à l'analyse de la matière. Bilan de 20 ans de recherches et perspectives', Aedificare, vol. 6, 2019, pp. 79-121; R. Vecchiatini, 'Historical Use of Metal Tie-Rods in the Italian Territory: Treatises, Essays, and Manuals through Four Centuries of History', International Journal of Architectural Heritage, vol. 13, no. 3, 2019, pp. 451-471.
[9] M. L'Heritier, Le fer et le plomb, (Note 8), pp. 79-121.
[10] Mauerer, Die Kunstdenkmäler des Kantons Basel-Stadt, (Note 3) p. 214.
[11] M. von Engelberg, Renovatio Ecclesiae. Die „Barockisierung" mittelalterlicher Kirchen, Petersberg: Imhof, 2005. pp. 166-186.
[12] $\lambda = \sqrt{\frac{A}{I_{min}}} \times l_k$; λ= slenderness ratio; A = diameter of the column; Imin = axial area moment of inertia, here assumed approximately as a circle; lk = length of the column.
[13] M. Maissen, 'Gewölbebau der Spätgotik in Graubünden' (Ph.D. thesis, ETH Zurich, 2020), pp. 167 - 168.
[14] S. M. Holzer, Gerüste und Hilfskonstruktionen im historischen Baubetrieb. Berlin: Ernst & Sohn, 2021. p.147.
[15] H.-R. Meier, D. Schwinn Schürmann, M. Bernasconi, S. Hess, C. Jäggi, A. Nagel, F. Pajor, Die Kunstdenkmäler des Kantons Basel-Stadt. Band X: Das Basler Münster, Bern: Gesellschaft für Schweizerische Kunstgeschichte, 2019. pp. 397-402.
[16] S. M. Holzer, Statische Beurteilung historischer Tragwerke. Band 1: Mauerwerkskonstruktionen, Berlin: Ernst und Sohn, 2013. p.19.
[17] Stettler, Die Kunstdenkmäler des Kantons Aargau, (Note 4) pp. 46-47.
[18] S. Ehrismann, 'Die spannende Geschichte der Orgeln in der Stadtkirche Aarau', Aarauer Neujahrsblätter, vol. 86, 2012, pp. 42-50.
[19] Schweizer, Die Kunstdenkmäler des Kantons Bern, (Note 5) p. 194-196.
[20] M. Schmelzer, Der mittelalterliche Lettner im deutschsprachigen Raum, (Note 1) P. 74.
[21] Schweizer, Die Kunstdenkmäler des Kantons Bern, (Note 5) p. 211-212.
[22] ibid., p. 209.
[23] Meier, Schwinn Schürmann, Bernasconi, Hess, Jäggi, Nagel, Pajor, Das Basler Münster, (Note 15) p. 141.

The so-called 'Palazzetto' in the Palazzo di Venezia Complex: A small construction history among the huge transformation events of the Rome centre in the early twentieth century

Caterina F. Carocci, Renata Finocchiaro and Valentina Macca
University of Catania, Italy

Introduction

The demolition of the Palazzetto di Venezia and its reconstruction in an area just about a dozen metres from the original one represents an example of those practices which took place in Rome at the beginning of the twentieth century in order to adapt some massive transformations inside the ancient urban fabric to the preservation of buildings regarded as particularly significant [1].

Despite the literature on the transformations that occurred from the last quarter of the nineteenth century in the most ancient area of the city being quite wide, the history of the Palazzetto di Venezia's 'relocation' has remained in the shade. The reason behind this can be recognised in the Palazzetto di Venezia's history belonging to the much wider context of actions aimed at realising the new colossal monument to celebrate Vittorio Emanuele II, first monarch of Italy and father of the nation, within which the Palazzetto's events – and the other ones carried out on similar buildings in the same area – represented a modest episode [2].

Nowadays, renowned studies dealing with the fifteenth-century building, the *Viridarium*, are available and refer to its relationship with both the adjacent Pietro Barbo's cardinalitial palace and the surrounding Medieval S. Mark's quarter, developed near the homonymous Basilica.

What the current literature is missing is the analysis of the procedures which marked out the Palazzetto di Venezia between 1885 and 1912 and, more particularly, the study of both the material and executive aspects which connected the actual building to its fifteenth-century antecedent.

A complicated administrative process – the length of which was mainly due to the broad group of participants involved in the operations – characterised the years preceding the beginning of the two building sites; they were conducted according to the parallel directives of reconstructing the new building in the image of the one which had to be demolished and reusing the stone elements belonging to the fifteenth-century cloister.

This contribution tries to fill this gap through the reading of the original documents held in the archives and the direct analysis of the rebuilt palazzetto – through architectural surveys and a few weakly destructive investigations – in order to outline the executive processes linked both to the demolition operations and the new construction ones.

From the pope Paolo II's secret garden to the 'Palazzetto di Venezia', headquarters of the Austro-Hungarian's embassy.

Built between 1466 and 1469, the *Viridarium* was conceived by the Pope Paolo II as a closed garden which allowed him to walk in the green while remaining in the very heart of the city; following a unique configuration – if compared to the architectural scene of Rome – it was originally independent of the adjacent St. Mark's palace. (Fig. 1) The building was

The so-called 'Palazzetto' in the Palazzo di Venezia Complex: A small construction history among the huge transformation events of the Rome centre in the early twentieth century

composed of a hanging garden placed above a basement level holding artisan shops. These last were accessible from the outside, while the actual garden – at over three meters above the surrounding squares and streets – was only accessible from the Pope's apartment, situated in the *piano nobile* of St. Mark's palace [3].

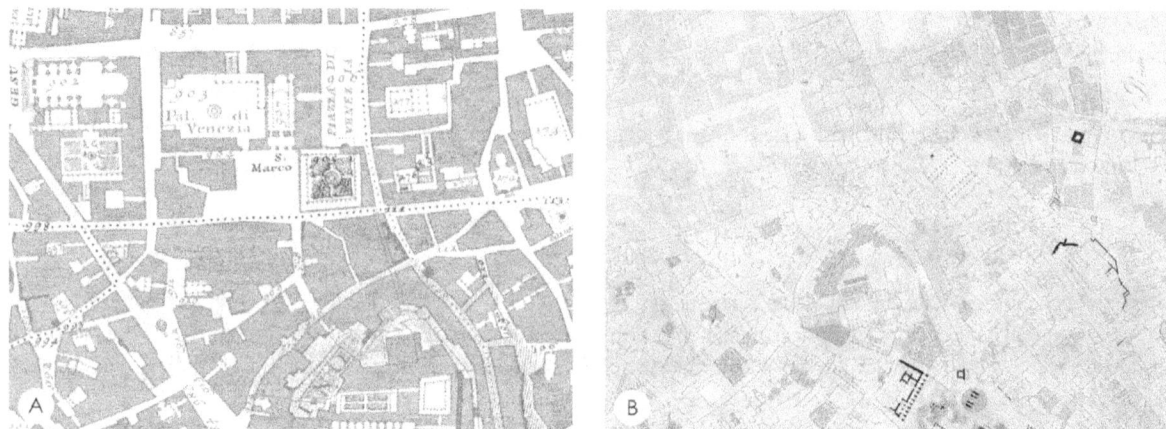

Figure 1: The area of Palazzo and Palazzetto di Venezia in the Nuova Topografia di Roma di G.B. Nolli, 1744 (A) and the Catasto Gregoriano, 1835 (B).

The masonry structure which enclosed the garden consisted of a two-level cloister open on both sides through wide arcades. The *Viridarium* was therefore a quite isolated space and, at the same time, completely permeable to sight from the surrounding public spaces. The cloister's spans were originally ten on each side; the first vaulted level had travertine octagonal pillars with capitals in acanthus leaves and curving corner volutes; the second level, with Ionic columns, was covered by a wooden gabled roof, as shown by the surveys carried out before the demolition. An embattlement crowned both the internal and the external walls.

The square plan of the inner garden turned into an irregular shape at the front overlooking the ancient *via Lata* to which the building was aligned [4]. This wing – which for this reason had a trapezoidal plan – held the sole spaces in the building having a residential function which were used by the Cardinal Barbo, the Pope's nephew.

The building was first subjected to major transformations under the Pope Paolo III (1535-49) when he decided to connect the *Viridarium* to the tower he had built for himself on the Capitoline hill. For this the Pope proposed the construction of a raised walkway supported by arches with the function of a real private footpath (see figure 1A); this was the period when most of the cloister's arcades were modified – closed or made smaller – deeply changing the peculiar permeability at sight of the garden and determining the change in name of the building, identified as 'palazzetto' since then. (Fig. 2)

Just a few decades later, Pope Pio IV (1499-1565) gave the ambassadors of the Serenissima (Venice) the St. Mark's complex (the main palace, to which the Paolo Barbo's palace belonged, and the Palazzetto di Venezia) provided that the titular cardinal of S. Mark's basilica maintained his residence. After the Treaty of Campoformio (1797) and the fall of the Republic of Venice, the entire complex passed to the French government. On the fall of Napoleon in 1814, the complex finally became property of Austrian government.

Figure 2: Piazza Venezia in a painting of F. Muccinelli 1781 (A) and piazza S. Marco in a drawing of V.J. Nicolle 1787 ca. (B)

Roma the Capital of Italy, the Vittoriano building site and the question of the Palazzetto di Venezia.

Connected to the period of great transformations in Rome – city expansion and the existing urban fabric's redefinition [5] – the events concerning the Palazzetto di Venezia were, as abovementioned, closely related to the construction of the Monument to Vittorio Emanuele II, first monarch of Italy.

After a period of uncertainty, the slope of the Capitoline Hill and namely that which overlooked the *Via del Corso* – the beating heart of the city at that time – was chosen for the realisation of the commemorative monument. This area, densely built-up by a thousand-year-old stratified building fabric, was to become the linchpin of the planned expansions on both sides of the Tiber. Despite the large quantity of demolitions which would have been necessary to make way for the new majestic building (not only minor architecture, but also churches and noble palaces), the special office for the Capital's Public Works and the specially established government committee persisted in the choice of this area on account of the importance that the building should have had in terms of symbolic value. As well as its commemorative purpose, the monument had to trace the architectural ideal of the 'national style'.

In 1884, Giuseppe Sacconi – the winner of the competition for the monument's project – defined the demolition works on the slope of the Capitoline Hill (among these the tower of Paolo III, the three cloisters of the Ara Coeli's Franciscan monastery and several residential blocks) and those necessary to redesign the foothill new piazza, symmetrically placed with respect to Via del Corso.

The site of the new piazza was marked out by an urban structure – clearly documented by the "Nuova carta di Roma" published in 1748 by Giovan Battista Nolli and the more recent Gregoriano land register – which consisted of two important adjacent squares clearly separated by the Palazzetto di Venezia's volume (see figure 1). The Torlonia palace was placed facing the Palazzetto, for which the demolition and the subsequent construction of a new building was planned in order to define the scenic space of the monumental backdrop.

As regard to the Palazzetto di Venezia, the project involved the reduction of its volume as much as the monument's perspective required with the subsequent definition of new facades. This intervention belonged to a *modus operandi* adopted up to that time for realising new roads or broadening the existent ones through the demolition of the existing buildings or their partial 'cut' (Fig. 3).

The so-called 'Palazzetto' in the Palazzo di Venezia Complex: A small construction history among the huge transformation events of the Rome centre in the early twentieth century

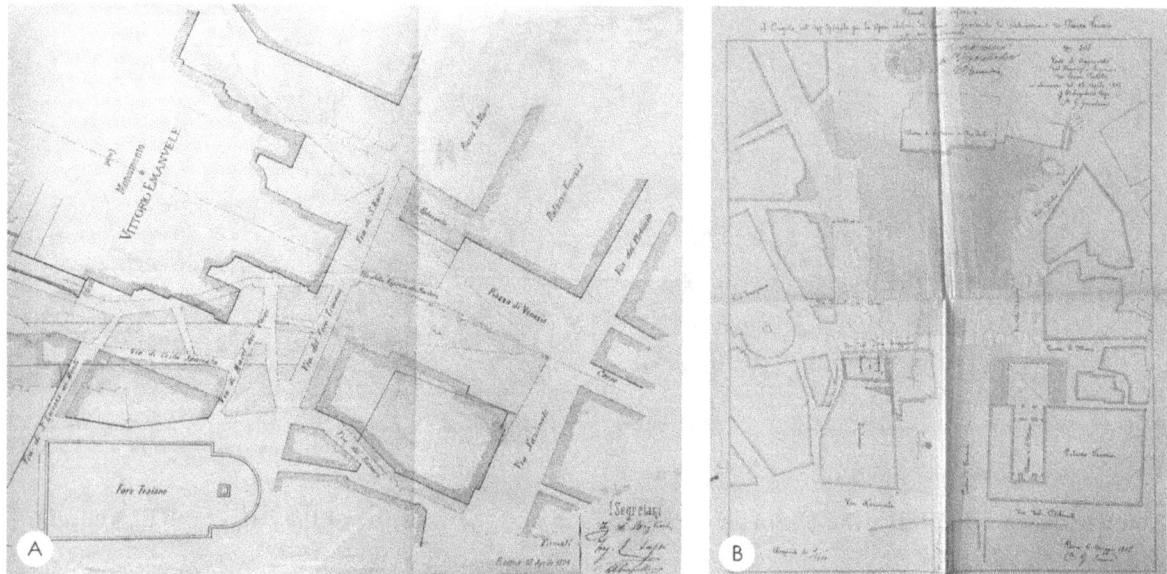

Figure 3: The first prevision for the cutting of a Palazzetto di Venezia's portion, 1893 (A); the Giuseppe Sacconi plan, 1887 (B).

The discovery of tunnels – as well as traces of the ancient Servian city wall – during the demolition, two years after the monument's construction site was launched, required in 1887 a thorough review of the project. The new proportions of the building and the subsequent enlargement of the construction area had significant consequences for the new Piazza Venezia's space, for which a new master-plan was drafted and then approved in 1897. The early prevision of partial – although considerable – expropriation of the Palazzetto di Venezia had ultimately turned into a total demolition and reconstruction [6]. The project had now to put together three different requests coming from the diverse participants in the operations: clearing the perspective of the monument under construction; symbolically preserving the Palazzetto, recognised as significant in the Italian architectural history; not depriving the Austro-Hungarian government of its property.

A close correspondence – held in the Italian central state archive in Rome – between the Ministry of Foreign Affairs, the Ministry of the Interior, the Ministry of Public Works, the Municipality of Rome and the Austro-Hungarian Embassy clarifies the difficulties in drawing up decisions about the Palazzetto's fluctuating fortunes. According to Sacconi's idea, the new building should have been built adjacent to the main palace and, to be exact, in correspondence with the St. Mark Basilica's building, for which the new Palazzetto would have assumed the role of forecourt. But the Austro-Hungarian government didn't accept this proposal because of the right of way which was necessary to allow free access to the church. The negotiations between the two countries, lead unofficially, proceeded slowly while in the meantime the demolition of the existing buildings and the elevation of the new monument were carried on. In 1899 a turning point was reached: the compensation amount awarded for the expropriation of the Palazzetto was fixed and the Austro-Hungarian government made a request for a specific area to build the new Palazzetto. This request was firstly considered too onerous by the Italian government, which took into account the possibility of a coactive expropriation instead, but reasons of international convenience, expressed by the Minister of Justice, suggested continuing friendly discussions.

In 1903, while the discussion on the Palazzetto's fortunes was becoming more and more urgent because of the progress of monument's work, no decision was yet made. The need to reach an agreement was finally clear in 1904 when, in order to complete the laying out of the square, all that remained was to purchase and demolish the building. It then became necessary to resume the suspended negotiations providing the approval of the abovementioned Austro-Hungarian government's provisions. The Italian government thus began the expropriations of residential blocks resting on the new Palazzetto's construction area. In 1906, along with the buildings' demolition, the Rome town council approved all the measures required to redefine the related road system: the Madama Lucrezia alley's suppression, changes in Via degli Astalli's layout and the expansion of the St. Mark square. (Fig. 4)

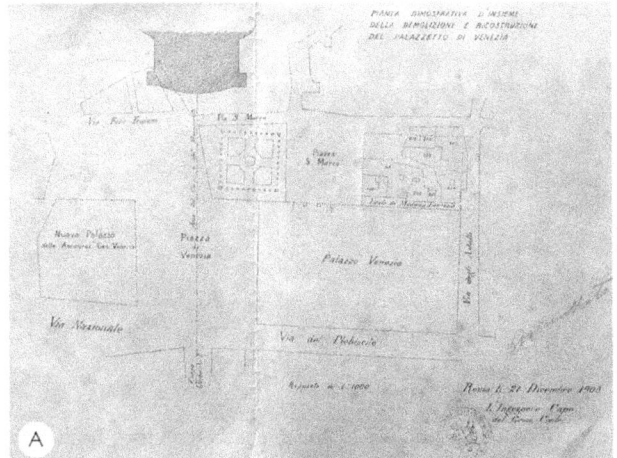 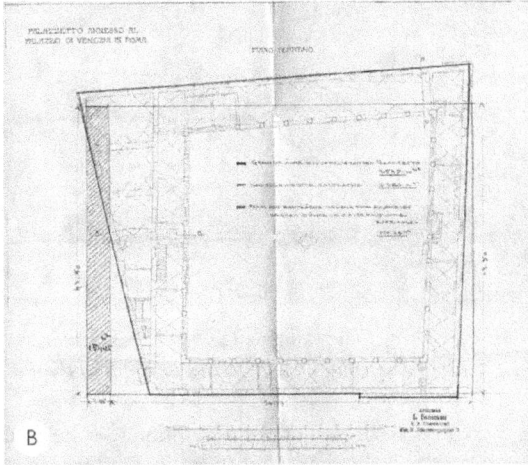

Figure 4: Preliminary plan for the Palazzetto di Venezia, 1903 (A). Survey elaborated before the starting of the demolition intervention (B).

After obtaining the approvals related to both the financial aspects and the assignment of the new construction area, the two governments signedan agreement aimed at formally regulating the building activities in June 1907 [7]. On the one hand, the Austro-Hungarian government committed itself to the demolition of the ancient *Viridarium* and the construction of the new Palazzetto di Venezia of an equal surface area; on the other hand, the Italian government was responsible for the expropriation and demolition of the existing residential blocks. The agreement also defined the methods and the times of the activities to be carried out: the Italian government had firstly to consign the area vacated after the blocks' demolition activities to the Austro-Hungarian government which, from that moment on, would have been committed to consign to the Italian government – within two years – the area vacated after the demolition of the *Viridarium*.

In early 1908 the blocks' demolition work began; despite the duration of the site being estimated at two months, only on October 1 was the area actually consigned to the Austro-Hungarian government.

In 1909 the Austro-Hungarian government appointed the architects Camillo Pistrucci, Jacopo Oblat and Ludwig Baumann to design and direct the work both on the demolition of the *Viridarium* and the construction of the new building. After solving some bureaucratic obstacles, a memorandum between the Municipality of Rome and the Austro-Hungarian government clearly defined the demolition works' procedures for the *Viridarium*. The greatest concerns were related to the possible superimposition of works to be performed on the ancient building and those necessary for the erection of Vittorio Emanuele's monument. Moreover, the celebrative monument had to be completed by the spring of 1911, on the occasion of its inauguration during the Great Universal Exhibition – which also corresponded to the fiftieth anniversary of the Italian Unification. These reasons required great care to avoid any interference between the two building sites.

All cautions were exercised in the demolition from the executive point of view. As regard to the walkway of St. Mark – whose demolition pertained to the monument's works supervisor – the operations firstly provided for leaving the last

The so-called 'Palazzetto' in the Palazzo di Venezia Complex: A small construction history among the huge transformation events of the Rome centre in the early twentieth century

arcade on site as a buttress for the *Viridarium*'s corner: it was finally removed after the fifteenth-century building's walls had been reduced to the height of the arcade itself. (Fig. 5)

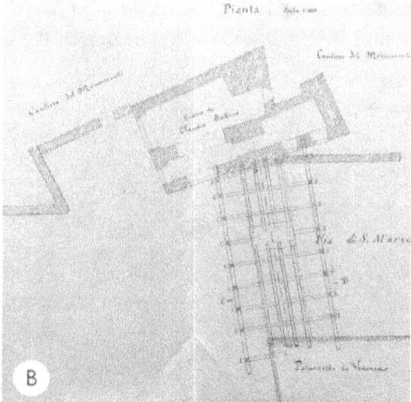

Figure 5: The walkway supported by arches connecting the palace and the Paul III's tower, 1839 (Pietrangeli 1978) (A); demolition project for the arch adjacent to the Palazzetto di Venezia, 1909 (B).

A further issue concerning the demolition was the requirement to produce appropriate documentation on the *Viridarium* because of its imminent disappearance [8]. Along with the request for an accurate survey, the Directorate-General for Antiques and Fine Arts – led at that time by Corrado Ricci – made further demands. Worried about the loss of the ancient building's material witnesses, Ricci proposed to carry out the analysis of the construction technique and of the original coloration in order to increase the knowledge of the history of architecture and to obtain a quite perfect reproduction of the ancient building through the construction of the new one.

In January 1910, when the project for the construction of the new Palazzetto was consigned to the Italian authorities the demolition works had not yet begun.

The demolition building site

Finally, in February 1910, the Austro-Hungarian government concluded an agreement with the Domenico Vitali company for the execution of the two construction sites: the Viridarium's demolition and the construction of the new Palazzetto. The delayed start of the works was probably due to the desire to begin them simultaneously; along with the advantages in terms of construction operations' costs, this choice probably allowed a better and faster management of the demolition materials, which had to be reused from the ancient Viridarium. Some agreements with the Municipality of Rome related to the permission to install a Decauville rail from the actual to the future Palazzetto's area and to provide for specific storage areas seem to confirm this hypothesis. (Fig. 6)

In this regard the possibility of using wide areas to methodically store the stone elements of the Viridarium's cloister assumed a quite significant role. These, according to the 1907 convention, had to be reused for the new Palazzetto in order to build a strong relation between past and present.

Figure 6: Palazzetto di Venezia demolition, 1910 (M.R. Coppola 2012). The Vittoriano monument construction site in progress (A) and the Biscia's tower covered by scaffolding (B).

Figure 7: Corrado Ricci's proposals to avoid the complete demolition of the XV century building.

Many disputes arose when the demolition work made visible the fifteenth-century cloister from Piazza Venezia. The debate in the press involved public opinion and the proposal put forward in August 1910 by Corrado Ricci was also made known via an essay by Gustavo Giovannoni, which was promptly published [9]. The reasons asserted by Corrado Ricci were based on a more conservative approach but also expressed a very precise observation on the stability of the Biscia's tower, to which the Viridarium was backed against. (Fig. 7a)

The opinions favourable to Corrado Ricci's proposal – to which the High Council of Fine Arts first and foremost belonged – was opposed by many other influential players so that, despite the increasing protests, the Italian government approved the continuation of the demolition works.

However, the issue on the stability of the Biscia's tower was still unsolved; so, it was decided to carry on some structural works before the removal of the *Viridarium*'s walls closer to the tower; in fact these last, conveniently reinforced, would have shored the high building during the strengthening intervention.

The so-called 'Palazzetto' in the Palazzo di Venezia Complex: A small construction history among the huge transformation events of the Rome centre in the early twentieth century

This represented the last chance for Corrado Ricci to save from the destruction at least a small part of the ancient building. In November 1910, Ricci proposed maintaining the double order of arches still in place and to proceed with their reorganization in the form of a loggia; this proposal would have avoided leaving visible the tower's rough basement on the other side, the S. Mark's façade. (Fig. 7b) Ricci's proposal also considered the executive issues related to the different configurations of the two buildings (the old one and the new one); in fact, in order to cover the same area and increase the covered spaces, the project of the new building included the reduction of the cloister. The proposal to leave in their original place the four ancient arches to form a loggia would have, among other things, returned a public function to the redundant stone elements [10].

In December 1910, the area was level to the surrounding roads but the fragments of the two cloister's arms closer to the Biscia's tower were still on site and under reinforcement. The final date for their complete demolition and the final liberation of the area was set for 15th February 1911. Pressures, indecisiveness and discordant viewpoints meant that on 10th February no decision had been taken concerning these last arcades. The same situation of uncertainty continued until the end of May but, in the meantime, the Austro-Hungarian government made it clear that it would not incur any additional costs for the recovery of the loggia. On the other side the Italian government had to come to terms with the time restrictions related to the inauguration of the monument to Vittorio Emanuele, scheduled for 4th June 1911.

The Palazzetto reconstruction site: where it wasn't, how it wasn't.

Often reduced in the literature to a simple relocation work, the project for the new Palazzetto was a far more complex process because of the involved symbolic connotations, material constraints and functional expectations. Spurning an impractical faithful reproduction of the ancient building, the Italian government's requirement for the new project was essentially that "… on the external facades and in the inner cloister the ancient building's style and the decorative apparatus' main features have to be respected …" [11].

The willingness of referring to the Viridarium's architectural language – firstly obtained through the reuse of the cloister's original elements – was accompanied by two further issues which heavily influenced the project definition: the connection with the southern wing of the main palace, which the Palazzetto had to join, and the urgent demand, expressed by the Austro-Hungarian government, to realize a real palace able to house the embassy's offices, instead of a simple four-sided cloister-enclosed garden.

Related to the latter question was the decision to decrease the number of the arcades – and so the overall size of the garden so as to place in the new building three wings of appropriate depth, the total area being equal. On the other hand, the new mutual relationship between the Palazzo di Venezia and the new Palazzetto introduced a twofold difficulty in the management of the different, and not modifiable, floor levels: those concerning the existing building and those dependent on the measures of the cloister's stone elements.

As confirmed by the consulted archive documents, the architects in charge of the project started elaborating it as early as 1908 and, long before the beginning of the Viridarium's demolition works, the new Palazzetto project was defined in detail.

The architect Camillo Pistrucci was entrusted with the management of the demolition works and the simultaneous organisation of the reconstruction operations.

On the day of the inauguration of the Vittoriano, the building was elevated with respect to the external roads by only one level, corresponding to the height of the internal courtyard in which the portico was to be established. (Fig. 8)

Figure 8: The opening day of the Vittoriano, June 4th 1911. The torre della biscia is still covered by the scaffolding (A), while the palazzetto reconstruction is ongoing (B).

Despite the lack of documentary sources on the peculiarities of the building site, we can here illustrate – not pretending to be conclusive – some information both from the memoirs of Camillo Pistrucci and the results of field surveys in which the authors took part in 2019. (Fig. 9)

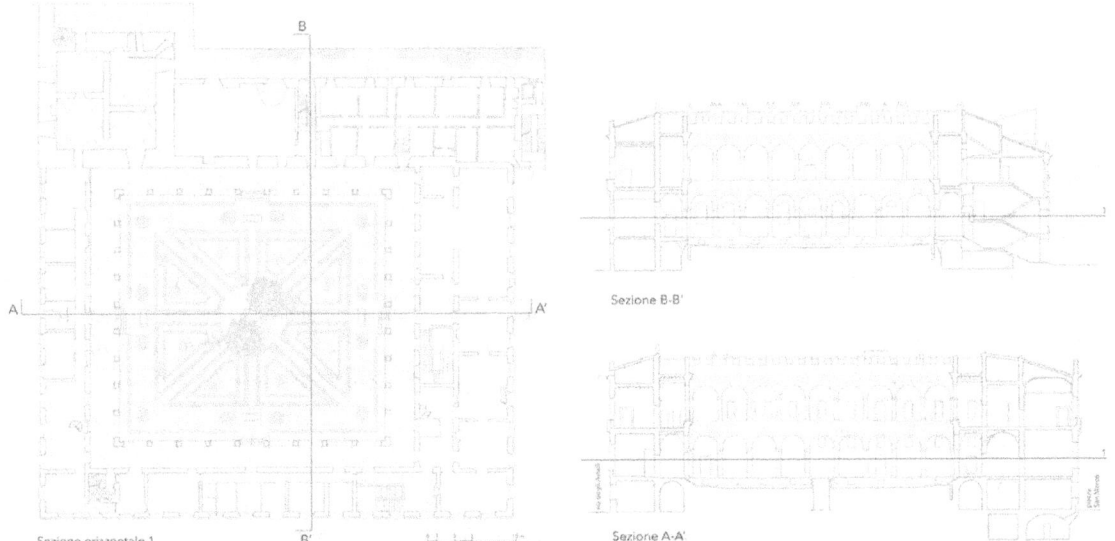

Fig. 9. Survey of the nowadays Palazzetto di Venezia.

The new Palazzetto is characterised by a clear masonry conception and the construction site used knowledge and methods belonging to the great masonry tradition; despite this, a clear modern execution emerges from the use of industrial materials – bricks and metal beams – which make up the structure, except, of course, for the arcades of the internal courtyard coming from the ancient Viridarium. The coexistence of both industrial material – cheaper and easier to assemble – and ancient stone elements introduced the necessity to conform the final aspect of the building to uniform architectural facies. The intended traditional effect is achieved through the use of decorative apparatuses which

The so-called 'Palazzetto' in the Palazzo di Venezia Complex: A small construction history among the huge transformation events of the Rome centre in the early twentieth century

dissimulate the horizontal structures in the most representative rooms while the metal roof and jack-arch floors are left visible in the utilities. (Fig. 10)

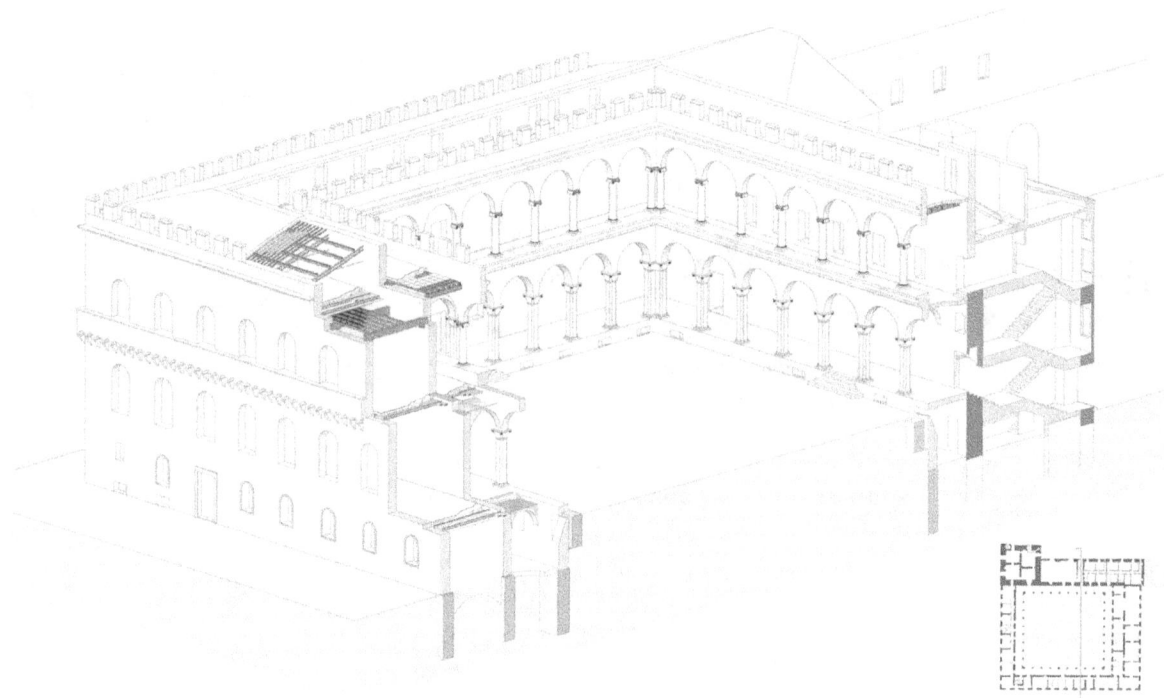

Figure 10: The new palazzetto and its relationship with the existing wing of palazzo di Venezia: a staircase manages the different floor levels' heights.

Some constructional features have been recognised from the analysis of the walls' arrangements and their connection's characteristics. The foundation plan is composed using extensive brick-vaulted substructures which locally define underground spaces accessible from the ground floor through specific stairs, recognisable from the outside by the presence of windows. The irregularity of the underground level's volume thus determined was probably due to the need to retain the possibility of creating as much space as possible and the obligation to preserve the archaeological findings of that area. The analysis of the masonry works and the connection of orthogonal walls showed a deep care in the realisation of the external corners and a less refined solution for the connection of the internal walls to the perimeter walls: the latter were the first to be built and had to be toothed to the former. This constructional sequence is probably due to the desire to first enclose the building area and then proceed to construct inside, minimizing the occupation of public property [12]. Thanks to a detailed study of the cloister's stone elements, it was possible to infer the technique used for their handling from the storage area to the subsequent installation at the works site. The use of specific construction machines is evidenced by the presence on each stone block of cavities, used to move the elements and doweled once assembly was complete. Numerous plaster repairs at the elements' corners and joints replace the absence of stone caused by damage when moving from the demolition site to the construction site [13].

Conclusion

Conceived within the background of Rome's designation as capital of Italy in 1871 and in the light of the consequent opposite requirements of innovation and conservation, the demolition of the fifteenth-century building and the reconstruction of a new Palazzetto only to a small distance from the previous one represents a small piece in the framework of the huge demolition operation conducted to make way for the monument devoted to Vittorio Emanuele II.

Of the large part of the building fabric demolished on that occasion, only a few buildings were rebuilt, including the Palazzetto di Venezia, whose reconstruction took place even before the great monument was finished. Reasons of international opportunity were crucial in this choice, which significantly complicated the progress of the work on the new Piazza Venezia.

This paper, through the examination of the published bibliography and the re-reading of archival documents – already known but studied until now only from the perspective of the great monument – has attempted to outline the specific framework of the vicissitudes of the *Viridarium* of the Pope Paolo II, of the decisions taken regarding its fate and of the construction sites that have decreed its position and current appearance.

References

This contribution comes from the study carried out on Palazzo Venezia in 2019 by the working group constituted by, in addition to the authors, arch. C. Circo, G. Cocuzza Avellino, prof. arch. C. Tocci, prof. eng. N. Impollonia. The authors thank arch. Sonia Martone, former director of the Museum of Palazzo Venezia in Rome.

[1] A. M. Affanni, 'Demolizione e ricostruzione della chiesa di S. Rita da Cascia' in L. Cardilli (Ed.) *Gli anni del Governatorato (1926-1944): Interventi urbanistici, scoperte archeologiche, arredo urbano, restauri*, Roma: Edizioni Kappa, 1995. pp. 131-137.
[2] M. R. Coppola, *La fabbrica del Vittoriano: Scavi e scoperte in Campidoglio (1855-1934)*, Roma: Istituto Poligrafico dello Stato, 2012; P. Acciaresi, *Giuseppe Sacconi e la sua opera massima: Cronaca dei lavori del monumento nazionale a Vittorio Emanuele II*, Roma, 1925.
[3] C. L. Frommel, 'Chi era l'architetto di Palazzo Venezia?' in S. Macchioni, B. Tavassi (Eds.), *Studi in onore di Giulio Carlo Argan*, Vol.3, Roma: Bonsignori, 1984; M. G. Barberini, M. De Angelis D'Ossat, A. Schiavon, *La storia del Palazzo di Venezia: Dalle collezioni Barbo e Grimani a sede dell'ambasciata veneta e austriaca*, Roma: Gangemi, 2011; A. Modigliani, *Disegni sulla città nel primo Rinascimento romano: Paolo II*, Roma, 2011.
[4] G. Mosca, 'Paolo II e il Viridarium del palazzo di San Marco a Roma: Nuove acquisizioni', *RR Roma nel rinascimento 2015*, Roma, 2016, ISSN 2036-2463. pp.379-400; M. Gargano, 'Paolo II e il palazzo di Venezia: considerazioni intorno all'architettura del Quattrocento a Roma', *RR Roma nel Rinascimento 2011*, Roma, 2011, ISSN 2036-2463, pp.279-302.
[5] I. Insolera, *Roma moderna: Un secolo di storia urbanistica 1870-1970*, Torino: Einaudi, 1993 (I ed. 1962); A. M. Racheli, *Sintesi delle vicende urbanistiche di Roma dal 1870 al 1911*, Roma, 1979; A. Ravaglioli, *Appunti per una cronologia di Roma Capitale 1870-1970*, Roma: Edizione del Banco di Roma, 1973; G. Miano, 'Roma: i piani urbanistici' in A. Restucci (Ed.), *Storia dell'architettura italiana: L'Ottocento*, Milano: Electa, 2005. pp. 272-295; M. Brancia di Apricena, 'Il quartiere di San Marco a Roma sulla base della documentazione otto-novecentesca: un'ipotesi ricostruttiva', *Bollettino d'Arte del Ministero per i beni e le attività culturali*, Anno 87, serie 6, fasc. 120, aprile-giugno 2002, pp. 21-48.
[6] Archivio Centrale dello Stato, Roma, Ministero dei Lavori Pubblici, Direzione Generale dell'Edilizia, Divisione V, Sistemazioni urbanistiche diverse, 1871-1927, b. 75.
[7] A. M. Racheli, 'Le sistemazioni urbanistiche di Roma per l'esposizione Internazionale del 1911' in G. Piantoni (Ed.), *Roma 1911*, Roma: De Luca editore, 1980. pp. 229-264.

The so-called 'Palazzetto' in the Palazzo di Venezia Complex: A small construction history among the huge transformation events of the Rome centre in the early twentieth century

[8] P. Dengel, M. Dvorak, H. Egger, *Der Palazzo di Venezia in Rom*, Vienna, 1909.

[9] C. Ricci, 'Pel Palazzetto di Palazzo Venezia', *Bollettino d'Arte*, VII, 1910, pp. 269-273; G. Giovannoni, *Relazione sulla proposta Ricci relativa al Palazzetto di Venezia in Roma*, Roma 1910.

[10] Archivio Centrale dello Stato, Roma, Ministero dei Lavori Pubblici, Direzione Generale dell'Edilizia, Divisione V, Sistemazioni urbanistiche diverse, 1871-1927, b. 74.

[11] C. Pistrucci, 'Memorie dell'architetto Camillo Pistrucci (1910-1914)' in M. G. Barberini (Ed.), *Tracce di pietra*, Roma 2008. pp. 373-388.

[12] Polo Museale del Lazio - Ministero per i beni e le attività culturali e per il turismo, '*REL.04 Report indagini specialistiche*', '*Elaborati grafici: Rilievo critico*' in *Studio del comportamento strutturale e analisi dello stato di conservazione, del degrado e dei dissesti di Palazzo Venezia e proposta di miglioramento anche in occasione di eventi sismici*, Progetto di rifunzionalizzazione del Palazzo, museo e biblioteca, programma triennale 2016-2018.

[13] R. Finocchiaro, *"Il Palazzetto di Palazzo Venezia. Studio delle vicende costruttive, analisi e nuovo allestimento dei reperti lapidei dell'ex Viridarium"* (diploma thesis, Scuola di specializzazione in beni architettonici e del paesaggio, Università La Sapienza Roma, 2021).

Contextualisation of the Timber Trade between the Sixteenth and Nineteenth Centuries in the Basilica of St Anthony, Padua

Martina Diaz

Institute of Construction History and Preservation (IDB), ETH Zurich, Switzerland

Introduction

Traces of timber trades such as scribed marks, pegs and notches are visible in the medieval and eighteenth-century domed roofs of the Basilica of St Anthony in Padua. The original Basilica worksite began in the 1230s and continued until the following century with the roofing system completion. The ongoing investigations are part of a research project developed by the Institute of Construction History and Preservation (ETH Zurich), under the direction of Prof. Stefan M. Holzer, in collaboration with the Delegazione Pontificia per la Basilica di Sant'Antonio in Padova and funded by the Swiss National Science Foundation (SNSF). In the absence of medieval archives, this project aims at identifying the parts of the original building and later transformations [1].

A doctoral research project addresses the study of the Basilica wooden roofs to trace the construction development. Historical sources provide little information on the six medieval timber superstructures. The first depictions of the domed roofing system are two bas-reliefs representing the Basilica in the first half of the fourteenth century and a fresco from 1382 by Giusto de Menabuoi inside the building. Moreover, the Visio Egidii written by Giovanni da Nono between 1263 and 1346 attests to seven domes. In the eighteenth century, some archives document the construction of the last dome above the Relics Chapel shortly after 1740 [2]. The main event reported in the historiography of the domes is limited to a disastrous fire that destroyed four domes in 1749: the cone of the Angel (d04), the dome of St James (d05), the presbytery dome (d06) and the choir dome (d07). According to eighteenth-century sources, the flames reached St Anthony's dome (d03) – on the north aisle of the transept – but quickly extinguished. As the burnt roofs were promptly rebuilt in the following years, three domes would have been preserved from complete reconstruction: the facade dome (d01), the intermediate dome on the nave (d02) and the dome of St Anthony (d03) [3]. The first dendrochronological analyses carried out in these three domes confirmed the preservation of part of the medieval structures, magnifying their importance worldwide.

Each dome is composed of an independent timber frame above the masonry shell supporting the outer cover. Except for the cone on the crossing, the bearing system consists of four main struts placed at right angles and connected to a central king-post. A system of lateral struts supports the horizontal collar-beams, while four concentric rings carry the ribs, on which lean the cover composed of wooden boards and lead plates (Fig. 1).

There are no carpenter marks related to the construction sequence of the frames. The presence of overlapped and nailed joints would suggest their onsite shaping on top of the building. However, numerous trademarks have been recorded in the domes rebuilt after the fire in 1749 and on replaced elements in the three intact domes.

Contextualisation of the Timber Trade between the Sixteenth and Nineteenth Centuries in the Basilica of St Anthony, Padua

Fig. 1 St Anthony Basilica: southern longitudinal section and eastern cross section (drawing L. Vandenabeele, author).

Alongside surveying and dating the timber structures, the present research aims at answering questions about the origin and trade of the timber supplied over the centuries to the Basilica of St Anthony. The first section of this paper introduces the findings obtained by laboratory analyses, archival research, onsite observations, and the importance of combining these results. The second section focuses on historical timber supply from the forests in the south-eastern Alps, down the rivers, towards the most prominent marketplaces. Based on a comprehensive literature analysis on historical floating routes in the Dolomites, alpine historical wood resources, and historical timber supply in Veneto, the regional trade's organisation is depicted. Furthermore, archival discoveries on Paduan timber merchants are contextualised in the regional trading routes. The third section brings into focus the use of trademarks. After describing historical marks in Veneto and the Italian Alpine regions, shipping marks found in the Basilica domes are interpreted.

Findings from laboratory analyses, archival sources and onsite observations

Xylotomous analyses have ascertained that all domes' superstructures were built in larch (*Larix decidua Mill.*). Moreover, dendrochronological dating has revealed numerous medieval elements in the three preserved domes, confirming that their current configuration largely corresponds to the original one [4]. From these results, it is likely that the reconstructions of the burnt domes followed the configuration of the original ones, aside from some simplifications. Moreover, the sample analyses have identified timbers presumably sourced from different forests, even within the same dome [5]. In general, the different ages of the trees at the felling date and the different growth trends of the examined samples show that they came from areas with different climatic factors and altitudes. Although it has not yet been possible to identify an unequivocal dendro-provenance of the trees, the results have contributed to recognising different origin areas. Comparative mean curves used as references have included dendro-chronologies from north-eastern Italy, Austrian Öetztal, Trentino South-Tyrol, and Italian-Slovenian regions. In this regard, the matches identified with the reference curves of other buildings are significant to identify medieval elements, particularly from the comparison with artefacts located in Verona, Venice, and the Belluno area. These results would suggest the exploitation of fluvial networks along the Brenta and Piave rivers, which have been historical transport routes for the forest resources located in the eastern Alpine regions. Indeed, rafting and free-floating timbers have been documented in these regions since Roman times for transporting wood to marketplaces such as Verona, Vicenza, Padua and Venice.

The study of archival documents of the church dating from the fifteenth century has provided rich documentation of the building between the medieval worksite and the reconstructions of the timber frames in the mid-eighteenth century. To map the timber consignments' provenance, research on purchase and administrative acts registered by the Veneranda Arca is ongoing [6]. Following the documented interventions' timeline, restorations took part in three pivotal stages during the sixteenth, eighteenth and nineteenth centuries [7]. At the present time, fifteenth-century records have shed some light on merchants' names from Padua active in the domes' reparations. Lastly, knowledge of their trade spheres depicted in previous studies has helped identify the supplying forests and trade routes.

As mentioned above, no trademarks have been found on the medieval elements dated by dendrochronological analyses. Among the dated signs, some correspond to the eighteenth-century post-fire reconstruction while others to nineteenth-century repairs. The similarity of marks recorded in different domes enables the linking of interventions that coincided. Their presence is thus also a preliminary criterion to identify replacements in the preserved frames. (Fig. 2)

Fig. 2 Cuneiform trademark in the eighteenth-century Angel cone (picture: author).

Historical wooden supply from the south-eastern Alps to Padua

Since Roman times if not earlier, timber trading in the subalpine area developed into local, regional, and interregional scales [8]. The forest resources included mainly spruce, beech-wood and larch. Between the early Middle Ages and the twentieth century, the main trading routes exploited the Brenta and Piave rivers and their tributaries towards Vicenza, Padua and Venice [9]. From the fourteenth century until modern times, the eastern pre-alpine and alpine sectors were divided into the three central powers of the Archduchy of the Habsburgs in the Tyrol County, the ecclesiastical principality of Trentino, and the Republic of Venice. Mountain natives did not manage the timber commerce in the

Contextualisation of the Timber Trade between the Sixteenth and Nineteenth Centuries in the Basilica of St Anthony, Padua

woodlands; this part was instead in merchants' hands from the Treviso area, the Duchy and Venice. Depending on territorial landowners, different administrative regulations were controlling the cuts.

In the fourteenth century, the mountain communities were structured in basic units called *Regole*, which operated until the end of Venice's authority in 1797. Each *Regola* had its own statute and ownership mark to brand timber. Over time, the communities started renting forest portions in exchange for annual fees to individuals or companies. From the fifteenth century onwards, the mountain regions of Cadore, Agordino, Ampezzo, Cansiglio, Primiero, Montello, Belluno, Feltre, Altipiano di Asiago, Patria del Friuli, and Istria were progressively included in the reach of Venetian brokers [10]. Due to the unruly forest exploitation and the city's essential needs, Venice established the Forest Rangers Office, called the *Provveditori sopra legni e boschi*, in 1464, followed by a series of stricter regulations for exportations that increased the control on private woodlands under Venetian ruling [11].

As from the sixteenth century, in the Archduchy of the Habsburgs, tree felling was subject to authorisation by the Chamber of Innsbruck, which managed the cutting permits and intermediary agents played representative roles for the merchants. These agents guaranteed transactions between the Germanic and regional markets by accessing the nearby customs offices and obtaining logging provisions, which were then resold in Italian cities, first and foremost Venice [12].

Forest exploitation depended on territorial power as well. In the woodlands under the Serenissima, the *consuetude* was to select and tag the mature trunks to provide high-quality timber required by the Arsenale and other institutional building-sides [13]. Officers by the Arsenal were sent to the forest to operate the most accurate selection. The forests authorities marked the selected logs with the official stamp. However, in the woodlands of Tyrol County, whole portions of forests could be harvested. The elements to be felled met standard sizes starting from 4.5 m height with an upper diameter of a Venetian foot corresponding to 34.77 cm, equal to 12 Veneto ounces [14]. This minor standard section was called *taja* or *taglia* in the Venetian dialect. The next marketable section was a 43.5 cm upper diameter, corresponding to 15 ounces. Due to the intensive exploitation of resources, from the seventeenth century onwards, the only forests still able to provide large quantities of timber were located in Cadore, Carnia and the Asiago plateau.

Between felling and downstream routes, the logs were usually debarked and hewn in sizes to facilitate transportation. Conveyance to waterways could rely on horses or wooden snow slides (*risine*). Floating started in spring. Along rivers and canals, infrastructures enabled sorting and streaming. In large rivers, barriers with diversions to stack logs consisted of a system of vertically sliding wooden gates and grates (*cidolo*). Another type of artificial floodgate allowed the damming of logs and the continuous flow of water along mountain streams (*stue*). Along the shores of larger rivers, the logs were assembled into rafts or directly sawn. The latter group was stacked, measured, and graded next to the mills, mainly located between Fonzaso and Valstagna along the Brenta, and between Perarolo and Longarone along the Piave [15]. Rafts assembly usually comprehend joined standard beams so that the smallest raft unit (*copola*) had a 4,2 m length, and a 5 m span reached flanking 18/20 elements. Longer logs could set on multiple-unit platforms built connecting head and tail basic rafts, reaching a maximal length of 30 meters (the so-called *rasi*) [16].

Direct wood trade routes towards Padua historically developed from the forests in Primiero, Tesino and Valsugana along the Brenta river that was connected to the city since the twelfth century by the Piovego canal [17]. Shipments of timber arrived in Fonzaso, where they were sorted along the riverbanks in the warehouses of the various merchants [18]. An alternative route involved channels along the Adige River, then into the Vanoi alpine stream and in the Cismon, to join finally the Brenta from the upstream station in Bassano. In the Brenta basin, the logs were conveyed by both untied floating and rafting, while only rafting is documented along the Cismon. Finally, an infrastructure of canals around Padua ensured the arrival of construction materials in the city centre via the Bacchiglione and the Piovego since the Middle Ages. (Fig. 3)

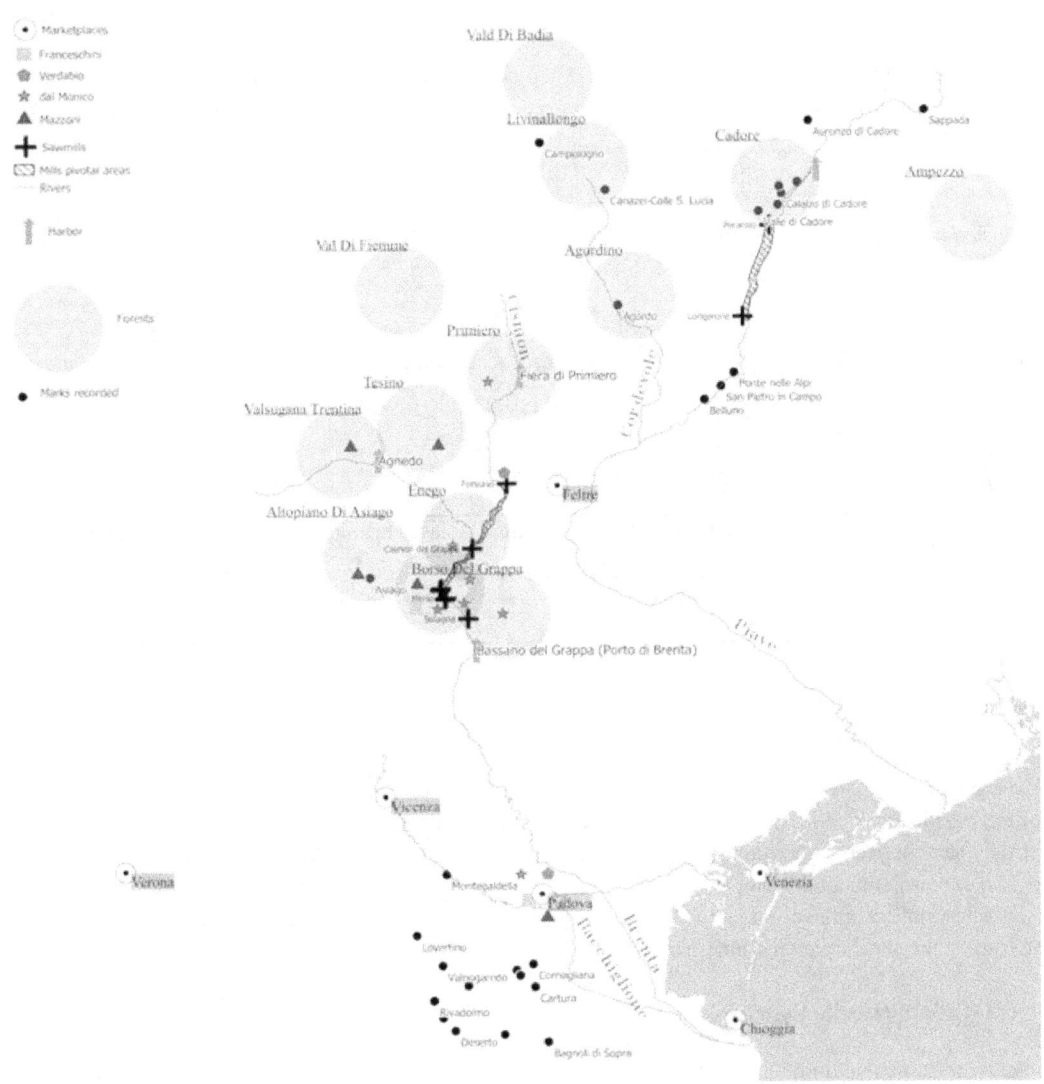

Fig. 3 Map with historical trade routes along the Brenta and Piave rivers, with historical forests, mills and Paduan merchants business areas (picture: author).

Timber suppliers in the Basilica at the end of the sixteenth century

Like Venetian merchants' business boost alongside the Piave River, Paduan brokers settled in the Brenta Valley, where they owned sawmills providing timber to the city. Information can be found in payment records in the fourteenth series, as well as in the acts registered in the second series of the Historical Archive of the Veneranda Arca di Sant'Antonio [19]. According to the so-far examined logbooks, different merchant's families from Padua played the role of timber suppliers for the roofs of the St Anthony Basilica at the end of the sixteenth century: Jacomo and Antonio dal Monico in 1562 and

1563, Lorenzo Franceschini in 1574 and 1582, Marco Mazzoni in 1584 and 1592, Nicolò and Bernardin Verdabio in 1591. Occhi has documented the business range of these traders' families through in-depth research in the historical archives in Bassano del Grappa, Vicenza, Venezia, and in the *Tiroler Landesarchiv Innsbruck* [20].

The families hold felling permits in Asiago, Enego, Borso del Grappa, Primiero, Valdibrenta, Tesino and in the Vanoi area [21]. Manufacturing processes took place in Fonzaso, Carpané, Cismon, Oliero, Merlo, and Valstagna (Table 1).

Table 1. Listed timber merchants and business aerials. (source: K. Occhi 2004).

Timber trader Families	Forest for tree felling	Sawmills
Dal Monico	Enego, Borso del Grappa, Primiero, Valdibrenta, Vanoi	Carpané, Cismon, Oliero
Franceschini	Valstagna	Carpané
Mazzoni	Valstagna, Tesino, Cismon, Asiago, Primiero, Valsugana, Val di Non	Fonzaso Oliero, Valstagna
Verdabio		Fonzaso

Bringing together the information, reveals that by the end of the sixteenth century the timber supply for repairs to the roofs of the Basilica arrived in the city down the Brenta. The merchants managed the trades differently, depending on whether they had cut licenses or purchased the consignments once brought downstream by previous actors. Eventually, they could also recruit mountain companies that operated in the cutting phase and provide successful timber downstream landing. Further similar archival research should also provide the list of actors active in the eighteenth and nineteenth centuries during the superstructures' later restorations.

Historical trademarks in Veneto

Shipping marks on floated timber has very ancient roots in the eastern subalpine region – they have been traced back to Roman times – until their decline in the twentieth century due to railways' development. Unfortunately, there is a lack of detailed literature on the topic in the Italian context [22]. The current knowledge comes from a handful of onsite investigations and sporadically published lists of ownership marks found in local archives.

During the trade process, logs could be marked at two moments. Firstly, in the mountains, the ownership marks were carved after selecting the trunks, during the distribution by the public officers to the private individuals or companies. An axe was used to remove the part of bark on which the mark was to be impressed with a small axe (*manarin*) or a traditional type of gouge (*zapín*), later replaced by a sharpened and curved iron tool (*fer de segnà*) (Fig. 4). Between the nineteenth- and the last century, forestry hammers with stamped owner's initials replaced the other tools [23]. Later, in the valley, in designated places near the mills (*stazi da segno*), ownership marks for floated timber were affixed after sorting and before floating [24].

Marks could represent merchants' identity, mills' addresses, or the communities that managed the forests exploitation [25]. In the first case, the marks expressed the merchant families' or trading enterprises' ownership. Most of those with ancient origin were cuneiform symbols that enabled the timber sorting at sawmills and docking channels even by illiterate operators. On the other hand, communities' acronyms consisted of abbreviations of two or more alphabetical and or numerical characters. Sometimes rafted logs may include both signs by the felling wholesaler and the trader. In other cases, the presence of just one mark could refer to a trader involved in the whole process, from the tree felling until the delivery on the marketplace. In similar cases, the merchant recruited lumberjacks companies and raftsmen who provided the material and operated the transport to the mills.

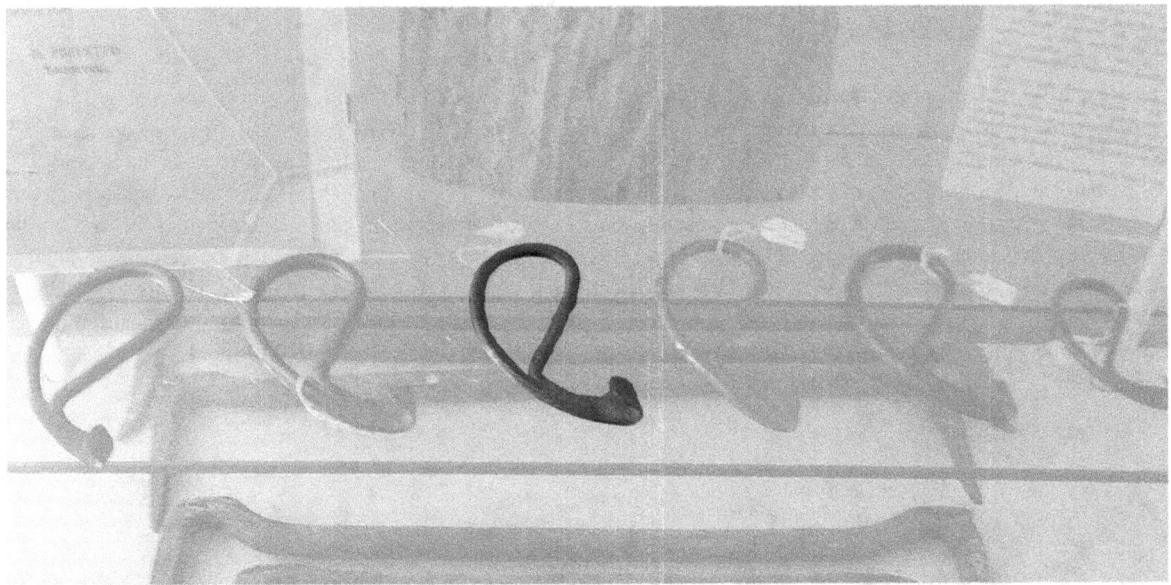

Fig. 4 Traditional tool to imprint marks on timber in the Rafting Museum in Codissago (picture: author).

Communities' legislations required the registration of all active marks in official lists, some of which preserved in local archives. The oldest list of signatures found in the Dolomites and the Basso Veneto date back to the fifteenth century. In other instances, ownership marks were used as signatures in sales contracts [26]. They were usually based on an original family's symbol further developed through signs and letters annexed over lineages. The ownership mark was hereditary from the head of the family to the eldest son, while the younger brothers inherited a variant as documented in other European cultures as well [27]. Hence, the initial signs evolved through increasing complexity over generations. Moreover, a gradual replacement of signs by alphabetical characters took place, which did not always correspond to the initials of the owner's name [28]. The latter greater spread of alphabetical characters among brands and communities acronyms could find reason in the more effortless reading required in printed documents.

Among the most important contributions in the Veneto area, Marcuzzi collected the marks already catalogued by previous studies and compared them with new findings. The study includes a comparison between marks collected between the Basso Veneto and Cadore and previous findings from Veneto, the Italian Alps, Switzerland and Western Germany [29]. From a map of these trading centres, it is possible to recognise Padua's central position between two clusters of marks he examined in Basso Veneto and Cadore. However, the resembling types of marks and the evolutions in isolated areas implied reiterations of the same tag in different contexts and times. For this reason, their interpretation must take into account other factors such as historical periods and trade routes.

Eighteenth and nineteenth-century trademarks in the reparations of the domes

Pegs, notches, and trademarks on timber elements in St Anthony basilica's superstructures bear witness to their rafting transportation. Marks can vary in characters, position and size. Although some persistent difficulties in tracing them back to the ownerships, few contribute to identifying timber provenance and historical interventions in the eighteenth and nineteenth centuries.

In the medieval domes of St. Anthony and the intermediate one above the nave, different marks remain challenging to interpret. Some of these consist of vertical, oblique and intersecting straight lines. In St Anthony's dome, a wedge-shaped mark appears in the reparations at the base of an original strut dated to the 1280s and on the horizontal beam above. (Fig. 5a)

Different types of marks have been detected in the cone of the Angel and in the other domes rebuilt after 1749. In particular, the B, X, L acronym recurs in struts and collar-beams located in the Angel cone, in St Jacob dome, in the presbytery one and in that on the choir. It has been also found in wooden elements at the base of struts in the St Anthony dome, helping identify their replacements (Figs 5b, 5c). In some cases, an additional cuneiform symbol emerges on the same beam. Although it is not a criterion for absolute dating of the elements, this alpha-numeric mark helps identify possible elements later than the medieval building site. Likely, they refer to operators involved in the reconstruction after 1749. Moreover, the previous research by Marcuzzi detected the same inscription as an ownership mark in buildings around Basso Veneto [30]. Furthermore, its spot sometimes on sawn sides of the beams, and the juxtaposition of the cuneiform mark mentioned above would refer to a merchant who acquired the timber consignment only after the hewing, thus already in the valley.

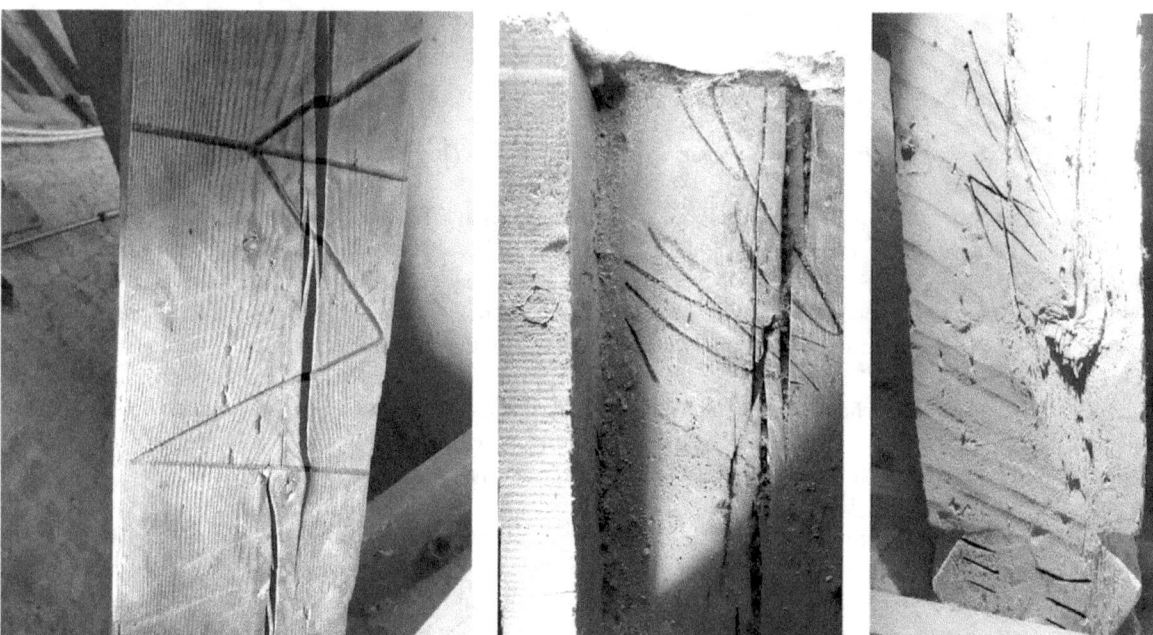

Figs 5a, 5b, 5c. Cuneiform mark on reparations in the medieval dome of St Anthony. BXL acronym in a base of St Anthony dome and in a strut in the choir dome (pictures: author).

Fig. 6 Cuneiform symbol in a rib of the Angel cone (picture: author).

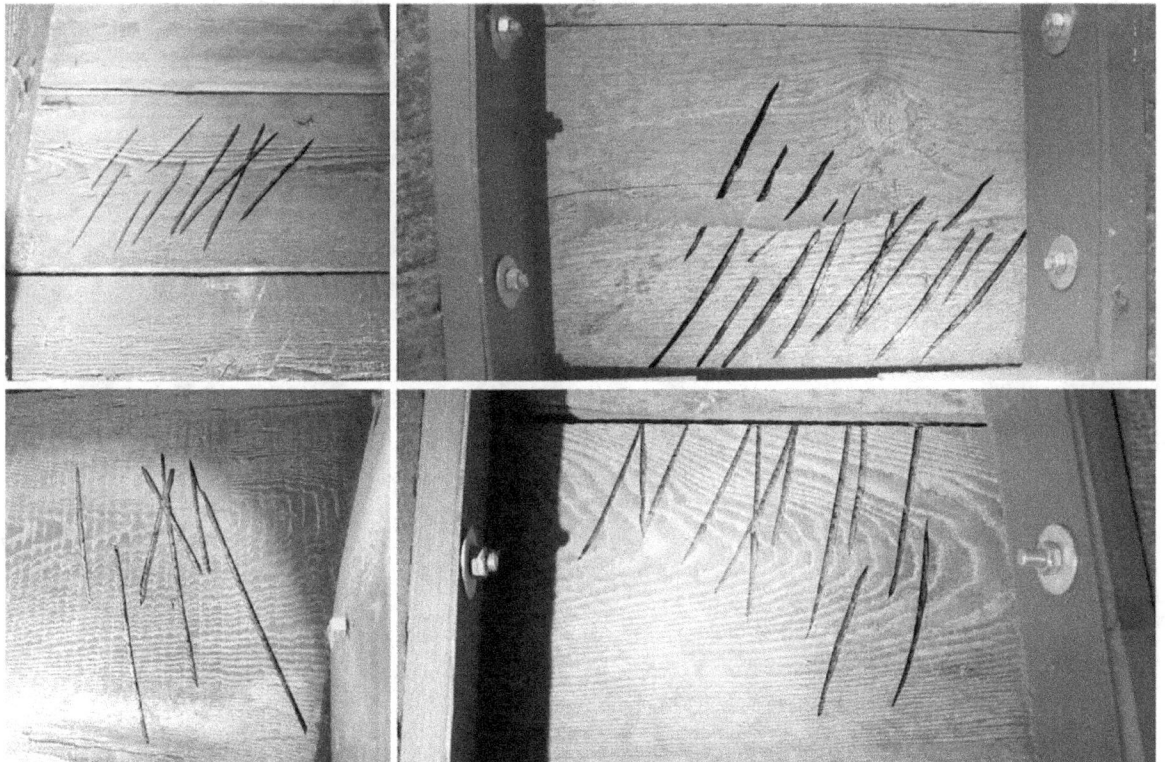

Fig. 7 Trademarks on nineteenth-century cover boards in the intermediate dome - upper row, in the St Anthony domes - lower row, left, and in the façade's dome - lower row, right (pictures: author).

Contextualisation of the Timber Trade between the Sixteenth and Nineteenth Centuries in the Basilica of St Anthony, Padua

As previously mentioned, it is not possible to codify unequivocally individual symbols because occurring in archival lists from different geographical contexts and historical periods. For instance, the above mentioned cuneiform mark could represent the ownership of Adriano da Piaza registered in Lorenzago di Cadore in 1699, as well as the one of Giuseppe Sebastiano Deppi registered in Domegge in 1777 [31] (Fig. 6). In this case, similar analogies leave open questions on the provenance from Cadore timberlands by the Piave.

From the accounting records of the nineteenth century, under the Austrian authority, documents report on partial replacements of the cover boards, king posts, rings and ribs in the three medieval domes, in the dome of St Jacob and the one above the presbytery. On the replaced boards, one can see acronyms that consist of three or more alphabetical, numerical and/or cuneiform characters. These include reiterations of the letters M, S, X and W, flanked by other characters akin to numbers. Sometimes the same mark occurs in several domes or on different elements of a single one. (Fig. 7)

Moreover, in replaced plates in the façade's dome, there are two inscriptions of analogy with those known from the northern European trades. (Fig. 8) Such diversity from the other local marks could be contextualised during the Habsburg domination for imported timber of limited sizes, such as the planking. However, more in-depth discussions on this subject are to be found elsewhere. Eventually, there is a three-symbol mark among the Relics dome's cover plates similar to tags used in the late 19th century by floating timber companies along the Piave [32]. (Fig. 9)

As it turned out, the post-eighteenth-century fire reconstructions, and the interventions in the late nineteenth century, could have involved timber supply down the Piave, likely from Cadore forests. A similar scenario would be not so unlikely accurate as in the mid-eighteenth century, with few others, the Cadore woodlands still provided large quantities of larch [33]. In addition to this, from the fifteenth century until 1797, Padua was a territory under Venice's republic. Timber purchase and other raw building materials mainly took place in Venice that strictly controlled the supply according to its constantly increasing demand.

Fig. 8 Inscriptions on replaced cover boards in the façade's dome (picture: author).

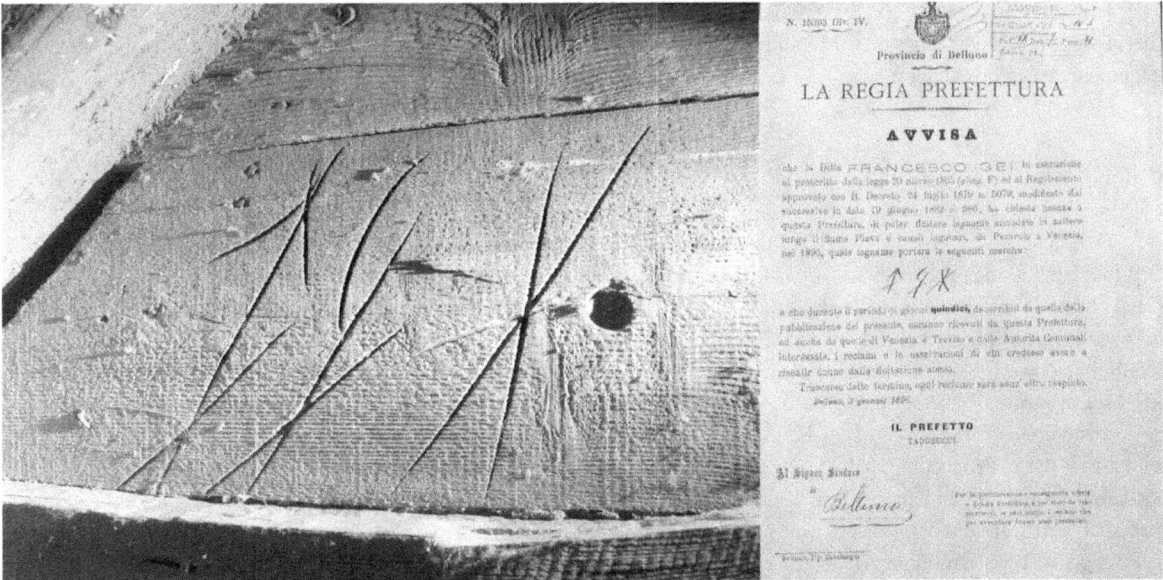

Fig. 9 Floating mark on a cover board in the Relics dome (picture: author), and similar one documented in 1896 along the Piave route, from Perarolo to Venice (State Archive of Belluno).

Conclusions

The research contributed to documenting the timber's dendro-provenance between the sixteenth- and eighteenth centuries during historical worksites in the timber superstructures of St Anthony basilica. It is possible to identify operators and trade routes involved over centuries through complementary investigations on archival documents and trademarks. In particular, from the two different types of findings (archival documents and marks), it comes out a possible shift of mountain sources and routes over centuries.

Archival documents have revealed the names of Paduan timber merchants active in the late sixteenth century, by the Cismon and Brenta water systems, involving consignments from the woodlands located in Primiero, Valstagna and Grappa in the Vicenza region, as well as Asiago, Valsugana and Tesino sectors.

Trademarks found in different domes identify replacements that occurred in the superstructures during the mid-eighteenth and the nineteenth centuries. In particular, the reiteration of the same marks contributes to date interventions occurred simultaneously in several domes. Furthermore, the comparisons of these marks with others recorded by previous research suggests the use of rafted timber along the Piave. If verified by further findings, this would mean a shift in the dendro-provenance of the timber supply in the history of the Basilica's domes towards woodland resources located in Cadore between the eighteenth and nineteenth centuries.

Further archival research should help to trace the timber batches used in the Venetian building sites between the sixteenth and twentieth centuries. Lastly, further research on historical timber traders and shipping marks along Brenta and Piave routes might help depict a broader scenario of the trade history of repairs in the medieval roofs of the Basilica in Padua.

Contextualisation of the Timber Trade between the Sixteenth and Nineteenth Centuries in the Basilica of St Anthony, Padua

Acknowledgements

This project is financed by the Swiss National Science Foundation (SNSF). The authors thank Gianni Paris Becher for sharing his valuable findings on ownership marks in the Dolomites and St Anthony's community for constantly supporting the onsite research with care.

References

[1] L. Vandenabeele, 'The Medieval Transformations of the Basilica of St Anthony in Padua based on an Analysis of the Original Brickwork', Proceedings of the 7th International Congress on Construction History, in press.

[2] A. Sartori, 'Il Santuario delle Reliquie della Basilica del Santo a Padova', *Il Santo - Rivista francescana di storia dottrina arte*, Vol. 2 no.2, 1962, pp.135-205. A. Sartori, 'Il Santuario Delle Reliquie Della Basilica Del Santo a Padova (continuazione e fine)' *Il Santo - Rivista francescana di storia dottrina arte*, Vol. 2 no.2, 1962, pp.289-335.

[3] G. Lorenzoni, *L'edificio del Santo di Padova*. Vicenza: Neri Pozza Editore, 1981. M. Salvatori, 'The Wooden Superstructures of the Domes of the St. Anthony 'S Basilica in Padua' in International Association for Shell and Spatial Structures (ed.), Proceedings of the International Congress Domes From Antiquity to the present, Istanbul, 1988, Instanbul: Mimar Sinan Üniversitesi, 1988. M. Salvatori, 'Strutture, vicende e restauri delle calotte lignee soprastanti le otto cupole in muratura della Basilica di S. Antonio di Padova.' in T. Gennaro (ed.), *Il restauro del legno*. Milano: Hoepli, 1989, pp.57-61. G. Bresciani Alvarez, *Architettura a Padova*. Padova: Il Poligrafo, 1999. B. Heinemann, *Der Santo in Padua: Raum Städtischer, Privater Und Ordenspolitischer Inszenierung*. Berlin: Verlag, 2012. G. Valenzano, 'Il Cantiere Architettonico Del Santo Nel 1310' in L. Bertazzo, L. Baggio (eds), *Padova 1310: Percorsi nei cantieri architettonici e pittorici della Basilica di Sant'Antonio*. Padova: Centro Studi Antoniani, 2012, pp.65-78. L. Baggio, L. Bertazzo, Padova 1310: *Percorsi Nei Cantieri Architettonici e Pittorici della Basilica di Sant'Antonio in Padova*. Padova: Centro Studi Antoniani, 2012. S. Ruzza, *La Basilica di Sant'Antonio. Itinerario artistico e religioso*. Padova: Centro Studi Antoniani, 2016.

[4] M. Diaz, L. Vandenabeele, S.M. Holzer, 'The Construction of the Medieval Domes of the Basilica of St Anthony in Padua', Proceedings of the 7th International Congress on Construction History, in press.

[5] O. Pignatelli, *Indagini dendrocronologiche sulle strutture lignee delle cupole della Basilica del Santo a Padova. I Lotto*. Unpublished report, 2020. O. Pignatelli, *Indagini dendrocronologiche sulle strutture lignee delle cupole della Basilica del Santo a Padova. II Lotto*. Unpublished report, 2021.

[6] Archivio della Veneranda Arca di Sant'Antonio. Series 2nd *Parti e Atti*, fasc. fasc.2-27, 1552-57. Series 14th *Mandati di pagamento (Registri)*, fasc.1-10, 1584-1593. Series 17th *Contabilità preparatorio e speciale*, fasc. 2068, 1865, fasc. 2069, 1866, fasc. 2075, 1867-68.

[7] G. Luisetto (ed.), *Archivio Sartori. Guida della Basilica Del Santo, Varie, Artisti e Musici al Santo e nel Veneto* (4 Vols). Padova: Centro Studi Antoniani, 1989. Vol.1, pp.109-123

[8] G. Fabbiani, 'Appunti per una storia del commercio del legname in Cadore', Rassegna Economica della Camera di Commercio, Industria ed Agricoltura di Belluno, no.10-12, 1959.

[9] S. Bortolami, 'Il Brenta medievale nella pianura veneta. Note per una storia politico-territoriale ' in A. Bondesan (ed.), *Il Brenta*. Verona: Cierre Edizioni, 2003, pp.209-238. P. Braunstein, 'De La Montagne À Venise : les réseaux du bois au XVe siècle', *Mélanges de l'école française de Rome*, vol.100 no.2, 1988, pp.761-99.

[10] K. Occhi, *Boschi e mercanti: Traffici di legname tra la Contea di Tirolo e la Repubblica di Venezia (Secoli XVI-XVII)*. Bologna: Il Mulino, 2006. M. Agnoletti, 'Il trasporto fluviale del legname nell'alta Valle del Piave (XIX Sec.)', *Nuncius*, vol. 10 no. 1, 1995, pp.193-209.

[11] Philipp, Braunstein, (Note 8) p.766.

[12] K. Occhi 'Mercanti e traffici nel canale di Brenta (1571-1702)' in D. Perco, M. Varotto (eds), *Uomini e paesaggi del canale di Brenta*. Verona: Cierre Edizioni, 2004, pp.55-94.

[13] R. Asche, G. Bettega, U. Pistoia, *Un fiume di legno. Fluitazione del legname dal Trentino a Venezia*. Scarmagno (TO): Priuli & Verlucca editori, 2010, pp..20-21. A. Lazzarini, *La trasformazione di un bosco. Il Cansiglio, Venezia e i nuovi usi del legno (Secoli XVIII-XIX)*. Belluno: Istituto Storico Bellunese della Resistenza e dell'Età contemporanea, 2006, pp.30-33. G. Corso, 'Nervesa Zateri. Gli Zattieri del Piave e l'arte de Zataria nei proverbi e nel folklore trevigiani' in Giavera Amministrazioni e biblioteche Comunali di Crovetta, Montebelluna, Nervesa, Volpago (eds), *Per Conoscere Il Montello*. Segusino: Segusino Stampa, 1990, p.61.

[14] G. Spada, 'Amministrazione e gestione della Regia Foresta di Somadida dal 1867 al 1915' in Circolo Vittoriese di Ricerche Storiche (ed.), Atti del Convegno Nazionale di Economia e Commerci delle Prealpi Venete (sec. XIII-sec. XX), Vittorio Veneto 2014, Godega di Sant'Urbano (TV): Dario de Bastiani Editore, 2014, pp.391-446.

[15] K. Occhi, 'Affari di Famiglie: Rapporti Mercantili Lungo Il Confine Veneto-Tirolese (Secoli XVI-XVII)', *Mélanges De l'École Française de Rome*, vol.125 no.1, 2013, pp.1-15.

[16] This are documented i.e. along the Piave in the 19th century. N. Di Lucia Coletti, 'Trasporti di grandi alberature sul Piave nell'Ottocento' in G. Caniato (ed.), *La via del Fiume dalle Dolomiti a Venezia*. Verona: Cierre Edizioni, 1993, pp.295-298. G. Šebesta, 'Struttura – Evoluzione della zattera ' in D. Perco (ed.), *Zattere, Zattieri e Menadàs. La fluitazione del legname lungo il Piave*. Castellavazzo: Tipografia Castaldi Feltre, 199, pp.177-216.

[17] E. Isnenghi, 'Il Governo del Fiume' in F. Selmin, C. Grandis (eds), *Il Bacchiglione*. Sommacampagna (VR): Cierre Edizioni, 2008, pp.302-17.

[18] G. Caniato, 'Commerci e navigazione lungo il Brenta' in A. Bondesan (ed.), *Il Brenta*. Verona: Cierre Edizioni, 2003. pp.255-270.

[19] https://archivioarcadelsanto.org/serie/mandati-registri-01/; https://archivioarcadelsanto.org/serie/parti-e-atti-01/

[20] Katja, Occhi (Note 10)

[21] *Ibid.* Roswita, Ascher, Giovanni, Bettega, Ugo, Pistoia (Note 13) p.84.

[22] L. Ciceri, L. Laszloczky (eds), 'I contrassegni individuali in Friuli', *Sot La Nape*, vol. 5, 1955, pp.3-10. C. Corrain, C. Corain, 'Segni grafici incisi su vecchie travi della casa rurale veneta', *Rivista di Etnografia*, vol. 20, 1966, pp.58-64. M. von Ostmann, 'Ursprung und Entwicklung der Hausmarkern', *Mitteil. Rhein. Veren. Volkskunde*, vol. 4, 1948, pp.1-4. K. K. A. Ruppel, *Die Hausmarke. Das Symbol Der Germanischen Sippe*. Berlin: Alfred Metzener, 1939. G. Marcuzzi, 'Segni di Casa del Basso Veneto e del Cadore', *Dolomiti*, vol. 15 no. 2. 1992, pp.47-64.

[23] I I. Domenico, 'I marchi di identità', *La Ricerca Folklorica*, no. 31. 1995, pp.53-66. G. Pais Becher, A. Martella, *Segni nelle Dolomiti Orientali*. Vittorio Veneto: Poligrafico Bianca e Volta, Comunità Montana Centro Cadore, 1998. Giuseppe, Corso (Note13).

[24] Pais Becher, Martella, p. 17.

[25] H. Tucci, 'Il marchio di casa nell'uso italiano', *La Ricerca Folklorica*, no. 5. 1982, pp.119-28.

[26] Pais Becher, Martella, (Note 23).

[27] Karl Konrad A., Ruppel (Note 25).

[28] Ciceri, Laszloczky (Note 22) p.4.

[29] G. Marcuzzi, (Note 25) pp.56-59.

[30] ibid..

[31] G. Caniato, (Note 16) p.282; Pais Becher, Martella (Note 26), pp.112-117.

[32] The State Archive in Belluno. Prefettura di Belluno, series Archivio Amministrativo, 8 january 1896.

[33] E. Casti-Moreschi, E. Zolli, *Boschi sella Serenissima: Storia di un rapporto Uomo-Ambiente*. (2 vols), Venezia: Archivio di Stato, 1988. Vol.2.

On The Origins of Hydro-Technics: The Gardens of Noisy (1570)

Bruno Bentz
Archaelogist, PhD (Omage), France

In the eighteenth century, all the great European gardens had spectacular water features due to the influence of the gardens of Versailles and Marly, which had amazed their contemporaries. From Peterhof (Russia) to La Granja (Spain), from Sadabad (Turkey) to Chatsworth (England), the art of water was at its most sumptuous. From then on, sumptuary hydraulics took on a special place in the art of gardens with its specialists, the fountain builders, contributing to the creation of the basins with their pipes. The large waterfalls, which were built in imitation of those of the French king, rivalled each other in length, height and decoration. Over time, the uses of water in gardens multiplied and diversified. These great gardens are the result of three centuries of creation, innovation and progress.

The Grandes Eaux of Versailles still attract huge crowds today. The success of this show is exceptional and is based on a 17th century creation which, for the most part, has preserved the original operation and water games. It is, in fact, first and foremost a hydraulic monument: here the water effects have been admired since the reign of King Louis XIV. The water brings an art of ephemerality that embellishes a garden built around clever perspectives, parterres, topiaries, vases, statues and various constructions, but a garden built first and foremost around the architecture of water. What is admired at Versailles, in the spectacle of the Grandes Eaux, are the basins and their water jets, i.e. the effects produced by the entire hydraulic system. However, there is no such thing as a result without technical means: for hydraulics, from catchment to jet, the production of the water masterpiece requires equipment and devices, in other words, hydro-technics.

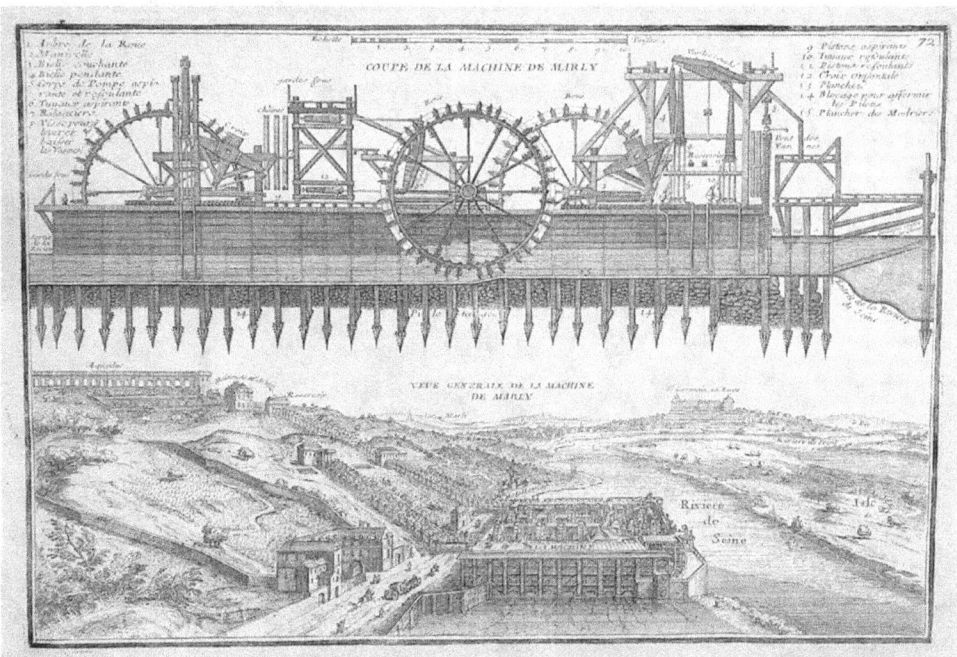

Figure 1: The Marly Machine, engraving, late 17th century (private collection)

At Versailles, the gigantic hydraulic network created for the gardens is difficult to quantify, depending on what is counted: the dozens of basins, the hundreds of kilometres of pipes or the thousands of nozzles. However, there was a problem feeding this elaborate system with enough water. This situation led to the mobilisation of many scientists, engineers, surveyors and technicians to find solutions for collecting and conducting the water in the surrounding area. Among the most daring ideas, we should mention the project to divert the Loire; the unfinished work on the aqueduct of the river Eure; and, finally, the damming up of the Rambouillet ponds which, by force of gradient, fills the great royal canal as far as Versailles. In addition, from the outset, mechanical installations were also used: the pump-mills of Clagny and then of the River Bièvre, whose flow was as weak as it was random. It was finally the creation of the Marly Machine, drawing from the River Seine, that completed the water catchment works [1]. The hydro-technical device used in this Machine was innovative as it allowed water to be raised to a height of about 150 m. This difference in level made it possible to reach the plateau overlooking the Versailles area, where storage reservoirs were dug from which the water could then be conveyed by a natural gradient network. The mechanism of this Machine was entirely set in motion by fourteen large paddle wheels which operated a series of piston pumps and linkages used, by sheer mechanical force, to carry the water off course over a long distance along the hillside in order to draw off the water in three stages. (Fig. 1) The Marly Machine was the ultimate technical achievement in the service of modern garden fountains, but in reality it was of no use to Versailles. By the time it was put into operation and the waters of the Seine finally reached Versailles in 1685, most of the fountains and waterworks had been completed and the time for great garden festivities had passed.

There was no new water feature at Versailles linked to the Marly Machine because the waters of the Seine arrived at Versailles in the Montbauron reservoirs in which the waters of the Rambouillet ponds were already stored. It is true that the Machine added to the reserves but it only enhanced the capacity of the network rather than being able to create new features. The only consequence of the creation of the Machine for the gardens of Versailles was to be able to prolong the duration of the spectacle of the Grandes Eaux which, formerly, accompanied the king's walk. In order to make the most of this abundant resource, there was a plan to double the size of the Montbauron reservoirs. This project was abandoned, probably because in the end it did not allow the creation of new features in the fountains of Versailles. In contrast, in the newly created gardens of Marly, near the Machine, the original hydraulic network were completely transformed [2]. The creation of the largest water features, the grand jet (Fig. 2) and then the cascades (Fig. 3), testifies to the success of these large-scale works.

Figure 2: Marly, the Grand jet (cl. B. Béranger)

Figure 3: Marly, la Rivière d'eau, engraving by Pierre Lepautre, ca 1710 (private collection)

Water treatises

The tradition of water features is closely linked to the development of the pleasure garden. It originated in the Italian villas of the 16th century, the most famous example being the gardens of the Villa d'Este. Between Georgius Agricola's treatise *De Ortu et Causis Subterraneorum* (1546) [3] and Bernard Forest de Bélidor's *Architecture hydraulique* (1737-1753) [4], knowledge of geology and physics, surveying, the circulation of liquids, the manufacture of materials, and the science of gears evolved considerably. Heir to the works of Antiquity and the Middle Ages, the development of hydraulics thus followed the course of technical progress, giving rise to both new achievements and new processes in a continuous analysis of means and ends.

Bélidor offers a complete panorama of the hydro-technical installations created for the gardens of Versailles, in particular the new cast iron pipes with their flanged and screwed joints and the wheels and mechanisms of the Marly Machine. The work of the academics now made it possible to calculate the flows and heights of the jets, thanks to Edme Mariotte and Jean Picard, while the brothers Paulus and Rennequin Sualem perfected the mechanical remote transmission from the German minesfor raising water from the Seine. At the same time, the first tests of a motorised machine were carried out for the water of the Maisons gardens drawn from the Seine, but the result remained imperfect for a long time.

Earlier, it was the works of Jean François, *La science des eaux* (1653) and then *L'art des fontaines* (1665) [5] that renewed our understanding of the water cycle and the means of collecting and conducting it. He mentions the existence at Noisy of a remarkable device, "where the fountain that makes the water jets has no other water for source than that of a higher pond and this pond none other than that of the rains that are reserved for this effect [6]". In fact, this reservoir was dug on the plateau dominating the site: only the rainwater could fill it. It could then supply all the garden basins by gradient flow. However, it is unlikely that this reservoir, located more than 600 m away from the garden fountains, was also used to produce the water jets.

The mechanics of the first machines for raising water are explained in the treatises by Salomon de Caus *Les raisons des forces mouvantes* (1615) [7] and Issac de Caus *Nouvelle invention de lever l'eau* (1644) [8]. The first pumps in Versailles applied these principles, in particular to pump water from the Clagny pond into the château's reservoirs. The first pump developed by Denis Jolly in 1664 was followed later by those of Claude Denis and Pierre Francine. They illustrate the progress being made in the manufacture of pumps and the various options using animal power (with one or two horses) or natural power (wind). The historian Pierre Matthieu reported in 1605 that an original machine had been tried out in Noisy:

> "The ancients were unaware of the industry of raising water higher than its source, and we and others would have remained in this ignorance without the ingenious and bold invention of Claude de Monconnis [...] who was the first to demonstrate it with admiration at the fountains of S. Germain en Laye & at the houses of the Maréchal de Retz at Noisy, & of the first President at Stains [9]."

The presence of Claude de Montconys in Noisy is not mentioned elsewhere. In 1599, he was appointed Superintendent of the King's fountains but his life and career are not well documented. Matthieu seems to be well informed, however, as he adds in the margin "The first proof of this invention was made in Rouen in the presence of the King, M. le Maréchal de Retz [Albert de Gondi] presented the inventor to H.M [10]." This meeting may have taken place in October 1596, when King Henry IV visited Rouen on the occasion of the Assembly of Notables, in which Albert de Gondi participated. This date is late for the work at Noisy, for which the role of Montconys remains uncertain, though his reputation as an engineer was established.

The Water Features at Noisy

Albert de Gondi acquired the property of Noisy in 1568 [11]. He was Count and then Duke of Retz, then became Marshal of France, making him First Gentleman of the Chamber of King Charles IX. His position at court was entirely due to the favour of the Queen Mother, Catherine de Medici, for whom he was one of the main advisors. Gondi was of Florentine origin and received important diplomatic missions, but he was also made responsible for supervising work on the royal buildings. Although he had lodgings in the Louvre and the Château de Saint-Germain, as well as his private mansion in Paris, he decided to build himself a pleasure house near the court. He had a small residence built in Noisy, with a villa built on a terrace surrounded by a wide dry moat overlooking extensive gardens with terraced flowerbeds. This layout is reminiscent of Italian gardens with, in addition, a pavilion decorated as a grotto.

The creation of the gardens of Noisy during the de Gondi period is attested to by several archival sources. In 1577, the Venetian ambassador Girolamo Lippomano, in the *Relazioni di Francia*, includes Noisy among the magnificent constructions around Paris:

> "where you can see arches, aqueducts, statues, gardens, parks, fishponds, and all the other amenities that you would expect from a royal building [12]."

By this time, the work was already well advanced, since Cambino de Cambini had already been entrusted with the upkeep of the gardens before 1575. It is possible that this gardener of Florentine origin participated in the earthworks. Another contract, signed in 1571 with a masonry contractor, Denis Courtin, for the walls of the castle entrance courtyard, also dates the start of the work shortly after the acquisition of the property.

During the recent archaeological excavations, new observations were made on the construction of the gardens [13]. The old terraces are still visible on the ground and can be clearly seen on a Lidar topographic survey. After the demolition of the buildings and all the visible masonry (walls of the terraces and courtyards), the site was integrated into the hunting park of the Château de Marly, and is still in a wooded area today. No construction has been carried out on the site, so that underneath a first layer of humus produced by the forest, there is still the backfill from the demolition covering some remains.

During the excavation of the grotto pavilion, built at the junction of two terrace levels, the foundations of the building were uncovered at a depth of about six metres. They were covered by the earthwork sands of the upper floor without any traces of reworking, which proves that the construction work was carried out before the terrace was built. The hydraulic pipes discovered under the grotto floor had therefore necessarily been laid at the beginning of the work. Similarly, when an old basin located in the middle of this high parterre was excavated, the drainage pipe was more than 2 m deep, in the earthwork, with no excavation trench above. It had therefore been laid when the parterre was laid out. The archaeological stratigraphy allows us to observe that the hydraulic network of the Noisy gardens was conceived at the same time as the initial project for the development of the site, i.e. between 1568 and 1570. (Fig. 4)

Figure 4: Noisy grotto, general view, 2019 (cl. I. Khmelevskikh)

According to the plans drawn around 1690, more than a century after the creation of the gardens, there were then six basins (in the middle of the upper and lower parterres on either side of the château, in the middle of the entrance courtyard and in the middle of the access ramps to the forest) decorated with water jets. (Fig. 5) The basin in the upper parterre of the grotto, rediscovered in 2020, still had a lead pipe with an opening in the centre of the basin to form a water jet. A piece of pipe from outside the basin was found in the backfill and measures 6 cm in diameter; the pipe in the basin invert

On The Origins of Hydro-Technics: The Gardens of Noisy (1570)

measures 5 cm in diameter and the outlet on the nozzle side is narrowed to 3 cm. (Fig. 6) The material used and this reduction show that this is an original pressure pipe, but we do not yet know its origin nor the height of the jet that was produced in this basin.

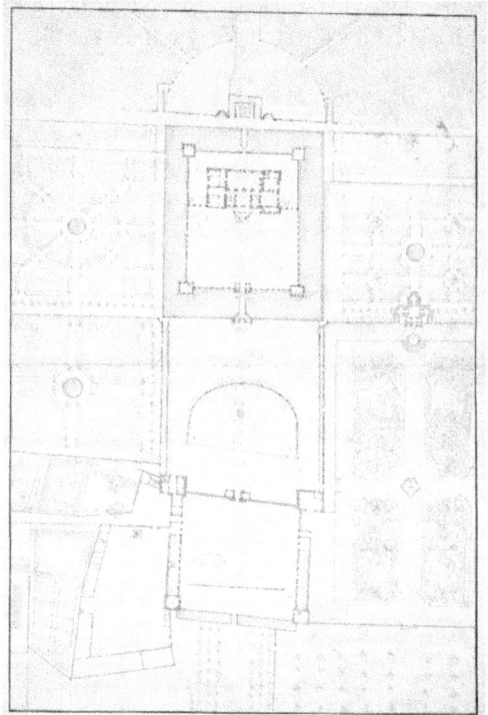

Figure 5: Noisy, Layout of the gardens, watercolour drawing, 1693 (Archives départementales des Yvelines, A 119)

Figure 6: Noisy, basin, lead pipe in the centre of the basin, 2020 (cl. Akane Hori)

Figure 7: Noisy, grotto, remains of two lead pipes, 2020 (cl. S. Chaumier)

Figure 8: Noisy, the water jet in the grotto, J. Marot, engraving, ca 1650 (private collection)

However, there was also a fountain inside the grotto. It was drawn by Jean Marot in his *Recueil des plans* (1656-1659)[14] in cross-section, and described by François Boulin in his *Description du chateau de Noisy* (1732)[15]. During the excavations under its former location, two lead pipes were still lying side by side in the grotto floor. (Fig. 7) These pipes measure 3 cm in diameter: one was used to form the jet of water coming out of the fountain, the other certainly served as an outlet at the bottom of the basin while creating a pressure pipe that could feed the jet of water in the basin of the low parterre of the last terrace. We know the height of the jet from the engraving (Fig. 8) and the description: it was about eight metres high and projected through an opening in the vault so it was visible in the parterre above. The discovery of the lead pipes in the foundations and the integration of the jet into the architecture of the grotto make it possible to date this exceptional hydro-technical arrangement to the time of the original construction.

The Water Jet in the Grotto

This eight-metre high water fountain was certainly a remarkable water effect for visitors to the gardens of Noisy, but it was also a great hydro-technical achievement. None of the great gardens of the French king had such an ornament. At Chambord, situated at the bottom of the plain, the calm waters of the Cosson dominated and had to be channelled to the edge of the garden. At the Tuileries, the garden was still rudimentary and the water supply was only installed in the following century. The old chateau of Saint-Germain had only the small surface flow of the Grand Cours aqueduct. Whereas, at Fontainebleau, the hydraulic network created under François I only provided water for a few fountains. Without abundant resources and significant water effects, the hydraulics of the French royal gardens were still poorly developed in the 16th century [16].

Among the various water features, vertical water was still difficult to implement, especially in gardens located on the plain or on the heights of a plateau. The use of mechanical means was necessary when the site did not have an elevated reservoir. The hydraulic treatises of the Renaissance offer a wide variety of drainage pumps, the main challenge of which is to pump water from a depth of about ten metres below ground and to discharge it. They were mainly intended for extracting discharge in mines or for sourcing domestic water. Adapting this mechanism, Jacques Besson, in the *Livre premier des instruments* (1571)[17], proposes a machine for raising water to the top of a tower. Agostino Ramelli, in *Le diverse et artificiose machine* (1588)[18], presents, on the one hand, two fountains with various water features and, on the other hand, a series of dewatering machines placed above wells and operating with cranks or vertical or horizontal wheels manually driven.

This mechanism is probably closest to the two suction pumps for the cisterns that were located in two pavilions at the northern end of the Noisy esplanade. They are mentioned in the accounts of repair work in 1693 and in the description of 1732: "in two of these pavilions there were wells of extraordinary depth with pumps to draw water more easily [19]". This water was probably intended for domestic consumption. Another pump is also mentioned in the archives: it was located in another pavilion, this time to the south of the esplanade, about 60 m from the grotto fountain. This pavilion was referred to as the machine pavilion.

This pavilion and its machine have left few traces in the archives. Nevertheless, it is likely that this pavilion housed the machine used to create the grotto jet. The ground floor and first floor were probably used as living quarters, while the basement, which was about six metres high, was built into the moat. A plan from the end of the 17th century indicates the presence of a well to domestic supply. This well was found during an archaeological excavation in 2019, however its depth could not be measured beyond two metres (Fig. 9). Among the debris left over from the demolition, only a few fragments of clay pipes confirmed the existence of an ancient hydro-technical device.

Two important observations could nevertheless be made. The basement room, mainly occupied by the well, had a level access to the bottom of the moat. Although this door was not original, this indicates the presence of a workroom at this level. Furthermore, it was observed that the circular well (1.5 metres in diameter) was not built perfectly in the centre of the room, whereas the entire architecture of the pavilion is built with symmetry and regularity. This imperfection can be explained by excavation work prior to the construction of the pavilion, which would have simplified the removal of the earth. This hypothesis reinforces the idea that the hydraulic network of Noisy was designed at the beginning of the construction programme.

Figure 9: Noisy, Pavillon de la machine, view of the well, 2019 (cl. B. Bentz)

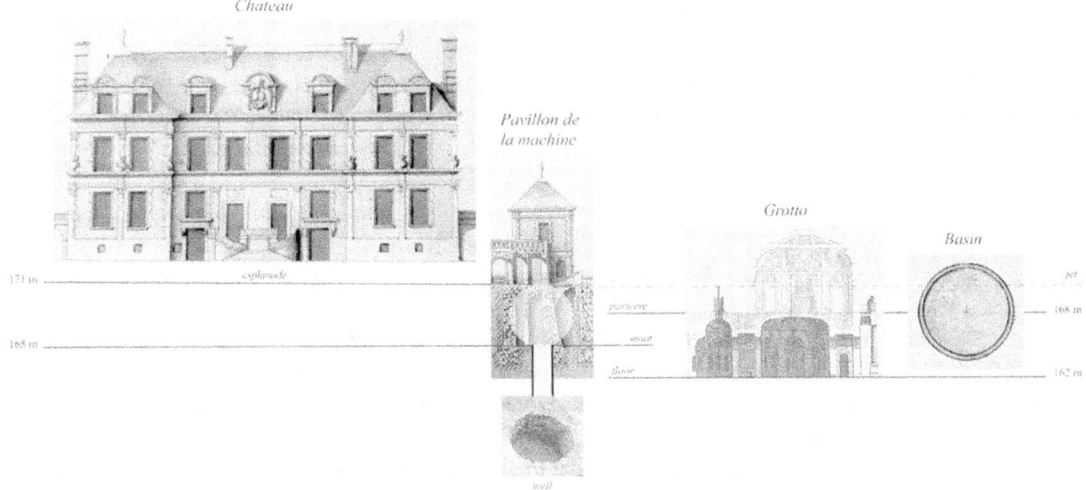

Figure 10: Noisy, graphic of the hydraulic devices

The hydro-technical device of the water jet of the Noisy grotto was perhaps associated with that of the basin of the high parterre. In fact, the two structures are close to each other and the altitude of the grotto jet could be equal to that of the jet from the high parterre basin, implying it could have a height of about 1.5 metres. In this hypothesis, the machine would have had to provide the same pressure for both jets. The position of the pavilion halfway between the level of the grotto and that of the high parterre was certainly an advantage: part of the pressure necessary to form the 8 m high water jet in the grotto was thus produced by a siphon. The machine therefore had to combine two functions: to draw water from the bottom of the well and then to force the water into a lead pipe under pressure. (Fig. 10) This performance was perhaps unprecedented [20].

At the same time, Jacques Androuet du Cerceau, in *Les plus excellents bastiments de France* (1579)[21], remarked on the water jet of the rock fountain in the garden of Diane at Chenonceau "of the height of three toises [approx. six metres] which is a beautiful and pleasant invention [22]". The hydraulic works of Chenonceau had been started in 1554 by the fountain-maker Cardin de Valence. This jet was produced by a natural slope from the fountain of La Roche situated above in a lead pipe; it was operated by a wooden pin blocking the pipe.

The creation of the Noisy gardens was also contemporary with the publication of Bernard Palissy's garden project in the *Recepte veritable* (1563)[23] in which music and water features play an important role. In particular with the use of the hydraulic organ imitating bird song which was to be found some time later in the Italian gardens or later in the grottoes of Saint-Germain. It is true that the jet in the Noisy grotto belongs to the tradition of surprise waterworks - since the outlet of the jet in the parterre of the upper terrace of the grotto was like a natural resurgence. However, it was based on an ingenious mechanism and produced an original effect that archaeological analysis has made it possible to partially reconstruct thanks to a few archival documents and the remains that escaped demolition [24].

References

[1] Unfortunately, the largest and most complete works on the Versailles hydraulic network are unpublished: F. Loyer, 'Les grandes eaux de Versailles. Étude des travaux hydrauliques de Louis XIV à Versailles pour la réalisation des grandes eaux', 2002; E. Soullard, 'Les eaux de Versailles', doctoral thesis in history, Université de Grenoble II, 2011.
[2] B. Bentz, 'Les Grandes eaux de Marly sous Louis XIV', *Marly art et patrimoine*, n° 4, 2010, p. 19-28.
[3] G. Agricola, *De ortu et causis subterraneorum*, Friben et Episcopius, Basel, 1546 ; I. Barton, 'Georgius Agricola's contributions to hydrology', *Journal of Hydrology*, n° 523, 2015, p. 839-849.
[4] B. Forest de Bélidor, *Architecture hydraulique*, Jombert, Paris, 4 vol., 1737-1753.
[5] J. François, *La science des eaux*, Hallaudays, Rennes, 1653 ; *L'art des fontaines*, Hallaudays, Rennes, 1665.
[6] 'où la fontaine qui fait les jets d'eau n'a point d'autre eau pour source que celle d'un estang supérieur, ny cet estang que celle des pluies qu'on réserve pour cet effet' : François, 1665, p. 32. I thank Aurélia Rostaing for bringing this reference to my attention.
[7] S. De Caus, *Les raisons des forces mouvantes avec diverses machines tant utilles que plaisantes ausquelles sont adjoints plusieurs desseings de grotes et fontaines*, Jan Norton, Francfort, 1615.
[8] I. De Caus, *Nouvelle invention de lever l'eau plus haut que sa source avec quelques machines mouvantes par le moyen de l'eau et un discours de la conduit d'icelle*, Londres, 1644.
[9] 'Les anciens avaient ignoré l'industrie de faire eslever & remonter les eaux plus haut que leur source, nous & les nostres fussions demeurés en cette ignorance sans l'ingénieuse & hardie invention de Claude de Monconnis […] qui le premier en a fait preuve avec admiration aux fontaines de S. Germain en l'Aye & aux maisons du mareschal de Rets à Noisy, & du premier Président à Stim.' : [P. Matthieu], *Histoire de France et des choses mémorables advenues aux provinces éstrangères durant sept années de paix, du règne du roy Henri IIII, roy de France et de Navarre*, Metayer et Guillemot, Paris, 1605, vol. 6, p. 265.
[10] 'La première preuve de cette invention fut faite à Roüen devant le Roy, M. le Mareschal de Rez [Albert de Gondi] présenta l'inventeur à S.M.' : Matthieu, 1605, p. 265.

[11] B. Bentz, 'Les jardins du château de Noisy', in: L. Gaugain, P. Liévaux et A. Salamagne (dir.), *La fabrique du jardin à la Renaissance*, Presses Universitaires François-Rabelais, Tours, 2019, p. 115-128.

[12] 'dove si veggono archi, acquidotti, statue, giardini, parchi, peschiere, e tutte quelle commodità in fine, che si ricercano a edificii regii' : M. N. Tommaseo, *Relations des ambassadeurs vénitiens sur les affaires de France au xvie siècle*, Imprimerie royale, Paris, 1838, p. 490-491.

[13] B. Bentz, 'Les grandes eaux de Noisy', *Marly, art et patrimoine*, n° 14, 2020, p. 29-42.

[14] J. Marot, *Recueil des plans profils et élévations des plusieurs palais chasteaux églises sépultures grottes et hostels bâtis dans Paris et aux environs*, Paris, [1656-1659], pl. 45-47 (plan, elevation and profile of the grotto of Noisy) ; K. Deutsch, *Jean Marot: Un graveur d'architecture à l'époque de Louis XIV*, De Gruyter, Berlin, 2015, p. 117-124, cat. p. 437-449, n° 53-55.

[15] Versailles, Bibliothèque municipale, G 280, p. 93-117, [F. Boulin], 'Description du chasteau de Noisy dans le grand parc de Versailles, entièrement démoly sur la fin de l'année 1732' (manuscript).

[16] G. Bresc-Bautier, 'Fontaines laïques de la première Renaissance française : les marbres de Tours, de Blois et de Gaillon', in : *Sources et fontaines du Moyen Âge à l'âge baroque*, Garnier, Paris 1998, p. 185-201 (see p. 190-192).

[17] J. Besson, *Livre premier des intrumens mathematiques et mechaniques*, Paris, 1571-1572.

[18] A. Ramelli, *Le diverse et artificiose machine*, Paris, 1588.

[19] 'il y avoit dans deux de ces pavillons des pui[t]s d'une profondeur extraordinaire avec des pompes pour tirer plus facilement de l'eau': Boulin, 1732, p. 103.

[20] It has hitherto generally been supposed that pump-driven fountains were a late seventeenth century invention, see James W.P. Campbell, 'The significance of John Theophilus Desaguliers's Course of Experimental Philosophy to the History of Hydraulics and what it reveals about the first pump-driven fountains' in J.Campbell, N.Baker, K.Draper, M.Driver, M.Heaton, Y.Pan, N. Ruamsanitwong and D. Yeomans (eds), *Iron, Steel and Buildings: Studies in the History of Construction, Cambridge: CHS, 2019*, 331-346, pp.342-343.

[21] J. Androuet du Cerceau, *Premier [et Second] volume des plus excellents bastiments de France,* Paris, 1576-1579.

[22] 'de la haulteur de trois toises [ca 6 m] de hault, qui est une belle et plaisante invention' : Androuet du Cerceau, vol. II, 1579, fol. 5v ; quoted (p. 141) by F. Boudon, 'Jardins d'eau et jardins de pente dans la France de la Renaissance', in J. Guillaume (dir.), *Architecture, jardin, paysage. L'environnement du château et de la villa aux XVe et XVIe siècles,* proceedings of the Tours conference in June 1992, Picard, Paris, 1999, p. 137-183 ; D. Brochier, 'Le chantier d'un jardin sur l'eau : l'exemple du parterre de Diane de Poitiers au château de Chenonceau (1551-1557)', *Livraisons de l'histoire de l'architecture*, n° 27, 2014, p. 9-19.

[23] B. Palissy, *Recepte véritable, par laquelle tous les hommes de la France pourront apprendre à multiplier et augmenter leurs trésors,* Berton, La Rochelle, 1563 ; J. Ferdinand, '"À l'imitation du souverain fontenier". Eaux et fontaines dans l'œuvre de Bernard Palissy', in R. Gorris Camos and alii (dir.), *Le salut par les eaux et par les herbes : medicina e letteratura tra Italia e Francia nel Cinquecento e nel Seicento*, Cierre Grafica, Vérone, 2012, p. 153-180.

[24] Translation: Helen Spraggett. Thanks to James Campbell for his review and advice.

The Seventeenth and Eighteenth Centuries (1600-1800)

How to Build a Dome

Stefan M. Holzer
Institute of Construction History and Preservation (IDB), ETH Zurich, Switzerland

Introduction

Although domes have been a recurrent theme in European architecture through the centuries from antiquity to the 20th century, the big rise of the dome as the key feature of the monumental church started only with Brunelleschi's dome of the cathedral of Florence (1420–36). While Brunelleschi's dome is strictly speaking an octagonal cloister vault like many other medieval and early modern domes, it already presented several aspects which distinguished it from most of the preceding domes: It is located very high above ground, and rests on a drum supported by large arches/squinches. By contrast, the domes of antiquity (of course excluding St. Sophia's in Constantinople) are typically 'directly' supported from the ground by a contiguous cylindrical or polygonal masonry structure. Medieval European domes – notably the domes or cloister vaults of Italian baptisteries – mostly followed this Roman model, with the exception of a few rather small domes on crossings of basilicas. Like the domes of some medieval baptisteries such as the one in Cremona, Brunelleschi's dome is essentially a thin-shell brick structure with a few ashlar reinforcements, while the Roman domes are typically built in massive 'opus caementicium', i.e. in thick rubble masonry employing a lot of mortar and inevitably necessitating fully lagged formwork.

Brunelleschi's dome is of course most noted for its free-hand erection without formwork. While this method continues to fascinate researchers until today, the prevailing focus on this single aspect tends to obfuscate the remaining and perhaps even more important challenges of dome construction: The high position of the early modern domes above ground (some 50 m to the cornice in Florence) made lifting and temporary storage of building materials a key issue. Furthermore, in Florence, the sheer mass of the building material and the size of some of the ashlar elements ruled out the classical medieval transport method by carriers via galleries and spiral staircases, and clearly called for more efficient worksite technology, including Brunelleschi's famous ox-driven elevator. However, historic lifting devices employed before the advent of the modern crane in the 20th century permitted only very limited rotation and horizontal movement of the load. Brunelleschi's construction therefore definitely required a spacious working platform at the base of the dome which allowed the accommodation of lots of workers and which was stable enough to move heavy pieces around on it horizontally.

The immense putlog holes for a cantilevering platform at the base of the dome are still visible on site (Fig. 1)[1]. They traverse the entire thickness of the masonry and were designed to receive timber scantlings of almost 60 by 60 cm (i.e. probably composite beams made up from four pieces), testifying to a very robust platform indeed. Probably, most modern reconstructions of this platform have grossly underestimated its actual size. Reinforced by raking struts from the gallery at the base of the drum, 13 m below, such a sturdy platform could easily have cantilevered 10 to 12 m towards the centre of the dome, as can be easily determined by a rough statical calculation. Such a spacious working platform, designed to last more than a decennium, also made the installation of the templates for form control easy, and it permitted setting up trestles for works at the lower sections of the dome. In the case of conventional dome construction with formwork, the formwork and its supporting truss could be erected with relative ease if such a platform was present at the base of the dome. On the other hand, the very fact that a dome of the size of Brunelleschi's could be erected without formwork indicates that one tends to over-estimate the role of the centring in dome construction. No matter whether the dome is erected in a free-hand approach or on formwork, it is typically built in successive self-supporting rings. Ironically, this makes a dome much easier to build than a barrel vault, and permits the application of much lighter centring.

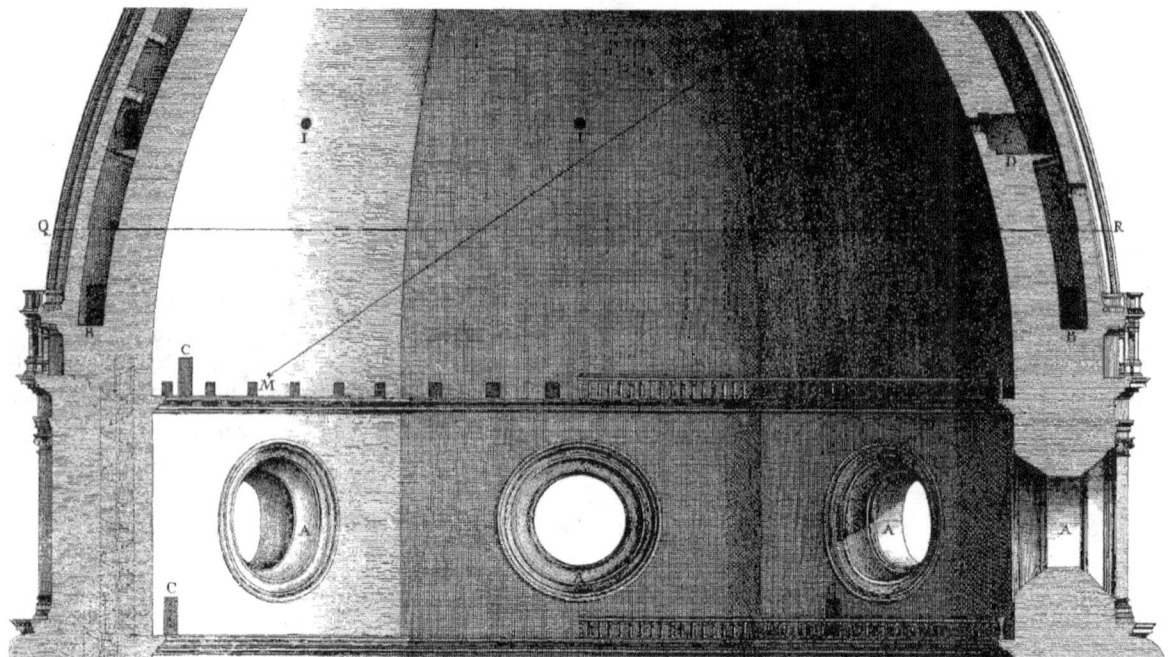

Figure 1. *Putlog holes at the base of Brunelleschi's dome of Florence cathedral. Engraving by Bernardo Sgrilli 1733, plate IX, detail.*

The remainder of the present paper will focus on a few well-documented examples of early modern dome construction where archival details about the scaffolding and centring are available. The attention is more on the "standard" baroque dome than on exceptional constructions like the cathedral of Florence or St. Peter's, Rome, where it is known that formwork was employed, but the available sources on the construction of the centring are in fact very fragmentary.

The question of dome construction has troubled architects and engineers for centuries. When Leonhard Christoph Sturm (1669–1719) wrote a special treatise on church architecture in 1718, he gave special emphasis to dome construction. In the preface to this work, he wrote: "As to building large domes, only very few people – particularly in Germany – know the key issues, let alone how to organize the worksite. In books, one also finds only very sparse instructions on this topic. The great Italian architects keep this knowledge among their arcana [2]." The present paper attempts to shed some light on this enticing enigma of construction history.

The Baroque

The dome was the most prominent 'leitmotif' of baroque architecture, particularly in 17th century Italy. None of the famous Italian architects of that century failed to design at least one significant dome. However, sources on how these domes were actually built are indeed difficult to find. It is therefore highly significant that one early case is documented in detail, namely, the church of Santa Maria della Salute in Venice. Recently, prof. Mario Piana has edited a letter written by the architect of that church, Baldassare Longhena, which was sent in 1649 to the principals, asking them to take care of the tender for the erection of the main dome [3]. Unfortunately, the drawings, which had originally accompanied this letter, are lost, but the letter contains detailed descriptions of all the members required to build the scaffolding and centring, so that the intended procedure of dome erection can nevertheless be reconstructed in detail.

The octagonal central space of the church (21.55 m diameter) had already arrived at the level of the principal cornice above the drum windows. What remained was to close the space by a (circular) brick dome. Longhena specified that the shell should be built on a continuous formwork made from spruce boards. The boards should be nailed to no less than 96 (i.e. twelve per side of the octagonal substructure) radial wooden arched ribs (each one 17.40 m in length), which Longhena suggested be constructed by three to four overlapping layers of sturdy boards nailed together. These radial ribs were to be fixed to laminated timber hoops both at the bottom and at the oculus of the dome. This primary formwork was to be supported by a truss that would rise another 12.50 m above the level of the cornice of the drum, in other words, up to the very top. The truss was to rest on an already established platform at the cornice level, carried by sturdy composite beams. The substructures of this platform were to be reinforced by additional struts. Longhena specified: "For safety, and to prevent this work from collapse, all struts shall reach from the floor of the church up to the already established platform [4]." In other words, the whole church was eventually filled with an impressive timber trestle, reaching from the ground up to the very top of the dome, quite unlike the fancy 'free-spanning' centring which was allegedly used for St. Peter's in Rome, according to Carlo Fontana [5]. When lagging of the 96 ribs was complete, Longhena himself would draw the outline of the dome's square coffers on it, the carpenters would build the templates for the coffers accordingly, and then the bricklayers would start to build the dome. Indeed, the huge shell with its thickness tapering from 80 to 50 cm was actually completed within just a few weeks.

Compared to Brunelleschi's 'minimalist' cantilevering temporary works, one may be surprised that the loads of the centring were carried to the very ground in the Venice church with its comparatively light dome. However, it appears that both the presence of a platform at cornice level and the direct support from below were current practice in the 17th century. Anyway, it is likely that a rough sketch showing the temporary works employed for the construction of Gian Lorenzo Bernini's domed church San Tommaso di Villanova in Castel Gandolfo can be interpreted in that sense [6](Fig. 2). At upper left, the wooden templates defining the shape of the dome and carrying the lagging are shown. However, in our context, the little drawing at the lower right is much more interesting: Obviously, it shows a simplified ground plan of the dome. A circle in the centre marks the lantern. Next to that circle, four small squares represent supports, which carry two orthogonal pairs of major beams spanning the entire interior of the dome. With a view to the other pieces of evidence shown in the present study, it becomes clear that the four supports are meant to rise from the very floor of the church to the base of the dome, where they support a large working platform carried by the four long beams. The circular templates for the dome itself are then erected on that platform, as shown on the bigger sketch in the upper left. That sketch includes a further interesting detail: It demonstrates that the lowest part of the shell is constructed in horizontal rather than conical courses of masonry, up to a certain level where the cantilevering rings were replaced by actual vaulting with radial joints.

For Filippo Juvarra's church of Superga near Turin, a preserved inventory of the timber employed in 1724 to erect the scaffolding of the cupola appears to indicate the use of a similar platform as Bernini's at Castel Gandolfo [7]. The inventory explicitly mentions four beams, each of almost 22 m length (7 Piedmontese trabucchi of 3.08 m). They are difficult to accommodate inside the dome with its diameter of slightly more than 22 m unless they spanned its entire interior and supported the principal platform, in a similar manner to Bernini's construction in Castel Gandolfo. In fact, it is stated in the archival record that the four beams were employed to carry a platform made from 110 boards, each 3.70 m long. This could not be anything else but the principal platform. In case the long beams were not used as the horizontal girders carrying that platform, they could at best have supported the platform vertically from below, again like in Bernini's design.

Further insight into the use of the platform at the base of the dome is provided by an interesting text written in the years between 1712 and 1725 by Giovanni Battista Nelli, then operaio of the cupola of the cathedral of Florence. The essay entitled Ragionamento sopra la maniera di voltar le cupole senza adoperarvi le centine was published posthumously in a collection of architectural texts in 1753 [8]. Even though Nelli's main topic is vaulting without formwork, he stresses explicitly the importance of solid scaffolding: "Therefore, instead of formwork, spacious, strong and commodious platforms are required in order to expedite the transport of all the materials required [9]." Nelli continues with a detailed description of the principal platform, which, in his case, is supported from the ground by a single strong wooden mast in the centre of the dome. Furthermore, Nelli states that the necessary trestles required to bring the bricklayers to their working place can then be erected on top of that solid platform.

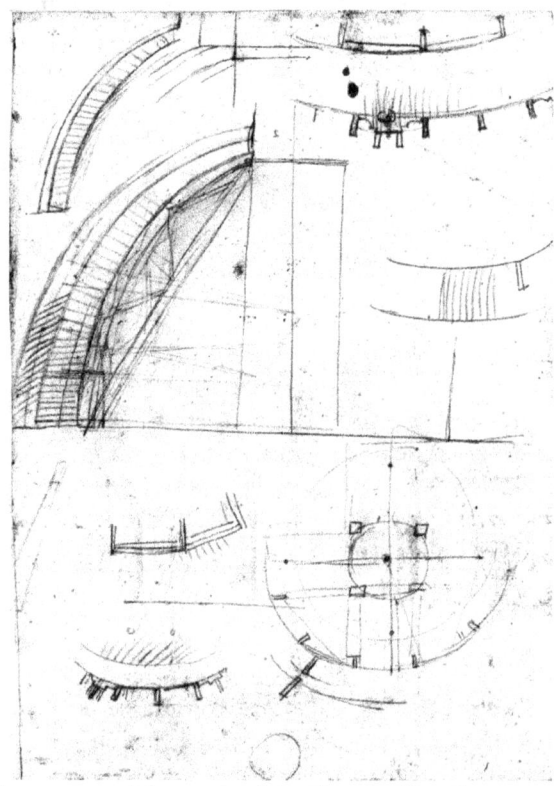

Figure 2: Sketches relating to the erection of the cupola of the Church of San Tommaso di Villanova in Castel Gandolfo. Gian Lorenzo Bernini, 1659. Biblioteca Apostolica Vaticana, Ms. Chig. P. VII, part I, fol. 13 v., here reproduced after Bauer/Wittkower 1931, plate 91, partly enhanced and redrawn by author.

Similarly, Leonhard Christoph Sturm, in his essay on church architecture cited in the beginning of the present article, also stressed the importance of a working platform, even in case of full formwork, for assembling the centring: "Such a centring cannot be erected unless the whole opening of the dome is covered completely or at least for the larger part of it, by a solid platform which is designed to carry a lot of workers and to permit them to walk on it and move the baulks around and lift them [10]." Sturm deserves a bit of mistrust since he also admitted that he had no personal experience with dome construction; furthermore, he suggested a fancy Serlio floor design for the working platform. In his figures, there is no word about direct vertical support of the platform from the ground. Rather, his work includes a plate showing a dome on a centring which rests on a platform that is supported from below by raking struts [11](Fig. 3).

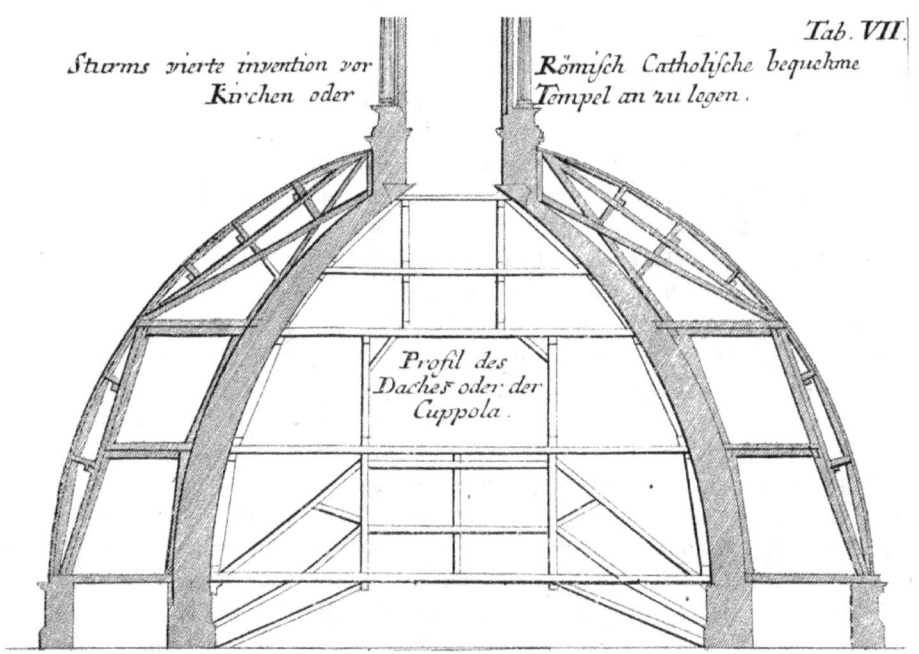

Figure 3. Section of a dome with the centering still in place. Engraving by Leonhard Christoph Sturm 1718, plate VII, detail.

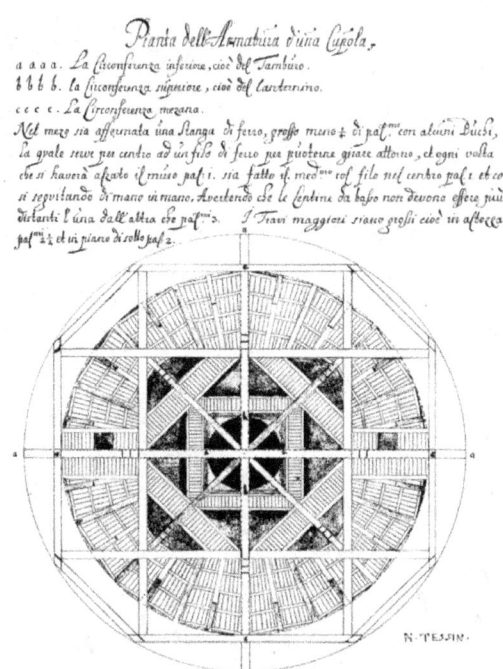

Figure 4. Zenithal view of a dome with scaffolding. Drawing by Nicodemus Tessin the Younger, Stockholm, Nationalmuseum, Cronstedt collection CC 749. Photo: Cecilia Heisser, public domain. Enhanced by author.

How to Build a Dome

Quite likely, the decision whether to construct the working platform in a free-spanning way or rather to erect it from the ground was strongly dependent on the absolute height above ground. For particularly slender cupolas, a free-span platform was probably more practical if more complicated to erect. It appears that Bernini's great contemporary Borromini in fact relied on such a platform when he erected the dome of Sant'Agnese in Agone in Rome, in 1655. The associated centring is depicted in an enigmatic drawing by Nicodemus Tessin the Younger [12](Fig. 4), who may have had access to original documents on the church during a study visit in Rome with Carlo Fontana in the 1680s. From the legend of Tessin's drawing, it does not become entirely clear whether the dome was built on formwork or not. On the one hand, the legend speaks about a dense arrangement of radial circular ribs, indicative of formwork; on the other hand, it also provides details about form control with a metal wire attached to an axis in the centre of the dome, related to free-hand erection. Be that as it may, the drawing definitely shows an interesting view of the working platforms, although it is not easy to understand: The drawing is apparently a reflected plan. At the base of the dome, a grid of orthogonal main beams (3 parallels in each direction) rests on the cornice via an octagonal array of wall plates. This grid of beams obviously constitutes the lowest level of the working platforms. Most of the boarding has already been translated to higher levels. Approximately at the height where the dome needs support and the masonry courses need to switch from horizontal to radial layers, a partly cantilevering platform is installed which rests on a star-shaped arrangement of beams spanning the entire width of the dome. Farther up there seem to be more platforms of the same type. Whether the various levels of platforms were to be supported vertically from below by struts is not entirely clear from Tessin's drawing. Small squares at the principal beams of the lowest platform probably indicate the ends of reinforcement lugs of the large beams, as suggested by the huge scantlings given in Tessin's legend (56 by 45 cm). The presence of the large platform (denoted by the term ponte reale) is attested by documents related to a trial of the contractors against the Pamphili family, the principals of the project: "First of all, one has to keep in mind that, in order to build this dome, a ponte reale was required which covered the entire extent of the dome, employing beams of unusual size, on which the winches for elevating the material were installed, which was then transported from hand to hand to the place where it was needed [13]." Indeed, Borromini himself noted that he left two rectangular openings at precisely that level "for the convenience of the masons who could easily move the material from inside to outside". Tessin's drawing shows two small platforms at the base level, which obviously served to install lifting devices (the only boarded parts of the lowest level of the scaffolding shown by Tessin).

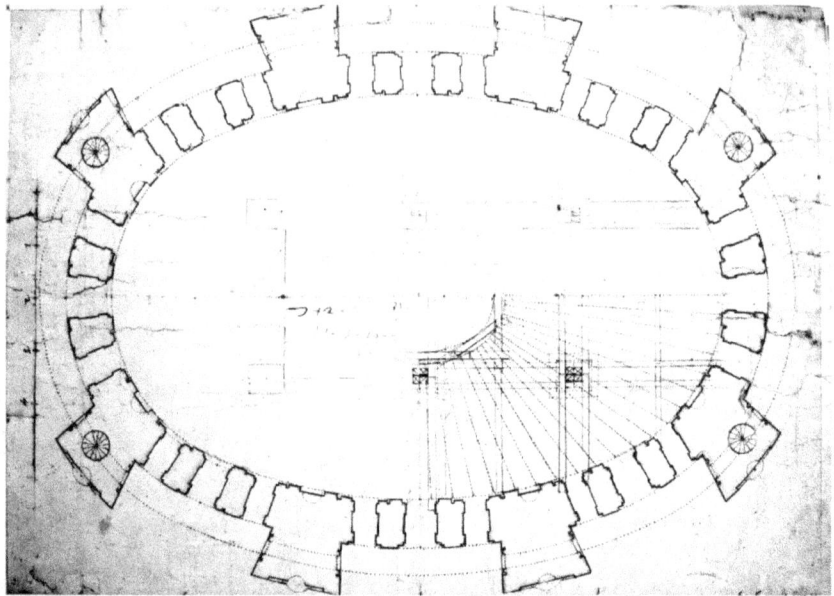

Figure 5. *Ground-plan of the drum of the oval dome of the basilica at Vicoforte di Mondovì. Drawing by Francesco Gallo, around 1729. Archive of the basilica. Photo: Martina Diaz, enhanced by author.*

The dome of the basilica of Vicoforte di Mondovì

So far, the reconstruction of the temporary works required for the domes has required a lot of guesswork. However, our assumptions are fully supported by the best documented construction site of a baroque dome, namely, the cupola of the basilica of Vicoforte di Mondovì in Piedmont [14]. That Marian pilgrimage church had already been begun in the late 16th century on a fancy large-scale oval plan with principal axes measuring 36 m and 24 m, respectively. However, the main dome to cover that oval nave was not even attempted then. The abandoned construction had to wait until 1728 when new plans for completion were prepared by Francesco Gallo. The dome was now to rise above a high drum added to the original project by Gallo. The falsework for the dome was erected in several steps between 1729 and 1731, interrupted by two winter breaks, but the masonry shell was finally erected swiftly in the fall of 1731, and de-centred in early 1732. The dome is unique in its oval plan. Shape control for an oval dome essentially requires formwork with a fully lagged surface.

In Vicoforte, the shape of the shell was defined by circular 'meridians' which, however, are not strictly radial in groundplan, nor orthogonal to the base oval (Fig. 5). The segmental shape of every single one of the eighty ribs carrying the formwork was constructed separately (or rather individually for every set of four identical ribs, due to symmetry), with different radii for each rib which were directly determined by the boundary conditions of a vertical tangent at the base and a uniform altitude at the oculus bearing the lantern (2 points plus one tangent uniquely determine the arch). The complicated centring was erected on a ponte reale that was once again resting on pairs of parallel principal beams. These beams in turn were supported by six temporary masonry piers rising from the floor of the church up to the cornice level. Fortunately, a whole set of drawings documenting the idea and the details of the temporary works has been conserved in the archives of the basilica.

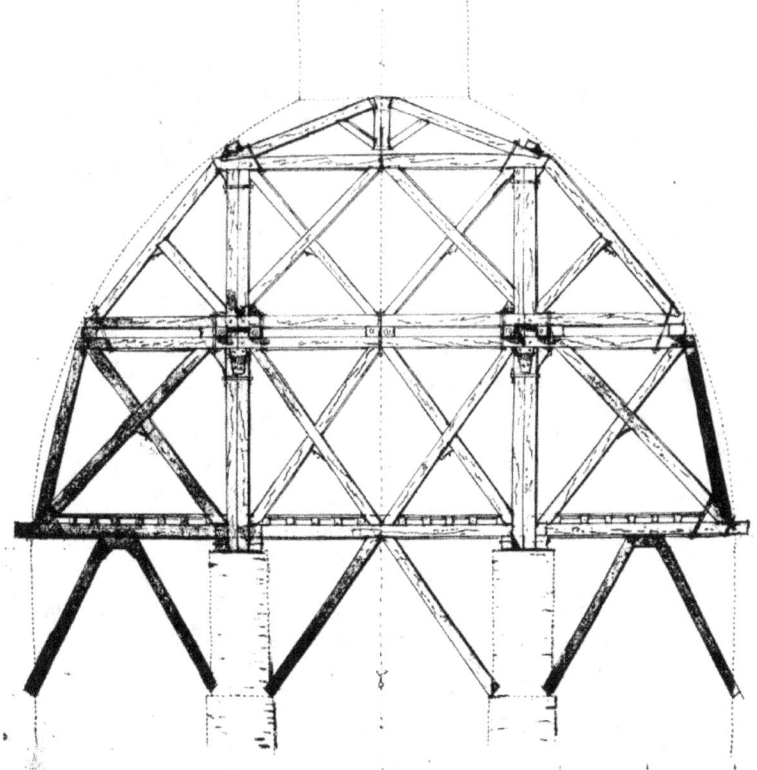

Figure 6. Transversal section of the centering of the dome of Vicoforte di Mondovì. Drawing by Francesco Gallo, around 1729. Archive of the basilica. Photo: Martina Diaz, enhanced by author.

How to Build a Dome

The drawings show that the masonry piers continued as wooden supports up to the masonry shell above the platform (Fig. 6). The truss supporting the formwork was diligently stiffened by diagonal windbracing. The ponte reale was obviously equipped with boarding throughout. This extremely robust and strong centring did not fail to attract the attention of contemporaries: The principle of Gallo's centring was published in two engravings a few years later in Giambattista Borra's treatise on vault erection.

Some 19th century sources

The great age of cupolas was already over when Gallo's dome was vaulted in 1731. However, a certain revival of dome construction happened in conjunction with the neo-classical style in the early 19th century. Among other projects, we note the various imitations of the Pantheon in Rome, e.g. Antonio Canova's memorial church in Possagno, the rotunda of Schinkel's *Altes Museum* in Berlin, or, last not least, the church *Gran Madre di Dio* in Turin, a relatively close copy of the classical model. For the latter project, a very interesting drawing has survived in the municipal archives of Turin [15]. The plan is dated February 26, 1829, and signed by the architect of the building, "professor Ferdinando Bonsignore" (1760–1843). According to the plan, the dome has (in modern units) a diameter of 21.21 m, and a perfect hemispherical shape. Like in Santa Maria della Salute in Venice, the dome is coffered, comprising 5 rings of 24 octagonal coffers each, or 120 in total. Evidently, the complex coffered shape required full lagging again. The drawing comprises two quarter sections of the dome, two quarter plans of the centring, and a plan for the layout of the lead cover (not discussed here).

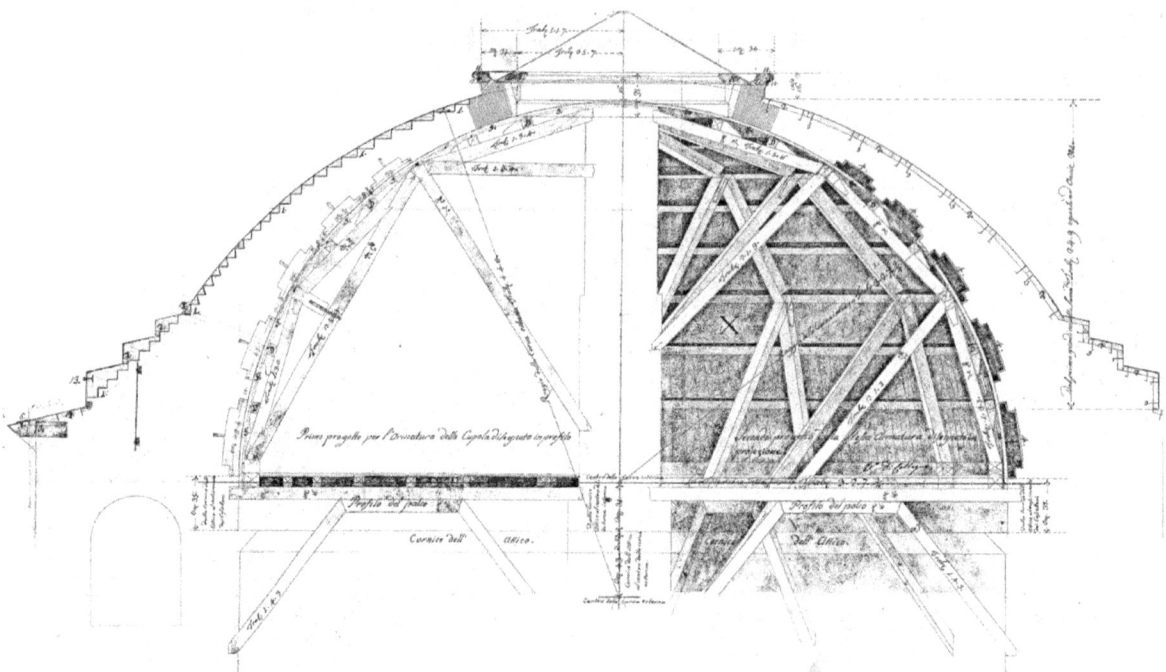

Figure 7. Two quarter sections of the dome of the church of Gran Madre di Dio, Turin. Drawing by Ferdinando Bonsignore, February 26, 1829, detail, enhanced by author. By kind permission of the municipal archives of Turin, TD 10.2.35.

The section (Fig. 7) shows two alternative layouts for the supporting truss. On the left side, the "first project" consists of twelve meridional ribs, each one composed of one raking strut supporting two arrangements of beams similar to a roof truss; on the right side, the circular section of the dome is approximated by three short straight beams, supported by oblique struts at each joint. In both cases, the actual lagging is carried by ring purlins running around the parallels of latitude of the spherical dome. The section also indicates the *palco necessario ai lavori inerenti all'armadura della Cupola*, or "platform required for the works erecting the centring of the cupola". The working platform is supported from below by a system of struts and straining beams.

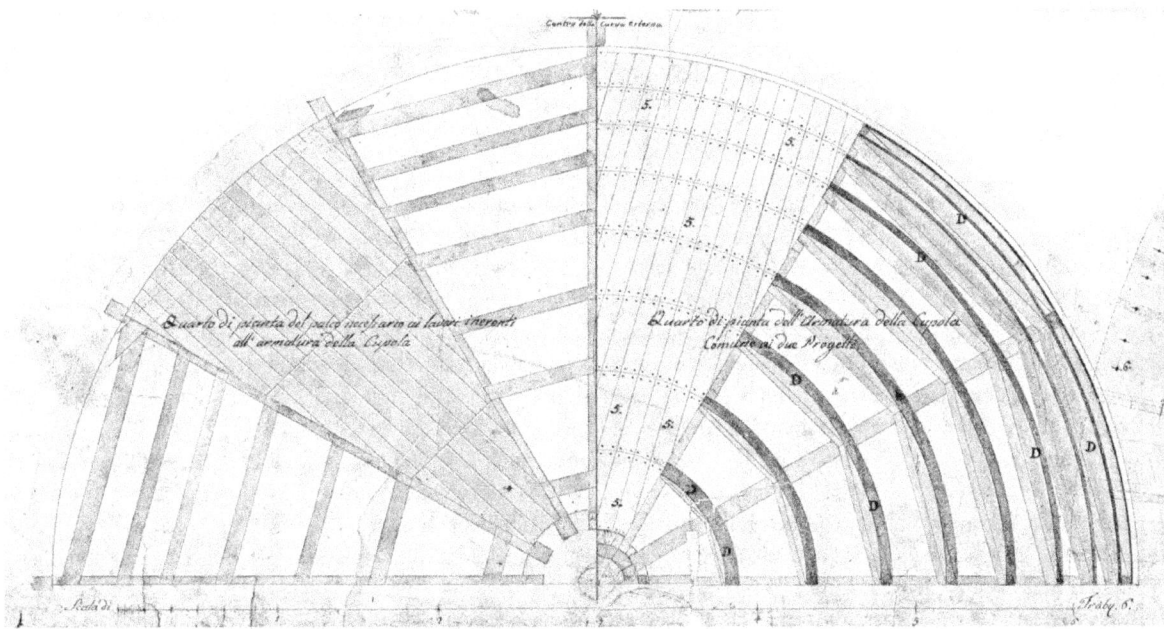

Figure 8. Two quarter plans of the dome of the church of Gran Madre di Dio, Turin. Drawing by Ferdinando Bonsignore, February 26, 1829, detail, enhanced by author. By kind permission of the municipal archives of Turin, TD 10.2.35.

The section and pertaining ground-plan (Fig. 8) reveal that these substructures rest on a central, axial temporary round pillar (according to the colour coding of the plan, a masonry one), which reaches up to the oculus and also receives the struts supporting the centres. The ground-plan shows (on the left side) the arrangement of the joists supporting the floor of the platform. On the right side, the layout of the lagging is shown, as well as the adaption of the ring purlins to the circular form by appropriate distance blocks. In the second project, the platform was to support the lower struts of the centring. Both of Bonsignore's designs are very similar to two centres for domes depicted in an almost exactly contemporary German treatise on carpentry (first edition printed in 1834), Georg Samuel Hörnig's *Sammlung praktischer Zimmerwerks-Risse*[16]. In Hörnig's designs, the platform again plays a key role, while it is supported by a central timber trestle or tower rather than a temporary masonry pillar.

Conclusions

The examples discussed have shown that the presence of a spacious and stable platform at the base of the dome was a key prerequisite for dome construction. Whether that platform was a free-spanning construction or directly supported from the ground depended on the special circumstances of the case. While free-spanning platform constructions were used for the cathedral of Florence and for the Panthéon in Paris (well known from Jean-Baptiste Rondelets engravings), it appears that the more common procedure – at least for cupolas at modest height above ground – was to build a temporary support for the platform in the middle of the domed space. Perhaps it is somewhat surprising that these temporary pillars were even built in masonry. The platform fulfilled a pivotal role in building the actual dome: It could be used to install lifting devices, move the material around on it, assemble the trusses and ribs of the falsework, and erect it. The construction of the actual supporting structure of the lagging was less important than one might expect at first sight, particularly since the loads to be carried by a dome built in subsequent circular ring courses of stones were rather moderate.

Acknowledgements

The friendly permit of the Municipal Archives of Turin to publish Figs 7 and 8 is gratefully acknowledged.

References

[1] B. Sgrilli, Descrizione e studj dell'insigne fabbrica di S. Maria del Fiore metropolitana fiorentina, Florence: Paperini, 1733. Plate IX.
[2] L. Ch. Sturm, Vollständige Anweisung, alle Arten von Kirchen wohl anzugeben, Augsburg: Wolff 1718. p.3: "Von dem Bau der grossen Kuppeln wissen die wenigste, sonderlich in Teutschland, was vor grosse und wichtige Bedencken dabey sind, viel weniger, wie man den Bau veranstalten müsse. In Büchern aber ist biß dato auch noch wenig dienliche Nachricht davon publiciret worden, und halten es die grössesten Italiänischen Bau-Meister noch unter ihren Arcanis."
[3] M. Piana, 'La cupola di S. Maria della Salute e i suoi restauri' pp.114-139 in: Storia e restauro. Studi, ricerche, tesi. Università IUAV di Venezia, Dipartimento di Culture del Progetto. Rome: Aracne, 2014.
[4] Cited after Piana, Cupola (note 3), p.136: "Per sicurazion di tale opera che non si rendi in nulla parte, però tute le armadure anderà da tera, cioè dal piano di essa chiesa fino sotto le cadene sudette sustenta detto pagiolo."
[5] C. Fontana, Il tempio Vaticano e sua origine, Rome: Buagni, 1694. p.321.
[6] H. Bauer and R. Wittkower, Die Zeichnungen des Gianlorenzo Bernini. Römische Forschungen der Bibliotheca Hertziana, 9, Berlin: Keller, 1931, pp.115–118 and plate 91.
[7] N. Carboneri, La reale chiesa di Superga di Filippo Juvarra, Turin: Ages, 1979, p.69 and p.188.
[8] G.B. Nelli, 'Ragionamento sopra la maniera di voltar le cupole senza adoperarvi le centine', pp.51-74 in B.S. Peruzzi, (Ed.), Discorsi di architettura del Senatore Giovan Battista Nelli, Florence: Paperini, 1753.
[9] ibid., p.57: "imperciocchè in luogo elle gran Centine, vi son da fare i Ponti amplissimi, forti, e comodi da trasportarvi per la più breve tutto il bisognevole della fabbrica."
[10] Sturm, Vollständige Anweisung, (Note 2), p.78: "Ein solches Bogen-Gerüste kan aber nicht wohl gerichtet werden / wenn nicht die Kuppel zuvor gantz / oder grössesten Theils mit einer solchen Decke überleget ist / daß die Zimmerleuthe in grosser Anzahl mit Handlangern darauf umlauffen / und die Balcken ziehen und heben können."
[11] Sturm, Vollständige Anweisung, (Note 3), plate VII.
[12] Stockholm, Nationalmuseum, Cronstedt collection CC 749.
[13] G. Eimer, La Fabbrica di S. Agnese in Navona. Römische Architekten, Bauherren und Handwerker im Zeitalter des Nepotismus, Stockholm: Almquist & Wiksell: 1970-71, vol.2, p.637: "In primis si deve considerare che per far detta cuppola è stato necessario a fare un ponte reale per levar tutto il vano della cuppola con legni non ordinarii sopra il quale si sono collocate le burbore per tirar sopra la robba, e da questo sono state transportate da mano in mano dove faceva bisogno."
[14] G. Zander, 'Su alcuni disegni di Francesco Gallo per le armature della cupola del Santuario di Vicoforte', Indice per i beni culturali del territorio ligure, vol.25/26, 1981, pp.19-30.
[15] Turin, Municipal Archives, Tipi e Designi, 10.2.35.
[16] G.S. Hörnig, Sammlung praktischer Zimmerwerks-Risse, 2nd ed., Dresden and Leipzig: Arnold, 1843.

Ornamental Hydraulics in the Arenberg Park of Enghien in the 17th Century: a possible link to Salomon de Caus

Gabriel Pirlet[1], Guido Schumacher[2] and Jean-Louis Vanden Eynde[3]
1: Architect, Rocaille Worker, Trainer
2: Art Historian-Musicologist, Organ Builder
3: Architect, Archaeologist, Professor UCLouvain

Background

The park of Enghien [1] was acquired in 1607 by Prince Charles of Arenberg and Princess Anne de Croÿ, when they wished to retire from the court life of Archduke Albert and Isabella, governors of the Spanish Netherlands in Brussels. They were 57 and 43 years old, respectively.

Figure 1: Portraits of Charles of Arenberg and Anne de Croÿ

Charles of Arenberg was chamberlain to Archduke Albert and carried out diplomatic and military missions on his behalf from 1598 to 1606. Anne de Croÿ was a lady in waiting of the Archduchess Isabella. She was the sister of Charles de Croÿ, governor of Hainaut, well known for the "Albums de Croÿ". When her brother Charles died, without an heir, Anne de Croÿ inherited all his titles and fortune.

Ornamental Hydraulics in the Arenberg Park of Enghien in the 17th Century: a possible link to Salomon de Caus

As soon as they settled in Enghien, the prince and princess undertook the creation of a new garden, instead of a new residence, and they gathered a fabulous botanical collection. Prince Charles died in 1616 and Princess Anne in 1635. After Charles's death, Anne ruled - Enghien alone and with an iron fist:

> 'In 1611, orange trees were brought from Brussels, grafts from Paris, firs from Spain as well as many plants and flowers. The provost from Tournai sent pheasants to populate the park, the abbot of Saint-Martin sent orange trees. Several flower gardens were created, and a gorgeous aviary filled with all kinds of singing birds [2] was built in one of them.'

> 'In 1620, the princess added new embellishments to her grotto. According to the records, this place was as interesting as it was rare and valuable since there were an organ, cuckoos, nightingales and other bird automata whistling and singing by means of water supplied to the grotto by a pump and pipes [3].'

Their eldest son, Léopold, suspected of having taken part in the *Nobles Conspiracy* against the Crown of Spain, was taken and kept in captivity in Madrid, where he died. He was posthumously pardoned and awarded the title of Duke.

The fifth son of Charles of Arenberg and Anne de Croÿ, Antoine (1593-1669), took over the office of chamberlain at the court of Brussels in 1606. When his father died in 1616, Antoine entered the Order of the Capuchin. He was also suspected of conspiracy and was sent into exile. He travelled around Europe and became friends with the Nuncio Fabio Chigi, future pope Alexandre VII (1655-1667). Antoine of Arenberg was staying in Rome at the time Alexandre VII had Bernini build Saint Peter's Square. When Antoine was cleared, he returned, became general of his order and designed the park of Enghien for his nephew (the son of Léopold) Léopold-François.

When Antoine entered religious life, he handed over all his belongings to his mother, including his library which was a witness of his knowledge of ancient philosophy, poliorcetics, mathematics, botany, astronomy and architecture. He owned, among others, The *Four Books on Architecture* by Andrea Palladio. He took the name of Father Charles of Brussels.

Hydraulic works in Enghien in the 17th and 18th centuries

We know about the "Fameux parc d'Anguien and its mouvements d'eau:" from the following sources

Written sources:

- The account of Father Charles of Brussels, designer of the Park, written around 1665 and intended for visitors [4]

- The description made by Nicolas Visscher, printer [5], to accompany a series of engravings printed in Amsterdam by Romeyn de Hooghe in 1685

- The Description du jeu des eaux des fontaines jaillissantes, bassins, réservoirs, conduits, décharges, aqueducs, écluses, written by the master of works of the city of Mons, H. Deseaublaux in 1787 [6]

- The Mouvement des eaux by the surveyor in charge H. Delulle in 1841 [7]

Illustrated sources:

- A series of supposedly anonymous engravings which should have illustrated Father Charles' account

- The series of etchings by Romeyn de Hooghe from 1685, entitled Villa Anguiana

- The plan associated with the Description by Deseaublaux in 1787

- The plan of the Mouvement des eaux by Delulle in 1841

Archaeological recording:

- Several investigations were led by architecture students from the Institut Supérieur of Architecture Saint-Luc in Brussels, supervised by the author of the project during the summers from 1993 to 1995

We consider that the topography and the geology of the park has not been altered since it was acquired by Charles of Arenberg in 1607.

The park is naturally supplied with water from a number of sources:

- From the East by the river Warelles, which has its source near the castle of Warelles at a height of 75 meters

- From the South East by the river Bourlotte, which has its source at the Champ du Cochet at a height of 77.5 meters at the top of the watershed, just before the Valley of the Senne, which flows into Steenkerque

- From the South by the stream of Maire-Bois (Tierne Farm, 85 m.) and by the stream of Balingue (Balingue Farm, 77.5 m.)

The last three join in Hoves and form the river Odru, which currently enters the park under the highway A8-E429 close to Park Farm. Collectively these sources represent a watershed of about five kilometres wide from East to West by six kilometres long from North to South.

Within the park, the valley of the Odru was landscaped with ponds which were, along the direction of flow;- the Grand Canal; the Mill Pond (adjacent to the castle farmyard); and the Dodane, the former city ditch. The lowest point of the park reaches 52.5 metres.

A small tributary from the East begins in the Duck Pond and feeds the Mirror Pond, the castle moat and the Mill Pond. Geologically, the ground consists of a five meter deep layer of silt, on a clay base fifteen meters deep, covering a sandy and permeable subsoil containing pressurized water. If a well is drilled, the water comes up nearly to the surface of the silt.

*Ornamental Hydraulics in the Arenberg Park of Enghien in the 17th Century:
a possible link to Salomon de Caus*

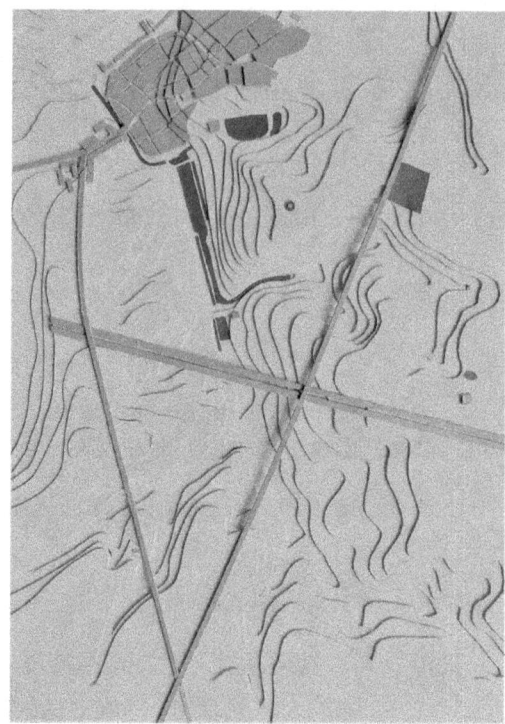

Figure 2: Plan and relief of the park of Enghien

Principles

Naturally storing water at the highest point

The Seven Stars circular basin was the first reservoir built in the park in 1661, at the highest point of elevation (72.5 metres). It has a surface area of 1018 m² and a water volume of 940 m³. It is fed by a spring, which seems paradoxical because of its altitude but is possible bearing in mind the screed of clay covering the layer of sand.

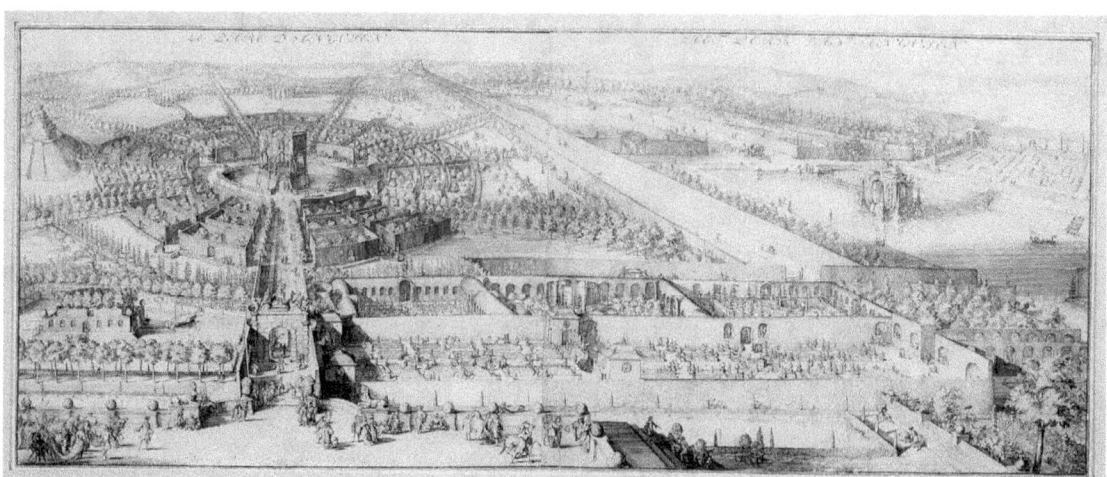

Figure 3: The pavilion of the Seven Stars and its circular basin, Romeyn de Hooghe, 1685

A large pond was created in 1673 on the Eastern plateau and was named after its designer, the canon Munoz [8] of Mons. It collects springs at an altitude of 70 metres and constitutes a water reserve of 200 x 250 x 2.5 m., that is 125,000 m³, whereas the highest point of the park is the Seven Stars Pavilion at an altitude of 72.5 metres.

Figure 4: The Munoz pond in the Eastern part of the park of Enghien, dried up nowadays

Artificially raising water

However, according to the engravings and records, two statues of river gods were situated at the entrance of the Seven Stars Pavilion and were pouring water from a vase into the basin. We have recovered the inlet lead pipes of these statues. For water to be pressurized at this location, it had to be coming from somewhere higher. A brick water tower was standing on the Western edge of the heptagonal park. At the top level below the roof, a lead water tank was filled by a pump that would draw water from a ditch, still visible today, and collect the overflow from the Seven Stars basin as well as some of the water from the heptagonal wood.

A similar water tower the South of the Mirror Pond still exists there but dates from the middle of the 18th century. The façades are brick linked by a crossed structure of beams on which lies a lead tank of 3.70 x 2.50 x 2 m., holding 18.5 m³. This tank was supplied from the Munoz pond by the principle of communicating vessels, whereas the one of the Seven Stars is above any possible natural supply.

Ornamental Hydraulics in the Arenberg Park of Enghien in the 17th Century:
a possible link to Salomon de Caus

Figure 5: The water tower called "le Fruitier"

Two types of pumps have been described in the texts. The first one specifically for the water tower near to the Seven Stars Pavilion:

> 'For the water of the tank be conducted to the top of the building n°48 by means of a first lower pump, then a second upper pump, into a lead lined tank located below the roof of the said building.
>
> A lead pipe comes out of this upper tank and brings water down from n°49 to n°50. There, a manhole and three taps lead water to three other lead pipes, one of which feeds the colonnade basin up to n°51 [9].'

The second description applies to the Mail:

> 'On the bottom of the Mail building n°68 was built a machine with a big wheel or drum moved by several men walking inside it. This movement activated three pumps to raise water through a pipe made partly of lead, partly of wood up to a lead tank, called the reservoir of this machine…'

The oldest elevated tank, dating back to 1636, is still hidden behind the fragmented pediments at the top of the Slave Gate and has a capacity of 4.90 x 4.90 x 1 that is 24 m³. This tank is fed by the overflow from the Seven Stars circular basin according to the principles of the communicating vessels. It is the reserve of pressurized water for the five enclosed gardens.

Figure 6: The Slave Gate, water tower.

Ornamental Hydraulics in the Arenberg Park of Enghien in the 17th Century:
a possible link to Salomon de Caus

Delivering pressurized water

The pipes conducting water from the tanks to its release are made either of:

- Lead, in the form of 4 to 6 millimetres thick lead sheets welded longitudinally

- Wood, as trunks drilled longitudinally, shaped to fit together and secured with iron rings

- Pottery, sections of glazed terracotta of about fifty-seven centimetres long, with male/female joints, sealed with mortar

The outflow pipes are different. They are made out of either masonry covered with stone flags or out of wood in the form of long crates held together by wooden harnesses, together with wooden flanges.

Figure 7: Excavation of the foundations of the Fountains Grotto, (Wallon Region, Directorate of Archaeology, under the supervision of te archaeologist Didier Willems, 1999)

Figure 8: Stoneware pipes with the Arenberg coat of arms. (Excavation of the Walloon Region, Directorate of Archaeology, under the supervision of the archaeologist Didier Willems, 1999)

Controlling the flow

The piping goes from one inspection chamber to another, each chamber being equipped with taps and switches:

> '36. Manholes with three taps for water intake through three leaden pipes around 32, 33 and 34 [10].'

These taps are made of brass or bronze and their heads are ring-shaped. They can also be found in the walls of the water towers, evidenced by continuous grooves in the masonry intended for the pipes and recesses inexplicable if not intended for the taps.

In the enclosed gardens, water was used sparingly and reused several times according to the principle of the communicating vessels for the Slave Gate, fountains in the Garden of Florets, circular in-and-out steps stairway and niches, and fountain in the Garden of Flowers.

Creating ornaments

Once water is pressurized, its simplest ornamental form is the water jet, vertical or oblique, shaped by a nozzle: straight, oblique or fan-shaped…Some nozzles are mobile, mounted on an axle and designed to move under the pressure of water, creating a spiral shaped water jet.

A water jets are used as *giochi d'acqua*, designed to trick visitors:

> 'The star-shaped cobblestones of this triumphal arch cover countless of fountains which surprise curious visitors and spray them when they least expect it [11].'

Ornamental Hydraulics in the Arenberg Park of Enghien in the 17th Century: a possible link to Salomon de Caus

'The second tap gives plenty of water by means of a lead pipe with eight little jets buried in the ground that covers the area of the theatre stalls, called the tricks, n°35 to surprise the spectators and make them wet.

A third tap, in the manhole n°34, can be turned on at any time to make water gush out of a lead pipe through five other jets hidden in the ground. It has the same tricky purpose.

In this manhole there is also a fourth little manual tap connected to a leather pouch which, leads to a copper nozzle that can be aimed in any direction to jet water up to seventy or even eighty feet. It was used to spray the people in the theatre, near the basin, at the tricks or anywhere nearby [12].'

Sometimes water is part of the architecture, like the small waterfalls of the circular in-and-out steps stairway linking the Garden of Florets to the Garden of Flowers:

'Going down the beautiful steps made equally of water and marble... Do not be trapped in the present, forget all about the past, look up behind and you will have the most varied and beautiful view you could imagine. The one of the two cabinets, the balustrade and the royal stairway with its facing gilded metal statues. You will also see sixteen niches divided by as many pilasters that support everything that lies above. The whole architecture is genuinely beautiful and its whiteness, highlighted by a background of azure mixed with green that appears to be many emeralds and turquoises, gives a very pleasant view on a large area and when the sun shines with all its brilliance, one's eyes can hardly bear its brightness.

Each niche is adorned with various ornaments made of shells or other curiosities from the sea and has in it centre a lion head fountain spilling water into a marble basin. The water flows by a marble canal alongside the alley with a gentle sound, which satisfies one's ear as much as the smell and the sight were satisfied in the garden, where the four lawns (I forgot to mention) are lined with low hedges and orange trees, as there can only be in the most beautiful gardens in the world [13].'

Figure 9: The circular in-and-out steps stairway between the Garden of Florets (above) and the Garden of Flowers (below)

Water jets can also be combined with statues. As stated previously, the statues of river gods at the entrance of the Seven Stars Pavilion were pouring water from the vases they were holding. At the centre of the Orange Trees Basin stands a fountain in typical renaissance style: a small water jet fills a round basin until water overflows around its entire circumference into a second basin held by the Three Graces, which overflows in turn into the larger basin.

> 'In front of the Pavillon du Mail stands the Water Spitter fountain, a more baroque figure: In front of this pavilion, on the avenue side, there is a statue above average height, with outstretched hands and raised head, who throws a big water jet from his mouth into a large, round stone basin, from which water overflows into another basin underneath [14].'

Figure 10: The Mail and the Water Spitter

Water flow can be used in a very unexpected way: a certain volume of water can only be displaced by moving an equal quantity of air. Therefore, we can compress air by filling in a closed volume with water or create a suction by allowing the water to flow out of a closed volume [15]. This principle was used at the top of Mount Parnassus, an artificial hill accessible through two helical paths (see Palladio) and topped by a hexagonal tower, topped itself by a statue of Fame:

Ornamental Hydraulics in the Arenberg Park of Enghien in the 17th Century: a possible link to Salomon de Caus

> 'At the top of this tower and mountain stands a Fame, who invites everyone with her trumpet that can be heard at great distances to come and see the place [16]

But the most remarkable hydraulic curiosity from the 17th century is the automata cabinet, of which we have two descriptions. The first one, is the more sensible:

> 'The second cabinet compares favourably with the first one and even outshines it by its ornaments and the beauty of the rock, embellished with many water flows. There are three castles, two of them shoot artillery fire and one defends itself bravely: there is no fire in these battle scenes, but water can hit the viewers if they are not careful. There are also six villagers who spend their time trying to shoot a bird on a long pole. The less skilful fail, others make it spin until one of them hits it. There is another (villager) shooting a duck, a water spitting dolphin and some whimsies.'

> 'In the grotto is also represented the fable of Pyramus and Thisbe [17] Pyramus is lying dead, and water gushes out of his wound up to the ceiling. Water jets also spring out of Thisbe wounds to form waterfalls, whose we mentioned before. The rock is dotted with several cupids mourning the death of the two lovers [18].'

The second description emphasizes the recreational use of water:

> 'A large garden divided in several beds of palms, whose branches and leaves interlace neatly and make many different patterns... At both ends of this garden are two lovely cabinets, even more remarkable from the inside where can be seen beautiful grottoes and fountains showing a thousand different moving scenes: uncommon statues representing Pyramus and Thisbe's death, all the technicalities of a castle siege, pole archery hunters, an aviary, etc. While curious spectators admire these rarities, fountains hidden under the cobblestones are switched on and wet them. And when they think of running out, others are ready to throw buckets of water in their faces...'

These works were popular in 1636 and the trend was introduced at the court of Brussels between 1605 and 1610 by Salomon de Caus, the hydraulics engineer invited by the archdukes Albert and Isabella. It should be noted that Charles of Arenberg and his son Antoine were chamberlains to the archduke, the first one until 1606, and the second between 1606 and 1617. It is reasonable to assume that the senior members of the court were knew and may have wished to emulate the latest innovations made in the archduke's gardens?

Searching for Precedents

Examples of hydraulic automata theatres from the 16th and 17th centuries are scarce. Only some visitors descriptions and drawings of the Italian gardens of Pratolino are known to us [19]. From the work of Alexander and Thomas Francini [20], who came from Pratolino to France, in Saint Germain-en-Laye, there only remain their descriptions and drawings to help picture spaces, which are now plain and empty. The same goes for the palatine garden of Heidelberg designed by Salomon de Caus, where architectural works are now emptied of the decor and the animated hydraulic automata, that made them famous. As for animated hydraulic mechanisms, some were restored or rebuilt by Rodney Briscoe; among others the organs in the gardens of the Villa d'Este in Tivoli (Rome) and in the Alcazar in Seville. Nowadays we can still visit the grottoes and the automata theatre in Hellbrunn (Salzburg, Austria), from 1613, and the precious pavilion of the villa Buonaccorsi in Potenza-Picena in the Marches (Italy), pre-1655. The last example, although the later, bears witness to an ancient tradition that was still alive in the second half of the 17th century, although slightly out of fashion. Nevertheless, by their size and the thaumaturgy of their movements, these works give an idea of what could have existed in Enghien. Moreover, their mechanics give valuable information on the craftsmen's skills and help us understand how manual or even pneumatic hydraulic automata work.

Salomon de Caus (Dieppe 1576- Paris 1626) travelled to Italy. Between 1597 and 1610 [21], he was invited in Brussels by the archdukes Albert and Isabella. He created several works in the Warande Park, known today as the Royal Park, below the palace of Coudenberg: basins, reservoirs, grottoes, rockery decors [22]. Between 1605 and 1610, he built a grotto animated with hydraulic automata.

> 'One goes up to this lovely place on a large square terrace with a big basin elevated on a pillar in its centre. From the basin flows clear water, which takes all kinds of shapes by means of the instruments fitted into the pipe. From there, one crosses a quite beautiful house, one room of which opens, through five monumental arched doors, onto a lawned terrace, from where is seen a gorgeous frontispiece with five porticos on a very wide platform artfully decorated with rockery and shells and adorned with twelve marble busts representing twelve Roman emperors.
>
> One reaches the place by a seven circular in-and-out steps stairway dotted with a countless number of pipes spraying water on people who do not expect it. The platform, cobbled in a rustic way, has nearly as many water jets as it has cobblestones. Each portico shows interesting rockworks, shells, water throwing figures of men, animals or fish. The one in the middle represents the Parnassus where all the figures throw water. In some of them, water is used to turn mills or to move working craftsmen as blacksmiths, sawyers, woodcutters, weavers and even cooks; at last, others present beautiful waterfalls decorated with birds, beasts and dragons throwing water. It is undoubtedly one of the most beautiful work of its kind, where water is handled with the most artistry and delicacy...[23]'

The account books also give an indication of the materials used [24]: 350 pounds of stones from England, 100 pounds of stones from India, a basket of sea plumes with eight big sea snails from Peru. The Frenchman Jean le Mesle provided beautiful stones, big orange shells, shells from Cape Verde, two hundred forty thousand mother-of-pearls and eight hundred porcelain shells. Guillaume Bernaerts delivered a wooden cyclops and three other stone figures, including a shepherd. Jérôme Duquesnoy delivered a few wooden figures, little birds. An organ was sent by the maker, Van der Elst. In 1611, Orpheus played a new music; birds moved in a new way. De Caus was paid six hundred pounds for motion generating devices [25]. All these descriptions give an idea of what could have been the decoration of the pavilion if it existed in the contemporary gardens of Enghien.

When he finished his project in Brussels, Salomon de Caus was hired between 1610 and 1612 by the Prince of Wales to work on the gardens of Greenwich, Somerset House and Richmond.

Later, he designed the Garden of Heidelberg for the Prince Palatine Frederick V, future king of Bohemia. After his employer's relocation, Salomon de Caus returned to France and benefited from the protection of the Cardinal of Richelieu.

Salomon de Caus has an impressive literary output. He published:

- la Perspective avec la raison des ombres et des miroirs (London, 1612)

- les Raisons des forces mouvantes avec diverses machines tant utiles que plaisantes ausquelles sont adjoints plusieurs desseign de grotes et fontaines (Frankfurt, 1615)

- Institution harmonique (1615), treatise on musical notation

- Hortus Palatinus (1620), in which he describes his creations and the other plans he had for the Garden of Heidelberg

- la Pratique et la démonstration des horloges solaires, avec un discours sur les proportions (1624)

Ornamental Hydraulics in the Arenberg Park of Enghien in the 17th Century: a possible link to Salomon de Caus

In his work *Les Raisons des forces mouvantes*, Salomon De Caus, describes a pneumatic organ driven by a hydraulic system. Paddle wheels operate bellows, which produce air. They also operate a musical drum, on which was "programmed" the madrigal score given by the Norman engineer *S. De Caus* [26].

There are a number of similarities between the features in Enghien and the work of Salomon de Caus:

- The circular in-and-out steps stairway described by Father Charles as a royal stairway made of marble and that has, by a very industrious way, as many fountains as it has steps...[27] Bramante invented the model when he designed the Cortile del Belvedere in the Vatican, but without fountains. Salomon de Caus made his own version in Heidelberg, where water flows from one basin to another, on every other step

- The aviary located on the island in the Mirror Pond, which combines the model of the Parnassus with the aviary in a clearing surrounded by birds

- The Mount Parnassus in Enghien, the double helical form of which was taken from Palladio but the topping of which, Fame sounding the trumpet, uses the depression principle explained by Salomon de Caus in his work *les Raisons des forces mouvantes*

- The cabinet of hydraulic automata, where the theory of *les Raisons des forces mouvantes* applies literally

- The solar clocks in the Garden of Florets, mentioned by Father Charles: in the centre of the four others (flower beds) are new solar clocks, surpassing the most ingenious: they show the time from many different sides, representing almost all the places in the world

- The Seven Stars Pavilion, which is both a solar clock and a perpetual calendar

The question remains, did Anne de Croÿ know Salomon de Caus? There is a clear connection: Salomon de Caus married Esther Pickart on March 19, 1606 in the parish church of Saint-Géry in Brussels. Their son, Guillaume, was baptized on February 24, 1607 in the parish church of Sainte Gudule [28]. Guillaume's godfather was Bertin Oudart Spinola and his godmother was Barbara Basselier. Bertin Oudart Spinola, count of Brouay, was married to Claire of Arenberg, seventh child of Charles of Arenberg and Anne de Croÿ.

Towards a Reconstruction

The inside dimensions of the automata cabinet in Enghien were 4,80 x 4,80 x 4,70 m. That is a cube with a side length of seventeen feet and each wall had a door or a window of seven feet wide (1,92 m.). Corners were then free to host four playlets, which redefined an octagonal central space with sides of eight feet. Therefore, the niches were four feet deep, that is +/-1,15m.

> 'The second cabinet compares favourably with the first one and even outshines it by its ornaments and the beauty of the rock, embellished with a lot of water movements [29].'

According to the text from 1665 written by the author of the project, Father Charles of Brussels, the pavilion was fully decorated and gave the visitor the impression of being inside a rock. The niches in the corners were probably arched and were animated by many water movements.

In these small grottoes were exhibited the popinjay or pole archery, Pyramus and Thisbe's death, a castle siege and, as described by Father Charles, a farmer shooting a duck and dolphins throwing water. In 1685, Nicolas Visscher described an aviary and its birds. Some unknown event might explain the change of decor in one of the niches but so could the disappearance of Anne de Croÿ's grotto, whose elements could have been recovered and reused.

The programme

The programme, through its scenes, affirmed the power of the patron: a scene illustrating the acquaintance with classical authors, a battle scene, a popular scene depicting the prince's skills with weapons and eventually a scene depicting nature. Indeed, the best way to show one's domination over things is to reproduce them. All these *intermezzi* ended with the watering of the spectators. That had two purposes: on the one hand, to break the enchantment before it was analysed and on the other hand, to exhibit a waste of water, symbol of life, as an "external sign of wealth".

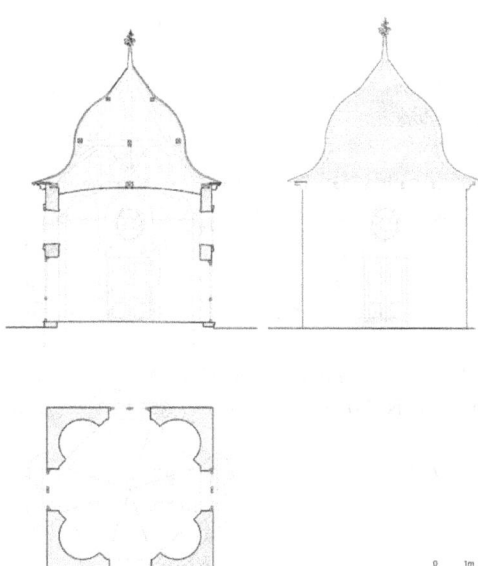

Figure 11: Plan, section and elevation of the Paintings Pavilion, one of the fourth identical pavilion on the corners of the Garden of Florets. On the plan is drawn the hypothetical layout of the niches in the Grottoes and Fountains Cabinet.

From the Pneumatics of Hero of Alexandria (1st century AD), translated in Latin by F. Commandino (1575)[30] and in Italian by B.Baldi (1589)[31] and G B. Aleotti (1647)[32], as well as from the descriptions written by Salomon de Caus in *Les Raisons des forces mouvantes* (1615)[33], we can say that two of the scenes were static and the two others were animated with automata.

Two of the grottoes were mainly animated by fountains: the castle siege and Pyramus and Thisbe's death. In contrast, in the ones showing the pole archery (popinjay) and the aviary, hydraulic automata needed a bigger space to house mechanisms, but also to allow someone to reach in and reset them.

The excavations carried out by the Walloon Region on the site of the Grottoes and Fountains cabinet revealed walls three meters high below the estimated level of the pavilion, suggesting a basement. This space was probably used to host

Ornamental Hydraulics in the Arenberg Park of Enghien in the 17th Century:
a possible link to Salomon de Caus

hydraulic mechanisms: valves, paddle wheels, gears and pulleys, as well as water and air tanks. A full resumption of the excavations may perhaps enable us to learn more about the water conveyance.

The scene of Pyramus and Thisbe's [34] death does not present any technical difficulty. It was probably a fountain statue, operated manually and occasionally by means of valves. The myth of impossible love was illustrated by fountains flowing from statues. Water gushes out of Pyramus's wound "*up to the ceiling. Water jets also spring out of Thisbe's wounds to form waterfalls, which we mentioned before. The rock is dotted with several cupids mourning the death of the two lovers* [35]". The author mentioned a fountain flowing up to the vault of the grotto, which corroborates the hypothesis of there being playlets.

The second grotto held: *"all the technicalities of a castle siege"*: *"there are three castles, two of them shoot artillery fire and one defends itself bravely: there is no fire in these battle scenes, but water can hit the viewer if he is not careful."* One can easily imagine a fortified castle being attacked by water jets from two armies of figurines and them striking back with water jets aimed not only at the attacking armies but also at the spectators. The water jets were probably simply operated by means of valves, manually and occasionally as it was for the previous scene.

The third grotto put on display a scene of: *"six villagers trying to shoot a bird attached to a long pole. Some, less skilful, fail, others make it spin until one of them hits it."*

The game of the "papegau/papegai" also called the "tir du Roy" or bird shooting was particularly widespread in this period. It was a good training exercise for crossbowmen. A target, originally a parrot replaced afterwards by a copy made of wood or cardboard, was placed on the top of a pole or a mast. Archers or crossbowmen had to use their skill to hit it and make it fall. The winner of the tournament was seen as a hero and received the title of "roy". He might represent a brotherhood or guild and receive its honours for one year. He was also exempted from some taxations, notably on wine.

For the record, the archduchess Isabella became "shooting queen" on May 15, 1615 in Brussels, and so was the princess Anne de Croÿ, the same year in Enghien. This shows the popularity of this game among all classes of society.

The representation of this game in its devoted grotto evokes the second problem raised in the second book of *Les Raisons des forces mouvantes* by Salomon de Caus: *"a drawing of a grotto, in which a ball is rising under the force of water"*. To this problem can be added the movement of one or several villagers, as it was suggested in the *theorem XL* proposed by G.B. Aleotti in his translation of the « *spiritali* » of Hero of Alexandria. It could also apply to the previous scene of the castle siege and explain why at one point spectators become the assailants' targets.

The descriptions of the fourth playlet or grotto of this cabinet are different from one author to another. In 1665, Father Charles of Brussels wrote the following: *"There is another (villager) shooting a duck, a water spitting dolphin and some other whimsies."*

Such a grotto is depicted in the second book of *Les Raisons des forces mouvantes* under *the problem XXVII*: *"A machine, by which will be featured Neptune, turning in circles around a rock, along with some other figures throwing water while turning".*

Figure 12: S. De Caus, Les Raisons des Forces mouvantes, Livre II, problème II

Figure 13: S. De Caus, Les Raisons des Forces mouvantes, Livre II, problème XXVII

Ornamental Hydraulics in the Arenberg Park of Enghien in the 17th Century:
a possible link to Salomon de Caus

In 1685, Nicolas Visscher describes an *"aviary, etc."* The decor of this grotto was probably modified. The aviary presents automata moved by a hydraulic organ, as proposed by Hero of Alexandria *(theorem XLIII and XLIIII* from the translation of the *"spiritali "* by G.B. Aleotti and by Salomon de Caus' applications, livre I, *problesme X et XVIII)*

'To imitate a natural bird song by means of water'

and XXIII

'To make several birds sing when an owl turns skyward and make them quiet when the owl turns around'

It is interesting to note that the problem had already been described by Philo of Byzantium at the end of the 3rd century BC and once more three hundred years later by Hero of Alexandria. The delightful trick of singing birds is a classic that was often used in creations of the 17th century: in the grottoes of the castle of Saint-Germain-en-Laye in 1598 [36], in the automata grotto of the castle of Outrelaize (Normandie) designed by Alexandre Francine in 1613 [37], not forgetting in the previously mentioned examples of the palace of Coudenberg in Bruxelles in 1605, and in Enghien in 1620.

New Attempts at a reconstruction

In February 2021, the organ builder Guido Schumacher (Eupen, Belgium) created a model of a "nightingale" according to the problems X and XVIII (in reality XXII) of book I from Salomon de Caus. Since there is no indication of scale in the treatise, he relied on the upper engraving of Plate XVIII for the proportions starting from a dimension that appeared realistic to him.

Here are the main dimensions:

- Upper tank 40 x 40 cm x 10 cm high

- Lower tank 40 x 40 cm x 12 cm high

- Distance between the 2 tanks: 30 cm

- Diameter of the pipe connecting the 2 tanks: 40 mm

- Diameter of the pipe feeding the "Rossignol" pipe: 20 mm

The trick is to create a small exhaust hole (3-4 mm) in the upper tank lid to prevent large air bubbles from rising up through the 40 mm pipe and then interrupting the singing of the nightingale. The nightingale sings for about twenty seconds.

The wind pressure, which results from the compression of the air by the water that fills in the upper tank, depends on the section of the connection tube between the tanks. It was 40 mm in the model built here. By opening this tube by about 30%, a constant pressure of about of a 75 mm water column is reached for 15 seconds. This pressure is in fact common in pipe organs. By fully opening the 40 mm tube, the pressure can even rise up to a 300 mm water column. In both cases the sound emitted by the whistle is continuous at first, while the pressure is still relatively low. The sound becomes modulating when the pressure is sufficient to cause the water level to ripple at the end of the whistle. The higher the pressure, the louder the sound and the more intense the modulation. The Rossignol pipe used in this test had a diameter of 12 mm and was 80 mm long.

To make a "Cuckoo", approximating the range of real cuckoos, one needs two pipes tuned at a minor third interval and with bodies of the following dimensions:

- Bass pipe: diameter 20 mm, length 113 mm
- Treble pipe: diameter 16 mm, length 96 mm

It could also work with narrower diameters, but in that case, the pipes should be a little longer. The organ builder does not know if real cuckoos all sing at the same pitch or if that pitch depends on the size of the birds. The recognizable characteristic of their song being the descending minor third, it can therefore be transposed.

The tap seen on the side of the downpipe was not recreated because the organ builder thought it was simply used to evacuate water. But in fact, it could/should also adjust the water flow and allow a better regulation of the water flow and pressure. The tank sides were made out of lead, which is relatively malleable. Salomon de Caus may have used a less pure alloy with some antimony or copper to harden it. These experiments show that the mechanisms hidden from the spectator were small and could be fitted under or behind the grotto.

Concluding Remarks

The need for a training course for ornamental plumbers

The Centre des Métiers du Patrimoine in la Paix-Dieu (Amay, Province of Liège, Belgium), supported by the Agence Wallonne du Patrimoine, wishes to organize a training course focused on ornamental plumbing. This discipline is sorely lacking in the restoration of hydraulic works in historic parks and gardens. Assistance was sought from hydraulic engineers of the Park of Versailles, who had themselves benefited from the teaching of André Heyen, an ornamental plumber from Liege. The Centre des Métiers asked the authors to think about the educational programme of this training course. We put forward the proposal that we should to start with the work of Salomon de Caus published in Frankfurt in 1615: *Les Raisons des forces mouvantes avec diverses machines tant utilles que plaisantes ausquelles sont adjoints plusieurs desseings de grotes et fontaines*. This treatise methodically expounds the physical principles and their implementation both mechanical and hydraulic. Starting with technically simple works, it gets more difficult as the "*problems*" get complex, ending with the creation of an organ as a final masterpiece.

The advantage of the Centre des Métiers du Patrimoine is that it can bring all the participants in a restoration project together: craftsmen (in this case the organ builder and a roofer specialized in lead roofing, a blacksmith, wood workers and a rocaille worker), art historians and archaeologists, architects and engineers, as well as the heritage administration. The training course is theoretical, practical and includes internships. It ends with the achievement of one of Salomon de Caus' problems.

There should be a place to display the masterpieces created in these training courses. Because of the significant network of hydraulic works in the Arenberg Park of Enghien dating from the beginning of the 17th century and the fact that there are still two ruined water towers, it was suggested that the city of Enghien might restore these buildings to exhibit the works made during the training courses and create a hydraulics museum in Enghien. The city of Enghien have agreed to take part in the project.

Ornamental Hydraulics in the Arenberg Park of Enghien in the 17th Century:
a possible link to Salomon de Caus

References

[1] Enghien is the second smallest city in Belgium and is located thirty-five kilometres East of Brussels, in the province of Hainaut, Walloon .
[2] LALOIRE Edouard, Histoire de la terre, pairie et seigneurie d'Enghien, Annales du Cercle Archéologique d'Enghien, T.VIII, 1914-1922, p.34.
[3] Idem, p.38
[4] F.Charles of Brussels, Briève description de la ville, chasteau et parc d'Enghien, Enghien, Annales du Cercle Archéologique d'Enghien, T.VIII, 1914-1922, pp.103-128.
[5] VISSCHER N., Villa Anguiana, Figure D, Amsterdam, 1685.
[6] DESEAUBLAUX H. Description du jeu des eaux des fontaines jaillissantes, bassins, réservoirs, conduits, décharges, aqueducs, écluses, AGR, Fonds d'Arenberg, Cartes et Plans n°1250.
[7] DELULLE H. Mouvement des eaux du Parc d'Enghien, 1861, AGR, Fonds d'Arenberg, Cartes et plans, n°1251.
[8] MATTHIEU E. L'étang Munoz à Petit Enghien, Annales du Cercle Archéologique d'Enghien, T.VI.1898/1907 pp.203-208.
[9] DESEAUBLAUX H. Description du jeu des eaux des fontaines jaillissantes, bassins, réservoirs, conduits, décharges, aqueducs, écluses, AGR, Fonds d'Arenberg, Cartes et plans n°1250.
[10] DELULLE H., Mouvement des eaux du Parc d'Enghien, 1861, AGR, Fonds d'Arenberg, Cartes et plans, n°1251.
[11] VISSCHER Nicolas, Villa Anguiana, Figure D, Amsterdam, 1685.
[12] DESEAUBLAUX H. Description du jeu des eaux des fontaines jaillissantes, bassins, réservoirs, conduits, décharges, aqueducs, écluses, AGR, Fonds d'Arenberg, Cartes et Plans n°1250.
[13] F.Charles of Brussels, Briève description de la ville, chasteau et parc d'Enghien, Enghien, Annales du Cercle Archéologique d'Enghien, T.VIII, 1914-1922, p.115.
[14] VISSCHER N., Villa Anguiana, Figure O, Amsterdam, 1685.
[15] This principle is used in Cassel, Park Wilhemshöhe, 1696. When many waters are released, two statues holding a trumpet or a horn start blowing until the water reserve is empty.
[16] F. Charles of Brussels, Briève description de la ville, chasteau et parc d'Enghien, Enghien, Annales du Cercle Archéologique d'Enghien, T.VIII, 1914-1922, p.127.
[17] OVIDE, Les métamorphoses, 4,43-166. Alors l'arme qu'il portait à la ceinture, il se l'enfonça dans le flanc et aussitôt, mourant, la retira de sa blessure brûlante. Il resta à même le sol, couché sur le dos et son sang jaillit bien haut. Ainsi lorsqu'un tuyau se fend, à cause d'un défaut du plomb, en sifflant il lance avec force à travers un petit trou de longs jets d'eaux qui déchirent et frappent l'air.
[18] F.Charles of Brussels, Briève description de la ville, chasteau et parc d'Enghien, Enghien, Annales du Cercle Archéologique d'Enghien, T.VIII, 1914-1922, p.113.
[19] ZANGHERI L. Pratolino, *il giardino delle meraviglie , documenti inediti di cultura toscana* volume X. Firenze, Gonnelli, 1987.
[20] MOUSSET A., *Francine créateurs des eaux de Versailles*, Paris,1930.
[21] DUVIVIER Ch. Notice sur un séjour de Salomon de Caus à Bruxelles, Revue d'Histoire et d'Archéologie, T.1. pp.1-17., Brussels, Devroye, 1860.
[22] MAKS Ch. S., *Salomon De Caus 1576-1626*, Paris, Jouve & Cie, 1935.
[23] HENNE and WAUTERS, *Histoire de Bruxelles*, T.III, p.330 et suivantes.
[24] De MAEYER D., *Albrecht en Isabella en de schilderkunst*, Bruxelles, 1955.
Acquis de la chambre des comptes C5547,5549 et Chambre des Comptes 27505, 27506, 27509, 275010.
[25] VANRIE A., De Philippe II à la fin du XVIII siècle, in *Le Palais de Bruxelles, huit siècles d'art et d'histoire, Bruxelles*, Crédit communal, 1991.

[26] In that respect, see the reconstruction made by André Heyen, Guido Schumacher and Yves Weinand, within a study of the « Technische Hochschule » of Aachen, Germany www.orgel-Schumacher.com abbaye de Michaelstein(D) machines fantastiques de Salomon de Caus.

[27] F. Charles of Brussels, Briève description de la ville, chasteau et parc d'Enghien, Enghien, Annales du Cercle Archéologique d'Enghien, T.VIII, 1914-1922, p.111.

[28] Register of births, Parish of Sainte Gudule, from 1605 to 1608, fol.V° in : MAKS Ch. S., Salomon de Caus, 1576-1626, Doctoral thesis, University of Leiden, 1935 p.129

[29] F. Charles of Brussels, Briève description de la ville, château et parc d'Enghien, Enghien, Annales du Cercle Archéologique d'Enghien T.VIII, 1914-1922, p 115.

[30] COMMANDINO F., *Heronis Alexandrini Spiritalium Libe*r, Urbino ,1575.

[31] BALDI B., *De gli automati overo machine se moenti*, libri due, Venezia, 1589.

[32] ALEOTTI G.B., *Gli artificiosi e curiosi moti Spiritali di Herone*, Bologna 1647.

[33] DE CAUS S., Les Raisons des forces mouvantes avec diverses machines tant utiles que plaisantes ausquelles sont adjoints plusieurs desseings de grotes et fontaines. Francfort, 1615.

[34] Pyrame et Thisbé, deux jeunes babyloniens s'aiment mais, leurs parents s'opposant à leur union, ils ne peuvent se voir que secrètement par une fissure du mur qui sépare leurs maisons. Ils décident un jour de fuir ensemble et se donnent rendez-vous au pied d'un mûrier, en dehors de la ville. Thisbé arrive la première mais, effrayée par une lionne, elle s'enfuit en abandonnant son écharpe qui est mise en pièces par l'animal. A son arrivée, Pyrame croit que son amie a été dévorée par la lionne et se poignarde de désespoir. Thisbé, revenue sur le lieu de rendez-vous, trouve Pyrame mort et se poignarde à son tour. La légende affirme que c'est pour cette raison que les fruits du mûrier qui, jusqu'alors étaient blancs, devinrent rouge sombre de tant de sang versé.
ROBERT P., Le Petit Robert des noms propres, Paris, 1994, p.1699.

[35] F. Charles of Brussels, Briève description de la ville, chasteau et parc d'Enghien, Enghien, Annales du Cercle Archéologique d'Enghien, T.VIII, 1914-1922, p.113.

[36] GOUJON A., *Histoire de la ville et du château de Saint-Germain-en-Laye, suivie de recherches historiques sur les dix autres communes du canton*, Saint-Germain ,1829.

[37] FAISANT E., Un témoin de la gloire des Francini : La grotte à automates du château d'Outrelaize. In Bulletin monumental, T. 175-4, Paris, 2017.

William Colles (1702-1770), Kilkenny Mayor, Entrepreneur, and Marble Necromancer

Dermot O'Dwyer
Department of Civil, Structural and Environmental Engineering, Trinity College Dublin

Introduction

William Colles (1702-1770) was an entrepreneur, inventor, mill owner and building contractor who lived in Kilkenny in the south-east of Ireland. William was the son of an English surgeon who moved to Kilkenny about 1690 and, through a friendship with the 2nd Duke of Ormonde, bought large estates of confiscated property [1]. In about 1730 he established the Kilkenny marble mills, which remained in the control of the Colles family until they closed in 1920. He was the grandfather of Abraham Colles (1773-1843) a leading Irish surgeon of the nineteenth century after whom the Colles fracture is named [2].

William Colles was a man of many talents. In his early life he was reputed to have written poetry, and throughout his life he participated in local administration. He was an Alderman, the city Treasurer, and was twice Mayor of Kilkenny city [3]. He owned and constructed a number of mills for the production of flax, flour and marble. He was central to the attempt to extend the navigation of the river Nore upriver from Inistioge to Kilkenny. William Colles was also a contractor who build many fine houses in the Kilkenny area and was contracted to construct the Kilkenny canal and the replacements for some of the principal masonry bridges across the Nore following the destruction of most of the bridges over the river in the flooding of 1763 [4]. He is was also identified as the person who constructed the current, third, Tholsel in Kilkenny [5]. A Tholsell is an Irish term for a type of building that functioned as a town hall, toll house, and courthouse. In this case it was the town hall raised on arches.

Many of William Colles' enterprises were significant and are worthy of detailed study. This paper concentrates on his development of machines to cut, bore and polish marble. Colles' work in this field is celebrated in Kilkenny, which is known as "The Marble City", but is little known elsewhere. It predates similar developments in the working of stone in the United Kingdom. Colles is a classic example of a highly talented entrepreneur who developed, or progressed, a technology largely independently of others, but who was part of the simultaneous technical advancements of the early industrial revolution.

Working of Stone in Ancient Times

Stone has been worked since antiquity [6]. It is appropriate to consider the achievements of the Egyptians, Greeks, Romans and other ancient civilisations before expressing amazement at the achievements of construction workers and engineers in later centuries. For example, Fontana's achievement in moving the obelisk in Rome about a quarter of a mile in 1590 is put into context by the more significant achievement of the Romans who transported it from Egypt and the achievements of the Egyptians who quarried, erected and transported it and other obelisks [7]. Similarly, Colles's achievement in boring water conduits from solid Kilkenny marble (a variety of limestone that appears black when polished) should be assessed against the Romans' ability to turn large columns on a lathe, the evidence of Roman and Byzantine water-powered mills for sawing stone, and later medieval marble mills [8].

The reference to Roman quarrying technology, and to Pliny in particular, is of particular relevance to William Colles's mechanical developments for the cutting, boring and polishing of Kilkenny marble. In his *Encyclopaedia of Natural History* Pliny describes the process by which marble is sawn [9].

> "The cutting appears to be done by iron, but really it is achieved by sand: the saw exerts pressure on the sand along a very thin line and it is the sand's movement to and fro that actually does the cutting."

This is the same basic process, albeit mechanised, that was used in Colles' marble mills.

Colles's other innovations

William Colles is most famous for his marble works, but he introduced innovations in many other industries. Tighe's 1802 account of the marble mills, written after William Colles' death, contains a description of his development of the machinery used in the mill, stating that, "He first tried a model in a small stream, and finding it succeed, took a perpetual lease of the marble quarry" [10]. This development and testing of prototype mechanisms is in keeping with the description of Colles' other works. Tighe described Colles as,

> "A man of great mechanical abilities and abounding in a variety of those eccentric schemes which mark original genius, though success only, in the eyes of the world can stamp them with rationality; one of which was an attempt to make dogs weave linen by turning wheels; …Such was the impression that his abilities made on the common people, that to this day his feats are proverbial among them, and they speak of him as a necromancer…He amused the populace by various devises, such as that of a musical instrument which played by itself, as it floated down the stream of the river, and many others,…He applied himself to the construction of useful machinery for different purposes; and invented a water mill and an engine for dressing flax, simple and efficacious, but now no longer used." [11]

Colles' interest in flax was significant. His entry in the dictionary of Irish biography describes the machinery he developed for processing flax and notes that in 1751 he was awarded a Dublin Society prize for the most flax grown [12]. Tighe states that,

> "Alderman Colles raised great quantities of flax; he invented a water machine to take off the bows of flax, and break them at the same time, which was attended by children, without danger of damage; and also an engine into which he threw the broken bows, and separated the light chaff from the seed, which was brought out finished and perfectly clean for sowing; these machines were plain and simple: he used a Dutch oven for drying Flax; and had it dressed by hand, instead of a mill, which he found injurious and wasteful." [13]

Colles also constructed, and operated, a three-storey flour and oat mill at Abbeyvale, a few hundred yards down-river from the marble works at Maddoxtown [14]. This mill was the largest industrial building in the country at the time of its construction in 1762 [15]:

> "…mills three stories high, whereby oats are shelled, winnowed from the shellings, ground to meal and shifted, by a regular and easy course of progression, and wheat is in like manner ground and completely dressed into flour, all of which are of a new, firm and convenient structure, many parts of which were invented by the petitioner [Colles] on much and long attention after several expensive trials with kilns and granaries necessary; and are fully supplied with water at all seasons of the year, and so much out of the reach of floods that they receive but little damage from the last extraordinary floods in that part of the country [16]."

The mill at Abbeyvale was one of a number of very large multi-storey mill buildings constructed in Ireland around this time, including the large mill at Slane completed in 1766 [17]. The development of these mills predate Arkwright's mill by about thirty years [18].

Detailed Description of Colles' marble works

The Kilkenny marble mills founded by William Colles continued in family ownership for many years and finally ceased operations in 1920 [19]. The full history of the marble works is described in detail by Hand [20]. Hand's thesis also covers William Colles' involvement in the Kilkenny Canal [21]. Kilkenny had a long history of marble quarrying and production and the Black Quarry, which was used as a source of marble by Colles was described by Bishop Roth writing in the seventeenth century [22].

William Colles' letter to the Dublin Society

The first mention and description of William Colles' marble works is his letter to the Dublin Society, a society that had been established in July 1731 by the members of the Dublin Philosophical Society with the aim of promoting improvements in animal husbandry, manufacturing, the sciences and other useful arts. The Dublin Society was later renamed the Royal Dublin Society, the name it is known by today. The letter, or a summary of it was written directly into the minutes at a meeting in February 1731. The text reads,

> "As I have seen a Paper inviting all Persons to comunicate to the Dublin Society, Improvements in Arts, & Manufactures, I thought it might not be unacceptable to let them know, That there being within ¼ of a Mile of Kilkenny, a Quarry of Excellent black marble, beautifully Veined, with great Variety of White, if tedious & expensive Methods of sawing, & polishing which, in the common Way, rendered the Trade for the said Marble less extensive that it might be, if wrought by a more expeditious Manner, induced me to try some Experiments in relation to sawing the same by an Engine, w[hi]ch appearing practicable, I obtained an Interest in the Quarry, & some Mills, on the River near adjoining thereunto, where I have now ten saws, w[hi]ch are moved by Water, & going night & day, & saw the Marble more true, and expeditious, than it can be otherwise be done, And have also erected an Engine that grinds the s[ai]d Marble with sand so as to fit it for polishing, whereby I employ upwards of thirty Hands in polishing & finishing Marble Chymney Peices, Tables, Cisterns, Mortars, Tombstones, & w[hi]ch I sell at more reasonable Rates, then heretofore they were sold.
>
> These Experiments Led me farther to the trying others, in relation to the Boring Pipes of the s[ai]d Marble, w[hi]ch I have brought to such Perfection, that I can bore Pipes of any reasonable Length from 2 to 10 inc[he]s Diam[eter]. fit for conveying water under Ground, or from the tops of Houses, for the Latter of which uses, some of them are set up at Mr. Sean Tighs Merch[an]t on Ushess Quay [23]."

This letter succinctly describes the nature of Colles's mechanical innovations in sawing, grinding and boring marble. The letter refers to the mills being adjacent to the quarry but may also refer to Colles's marble works at Abbeyvale, also called Maddoxtown. Colles is thought to have started his marble works at Maddoxtown, which is about two miles down-stream from the Black Quarry, in the 1730s [24].

Unfortunately, there are no surviving drawings of the machinery developed by Colles to saw, bore, true, grind or polish marble. However, Ramelli's 16th century text (Fig. 1), shows an animal-powered marble saw [25] that probably shows the key components of Colles' saw. Such illustrations show the key concepts involved in a mechanism but would not be sufficiently detailed to build the machine unless one was an experienced mill wright. This illustration shows a gearing system, a crank, a saw frame and a method of adjusting the motion of the saw frame relative to the stone that is being cut. Ramelli's text also contains images of similar water-driven saws.

Figure 1: Animal-powered marble sawing mill from Ramelli 1588 [25].

The boring of marble pipes was probably achieved by a mechanism similar to the machine for boring wooden pipes illustrated by Isaac de Caus, (Fig. 2) [26]. A surviving piece of Colles' marble piping shows a female socket similar to the coupling system used in the timber pipes shown in the background of de Caus' illustration [27]. In practice it is difficult to build a machine to bore long pipes with precision. Similar machine arrangements were used to bore or true cannons but it was not until Wilkinson improved boring technology in 1775 that precision boring of metal cylinders was achieved [28]. Colles' achievement in being able to bore limestone pipes is impressive.

Two further accounts of the marble mills at Maddoxtown and of Colles' mills adjacent to the Black Quarry date from the time of William Colles. The first comes from *A tour through Ireland...by two English Gentlemen*, William Chetwood and Philip Luckombe, which was published in 1748 [29]. Their account of Colles' mills, was summarised by Tighe but is short of technical details. They describe seeing warehouses full of "such a diversity of chimney-pieces, cisterns, buffets, vases, punch-bowls, mugs of different dimensions, frames for looking glasses, pictures, etc." This combined with a newspaper advertisement for Colles' marble products confirms that he was turning a variety of smaller marble items at his mills [30]. Production of these products and of the bored pipes seem to have ceased by 1802 when William Colles' grandson, Richard Colles, had ownership of the mills.

Figure 2: Illustration from Isaac de Caus' text on mechanical devices [26]

Hugh Dawson's account of Colles' grinding Mill

The second account of the marble mills is far more detailed. This account is by Hugh Dawson, from near Kilkenny, who gave a description of the Black Quarry and the marble mills to the Physico-Historical Society. This society was founded in 1744 but was wound up by 1752. It was founded with the objective of publishing county surveys covering industry etc. Dawson's unpublished account is held in the Robinson Library in Armagh. The following extracts are taken from Hand's account of these manuscripts [31].

Dawson states that Colles had erected mills on the river Nore where iron saws moved by two waterwheels sawed the marble "with Much more Expedition and Truer than by Mens Hands". This adds little to the picture painted by Colles himself, however; Dawson also includes an interesting description of Colles' system for truing the marble blocks. This involved first grinding one surface of the block, presumably a cut face, flat. Dawson states that the blocks were:

> "Ground to bring it truly out of winding by a waterwheel fixed horizontally which is moved by a current passing by one side of the wheel while the rest wades in an eddy:"

Horizontal waterwheels had been in use in Ireland since early Christian times but Dawson's description of the wheel being moved by a current passing by one side of the wheel while the rest wades in an eddy may not tally with the traditional horizontal mill described by Rynne [32]. The text suggests that the mill building straddled a channel or mill race. Above the waterwheel,

> "Is a circular bed of the sawed marble of 27 feet in diameter laid level and bedded in sand on which are laid a parcel of marble Slabbs Less than the Breadth of the Bed w[hi]ch by an arm Passing from the Shaft are Moved Round over the Bed and by a Small wheel fixed on said arm are so Shifted to and from the Center That they Every round change their Possision so as to Make no Hollows In ye Bed"

Both the blocks that make up the circular bed and the "parcel of marble Slabbs" are being ground flat. This would have required considerable care when laying the blocks in the circular bed in the sand bedding. If the arm that projected from the drive shaft had simply dragged the upper blocks in a circle over the bedded blocks, then the lower blocks would not have been ground flat. Instead circular paths would have been worn into the lower bed and the bottom surface of the upper blocks would have been ground to match. For the mechanism to work it was essential that the blocks moved both circumferentially and radially. Figure 3 shows a simple potential mechanism that tallies with Dawson's description. A is the shaft, shown rotating anti-clockwise, B is the arm, C the small wheel, D is a "wheel" that surrounds the shaft but doesn't rotate and E is a belt or chain to which the marble pieces are attached. There are many other methods of achieving the required motion: there is no implication that the mechanism described is the method Colles used.

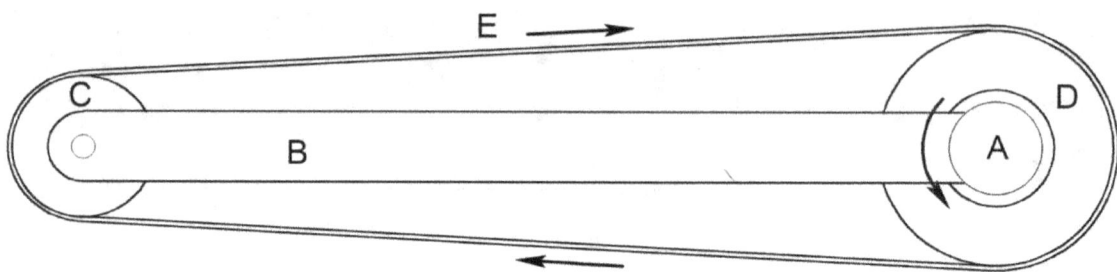

Figure 3: Mechanism to move blocks both radially and circumferentially.

Dawson commented on the time that it took to grind the blocks,

> "the Bed Stones take a fortnight or 3 weeks to Rubb Sufficiently but the Upper Stones w[hi]ch are always In Motion are Rub'd twice in a Day Here the Marble after being Rub'd on the fface is alsoe Rub'd on the Edges w[hi]ch Makes It as True as if Chiselled and free from Gapps:"

This makes sense as the upper blocks are constantly in motion whereas the lower bed is only ground when the upper blocks pass. Dawson also describes the next step in the process whereby the blocks are honed to remove the sand tracks. This confirms that, as one would expect, a sand slurry was used in the trueing process and further, that Colles did not attempt to rotate the upper blocks as they were dragged across the lower bed. Dawson describes the honing process thus,

> "where 3 or 4 Peices being Laid Side by Side there and fixed on Each of Them a piece of a Kind Greet Stone Called Black Hone found at a place called Chappel in the Libertys of ye City of Kilkenny which being moved by ye Mills Backwards and forward the whole Length of the Marble Slabb Takes out ye Tracks of the Sand & Leaves the Marble Smooth Skin'd and Black:"

The description of the grit stone as been moved back and forward by the mill implies that a crank was used to turn the rotary motion of the mill wheel into a back and forward motion in much the same way as the saw frames would have been moved. Dawson describes a final polishing sequence with emery and putty that is again driven by the mill and which achieves a finish on the flat surfaces, "no hand being able to give it a Higher Gloss that this do's" in a manner similar to the honing machine.

Dawson also comments on

> "Boring Pipes of Marble…and Making Pumps for all w[hi]ch uses they are Excellent He alsoe Turns & Polishes Marble Punchbowls, by the Same Mills. and Has thereby Made Engines for Extinguishing fires In one Solid Stone of 2ft 2in Long 1ft 10 In Deep and 1 foot 1 Inch Broad w[hi]ch Is a Valuable Improvement of these Kinds of Engines being less In Bulk more Durable Incapable of Rusting & Subject to fewer Repairs."

Dawson too makes the comment that Colles' mills were his "own Invention & Contrivance".

This combined with the description of the items in Colles' warehouses by the English gentlemen confirms that Colles was using a lathe to turn marble items and was still boring pipes in the late 1740s. The description of the pump cylinder block is interesting.

Tighe's account of 1802

The final description of the eighteenth-century mills from comes from Tighe, who published his account in 1802. William Tighe's *Statistical Observations relative to the County of Kilkenny* was addressed to the Dublin Society and was described as being made, for their consideration and under their direction [33]. By this time William Colles had died, and the mill was being run by his Grandson Richard Colles. Tighe gives a lot of information on the operation of the mills in general including details of costs and the quantities exported abroad. By Tighe's account some course work was finished at the Black Quarry close to the city with some of the blocks being split in the town by handsaws and a little polished work and the cutting of tomb-stones. However, the principal work was carried out at the marble mill at Maddoxtown, requiring the marble to be drawn across John's bridge. Tighe noted that the Carrara marble was also being imported and worked at the marble mills.

Tighe describes the Maddoxtown marble mill as having one wheel, ten feet in diameter and with twelve floats or ladles. A crank at one end of the wheel's shaft moved a frame containing twelve saws, and it was described as doing the work of about twenty men. Another crank at the other end of the wheel's axis drove a frame of five polishers, which did the work of about ten men. There was a further note that Mr. Colles had recently fitted a frame beneath the polishers with eight saws. The power of the machine was found to the equal to the additional frame. Tighe reported that the strength of the stream did have some effect on the working of the wheel, but not much, and the mill could reliable do the work of forty-two men daily. Tighe reported that the mill is stopped at night as constant attention was required to supply the saws with sand and to attend the polishers. This differs from the original night-and-day descriptions of William Colles and the English gentlemen. Tighe gives information on the marble saws stating that,

> "The saws are made of soft iron, and last about a week; they are constantly supplied with water and sand, the latter is taken out of the bed of the Nore, well washed and riddled until nothing remains but very fine and pure siliceous particles. A saw cuts ten inches in the day, and twelve when the water is strong; it would require two men to do the same with a hand-saw [34]."

His description of the honing and polishing of the marble describes three stages: first boys use a cove-stone, a brown sandstone imported for Chester; next it is polished with a hone-stone, which is "a smooth nodule of the argillaceous iron ore, found in the hills between Kilkenny and Freshford", and finally it receives its last polish in the mills with rags and putty.

By 1802, it seems that the production of smaller turned items and the boring of pipes had ceased. Tighe's account is of particular importance with regard to Colles' marble water pipes and may explain this sessation. Tighe states that Colles' plan to supply Dublin Corporation with, "bored marble tubes, as pipes for distributing water through the city, was defeated only by a combination of pump-borers and other mechanics, who rose in a mob and destroyed them on their arrival".

This reaction to the progress of the industrial revolution predates the activities of the Luddites in the 1810s by many decades.

Although William Colles, the founder of the marble works, was clearly particularly mechanically gifted it would be a mistake to assume that his facility with machines was the key to the development of the mills. Kilkenny had a very long tradition with milling that dated back to the coming of the Normans in the twelfth century. Part of the original Norman contingent comprised Flemish speakers who brought milling technology from the Netherlands [35]. Later accounts of the mills, and a study of the ordnance survey maps, show that the mills at Maddoxtown were repurposed many times by the later family, showing that the expertise to modify the works as necessary was available [36].

Sherrard and Brownrigg 1777 Survey of Millmount

Figure 4 shows a 1777 survey of the marble works at Maddoxtown by Sherrard and Brownrigg [37]. The survey was commissioned by William Colles (1745-1779) who designed and built Millmount at Maddoxtown and who was the son of the original William Colles. William Colles (1745-1779) was educated at the Shackelton's Quaker school in Balitore [38].

Figure 4: Survey of Mill-Mount house and the marble works by Sherrard and Brownrigg [37].

The survey shows three mill buildings. The mill on the left was the marble sawing mill. That in the centre was originally an old flour mill associated with an Abbey that was located at Maddoxtown. It is shown in William Petty's Down Survey of 1655-1656. The mill on the right of the survey is William Colles' three-storey Abbeyvale mill. By the time Tighe was writing in 1802 the central mill was a paper mill and later accounts showed that it was subsequently used as the main marble sawing mill. The marble works remained in the ownership of the Colles family until 1920 when the mills closed. The mills are in the parish of Clara and a recent social history of the parish gathered accounts of the last workers at the mill and their families [39]. They described a system of horse-drawn railways operating between the mills and the publication also includes a sequence of photographs taken from the marble mills' catalogue that illustrate some of the stages in the quarrying, transportation and sawing of the marble shortly before the marble works closed.

William Colles' contractor and the Kilkenny canal

William Colles was also a successful building contractor who constructed many fine houses and bridges in the Kilkenny area [40]. The skills necessary to operate a quarry, undertake building works and develop machinery are complementary.

William Colles was at the heart of promoting, planning and constructing the Kilkenny canal. He was involved with the canal throughout the second half of his life and his death coincides approximately with the end of substantial works on the canal [41]. The history of the Kilkenny canal has been detailed many times but deserves further work on its engineering aspects. This paper gives brief summary of William Colles' involvement.

The river Nore, which flows through Kilkenny, is navigable upriver from New Ross as far as Inistioge but from Inistioge to Kilkenny the river has sections of shallow rapids. Despite this shallow-draft flat bottomed local "cots" were used to ferrying goods by hauling them upriver [42].

Colles was actively involved in an official capacity in promoting the canal [43]. He was not a disinterested party because his marble produce was being transported to Dublin and exported to England and Scotland. A canal from Killkenny to Inistioge would have been of considerable advantage in reducing Colles' transportation costs as it would have facilitated transporting the marble by river to New Ross or Waterford and would have tied Kilkenny to the Barrow Navigation and Dublin. In the absence of the canal, Colles had to transport his goods by road to Leighlinbridge, which was on the Barrow navigation. The construction of the Kilkenny canal would also have linked the Black Quarry, and his mills adjacent to the quarry, with the marble mills about two miles down-river at Maddoxtown.

Construction of the canal was begun in 1755 to the design of William Ockenden, who was involved in many of the canals being constructed at the time [44]. Unfortunately, Ockenden proved to be a poor engineer and many of his canals experienced problems. At the time the Irish Parliament wanted to minimise the amount of the surplus funds that were sent to the English Exchequer. Thus, the political circumstances facilitated the initial funding.

Ultimately the Kilkenny canal was a failure and the general consensus is that one of the primary causes was the decision to start work on the canal to Kilkenny and work downriver. Colles is usually blamed for pushing this approach. The reason given at the time was that construction costs would be minimised as the quarries and other building materials were located in Kilkenny and the cost of moving materials would be minimised. The second reason, which is often surmised, is that once substantial works had been completed it would be easier to lobby for additional funds so that the money already spent would not be wasted.

The actual progress in the construction of the canal is difficult to assess. There is clear evidence of a level of purposeful misreporting of progress as part of the overall attempts to continue to secure funding [28]. However, there is physical evidence to support the accounts that the canal was constructed as far as Bennetsbridge. Thus, the map that was published in the Journal of the Irish House of Commons, (Fig. 5), can be taken as an accurate account of the route of the canal and the location of the locks that were constructed [45].

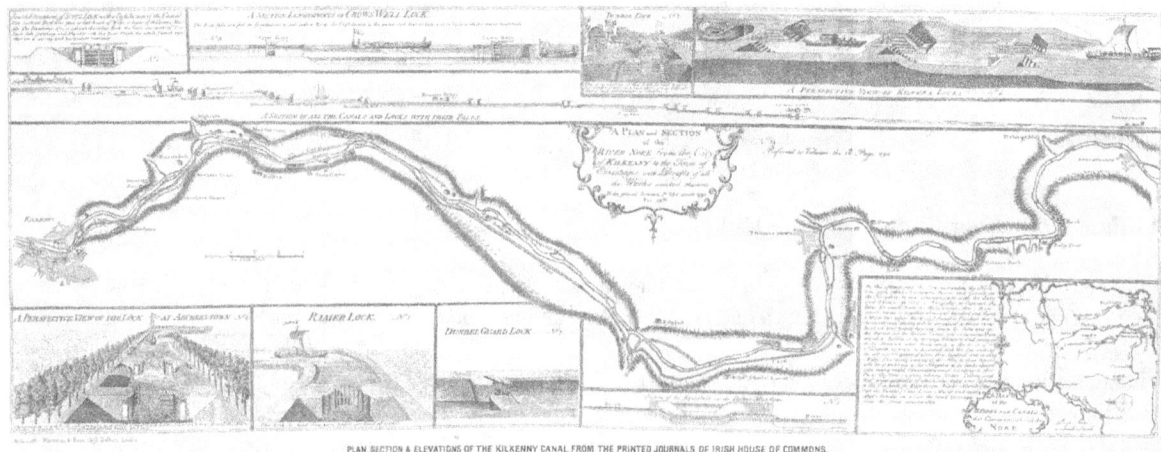

Figure 5: Plan of the Kilkenny Canal from the Journal of the Irish House of Commons [41]

In 1763 there was a very significant flood on the Nore that washed away most of the masonry arch bridges including both of the Bridges in Kilkenny city [46]. The Clara Heritage Society publication contains a letter written by William Colles immediately after the flood that lists the bridges that were swept away and commenting on the damage to the canal [47]. Today the Nore has a collection of particularly fine masonry arch bridges that were all constructed to replace those lost in 1763 [48]. The considerable expense of replacing so many bridges took from the funding that was earmarked for completing the canal and Colles, who was the contractor for the canal, and George Smith, who had taken over as the engineer for the canal on Ockenden's death, were diverted to the reconstruction of the bridges.

Figure 6: Green's Bridge designed by George Smith and constructed by William Colles.

Green's Bridge, (Fig. 6), which is based on Palladio's drawings of the Bridge at Rimini, was designed by George Smith and constructed by William Colles [49]. This was the event that appears to have ended the canal works.

Although contemporary accounts state that the canal works were not adversely affected by the flooding this may not be correct. Furthermore, the major flood of 1763 was followed by a number of severe floods in the next few decades [50]. The locks were largely of earthen construction and David Chapman's estimate for a renewed and extended navigation in 1787, which is included as an appendix in Tighe, includes significant work repairing and dredging the canal [51]. Chapman's commentary also highlight that some aspects of the original canal were poorly designed.

Conclusions

William Colles was an entrepreneur of considerable mechanical ability. He applied this ability to flax production, milling flour and oats and working marble. His mechanical skills also extended to contracting and he is associated with the construction of significant bridges and buildings. His development of marble water pipes was notable not only as a novel technology, but also as an early example of "Luddite" resistance. Colles' inventions are significant as an example of how new building technologies emerged in the eighteenth century. When writing about the construction of three-storey mills in Ireland in the 1760s, when large scale mills were few, Cullen commented that they could be regarded as the precursor of the textile mills which became common in the 1770s and later [52].

Colles was a particularly skilled mechanic. However, others were also progressing rapidly in the same fields at the same time. Thus, the reason for the rapid technical developments were not due to Colles' mechanical genius alone. The machines that Colles developed were not all new inventions and the early reference to his production of a music-playing machine, when taken with some of the other mechanisms he produced, suggest that he may have had access to one of the sixteenth or later mechanics texts that showed such machines. This is not to detract from Colles' skill, but simply to acknowledge that his skill-set was not unique.

In Colles' letter to the Dublin Society written in 1731, he makes the point that his motivation in developing his marble mill was the realisation that he could reduce the cost of producing finished marble by developing machines. This clearly shows the role of economics in allowing the adoption of new technologies. Similarly, his construction of the three-storey mill at Abbeyvale was a direct response to the introduction of the Irish Parliament's corn bounties in 1758. The example of William Colles' reinforces the idea of the spontaneous development or reinvention of technologies when the economic conditions are ripe.

References

[1] K. M. Lanigan & G. Tyler, eds., *Kilkenny: its architecture & history*, Kilkenny: An Taisce, Kilkenny Association, 1977.
[2] C.J. Woods in *Dictionary of Irish Biography*, ed. by James McGuire and James Quinn, 9 vols., Cambridge: Cambridge University Press, II, 2009, pp. 665-666.
[3] W. Tighe, *Statistical observations relative to the county of Kilkenny: Made in the years 1800 & 1801*. Dublin: Graisberry and Campbell, 1802.
[4] Dictionary of Irish Architects, entry of William Colles' works, retrieved 02/04/2021, https://www.dia.ie/architects/view/1187/COLLES-WILLIAM%5B1%5D%2A#tab_works; Lanigan and Tyler, Kilkenny, (Note 1).
[5] Archaeological Impact Assessment, Proposed Restructuring and Renovation of the Tholsel (RMP KK019-026061), High Street/St Mary's Lane, Kilkenny, Kilkenny Archaeology, 18E413, December 2018; Lanigan and Tyler, *Kilkenny*, (Note 1).

[6] J.P. Oleson, ed., *The Oxford Handbook of Engineering and Technology in the Classical World*, Oxford: Oxford University Press, 2008.

[7] D. Fontana, *Della traspolieatione dell'obelisco Vaticano et delle fabriche di papa Sisto V. Libro Primo*, Rome, 1590.

[8] Pliny the Elder, *Natural History, A Selection: Translated with an Introduction and notes by John F. Healy*, London: Penguin Classics, 2004; P. Kessener, 'Stone Sawing Machines of Roman and Early Byzantine Times in the Anatolian Mediterranean', *ADALYA*, XIII, 2010, pp. 283-303; F. V. Sánchez Martínez et al., 'Marble cutting processing used in 16th century for building the "El Escorial" monastery altarpiece', *Procedia Manufacturing*, 13, 2017, pp. 1381-1388.

[9] Pliny the Elder, *Natural History*, (Note 8).

[10] Tighe, *Statistical observations relative to the county of Kilkenny*, (Note 3).

[11] *Ibid*.

[12] Woods in *Dictionary of Irish Biography*, (Note 2).

[13] Tighe, *Statistical observations relative to the county of Kilkenny*, (Note 3).

[14] C. Rynne, Industrial Ireland 1750-1930: An Archaeology, Cork: Collins Press, 2006; L.M. Cullen, 'Eighteenth-Century Flour Milling in Ireland', *Irish Economic and Social History*, vol. 4, 1977, pp. 5–25.

[15] Woods in *Dictionary of Irish Biography*, (Note 2).

[16] Cullen, 'Eighteenth-Century Flour Milling in Ireland', (Note 14).

[17] Rynne, Industrial Ireland 1750-1930, (Note 14); Cullen, 'Eighteenth-Century Flour Milling in Ireland', (Note 14).

[18] Rynne, Industrial Ireland 1750-1930, (Note 14).

[19] J. C. J. Murphy, "The Kilkenny marble works", *Old Kilkenny Revue*, ii, 1949, pp. 14–19.

[20] Tony Hand, "'Doing Everything of Marble wch can be Done with it': some descriptive accounts of the Kilkenny Marble Works", *Irish Architectural and Decorative Studies*, 11, 2008, pp. 74-99; T. Hand, *The Kilkenny Marble Works: A Family Business Enterprise*, PhD Thesis submitted to the History of Art and Architecture Department, Trinity College Dublin (TCD Thesis 9650.2), 2012.

[21] Hand, *The Kilkenny Marble Works*, (Note 20).

[22] W. Carrigan, and Most Reverend Dr. Brownrigg. *The History and Antiquities of the Diocese of Ossory*, 4 vols., Dublin: Sealy, Bryers & Walker, 1905.

[23] W. Colles, 'Letter of William Colles of Abbeyvale to the [Royal] Dublin Society', RDS Archives, *Minute Book 1*, 3rd February, 1731/2.

[24] Tighe, *Statistical observations relative to the county of Kilkenny*, (Note 3).

[25] Agoarino Ramelli, *Le Diverse Et Artificiose Machine Del Capitano*, Paris, France, 1588.

[26] Isaac de Caus, *Novvelle invention de lever l'eau plus haut que sa source avec qvelqves machines movvantes par le moyen de l'eau, et un discours de la conduite d'icelle ...*, Londres, 1657.

[27] Hand, *The Kilkenny Marble Works*, (Note 15).

[28] E. A. Forward, 'The Early History of the Cylinder Boring Machine', *Transactions of the Newcomen Society*, 5:1, 1924, pp. 24-38.

[29] W. R. Chetwood and P. Luckombe. *A Tour Through Ireland. In Several Entertaining Letters.: Wherein the Present State of That Kingdom Is Consider'd... By Two English Gentlemen.* London: J. Roberts, 1748.

[30] Advertisement by William Colles, *Dublin Journal*, Tuesday 7th, 1734, p. 2.

[31] Hand, *The Kilkenny Marble Works*, (Note 15).

[32] Rynne, Industrial Ireland 1750-1930, (Note 14).

[33] Tighe, *Statistical observations relative to the county of Kilkenny*, (Note 3).

[34] *Ibid*.

[35] Carrigan, *The History and Antiquities of the Diocese of Ossory*, (Note 22).

[36] The Clara Heritage Society, *Clara County Kilkenny: A Social History of People and Places in the Parish*, Kilkenny: The Clara Heritage Society, 2006

[37] T. Sherrard and J. Brownrigg, *A Survey of Mill-Mount in the Parish of Black-Rath, Barony of Gowran and County of Kilkenny: The Estate of William Colles, Esquire*, (recently gifted to the Geology Museum, Trinity College Dublin,

Mrs. Alexandra Mallaghan, whose uncle, Michael O'Dwyer, owned The Rocks, Millmount and the disused marble works in the 1960s), 1777.

[38] M. Leadbetter, *Leadbetter Papers*, London: Richard Davis Webb, 1862.

[39] The Clara Heritage Society, *Clara County Kilkenny,* (Note 36).

[40] Dictionary of Irish Architects, (Note 4).

[41] R. Delany, *Ireland's Inland Waterways: Celebrating 300 Years*, Belfast: Appletree Press, 2004; N. Stopford, 'The Kilkenny Canal 1755-1786', *Old Kilkenny Review*, 1954, pp. 25-29; P. Watters, 'The History of the Kilkenny Canal', *The Journal of the Royal Historical and Archaeological Association of Ireland*, vol. 2, no. 1, 1872, pp. 82–98.

[42] Delany, *Ireland's Inland Waterways,* (Note 41).

[43] Watters, 'The History of the Kilkenny Canal', (Note 41).

[44] Delany, *Ireland's Inland Waterways,* (Note 41).

[45] Watters, 'The History of the Kilkenny Canal', (Note 41).

[46] P.M. Egan, *The Illustrated Guide to the City and County of Kilkenny*, Kilkenny: P.M. Egan, 1884.

[47] The Clara Heritage Society, *Clara County Kilkenny,* (Note 36).

[48] T. Ruddock, *Arch bridges and their builders, 1735-1835*, Cambridge: Cambridge University Press. 1979.

[49] *Ibid*; A. Palladio, *I quattro libri dell'archittettura [The Four Books of Architecture]*. Venice. 1570.

[50] Tighe, *Statistical observations relative to the county of Kilkenny,* (Note 3).

[51] *Ibid.*

[52] Cullen, 'Eighteenth-Century Flour Milling in Ireland', (Note 14).

The Behaviour of Tile Vaulted Structures in Spanish Military Engineering

Cinta Lluis-Teruel, Iñigo Ugalde-Blázquez, Josep Lluis i Ginovart and Zahra Hadji
Universitat Internacional de Catalunya. School of Architecture UIC Barcelona

Introduction

Art historians George Roseborough Collins (1917-1993) [1] and Turpin Chambers Bannister (1904-982) [2] made known in the *Journal of the Society of Architectural Historians* (1968), the unique typology of construction with *bóvedas tabicadas* and brought them closer to the international debate of architectural history. They treated with special emphasis Rafael Guastavino Moreno (1842-1908), a key figure in understanding the transfer of the cohesive construction of European tradition to the United States of America, produced after the Chicago fire (1871).

In the *Essay on the Theory and History of Cohesive Construction* applied especially to the timbrel vault (1892) [3], he defined cohesive construction as one that is carried out by assimilating different materials through the use of mortars, compared to what he calls mechanical construction, which works by gravity and demonstrated knowledge that the construction system was used in the Corona de Aragon region [4], on the Iberian Peninsula, since the 14th century [5].

The Duke of Belle-Isle and the Count of Espié had known in their crusades of the War of Succession (1701-1715) *la voûte à la Roussillon*. These tile vaults were well received throughout Europe as well as in Spain (where they were well-known since the 14th Century) thanks to the dissemination of the texts of the Count of Espié (1754) and Pierre Patte (1777). We determine what use the tile vaults had from the point of view of military construction, favoured by their supposed mechanical qualities, and what the repercussion was among Spanish military engineers in the 18th Century, on the base that the location of the projects carried out through this technique by military engineers in Eastern Spain coincides with the places where a specialized workforce already existed, and that people in those places already knew such construction technique. In Spain, the work of the Count of Espié had more influence among the architects of the Royal Academy of San Fernando, than among the Military Engineers of the Academy of Mathematics of Barcelona.

The study is limited to the interpretation of the graphic representations of the projects of the engineers belonging to the Collective Catalogue of the Collections of Maps, Plans and Drawings of the State Archives of the Ministry of Culture, and the Collection of Maps, Plans and Drawings of the General Archive of Simancas, as well as the map library of the Ministry of Defence together with the consultation of the General Archive of Segovia, the General Military Archive of Madrid and the Naval Museum of Madrid.

The Rediscovery of the voûte à la Roussillon or volta de maó

Félix François, Count of Espié, had presented a Project of Military School (1751) to Louis XV of France (1710-1774), later published as *Réflexions du Comte sur l'établissement de l'École militaire* (1756) [6]. In this parenthesis, he published *the Manière de rendre toutes sortes d'édifices incombustibles* (1754), which he said, provided instruction for the use of tile vaults to safeguard strongholds from enemy the fire [7] (Fig. 1a).

The Spanish translation, *Modo de hacer incombustibles los edificios* (1776), was made by Joaquín de Sotomayor Cisneros y Sarmiento (f. 1776) [8]. Despite this, the tile system was questioned by the Académie Royale d'Architecture (1747) owing to the demand of the Capuchin Fathers for the construction of the Montauban convent, even though they recognized that the technique had already been introduced by this Order in the convent of Castelnaudary in Languedoc [9]. The discussion of monolithism and the thrust of tile vaults between the Count of Espié and the answer of Ventura Rodríguez (1717-1785) in the *Censura de la trabajo de Sotomayor* (1776) has been widely disseminated [10] [11]. The fire behavior of these vaults was to be one of the arguments in favor of the so-called cohesive construction by Rafael Guastavino Moreno (1842-1908) in the *Essay on the Theory and History of Cohesive Construction* applied especially to the timbrel vault (1892) [12].

This last defined it as the one that is carried out by the assimilation of different materials, compared to what he calls mechanical construction that works by gravity, usually used by military engineers [13] (Fig. 1c).

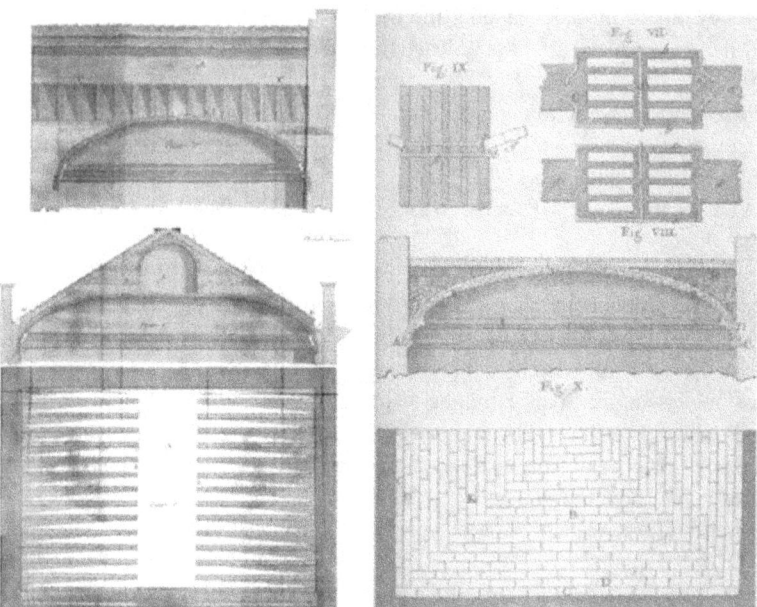

Figure 1: Tile vaults; a) Count of Espié (1765); b) Pierre Patte (1777), c) Rafael Guastavino (1892)

Félix François, Count of Espié, and the Academia de Bellas Artes de San Fernando

Diego de Villanueva (1713-1774) was the Director of the Architecture Department at the San Fernando Academy of Fine Arts (1756) and spread his doctrine in the *Colección de diferentes papeles críticos sobre todas las partes de la Arquitectura* (1766) [14]. In his Letter 1, he cites as reference authors the Abbè Marc-Antoine Laugier, (1713-1769) and P. Lauguier (1745). In his *Essai sur l'architecture* [15], a work also structured as letters, he addresses similar topics. He also cites the *Mémoires critiques de l'architecture* (1702) by Michel de Frémin (f. 1686), the *Mecure de France* (1747) and the Letter VII to Amadée Francois Frezier.

In the text of the Letter No.VI "On the art of manufacturing; and fraud against the Workers", similar to Abbè Laugier's one (1745), he quotes the Count of Espié. His work specifies that the *Comble Briqueté* were buildings roofed without the use of wood or iron, only with flat bricks, laid with plaster, lime and sand mortar and built on *Voutes Plates*. As a military man, he referred to this type of construction to safeguard strongholds, warehouses and arsenals from fire. It also concluded that this type of construction did not produce thrusts since the partitions of the tabs performed the function of bracing, causing a monolithic structural operation. In the translation of the work of the Count of Espié by Joaquín de Sotomayor (1776), additions were made to what was known in the *Observations sur l'Architecture* (1765) by Marc-Antoine Laugier (1713-1769). In the censorship of the work, Ventura Rodríguez (1717-1785) addressed the thrust of the vaults, contradicting Espié whose theory and effect of the thrusts had already been described by Fray Lorenzo de San Nicolas (1593-1679).

Illustrated knowledge of the military engineers of the 18th century

King Felipe V (1683-1746) was to appoint Jorge Prosper Verboom (1665-1744) General Engineer and Mateo Calabro (1680-1748) director of the Academy of Mathematics of Barcelona (1720-1738), a position that was held later by Pedro de Lucuze and Ponce (1692-1779) between (1738-1779). In the curricula of the Academy under Calabro (1724), Verboom (1739) and Pedro de Lucuze (1738) (16) the texts were *The first six books of the geometry of Euclides* (1576) by Rodrigo Zamorano (1542-1620), the *Nouveaux Éléments de géométrie* (1667) by Antoine Arnauld (1612-1694), *La geometrie des lignes et des surfaces rectilignes et circulaires* (1712) by Jean-Pierre de Crousaz (1663-1750), *Mathemático* (1707-1715) by Tomás Vicente Tosca (1651-1723), *le Nouveau cours de Mathématiques* (1725) by Bernard Forest de Belidor (1698-1761) and the *Traité d'Architecture* (1714) by Sébastien Le Clerc (1637-1714). The Royal Military Academy of Mathematics of Barcelona printed some texts on its own initiative. Thus, the works of John Müller (1699-1784*), A treatise containing the elementary part of fortification, regular and irregular* (1755), of Miguel Sánchez Taramas (1733-1799) published as *The Principles of Fortification* (1772) and Pedro de Lucuze and the Military Notions or Supplement to the Principles of Fortification (1781) by José Ignacio de March (f. 1781). Another educational resource were the compulsory notes collected by the students of the Academy on the Treaty VIII of Civil Architecture dictated by Pedro de Lucuze in the period (1739-1779)

Among the architecture books, there were the Vitruvio editions: Sabatini had Cesare Cesariano's edition (1521) and Claude Perrault's called *Les dix livres d"architecture de Vitruve*, (1673) and together with Verboom and Hermosilla he also had, from the translation of José de Castañeda (1766), published as *Compendio de los diez libros de Arquitectura de Vitruvio* (1761). We know that Cermeño owned an edition of Serlio and Verboom of the *Extraordinario Libro di Architettura* (1551). Also, Sabatini owned an edition of the *I quattro libri de l"Architettura* (1547) and of *Tutte l'opere d'architettura* (1584), completing his library *I quattro libri de l"Architettura (1570) by Palladio, Le due regole della prospettiva pratica* (1583) by Vignola and *Dell'Idea dell'Architettura Universale* (1615) by Scamozzi.

As for French treaties, Verboom had the *Cours d'architecture qui comprend les ordres de Vignole* (1691) by Agustín-Charles d'Avilier , in the Sabatini library were *les Ordonnance des cinq espèces de colonnes selon la méthode des Anciens* (1683) by Perrault, *La théorie et la pratique de la coupe des pierres* (1737-1739) by Frezier, *Mémoires sur les objets les plus importants de l'architecture* (1769) by Patte and the *Cours d'architecture* (1771- 1777) by Blondel and Patte

Tile vaults of the military engineers of the 18th century

This construction system of tile vaults was executed through the combined action of layers of thin brick tiles. The first of these ceramic sheets that forms the soffit was made with plaster paste, while the others could also be made with lime mortar. The slats were arranged in a plank and tangent to the guideline of the vault and the upper ones were placed in a joint and in different directions. The main characteristic of this type of construction was the use of plaster as a binder. This material, kneaded with water, involves rehydration and reacts with an increase in temperature, resistance and initial volume in a short time. Its use was reserved for the covering of warehouses, domes, construction of floor support and stairs.

We can compare the difference between bricks and masonry vaulted construction in the two designs for the dome of the church of the citadel of Barcelona. A first project (c.1717), by an unknown author [MPD, 02, 047] [1], was made with stonework (Fig. 2a), while the later in essay (1724) by Francisco de la Pierre (f. 1690-1760) [MPD, 16, 024], was made with a tile vault (Fig. 2b). In the sections, it is possible to observe the great difference in thickness and, therefore, the great difference between the masses and counteracting thrusts.

Figure 2: Citadel Barcelona; a) Anonymous, masonry dome (c.1717); b) F. de la Pierre, tile vault (1724).

The difference in the construction systems can be verified in the two projects drawn up by Carlos Berenguer (1698-1756) for the construction of a sentry box in Alicante: "Plano, y Perfil de una Garita que se propone executar inmediato al Almazén de Polvora para su custodia" (1751) [MPD, 06, 167] and "Perfil, y Vista de Una de las garitas proyectadas de Piedra de sillería, para la Plaza de Alicante" (1752) [MPD, 06, 161].

Between the two, the different speed of execution is evident in the term "execute immediately" for the tile vault, compared to "ashlar stone". The latter is more resistant, but it presents a great difference in terms of the material availability and the execution period. These systems were also used for small vaulted constructions such as the guardhouse or the dome of a chapel. That was the case of the project for the Chapel on the Muelle de Levante in Malaga (1727) by Juan de la Feriére (f. 1724-1737) [MPD, 29, 091] (Fig. 3a) and [MPD, 08, 197] (Fig. 3b).

Figure 3: Chapel in the Muelle de Málaga (1727), by Juan de la Feriére; a) [MPD, 29, 091]; b) [MPD, 08, 197]

Tile vaults in church buildings

Since the 17th century, there was a practice in civil architecture to use the tile vault to cover the naves in religious buildings. The system, subjected to its own weight and a maintenance overload, has less thrust and cracks than churches built with masonry. Above these vaults, the roof of the buildings presents different types of sloping or flat roofs.

Figure 4: Vaults under roof; a) Flat and sloping Barcelona [MPD, 08, 104]; b) El Ferrol gabled [MPD, 15, 017].

This is the case of the flat and inclined roof in the project for the end of the choir of the church of the Citadel of Barcelona (1718) by Alejandro de Rez (f. 1710-1729), [MPD, 08, 104], (Fig. 4a), it is also the case of the sloping gable roof of the new parish of San Julián in El Ferrol (1764) by Pedro Ignacio de Lizardi (f. 1760-1775), [MPD, 15, 017] (Fig. 4b).

Tile domes

Military architecture gathered the symbolism of the domes used in religious architecture and used them as elements of representation of hegemony within some military enclosures, as can be seen in different projects for the Barcelona arsenal. For example, in Jorge Próspero de Verboom's (1665-1744) Profile of the entire building cut on the BHI line of the horizontal plan of the Arsenal to be built in the citadel of Barcelona (1717), [MPD, 14, 003] (Fig. 5a), or later in the design (1730) by Andrés de los Cobos, (f. 1700-1737), [MPD, 18, 004] (Fig. 5.b) that also appears unsigned [MPD, 18, 005] as a duplicate required by the Ordinance of 1718.

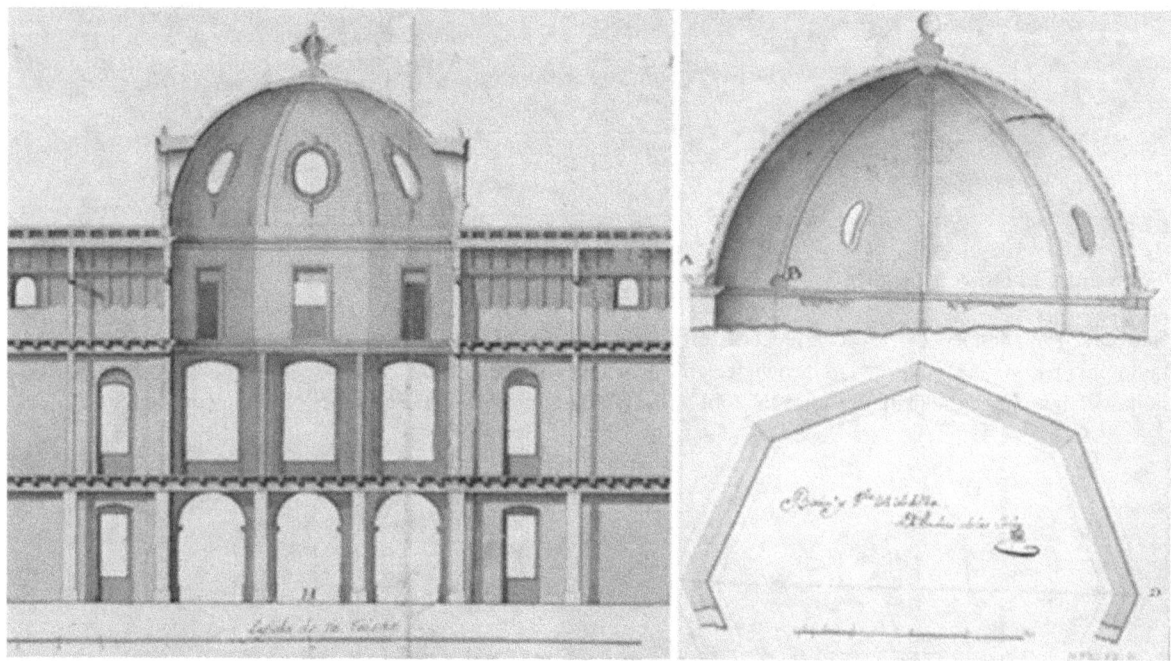

Figure 5: Domes for Arsenal de Barcelona; a) Jorge Próspero de Verboom (1717) [MPD, 14, 003]; b) Andres de los Cobos (1718) [MPD, 18, 004]

Tile vaults in slabs

The types of forging in military buildings were very varied. Although the most widely used was the ceramic vault between wooden beams, there were projects with wooden floor slabs or edge brick vaults. We have evidence of the use of tile vaults in the Lonja Barracks in Barcelona (1741), [MPD, 18, 091] by Miguel Marín (f. 1718-174), with details of the specific section of the project [MPD, 18, 091]. A very particular case are the vaults of the "Plano, Perfil y Elevación del cuartel nuevo de Caballería, unido a la Real Academia de Matemáticas en la Plaza de Barcelona, capaz para un Escuadrón" (1759) by Pedro Martín Cermeño (1722-1792), [MPD, 10, 012] In this project, the main vaults are locked to the arches by means of tabs on their rear side. These elements, located symmetrically on the main vault, are built in the shape of a jumble, although they are somewhat sloping and also serve to support the flooring.

Tile vaults in stairs

One of the elements that has lasted and that has survived to our day is the tile staircase disseminated by Manuel Fornés Gurrea (1777-1856), in his *Observaciones sobre la práctica del arte de edificar*, [fol 19-22 (1841)] (44). The use of this system by unloading an arc curve allows great flexibility in setting out different runs of stairs. On the other hand, the rehydration of the gypsum mass causes crystallization to take place with a rapid hardening of the material, which allows a very fast execution owing to the shortage of auxiliary elements. This would be the case of the project of the Cut Profile in the LMN line of the Arsenal that has to be built in the Citadel of Barcelona (1717) by Jorge Prosper Verboom (1665-1744,) [MPD, 14, 002] (Fig. 6a).

Figure 6: Detail of vault stairs; a) Jorge Prosper Verboom (1717) [MPD, 14, 002]; b) Miguel Marín (1740) [MPD, 07, 128]

If the previous project started with a staircase with straight sections, we have also been able to analyze the design of a helical staircase designed by Miguel Marín (f. 1718-1742). Its first version under the title *"Perfil de la Linterna según la línea C. D. de los muelles proyectados en Barcelona, con sus baterías a la cabeza, cuerpos de guardia, almacenes de pólvora y cisternas"* (1740), [MPD, 07, 013] (Fig. 6b) was subsequently rectified as Elevation of the lantern with that of the elliptical battery according to the dotted line RS (1743), [MPD, 07, 128]. In both cases, a form, similar to that of the staircase initially projected, was maintained.

Vault thrusts

The revision of the theory of the Count of Espié (1765) on the monolithism and the thrusts of the tile vaults was already answered by Juan de Herrera (1776), but we have previous evidence in which there is proof of knowledge from the Spanish engineers on the abutment of these vaults. This is the case of the Orihuela Barracks project (1747) by Pedro Torbe, (f. 1743-1772) in a first section of August 3rd, carried out by the access to the barracks: *"Perfil cortado según la línea A.BB, y C. del Cuartel de Orihuela"* (1747), [MPD, 27, 062] (Fig. 7).

Subsequently, there was a modification of the section, dated October 21: "*Perfil de una de las Alas del Quartel de caballeria, el que representa la nueba disposicion de su cubierta, y juntamente la Abitacion que quedara para los soldados, y Omenages a la Tropa*" (1747), [MPD, 67, 080]. In the explanation of this modification was specified: "8, Encased to receive the roof, and together they serve to abut the barrel of the *Bobeda* of other *Attics*. In the first place, a more slender and steeper section of the roof can be seen in the modification, and secondly, the definition of the cladding with the specific function of operating as the tabs to tie down this type of vaults.

Figure 7: Orihuela Barracks, Pedro Torbe (1747). Push vaults, [MPD, 27, 062], [MPD, 67, 080].

Fireproof vault

A knowledge of the fireproofing properties of tile vaults is manifested in the texts of the Count of Espié (1765) of Sotomayor (1776) or of Patte (1777), and is quoted verbatim in that of the "*Proyecto del Cuartel de la Puerta de los Pozos dirigido a Sabatini*" (1794): Plan and profile of a new way to build an Infantry Barracks in accordance with the modern and advantageous footing of the method that has been followed up to now, [AGMS [2]. Signature: 3rd / 3rd / File 577]. The barracks were located at the door of the snow wells of Madrid, and refers to Francisco de Sabatini as Director and General Commander in ownership of roads, bridges, buildings of civil architecture and irrigation and navigation channels, and Inspector General of the Academies and Fortifications branches (1791-1797) and also as a designer of some of the Gates of Madrid and as a connoisseur of Patte's text (1777) in his library. The project legend indicates the advantages of the new metric and constructive system:

Non-defensive construction of the military engineers of the 18th century

In the formative treatise of engineers, the construction of non-defensive elements was addressed. This was indicated by the translation by Miguel Sánchez Taramas (1733-1799) of the title *A treatise containing the elementary part of fortification, regular and irregular* (1755) by John Müller by *Tratado de fortificación, ó Arte de construir los edificios militares, y civiles* (1769). This work dedicates Section XIX to powder magazines and Section XX to barracks, arsenals and hospitals. Regarding the barracks, it qualified those dedicated to the Cavalry Corps due to the specific need for the construction of the stables with respect to the other weapons. Miguel Sánchez Taramas introduced some Additions for the Iberian readaptation of John Müller's treatise with its own constructive characteristics. For its part, *The Principles of Fortification* (1772) by Pedro de Lucuze, makes reference in its Chapter XIX to the Main Buildings which it defined as military buildings: the General Staff quarters, barracks, pavilions, hospitals, food stores and ammunition, church and cistern, considering them constructively as a simple type or as a bomb-proof type.

Quarters

In the additions of Miguel Sánchez Taramas (1733-1799) to the Tratado de fortificación, ó Arte de construir los edificios militares, y civiles (1769), reference is made in Plate No. 7 to the project of the Reus Cavalry Barracks by Juan Martín Cermeño (1700-1773) entitled "Plano ynferior del quartel y pavellones que se esta executando en la Villa de Reus capaz de 700 ynfantes, un esquadrón de cavalleria y los correspondientes oficiales, cuio proyecto se deve seguir igualmente en los de Valls y Villanueba de la Geltrú" (1751) [MPD, 20, 028]. Both the project and the text became a prototype to be followed in order to be reproduced as a typological model. Regarding tile construction, Miguel Sánchez Taramas said:

> *This is clearly manifested in the interior structure of the Building, the nature of its Vaults (which are partitions, and built by Arista), the arrangement of the Stairs, the magnitude and number of the Arches and Pillars of the Corridors, the formation of the Armor* [fol-384-385 (1769)].

In this same year, Juan Martín Cermeño carried out the Project of a Quartel that requested the erection of the Villa of Villafranca de Panades, for two Cavalry Squadrons or a Ynfanteria Battalion with corresponding Pavilions for officers [MPD, 08, 136] (Fig. 8a). The section of the project is identical, although symmetrical, to that of the text of the Tratado de fortificación, ó Arte de construir los edificios militares, y civiles (1769) (Fig. 8.b). Consequently, it is a matter of systematizing a typological model both from the formal distribution of the building and from the building construction point of view through the use of ceramic masonry in walls, pillars, arches and tile vaults.

Fig. 8. a) Villafranca Penedés Barracks, Juan Martín Cermeño (1769) [MPD, 08, 136]; b) Reus Cavalry Barracks Section Fortification Treaty (1769)

The system was previously used by Nicolás Agustín Bodin y de Bellet (f. 1718-1753) for the construction of barracks, as is the case of the "*Planta y dos perfiles del cuartel de Alicante que se proyecta*" (1739) [MPD, 25, 095] and of the "*Plan, Profiles and elevations of a Quartel de Cavallería for abating 200 soldiers*" (1741) [MPD, 10, 092].

Stables

While the barracks for the accommodation of troops had to be housed near the bastions, the location of those for cavalry were governed by the usefulness of the horses and required particularly the supply of water for their hygiene and maintenance. Therefore, its location was relegated to this need. The layout of the stables was determined in two ways: one for the stables and the other for the circulation and maintenance of the horses. In cases where the stables had only one floor, they were covered by tile vaults, as shown in the projects by Pedro Torbe (f. 1743-1772 *""Plano inferior del Cuartel de Caballería que se está construyendo extramuros del Arrabal de la ciudad de Orihuela, Proyecto de aumento de Caballerizas""* (1747), [MPD, 27, 061] and "*Plano del fuerte llamado San Carlos, situado en la Costa de Levante de la Ciudad de Málaga*" (1796) [MPD , 65, 029] by Fernando Pirez (f. 1788-1801).

Grocery stores

Pedro de Lucuze said that warehouses had to be built in dry places, distributed and not very far from the barracks. This is particularly so of the project for a salt warehouse in Zaragoza which, due to the special conditions of the condiments and the need to be housed in a place with low humidity, was built by use of a tile system. The project was by the engineer Narciso Brer y Miró (f.1769) and was entitled "Plano y Perfil del Almacen de Sal que se propone en el Lugar de Remolinos del Reyno de Aragon" (1769) [MPD, 68, 097].

Main buildings

In Pedro de Lucuze's instructions, the existence of representative buildings located in the main square of the arsenal or the fortified squares is referred to. As examples of tile constructions in these forms of construction we have the project by Juan Caballero (1713-1791) for the Cadiz Customs Office (1769), [MPD, 14, 025] (Fig. 9.a) or the Sala de Armas del Ferrol (1769) [MPD, 51, 019] by Julián Sánchez Bort (1725-1781). (Fig. 9b).

Fig. 9 a) Cadiz Customs Juan Caballero (1769) [MPD, 14, 025]; b) House of Arms Ferrol Julián Sánchez Bort (1769) [MPD, 51, 019].

Hospitals

John Müller sized the Hospitals according to the garrison of the square, using the criterion of one bed for every hundred soldiers. For his part, Pedro de Lucuze advocated his situation within the Plaza Fuerte, being secluded and close to a place with a water supply. For this type of building with a structure similar to that of the barracks, is an account of the project for the Hospital de Algeciras (1745) [MPD, 27, 059] by Loren-zo de Solís (1693-1761).

Churches

The churches of the fortified enclosure, according to John Müller and Pedro de Lucuze, must occupy the main site of the square, near the Governor's house. The chapels were also projected as an auxiliary element within hospitals, for spiritual assistance to the sick or wounded. Among these projects is the "Planta, Elevación y Corte interior de la Obra más proporcionada que puede hacerse en la Iglesia de San Bernardo Extramuros de Toledo" (1748), [MPD, 09, 038] by José Hernández Sierra (c.1705-1782) as well as Interior representation of the parish church projected for the new city of Ferrol; Main façade for the same church (1763) by Julián Sánchez Bort (1725-1781), [MPD, 05, 053] and other projects for arsenals such as Ferrol (1764) [MPD, 05, 055 .] by Pedro Ignacio de Lizardi (f. 1760-1775) (Fig. 10a) and that of La Carraca de Cádiz and its church (1785) [MNM, Sig. MN-P-2E-36] by Francisco Autrán de la Torre (1736-1792) (Fig. 10b).

Fig. 10. Church for Arsenals a) Ferrol, Pedro Ignacio de Lizardi (1764) [MPD, 05, 055.]; b) Cádiz, Francisco Autrán de la Torre (1785) [MNM, Sig. MN-P-2E-36]

Conclusion

The Corps of Military Engineers used tile vaults as a local construction system of skilled labor used in the Iberian Peninsula since the 14th century for the construction of domes, vaults and staircases. An example of this is the project for the Cuartel de Caballería de Orihuela (1747), [MPD, 27, 061] which preceded the publication of the Count of Espié (1754) and was contemporary with the Castle of Bizy (1740). Miguel Sánchez Taramas (1769) recommended tile construction for the Barracks of Reus (1751), noting that this system had already been used by Nicolás Agustín Bodin and de Bellet in the barracks of Alicante (1739) [MPD, 25, 095] and Orihuela (1741) [MPD, 10, 092] `

The tile construction was used in the Plan of the Citadel of Barcelona, developed by Jorge Prospero Verboom. He used it himself in the dome of the Arsenal (1717), [MPD, 14, 003] (Fig. 10a) while Andrés de los Cobos [MPD, 18, 004] (Fig. 10b) and Francisco de la Pierre (f. 1690-1760) [MPD, 16, 024] (Fig. 6b) also used it at the same time. His projects preceded the Royal Ordinance of 1718 and the teaching at the Barcelona Academy of Mathematics (1720). Construction with tile vaults was common in civil construction, throughout the Spanish Levante where most of these projects are located. Therefore, there was a rapid assimilation, from the beginning of the creation of the Corps of Military Engineers, of the use of this construction system that had been used in this territory for more than three centuries.

Abbrevations

[1] MPD: Mapas, Planos y Dibujos del Archivo General de Simancas.

[2] AGMS: Archivo General Militar de Segovia

[3] MNM: Museo Naval de Madrid

References

[1] G.R. Collins, 'The transfer of thin Masonry Vaulting from Spain to America', *Journal of the Society of Architectural Historians*, Vol. 27 No. 3, Oct., 1968, pp. 176-201.
[2] T.C. Bannister, 'The Roussillon Vault: The Apotheosis of a "Folk" Construction"', *Journal of the Society of Architectural Historians*, Vol. 27 No. 3, Oct. 1968, pp. 163-175.
[3] R. Guastavino, *Essay on the Theory and History of Cohesive Construction applied especially to the timbrel vault*. Boston: Ticknor and Company, 1892, pp. 45.
[4] M. Gómez-Ferrer, 'The origins of tile vaulting in Valencia', *Construction History*, vol. 24, 2009, pp. 31-44.
[5] A. Zaragozá, 'Towards a History of the Tabicadas Vaults' in A. Zaragozá et alt. (Ed.), *Proceedings of the International Symposium on Tabicated Vaults*, Valencia 26, 27 and 28 of May 2011, Valencia: Universitat Politécnica de Valencia, 2011.
[6] F.F. D'Espié, *Réflexions du Comte D. Offcier d'Infanterie, Chevalier de l'Order Royal & Militare de St. Louis, sur l'établissement de l'École militaire*. (S.I.), 1756.
[7] F.F. D'Espié, *Maniere de rendre toutes sortes d'édifices incombustibles; ou Traité sur la construction des voutes faites avec des briques & du plâtre dites voutes plates; & d'un toit de brique sans charpente appelé comble briqueté*. Paris: Duchesne, 1754, pp. 2-12.
[8] J. Sotomayor, *Modo de hacer incombustibles los edificios, sin aumentar el coste de su construcción extractado del que escribió en francés el conde D'Espie, ilustrado por Joachin de Sotomayor Cisneros y Sarmiento*. Madrid: En la oficina de Pantaleón Aznar, 1776.
[9] H. Lemonier, *Procès verbaux de l'Académie royale d'Architecture 1671-1793*. Paris: Armand Colin, 1929, T. VI, pp.74-82.
[10] S. Huerta, 'La mecánica de las bóvedas tabicadas en su contexto histórico, con particular atención a la contribución de los Guastavino' in S. Huerta (Ed.), *Las bóvedas de Guastavino en América*. Madrid: Instituto Juan de Herrera, CEHOPU, 2001, pp. 87-112.
[11] J. L. González Moreno-Navarro, (2004). 'La bóveda tabicada: pasado y futuro de un elemento de gran valor patrimonial' in A. Truño (Ed.), *Construcción de bóvedas tabicadas*. Madrid: Instituto Juan de Herrera, 2004, pp. XI-LX.
[12] R. Guastavino, *Essay on the Theory and History of Cohesive Construction applied especially to the timbrel vault*. Boston: Ticknor and Company, 1892, pp. 45.

[13] S. Huerta, 'La construcción tabicada y la teoría cohesiva' in *Escritos sobre la construcción cohesiva y su función en la arquitectura*. Madrid: CEHOPU, Instituto Juan de Herrera, 2006, pp. XV-LX.

[14] Diego de Villanueva, *Colección de Diferentes Papeles Críticos sobre todas las partes de la Arquitectura*. Valencia: Benito Monfort, 1766.

[15] M. A. Laugier, *Essai sur l'architecture*. Paris: chez Duchesne, rue S. Jacques, au Temple du Goût. M. DCC. LIII. avec approbation & privilege du Roy, 1753.

[16] J. Carrillo de Albornoz, 'Els plans d'estudi a l'Acadèmia de Matemàtiques i el seu funcionament intern' in J. M. Muñoz (Coor.), *L'Acadèmia de Matemàtiques de Barcelona. El llegat dels enginyers militars*. Madrid: Ministerio de Defensa, 2004, pp. 103-115.

Pioneering Education for a Unique Engineering Profession – British Military Engineers

Nicholas A. Bill
St Peter's College, University of Oxford, UK

Introduction

Whilst much has been written about the early history of the civil engineering profession and its systems of education, comparatively little has been said regarding military engineers. The trajectory of their profession, influenced largely by their pioneering systems of education, saw military engineers play a crucial role in the development of science, engineering, and construction practices across the British Empire.

British military engineers were extensively involved in building and engineering projects throughout the nineteenth century and operated at the vanguard of imperial expansion. During peacetime, successive governments, both at home and in the colonies, used their expertise in science and engineering to further economic and technological development within their respective territories. Amongst their numerous responsibilities, military engineers were charged with developing infrastructure that helped establish new colonies, often years before civilian engineers and architects arrived.

Most territories fell under the domain of the Royal Engineers. Established in 1717 under the control of the Board of Ordnance, the Royal Engineers were responsible for providing scientific and engineering support to the British Army. Together with the Royal Artillery, they became known as the "Scientific Corps" and were a vital instrument to the Board of Trade. They served on numerous royal commissions and advised Parliament on issues concerning infrastructure projects. Moreover, they facilitated direct governmental intervention in the business of railways, providing an exclusive source of inspecting officers for Her Majesty's Railway Inspectorate until the 1960s.

Prior to 1862, British India remained under the control of the East India Company, which fielded three essentially private armies to defend the Company's interests and control the Presidencies (Bengal, Bombay and Madras), each possessing their own corps of engineers. These were used extensively in public works and have left behind a rich architectural legacy ranging from railways stations to cathedrals. Despite their separation, officers in British India maintained close contact with the Royal Engineers, collaborating on several projects before they were ultimately absorbed into the latter when the Crown asserted direct control.

British military engineers could rise to these challenges owing largely to their innovative and pioneering system of education. Whilst their civilian counterparts embarked upon a haphazard system of unregulated apprenticeships, military engineers enjoyed a more structured and systematic approach to their education, which was provided by some of Britain's finest scientific minds. Subject to continual reforms, it was designed to equip officers with the necessary skills to operate effectively in isolated colonial outposts. Furthermore, their continued professional development was supported through their own series of publications and the establishment of libraries at key strategic locations around the empire.

This paper focuses on the pioneering education of British military engineers at Woolwich, Addiscombe and Chatham, during the late-eighteenth and early-nineteenth centuries, particularly their training in design and building construction. Drawing comparisons with civilian engineers, it will demonstrate how they developed an institutional locus, furthering engineering science.

Royal Military Academy, Woolwich

Attempts to formalise military education began with the foundation of the Royal Military Academy, Woolwich, in 1741. Affectionately labelled "The Shop", owing to the use of converted workshops at the Royal Arsenal, the academy was the first military and technical school in the British Empire [1]. As stated in its Royal Warrant, its purpose was to educate cadets "In the several parts of mathematics necessary to qualify them for the service of the artillery and the business of engineers [2]." Essentially the principles of gunnery and fortifications. Intrinsically linked, prospective officers for both the Royal Artillery and Royal Engineers initially received the same training before being allocated into each service based upon their final examination scores, with those scoring the highest marks commissioned into the Royal Engineers.

Recruitment and Admission – Tentative Steps towards Meritocracy

Until 1855, nomination for a cadetship was at the sole discretion of the Master-General of the Ordnance [3]. Despite this system of patronage, cadets were still required to pass an examination before receiving their commission, the first branch of the British Army to impose such a requirement. In contrast, officers entering regiments of the line received their commissions via a system of purchase, rather than meritocratic award. Coupled with relatively low pay, this represented a significant and intentional financial barrier to entry. Moreover, prior to the establishment of Royal Military College at Great Marlow and High Wycombe, some 60 years later, infantry and cavalry officers were not required to undertake formal military training [4].

The system of patronage still required cadets to possess sufficient social connections. Consequently, cadets reflected the general pattern of army officers with respect to their social origins, although not usually the most affluent. Cadets came from all corners of the United Kingdom and the colonies. However, the Scots were over-represented by proportion of their population. Prior to 1855, many came from military families or those in the civil service, with almost all educated at notable schools or under private tuition [5]. Every cadet was literate and arrived with some knowledge of mathematics and the French language, as reflected in the content of the entrance examination [6].

Entry into the civil engineering profession presented similar financial and social barriers. Other than those who were entirely self-taught, young men wishing to receive instruction from established civil engineers, were typically required to pay a premium towards their education, in a system of unregulated apprenticeships known as pupillages [7]. No formal examinations were required, either at the beginning or end of their training, other than the exam necessary to obtain membership of the professional institutions. Hence, the quality of instruction varied significantly.

After 1855, following the dissolution of the Board of Ordnance, nominations were replaced entirely by open competitive entrance exams, with the intention of widening access and attracting the best candidates [8]. This ended the days of boys as young as 14 being admitted on the basis of family privilege, with the age limit raised, the mid-nineteenth century saw a new generation enter Woolwich, including university graduates [9].

Professors and Tutors

Despite its military function, most professors and tutors at Woolwich were civilians, except for those conducting classes focused on practical gunnery or other aspects related to soldiering. Mostly academic in nature, they represented some of Britain and Ireland's finest mathematicians, scientists, and indeed artists (see Table 1).

Table 1: Notable Civilian Professors and Tutors at the Royal Military Academy, Woolwich

Professor/Tutor	Subject	Service
John Müller (1699 – 1784)	Artillery and Fortification	1741 – 1766
Thomas Simpson (1710 – 1761)	Mathematics	1743 – 1761
Paul Sandby (1731 – 1809)	Drawing	1768 – 1799
Charles Hutton (1737-1823)	Mathematics	1773 – 1807
Isaac Landmann (1741-c.1829)	Artillery and Fortification	1777 – 1815
Adair Crawford (1748 – 1795)	Chemistry	c.1788 – c.1890 (Professor)
William Cruickshank (d.1811)	Chemistry	1788 – 1804 (Assistant to Crawford)
Lewis Evans (1755 – 1827)	Mathematics	1799 – 1820
Peter Barlow (1776-1862)	Mathematics	1801 – 1847
Olinthus Gilbert Gregory (1774-1841)	Mathematics	1802 – 1838 (Professor from 1821)
John MacCulloch (1773 – 1835)	Chemistry and Geology	1803 – ?
Thomas Myers (1774 – 1834)	Mathematics	1806 - ? (Professor)
Samuel Hunter Christie (1784 – 1865)	Mathematics	1806 – 1854 (Professor from 1838)
John Bonnycastle (1751 – 1821)	Mathematics	1807 – 1821
Michael Faraday (1791-1867)	Chemistry	c.1820 – 1852
Thales Fielding (1793 – 1837)	Drawing	1828 – 1837
James Marsh (1794 – 1846)	Chemistry	1829 – 1846 (Assistant to Faraday)
Thomas Simpson Evans (1777 – 1818)	Mathematics	c. .1830 – 1810 (Assistant to Evans)
William Rutherford (1798 – 1871)	Mathematics	1838 – 1865
Sir Frederick Able (1827-1902)	Chemistry	1852 – 1888
James Joseph Sylvester (1814 – 1897)	Mathematics	1855 – 1870
John Callow (1822 – 1878)	Drawing (Landscapes)	1861 – 1865
Aaron Edwind Penley (1807 – 1870)	Drawing	1861 - 1870
Francis Bashforth (1819 – 1912)	Applied Mathematics	1864 – 1872
Morgan Crofton (1826 – 1915)	Mathematics	1870 – 1884
Sir Alfred George Greenhill (1847 – 1927)	Mathematics	1876 – 1908

The Academy's first headmaster was John Müller (1699–1784), a German immigrant with no practical military experience, who was apparently appointed on the strength of his publication, *A Mathematical Treatise* (1736), which he dedicated to the Master-General of the Ordnance [10]. During his tenure as Professor of Fortifications and Artillery, Müller authored numerous textbooks that purposely went beyond pure mathematics and mechanics. His books presented theoretical solutions for practical problems of structural engineering encountered during the construction of fortifications.

They included theories for masonry arches, strength of beams, and of earth pressure and stability of retaining walls. Further works also covered navigational astronomy, ballistics, hydraulics, and pneumatics [11].

Müller's efforts, together with those of Thomas Simpson (1710–61), Charles Hutton (1737–1823) and Isaac Landmann (1741–c.1829), established the philosophy in which applied mathematics and mechanics were developed deliberately and systematically. Thus, an institutional locus was established at Woolwich, where such endeavours found patronage. In addition to their instruction, many of Müller's successors also produced numerous textbooks based upon original research in mechanics [12].

Arguably the most influential of these publications was an *Essay on the Strength and Stress of Timber* (1817), produced by Peter Barlow (1776–1862). Barlow claimed that his study was commissioned by General William Mudge (1762–1820), then lieutenant-governor of the Royal Military Academy, for the purposes of educating cadets and officers. Although Barlow's work was flawed and subject to later criticism, it proved extremely popular throughout military and civilian circles, seeing five editions in Barlow's lifetime alone, with further revisions after his death.

Lesser-known publications include those by Hutton. His treatise *The Principles of Bridges* (1772) was inspired by his predecessors' involvement in the Blackfriars Bridge (1769) controversy, together with the spate of bridge failures at that time. As with Barlow, his work suffered from flaws that were typical of his time. Hutton attempted to apply the elementary laws of statics to analyse statically indeterminate structures, without appreciating that they could not be solved. Nevertheless, such early attempts sometimes yielded results that were sufficient for practical applications and were probably used in actual design practice [13]. Moreover, these efforts stimulated further research, fuelled by interactions between a growing group of likeminded men, which foreshadowed the professionalization of engineering [14].

In contrast, civilian engineers were yet to develop such a locus, although an attempt had been made in 1771 with the founding of the Society of Civil Engineers (later the Smeatonian Society of Civil Engineers). Bringing together prominent engineers, in addition to instrument-makers and other craftsmen, its effective early membership was maintained for many years at about twenty. Whilst they managed to amass a substantial collection of brooks, drawings, and reports [15], they remained silent on the education of engineers and over time the society became little more than a dining club. Eventually its perceived failings led to the foundation of the Institution of Civil Engineers in 1818, where prominent military engineers would play an active role throughout the nineteenth century.

Course Structure and Content

The course at Woolwich was broadly divided into two components, one theoretical and a second practical, both lasting up four years and undertaken concurrently. Cadets were divided into classes based upon their levels of competence, as judged by the professors, to ensure each cadet saw a steady and efficient progress [16].

The content was provided through a series of lectures and practical demonstrations, as in the case of gunnery and surveying. Cadets were assessed by both oral and written exams set by the professors. In addition, each cadet was issued with blank notebooks which were inspected monthly [17].

The theoretical course comprised of a Course of Mathematics and a Course of Fortifications. The mathematics included the topics of: Arithmetic, Algebra, Logarithms, Geometry, Application of Algebra to Geometry, Trigonometry, Heights and Distances, Analytical and Descriptive Geometry, Conic Sections, Spherical Trigonometry, Mensuration, Differential and Integral Calculus, Mechanics, Hydrostatics, Hydrodynamics, and Pneumatics. It was intended that the application of these principles was shown in the Professor's Course of Lectures on Natural Philosophy, with further examples of their application demonstrated throughout the practical classes [18].

The Course on Fortifications included further elements of geometry, together with theoretical and practical drawing, including perspective and measure drawings. Cadets were tasked with copying existing drawings and drafting new ones, using views around Woolwich and surrounding areas as a source. Drawing work extended to the preparation of plans, sections and elevations of ordinary buildings, annotated with colour to indicate the different materials and the technical names of each component [19].

The practical course involved exercises in surveying, gunnery and drills, in addition to instruction on riding and fencing. This "practical" course also included further lectures on chemistry, geology and metallurgy [20].

Language skills were also a key component. French was compulsory throughout with later decades offering the choice of Hindustani or German [21], before expanding to include Italian, Spanish and Russian [22]. According to Sir Francis Bond Head (1793–1875), Hindustani was rarely chosen, whilst entrance exam results continually exhibited a poor grasp of foreign languages upon entry [23]. Considering British schools were dominated by classical education, Woolwich provided officers with an ability to read and understand foreign texts, as evidenced by their numerous translations, an opportunity which seemed lacking in many of their civilian counterparts.

Effectiveness of Training

Whilst the provisions at Woolwich appear impressive on paper, experiences during subsequently military campaigns, particularly the Peninsula War (1807–14), exposed severe deficiencies, with the effectiveness of young officers heavily criticised. Moreover, those reflecting upon their service noted how ill-prepared they were for their range of duties, notably in the construction of buildings [24]. The exercises at Woolwich ultimately fell short of specific training in structural engineering and general architecture. Instead, such emphasis on mathematics reflects the Continental influence of the academy's early professors and moreover, the theoretical origins of bastion and star fortifications that attempted to circumvent advances in artillery and ballistics.

Regardless of its failings, Woolwich still represented the first attempts at the systematic instruction of engineers in the British Empire and moreover, provided the model for future military schools.

East India Company Military Seminary, Addiscombe (1809–61)

In British India, officers needed for the engineering corps were initially drafted from the infantry [25]. Finding this system unsatisfactory, the East India Company sought assistance from the Crown, eventually reaching an agreement whereby the Company paid for their cadets to study at Woolwich. This arrangement lasted until 1809, when the East India Company Military Seminary was founded at Addiscombe, Surrey.

Modelled upon Woolwich, Addiscombe was originally intended for the education of engineering and artillery officers. In 1827, however, it began admitting cadets for "general service", morphing into a hybrid of Woolwich and Sandhurst.

With no system of purchase in the East India Company's armies, admission followed the patronage system of nomination confirmed by a qualifying examination. Cadets were entirely gentlemen, many of whom came from families with relations already serving in India, ether in the civil service or the military. As with the Royal Engineers, a signification proportion were recruited from Scotland [26]. However, most recruits were of lower social standing. Despite evidence that some suffered from occasional prejudice, collaborations on later publications demonstrate that officers from both services enjoyed mutual respect at a professional level [27].

Professors and Tutors

Like Woolwich, most of the professors at Addiscome were civilians, including many prominent mathematicians and scientists (see Table 2). In later decades, officers returning from India provided instruction on surveying and fortifications.

Table 2: Notable Civilian Professors and Tutors at the East India Company Military Seminary

Professor/Tutor	Subject	Service
James Andrew (c.1774 – 1833)	Superintendent	1809 – 1822
John Shakespear (1774 – 1858)	Hindustani	1809 – 1829
Joseph Bordwine (d.1835)	Fortifications	1809 – 1835
William Frederick Wells (1762 – 1836)	Drawing	1813 – 1836
John MacCulloch (1773 – 1835)	Chemistry and Geology	1814 – 1835
Jonathan Cape (1793 – 1868)	Mathematics	1822 – 1861
William Sturgeon (1783 – 1850)	Science and Philosophy	1824 – 1850
Theodore Henry Adolphus Fielding (1781 – 1851)	Drawing	1826 – 1850
Charles Bowels (later Shakespear)	Hindustani	1829 – 1859
John Frederic Daniell (1790 – 1845)	Chemistry	1835 – 1845
John Christian Schetky (1778 – 1874)	Drawing	1836 – 1855
Alfred Wrigley (1818 – 1898)	Mathematics	1841 – 1861
David Thomas Ansted (1814 – 1880)	Geology	1845 – 1861
Edward Solly (1819 – 1886)	Chemistry	1845 – 1859
Aaron Edwind Penley (1807 – 1870)	Drawing (Later at Woolwich)	1851 - 1861
John Callow (1822 – 1878)	Drawing (Later at Woolwich)	1855 – 1861
Edward Frankland (1825 – 1899)	Chemistry	1859 – 1861

Course Structure and Content

The course at Addiscombe lasted only 2 years and placed mathematics above all other subjects, occupying an average 22 hours of the 54-hour academic week [28], and dominated the final examination with the emphasis increasing over time [29]. Taught through the tutorial system, the entire course covered mathematics (including natural philosophy), fortifications, artillery, military drawing and surveying, landscape drawing (and later photography), military tactics, religious instruction, and languages [30].

The course of mathematics included topics of: Algebra, the Binomial Theorem, Logarithms, Differential and Integral Calculus, Geometry (Planes and Solids), Analytical Geometry (including conic sections), Trigonometry (Plane and Spherical), and the analytical investigation of Trigonometrical Formulae. Further topics included: Natural Philosophy, Statics, Dynamics, Hydrostatics, Hydrodynamics, and Astronomy [31].

The course of Military Drawing and Surveying comprised the operations of laying down a skeleton map trigonometrically. Cadets were then instructed on how to fill in by aid of the compass route surveying, reconnaissance, levelling with spirit levels and barometers. The relatively minor course of Landscape Drawing covered the Elements of Perspective, Landscape, and Figure Drawing [32].

The languages covered at Addiscombe included French, Latin and Hindustani. The French course included the study of French works on military science, whilst Latin focused on selections of historical works. Lessons in Hindustani were intended to provide cadets with the ability to communicate with their subordinate workforce when they arrived in India.

Further lectures were given in Geology, Chemistry, Artillery, and additionally, the steam engine, and the application of mechanical powers to machinery.

When studying fortifications, Cadets were instructed in sand modelling, conducted within a covered building erected for the purpose, 60 feet long by 50 feet wide. First introduced in 1839, by then Assistant Professor of Fortifications Lt. Cook, R.N., F.R.S., this technique would see wider applications by officers in the design of large-scale infrastructure works across India and Egypt [33].

Effectiveness of Training

Despite its ambitions and the considerable expense outlaid by the East India Company, the failings at Addiscombe were legion, falling well behind the standards set at Woolwich. Discipline was problematic throughout the first decades, culminating in a culture of corruption [34]. Demand for engineers across India meant that the Company repeatedly selected cadets who failed to meet the required standards and would otherwise be sent to the artillery or infantry [35].

The standard of education was also questionable, as were the appointments of some professors. Possibly the most farcical was that of Charles Bowles. Appointed Assistant Professor of Hindustani at the age of 19, barely older than some of the senior cadets, Bowles had never been to India nor heard the language spoken [36]. It is therefore unsurprising that cadets hated their classes and failed to pick up the language before reaching India. Despite several efforts by the Company to improve the language skills of their officers, it is arguably one of Addiscombe's greatest failings. Especially, as the inability of many officers to fully understand their indigenous subordinates contributed to the Indian Mutiny (1857), which ultimately saw the East India Company lose control [37].

Any attempts at developing an institutional locus dedicating to furthering Indian engineering failed and Addiscombe was deemed surplus to requirements. The school closed its door to new cadets in 1858 when the Crown began absorbing the East Indian Company's engineers into the Royal Engineers.

Royal Engineer Establishment, Chatham (School of Military Engineering)

Rather than overhaul Woolwich, it was thought that the practical skills could be improved by introducing a two-stage system of education, whereby cadets would continue to receive a foundation in theoretical knowledge at Woolwich before progressing to a new establishment that focused entirely on the latter. In 1812, the Royal Engineer Establishment was founded at Chatham to provide the Royal Engineers with that second stage. Lasting approximately 18 months, the course was also offered to the East India Company's cadets, who joined after their initial training at Addiscombe.

Chatham owes its foundation and early development to the endeavours of General Sir Charles William Pasley (1780–1861), a veteran of the Peninsula War who gained first-hand experience of the deficiencies of training in military engineering. Pasley spent his early career employed in the construction of fortifications, before taking part in the Walcheren Expedition (1809), where he suffered severe injuries. Rendered incapable of further active duty, he used his convalescence for reflection and personal development, learning the German language and writing various treatises [38]. In 1810, Pasley and Sir John Fox Burgoyne (1782–1871) formed the 'Society for Producing Useful Military Knowledge', a small group of Royal Engineers intent on encouraging the theoretical and practical studies in military engineering. They formed the nucleus of a new generation of officers with their own ideas of what needed to be done, starting a trend that inspired later generations and characterised the nature of reform in the coming years.

Pasley's philosophy on education was to establish a system of self-instruction. Largely inspired by the work of the educationalist, Andrew Bell (1753–1832), Pasley was first motivated to improve skills related to military works in the field, especially amongst the sappers and non-commissioned officers [39]. As such, the early curriculum was geared towards that purpose. Later he would turn his attention to the knowledge gap surrounding the Corps' peacetime duties. Himself an advocate of employing the Royal Engineers in the construction of public works, the need to improve skills became pressing when the Board of Ordnance resumed responsibility for the construction and maintenance of barracks in 1822.

Architecture and Construction Technology

Many issues the Royal Engineers faced were the result of the divisions between the professions and the building trades. When Chatham was founded, architecture as a profession was predominately the pursuit of gentlemen who would write on the subject or subscribe to architectural publications [40]. Where architects were employed, they did not provide detailed drawings that would be expected of the same professionals today. Hence, there was a greater reliance upon the skill and knowledge of the clerk of works and tradesmen to produce the required details [41]. The key issue that the Royal Engineers faced in the early-nineteenth century is that they were a corps that consisted entirely of officers who were not in regular command of a troop of skilled artificers. Therefore, the deficiencies in their practical knowledge had greater consequences. Recognising this problem, the Board of Ordnance issued an order in 1825 that a course of Practical Architecture should be instituted at Chatham [42]. It became the first formalised educational programme in architecture and building construction found anywhere in the British Empire.

As Chatham's director, Pasley attempted to address this issue through the production of his textbook *Outline of a Course of Practical Architecture* (1826). Filled with numerous sketches of building details it focused mainly on traditional construction in masonry, partially brick. Contrary to suggestions by its title, Pasley did not attempt to outline rules for proportioning buildings and outright avoided discussion on decoration, which he regarding the reserve of 'professed architects' [43]. Instead, training in design involved copying architectural drawings from books and plans before exercises in measurement. Using published price books, cadets were expected to draft estimates for the expense of buildings based upon the drawings and specifications [44]. Considered sufficient to design common military buildings such as barracks, hospitals, and storehouses, Pasley's book inadvertently helped cement the Royal Engineer's reputation for designing dull buildings whilst furthering a dependence upon pattern books that is observed in the early public works of British India.

Pattern books, exemplified by the works of William Pain (1730–90), Peter Nicholson (1765–1844), and Thomas Tredgold (1788–1829), attempted to bridge the gap in technical knowledge between building trades and design professionals, primarily for the benefit of the latter. Largely following their format, Palsey acknowledged the assistance of some of the most eminent civil engineers and builders in the preparation of his textbook [45]. However, much of its content was undoubtedly based upon his extensive experimental works conducted at Chatham.

Indeed, developing experimental science in construction was a crucial objective of the Establishment. Building upon the efforts of Müller at Woolwich nearly a century earlier, Chatham provided the Royal Engineers with a place to carry out investigative work, furthering the development of rational design. Crucially, its instructors instilled the virtues of such methods and disseminated the necessary skills to its cadets who formed the basis of the next generation. Two key protagonists were Sir William Thomas Denison (1804–71) and Richard John Nelson (1803–77). Denison published numerous scientific and technical papers throughout his career and was instrumental in establishing the Corps' leading technical journal in 1837, Papers on Subject Connected with the Duties of the Corps of Royal Engineers. Similarly, Nelson was a prolific author and keen advocate of self-instruction, publishing guidance for junior officers serving in remote locations.

Mid-Nineteenth Century Reforms

By the mid-1850s, however, the effectiveness of military engineers was again brought into question. The Crimean War (1853–56) exposed severe deficiencies across all levels within the British Army, from outdated tactics to the shambolic care of wounded soldiers and drew attention to these conditions at home. Reporting in 1861 and 1863, the newly formed Barracks and Hospitals Commission published a damming critique of construction and state of military buildings, for which the Royal Engineers were responsible. In 1855, the Board of Ordnance was abolished, and the Royal Engineers placed under the newly formed War Department. Shortly after, the Indian Mutiny (1857) saw the collapse of the East India Company and preparations were made to transfer its forces to the Crown. Doubling in size, the Royal Engineers were now faced with the challenges of public works in British India, whilst needing to address their existing shortcomings.

Commissions focusing on military education carried out in 1857 and 1862 concluded that whilst the theoretical education of officers was sufficient, their practical education was inadequate. Owing to the division of training between Woolwich and Chatham, the critique was targeted at the latter. Despite Pasley's earlier efforts, the Royal Engineers appeared incapable of educating their own. Moreover, the Establishment he founded appears to have gone into decline following his departure. Major-General Edward Renouard James (1833–1909), who entered Chatham in 1851 [46], later claimed that "the average man left Chatham incapable of designing or superintending the erection of the simplest work [47]." Whether an exaggeration of not, action was taken, and the commissioners' recommendations implemented. Under the new direction of Sir Henry Drury Harness (1804–83), officers such as Henry Wray (1826–1900), Henry Cooper Seddon (1837–1911), and Henry Young Darracott Scott (1822–83) arrived at Chatham. They brought a fresh impetus and practical experience of erecting public buildings, especially Wray who reformed teaching practices with a firm idea of an officer's role in design [48]. Moreover, these officers did much to advance our understanding of material science through experimental work that they disseminated through their own technical manuals.

In later decades, Chatham established a series of schools, focusing on the diverging specialisms that were developing in the civil sphere. These included the schools of Estimating and Construction, Surveying, Electricity, Telegraphy, and Balloons. Each played host to rotor of guest civilian lecturers who were brought in to provide up-to-date knowledge of the latest developments in civilian engineering and technology.

The Royal Engineer Institute – Focus on Military Science

Reform resulting from military calamities would eventually have a detrimental effect upon the Corps' wider contributions to science and engineering. By the 1870s, a view had developed within the army, which according to Captain W. A Ross of the Royal Artillery, thought that "scientific study of almost any kind, is derogatory to their military character [49]". The foundation of the Royal Engineer Institute at Chatham, with its remit to focus specifically on military science, signalled an intent towards that direction. Moreover, the army's inability to provide enough engineers for the public works programmes across the empire would see them relieved of those duties.

In the latter decades of the nineteenth century, military education went from a broad-based engineering education towards an explicitly martial nature. Whenever conflict for space within the curriculum arose, aspect focusing on civil works were sacrificed [50]. Some leading officers continued to advocate the benefits of scientific study, beyond those immediately necessary for carrying out military duties, and repeatedly push back against the countermovement of masculinity. However, their efforts were largely in vain.

Summary

From their foundation in 1741, the education of the Royal Engineers and their Indian counterparts consisted of a structured curriculum, intent on developing a solid understanding of mathematics and scientific principles. In contrast, civilian engineers who were not entirely self-taught were educated through non-structured, un-regulated apprenticeships. Whereas civilian engineers developed their expertise based upon observation, precedence, trial-and-error and manual dexterity, military engineers were early proponents of rational design methods.

Efforts at Woolwich, Addiscombe and Chatham helped establish an institutional locus that furthered the engineering sciences, especially materials science. They nurtured ideas, provided facilities to carry out research, and the means to disseminate their findings through their own publications. No equivalent establishment was available to civilian engineers in the nineteenth century.

Both civilian and military engineers acknowledged their own deficiencies, however, the latter were more open to reform. Throughout the nineteenth century, military engineers sought to improve their practical knowledge and learn from their mistakes. Moreover, they readily adopted knowledge and technology from overseas. In contrast, civilian engineers were slow to embrace theoretical developments, holding the firm belief that British civilian engineers were the envy of the world, by virtue of the fact they were in such high demand. Furthermore, the British education system remained largely rooted in classical education and lagged behind European countries with regards to science.

Ultimately, the shift from apprenticeships to university-based education, followed by post-graduate qualification through experience, saw the civilian engineering profession adopt the two-tier system that the military developed over 100 years ago.

References

[1] F. G. Guggisberg, *The Shop: The Story of the Royal Military Academy*. London: Cassell & Co., 1900.
[2] Royal Warrant, 30 April 1741. Quoted in: Douglas William Marshall, The British Military Engineers 1741-1783: A Study of Organization, Social Origin, and Cartography. PhD Thesis, University of Michigan, 1976, p.87.
[3] Sir Francis B. Head, *The Royal Engineer*. London: John Murray, 1869, p. 1
[4] John Black, *The development of professional management in the public sector of the United Kingdom from 1855 to 1925: the case of the ordnance factories*. PhD Thesis, The Open University, 2000, p. 52
[5] This assessment is based upon an analysis of published obituaries and memoirs of numerous Royal Engineers.
[6] Douglas William Marshall (see note 2).
[7] Fleeming Jenkyn, 'A Lecture on the Education of Civil and Mechanical Engineers in Great Britain and Abroad', In: Institution of Civil Engineers, *The Education and Status of Civil Engineers in the United Kingdom and Foreign Countries*. London: 1870, pp. 198-204.
[8] Claire Jean Cookson-Hills, Engineering The Nile: Irrigation and the British Empire in Egypt, 1822 – 1914, PhD Thesis, Queen's University (Kingston, Ontario), 2013, p. 62.
[9] H. Moseley, H., *Report on the Examination for Appointments in the Royal Artillery and Engineers, Held at King's College, London on the First of August, 1855, with Copies of the Examination Papers*. London: Harrison, 1855.
[10] John Müller, *A Mathematical Treatises: Containing a System of Concic-Section; With the Doctorine of Fluxions and Fluents, Applied to Various Subjects*. London: T. Gardner, 1736.
[11] Harold I. Dorn, *The Art of Building and the Science of Mechanics: A Study of the Union of Theory and Practice in the Early History of Structural Analysis in England*. PhD Dissertation, Princeton University, 1970, p. 142.
[12] ibid., p. 148.
[13] ibid., p. 151.
[14] ibid., p. 151.
[15] A. W. Skempton and Esther Clark Wright, 'Early members of the Smeatonian Society of Civil Engineers', *Transactions of the Newcomen Society*, Vol. 44, No.1, 1971, pp. 23–47.
[16] Lt. Col. William Yolland, Lt. Col. Symth, The Rev. W. C. Lake, *Report of the Commissioners Appointed to Consider the Best Mode of Re-Organising the System for Training Officers for the Scientific Corp*. London: HMSO, 1857, p. 289.

[17] John Michael Weiler, *Army Architects*, PhD Thesis, University of York, 1987, p. 8.
[18] Lt. Col. Yolland, et. al, (note 16), p. 289.
[19] John Michael Weiler (note 17), p. 9.
[20] ibid., p. 8.
[21] Lt. Col. Yolland, et. al, (note 16), p. 266. Sir Francis B. Head (note 3), p. 13.
[22] Captain Walter H. James, late R.E., 'Military education and training', *Royal United Services Institution Journal*, Vol. 26, 188), pp. 369-95.
[23] Captain Walter H. James (note 22), p. 372.
[24] Anon. *Our Military Engineers: Being an Inquiry into the Present State of Efficiency of the Corps of Royal Engineers.* London: Judd & Glass, 1860.
[25] Colonel H. M. Vibart, *Addiscombe – Its Heroes and Men of Note.* Westminster: Archibald Constable & Co., 1894, p. 1.
[26] A. Cameron Taylor, *General Sir Alex Taylor G.C.B., R.E, His Times, His Friends, and His Work.* Vol. 1. London: Williams and Norgate, 1913, p. 3
[27] John Michael Weiler (note 17) p 5.
[28] Major William Broadfoot, 'Addiscombe', *Blackwood's Edinburgh Magazine*, Vol. 153, 1893, pp. 647-57.
[29] Colonel H. M. Vibart, (note 25), pp. 154-155.
[30] Lt. Col. Yolland, et. al, (note 16), p. 266.
[31] ibid., p. 266.
[32] ibid., p. 266.
[33] Colonel H. M. Vibart, (note 25), p. 131; Claire Jean Cookson-Hills (note 8), p.65-6.
[34] Major William Broadfoot (note 28), p. 653.
[35] Lt. Col. Yolland, et. al, (note 16), p. 269
[36] Colonel H. M. Vibart, (note 25), p. 95.
[37] J. M. Bourne, 'The East India Company's Military Seminary, Addiscombe, 1809 – 1858', *Journal of the Society for Army Historical Research*, Vol. 57, No. 232, 1979, pp. 208-10.
[38] Captain H. W. Tyler, 'Memoir of the late General Sir C. Pasley, K.C.B., R.E.', *Papers on Subjects Connected with the Duties of the Corps of Royal Engineers, New Series,* Vol. 12, 1863, pp. i – xv.
[39] Colonel Bernard R. Ward, *School of Military Engineering, 1812-1909*, Chatham: Royal Engineers Institute, 1909, p. 9.
[40] David T. Yeomans, 'Early carpenter's manuals 1592 – 1820', *Construction History*, 2 (1986), pp. 13 – 33.
[41] ibid., p. 29.
[42] Colonel Bernard R. Ward (note 39), p. 16.
[43] Shanti Jayewardene-Pillai, *Imperial Conversations: Indo-Britons and the Architecture of South India.* New Delhi: Yoda Press, 2007, p. 181.
[44] Charles William Pasley, *Outline of a Course in Practical Architecture*, Chatham: 1862, p. 1-12; John Michael Weiler (note 17), p. 13-14.
[45] Charles William Pasley (note 44), p. 2.
[46] Colonel R. H. Vetch, 'Memoir: Major-General Edward Renoud James, Royal Engineers', *Royal Engineer Journal*, Vol. 12, No. 3, 1910, pp. 191-206.
[47] Quoted in: Colonel Bernard R. Ward (note 39), p. 19.
[48] Colonel Bernard R. Ward (note 39), p. 19.
[49] Captain W. A. Ross, late R.A., 'The cultivation of scientific knowledge by regimental officers of the British Army,' *Royal United Service Institution*, Vol. 16, 1873, pp. 774-81.
[50] Claire Jean Cookson-Hills (note 8), p.71.

The social status of Parisian building contractors in the 18th century. A hierarchical and ambitious professional "body": between nobility and destitution

Robert Carvais
Legal Historian, CNRS, Centre de théorie et analyse du droit, France

It has long been customary to confuse the functions of different people engaged in the building trade from the early modern period to the 19th century in France. Is it possible for clear distinctions to be drawn between the different types of builders, contractors, architects, and engineers concerned? For example, has the law, thanks to the Civil Code of 1804, has in terms of liability retained the ambiguity of the Ancien Régime This misunderstanding has had numerous consequences on several fronts: economic, legal, and social. This will thus be the starting point of our reflection.

Our previous research on the right to build under the Ancien Régime, and more specifically on the Chamber of the Building Trades (Chambre des Bâtiments), has shown that the building contractor could be defined, simply, according to two criteria: mastery and contract. As a holder of one of the building masterships overseen by a guild, the contractor is contractually bound to his client to complete a construction project [1]. This definition gives rise to a specific legal status where rights are the counterpart of certain obligations, where privileges compete with responsibilities, and where financial risks legitimize profits [2]. Having defined and framed the building contractor in this way, we now need to consider how he is represented in society and, more specifically, his place within his own professional group.

During our research, it became clear that, under the Ancien Régime, building contractors constituted a 'transversal' group in French society, that is one containing both elites and lowly earners. Their main social activity was the creation of self-norms through the guild jurisdiction which they directed and to whose authority they were all subject. At the time, the specificity of the construction sector lay in the fact that it involved several institutions simultaneously and in superimposition with one another: a justice system and a police force embodied by the Chambre des Bâtiments; multiple trade communities (masons, carpenters, plasterers, etc.) who all recognized that they belonged to the same world, the building trades; and a large number of private or public construction companies governed by the principles of the emerging liberal economy, the rules of private and commercial law.

However, this superimposition of institutions should not distract us from the fact that "it is in the social processes - rather than in the institutions - that the analyses of law and order in a society must be anchored" [3]. Studying the practice of these institutions will shed light on the foundations of the social status of contractors who had to learn to reconcile the pursuit of profit with respect for public interest.

In the face of free competition in the construction market, contractors clung to the privilege of a monopoly. Only masters of a trade were allowed to undertake work. The relentless search for quality was paramount. This was symbolized by the production of a masterpiece, the gradual establishment of new construction law, and the ongoing search for the perfect building, even if this meant preventing defects, rectifying them, and repairing this or that defect. The desire to maintain constant control over the product of work legitimized the maintenance of a hierarchy among contractors. This is even more the case in our field of interest since it involves a specific system of justice for construction and expertise, which is particularly important. Hierarchy is inherent to the structure of the guild. "[I]n the exercise of the profession [this] was

The social status of Parisian building contractors in the 18th century.
A hierarchical and ambitious professional "body": between nobility and destitution

also extended by a *cursus honorum* within the communities which gave masters access to the offices of syndics, adjuncts and experts. These offices, often the prerogative of the most important artisanal dynasties, represented the public recognition of either a high level of professional skill or a recognized economic and social prestige" [4].

Nevertheless, this hierarchy of different building contractors was tempered by the classic solidarity observed within the trades themselves. This derived from the traditions of a collective ritual sacralised by the corporative institution, such as the corporative assembly and its organizational rules; membership of a specific fraternity; the place occupied at both ordinary and police hearings of the Chambre des Bâtiments; and the rank in the solemn processions of the constituted bodies. We will examine this tempered hierarchy first of all.

In parallel with this hierarchy, however, which was imbued with a character of solidarity, abuses of injustice, clientelism and favouritism did occur in the building sector in the 18th century in the search for profit, probably through the influence of public buildings and works. The building contractor was torn between respect for the initial and pure morality of guild privilege and abuses of it: a system that valued not just work well done but also social and financial success. At times, such success was achieved through the violation of guild regulations or at least actions bordering on illegality, as well as abuses of all kinds. The contractor's relentless ambition, his primary obsession, remained his quest for success, whatever the cost. Within the context of developments in rental property under Louis XV, the completion of quality work was not enough to satisfy the contractor's need for money. Gradually, the building contractor became a true businessman, attached to the guild values that had nurtured him, but attracted by a thirst for easy profit. Many pamphlets and court cases denounce this state of affairs. The search for this "lost paradise" led some contractors to their own demise.

By what means did masonry contractors succeed in their profession, or, in some cases, face bankruptcy? In the second part of this paper, we will examine the two key words relating to their success, "glory" and "money", as they applied to the practice of their profession.

Hierarchies and the expression of solidarity

The guild system is ambiguous: on the one hand, it implies a superimposition of different hierarchies, while on the other hand it implies a redeeming spirit of solidarity.

The construction of a hierarchy

Archival research reveals that several hierarchies existed among building contractors. Firstly, let us consider the position of the different groups of contractors within the *Chambre des Bâtiments*. In a memorandum concerning the jurisdiction of masonry in 1707, Master General Jomard describes the composition of the court, naturally placing the judges at the top. He classifies the personnel involved in precise terms: the three or four master generals, the two counsellors, the five attorneys, the three bailiffs, the chief clerk and his assistant, the collector of spices and vacations, the controller, and finally the syndic in office. After the magistrates, the first contractor only appears in the 7th rank as the syndic of the master masons' community, playing the role of a king's prosecutor [5].

Almost a quarter of a century earlier, a notarized compromise drawn up to settle disputes and lawsuits between the communities of master masons and the community of sworn masons (*jurés-maçons*) or experts regulated the location of these two groups of contractors [6]. The hierarchy at the judicial level was thus as follows: 1) the judge; and 2) and 3), on the same level, the syndic and adjunct of the community of master masons, who served as public prosecutors, and the sworn masons, who always ensured, where necessary, that a replacement was found for an absent judge if the hearing was a police hearing, a fourth row was established below with the masters of the visit. Regarding visits to building sites by the building police, the hierarchy was identical to the previous one, with the exception of the following clarification: the 4th rank contained the master masons, contractors, and the sworn masons appointed by order of seniority [7]. The hierarchy relating to the reputation of the contractors, on the other hand, comprised three ranks: 1) the judges; 2) the expert or sworn masons; and 3) the contractors, by order of seniority, with the additional criterion of whether or not they worked for the King's works. Those employed in the Royal Buildings were often considered to be privileged, benefiting from certain special favours [8].

Finally, with regard to the community of master masons, the hierarchy was as follows: 1) the judges, the true masters of the community; 2) the syndics and adjuncts, permanent representatives of the community before all administrative judicial authorities, etc.; 3) the council of twelve elected deputies, which constitutes the office of the community in charge of deciding on delicate, urgent, or even general questions concerning the company; and 4) the master masons, according to their rank within the community [9].

Research undertaken at the archives of the *Chambre des Bâtiments* clearly demonstrates that the masonry contractors were well aware of the different classifications that placed them in a specific rank, according to their specific situation, and that they were quite content with this situation [10].

Thanks to the combination of these four hierarchies of building contractors, we have been able to reconstitute four levels of prestige and fortune in the profession. These are as follows, and will be studied one after the other, in descending order: 1) the three master generals, judges of the *Chambre des Bâtiments*; 2) the fourteen administrators of the community in the persons of the syndic and the adjunct and of the council of the twelve deputies; 3) the expert-contractors; and finally, 4) the master mason contractors.

1/- "Les Maîtres généraux des Bastiments du Roy, Juge et Garde de la Juridiction royale des Bastiments, ponts et chaussées de France, establie au palais à Paris et en la ville Royale de Versailles".

This was the official title of their office at the beginning of the 18th century. These individuals were first and foremost contractors, since they had to be masons. And as architects and project managers, they produced a large number of buildings. There were three of them and from 1645 onwards, they exercised their magistracy alternately every third year [11]. Hearings were not held every day and the judicial holidays gave them time to attend to their business. Despite some abortive attempts to the contrary, they always retained their original function as master masons. There were a few exceptions to this in the second half of the 18th century, however, when some master generals only had a legal background [12].

Their main role was to exercise justice and police their fellow men. They exercised a justice of peers, centred on carrying out the building business. They alone developed an 'esprit de corps' which would exclude any 'intruder' who was not considered to belong to the world of construction. Five large families of architect-contractors provided the of the Master-Generals: the Marchands for 26 years; the Villedos for 23 years; the Delespines for 33 years; the Tricots for 9 years; and the Beausires for 68 years.

The function of judge was passed down from father to son, from son to father, or from brother to brother. Such figures were procedural, speculative, and somewhat authoritarian but retained a certain sense of public service and honour. In their role as judges, the master-generals played a key role in understanding the history both of Parisian construction before the Revolution and of the building trade. They also played a central role in the process of controlling building sites through police visits and in granting aspiring masters the final license to proceed in their work. Entrepreneurial licenses were issued upon their judgement. They confirmed the appointment of the community management and regulated it.

The social status of Parisian building contractors in the 18th century.
A hierarchical and ambitious professional "body": between nobility and destitution

2/- The syndic, the adjunct, and the twelve deputies:

This group, made up of fourteen people, managed and ruled the building contractors' guild: a syndic, an adjunct and 12 deputies. They were, of course, contractors. The syndic and the adjunct, were each elected for one year by their peers in a general assembly [13], serving as the representatives of all contractors. The functions they exercised were substantial and of an administrative, accounting, and judicial nature, but they were also short-lived. The management of the community's current or urgent affairs was entrusted to the office. This office was made up of the twelve deputies [14], who were re-elected every year in increments of six [15]. This team was accountable when it left office. The team's legitimacy derived from its democratic election in the General Assembly. The elected members were chosen by all their colleagues as representatives of the members of the community. They were deemed to be in possession of all the necessary qualities to: serve as intermediaries with the public authorities; defend their financial interests, among other interests, since they were entrusted managing the budget; confront the forced monetary appeals of the king; and demonstrate the technical competence of the contractor and the benefits of the building company to the public and the owners, to provide the people of Paris with a defence against the malfunctions fought against by the police, which they oversaw [16]. Let us not forget that the syndic and the adjunct acted as public prosecutors at police hearings. At their request, the master general would decide for or against prosecuting a contractor or journeyman who had failed to respect the building regulations. In addition, they were responsible for most of the judges' ordinances on construction.

Although they were restrictive, these functions presented many advantages, of which their holders were aware when they voluntarily put themselves forward as candidates. Once elected, they enjoyed a reputation that placed them among the elite of the profession in the eyes of the public, thanks to the publicity surrounding their election.

In addition to the syndic and the adjunct, the restricted assembly, which represented the whole community in its decisions [17], was made up of twelve deputies. These deputies were distributed as follows: two sworn masons; two former syndics who had knowledge of the previous affairs and were selected from the twelve oldest; the last two syndics to have left office after the presentation of their accounts and who were aware of the new affairs; and, finally, six "modern" and young masters, including a privileged master of the hospital of the Trinity, selected by his fellow-members [18]. The presence of holders of the office of sworn mason among the twelve deputies naturally caused a conflict of propriety. The assembly needed to resolve this with skill, recognizing the pre-eminence of the sworn masons (3rd rank) over the simple contractors (4th rank) [19].

3/- Expert contractors:

This is a group of privileged master masons whose office granted them a certain entitlement to control the activity of building tradesmen. Elected since the Middle Ages by the members of the mason community, two Edicts successively modified their status as experts: in 1574 they became office bearers and in 1690 the post of the expert was opened up to the bourgeois [20].

In 1572, these sworn masons, who had untaken an oath to fulfil their official obligations, were tasked with carrying out visits to and estimates of all the buildings, and overseeing the divisions of inheritance and measures (toisés), which their auxiliaries, the clerks of the building, recorded in their minutes and reports. In 1690, their jurisdiction was extended to all the towns in the kingdom and to "all visits and reports on works, both amicably and by court order". They then held a monopoly over building appraisals.

Expert contractors [21], who were relatively few, numbering between twenty and thirty in the 18th century, easily became rich thanks to their double source of income. On the one hand, they earned a salary as experts, and on the other they benefitted from the profits of their building businesses. Moreover, in the complex web of administrative, police, and even judicial mechanisms that characterised the community of contractors, experts took up strategic positions, acted as sponsors for aspiring masters during the preparation of the masterpieces, overseeing the regular police visits in the capital, and replacing the master generals, *ex officio*, in the event of absence or prohibition of their office. As such, they constituted an elite group situated above simple contractors. Causing numerous conflicts with other competing privileged categories, they felt more connected with their own community than with that of the master masons. More so than mastery, holding an expert's office rendered expert contractors special, more competent and therefore more renowned.

4/- Master builder contractors:

Finally, the bottom category of the hierarchy comprises all sorts of contractors, from the renowned to the unknown. It includes those who built up quite a fortune by taking on a significant number of buildings, to those who never had the chance to be anything other than a construction maintenance craftsman, remaining in the service of other, more influential colleagues. Within this heterogeneous group, the category of contractors for the King's Buildings stands out, particularly during the reign of Louis XIV and the great construction projects of Versailles and Saint-Cloud. Such individuals were often called upon to "settle accounts between two parties" [22]. The court undoubtedly considered them to be outstanding business managers and put their skills to good use. Protected by the royal power for whom they served, and even rubbing shoulders with the king's greatest architects at a lower rank, they were assured, if not of a certain wealth, at least of a certain notability.

Based on our current knowledge, the number of Parisian contractors seems to have increased in the 18th century from around 150 at the beginning of the century to nearly 300 in around 1750. Following some ups and downs, the number reached nearly 400 by the end of the century. As for the privileged, they remained very few in number, as did the sons of masters.

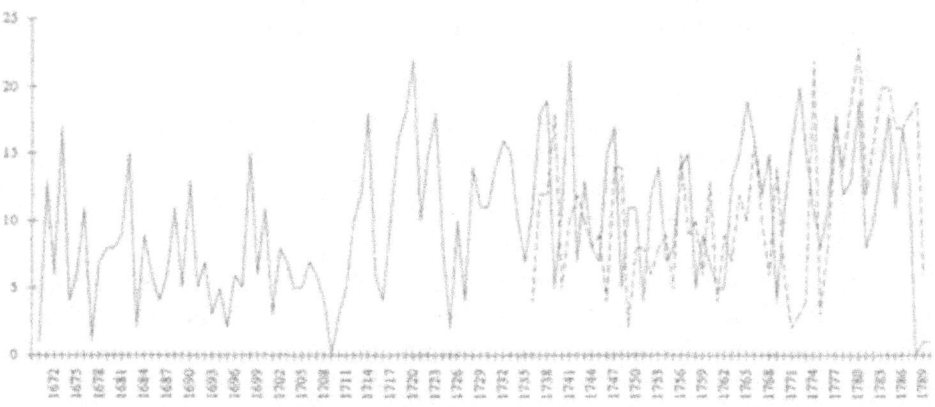

Figure 1: Evolution of the number of aspiring masons from 1690 to 1790 (solid line: after A.N. Z1J and dotted line: after A.N. Y)

The graph of new contractors by year shows three trends (Fig. 1): from 1670 to 1710, there was a significant and constant drop in new entrants; from 1710 to 1770, there was a fairly high and regular retention of new masters, albeit with some peaks and troughs; and from 1770 to 1787, there was a period of stability despite a tendency to see a rise in the number of aspiring masons received with the approach of the Revolution, which would liberate the system from the corporate shackles. The political awareness of aspiring members appears to have been raised at a late stage. In 1789 and 1790, the

The social status of Parisian building contractors in the 18th century.
A hierarchical and ambitious professional "body": between nobility and destitution

virtual absence of receptions heralded the imminent upheavals. In the graph created from the registers of the King's prosecutor in 1776 (when this source became reliable), the trend is clearly upwards [23].

The master masons and their solidarity

We must not forget that this group of building contractors also included the most disadvantaged, who bestowed an apparently pitiful general financial state upon the community: an assembly of 14 July 1710 mentions that "a petition will be made to Monseigneur d'Argenson to represent to him the state of the aforementioned community and to ask him to give him sufficient time to represent to Monseigneur le Contrôleur général the impossibility in which the aforementioned community is to pay (the sum of 12,000 livres and the 2 sols per livre)" [24], its state being reduced to a point where the majority of the masters are obliged to abandon their families for lack of funds because of the hardships of the times" [25]. Even if the reality was often different, particularly with regard to the community's finances, which were never in deficit despite the heavy toll regularly demanded by the monarchy, the fact remains that the apparent poverty and distress of certain contractors legitimised an exemplary solidarity in more than one respect, despite this harsh four-level hierarchy, where contractors often needed to jostle for their position. This is firstly because it was spontaneous, reminiscent of the guild spirit, but also because it was established between all levels of the hierarchy. Bridges of mutual aid, not necessarily financial, were built across the four ranks of contractors. There are many examples of these manifestations of solidarity.

The assembly of 26 July 1736 mentions that a contractor had lent money to the community and provides for his widow being reimbursed with 60 livres that were still owed, "to cancel a contract for three livres of annuities that the community owes them" [26].

More often than not, the Company of Master Masons provided for extreme needs, and "the caducity which prevents them from earning", of some of its members by granting them a lump sum of 10 or 12 livres per month until their death [27]. It would also temporarily lend a contractor who had been imprisoned the sum of 15 livres per month, "to serve as assistance" [28], or support a contractor's widow in their old age by providing them with a monthly sum of 15 livres [29].

A spirit of solidarity also characterised justice enacted between master masons as well as those set to occupy the position. The presence of two judges at certain hearings in 1695 can undoubtedly be explained by a former magistrate's desire to help the new holder of the office of alternative Master General, François Jomard, who had just been appointed [30]. Jean Aumont, still a simple contractor at the time, managed to have his case heard by his future fellow master generals and was relieved of his responsibility for a collapse in a building he had overseen [31].

The legal concept of solidarity was often invoked before the Chambre des Bâtiments between parties to a lawsuit. In principle, it was only used if the defendants in a liability action occupied the same rank within the professional hierarchy: if, for example, two contractors were bound by a sharecropping contract, the sentence would be joint [32]. On the other hand, this was not the case between a master mason and his fitter in relation to a failure to pay for stone [33]. Similarly, the same solidarity has been retained with regard to an owner in the context of liability for the non-use of his house which had been left under construction for too long [34].

This idea of solidarity between the different classes of the same contractor was sometimes threatened by a malicious complacency towards bourgeois clients who were victims of the work of a certain master mason. Master generals were surprisingly tolerant and flexible when assessing the work of one of their fellow master masons, a former syndic of the community, in a dispute with the project owner. While they did not go so far as to discharge the contractor in question "by grace and without drawing any conclusions" with regard to an "overhang" which they nevertheless deemed "beautiful and solid" [35]?

While this multifaceted solidarity may attenuate the somewhat feudal aspect of the professional hierarchy of Parisian building contractors, it also clearly demonstrates that, whatever their status, such contractors all pursued a singular quest for success during their entrepreneurial careers. We will now turn our attention to this quest in order to understand the mechanisms and means of achieving it.

The quest for success: working, making a fortune, and having "rank"

Exercising their profession allowed contractors to pursue a single goal: rapid success [36], the attributes of which were without question at the time, "glory and money" [37]. Being rich and holding a rank in society could have been the motto of Parisian building contractors. They entered this vicious and infernal circle which led them from fortune to recognition, from recognition to new estimates and contracts, and thus to new profits.

Business

According to what Le Camus de Mézières attributes to the architects whom "those who want to build" must choose, building contractors possessed "the minimal knowledge on business" [38]. As their main activity was their work, they undertook building projects in excess. Two archives in particular shed light on the professional activity of building contractors: firstly, the bankruptcies held at the Archives de la Seine. For example, we studied, fruitfully, the register of the companies of Edouard Jean Leboullier, master mason and contractor of the buildings of Paris, who received his master's degree in 1718. From 20 May 1719 to 10 March 1727, the register lists, successively, the type of work carried out (new buildings or repairs), the location of the building site, and the name and title, if any, of the master builder [39]. In addition, it contains marginal indications as to whether or not the work was completed and whether the contractor had been paid. In a note, he indicates "that the articles contained in the present register not crossed out and not declared paid which are not included in the state of what is due, are matters which still remain in the works and are not finished and matters of which the works are finished but of which I do not have yet rested from memory and on which works I received a number of sum and account by means of which I think to be almost paid except to count". We have provided a summary of this register in Table 1 below:

Table 1: Quantitative statement of the undertakings carried out by Ed. J. Leboullier, master mason in Paris between 1719 and 1727

Year	No. of new buildings and/or repairs	No. of new buildings and/or repairs, achieved and settled in 1727	No. of repairs	No. of repairs achieved and settled in 1727
From May 1719	2	2	7	3
1720	3	0	13	11
1721	2	2	21	18
1722	2	2	24	22
1723	3	2	18	17
1724	3	1	25	23
1725	1	0	21	13
1726	0	0	20	17
Until March 1727	0	0	3	1
	16	9	152	125

The social status of Parisian building contractors in the 18th century.
A hierarchical and ambitious professional "body": between nobility and destitution

On average, this contractor built two to three new buildings per year and carried out about twenty repairs. We have no detailed information on the contracts in question. However, one of the causes of his bankruptcy was probably the fact that five large building sites, not to mention the last ones begun in 1725, failed to pay several workers after the work had begun, if it was ever completed.

A global analysis of the cases of bankruptcy among building companies would inform us as to the total volume of their businesses and the reasons why they failed. Here too, individual examples are not representative, since the financial differences between individual contractors are so great. Even if the balance sheets are somewhat lower than 10,000 livres, some show some intense activity [40]. We believe that, even if most of the creditors of bankrupt contractors consist of large sums of money unpaid by the owners of the works undertaken, and apart from the seasonal nature of the building trades [41], the main cause of bankruptcies in the building trade lay in the lack of "financial resources" to cover the expenses required by the trade: not only the payment of workers, but above all, and in a greater proportion, the purchase of supplies and raw materials that the contractor was obliged to finance in advance.

Moreover, other symptoms of the contractors' financial difficulties can be seen in the actual seizures of their offices of experts, which can frequently be found in the judicial archives of the masons [42]. They would use their office as a guarantee to make up for temporary cash flow difficulties and to enable them to continue their business wisely.

The other archive, which provides an indication of the activity of building contractors, is scattered across the series of the A.N. Z/1j/1-255 (Chambre des Bâtiments). These are the declarations imposed on building contractors by the authorities [43]. Of these declarations – which, over time, the owners, the journeymen masons and finally the master mason contractors had to make on construction projects they were planning – only the last category seems to be reliable for counting Parisian building sites. However, this source only exists for the years 1782 to 1787, and even then it is incomplete, in the registers listed as Z/1j/1743 in the National Archives [44]. For the complete years, we can draw up Table 2 below. This shows us that at the time, the 310 Parisian contractors started an average of 360 building sites each year (!).

Table 2: Number of Parisian building sites from 1783 to 1786.

Year	No. of Parisian building sites
1783	394
1784	367
1785	346
1786	342

During the 18th century, masonry contractors were so overloaded with contracts that they often delivered their buildings late. The Chambre des Bâtiments did not hesitate to inflict damages to sanction such practices, which were embarrassing for the owner or tenant. Their priority was always construction, regardless of any parallel activities they might have been carrying out, even if such activities were in the interests of their community. As soon as their presence was required simultaneously on one of their building sites and in another place they would always choose their building site. For example, for the master general the building site would take priority over a hearing, for the syndic, his adjunct or the deputy, it would be prioritized over a general assembly, and for the police, it would take precedence over a visit. Most often, of course, they managed to combine their activities in such a way that they did not interfere with each other. They believed that anything that might have hindered the construction of the buildings for which they were responsible was to be avoided: lengthy trials were costly in procedural terms. The increase in the number of expert reports and site visits was a source of dissatisfaction, about which they often complained.

The archives show a great variety of situations, and a wide range of levels of wealth. To start a healthy building business, the contractor needed to have a financial base of about 2000 to 2500 livres. To inspire confidence, they needed to frequent the useful networks that maintained their assets (for example during, appraisals), to fight against the competition of newly appointed architects by revealing their incompetence, to accept and even contribute to the standardisation of new economic and legal knowledge, and to conquer the market for the construction of new buildings. The most far-sighted individuals ensured the creation of construction companies centred on the distribution of financial dangers, such as through subcontracting or associations [45]. However, contractors' most lucrative activity remained speculation through allotments, i.e. subdivided plots of land [46] and the construction of "turnkey" buildings. Others were tempted by innovation. While the search for profit is almost inescapable in the building profession in general, it is even more accentuated in the field of public works. In his Dictionnaire de jurisprudence et des arrêts, Prost de Royer writes: "As for buildings, they have become, especially in recent times, an abyss in which speculators, owners and even contractors have been lost, due to the difficulty of calculating accurately, the high cost of materials, and the perpetual illusion that artists and workers are, seeing only their own fortune and caring little about the ruin of their client. - Administrations are even more likely to be deceived and are more unfortunate: 1/ in that the care of the administration cannot equal that of personal interest; 2/ in that contractors, workers and suppliers, always greedy, are more audacious and less scrupulous, when they have to deal with any administration; convinced that there is no harm, because they only take over, and with whom, they say, would we make our fortune? " [47]

The glory of 'rank'

Alongside money, fame was the queen of virtues for the building contractor. One of the only ways for building contractors to achieve "glory" was to be elected as an adjunct, and therefore syndic, of their own community [48], or even simply to become one of the deputies responsible for representing all the members of a restricted assembly. For contractors, being elected by one's peers constituted a sign of recognition and pride, which they could use to their advantage. The multiplication of the election mechanism in this community made it 'avant-garde' in this field. In his *Répertoire de jurisprudence civile, criminelle, canonique et bénéficiale*, Guyot notes that, "the community of master masons was the only one whose affairs were managed by deputies, and that this form, prescribed in the past by the general judges, seemed so wise that it has since been applied, by the edict of 1776, to all the other communities, because the disadvantage of provoking a general assembly for each case, where there is almost always too much confusion, was felt" [49].

Provided that the election is held under optimal conditions, allowing individuals to help oversee and manage their professional organization, gives a key advantage which proves central to their success. Indeed, what would have been the point of being elected syndic or adjunct, or even deputy, by an assembly characterised by its absenteeism. Awareness was raised among the community by the contractors in 1738. The records of these elections have been passed down to us through the Masons' Court.

The social status of Parisian building contractors in the 18th century.
A hierarchical and ambitious professional "body": between nobility and destitution

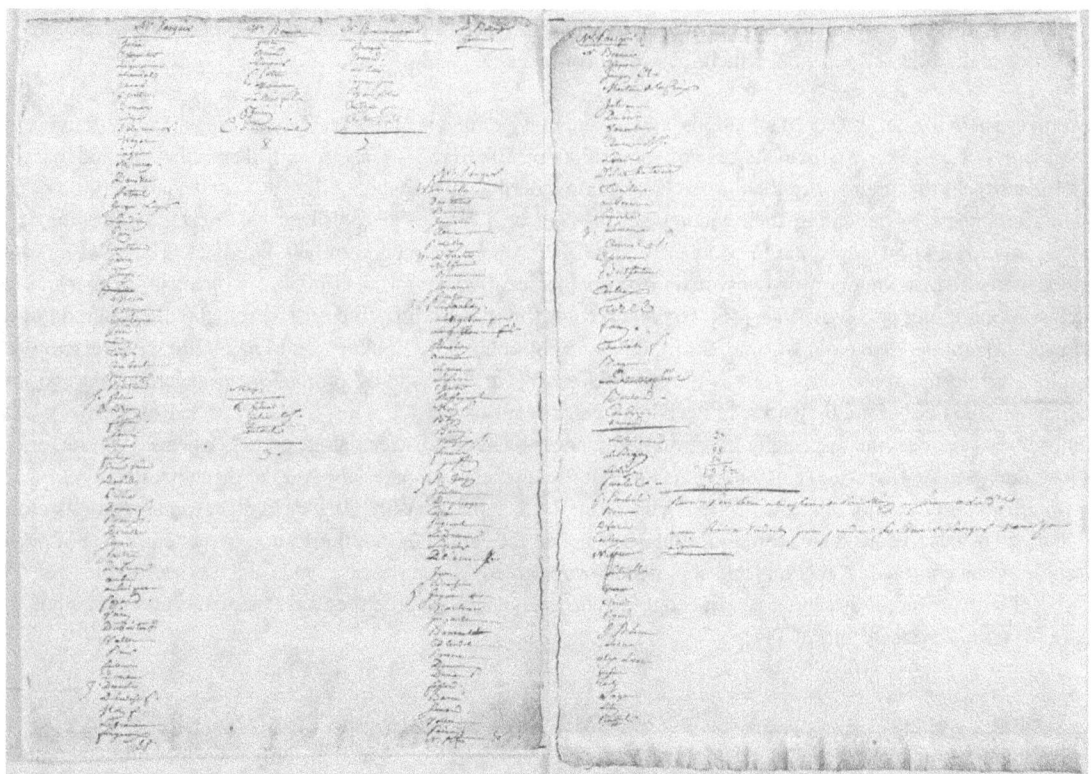

Figure 2: Example of a voting page for the election of an adjunct on 17 August 1764 (in A.N. Z/1J/139, recto-verso).

For all the elections, we have drawn up Table 3 below:

Table 3: Reconstitution of the votes in the elections of the adjunct to the syndic of the masons' community (1724-1775)

Years	Registered voters	Voters	Participation rate (%)	Abstention rate (%)	No. of Candidacies	Votes obtained by the elected adjunct	% of votes for the elected adjunct
1724		56					
1725	260	54	20.77	79.23	"2"	40	74.07
1726	260	120	46.15	53.85	"5"	71	59.07
1727	200	97			"2"	76	78.35
1728		101			"2"	86	85.15
1729	208	106	50.96	49.04	"2"	54	50.94
1730		54			3	27	50.00
1731		47			4	30	63.83
1732		75			3	50	66.67
1733	245	123	50.20	49.80	4	52	42.28
1734		107			5	52	48.60
1735		94			4	86	91.49
1736							

1737		86			5	30	34.88	
1738	204	172	84.31	15.69	5	145	84.30	
1739	234	150	64.10	35.90	4	88	58.67	
1740	240	188	78.33	21.67	8	125	66.49	
1741		179			8	109	60.89	
1742	262	201	76.72	23.28	5	100	49.75	
1743	246	203	82.52	17.48	9	96	47.29	
1744	234	194	82.91	17.09	5	147	75.77	
1745	257	206	80.16	19.84	9	125	60.68	
1746	231	206	89.18	10.82	6	158	76.70	
1747	240	223	92.92	7.08	4	179	80.27	
1748	284	203	71.48	28.52	3	195	96.06	
1749		215			5	144	66.98	
1750								
1751								
1752	280	209	74.64	25.36	10	169	80.86	
1753	243	203	83.54	16.46	2	200	98.52	
1754								
1755		82			4	68	82.93	
1756		187			5	126	67.38	
1757		156			4	112	71.80	
1758		137			3	130	94.89	
1759		143			6	114	79.72	
1760		153			7	89	58.17	
1761		139			8	99	71.22	
1762	275							
1763		162			4	135	83.33	
1764		174			4	156	89.66	
1765		178			3	156	87.64	
1766		205			4	115	56.10	
1767		182			5	120	65.93	
1768		120			3	91	75.83	
1769		152			5	103	67.76	
1770		130			3	128	98.46	
1771	305	209	68.52	31.48	5	198	94.74	
1772		171			3	85	49.71	
1773		230			7	110	47.83	
1774	335	175	52.24	47.76	5	89	50.86	
1776	330	189	57.27	42.73	4	107	56.61	

The social status of Parisian building contractors in the 18th century.
A hierarchical and ambitious professional "body": between nobility and destitution

Figure 3: Evolution of the number of registered voters and voters in the elections of the adjunct to the syndic of the master masons' community (1724-1775)

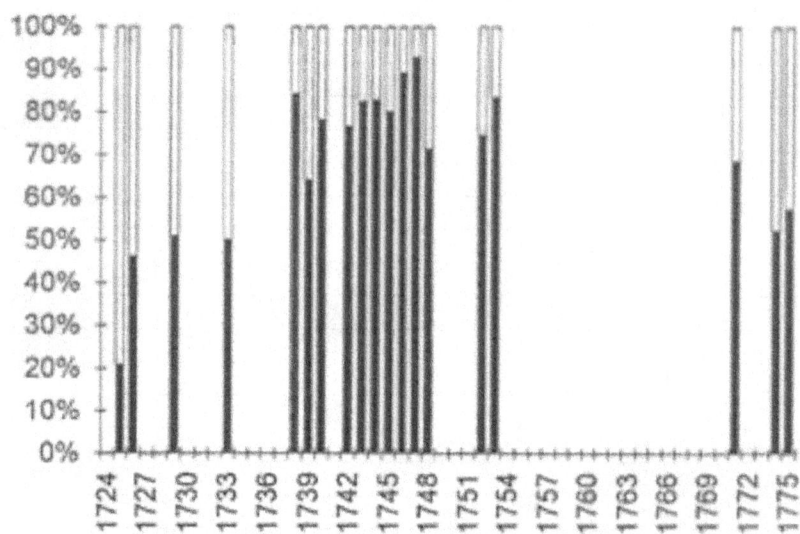

Figure 4: Histogram of the participation/abstention rates in the elections of the adjunct to the syndic of the master masons' community - 1724-1775 (abstention rate in white / participation rate in black)

From 1724 to 1737, an average of 85 out of every 243 master masons, *i.e.*, barely 35% of the contractors, voted to elect the leaders of their community. From 1738 to 1753, the average number of voters rose to 80%, before falling to 70% between 1754 and 1777 (Fig. 3 and 4). The same phenomenon can be seen in relation to the number of candidates. This number rose from four in the first period to five or six on average thereafter (Fig. 5). After 1738, the deputy was most often elected by an absolute majority of more than 60% in more than 75% of all cases (Fig. 6). A closer look at the records of these elections as a whole allows us to study the differences in candidacies. To succeed, 37% of the candidates had to run once, 27% had to run twice, 19% had to run three times, and 18% had to run seven times.

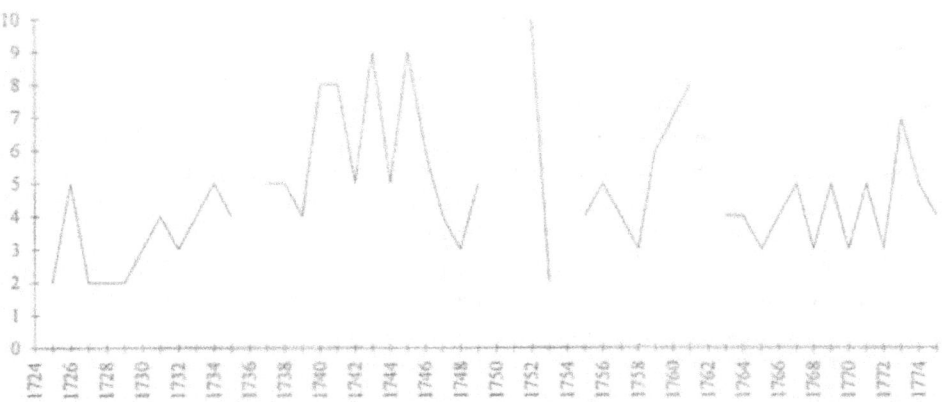

Figure 5: Evolution of the number of candidates for the election of the adjunct to the syndic of the master masons' community (1724-1775)

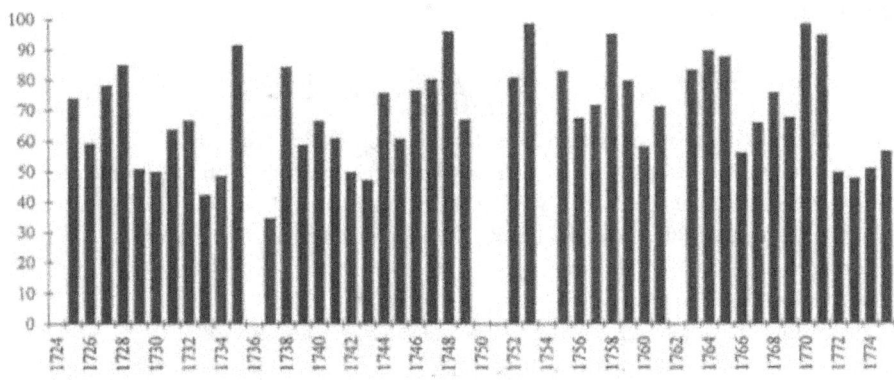

Figure 6: Evolution of the percentage of votes cast for the elected adjunct to the syndic of the master masons' community (1734-1775)

When a contractor did not achieve his moment of glory by being elected head of his community, he would sometimes try to reach a higher rank by all means possible. This was the case for Jean Pinard, who, disappointed at having been refused the position of syndic of the community, even though he had been elected deputy in 1707 as he also belonged to the community of expert contractors, acquired the position of alternative master general of buildings in 1751, thereby achieving his goal.

The social status of Parisian building contractors in the 18th century.
A hierarchical and ambitious professional "body": between nobility and destitution

Recognition from one's peers was only acquired through time. A contractor could only expect to be elected adjunct to the syndic after about twenty years of unblemished practice. The example of Pierre Convers is classic in this regard. Born on 2 September 1705, Convers was received as a master in August 1729, at the age of 24. He was successively elected administrator of the confraternity in 1751, and adjunct to the syndic in 1753, at the age of 48. He was elected syndic at the age of 49, after 25 years as a contractor. His election was almost a reward for merit.

The Parisian building contractor evolved admirably within the strict corporative fabric of the Ancien Régime, effectively supported by his peers within the legal and technical framework of the *Chambre des Bâtiments*. Those in the construction field naturally rubbed shoulders with those in the world of business. From the 17th century onwards, buildings were made not only for living in but also speculatively. During his professional career, contractors would encounter many pitfalls such as their random, difficult passage through the various stages of the hierarchy that characterised their working environment. Few of them would reach the magistracy of masonry; others would be satisfied with honourable intermediate levels or simply accept the benefits of an ordered solidarity. They did not all become powerful and/or wealthy, even though overall the construction activity was a proven growth sector, creating wealth.

We will close this study on building contractors in the 18th century with three general reflections. First of all, and particularly with regard to the contractor's social status, we are convinced that, despite certain misleading appearances, the strength of the building world lay in its ability to remain united at all times. For, although it comprised several guilds, the world of construction was united, as the history of the *Compagnonnage* [50] reveals. This true unity enabled those involved to innovate in a delicate area: the representation of the profession through democratic elections. No other trade in any field that we know of had done this at the time. This essential novelty, this quasi-revolutionary behaviour, prefigured the elective system of national representation that came after the Revolution. It should be noted here that no election in the close-knit world of building was contested. This also demonstrates an exemplary political maturity which enabled the building field to pass – without too much turmoil – from trade to profession, and from guild to the freedom of enterprise at the dawn of the 19th century.

Secondly, and more generally, it should be emphasised that the concept of the contractor could not have been studied without the archives passed down by the *Chambre des Bâtiments*, whose sentences from the 16th century onwards could only be appealed before the Parliament of Paris. An examination of these papers, which reveal the tumultuous, procedural social lives of contractors and other construction workers, helps us understand how this form of justice allowed both judicial and jurisdictional practices to become sources of law. Here again, we agree with Simona Cerutti when she writes about trade justice in Turin in the 17th and 18th centuries: "this presupposes that legal rules are inscribed in the practices of individuals and, consequently, does not attribute any supreme authority to the 'specialists in law' in the field of judgement, considering instead the judgement of the 'laity' to be legitimate." [51] Might it then be possible to question the assumption that, in Ancient Law, jurisprudence could never be considered as a source of law, or only rarely? The regulations issued by the jurisdiction of masonry were nonetheless norms, even though this was not run by professional magistrates, but by construction workers. Ordinary life – or, more precisely, trade, industry, economic life, in short – have contributed to the creation of norms outside of state institutions by summary justice in the hands of non-lawyers, institutions that have more or less distanced themselves from central power [52].

Finally, any research similar to ours must lead to a methodological reflection. From our example, we realised that it would be appropriate to develop micro-historical studies on specific, isolated social and professional groups by cross-referencing, where possible, normative and practical legal sources (e.g., court decisions, contracts, arbitrations, etc.), economic sources (bankruptcy files, order books, archives of companies to be solicited), and social sources (guild papers: minutes of general assemblies, statements of finances, etc.). As such, the history of labour law and that of social law would become a new, privileged field of research for lawyers, a field they have too long overlooked. Moreover, for the protohistoric industrial period, it is essential to develop the history of the economic fields of social groups, which are little known and difficult to locate, in order to measure economic activity accurately. The economic history of this period remains very sketchy to this day. Studying a subject from a multidisciplinary perspective remains a major asset for any historical research.

References

[1] R. Carvais, 'La force du droit. Contribution à la définition de l'entrepreneur parisien du bâtiment au XVIIIe siècle', *Histoire, économie et société,* 1995/2, pp. 163-189.

[2] R. Carvais, 'Le statut juridique de l'entrepreneur du bâtiment dans la France moderne', *Revue historique de droit français et étranger,* 74 (2), April-June 1996, pp. 221-252.

[3] S. Cerutti, 'Normes et pratiques, ou de la légitimité de leur opposition', in B. Lepetit (Ed.), *Les formes de l'expérience. Une autre histoire sociale,* Paris, Albin Michel, 1995, pp. 126-149 and the corresponding notes, pp. 322-326.

[4] H. Burstin, 'Conditionnement économique et conditionnement mental dans le monde du travail parisien à la fin de l'Ancien Régime, le privilège corporatif', *History of European Ideas,* 1982, vol. 3, n° 1, pp. 26-27.

[5] Bibliothèque nationale de France (referred to hereafter simply as BnF) Joly de Fleury 2400, Cartons Blancs, fol. 100.

[6] BnF Ms fr. n.a. 3357, fol. 89-91 v°, 12 octobre 1657 : « Que ledit juré du roy ès oeuvre prendra sa place dedans l'auditoire de ladite justice les jours des audiences sur les sièges en retour dudit maître des oeuvres du costé droit et les autres jurez sy aucuns sy trouvent se mettront du mesme costé et le syndic desdits maîtres maçons et l'ancien Bachelier prendront leur place sur les sièges en retour du côté gauche et les maîtres de la recherche à leur place ordinaire et autres maîtres s'il s'en trouve ».

[7] Archives nationales (referred to hereafter simply as A.N.) Z/1j/134, fol. 121, 1691.

[8] A.N. Z/1j/186, fol. 7 v, 19 June 1693, granting of a debt remission; A.N. Z/1j/188, fol. 4 v, 24 July 1697. *Idem*, A.N. Z/1j/192, 8 May 1679.

[9] The rank of the contractor in his guild is so important that it makes it possible to determine his seniority, his turn in the police force, his respectability, his propensity to be elected to the leadership of the guild.

[10] There are many examples: Procès-verbaux de J. Beausire, expert, 13 January 1775, A.N. Z/1j/227; A.N. Z/1j/222, 4 December 1726. On 4 December 1726, the *Chambre des Bâtiments* discharged Jean Aumont, masonry contractor, future master general, of the accusation of liability for having compressed the extra height of a shed. He managed to convince the judge that the plaintiff tenant of the site, a carpenter by trade, was guilty of having stored too much wood upstairs (A.N. Z/1j/222). Would the court have acted in this way if the contractor, even a mason, had not belonged to a 'privileged' class?

[11] From then on, three offices of master general were held in turn by an ancient officer, an alternate, and a triennial.

[12] Maugis was an attorney at the Châtelet, Boiesnier de Bardy was a lawyer, Léonard-Pierre d'Osmond was an architect-expert-bourgeois, and Pierre Caron, in addition to his title of lawyer, was a king's architect. Jean-Baptiste Beausire, Gabriel Chireix and Jacques Vinage were architects.

[13] The second succeeded the first, and each adjunct thus served for two years, one year as adjunct and the following year as syndic with a newly elected adjunct.

[14] From 1776, there were 24 deputies.

[15] Each one thus remained in the role for two years.

[16] *Cf.* the formula of the oath of the syndic and the adjunct in front of the *Chambre des Bâtiments* in Art. XII of the last statutes of the community of master masons in 1782: "To take care of everything concerning the policing of the buildings, solidity, good construction and public safety". An additional commitment was required from the King's Prosecutor before the Châtelet to authorise their entry into office: "To perform their duties well and faithfully, with regard to the internal policing of the community and the administration of its revenues" in A.N. Z/1j/153, fol. 10, 4 October 1782.

[17] Order of the Master General of 18 August 1741, Archives de la Préfecture de Police, Coll. Lamoignon, t. XXXIV, fol. 658-663 v° or A.N. Z/1j/112.

The social status of Parisian building contractors in the 18th century.
A hierarchical and ambitious professional "body": between nobility and destitution

[18] Arrêt du conseil portant homologation de la délibération de la communauté du 5 mai 1759, en date du 18 avril 1762 in *Recueils de pièces contenant divers objets de réglemens pour l'administration de la communauté des maîtres-maçons, entrepreneurs des bâtiments de la ville et faubourgs de Paris...*, Paris, 1762, BnF F 13023, pp. 26-31.

[19] A.N. Z/1j/237, 30 March 1753: "It was ordered that at the assemblies of the twelve and for the business of the community, the rank of each of the twelve would be regulated and determined and the votes and signatures received firstly from the syndics and adjuncts, then from the experts contractors who would be appointed to be of the twelve and finally from the other master masons divided up and appointed by the twelve according to the order of their reception".

[20] R. Carvais, "Creating a Legal Field: Building Customs and Norms in Modern French Law", in K.-E. Kurrer, W. Lorenz and V. Wetzk (Ed.), *Proceedings of the Third International Congress on Construction History*, Cottbus, Brandenburg University of Technology, 2009, pp. 321-328.

[21] From 15 sworn masons and 8 sworn carpenters in 1576, this number rose to 30 sworn masons and 18 sworn carpenters, *i.e.*, 48 experts in 1639, followed by 50 experts divided into two columns of 25 expert contractors and 25 bourgeois expert architects in 1690. From 1693, there were 30 officers per column.

[22] A.N. Z/1j/186, fol. 6, 22 April 1693.

[23] Over nearly 12 years, the annual average of reception was 17.

[24] "For the reunion of the offices of treasurer receiver of the money belonging to the said community, of the office of visiting controller of weights and measures and of the office of clerk to register letters of mastery, patents of apprenticeship, election of adjunct to the syndic, treasurer agent of the affairs of the said community and confirmation of the heredity of the offices of auditor and examiner of accounts."

[25] Bibliothèque de l'Assemblée nationale (referred to hereafter simply as B.A.N.) CZ11 31, fol. 6.

[26] B.A.N. CZ11 31, fol. 14 r°.

[27] B.A.N. CZ11 31, fol. 7 r°, general assembly of 27 February 1723; B.A.N. CZ11 31, fol. 27, 8 November 1754; B.A.N. CZ11 31, fol. 30, 16 April 1755.

[28] B.A.N. CZ11 31, fol. 8, 19 January 1724.

[29] B.A.N. CZ11 31, fol. 25, 26 July 1736.

[30] A.N. Z/1j/37, fol. 53 v°, 1695.

[31] A.N. Z/1j/222, 4 December 1726.

[32] A.N. Z/1j/221, 12 February 1724.

[33] A.N. Z/1j/200, 17 September 1688; see, however, the case of a joint liability declared between a master mason and his companion responsible for faulty workmanship and ordered to pay damages to the owner of the building in question (A.N. Z/1j/200, 26 March 1688).

[34] A.N. Z/1j/206, 21 September 1697.

[35] A.N. Z/1j/145, fol. 23, sentence of 18 October 1771.

[36] The contractors responsible for embezzlement did not hesitate to take offence at the accusations made against them, speaking of insults to their honour. (BnF 4° Fm 24084, *Mémoire pour les Supérieurs et Communauté des Pères Théatins, demandeurs, contre le sieur Bonneau, Maître Maçon, défendeur*, s.d., p. 10).

[37] The expression comes from a passage by Frémin in his *Mémoires critiques d'Architecture*, Paris, 1702, p. 173. It is used by this author in relation to workers, whom he tends to confuse with building contractors. The expression is reused by Françoise Fichet-Poitret, 'La gloire et l'argent - Architectes et entrepreneurs au XVIIe siècle', *Revue française de sociologie*, X, 1969, pp. 703-723.

[38] *Le guide de ceux qui veulent bâtir ; Ouvrage dans lequel on donne les renseignements nécessaires pour se conduire lors de la construction, & prévenir les fraudes qui peuvent s'y glisser*, Paris, 1786, 2 vols, t. I, p. 42.

[39] Archives de la Seine (referred to hereafter simply as A.S.) D5B6 638.

[40] *Cf.* A.S. D4B6 7 doss.314: bankruptcy of Louis-François Roquet, 13 March 1747: assets = 208,441 livres; liabilities = 182,363 livres.

[41] Weather conditions could be a reason for the momentary failure of a business.

[42] That of J. Beausire seized by decision of 17 January 1703 (A.N. Z/1j/53, fol. 54 r), of Jacques Lepas-Dubuisson by decision of 28 January 1706 (A.N. Z/1j/58, fol. 47 v et seq.), and of Pierre-Nicolas Delespine by decision of 29 May 1716 (A.N. Z/1j/69, fol. 44).

[43] See our paper 'La force du droit', (Note 1) pp. 177-178.

[44] It is not easy to read because it was compiled half chronologically and half in the alphabetical order of the names of the contractors.

[45] M.-A. Moulin, *Les maçons de la Haute-Marche au XVIIIe siècle*, Clermont-Ferrand II, Publications de l'Institut d'Étude du Massif Central, 1986, fasc. XXIX, p. 151. A study of the legal means offered to contractors to guarantee financial disbursements remains to be undertaken.

[46] J.-L. Harouel, *L'Embellissement des villes. L'urbanisme français au XVIIIe siècle*, Paris, Picard, pp. 174-179. "Fr. Monnier believes that speculation should not be given a moral connotation insofar as the State favours it, particularly in order to subdivide the large Parisian plots. Moreover, the word 'speculation' is from the 19th century. In the 18th century, you couldn't build without a speculator. We can distinguish three main types of speculator at that time: on the one hand, financiers and contractors who were really looking to make money; on the other hand, owners who had large gardens or private mansions that they could no longer maintain and who deliberately chose to subdivide land to improve their financial situation; finally, religious communities who owned huge plots of land in the city - originally designed to protect them from the movements of the city and which gradually lost their original purpose, as the city was becoming so much more demanding - and also subdivided them. Discussion during the colloquium on 'Brongniart, Architecte et Urbaniste de 1770 à 1815. I - L'Hôtel particulier et la maison dans la ville de la fin du XVIIIe siècle à la fin de l'Empire', *Cahiers du C.R.E.P.I.F.*, n° 18, March 1987, p. 91.

[47] Lyon, volume 3, 1782, V° administration, p. 857.

[48] One is elected adjunct for one year and automatically becomes syndic the following year.

[49] 1785, t. XI, V° *Maçonnerie*, p. 65.

[50] Even if the guild and companionship in reality have nothing to do with one another, the two institutions have something intangible in common, perhaps this very idea of solidarity.

[51] S. Cerutti, "Normes et pratiques", (Note 3) p. 137.

[52] It would certainly be interesting to draw up a comparative table of the two judicial institutions studied at the same time: the Turinese justice of trades, and the Parisian jurisdiction of the masons, if only in terms of the summary procedure that they shared. Read, by the same author, *Giustizia sommaria. Pratiche e ideali di giustizia in una società di Ancien Régime (Torino, XVIII secolo),* Gian Giacomo Feltrinelli Editore, Milan, 2003. This important book has just been published in French, *Justice sommaire. Pratiques et idéaux de justice dans la Société d'Ancien Régime (Turin, XVIIIe siècle)*, Paris, EHESS, 2021.

Long Nineteenth Century (1800-1914)

Time to Re-Evaluate? – New Findings on the Application of the Hennebique System in Germany

Geraldine Buchenau and Sabine Kuban
Landesamt für Denkmalpflege im Regierungspräsidium Stuttgart, Germany

Introduction of Reinforced Concrete in the Southwest of Germany

The state of Baden-Württemberg is located in the southwest of Germany, founded in 1952 by merging the post-war states of Württemberg-Baden, (South) Baden and Württemberg-Hohenzollern (Fig. 01). Each of the three original states had been part of the German Empire since unification in 1871. When investigating the introduction of reinforced concrete in this part of Germany, additional boundary conditions that apply (building law, authorities, etc.) due to the different social and political developments need to be kept in mind. The initial situation for the industrial revolution was significantly different in Germany compared to Great Britain. One reason for the delayed development in Baden and Württemberg was territorial fragmentation. At the beginning of the 19th century, industrialisation initially proceeded more rapidly and successfully in the Grand Duchy of Baden than in Württemberg. Baden was located in a relatively convenient position, with the Rhine plain offering an excellent traffic route, including a railway line constructed between 1840 and 1863. Many entrepreneurs with financial resources from France and Switzerland came to Baden from 1836 onwards, to establish at least a branch of their companies in one of the German states in order to benefit from the advantages of the unified customs territory.

Figure 1: Historical map showing railway connections 1849, marked in grey are the states Baden, Württemberg and Hohenzollern. Scan: Based on Railway map 1849 with additional information

*Time to Re-Evaluate? – New Findings on the
Application of the Hennebique System in Germany*

In 1838, Gustav Leube (1808–1881) founded Germany's first cement factory in Ulm (Württemberg) for the production of Roman cement. The founding of quite a number of other cement factories in the region soon followed [1]. The 1860s are considered the pioneering years of the cement industry in Württemberg [2]. Cement factories were also built in Baden during this gold-rush-like period, first in Mannheim and shortly afterwards also in Heidelberg [3]. The Portland cement factory in Heidelberg was founded in 1874 and is still in operation today under the name HeidelbergCement.

The spread of concrete construction, however, was hampered by the variable quality of Portland cement until the early 1870s. In 1868 the scientific work of the Berlin chemist Wilhelm Michaëlis finally established the foundations for the production of Portland cement [4]. Michaëlis was the first to provide precise information about the most favourable composition of the raw material mixture for artificially produced Portland cement. Based on his theses, the first cement standard was issued in 1878 and made mandatory for public building projects. As a result, demand for Portland cement rose sharply in the German Empire in the mid-1880s. With the standardisation of Portland cement, confidence in the newly developed binder ultimately grew.

From an early stage, concrete was used to construct buildings in Germany [5]. One of the oldest concrete houses in Germany is a railway caretaker's house near Blaubeuren (Württemberg), which the Leube brothers built in 1868 using Roman and Portland cement. They wanted to prove the usefulness of cement for building. Also residential buildings (Fig. 02) and even large-scale factory buildings were built using this material. The history of concrete buildings in the southwest is quite diverse.

Figure 2: Early example of a concrete town house called Villa Merkel (Württemberg). Photo: Iris Geiger-Messner LAD 2021.

With the knowhow to build larger concrete buildings and with the development of building with reinforced concrete under the influence of the Monier patent, it was only a question of time before reinforced concrete was properly introduced as a building material. The location of the Monier patentees, Freytag & Heidschuch in Neustadt an der Haardt in the southwest and Gustav A. Wayss in Berlin in the northeast of the German Empire, defined two poles in the development of reinforced concrete. Beginning in Berlin the first reinforced concrete structures were built in 1887, the same year in which a first design theory was published [6], but the realisation of larger buildings using a skeleton frame was only achieved after 1900.

After the expiry of the German Monier patent in 1894, there was no uniform theory about the bonding effect of concrete and iron. Construction companies used reinforced concrete according to their own construction designs and load tests. Above all, the companies Wayss & Freytag (founded in 1893) and Dyckerhoff & Widmann (founded in 1865) significantly advanced the use of reinforced concrete in southern Germany. However smaller regional companies, such as Brenzinger & Cie. from Freiburg, also played a part.

It is generally agreed that François Hennebique (1842–1921) was responsible for the decisive impulse in favour of reinforced concrete in the early 1890s. Hennebique was a French entrepreneur who created a system for reinforced concrete without formal academic training. He connected ceilings, beams and columns into a single unit and thus created the foundations for the widely used reinforced concrete construction method that bears his name. Hennebique had applied for patents in numerous countries from 1892, for example in Switzerland in 1893. These patents, as well as publications in his own journal Le Béton armé, accelerated the spread of his system. Ultimately, he became widely recognised through his presentations at the 1900 World's Fair in Paris.

The history of François Hennebique, his company and his significant contribution to the history of reinforced concrete have been the focus of various investigations over the past 30 years [7]. Based on patent rights and a specific business scheme, Hennebique's company and a network of concessionaires with permanent licence contracts greatly influenced the introduction of reinforced concrete in Europe. Hennebique only granted execution rights to his licensees. He reserved for his own office the technical processing tasks associated with projects and the preparation of construction drawings in exchange for ten per cent of construction costs. There were also a few concessionaires in Germany. Eduard Züblin (1850–1916) took over the general agency of Hennebique's system for southern Germany in 1898, when he settled in Strasbourg and founded his concrete construction business Ed. Züblin. However, as the paper will highlight, even earlier applications of reinforced concrete in the southwest of Germany included a number of applications based on the 1892 Hennebique Patent. A fine example is situated in Dinglingen/Lahr (Baden), a small town between Strasbourg and Freiburg im Breisgau, close to the river Rhine and with an early railway connection.

The Eckenstein Malting Factory in Dinglingen/Lahr

The malting factory in Dinglingen was one of the most modern malting plants at the end of the 19th century. The original building had been built in 1889, when the area around Lahr had developed into one of the best barley and hop growing regions. For a long time, hop growing was curbed by the authorities in favour of viticulture and so did not become established in Baden until the middle of the 19th century. As a result of the rising population, beer consumption also increased steadily in the late 19th century. In the euphoria, the former brewer Louis Stauffert had built the malting plant in Dinglingen in 1889 [8]. However, the factory owner had overstretched himself financially and quickly had to sell the plant. The malting factory was located in the same neighbourhood as a number of important breweries. The director Eduard Eckenstein of the Schweizer Gesellschaft für Malzfabrikation Basel (Swiss Malt Manufacturing Company, Basel) therefore had a great interest in the Stauffert malting plant. Consequently, Eckenstein bought the plant 1893 as one of five branches in the best barley regions of Europe. The building was extended in 1895 and mechanised a little later. State-of-the-art turners and kilns were purchased and installed in the newly built reinforced concrete extension [9]. By 1927 the company had become the largest malt production company in Europe with five factories spread across Europe. The malting factory in Dinglingen still stands, little changed. It continues to produce malt under the name Malzfabrik Eckenstein & Co. GmbH, Lahr-Dinglingen. The air raids on Dinglingen in 1945 caused little more than glass damage to the malt house [10].

Contractor

The building company Brenzinger & Cie. of Freiburg im Breisgau was commissioned to carry out the reinforced concrete work for the extension of the malting factory in 1895 [11]. Founded in 1872 by Julius Brenzinger (1843–1924), the company had initially specialised in the manufacture of cement ceilings and slabs in the 1870s. At that time, Brenzinger's company bore the additional designations "Cementwarenfabrik, Betonbau-Unternehmung, Stuccatur- und Asphalt-Geschäft" (cement products factory, construction company, stucco and asphalt business) [12].

The installation of a sewer system in Freiburg im Breisgau in the 1880s led to the company receiving important orders for the production of cement pipes. At the same time, concrete building construction developed with the building boom in Freiburg. Thus, Julius Brenzinger, a trained stonemason and sculptor, also began to produce artificial stones as imitations of natural stones. In 1893 he gained national attention with his artificial stone production when he was commissioned by the Portland-Cementwerke Heidelberg-Mannheim to deliver an impressive collection of artificial stones for the World Exhibition in Chicago [13].

The construction company had already started using reinforced concrete in construction in the early 1890s. However, the factory in Dinglingen was its first larger building structure using reinforced concrete. Julius Brenzinger was particularly interested in concrete technology [14]. In 1898 he became co-founder of the Fachverein für Beton (Professional Association for Concrete), later known as Deutscher Beton-Verein (German Concrete Association). As chairman of the association, he regularly attended its meetings in Berlin. At this time Brenzinger used the Hennebique system, but later on he also used the Monier system [15]. It is not known how the company actually gained its knowledge of the Hennebique system. According to Hennebqiue's company publication Le béton armé, Brenzinger was never listed as official concessionaire [16].

The first decades of Brenzinger & Cie. were characterised by growth as well as technical and artistic excellence. Julius Brenzinger already employed 140 people at the turn of the century when his son Heinrich (1879–1960) joined the company. By 1912 the construction company had almost 400 employees at various locations. The construction of bridges, elevated reservoirs, hydroelectric power plants, water towers, large factory buildings, hotels, sanatoriums and churches brought considerable inspiration and promoted reinforced concrete construction during the period when this construction method was flourishing. The Technical University of Karlsruhe awarded Julius, and later Heinrich, Brenzinger honorary doctorates for their achievements, and the Deutsche Beton-Verein named Julius Brenzinger an honorary member. The company's last significant buildings included large construction projects during the reconstruction period. In 2008 Brenzinger & Cie., now managed by the fourth generation of the Brenziger family, was transformed into a real estate company.

Architect

The design for the extension was carried out by the Freiburg architect Johannes Flink, who specialized as a brewery architect under the company name J. Flink & Cie [17]. Unfortunately, personal information about Flink is very scarce. His name and address were still listed in a Freiburg im Breisgau address book of 1922 [18].

The Building

The company premises of the still-functioning factory include a number of buildings from different times. However, the original building from 1889 still dominates the complex. It is a five-story high (about 22 metres) masonry building with an elaborate décor using different coloured bricks and pilaster strips. The decorative triangular gables were destroyed in the 1950s. The rectangular layout features an east–west orientation, with sidewalls 32 metres in length and gable walls about 19 metres long. The factory building and the extension were originally sloped with earth to protect them from heat. (Fig. 04)

From the beginning, the building enjoyed a connection to the nearby railway station. From there, after reloading into smaller carriage waggons the malt was delivered directly to the factory to be processed. (Fig. 03) This railway connection no longer exists, and delivery and collection are now solely by lorry.

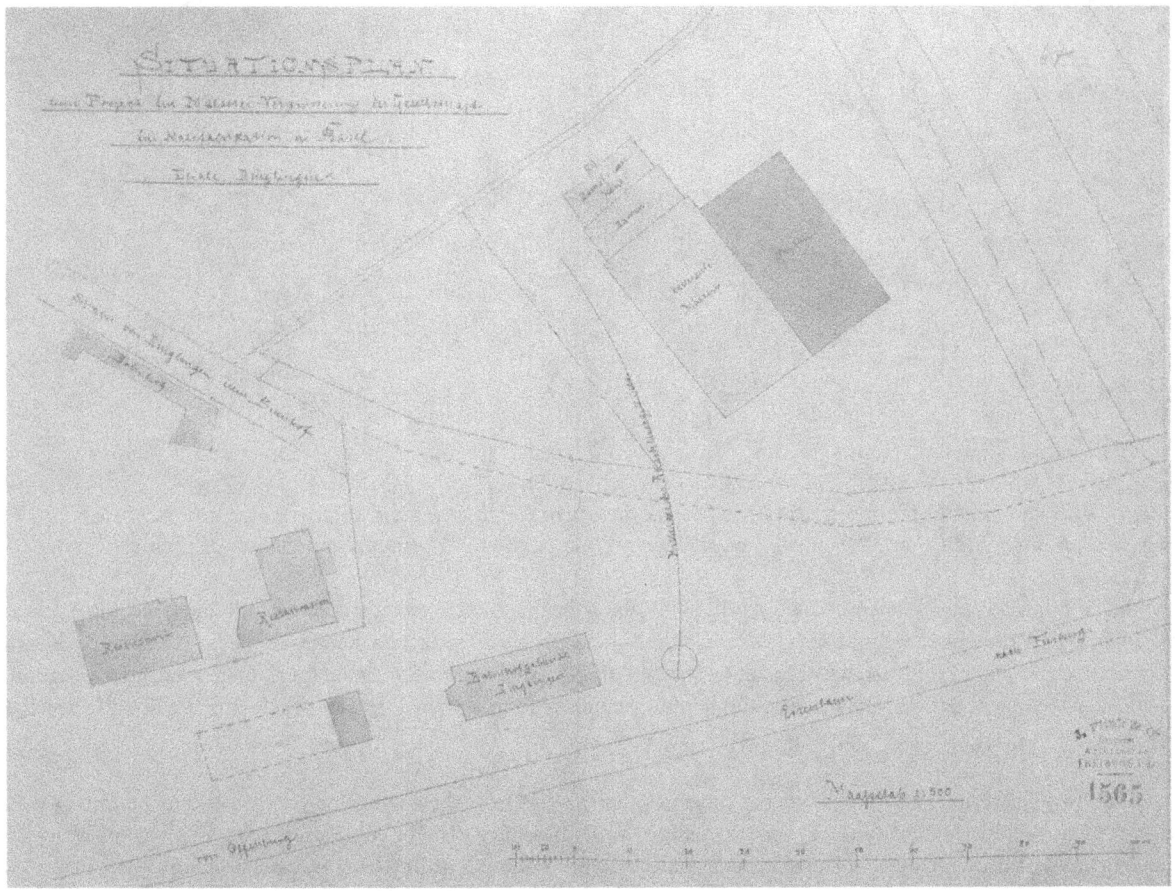

Figure 3: Map of the company property (the reinforced concrete extension is marked) as part of the building application of 1895. Photo: Kuban. Lahr Building Authority Archive.

*Time to Re-Evaluate? – New Findings on the
Application of the Hennebique System in Germany*

The extension of 1895 to the south side of the factory building (Fig. 03) connects to the main building via a doorway on each floor. Contrary to the drawing of 1894 (Fig. 03) the extension was two-storeyed, of which only one storey was above ground.

Figure 4: Drawing of the northwest façade of the malt factory in Dinglingen/Lahr. Photo: Wirtschaftsarchiv der Universität Basel, SWA H / Ba 501 Businessreport of the Gesellschaft für Malzfabrikation Basel, (presumably 1894).

In the building permit documents (dated April 1895), the structure is referred to as a cellar building. According to the accompanying drawings, both storeys were planned underground. The actual height of the earthen slope is not documented (compare Fig. 04 and Fig. 05). The building permit application includes a floor plan and a section. Unfortunately, more detailed drawings of the reinforcement, its form, dimensions and positioning are not documented [19].

The following descriptions are based on the construction drawings from the application for the building permit, as well as on findings from an onsite investigation focussing on the basement. The building itself covers an area of about 23 metres in width and 32 metres in length. The distance between floor and ceiling level is about 3 metres in both storeys. The top storey (i.e. the ground floor) has an incline of the ceiling level to the south.

The interior layout from north to south includes three rows of reinforced concrete columns 5 metres apart. Each row (from east to west) consists of five columns with a distance of 5.10 metres between each column. (Fig. 06) The columns on the upper floor have a dimension of 35 by 35 centimetres, while the columns in the bottom floor have a dimension of 41 by 41 centimetres.

The ceiling structures on both floors include three different beam types, with types two and three running perpendicular to type one. The following description concentrates on the basement structure. Here the primary load-bearing beams have a dimension of 18 by 33 centimetres and run east to west in the axis of the columns. Their supports at the columns as well as at the outer walls show haunches. The secondary and tertiary beams run north to south. The secondary beams also run in the axis of the columns and have a dimension of 18 by 24 centimetres. Their supports also show haunches. It should be noted that the built dimensions of the haunches, both with the primary and the secondary beams, show a length of 88 centimetres. Thus they are much larger than originally planned. The tertiary beams run north to south in between the column axes and have a dimension of 18 by 27 centimetres. These beams have a rectangular form without haunches. The ceiling between the basement and ground floor has a thickness of 10 centimetres.

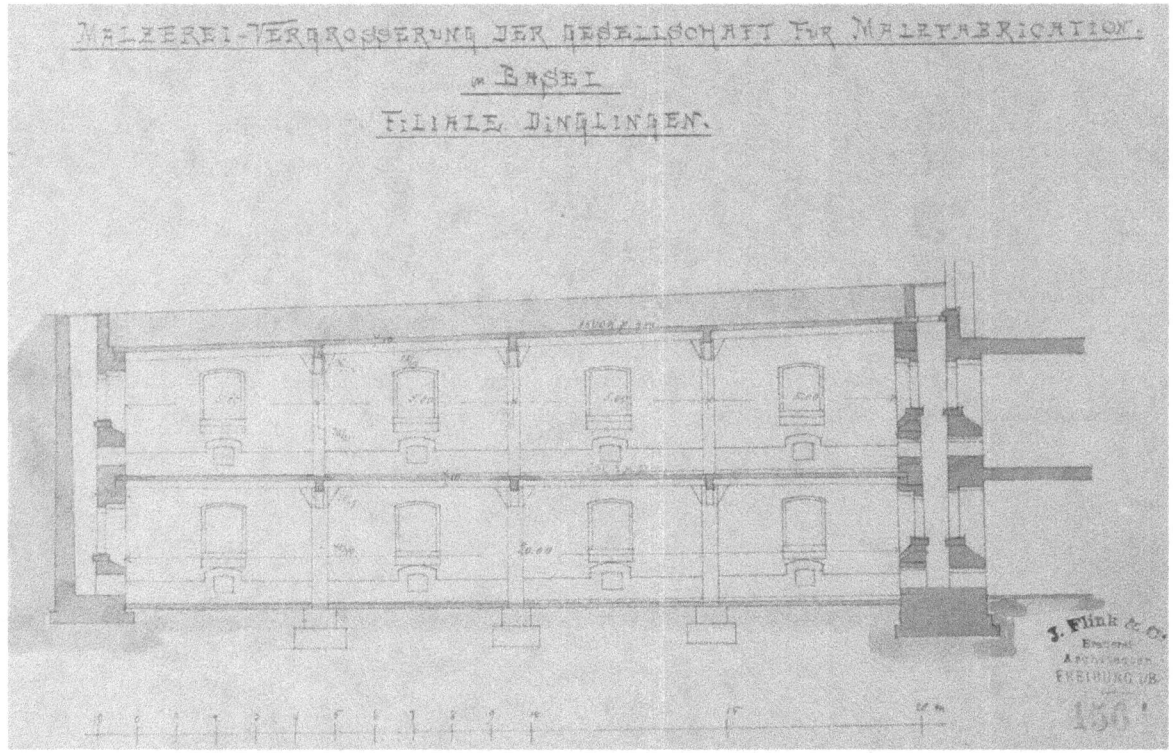

Figure 5: Section drawing (north–south orientation) as part of the application of building permission, 1895. Photo: Kuban. Lahr Building Authority Archive.

Brenzinger had obviously used information from the Hennebique system when building the extension to the malt house. In his company brochure, and later in a company chronicle to celebrate the company's 50th anniversary in 1922, he gladly listed the malthouse as a reference, describing it as using reinforced concrete ceilings in Hennébique construction, executed in 1895 (Fig. 07) [20]. And although the building records do not include a direct reference to Hennebique, the structure itself gives definite proof.

*Time to Re-Evaluate? – New Findings on the
Application of the Hennebique System in Germany*

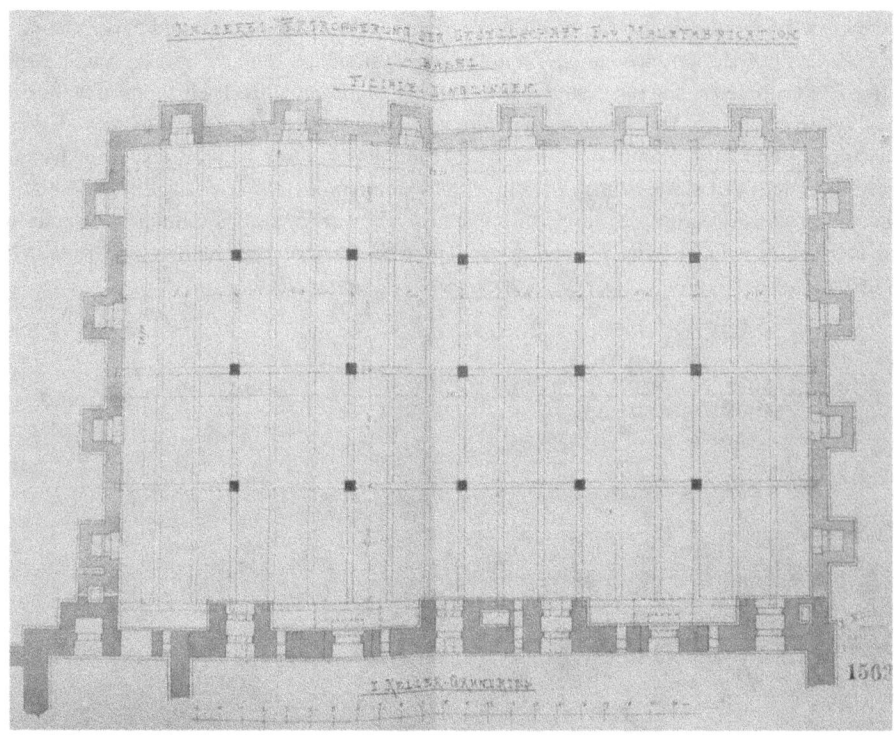

Figure 6: Ground floor plan, with the 15 columns highlighted as part of the application of building permission, 1895. Photo: Kuban. Lahr Building Authority Archive.

Figure 7: Interiour of the extension of the malt factory. Photo: Company chronicle for the 50th anniversary of the Brenzinger Company (1922), Badisches Landesmuseum Karlsruhe Außenstelle Südbaden: BA 2000-01514_Scan01_LABW_Staufen.

The Hennebique System

The Hennebique system is known for its flat iron stirrups, designed to absorb sheer forces and hold the longitudinal iron reinforcement in position. These, as well as round shaped reinforcement bars, were part of the design from the start. However, the composition of the reinforcement evolved over time [21].

By rigidly connecting the vertical columns with horizontal ribs and beams, a monolithic structure was created. The external shape consists of beams connected with haunches, a longstanding characteristic of monolithic reinforced concrete constructions that is generally associated with Hennebique. In order to compensate overlapping stresses and the supporting moment of crossing beams, haunches were included in the structure.

Wilhelm Ritter (1847–1906), Professor at the Eidgenössisches Polytechnikum in Zurich, sketched the course of forces in such a reinforced beam in 1899 through an analogy to the truss girder [22]. Even before, and around the same time as the malting factory was being built in Dinglingen/Lahr, the engineer and contractor Armand Favre (1859-1899) from Zurich had presented the advantages of the Hennebique system in an article in the Swiss construction journal Schweizerische Bauzeitung in February 1895 [23]. The reinforcement at the malting factory in Lahr/Dinglingen was designed accordingly.

Initially, Hennebique's reinforced concrete structure was supported with masonry perimeter walls. [24] Hennebiques T-beam system was the common for high loads and large spans [25]. For higher loads, round iron reinforcement bars were placed close together and even several times on top of each other. For large spans, secondary beams perpendicular to the main beams were common. Hennebique arranged longitudinal reinforcement bars in the columns in combination with flat iron strips as transverse connections to secure their position [26]. These horizontal, perforated flat iron strips, were a characteristic of Hennebique and gave the longitudinal reinforcement bars support during concreting. (Fig. 10 left)

The Malting Factory and its Reinforcement

Neither the original structural calculations nor the reinforcement design for the malting factory are documented, and it is not clear if and in what way François Hennebique and his company were directly part of this building project [27]. However, the findings in the malting factory seem identical to the flat iron stirrups used in the Hennebique system. (Fig. 08)

Figure 8: Stirrup for ceiling reinforcement found at the malting factory. Photo: Buchenau 2020.

As a result of aging and the corrosion of the reinforcement, the building structure nowadays lacks parts of its concrete cover and thus allows a direct investigation of the reinforcement of the ceiling, beams and columns. (Fig. 09) The ceiling slabs (10 centimetres) in both storeys have small round bars (ø 6 millimetres, 25 centimetres apart) spanning one-way between the tertiary beams, as well as small stirrups (Fig. 08). The stirrups in the ceiling slabs are made from iron strips with a thickness of 2.5 millimetres and a width of 20 to 23 millimetres. Bent to shape, each stirrup has a height of about 9 centimetres, leaving a concrete cover of about 0.5 centimetres at the top and bottom of the ceiling slab.

All the beams have longitudinal round bars with a diameter of more than 30 millimetres, positioned along the bottom flange and larger stirrups. The stirrups in the beams are also made from iron strips but with a thickness of 3 millimetres and a width of 40 to 47 millimetres. The height of these stirrups remains unclear as their ends are encompassed from the ceiling slab. Along the length of each beam, the stirrups are positioned with a distance of about 15 centimetres. (Fig. 09)

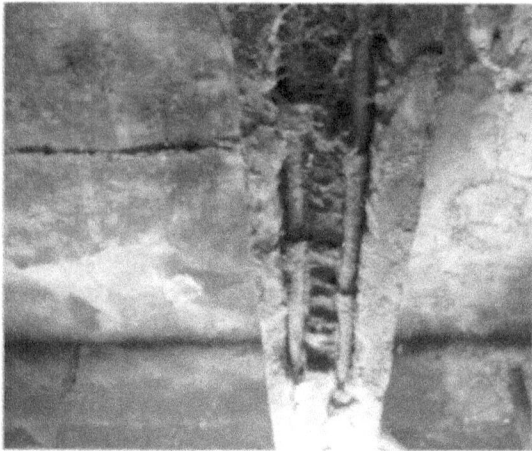

Figure 9: Details of the basement structure in its current state. Photo: Buchenau 2020.

The beams underneath the ground floor ceiling slab have up to four bars in the bottom layer and additional bars in a second layer around the middle height of the beams. The beams in the basement have only two bars each, in a single bottom layer. This obvious difference of the reinforcement ratio can be explained through the original design. The records show that the ground floor ceiling was designed for a live load of 15 kN/m² (resembling a significant cover of earth) while the ceiling between basement and ground floor was designed for a live load of only 2.5 kN/m². (Fig. 05)

The columns have round bars (ø 23 millimetres) as longitudinal reinforcement and horizontal stirrups with a spacing about 65 centimetres. The column stirrups are made from iron strips with a thickness of 5 millimetres. (Fig. 10)

Interestingly, the constructed structure almost perfectly matches a design made for a warehouse in Antwerp in 1894 by Henri Hertogs (1861–1930), a Belgian architectural engineer [28]. Both projects prematurely incorporate the system Hennebique patented only in 1896. Even more astonishing is the fact that the first design drawing for the project in Antwerp predates contact with the Hennebique company office. The Antwerp design was never executed, making the building in Lahr/Dinglingen an even more precious temporary witness.

Figure 10: Reinforcement details of a column according to Ritter (left) and as built (right). Scan (left): from Hennebique com- pany magazine Le Béton Armé, Jul.1899, p. 13; Photo (right): Kuban 2020.

Conclusions

The malting factory structure in Lahr/Dinglingen seems to be the first 'Hennebique' structure in the German Empire [29] and maybe even one of the first in Europe still intact and in existence. Built in 1895 it predates so far the oldest known Hennebique construction in Germany by almost three years [30]. Comparatively smaller in size it nevertheless includes the Hennebique reinforcement system. It also seems to be one of the first multi-storey building structures made with reinforced concrete. The malt house extension was built by the medium-sized construction contractor Brenzinger & Cie. of Freiburg im Breisgau, apparently without a documented connection to the Hennebique's main office in Paris. However, there must have been some kind of influence from François Hennebique through his construction company, since the structure includes significant characteristics of the Hennebique system.

Julius Brenzinger was never an official concessionaire of the Hennebique patent. But with the company's location close to Switzerland and France, and a Swiss owner for the building project, it seems very likely that the Hennebique patent was an influence. For example, the Swiss engineer and Hennebique representative Samuel de Mollins from Lausanne disseminated the construction method as early as 1893 in the journal Bulletin de la Société vaudoise des ingénieurs et des architectes, showing section drawings of a multi-storey structure [31]. The design shown in the article includes specific characteristics that can also be found in the built structure. Yet, further research is necessary in order to analyse Brenzinger's company business organisation in more detail and also to evaluate possible influence on building with reinforced concrete in the neighbouring regions.

Given its importance, the Brenzinger & Cie. company should be mentioned alongside companies like Hennebique concessionaires such as Martenstein & Josseaux and Züblin [32], or the licensee Max Pommer [33]. All three started as local building contractors. However, they began building larger reinforced concrete buildings only in 1898 – significantly later. These projects included the former warehouse building in Strasbourg as well as buildings such as the Adlerwerke in Frankfurt am Main and the Röder printing company in Leipzig. The last building is still preserved. In conclusion, the case study presented in this paper shows that Hennebique was to some extent successful in Germany at an early stage.

Perhaps this success did not take the form of profitable patent fees, but in any case his influence on developments in the German building industry began earlier than has been thought in form of knowledge transfer.

References

[1] G. Buchenau, M. Hascher, 'Zementfabriken als Industriedenkmale', *Die Denkmalpflege*, vol.77, no.1, 2019, pp. 44-53.
[2] O. Kehm, 'Die Entwicklung der Oberschwäbischen Zementindustrie', *Zeitschrift für die gesamte Staatswissenschaft*, 1907, Tübingen: Verlag der H. Laupp'schen Buchhandlung, pp. 54-82.
[3] D. Cramer, '*Die Geschichte von HeidelbergCement. 140 Jahre Baustoffproduktion*' Heft 8, Hrsg. HeidelbergCement AG, 2013
[4] W. Michaëlis, *Die Hydraulischen Mörtel Insbesondere Portland-Cement in Chemisch-Technischer Beziehung für Fabrikanten, Bautechniker, Ingenieure und Chemiker*, Leipzig: Verlag von Quandt & Händel, 1869.
[5] G. Buchenau, 'Beton und seine Wachsende Rolle in der Denkmalpflege', *Denkmalpflege in Baden-Württemberg*, vol.46, 2017, pp. 29-35, 208-214, 306-311; vol. 47, 2018, pp. 55-60.
[6] S. Kuban, 'Innovation and Standstill: Early Application and Development of the Monier-System in Berlin', pp.431-438 in B. Bowen, T. Leslie, J. A. Ochsendorf, D. Friedman (Eds.), Proceedings of the Fifth International Congress on Construction History, Chicago 2015, Chicago: Construction History Society of America, 2015.
[7] One of the first of these investigations is Gwenaël Delhumeau, 'Hennebique and Building in Reinforced Concrete around 1900' in V. Gregotti, L. Ravanel, M. Culot, G. Delhumeau (Eds.) *Rassegna (Reinforced Concrete: Ideologies and Forms from Hennebique to Hilberseimer)*, pp. 15-25; Gwenaël Delhumeau, Jacques Gubler, Réjean Legault, Cyrille Simmonnet, *Le Béton en Représentation*. Hazan Paris,1993; and Gwenaël Delhumeau, *L'Invention du Béton Armé: Hennebique 1890–1914*. Edition Norma Paris 1999. More recently the publication by Stephanie Van de Voorde of *Hennebique's Journal le Béton Armé: A Close Reading of the Genesis of Concrete Construction in Belgium* (pp. 1453-1461 in K. E. Kurrer, W. Lorenz, V. Wetzk (Eds.), *Proceedings of the Third International Congress on Construction History*, Cottbus 2009, Cottbus: Neunplus 1, 2009) concentrates on Belgium and investigates the company magazine *Le Béton Armé*..
[8] W. Caroli, *Dinglingen: Das Dorf am Schutterlindenberg, Eine Ortsgeschichte*, Ort: Bärenfelser-Verlag 2011.
[9] Wirtschaftsarchiv Basel SWA H / Ba 501, company publication, *Geschichtliche Notizen über die Gesellschaft für Malzfabrikation (Malterie Franco-Suisse) der verehrten Kundschaft anlässlich der Internationalen Ausstellung zu Mailand 1906 gewidmet*. Firmenbroschüre;
[10] Caroli, *Dinglingen* (Note 8).
[11] Company publication Brenzinger & Cie. Beton- und Eisenbeton-Bau, Cementwaren-Fabrik, Freiburg im Breisgau ca. 1915.
[12] Musterbuch der Firma Brenzinger & Cie. not dated.
[13] Company Calendar by Brenzinger & Cie. published in 1922.
[14] Brenzinger was very active in the Beton-Verein. This can be interpreted as a significant interest in reinforced concrete and the building technology in general.
[15] *Bericht über die 6. Hauptversammlung des Deutschen Beton-Vereins*, Berlin: Verlag Thonindustrie-Zeitung, 1903
[16] The Hennebique company magazine *Le béton armé* is available online - https://lib.ugent.be/catalog/ser01:000895607 (last checked 10th of March 2021).
[17] The drawings as part of the application of a building permission include a company stamp indicating this specialisation.
[18]https://adressbuecher.genealogy.net/addressbook/547461461e6272f5cfece02e?start=..&sort=lastName&offset=5775&max=25&order=asc (last checked on 5th March 2021).
[19] Lahr Building Archive, building record including the 1895 building permit for the property at Wilhelmstr. 1-2 in 77922 Lahr-Dinglingen.
[20] Badisches Landesmuseum Karlsruhe Außenstelle Südbaden: BA 2000-01514_Scan01_LABW_Staufen.

[21] Armande Hellebois, 'Theoretical and Experimental Studies on Early Reinforced Concrete Structures: Contribution to the analysis of the bearing capacity of the Hennebique System' (Ph.D. thesis, Université Libre de Bruxelles, 2013) gives a detailed account on the evolution of the Hennebique System with a focus on the reinforcement.

[22] Wilhelm Ritter, 'Die Bauweise Hennebique', *Zürich Schweizerische Bauzeitung*, vol.33/34, no.5, 1899, pp. 41-43, no. 6, pp. 49-51, 59-61.

[23] Armand Favre, 'Einiges über den „Béton Armé" nach dem System Hennebique', *Schweizerische Bauzeitung*, vol.25/26, no.5, 1895, pp. 31-32.

[24] *Bericht über die 5. Hauptversammlung des Deutschen Beton-Vereins*. Berlin: Verlag Thonindustrie-Zeitung, 1902

[25] Carl Kersten, *Der Eisenbetonbau – Teil 2: Anwendungen im Hoch- und Tiefbau*, 4. Aufl., Berlin: Ernst & Sohn Verlag, 1909

[26] Carl Kersten, *Der Eisenbetonbau – Teil 2: Anwendungen im Hoch- und Tiefbau*, 3. Aufl., Berlin: Ernst & Sohn Verlag 1906

[27] As indicated before, there is no mention of Brenzinger as a concessionaire in *Le Béton Armé*. The magazine archive is available via https://archiwebture.citedelarchitecture.fr/ (last checked on 16 March 2021). It does not include any information on this specific building project.

[28] Ine Wouters, Stephanie van de Voorde, Marianne De Fossé, Inge Bertels, 'Built to Stock: Versatility of Hennebique's Urban Warehouses in Belgium (1892-1914)', in I. Wouters, S. Van de Voorde, I. Bertels, B. Espion, K. De Jonge, D. Z. (Eds.), *Building Knowledge, Constructing Histories: Proceedings of the Sixth International Congress on Construction History*, Brussels 2018, Leiden: CRC Press. Taylor and Francis Group, pp.1383-1391.

[29] Alexander Kierdorf, 'Why Hennebique Failed in Germany: Strategies and Obstacles in the Introduction of a New Construction Technology in K. E. Kurrer, W. Lorenz, V. Wetzk (Eds.), *Proceedings of the Third International Congress on Construction History*, Cottbus 2009, Cottbus: Neunplus 1, 2009, pp. 897-901.

[30] Stefan W. Krieg, 'Max Pommer and the Oldest Known Hennebique Construction in Germany: A Printer's Shop in Leipzig' in K. E. Kurrer, W. Lorenz, V. Wetzk (Eds.), *Proceedings of the Third International Congress on Construction History*, Cottbus 2009, Cottbus: Neunplus 1, 2009, pp. 911-918.

[31] Samuel de Mollins, 'Le Béton de Ciment Armé', *Bulletin de la Société Vaudoise des Ingénieurs et des Architects*, vol.19, no.6, 1893, pp.105-107.

[32] According to the Hennebique company magazine *Le Béton Armé*, available online - https://lib.ugent.be/catalog/ser01:000895607 (last checked 10th of March 2021).

[33] Thomas Adam et al, *Max Pommer: Architekt und Betonpionier*, Beucha: Sax 1999; Krieg, *Max Pommer* (note 31).

Agrarian Capitalism and The Cost of Building in Antebellum Virginia

Clifton Ellis
Texas Tech University

The antebellum period in the United States of America is defined as the period between 1815 and the outbreak of the American Civil War in 1861. This paper seeks to reveal the causal links between intention and architecture in the American South during the antebellum period and the implications and legacies of an environment built with enslaved labor. A study of the actual construction costs of antebellum building campaigns can consider both the monetary and human cost of construction of enslaved labor. The focus of this study is the Greek Revival mansion house (Fig. 1) that James Bruce, a Virginia tobacco planter in Halifax County, completed at his Berry Hill plantation in 1845 [1].

Figure 1: Berry Hill Plantation, Halifax County, Virginia (Virginia Department of Historic Resources)

James Bruce enslaved more than 400 African Americans on his four Virginia plantations. Both the manuscript documentation and the surviving buildings of his home plantation, Berry Hill, are evidence of the human cost of agrarian capitalism; such building campaigns exacted not only a monetary cost, but also a human cost. The cost of one enslaved worker's labor is fully documented in original sources, as is the cost of housing that enslaved worker. The cost of an enslaved worker can readily be compared to the cost that Bruce incurred of employing a tutor, an overseer, a clerk, or to the cost of a marble fireplace mantle, a silver-plated doorknob, a dining room sideboard.

The mansion house that James Bruce completed at his Berry Hill plantation in 1845, had a final cost of $35,432.00. At 9,000 square feet, the house was two-and-a-half times larger than the Halifax County courthouse (Fig. 2) that the master builder, Josiah Dabbs, had finished in 1838. Berry Hill stood in the landscape of Virginia as the largest and finest example of Greek Revival architecture of the period, and more importantly to this discussion, as a testament to the profitability of an agrarian system of capitalism based in slavery [2].

Figure 2: Halifax County Courthouse (Virginia Department of Historic Resources)

On March 15, 1842 James Bruce paid $3,000 to master builder Josiah Dabbs, who began work immediately, following the drawn plans and detailed descriptions according to the contractual agreement that Bruce and Dabbs had signed the previous month. Dabbs had the building ready for occupancy by November of 1843 and the Bruces were settled in their new house by Christmas of that year. Although Dabbs had finished most of the work on the house within eighteen months, he continued to work on outbuildings and the house itself for another year. During the entire building campaign Dabbs was responsible for procuring materials and for employing and supervising brick masons, stone masons, carpenters, blacksmiths, tinsmiths and general laborers. The most important members of his work force were skilled white laborers like the brick masons James and Joseph Whitice, who had experience with large building projects. Master carpenters and master masons often served as what today would be called general contractors. James Whitice, in partnership with carpenter William Howard, had built the large brick courthouse for $8,000 in neighboring Mecklenburg County between 1838 and 1842. The resemblance between Mecklenburg's courthouse (Fig. 3) and the house at Berry Hill plantation is striking. Comparable in scale and dimension, the most striking similarity of the two buildings is the temple front motif. The difference lies in the Ionic order of the courthouse and the Doric order of Bruce's house. Whitice no doubt understood the monumental nature of the building project at Berry Hill. Dabbs also employed two stone masons, George and Enoch Taylor, along with their assistant William Coarse to locate, quarry, and dress the granite. Except for their work at Berry Hill, the careers of these stone masons is unknown. Many other craftsmen, both free and enslaved craftsmen, who worked at Berry Hill remain nameless [3].

Figure 3: Mecklenburg County Courthouse (Virginia Department of Historic Resources)

Dabbs, the Whitices, and the Taylors supervised both skilled and unskilled, free and enslaved laborers. Unskilled laborers would be employed for such tasks as felling and hauling timber, preparing clay pits for bricks, and hauling brick and stone. Skilled free laborers included apprentices and journeymen. Apprenticeships were unregulated in antebellum Virginia, and advancement to journeyman was an informal rite, based on the artisan's reaching the age of majority and his experience. Journeymen generally possessed the same skills as their employer but lacked the capital to operate independently as a general undertaker. Most journeymen worked for daily wages. William Coarse was described as the assistant to stone masons George and Enoch Taylor, but he probably was serving an apprenticeship. He worked for $.50 a day, while his employers each made $1.50 per day, the equivalent of $300 annually. By comparison, James Bruce paid the overseers of his four plantations $.96 per day, or $240.00 annually, plus housing. Bruce paid his clerk and children's tutor, skilled professionals, $1.60 per day, or $400.00 annually, plus housing. Although skilled workers such as stone masons were well compensated, the high rate of pay might reflect the short-term nature of the building season, and possibly fluctuations in the economy; if for example the stone masons had only seasonal work, they might charge more during the building season [4].

Slave owners who rented out their skilled slaves could often command wages equal to those of free skilled laborers. Masters often sent both skilled and unskilled slaves to cities like Charleston, South Carolina where they were to hire themselves out, often negotiating their own contracts. Under these circumstances, slaves were allowed to keep a portion of the wage they had contracted. In the countryside, however, there is little evidence that slaves who were rented out were given any portion of the contracted amount. At the time that they built Berry Hill, Josiah Dabbs owned eleven slaves and James Whitice owned ten. The stone masons appear to be the only free labor that Dabbs hired, so the entire workforce that Dabbs and Whitice brought to the site was fourteen skilled and unskilled laborers. There is no evidence to suggest that Dabbs or Whitice supplemented this initial workforce by hiring additional skilled or unskilled slave labor. Some clients did on occasion loan their slaves to Dabbs as a form of payment for his services, but there is no indication that Dabbs or Whitice had such arrangements with Bruce while working at Berry Hill [5].

James C. Bruce owned two slaves trained as carpenters and one trained as a mason, and it is possible that when their skills were not required on one of his other plantations, these slaves worked alongside the white and enslaved laborers at Berry Hill. Bruce did, however, hire from his stepmother a slave, John Royall, who was trained as a carpenter. Bruce paid his stepmother $125 for Royall's skills for one year beginning in December of 1842. Bruce's stepmother did not give her stepson a discount on the hire cost -- $125 was the going rate for a skilled slave during the late 1830s and early 1840s. It is not known if Royall worked on the construction of Berry Hill mansion house or if he was hired for other building projects that were going on concurrently. The point is that, although the purchase price in 1842 for such a skilled slave such as Royal could be as much as $450, the slave's owner could expect to realize a substantial return on that $450 investment by hiring out a skilled slave. Likewise, anyone who hired a skilled slave was paying much less than they would for a free skilled laborer [6].

It is unlikely, however, that Bruce used any of his own slaves as unskilled labor for the building of his house. During the construction of Berry Hill, Bruce sold his 1500-acre Wolf Island Plantation in Caswell County, North Carolina because he did not have enough hands to work it. In fact, Bruce struggled during the early 1840s with a labor shortage on his four plantations and his other businesses, and he required the labor of more slaves than the 400 that he owned. When he began making improvements to the drainage system at Berry Hill, Bruce had to hire ten slaves from his neighbors to dig ditches ('ditchers'), paying their owners $4.00 per month for each enslaved worker, and he paid Thomas Webb $135 to oversee these ditchers. Even if Bruce's house had been constructed entirely with free white labor, the slaves who worked on his plantations, in his mills, on his boats, and the slaves who toiled for the Roanoke Navigation Company in which Bruce owned stock, all contributed directly to the resources that Bruce commanded, making such a building campaign possible [7].

Regardless of the status of his workforce, Dabbs was responsible for the quality of all his workmen and he was held accountable according to the contract. After assembling his workforce, Dabbs directed the brick masons to begin work [8]. Having finished the courthouse a few months before, James Whitice already had a group of skilled enslaved brickmakers and masons ready to begin work immediately and he would have been well prepared to undertake work at Berry Hill. Whitice's masons began work on the foundation while brickmakers prepared clay pits for making more brick. The Whitices evidently began work immediately for by August of 1842 they had laid the foundation and begun building the walls of the house. By March of 1843, when they had finished the walls and installed the windows, construction of the roof was ready to begin [9].

For the roof over the main block of the house, Dabbs supervised the carpenters in building a principal rafter roof system supported by king posts that span the sixty-four foot breadth of the house. Both Dabbs and the Whitice brothers were familiar with this roof system since they had employed it in their courthouse constructions. The largest structural members, the king posts and the principal rafters, were hand hewn on the site. Bruce operated a sawmill that had a water-powered reciprocal saw at Meadesville, a hamlet on the Bannister River about fourteen miles north of the plantation. This mill was managed by his slave whom Bruce called 'Meadesville Joe,' dealt with customers to the mill and who oversaw the four other slaves Bruce assigned to the mill. Because of the increased production of wood for the construction of the mansion house, Bruce hired from neighbors two enslaved workers, Pleasant and Bob, for $25 per year. Meadesville

Joe supervised the cutting of joists, rafters, beams, and the common rafters, as well as the studs framing the partition walls of the first and second floors. By June of 1843 tinsmiths were installing the roof and gutters [10].

By the fall of 1843, Berry Hill mansion house had assumed the Grecian temple form that Bruce had envisioned from the beginning, and in March of 1844, two years after construction began, Dabbs and Bruce began settling accounts. In the final reckoning, James C. Bruce paid Josiah Dabbs the balance he owed, $27,141.00 for his house -- a princely sum in 1844, the same year that Bruce paid his overseer at Berry Hill an annual salary of $325.00 [11].

Although the house seems to stand aloof and isolated on its hill, it was in fact the center of an extensive and bustling agricultural enterprise. This large operation required numerous structures of its own and Bruce oversaw the construction and placement of all the requisite outbuildings that supported the main house. Tobacco barns were essential to the operations of Berry Hill, and although none survive on the property, carpenter Isaac Smart built two for $128.00 each. Wheat was the second largest cash crop grown at Berry Hill and in 1844 master carpenter Pleasant Headspeth built a granary at Berry Hill for $1,089. Corn was a staple for Bruce's family, his slaves and his livestock, and Josiah Dabbs charged $630.00 to build a substantial corn house the same year he built the granary. The smoke house, completed by Dabbs in 1845 at a cost of $150.00, was one of the most important buildings because it held the cured meat that the entire plantation consumed over a year's time. Bruce placed it in the rear yard of the main house where he could keep a watchful eye on it. The two large barns that Bruce built for livestock no longer stand, but the foundations of the substantial stable which measured thirty feet by sixty feet survive near the corn house. Dabbs built the stable for $1,156.00. All of these utilitarian structures were dispersed through Berry Hill's landscape, located for convenience on the road that bisected the plantation.

Berry Hill slaves were an active, influential force that James Bruce had to consider when planning his plantation. Berry Hill slaves appropriated the southeast corner of the plantation as a burial ground, a location that was well beyond white surveillance. Space at Berry Hill was as fluid as it was static. Both households, black and white, carried on a domestic life in discreet, well-defined spaces enclosed by wood, brick, and stone. Yet the yards, the fields, and the woods constituted another space which blacks and whites claimed, abandoned, surveyed, and contested daily. Berry Hill plantation, like any plantation in the antebellum south, comprised a landscape that was simultaneously simple and comprehensible, yet complex and inscrutable.

The stone slave houses that James Bruce and his slaves built between 1853 and 1855 were a crucial aspect of this landscape. Compared with most slave houses that survive from the antebellum period, these stone slave houses are substantial and capacious dwellings. The quality of these slave houses and their placement in the landscape are significant for what they indicate about James Bruce and his notions of slave management. James Bruce spent ten years arranging his plantation landscape before he considered more thoughtfully the living conditions of his slaves. In February of 1853 Bruce wrote to his son Alexander quote:

> I have put up an overseers house and kitchen of stone with Alec as my principal and Sam, old Darby and Harris for aids. We think it shows talent and energy for a first effort. I shall next build a cook's house of stone with two rooms one for cooking for the people, the other for cook and family to live in. It will be placed where the road crosses the pond branch below Viny's house [12].

This letter is significant because it indicates the location of the overseer's house which is well beyond the view from any slave house. Perhaps most important, this letter mentions the names of the slaves who built the houses. Sam was one of two slave stone masons at Berry Hill. Old Darby and Harris are listed as carpenters in Bruce's slave inventory. And Alec, although not trained in building trades, was a trusted slave who traveled with Bruce and who presumably possessed some organizational skills that Bruce valued in his building campaigns.

The Cook's House (Fig. 4) that Alec, Sam, Old Darby and Harris built is one of two types (Fig. 5) found at Berry Hill. It measures twenty feet by thirty-eight feet and its stone walls are, on average, one-and-a-half feet thick. A stone wall partition with a paneled door divides the structure into two heated rooms, each measuring approximately seventeen feet square. Each room has an exterior door on the east wall and a glazed window on the west. Above stairs are two more rooms, divided by a wood partition, one with a small firebox. Each of these rooms is lighted by two small windows that flank the small fireplace. Bruce built the kitchen adjoining the north wall of the slave house. It measures approximately fifteen feet square and has access only through a door on the east wall. A window on the west wall lights the interior. The firebox is small but large enough for the cook to prepare the simple meals that that slave children would take to the field hands at mid-day.

Figure 4: Cook's House at Berry Hill Plantation, Halifax County, Virginia (author)

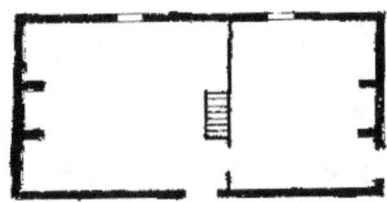

Slave house, plan type #1, 1853, Berry Hill plantation, Halifax County, Va.

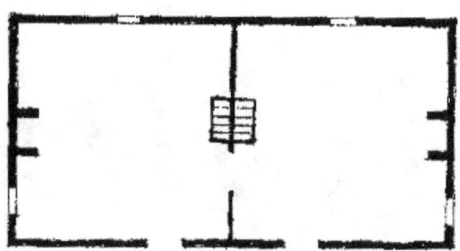

Slave house, plan type #2, 1853, Berry Hill plantation, Halifax County, Va.

Figure 5: Two types of slave housing at Berry Hill Plantation, Halifax County, Virginia (author)

The second type of slave house at Berry Hill is a variation on the cook's house -- slightly smaller, with different fenestration. The slave house near the small pond and just outside the stone wall surrounding Bruce's mansion house belonged to his butler, Ellick Pamplin. (Fig. 6) It measures eighteen feet by twenty-eight feet and its stone walls are one-and-half feet thick. A wood partition probably divided this structure into two rooms on the first floor. The larger room has a fireplace that measures three feet wide and is large enough to cook in. The other fireplace measures only one-and-a-half feet wide and was probably used only for heating the small room it served. Each of these rooms has an exterior door. The smaller room has a door on the gable end while the larger room has a door centered on the east elevation parallel with the ridge line. Each room also has a window on the west elevation. Although no evidence for a stair exists, the two small windows flanking the western chimney stack indicate that an unheated garret above stairs was occupied as well.

Bruce built at least eight of these single-family houses at Berry. Josiah Dabbs had built 8 brick slave houses for Bruce at another plantation, Morotock, for approximately $280 each. Feeling confident that the skills of his enslaved carpenters, stone masons, and brick masons could be put to use with results as good as those of Dabbs, Bruce assembled a workforce of skilled and unskilled slaves and commenced a building campaign at Berry Hill plantation. In building these stone slave houses, Bruce's slaves increased the value of Berry Hill plantation by $2,228, no small sum considering that Bruce paid the oversser at Berry Hill $325.00 that same year. The $2,228 value that Bruce's slaves produced easily equaled the amount that Bruce paid for those slaves on the auction block.

Figure 6: Ellick Pamplin's House at Berry Hill Plantation, Halifax County, Virginia (author)

When in 1852 Bruce made his inventory of the 109 slaves he held at his Berry Hill plantation, he counted seventeen families, so these eight single family houses probably supplemented the existing slave houses that are known to have existed on the plantation. Levi Pollard a slave on Charles Bruce's Staunton Hill plantation described a house similar to the ones that James Bruce built, explaining the room arrangement and how his family occupied those spaces.

> We had us a two-story house. Of course upstairs you couldn't stand up straight because the roof cut the sides off. Part of the children stayed up there. There was two rooms downstairs. One was the kitchen, and mammy and pappy and the other children slept in that other room. Some slept in the kitchen, too. There were fourteen children in all [13].

A family with fourteen children would find Bruce's stone slave houses crowded, to be sure. Yet, these slave houses averaged 760 square feet of living space on the first floor, which was considerably more than the 256 square feet of the average slave house in the antebellum South. In both materials and space, Berry Hill slave houses were unusually substantial and well-built and provided a level of comfort that characterized what would seem to be one of the most benevolent of plantation regimes of the antebellum period [14].

Bruce's efforts to create arcadian idyll with his Grecian temple, stone slave houses, and full complement of well-built, substantial farm buildings disguised a hard fact. At his home plantation, Berry Hill, Bruce knew his 109 slaves by name. But he owned more than 400 slaves. James Bruce had so many slaves working at various tasks and locations that it was impossible for him to have any meaningful interaction or understanding for their welfare. In at least one instance he literally lost track one slave, Connie. Bruce's father, James Bruce Sr. and his business partner, Thomas Hagood, had acquired Connie sometime before 1820 in a foreclosure when they were in business as Bruce and Hagood. Evidently Bruce and Hagood had hired the woman out. By 1857, nineteen years after the death of James Bruce Sr., Connie had been lost in the shuffle and her 'guardian' John Forbes wrote to James C. Bruce that the old woman Connie owned by Bruce and Hagood is still at my house and wishes to remain with me. I have kept her up to the first of January for $20.00 per annum at which time I informed Dr. Atkisson that I would have to charge more. Dr. Atkisson said he wished her to continue whre she is and that you would do right. The old woman is almost helpless and needs waiting on. I thought $30.00 per year would not be too much and I can keeper for that as she wants to stay. I haven't received anything for the last two years and being pressed for money, if it suits your convenience, I would be glad [15].

In executing his father's will, Bruce had left Connie in the employ of the man who originally hired her. Rather than assume direct responsibility for Connie when she became infirm, Bruce arranged for her to stay under the care of Forbes. Like his father, however, Bruce found owned so many enslaved individuals that he forgot about Connie's existence altogether. In March Bruce paid Forbes the money due him, but Forbes wrote again in August, this time informing him of Connie's death and charging him $3.50 for providing her a shroud and coffin and $1.56 for digging her grave [16].

James Bruce was keenly aware of the economic forces that were shaping antebellum Virginia, and he spent his life shrewdly building an agricultural and business empire that reached far beyond his home in Halifax County. He was a man who was in control of his destiny. Old Connie, on the other hand, knew little of the machinations of the market economy, except that much of that economy depended on the forced labor of people like herself. Old Connie spent her life in the constant knowledge that powerful people like Bruce could go bankrupt or die, leaving her fate in the hands of yet another master or mistress. The substantial and permanent stone houses that Bruce's slaves built masked the very nature of a world organized around agrarian capitalism, a nature that was volatile, unpredictable, and rife with the anxiety and fear of those whose labor built that world [17].

References

[1] This paper draws upon the original source material of the Bruce Family Papers, which are held at the University Virginia Library. Over the course of a calendar year, these documents were mined for evidence of James Bruce's architectural legacy.
[2] Account of James C. Bruce with Josiah Dabbs, Bruce Family Papers, University of Virginia, Business Papers 1844.
[3] Gilliam, Gerald T. "Josiah Dabbs: Carpenter and Contractor." *The Southsider,* vol. 5, no. 1, Winter 1986; Josiah Dabbs & Co., Accounts (1837-1845), and Dabbs, McDearmon & Co., Accounts (1839-40), in possession of Mrs. David McGehee, Halifax County.
[4] On builders, apprentices, and journeymen see: C. W. Bisher, C. V. Brown, C. R. Lounsbury and E. H. Wood, *Architects and Builders in North Carolina: A History of the Practice of Building,* Chapel Hill: University Press of North Carolina, 1990, pp. 33-38, pp. 93-97; and Richard Charles Cotes, "The Architectural Workmen of Thomas Jefferson in Virginia," PhD Dissertation, Boston University, 1986, 80-109. Wages for George and Enoch Taylor and for Bruce's overseers, clerk, and tutor are listed in the Bruce Family Papers (BFP), University of Virginia, (UVA), Business Papers (BP) 1842 and 1843.
[5] H. Greene, H. S. Hutchins, Jr. and B. E. Hutchins, *Slave Badges and the Slave-Hire System in Charleston, South Carolina, 1783–1865,* Jefferson, NC: McFarland, 2004.
[6] On slave labor in the building trades in antebellum Virginia, see: Bisher, et al, Architects and Builders, 99-102; and Cotes "Architectural Workmen", 97-99. Also see Catherine W. Bishir, "Black Builders in Antebellum North Carolina," North Carolina Historical Reivew 61, no.1 4 (Oct. 1984), 423-61. A list of Bruce's slaves is in "Register of Negros" BFP, UVA, Box 13. Dabbs's experience with slave labor is described briefly in Gilliam, "Josiah Dabbs", 16. Bruce inherited John Royall after the death of his step-mother and in his list of skilled slaves, he identifies John Royall, Jacob, and 'Cheeseman' as carpenters. See James C. Bruce (JCB) to Elvira Bruce, Dec. 27, 1842, BFP, UVA, BP 1842; and "Register of Negros" BFP, UVA, Box 13. For the average price of skilled and unskilled slaves during the period of 1804 to 1862, see MeasuringWorth.com, Measuring Slavery in 2020. https://www.measuringworth.com/slavery.php accessed 06/05/2021.

[7] In a letter to William Price, Bruce offered to sell his Wolf Island plantation stating he did not have enough hands to work it. JCB to William Price, April 18, 1842, JCB Letterbook, BFP, UVA. Bruce sells the 1500-acre plantation to Price on April 30, 1842. See Caswell County, North Carolina Deed Book FF, p. 810. In 1847, Bruce hires slaves to dig drainage ditches at Berry Hill indicating that he still has a shortage of labor. See various receipts for hire of slaves BFP, UVA, BP 1847.

[8] Letters indicate that the Bruces moved into the house during the first week of November 1843. See Sarah Bruce to Charles Bruce, October 6, 1843, and Elvira Clark to Charles Bruce, BFP, Virginia Historical Society. Receipts for finished work also indicate the progress of the building campaign at Berry Hill. See: Receipt, Josiah Dabbs to JCB, March 15, 1842, BFP, UVA, BP 1842. Receipts, Josiah Dabbs to JCB, November 8, 1843 and December 25, 1843, BFP, BP 1843, UVA. Receipts for services rendered by Dabbs and other akilled laborers and for the hire of skilled slave masons are in BFP, BP for 1842-46. Bruce also owned slaves who were skilled as stone masons, brick masons, carpenters, and blacksmiths who presumably worked on the building projects at Berry Hill. See Slave Book, Berry Hill, 1841, BFP, UVA, 2692-c, vol. 6.

[9] On the Whitices's work at the Mecklenburg County courthouse see John O. and Margaret T. Peters, Virginia's Historic Courthouses, (Charlottesville: University Press of Virginia, 1995), 78-79; and "Mecklenburg County Courthouse," VDHR file no. 173-6. On the Whitices's work at Berry Hill see JCB to EWB, August 8, 1842: Bruce instructs his clerk to check on the progress of the walls and quality of the brick and the lime in the mortar; See also a performance bond in the amount of $25,000 dated May 29, 1843 that Joseph and James Whitice co-signed with Josiah Dabbs to James C. Bruce guaranteeing that work would be 'well and faithfully' executed: BFP, UVA, FP 1843. The brick for Berry Hill was hand made. For more on nineteenth-century brickmaking see: Bill Weldon, "The Brickmaker's Year", in Earl L. Soles, Jr., ed., The Colonial Williamsburg Historic Trades Annual, Vol. 2, (Williamsburg: The Colonial Williamsburg Foundation, 1990), 1-41; Bricks were handmade in Virginia throughout the antebellum period. Thomas Jefferson estimated that two men could mold 2000 bricks per day. In 1819 the first patented brick-molding machine operating near Washington D.C. molded 30,000 bricks in a twelve-hour day. There is no evidence to suggest that such machines were in used in southside Virginia during the antebellum period. For the mechanization of the brickmaking industry in the United States see: Harley J. McKee, "Brick and Stone: Handicraft to Machine", in Charles E. Peterson, ed., Building Early America: Contributions toward the History of a Great Industry, (Radnor, Pennsylvania: Chilton Book Co., 1976), 74-96.

[10] Dabbs charged Bruce for hauling materials from Dixon's Mill. See: Receipt, JD to JCB, June 15, 1843. Large structural members for framing continued to be hand-hewn in Virginia well into the second half of the nineteenth century. Smaller structural members like studs and rafters were often prepared at sawmills using reciprocal saws powered by water. By 1820 three sawmills were in operation in Halifax County. See: Census of Manufactures, Halifax County, Virginia, 1820. While smaller framing members were mechanically sawn, lath for plastering continued to be hand-riven. Lath at Berry Hill is hand-riven. Dabbs billed Bruce for four bushels of "coal for tinners" indicating that the tin roof was in place and that the tinsmiths were using the coal to heat the solder for the roof work. See: Receipt, JD to JCB, June 5, 1843, BFP, FP, 1843. See also Waits Report. p 11.

[11] Account of James C. Bruce with Josiah Dabbs, BFP, UVA, BP 1844.

[12] BFP, Box 14, Feb. 17, 1853.

[13] C. L. Perdue, Jr., and T. E. Barden, *Weevils in the Wheat,* Charlottesville: University of Virginia Press, 1991, p. 227. Taken from the records of the Federal Writers' Project of the 1930s, these interviews with one-time Virginia slaves provide a clear window into what it was like to be enslaved in the antebellum American South.

[14] L. McKee, "The Ideals and Realities Behind the Design and Use of 19th Century Virginia Slave Cabins," in A. E. Yentsch and M. C. Beaudry, eds., *The Art and Mystery of Historical Archaeology: Essays in Honor of James Deetz*, London: CRC Press, 1993), p. 198.

[15] John Forbes to James C. Bruce, Feb. 25, 1857, BFP, UVA.

[16] Receipt, John Forbes to James C. Bruce, March 7, 1857. John Forbes to James C. Bruce, Aug. 30, 1857, BFP, Business Papers 1857, UVA.

[17] ibid.

The Madrid-Delicias Railway Station: between formal and technological innovation in the 19th century Iberian Peninsula

Gian Marco Prisco
Scuola di Specializzazione in Beni architettonici e del Paesaggio, Università degli Studi di Napoli Federico II, Italy

Introduction

The experience of Modernity is linked to the process of social modernization which takes roots in the development of science and technology, together with the rationalization and industrialization of production [1]. Among other technological developments, the use of iron as a construction material became central in the architectural discussion since the early nineteenth century. Iron brought - on a technological side - new construction techniques and processes, challenging the traditional discipline and inspiring a new aesthetic, made by light structural form with slender proportions [2]. Contrasting the Academic praxis, iron was viewed as a symbol of modernity, particularly because of its ability to permit the creation of large public spaces, promising a technological utopia and a new, modern architecture.

According to Karl Bötticher, iron should have represented the dawn of a new, higher historical level, "a new way of designing", evolving from the characteristic of material and technique [3]. This link with the physical reality represents the same working premises of architecture, based on "static principles" and "materials relations". In this way, styles may be considered "evolutionary stages" of an history that would certainly not end with the eclectic style parade shown on the outer shell of buildings by Classicists and Neogothicists [4].

Later on, Walter Benjamin, in his Theory of Cultures [5], pointed out the significance of iron and the importance of new material objects in the experience of modernity as a source of dialectic imagination [6], a precipitator of change in multi-faceted architectural and social phenomena.

It is impossible, in fact, to ignore the larger socio-cultural and environmental implications that iron construction brought about. The modern industrial culture has produced its own landscape vision which, through craft areas, suburbs and residential construction, imposes itself, especially in times of crisis, through terms of emptiness and absence. The contemporary need to rethink the land use leaves an unsolved issue not only spatial, but temporal: the absence of knowledge and memory of a large part of the territory and thus of a part of one's everyday life.

These signs represent the latest stratification of the contemporary landscape, a complex of buildings and newest remains of the Industrial Era that dwell in a void between past and present. The research on the Madrid Delicias Railway Station aims at recognizing the building and its constructive evolution in the overall context of the social, cultural, and economic transformations of the Spanish capital in the second half of the nineteenth century. (Fig. 1)

Building the Modernity. The Madrid-Delicias Railway Station between Formal and Technological Innovation in the XVIII Century Iberian Peninsula

Figure 1: (left) Exteriors of the Delicias railway station, Émile Cachelièvre, 1880. Photo by the author
(right) Interiors of the Delicias railway station. Detail of the iron structure, Émile Cachelièvre, 1880. Photo by the author

Iron Constructions between Structural and Architectural Composition

While in England the first approach to this new material involved mainly the bridges, in continental Europe roofs were the principal research field of iron technology. Metal covering represented a versatile and cheaper alternative to stout timber sections, together with the guarantee of fireproof performances. Since 1786 it was conceived as metallic solution for Victor Louis' *Théâtre-Français* in Paris, starting a research which would have reached its climax in the pavilions for the Universal Exhibitions of 1878 and 1889.

As a result of the Industrial Revolution, iron in architecture and engineering reached the Iberian Peninsula and, particularly, Spain, in the mid-nineteenth century. Although the first examples were industrial facilities, it was in the architectural design that its application represented a revolution in the construction of large buildings and, among them, of railway stations. These buildings stand out from traditional and monumental architecture, as Felix Cardellach Y Alives [7] argued in one of his numerous writings on the aesthetics of new industrial architecture at the beginning of the 20th century:

> "This new architecture will have different aims from the monumental one that can be identified in a strongly industrial and productive character, not limiting itself to the 'factory' alone, but extending this vision to all those buildings constructed or adapted to any branch of industrial production, such as the transport sector, in which the railway stations are located".

A characteristic element of this architecture will be the creation of new construction types, as consequence of the scientific and production processes. Through the use of new materials, it was possible to build architectural skeletons capable of creating diaphanous and flexible spaces, in which the use of the foundry column and the metal carpentry played a key role within the architectural and structural composition. In the same way, it was developed a new language for the exterior, using elements and a formal code which, while relying on classical styles, were detached from the academic architecture of that period.

The Challenge of a New Architectural Typology: the Railway Station

Railway stations, as claimed by Pruneda and Arangoiti [8], represent one of the great typological contributions of the nineteenth century, identifying - in a certain way - the same idea of progress. These constructions can be distinguished generally by terminal and passing stations, although it is also possible to make distinctions based on the number of buildings that make up the station complex and the relationships between the large space of the rails and the façade of the building.

When choosing the construction site for these buildings, bringing them as close as possible to urban centres was a priority, regardless of the need for large open spaces. The railway stations, in this way, usually were built in an almost tangent form to the consolidated urban centres [9]. Stations built in the nineteenth century were generally placed on city limits – as is the case of the Delicias Station – and nowadays, due to the cities' growth, have become central areas of the urban surroundings.

Stations can be divided into different types, regarding their location within the city: central, perimetral or external to the urban centre [10]. These differences can also be founded in the dichotomy between the so-called English and French model. If the former one places the station as close as possible to the city centre, in France, on the contrary, peripheral sites are chosen, connected by a layout of ring roads. It is certain that stations would soon become points of reference for cities, a strategic and focal element, what Kevin Lynch would have called a 'node' or 'nucleus' [11], in his book *The Image of the city*.

The methodological difference between English and French approach was even more evident in the image of the station itself. The façades of the great European railway yards follow two distinct models: the first one, in which railway activities are concealed behind buildings that camouflage themselves in the urban fabric, with offices or hotels in Anglo-Saxon style; and another one, common in France, where the view from the station's patio was implicitly allowed. In this second approach, it seems as if there is a desire to expose the large space hidden inside the station and the life it generates. Paradigmatic examples of such views are the St. Pancras Station in London and the Gare du Nord in Paris.

In Spain, the French trend was predominant – because of the influence of the *École des Ponts et Chaussées* and the work of its technicians in this country – and the Delicias Station represented one of the clearest examples of this approach. Its large glass façade reflected the forms of interior space and the image of a diaphanous, modern dimension, outcome of the technological processes and capturing the *zeitgeist* of the Industrial Era. (Fig. 2)

Figure 2: Exteriors of the Delicias railway station, Émile Cachelièvre, 1880. Photo by the author

In addition to these aspects, Sobrino Simal [12], proposes to add further themes such as the spatial organization and the station's impact on the urban fabric, in relation to its formal social and anthropological contributions. These elements would have produced radical changes on the image of the city, as stressed by the emblematic evolution of Madrid in this period.

Drawing a New Urban Landscape: the Case of Madrid

In the second half of XVIII century Madrid still looked like a centre closed in its fortified walls. It was only during the reign of the King Charles III that the city was enriched by an accurate study of the access roads to the urban area. One of them was the so-called trident configured by the Paseo de las Delicias, the Paseo de Santa Maria de la Cabeza and the Ronda de Atocha. This scheme followed the layout of the baroque trident or 'patte d'oie', used in the reconfiguration of Sixtus V's Rome and passed on to landscape design, as in the case of the Versailles gardens of Andrè de la Notre: in the cartography of that time, it appeared as an organised but nevertheless peripheral and semi-rural area, a popular zone where the transition from the city to the banks of the Manzanarre took place. This structure remained unscathed until the mid-nineteenth century: by this moment, urban growth, technological advancement and the arrival of the railroad ensures that the agricultural landscape would be converted into the city's new expansion zone.

In 1857 Carlos Maria de Castro was commissioned to carry out a study for the extension of the capital: the Proyecto del Ensanche de Madrid [13] juxtaposed a large enveloping surface from the north-east to the south-east of the historical city, organizing the space through an orthogonal north-south grid.

The ordering element of the space was the rectangular block alternated with road axes and, in strategic points, squares or public buildings. The de Castro's plan had a strong social logic, identifying distinct zones for different strata of the society. Among the various neighbourhoods designed by de Castro, the Arganzuela-Delicias district would have a predominant industrial and working-class vocation, consolidated by the arrival of the railway fabric that determined its productive development.

The Delicias Railway Station

On 30 March 1880, King Alfonso XII and Queen Maria Cristina inaugurated the Madrid-Delicias station, as reported by the press of the time [14]. This station was built as the head of the railway line from Madrid to Ciudad Real by the *Compañía de los Ferrocarriles de Ciudad Real a Badajoz* (CRB) three years after the opening of the first railway line on Iberian soil, the Barcelona-Mataró, instituted in 1848. (Fig. 3)

This station, together with those of Atocha and Norte-Prince Pio, were an integral part of the so-called triad of stations in nineteenth century Madrid. The Madrid-Delicias station, even if related to the more recent line, was the first monumental station to be built as such - unlike Atocha, which had already been in operation since 1851, but simply as a dock [15].

Delicias became the Lisbon-Madrid line terminal, starting immediately with passenger and freight services and, in 1885, with sleeping cars and large European express trains. The most famous train to run on its tracks was the Sudexpreso, inaugurated in 1887, which connected Lisbon, Madrid, Paris and London on a weekly basis. The influx of passengers was such that, in the following years, the service increased its frequency to three times a week. The Lisbon-Madrid line was in operation for many decades, experiencing great changes but always being the most prestigious service offered by the Delicias Station [16].

Figure 3: Engraving of the Delicias railway station's inauguration, March 30, 1880. Author: Juan Comba. Spanish and American Illustration Magazine, 8-Apr-1880. Archivo Historico ferroviario, Madrid

The project was designed by the French engineer Émile Cachelièvre, *Ingeniero Jefe de la Costruccion*, according to the archival documentation, in collaboration with Spanish engineers José Antonio Calleja, Santiago Bausá and Bonifacio de Espinal [17].

The first documentary references to the Madrid-Delicias Station - also defined as 'Madrid Station' or 'Ciudad Real Station' - will be found at the *Archivo General de la Administraciòn* di Alcalà de Henares (AGA). In the memorandum of 1875 - approved, with conditions, on 16 August 1877 - in addition to simple data on the location and site, were recorded two calculations showing the estimated costs for the station, respectively of '1,574,532 pesetas' and '224,980 pesetas for the material' [18], an amount proved to be underestimated during the construction phase. Nevertheless, the most interesting aspect reported by the document stresses the role of Delicias, for which "the status of Royal Court station, the most important on the Madrid-Ciudad Real line, implies the need for a specific project".

By the report of 22 January 1878, approved on 23 July of the same year, it can be deduced that it was finally decided to place the station near to the Paseo de las Delicias, which gave the station its name [19]. Several factors were taken into account regarding this choice: firstly, its proximity to the ring road that linked Atocha and Principe Pio stations since 1863; secondly, that it had good passenger and facilities transports; and lastly, its proximity to the city centre and Puerta del Sol.

The railway yard organisation was divided into three areas, according to their use: passenger service, freight service and operational service. These included, in terms of importance, the construction of the Passenger Building or '*Nave de viajeros*', which was the most representative of the entire complex.

The group of drawings [20] at the *Archivo Historico ferroviario-Museo del Ferrocarril* dated on 12 October 1878, confirms the correspondence of the present building with the original project. On 2 December 1878 the engineer Santiago Bausá reported a general description and a memorandum on the construction materials defined as "materials imported from abroad, free of rights". According to the *Diario Ilustrado* "On 28 December 1878, construction began on this

Building the Modernity. The Madrid-Delicias Railway Station between Formal and Technological Innovation in the XVIII Century Iberian Peninsula

remarkable work, the first of its kind in Europe, comparable only to that of Orleans, in France, but not quite as beautiful" [21].

In turn, the *Annales de la construccion y de la Industria* informs us that in February 1879 the station was under construction, adding that the "metal skeleton is already in Spain and will start to be assembled in a few days" [22], referring to the metal trusses reinforcing the central nave of the passenger building. This information can be corroborated by Hebert's photograph entitled "1 June 1879", in which it is possible to see how the construction of the station was already advanced on that date, particularly regarding the covered platform No. 1, which appeared to be almost finished, unlike the passenger building which was still under construction. The metal elements of the central structure, which would support the double-pitched roof would, were already standing, as well as the iron pillars visible in the lateral areas. (Fig. 4)

Figure 4: Status of the construction works on 1 June 1879. Photo: Pedro Martínez de Hebert. Archivo Historico ferroviario, Madrid

The Passenger Building suffered some modification during the construction phase in terms of materials, in order to achieve greater economy. Thus, for example, pressed bricks were used only in the exteriors, preferring ordinary bricks, finished with plaster, in the interiors. This fact produced a contrast between the polychrome brickworks of the urban façades and the minimalism of the railway's area, creating a contrast with the polychrome brickworks in exterior façades. The zinc ornaments were also replaced by wrought or cast-iron ones, while the slate roof planned for the large central nave was substituted by a simple roof of corrugated and galvanised metal sheet. Although this last material was more expensive than slate, the construction process resulted easier in terms of time and work. The slate covering was kept just in the side pavilions, whose elevations became examples of the rational use of materials and structural clarity.

These changes did not affect the functional organization and the general layout of the Passenger Building, whose architectural type consisted of two parallel side pavilions, one for departures and one for passenger arrival, divided in the middle by rails and docks covered by a steel and glass structure from the Fives-Lille factory. (Fig. 5)

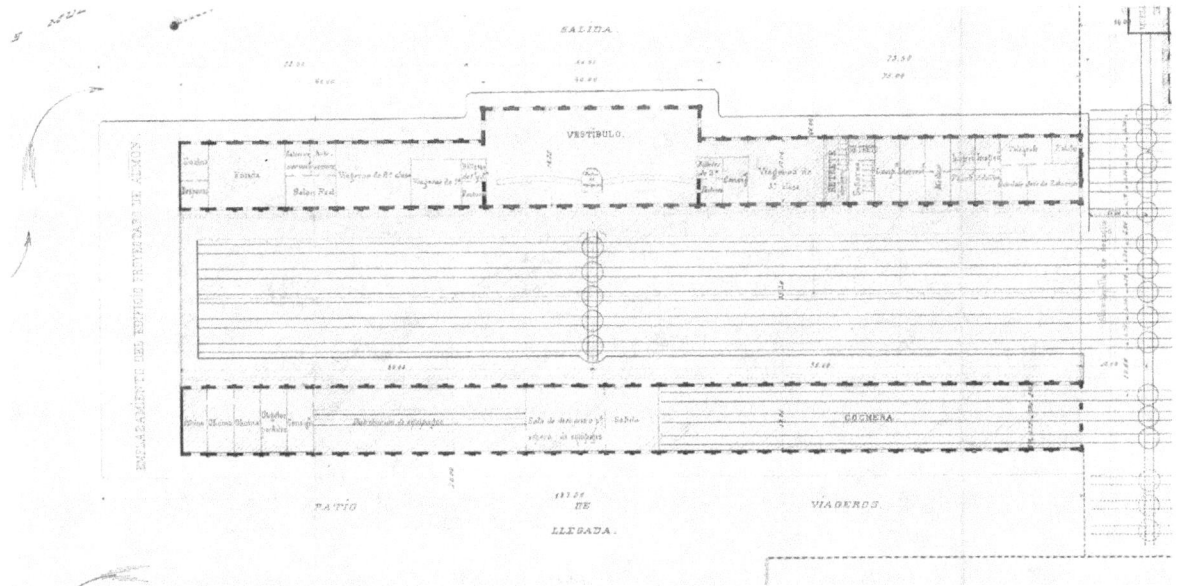

Figure 5: Plan of the Delicias railway Station, 2 Aug.1879. Author: Émile Cachelièvre. W_1001_001, Archivo Historico ferroviario, Madrid

This building, which was created with an industrial and functional character, is part of the iron and glass construction culture of the nineteenth century, recognisable in the structural clarity and employed materials. It became a clear example of the historical, artistic and cultural heritage of nineteenth century Spanish industry, combining the harmony of forms with functionality and technological innovation for which it was built.

The Delicias station would be in operation for about a century, until the suspension of passenger and freight services in 1969 and 1971, the year in which the railway yard closed definitively, diverting the rail services to Extremadura and Lisbon to the Atocha station.

Critical Realism: Constructive Interpretation of a New Industrial Approach

The main and central area of the station was accommodated the tracks, where the arrival and departure of trains took place. The smoke generated by coal-fired steam locomotives demanded high and appropriately ventilated spaces. This gave rise to the large metal covers protecting trains and passengers from the inclemency of weather and which, at the same time, achieved a diaphanous and luminous space, becoming a topical element of the 'station' concept. These iron and glass constructions avoided the use of massive load-bearing structures in favour of large spaces and clear elements, left visible, acquiring a formal dignity.

The possibility of huge, open spaces represented a real challenge for the technicians of the nineteenth century, who experimented new forms of iron frameworks in the great Exhibitions held throughout those years. The first structural system to be tested was developed by the French engineer Camille Polonceau in 1839 and then used for the pavilions of the Universal Exhibitions in 1855 and 1867. The gable roof consisted of two inclined beams and a central tie, in tension. This scheme, characterised by its lightness and simplicity of construction, represented one of the most interesting ideas introduced in the design of wide span structures. (Fig. 6)

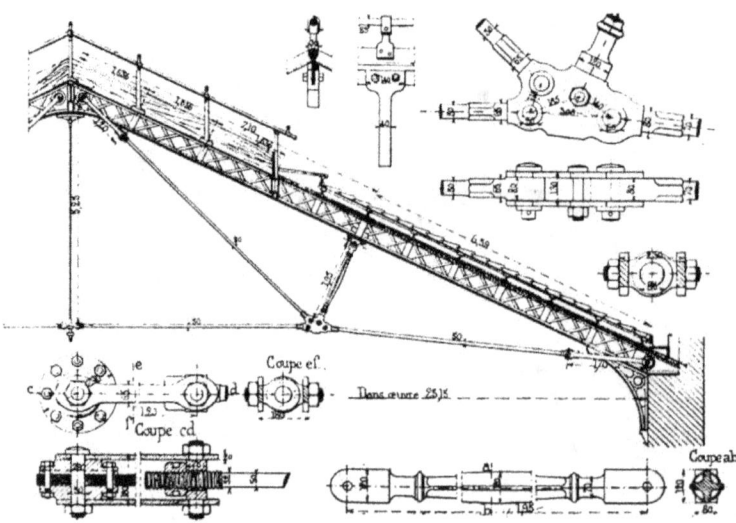

Figure 6: The Polenceau truss beam, in Architecture et Constructions civiles: Charpenterie métallique, Volume 2, 1894, p. 236. Author: J. Denfer

Afterwards, a leap forward was made by the engineer Henry De Dión -at that time president of the *Société des Ingénieurs Civils*- who highlighted the rapid evolution of iron technology in structures by proposing a calculation model in 1877 which achieved a new constructive solution. His project for the Galerie des Machines at the Paris Exhibition in 1878 superseded the classic Polonceau system for a truss made by iron prefabricated elements which formed a whole with the supporting structure, constituting a unique framework linked to deep foundations. (Fig. 7)

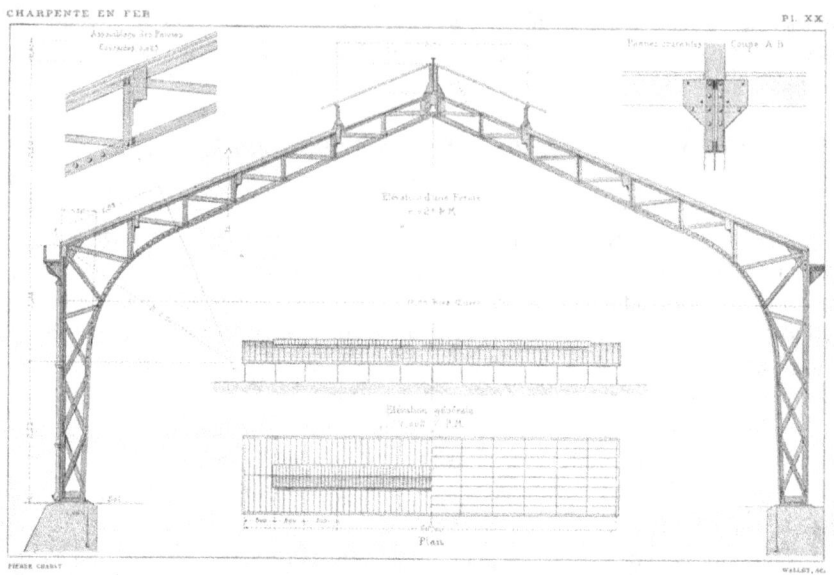

Figure 7: The De Dion truss beam, in Cours de dessin géométrique, 1885, p. 423. Author: Pierre Chabat

This constant research continued, culminating in the revolutionary construction of the *Galerie des machines* of the great Paris Exhibition in 1889 realized with a complex of articulated arches by the architect Charles Louis Dutert and the engineer Victor Contamin.

In Spain the technological evolution of the stations also hides a strong rivalry between the train concessionary companies, which tried to propose on each occasion more daring solutions than those known up to that time. In a certain way, they recall the struggle of the medieval cities through the heights reached by their cathedrals which acquired, in the industrial city the iron expression of the railway station [23]. Exemplary, in this sense, is the case of Madrid with its three main stations of Delicias, Norte-Principe Pio and Atocha, in which is effectively possible to trace that attempt to overcome allowed only by a constant update in the application of construction techniques. These three stations belonged to different companies and, as such, each one tried to develop its own unique image, and to reflect the economic potential of the line.

The French engineer Émile Cachelièvre, who worked for the Madrid-Ciudad Real Company, conceived for the Delicias Station the latest innovation in construction techniques of the time. The structure was made by a sequence of 18 De Dion metallic truss beams which forms a whole with the supporting pillars, realizing for the very first time in Spain a covered large space without any kind of braces or buttresses. (Fig. 8)

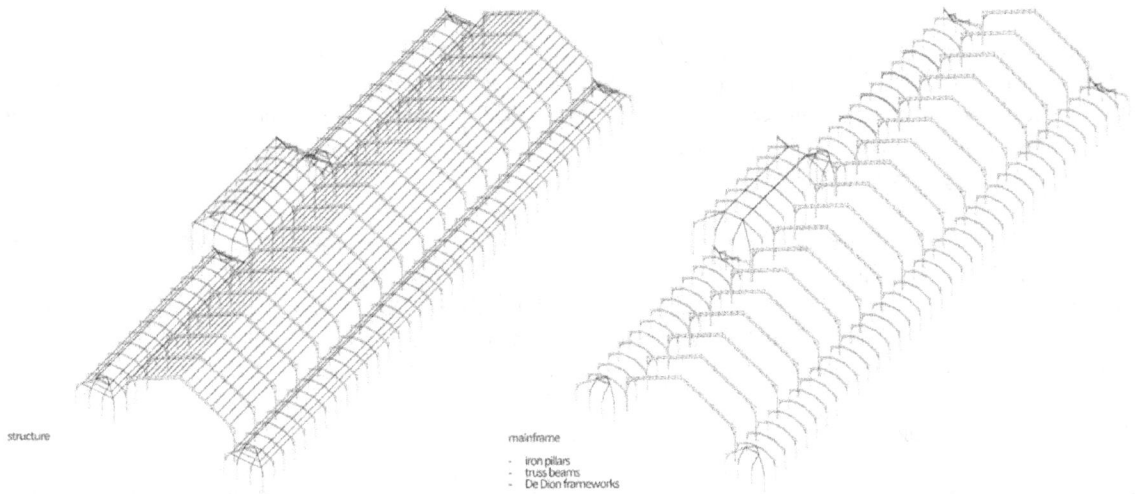

Figure 8: Scheme of the general iron structure (right) and of the mainframe (left) of the Delicias railway station. Drawing by the author.

The sequence of the De Dion's experience in the *Galerie des machine* (1878) and the Cachelievre's project for the Delicias railway station (1879), increase even more the historical and constructive value of the Madrid example, especially if we consider the loss of the Parisian model. The parallel between the two buildings extends up to the spatial dimension: both the two halls have a span of 35 m and a very similar height, being 25m in Paris and 22.5m in Madrid. These similarities were also founded in the construction process, if we take into account that the Spanish frameworks - as well as the 1878 *Galerie* - were made in France by the well-known company Fives-Lille and assembled under the direction of the same engineer, Paul Vazeille [24]. According to the documents of that time, the building was described as "completely stable and solid (...) and it can also serve as a guarantee that the construction company that will realize the structure is the same one that did it in the Exhibition Palace (1878) and that, therefore, already has the necessary experience" [25]. (Fig.9)

Building the Modernity. The Madrid-Delicias Railway Station between Formal and Technological Innovation in the XVIII Century Iberian Peninsula

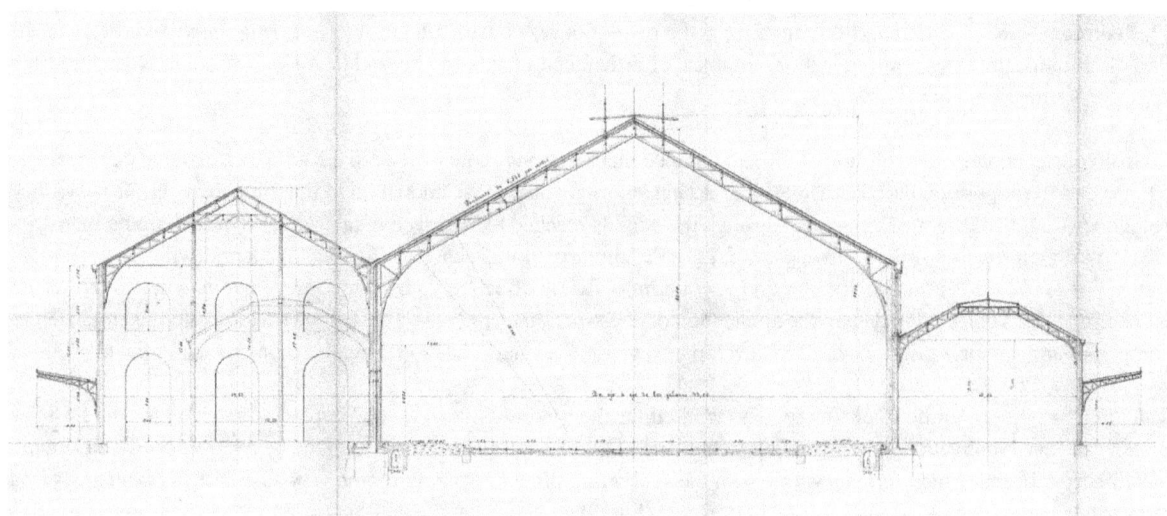

Figure 9: Constructive section of the metal framework in the Delicias railway station, 2 Aug. 1879. Author: Émile Cachelièvre. W_1001_005, Archivo Historico ferroviario. Madrid

This project had a great impact on the Madrid railway industry of that time. The introduction of De Dion system in Delicias led to a modification in the initial project of the Northern Iron Road Company for the Norte-Principe Pio Station (1888) carried out by the French engineer Mercier. Here the classical Polonceau scheme was abandoned, transforming the pairs as well as the ties into bolted reinforced beams with a curved development which joined the iron pillars that supported it, achieving forty metres of span.

Finally in the project of the Atocha Station (1892) - terminal of the Madrid-Zaragoza-Alicante company - the Spanish architect Alberto de Palacio built a large framework which bears a great resemblance to the 1889 *Galerie des Machines,* but with a parallel which remained merely formal. He still used, in fact, De Dion system to build an inner diaphanous space that exceeded any other ones of Spanish pre-industrial architecture becoming one of the last and extreme experiences of this system, before the revolution of the articulated trusses by Contamin.

Between Past and Present. The Architecture of the Engineers

The shapes and volumes of the nineteenth century stations were based on clear aesthetic principles such as proportion, rhythm and symmetry: a minimalist composition that would also be reflected in the façades, characterised by repetition and sequence, recurring throughout the so-called 'architecture of engineers'. While the large metal roof was one of the main fields of engineering experimentation at the time, the architects' contribution would be focused, in many cases, just on the stylistic approach of the forms given to this new typology.

From a formal point of view, the need to find a language for the new architectural typology meant the attempt to reach a compromise between the simplicity of industrial forms or the complexity of styles borrowed from the repertoire of eclecticism prevailing at that time.

This dichotomy also manifested itself in the choice of the exterior cladding, especially in the case of buildings that conveyed their innovative scope and productive vocation in the elevations through the combination of iron with bricks. Once again, France saw the birth of this trend: the brick - used until then as a structural element inside the load bearing walls, covered with stone slabs - emerged on the outside, acquiring a marked formal character. The renewed interest in the possibilities of this material was definitively confirmed by one of the most important buildings of the time: the *Les Halles* market in Paris.

Designed by the architects Victor Baltard and Felix Callet in different phases - between 1854 and 1866 - the complex consisted of a series of large rooms supported by metal structures and paired externally by brick walls with red and yellow blocks arranged in lozenges. The use of bricks had a double reason: on one hand it allowed a rapid execution and guaranteed excellent fireproof properties, while on the other hand it allowed 'the structural rationalism' theorized by many authors of the time. Viollet-le-Duc himself, inside his Entretiens sur l'architecture [26], inserted numerous schemes of iron and brick buildings, basing his theories on the constructive clarity embodied in Gothic architecture, laying the foundations for the architecture of the future. This multiplied the manuals [27] in which, through brightly coloured illustrations, architects tried to promote a new style combining polychrome surfaces with different materials in distinct shapes.

In Spain this architecture took the forms of the so called Mudejar art, characterized by exposed brickwork which created consistent geometric motifs. In 1859, in a speech at the San Fernando Royal Academy of Fine Arts, archaeologist José Amador de los Ríos used the term 'mudéjar' for the first time to describe Christian churches and palaces built using techniques and decorative elements reminiscent of those of Hispano-Islamic architecture (like tiles, plasterwork, horseshoe arches, etc.) [28]. Since then, its status as a composition of all the styles that co-existed on the Iberian Peninsula by the end of the Middle Ages has led intellectuals to consider it as the only purely Spanish style.

With the construction of the Spanish Pavilion by Agustín Ortiz Villajos for the 1878 *Exposition Universelle* in Paris, the Neo-Mudéjar architecture began to be associated with Spain's particular idiosyncrasies. The pavilion's façade combined elements from the Alhambra's Court of Lions with elements from important Christian buildings such as the Royal Alcázar of Seville, Puerta del Sol gate in Toledo and the Cathedral of Tarragona, in an extreme synthesis of the Iberian art [29]. The external aesthetic code of the Delicias Station fully responds - with its complex decorative patterns - to the principles of this style. In this period, in fact, Neo-Mudéjar emerged as the style that best suited industrial architecture [30]. It turned necessity into a virtue by embracing the beauty of exposed brick and its enormous range of practical and decorative possibilities, building an entire imaginary for the new bourgeois class. (Fig. 10)

Figure 10: Detail of the north elevation. Delicias railway station, 2 Aug.1879. Author: Émile Cachelièvre. Archivo Historico ferroviario, Madrid

Conclusion

Thus, iron construction brought about fundamental changes in the traditional architectural production and thinking as well as in the disciplinary boundaries within architecture. It could even be argued that the development of iron construction and the transformation of architectural discourses on iron since the nineteenth century literally represented the history of modernity in architecture.

There are several conclusions to be drawn from this study. Thanks to the organization of great events like the Universal Exhibitions we witness a real 'cultural globalization' that involved the iron construction field during the nineteenth century. This transmigration of knowledge is strictly connected with the spread of construction manuals at that time - in which the construction systems appeared in detail, including tables and calculations of the profiles, depending on the spans – together with the work of technicians and companies that operated in different countries throughout Europe, sharing their know-how. Moreover, it is necessary to underline the continuous overcoming of models, a constant search of more innovative and effective solutions in a positivist confidence to the progress that drove the technicians of that time in their research. The improvement in the use of iron through a new truss morphology puts the Delicias Station into an international perspective, stressing on its importance in the definition of a construction history of the building techniques in the nineteenth century.

As argued by Giedion, "History is not simply the repository of unchanging facts, but a process, a pattern of living and changing attitudes and interpretations, deeply part of our nature…For planning of any sort our knowledge must go beyond the state of affairs that actually prevails. To plan we must know what has gone on in the past and feel what is coming in the future. This is not an invitation to prophecy, but a demand for an universal outlook upon the world" [31].

The knowledge of these spaces appears to us fundamental in the study and conception of the future cities: they must be studied in their material and social essence, in the construction of new relationships with the urban space.

References

[1] R. Banham, *Theory and Design in the First Machine Age*, London: The architectural Press, 1960.
[2] S. Lee, 'Technology and form: iron construction and transformation of architectural ideals in nineteenth century France, 1830-1889' (Ph.D thesis, Massachusetts Institute of Technology, 1996).
[3] S. Giedion, *Building in France, Building in iron, building in ferroconcrete*, Santa Monica: Getty Center for the History of Art and the Humanities, 1995, p. 6.
[4] ibid., p. 7.
[5] W. Benjamin, *Paris, the Capital of the Nineteenth Century*, New York: Schoken Books, 1986, pp. 148-149.
[6] S. Buck-Morss, *The Dialectics of Seeing: Walter Benjamin and the Arcades Project*, Cambridge: MIT Press, 1991.
[7] I. Aguilar Civera, 'Entretiens sobre arquitectura industrial. Conferencias pronunciadas por F. Cardellach en la Universidad de Barcelona. Curso 1907-1908', Ars Longa, Cuadernos de Arte, n° 4, 1993, pp.21-35.
[8] J. A. Pruneda – I. Barrón De Arangoiti, Estaciones europeas, Barcelona: Lunwerg, 2005
[9] Allison, T., 'London Railway Goods Depots, 1835-1905: Land Factors and Building Design', *Construction History*, Vol 35, n° 1, 2020, pp.51-86.
[10] N. Pevsner, *Storia e caratteri degli edifice*, Roma: F.lli Piombi, 1986.
[11] K. Lynch, *L'immagine della città*, Venezia: Marsilio, 1982.
[12] J. Sobrino Simal, *Arquitectura industrial en España (1830-1990)*, Madrid: Cátedra, 1996, p. 367.
[13] VV.AA. , Cartografía básica de la ciudad de Madrid. Planos históricos, topográficos y parcelarios de los siglos XVII-XVIII-XIX y XX, Colegio Oficial de Arquitectos de Madrid , Madrid, 1979.
[14] E. Echegaray Eizaguirre, 'Ferrocarril de Madrid a Ciudad Real. Inauguración de la estación definitiva en Madrid', *Revista de Obras Públicas*, no.27, 1880, pp. 256-259.

[15] N. Torres Ballesteros, *La Estación de ferrocarril Madrid-Delicias (1875-2011): arquitectura, usos y fuentes documentales*, Madrid: Fundación de los Ferrocarriles Españoles, 2010.
[16] J. P. Esteve García, *El ferrocarril Madrid-Ciudad Real-Badajoz: Historia del primer acceso ferroviario a Portugal*, Barcelona: Lluis Prieto, 2008.
[17] A. Escobar, 'Inauguración de la Estación del ferrocarril Madrid-Ciudad Real y Badajoz', *La Ilustración Españolay Americana*, 8 Apr. 1880, p. 221.
[18] Archivo General de la Administraciòn di Alcalà de Henares (A.G.A.), IDD (04) 36, 'Libro 3699' TOP. 46/42.101-47.306.
[19] A.G.A. , IDD (004)31, Caja 25/2396.
[20] A.G.A., IDD (04)32, Caja 25/2085.
[21] 'Estación definitiva de la línea de Madrid á Ciudad-Real y Badajoz', *Diario Ilustrado,* no.4, 1 Apr. 1880
[22] E. M. Repullés y Vargas, 'Inauguración del ferrocarril directo de Madrid a Ciudad Real', *Anales de la Construcción y de la Industria,* no. 3, 1879, p.37.
[23] P. Navascués Palacio, Las estaciones y la arquitectura del hierro en Madrid, *Catálogo de la Exposición sobre Las estaciones de Madrid y su incidencia en la ciudad,* Madrid: COAM, 1980.
[24] P. Navascués Palacio, *Arquitectura e ingeniería del hierro en España (1814-1936)*, Madrid: Fundación Iberdrola, 2007, pp. 41-102.
[25] Archivo General de la Administraciòn di Alcalà de Henares (A.G.A.), IDD (04)32, Caja 25/2085.
[26] E. E.Viollet-le-Duc, *Entretiens sur l'architecture,* Paris: A. Morel, 1872.
[27] J. Lacroux – C. Detain, *Constructions en briques: la brique ordinaire au point de vue décoratif,* Paris: Ducher, 1878.
[28] J. Amador De Los Ríos, *El arte mudéjar en la arquitectura*, Granada: J. M. Zamora, 1859.
[29] C. Álvarez Quintana, 'Apuntes para una estética de la arquitectura industrial del siglo XIX', *Ábaco*, no. 8, 1996, pp. 47-56.
[30] I. Aguilar Civera, *El patrimonio arquitectónico industrial,* Madrid: Instituto Juan de Herrera, 1999.
[31] S. Giedion, *Space, Time and Architecture: The Growth of a New Tradition*, Cambridge: Harvard University Press, 2009, p. 6.

Plate Girder Bridges in Andalusia, 1850-1910. The Spread of an Unusual Genre of Iron Bridges

Antonio Burgos Núñez and Maxwell Adrian Kite
University of Granada, Spain

Introduction

After their remarkable appearance in Great Britain around 1850, the use of plate girder bridges spread rapidly throughout many countries. However, compared to the popularity of iron truss bridges, their acceptance was low and they were generally rarely used from the 1870s.

Nonetheless, such bridges were used for quite some time in Andalusia, the southern region of Spain. Between 1850 and 1910, about ten projects for bridges of this type were submitted, most of which went on to construction.

In this interesting group of bridges, especially in the earlier ones, British iron construction had a notable influence, both in design (through the experiences of Fairbairn and Hodgkinson, and Fairbairn, which were followed with interest by Spanish engineers) and in construction, some of the bridges being manufactured in the United Kingdom and later taken to Spain.

This paper aims to report on the history of these original bridges, exploring all different perspectives.

The Emergence of Tubular and Plate Girder Bridges

The earliest iron bridges were built at the end of the 18th century mainly in Great Britain (Coalbrookdale, 1776; Buildwas, 1796; Sunderland 1796), but also in Germany (Laasan, 1796) and France (Louvre, 1803) [1].

They were all made with cast-iron elements, following models taken from traditional bridges: wooden piece truss and voussoirs vaults [2].

Some experimentation in cast iron bridge construction was seen in the first three decades of the 19th century. In 1819 Sir John Rennie built the Southwark bridge which comprised three arches, each of 64 metres in length. For his part, French engineer Polonceau introduced a new concept using hollow profiles for the arches [3].

In the first half of the century, innovations in design came in the form of suspension bridges, which were pioneered in Europe by the great Telford on the Menai Bridge. The success of this led to other suspension bridges, notably those at Clifton (by I.K. Brunel) and the famous chain bridge over the Danube between Buda and Pest, built by the Tierney brothers [4].

Also at this time in France, the use of this type of bridge increased greatly, to which was contributed both the work of Henri Navier for its technical design and the constructive impulse from the company of the Seguin brothers. Many bridges of this type were built during this period in France and other countries, including Spain [5].

Plate Girder Bridges in Andalusia, 1850-1910.
The Spread of an Unusual Genre of Iron Bridges

The railway network was then expanding, which necessitated the rapid construction of many bridges. Suspension bridges were soon ruled out as a result of some notorious collapses. Initially, the traditional methods of construction such as masonry or brickwork arches continued to be used, but they had important limitations of spans and cost (especially due to the falsework required for erection).

Thus, the railway engineers who were faced with these new problems, not the least being the time factor, reverted to the most elementary type of bridge: the simple beam - the log placed across the stream by primitive man.

In 1820, Ithiel Town, a builder from New Haven (USA) patented a new type of bridge in such a way. It was made of wooden planks crossed in a diamond pattern and fastened with wooden pins [6].

During the early rush of railway construction, Town timber bridges were largely built, sometimes to save time and many of them not as a definitive solution.

Nevertheless, engineers quite naturally found the solution: a simple transposition from this timber structure to cast and wrought iron with which they were familiar and was then being commercially produced.

In the 1850s the process to produce wrought iron was much improved and finally the industry could provide plates, angles, tees, etc. It was then possible to make beams of a large size for use in bridges by riveting together these sections [7].

The idea was first adopted by Robert Stephenson in 1845-50. After small beginnings with short spans of under 10 metres (like the river Nene bridge at Wisbech [8]), he decided to build a wrought-iron bridge of great magnitude and singular novelty for the railway crossing of the Menai Straits. The Britannia bridge was designed by Stephenson and Sir William Fairbairn with the assistance of Professor Eaton Hodgkinson, the mathematician, to provide a stiff decked bridge for train loading [9].

It was an original design, drawn from a wide range of investigations, including the use of scale models. Apart from the drawing of the major section of the bridge, new processes of physical construction had to be elucidated, and empirically the positive structural performance of continuous spans deduced.

The Britannia Bridge (completed in 1850) represented an amazing advance in bridge-building. It was the forerunner of the tens of thousands of plate-girder bridges that can be seen all over the world today [10]. Stephenson, Fairbairn and Hodgkinson had originated a new era in bridge-building with the plate girder based on an entirely novel principle of construction [11].

However, despite their originality, plate-girder bridges did not have a long life [12]. Barely a decade later, they had virtually disappeared from the scene, replaced by an iron Town lattice girder. These were much cheaper and more aesthetically pleasing. In the last third of the century, engineers turned to triangulated beams (Warren, Howe, Pratt, etc.), incorporating increasingly complex configurations (cantilever) and again resorting to arches.

Nevertheless, in the south of Spain, tubular and plate-girder bridges did have a notable development. Only two years after the construction of the Britannia Bridge, Stephenson and Fairbairn's advances were quickly accepted and they were used in the design of a bridge in the city of Málaga. Before long, the first bridge of this type was built, which was followed by many others. Some of them were even built in the first decades of the 20th century.

The Alameda tubular bridge in Málaga, by Diego Ramírez (1852)

In the mid-19th century, Malaga was a city in expansion, one of the most important in Spain [13], where a thriving economic activity based on commerce and an incipient metallurgical industry was driving the realisation of remarkable urban development.

In the style of the large European cities, new areas of this bourgeois city were laid out, which included several bridges over the Guadalmedina River, which traversed the city.

Malaga was a cosmopolitan city, receptive to modern advances and ideas. It is not surprising, therefore, that when the construction of the new bridge was considered, eyes were turned towards the extraordinary British innovations:

'The whole world now admires as one of the wonders of this century the construction of the Conway and Britannia bridges, and engineers of all nations, following the path opened by Stephenson and Fairbairn, are adopting with a predilection for their work a system which combines the strength and rigidity of fixed bridges with the cheapness, lightness and low material requirements of suspension bridges [14]'.

Diego Ramirez, the engineer responsible for the new bridge, proposed a structural solution consisting of two main 1,80 x 0.70 metre tubular beams made up of riveted wrought iron plates, with the deck below (Fig. 1).

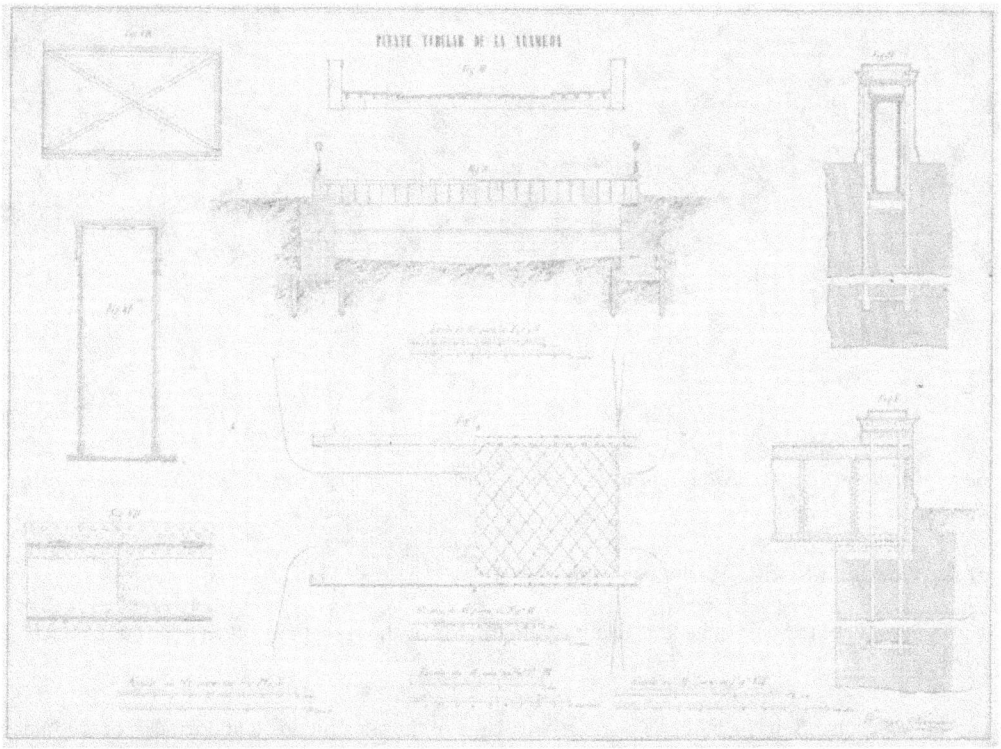

Figure 1: Original drawing of the Alameda bridge in Málaga. Diego Ramírez, engineer. 1852. Archivo del Ministerio de Fomento, Spain.

Plate Girder Bridges in Andalusia, 1850-1910.
The Spread of an Unusual Genre of Iron Bridges

Inspiration from British models also reached the structural design. Ramirez relied on the empirical formulae deduced by Fairbairn from his experience on the Conway and Britannia bridges [15].

The bridge was built with a significant modification, that being a central pier, leaving it with two continuous spans [16].

It remained in use until 1910. By then it was in a very bad condition, with a large number of its plates affected by corrosion (it was located near the coast). Curiously, considering the fact that the original configuration of iron plate girders was then already anachronistic, the original metal part was replaced. The new bridge, designed by the engineer Eduardo Franquelo, lasted until the 1960s (Fig. 2).

Figure 2: Second bridge of La Alameda (Tetuan) in Málaga. Built in 1910 by the engineer Eduardo Franquelo. Archivo Histórico Provincial de Málaga.

Bridges of the Córdoba-Sevilla Railway (1858-1860)

The railway was introduced to Spain quite late, relatively. In the 1850s, the main lines began to be built, mostly promoted by foreign companies.

A consortium of French and Belgian entrepreneurs was in charge of the construction and operation of the important line from Seville to Cordoba, which ran along the Guadalquivir River Valley [17]. Built between 1857 and 1860, it comprised four plate girder bridges each with single or two continuous spans as well as the superb 154 metre bridge over The Guadalquivir River in Lora del Río, formed by eight continuous spans upon cast-iron cylindrical piers [18].

All these bridges were designed by the English Engineer Joseph Lane Manby, who was working in association with the French building company Savalette [19] (Fig. 3).

Figure 3: Some of the bridges of Córdoba-Sevilla Railway, designed by the engineer Joseph Lane Manby (1858-1860). Biblioteca Virtual de Andalucía.

The River Víboras iron bridge (1863)

Once the conflicts that had destabilised the country in the first half of the 19th century were over, the Spanish Government was able to push ahead with the deployment of the national road network from 1860 onwards.

To assist the engineers in charge of designing and building these new roads, they set up technical commissions to study the standard elements.

Thus, a commission of three civil engineers (Lucio del Valle, Víctor Martí, Ángel Mayo) was charged with introducing the new iron bridges in Spain. The plate girder bridges were adopted by then as the main design concept and in the early 1860s a number of bridges of this type were built all over the country.

Plate Girder Bridges in Andalusia, 1850-1910.
The Spread of an Unusual Genre of Iron Bridges

One of the most significant was the Víboras river bridge, included in the road that was to link the cities of Jaén and Granada. Of all the bridges designed by the commission of engineers, it is the only one that has survived to the present day (Fig.4).

Figure 4: River Víboras iron bridge, which nowadays is still in use. Del Valle, Martí and Mayo, engineers.

This 60 metre bridge (in two continuous spans) was designed using new rational theories of Strength of Materials, developed in the first half of the 19th century (Fig. 5).

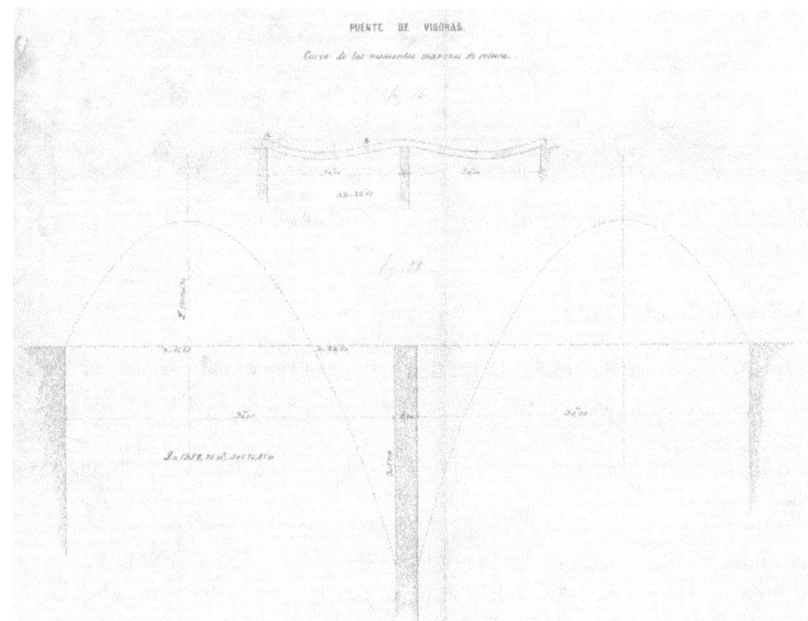

Figure 5: Bending moment diagram calculated for the iron bridge of river Víboras. Archivo General de la Administración, Spain.

The British contribution to this bridge was also very important. Its metal part was manufactured by the company John Butler Iron Works, from Staningley (near Leeds). It was transported by ship to Seville port and moved later to Jaén on an arduous three-month journey through the Spanish countryside. Finally, the two spans that formed the bridge were assembled and mounted over the masonry supports in September 1863. This operation was carried out by technicians sent out by John Butler's company [20].

The design of the superstructure was utilised as a model for all of the bridges of this type that were built later. It consisted of an upper deck supported on two main beams (plate girder in double Tee section). The interior of the bridge was reinforced with X bars (Fig. 6).

Figure 6: Superstructure of Víboras bridge

Plate girder bridges of the last quarter of 19th Century

The river Víboras bridge had a great impact on the design of bridges in this region of Spain between 1685-1875. In this period, four similar road bridges were drafted in the provinces of Jaén and Almería (Fig. 7).

Plate Girder Bridges in Andalusia, 1850-1910.
The Spread of an Unusual Genre of Iron Bridges

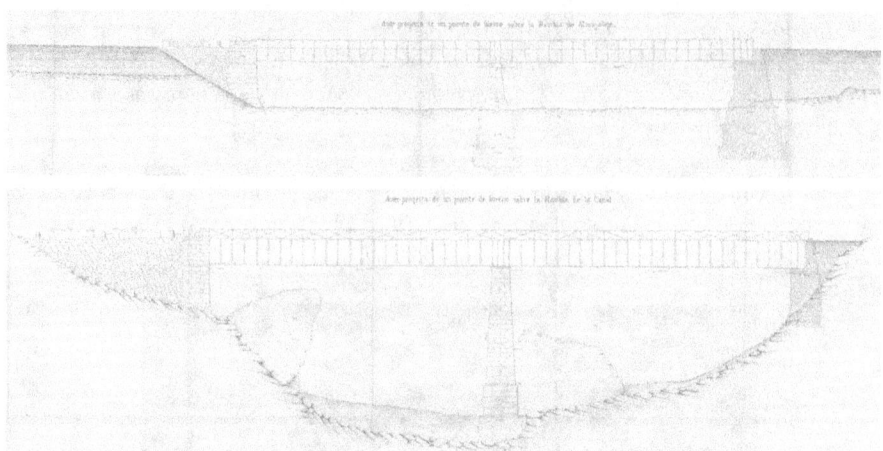

Figure 7: Preliminary drafts of Rambla de Almajalejo and Rambla de la Canal bridges, 1876. Province of Almería. Rafael Moreno Levenfeld, engineer. Archivo General de la Administración, Spain.

But the success of this design was as brief as it was sudden, none of these bridges ever being built with plate girders. From 1875 onwards, the Town lattice truss became practically universal in road bridges, while on the new railway lines, foreign engineers began to introduce triangulated girder models. Masonry arches, for their part, were also brilliantly used in road bridge construction.

However, the plate girder bridges did not disappear completely, at least in the eastern part of Andalusia. The insistence of a Spanish engineer, José María Iturralde, prolonged its validity in this region until the arrival of the 20th century. In 1881 he designed the bridge over the river Guadalimar (Province of Jaén). It had three 30 metre continuous spans (Fig. 8). Problems with the foundations of the supports delayed their materialisation until 1889. In this case, the metal parts were manufactured by a Belgian company.

Figure 8: Original setting of the bridge over Guadalimar river, province of Jaén, 1889. José Iturralde, engineer. The University of Granada Library.

The engineer Iturralde was a convinced advocate of this type of bridge [21], and he insisted on its use until nearly the 20th century. In 1891 he applied exactly the same design for the bridge at Galera, in the province of Granada.

Both bridges are still in use nowadays. The one in Galera is in the same condition as when it was built. However, the Guadalimar Bridge was reinforced in the 1940s, two warren beams being added under the deck of each span, giving it the unusual structural configuration it has today (Figure 9).

Figure 9: Guadalimar (left) and Galera (right) bridges, nowadays. J. Iturralde, engineer.

The Veguetas bridge, on the Sierra Nevada Tramway line (1925)

The swan song of plate girder bridges in Andalusia was the Veguetas bridge, built-in 1925 for the tramway line from Granada City to the mountains of Sierra Nevada.

This was an innovative infrastructure, in which reinforced concrete was used to build all of the bridges on the tramway. Its project was presented in 1924 [22].

However, as a concession to the previous tradition, an iron bridge was included in its layout: a single 15 metre span over both masonry arch supports (Fig. 10).

Figure 10: The Veguetas bridge, on the Sierra Nevada Tramway line. Carlos Morales Lahuerta, engineer. Archivo Histórico Provincial de Granada.

Interestingly, this last realisation of plate girder bridges reiterated the primitive configuration of the pioneers: a deck upon two main beams with double T-section, made up of riveted wrought iron plates.

The tramway was closed in 1974, a major part of which, including Veguetas Bridge, is now under the water of a modern reservoir.

Conclusions

The concept of plate girder bridges was especially followed in the south of Spain during the second half of the 19th century.

Originally the design of these bridges was made using models and empirical knowledge developed by British Engineering.

British ironwork companies manufactured some of these bridges and then Spanish engineers undertook their design, applying the rational principles of the Strength of Materials.

More than a century after their construction, many of these bridges are still in use, proving the validity of their design and construction.

References

[1] H. G. Tyrrell, Bridge Engineering, Chicago: Published by the autor, 1911, pp.151-155.
[2] E.M. Gauthey, Traité de la construction des ponts, Lieja: Chez Leduc, 1843, p.112.
[3] J. Sganzin, Cours de constructions, Bruxelles: Bruylant-Christophe &Compagnie, éditeurs, 1867, pp.60-62.
[4] E. De Maré, Bridges of Britain, London: Batsford, 1954, p.62.
[5] B. Lemoine, L'Architecture du Fer, Seyssel: Éditions Champ Vallon, 1986, p.226.
[6] R. S. Kirby, Engineering in History, New York, MacGraw-Hill, 1956, p.226.
[7] W. Fairbairn, On the application of cast and wrought iron to building purposes, London: John Weale, 1854, pp.192-193
[8] G. Roisecco, L'architettura del ferro. L'Inghilterra (1688-1914), Roma: Bulzoni, 1972, p.246.
[9] C.M. Norrie, Bridging the Years: A Short History of British Civil Engineering, London: E. Arnold, 1956, p.121.
[10] H. S. Smith, 'Bridges and tunnels' p.505 in Ch. Singer (Ed.) A history of technology, Oxford: Oxford University Press, 1958.
[11] Norrie, (Note 9) p. 123.
[12] M. Aguiló, Forma y tipo en el arte de construir puentes, Madrid: Abada, 2008, p108.
[13] J. A. Lacomba, 'Economía y recuperación comercial: Málaga en torno a 1862', Estudios Regionales, n.o 40, 1994, p.326
[14] D. Ramírez, Proyecto de Puente de la Alameda, hoy de Tetuán, 1852, Archivo Histórico Provincial de Málaga.
[15] W. Fairbairn, An account of the construction of the Britannia and Conway tubular bridges, London: John Weale, 1849, pp.268-283.
[16] E. Franquelo, 'Informe del puente de Tetuán sobre el río Guadalmedina en Málaga', 1908, Archivo Histórico Provincial de Málaga.
[17] D. Cuéllar, 150 años de ferrocarril en Andalucía: un balance, Sevilla: Consejería de Obras Públicas y Transportes, 2008, pp.92-95.
[18] C. Santigosa, Album del viajero por el ferrocarril de Córdoba a Sevilla, Sevilla: Imprenta y litografía de las novedades, 1861, pp.26-27.

[19] Unknown, 'Obituary. Joseph Lane Manby, 1814-1862', in Minutes of the Proceedings of the Institution of Civil Engineers 22, 1863, pp. 629-30.
[20] 'Construction proceedings of the Víboras bridge', 1863, Archivo Histórico Provincial de Jaén.
[21] J. M. Iturralde, 'Tramos metálicos para el puente del Guadalimar, en la carretera de Bailén a Baeza, provincia de Jaén', Revista de Obras Públicas, 15 de junio de 1886.
[22] C. Morales Lahuerta, 'Proyecto de Tranvía Ferrocarril de Granada a Sierra Nevada', 1924, Archivo General de la Administración.

Timber frame system after the western influence on the houses of Istanbul

Saniye Feyza Yagci Ergun[1] and Manfred Schuller [2]

1: Istanbul Technical University, Faculty of Architecture, Department of Industrial Design, Turkey
2: Technical University of Munich, Department of Architecture, Chair of Building History, Building Archeology and Conversation, Germany

Introduction

Wooden houses have a special significance on the Ottoman architectural heritage. Although certain characteristics and the cultural spirit were mainly preserved, various features of the houses were transmuted throughout the years. Also, the structural system of the wooden houses is varied upon the region and the period of construction. There are many studies mentioning the classifications including log houses, different kinds of "*hımış*" and "*bagdadi*" techniques [1][2][3]. The timber frame system, which is typically interconnected with *"Bagdadi"* method, is generally found in Istanbul and its spheres of influence [4]. The timber frame system without infill is a lightweight structure providing economic, practical and speedy solutions. It allows more open areas. As the structure became lighter, span lengths and spaces could be enlarged. Consequently, dimension of houses, as well as the sizes and number of the windows were increased [5]. Traditional knowledge about the material, ease of supply, economic advantages, earthquake threat and the cultural habits contributed to the intense popularity of the usage of timber structures in residential buildings. In accordance with the importance and the cosmopolitan structure of the city, there was a huge variety of houses in Istanbul. Flamboyant and eye-catching examples of timber buildings were built in different parts of the city. Wooden structures were explicitly remarkable on the urban texture of Istanbul until the mid-20th century.

This article focuses on the timber frame system of the Ottoman houses in Istanbul from period between the nineteenth century and early twentieth century. More than 750 wooden residential buildings were seen on site during the years 2014-2019 and the structural system could be observed in at least 20 of them. The statements are mainly based on the site investigation and measurements of numerous authentic elements from the timber houses built at the last period of the Ottoman Empire. As the number of the preserved buildings and original elements gradually decrease, the observations on site encompass importance. Usually structural systems are the least documented part of the structures, because they are enveloped and invisible to the users. Within this study, besides the visual and written explanations about the system, dimensions of the wooden elements and sizes of the gaps are given in tables for objective comparisons.

Lightweight system and joints

The timber frame structure of the houses of Istanbul is typically raised above a masonry ground. Thus, basements and/or ground floors are generally built in brick or stone masonry. Main load bearing elements of the timber structure are the bearers and posts, which commonly have square-like section. Floor joists sit above the bearers and the diagonal braces help to provide rigidity to the structure. Moreover, thin horizontal and vertical timber elements are placed at the gaps between the load bearing posts. Timber headings enlarge the mating surfaces and support bearers of the upper floor.

According to the application of the beams and posts, timber frame systems are categorized into four different types [6]. However, single based system is the most typical type. Therefore, all the data presented in the article mainly represents this type. In Figure 1 and 2, single based structural system can clearly be seen. In a point of fact, although it does not reflect the traditional and common method, the exceptional type like timber grid structure can be encountered in few very late examples.

Figure 1: Single based timber frame system from a house in Sarıyer

Figure 2: Timber frame system of a house in Bakırköy

At least one post is placed on each corner of a building. The number of vertical posts depends on the number of floors, all of them are positioned on the same vertical line. Distances between the parallel elements, such as posts, studs and noggings can vary depending on the project. In general, posts are placed on the line through the walls and their array with gaps is arranged based on the durability of the system and the design of the structure. Noggings and studs were added in anywhere needed as their place was probably decided on site by the rule of thumb. Timber is also used for the structural system of the roofs. Timber rafters are nailed to the ridge beam and often supported by the purlins. Thus, the load is distributed always toward the plates. Through the extension of the rafters, eaves are generated. The wooden roof structure is covered with boards both inside and outside. The upper boards create a suitable surface under the final covering and also help to protect the structure from the weather. Under boards provide clear finishing for the interior and enable decorative ceilings. Unlike many European examples, the wooden roof structure is invisible to the users. While the upper boards are nailed directly above the rafters, the interior boards are nailed down to the additional horizontal timber elements (Fig.4). The spaces, where the roof structure is observable, are mainly structured to be used as a repair room or as a warehouse.

Figure 3: Structural system inside the walls

Figure 4: Roof structure and the plates

Timber frame system after the western influence on the houses of Istanbul

Joinery methods of the timber structural system are mainly simple and all the joints are nailed. As the flexibilty had a great significance to the structures in the city with a threat of earthquake, nailed connections were preferred. Although several other techniques are mentioned in literature, basic nailed joinery is the most popular and common method applied for the houses. Probably locked joinery was used in rather small architectural elements. In the structural system, even the most basic form of connections, such as bringing elements together just with small notch or without any chipping can be encountered. Moreover, several types of lap joints, basic butt and beveled pieces are often found. At the joints, where more than two elements are connected, combinations of the traditional simple methods are used. Several examples of the joints are given in Figures 5-8.

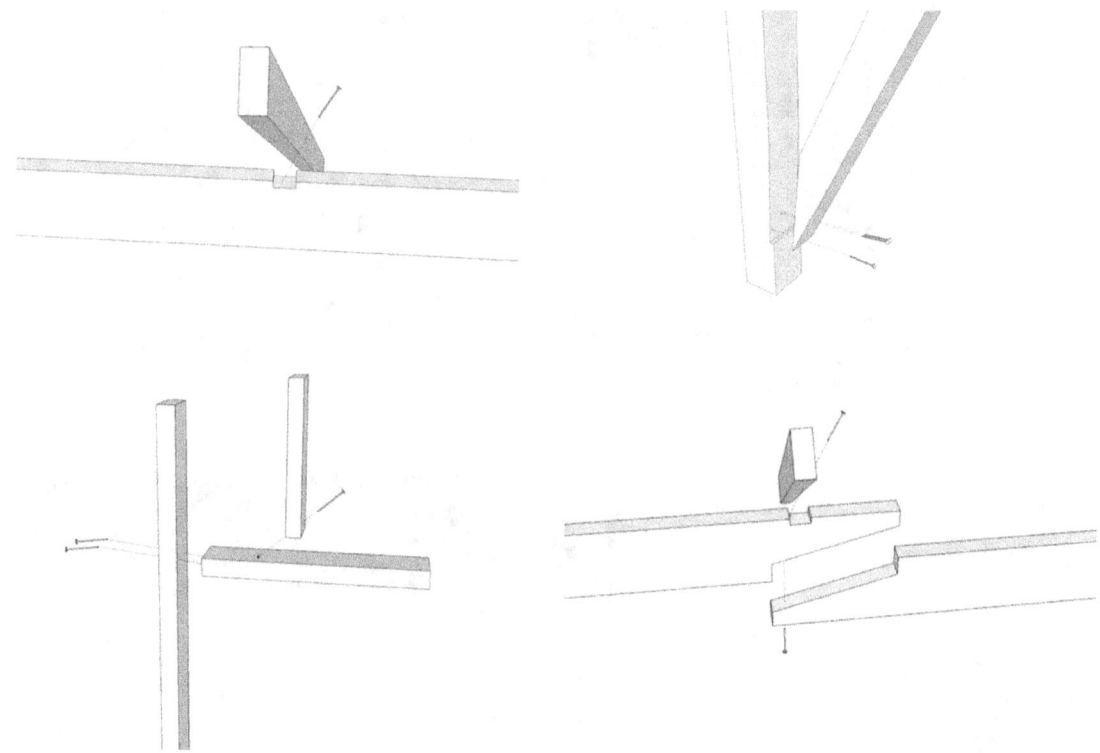

Figures 5-8: Example of a joint bringing two elements together

It has to be underlined that the nails play an important role in timber houses. They are not only used for strengthening the connections of the structural parts, but also in small decoration elements. Therefore, different sized nails are utilized associating with their purpose. All nails are made of metal. Both wrought iron and also factory produced small wires were found on the researched sites. Reused timber pieces and later renovations might also have introduced older or newer types of the nails into the structure. As a general rule, thick and strong nails were used for the load bearing elements and tiny as almost invisible ones were kept for the façade ornaments. To avoid the risk of danger, any kind of exposed nail end was twisted. Furthermore, the role of the craftsman on the decisions for the nailed joints has to be emphasized. There were no standardized systems for the application of the connections and usage of the nails. They were mainly decided on site and formed by hand tools. The number or direction of the nails used in the same type of joint can vary. Thus, it is quite obvious that function, visual quality, safety and playing by ear through the knowledge of the craftsmen have played important roles on the nailing tradition [7].

Exterior and interior spaces

Facade claddings are among the very specific characteristics of wooden houses of Istanbul from the last period of the Ottoman Empire. Horizontal timber elements differentiate them from many Anatolian and European houses. The tradition of the horizontally placed hand-cut timber boards dates back to the beginning of the eighteenth century and because it was only used for the seaside mansions, this specific type is known as *"yalı baskısı"* meaning the stamp of the seaside mansion. The facades were protected from water leakage by the nailed overlapped boards. *"Yalı baskısı"* was broadly used between late 18th century and early 19th century [8]. In the second half of the 19th century, timber boards with half grooved connections and tenon mortises appeared in the architectural atmosphere of Istanbul. Moreover, establishment of a timber factory in Istanbul enabled the production of machined claddings by the end of the 19th century.

Different types of boards including *"yalı baskisi"* or machine shaped claddings can be still seen in Istanbul. In addition to characteristic horizontal boards, with the influence of European architecture vertically placed claddings are found. However, they are always combined with horizontal ones and are usually incorporated for decoration at the upper part of the facade. The horizontal timber claddings are approximately 1-3 cm thick, however, their width varied in a wider range between 10 and 32cm. With increased width, commonly over 20-24cm, lines were printed to convey the impression of narrow cut boards [9]. Timber planks were always protected from fast deterioration by the application of a coating. Besides, their visual perception was remarkable with vivid colors. Colors like red, yellow, blue, white or beige were frequently used. Even on the neglected houses, which are remained in original wood color, traces of vivid paint from early days can be observed.

Interior sides of the walls are covered with the *Bagdadi* laths, plaster and color, while timber cladding boards are applied on the exterior side. *Bagdadi* is the name of a common technique, which enables the creation of a suitable surface for plaster and paint above the timber framed walls. The elements of the timber structure provide a base whereon thin laths are placed horizontally and nailed. This surface is then coated with 1-3 cm thick plaster. The Bagdadi technique can be categorized in two distinctive types by observing the separation of the laths. The first type shows evenly cut thin elements which are separated by small gaps and nailed regularly. The second type, however, shows irregularly split timber laths with varying gaps and fractures. Although rather uncommon, both types are sometimes observed within the same room or even on different parts of the same single wall. In these rare cases at the specific areas, a probability of a previous restoration work has to be kept in mind.

Although Bagdadi method is dominantly found on the timber frame structures, another similar application method can be occasionally encountered. In this method, which came in after the end of the 19th century, galvanized wires were used instead of timber laths. They were nailed to the timber structural elements for the same purpose of the *Bagdadi* laths [10].

Dimensions

After a comprehensive investigation on site and measurements with traditional methods, a general dimensional range has been found. All the measurements including the extreme bounds were taken into consideration and counted in the research rather than recording only the average numbers. Besides the gaps between the same types of elements (Table 1), short and long edges of the various structural timber elements are presented (Table 2 and 3).

The distance between main posts was stated between 1.5 and 2.0 meter on the published lecture notes of Ali Talat from 1911, while it was found at the range 96-239 cm on the site measurements [11]. Furthermore, the same source claims that the studs were placed with 20-30 cm gaps, but they are measured between 16 and 50 cm on the preserved authentic examples. Published data reflects a narrow scale than the actual findings, but it probably reflects the most common or the ideal numbers.

	Rafters	Posts	Floor Joists	Studs
Distance in cm:	29-53	91-239	28-50	16-50

Table 1: Gaps between the same types of elements [12].

In Table 2, width and height the original timber elements are presented. As the length of the elements vary in a wide range up to the span size and also design of the dwelling, they were not added to the classifications. All the sizes were measured on site with the metric system, but it should be emphasized that old unit system was still being used at the time those buildings were constructed. Although the metric system was first approved in 1869 at the Ottoman Empire period, the old system was not totally left. Both types of measurement system can be encountered, under different laws from different years until the permanent reform at the year 1931. Cross-section sizes of the timber elements became smaller after the mid-19th century. As an example, it is reported that the king posts were minimum 30 x 30 cm and the posts of a seaside mansion in Boyacikoy were 40 x 40 cm [13]. Nevertheless, among the researched objects any structural element in such a big size was not seen.

Timber Elements	Short Edge (cm)	Long Edge (cm)
Posts	8-14	10-16
Braces	8-12	9-15
Bearers	7-13	11-15
Floor joists	3-6	12-22
Noggings and Studs	3-5	7-15
Bagdadi laths	0,5-1,5	1-4

Table 2: Sizes from the cross-sections of the timber elements according to the on-site measurements [14].

Width and height of the timber elements of the roof structure are given in Table 3. Although hip rafters are put in a separate classification, sizes of the jack rafters and king commons are given under the group of "common rafters", because their character and dimensions are very similar.

Timber Elements of the Roof Structure	Short Edge (cm)	Long Edge (cm)
Roof Studs	5-12	10-15
Hip rafters	5-6	15-22
Common rafters	3,5-6	10-14
Purlins	4-11	14-22
Ridge Boards	5-6	16-21

Table 3: Sizes from the cross-sections of the timber roof elements according to the on-site measurements [15].

Sizes of lumber with the types of the wood used in the second half of the 19th century are published in a text book named "Usul-I Kesf-I Mimari" [16]. They are given below in Table 4 to provide another comparison. However, it has to be kept in mind that the names of the elements on the published data are different from current usages. The lumber was identified in detail closely related to the sizes and the original meaning was lost after the change in the measurement system. Direct translation of the data may cause confusion. Therefore, the data was regrouped and simplified. As an example, nearly 5-10 different sizes of lumber of the same usage were put under the same group. Moreover, although the metric system was already approved at that time, "zira" and "parmak" are the units of measurement on the published data. Zira is equal to 0,758 m and parmak is 3,1582 cm. They were converted to the metric system in Table 4 for better understanding and original units were also presented for exact accuracy.

When the results of the Table 2 are compared with the lecture notes (Table 4), the cross-section sizes of the lumbers appear in a wider range. As the onsite measurements reflect the end sizes of the timber pieces, having sizes smaller than the uncut lumber is an expected result.

Usage	Type of Wood	Length		Width		Height	
		Zira	meter	Parmak	cm	Parmak	cm
Corner post and buttress	Oak	5-12	**3,8-9,1**	3-12	**9,5-37,8**	6-12	**19-37,8**
Bearer (horizontal element)	Oak	6-12	**4,6-9,1**	3-5	**9,5-15,8**	1-4	**3,2-12,6**
Brace (diagonal element)	Pine	6-15	**4,6-11,4**	3-12	**9,5-37,8**	1-12	**3,2-37,8**
Floor joists and bearers	Hornbeam or oak	5-10	**3,8-7,6**	3-8	**9,5-25,3**	1-3	**3,2-9,5**
Bagdadi laths, Ceiling and the rooftile underlayment	Pitch pine or other kinds of pine	2-5	**1,5-3,8**	3-7	**9,5-22,1**	1/6-1/2	**0,5-1,8**

Table 4: Types and sizes of the lumbers used during the second half of the 19th century. The data is generalized and the size ranges correspond to the data from various pieces [17].

Role of the influences

The influence of the European styles was mainly realized at first view on the façade layout and ornaments. However, there is an indirect impact of the westernization on the structural system. It is quite obvious that after the 19th century, a special importance was devoted to the exterior decoration of the houses in accordance with the increased popularity of the western styles. The visual meaning of the structural system lost its significance especially in Istanbul, because they were enveloped and became non-visible to the users. Gradually, the system became lighter. On the other hand, the transformations always trigger another issue. The effects were bidirectional. As the structure became lighter, it enabled the creation of more open spaces. In this way, bigger houses with larger windows could be constructed. As the freedom on the design and façade surfaces increased with the lightweight structure, architectural environment became more suitable for applying new trends.

Furthermore, the timber frame structural system of houses in Istanbul has several similarities with the balloon frame and platform frame. Although they were applied in almost at the same period of time in USA and Ottoman Empire (or maybe earlier in Ottoman Empire), the distances between the geographical locations reduce the probability of an interaction. There may be some coincidences, as the timber is one of the oldest and basic construction materials of humanity. But, also a kind of interaction has to be thought. At this point, it needs independent detailed research for clarification.

Conclusion

Authentic timber elements of houses of Istanbul are gradually disappearing. Not only the urban metropolitan conditions and changed lifestyles, but also through deterioration through lack of maintenance and wrong interventions he loss of their original form. Visual documentation of the houses is rather easy with various techniques, but the structural system is the least documented part. Within this paper, timber frame structure without infill and the Bagdadi method is explained in detail. Moreover, dimensions of the structural elements, distances between the same type of elements on the frame system and joint techniques are presented. Quantitative findings on site are compared with the published data. Role of the influences are discussed. Observations from hundreds of houses were used for the statements made in the article. To sum up, it is aimed to shed a light to the present status that may lead to further studies on timber structures.

References

[1] Oztank, N. Traditional Wood Turkish Houses and Structural Details. 10th World Conference on Wood Engineering. Miyazaki, Japan, 2008, p.235.
[2] Aras, F., Timber-Framed Buildings and Structural Restoration of a Historic.
Timber Pavilion in Turkey, International Journal of Architectural Heritage: Conservation, Analysis, and Restoration, 7:4, 2013, 403-415, DOI: 10.1080/15583058.2011.640738
[3] Güçhan N. Ş., History and Characteristics of Construction Techniques Used in Traditional Timber Ottoman Houses, International Journal of Architectural Heritage, 12:1, 1-20, 2018, DOI: 10.1080/15583058.2017.1336811
[4] Çobancaoğlu, T., "Türkiye'de Geleneksel Ahşap Ev Yapı Sistemlerinin İrdelenerek Gruplandırılmasına Yönelik Bir Değerlendirme", Tasarım Kuram, Volume 2, Issue 3, 2003, pp 27-42.
[5] Eldem, S.H., Turkish Houses Ottoman Period, T.A.Ç Vakfı: Istanbul, Volume: I, 1984.
[6] Eldem, S. H., Yapı, Birsen Yayınevi, Istanbul, (publication year is not written on the book).
[7] Ergün, S. F., The European Influence on the Ottoman Timber Residences in Istanbul, Technische Universitaet München, Unpublished doctoral thesis, München, 2020.
[8] Eldem, S. H., (Note 5).
[9] Yagci, S. F., Historic wooden houses of Istanbul with the influence of European styles, Proceedings of 4th WTA International PhD Symposium, Delft, Netherlands, ISBN: 978-90-79216-19-2, 2017, pp.65-74.
[10] Acar D. and Mazlum D., Timber-framed Houses Built for the Court Members after the 1894 Earthquake in Istanbul: Rationalization of Construction Techniques, International Journal of Architectural Heritage, 10:5, 604-619, 2016, DOI: 10.1080/15583058.2015.1045995
[11] Acar,D., 2017 referring the Ottoman source "Talat, A., Mühendis Mektebinde Tedris Olunan Ahşap İnşaat [Timber Construction Lecture Notes] (Istanbul, 1911), p. 104 in the article with DOI: 10.1080/13556207.2017.1330384.
[12] Ergün, S. F., thesis, (Note 7), p.181.
[13] Eldem, S. H., (1987) Turkish Houses Ottoman Period, T.A.Ç Vakfı: Istanbul, Volume: III.
[14] Ergün, S. F., thesis, (Note 7), p.182.
[15] Ibid.
[16] Günergun, F., 'Mekteb-i Harbiye'de Okutulan Mimarlık ve İnşaat Bilgisi Dersleri için 1870'li Yıllarda Yazılmış Üç Kitap, in Afife Batur'a Armağan-Mimarlık ve Sanat Tarihi Yazıları, ed. A. Ağır, D. Mazlum and G. Cephanecigil, Literatür Publication, Istanbul, 2005, p. 156.
[17] Ergün, S. F.,thesis, (Note 7), p.185.

Faulty Figures and Paper Technologies: Cost Estimating in Late Nineteenth-Century America

Chelsea Spencer
Massachusetts Institute of Technology

Introduction

In the late nineteenth century, a new genre of book began to be published for a new readership of building professionals in the United States. This was the building-cost estimating handbook, or estimator, and it was a response to uncertainties that arose from changing practices of valuation and new modes of knowledge production and circulation that were crucial to the development of the nascent American building industry. This paper focuses on two early examples of this genre, seeking to understand for whom these books were published, from what sources their contents were derived, and how their appearance and circulation in the United States in the last decades of the nineteenth century reflected changing social and cultural conditions in the American building trades during the coalescence of general contracting. I suggest that closer attention to estimating as both a practice and a body of knowledge that depends on the circulation, storage, and analysis of quantitative and qualitative information can help us better understand the circumstances that both enabled and were reshaped by the advent of the American general contractor [1].

Old Price and New Markets

The correct way to estimate the cost of prospective building projects became a subject of consternation and debate among American builders and some architects in the 1870s. In the pages of monthly trade journals like *American Builder* and *Carpentry and Building*, correspondents from across the industrialising regions of the United States complained of an increasingly chaotic building market, as experienced builders found themselves competing for work against men of no particular qualifications beyond 'a good opinion' of themselves [2]. As historians of nineteenth-century building culture in the United States have shown, the pressures of market competition had already begun to reorganise the political economy of artisanal work in the antebellum era, forcing even master craftsmen to use percentage discounts to bend the stability of 'old price' to market forces [3]. After the end of the Civil War, however, a far more extensive and integrated building market was created, as communication and transport networks drew builders and contractors out of their local markets and into closer competition with one another. At the same time, periodic financial booms and busts rippled across the country, encouraging speculative building, destabilising prices, and in lean times stiffening competition. Advertisements for estimates on major building projects brought in ever greater numbers of submissions, not just from local builders but also from building concerns stationed a considerable distance from the proposed building site. And as these calls for competitive price proposals received responses from contractors large and small, near and far, experienced and inexperienced, responsible and reckless, the wide range of prices for the same project brought the question of estimating expertise into view. For builders, vast discrepancies between estimates—but especially the recklessly low underestimates, or 'plungers', as some called them—represented an existential threat to the entire industry. A single untenably low bid took work away from more competent or responsible builders, often bankrupted the winner of the contract, and sometimes ended in the collapse of the project. Moreover, as many pointed out, disparate estimates left a bad impression on America's capitalists (builders' ideal clients), for the lack of agreement over price suggested not merely a failure of precision but also a lack of competence in matters of business among builders generally. One *Carpentry and Building* correspondent yearned for a day when contractors 'shall be so thoroughly educated by their mechanical journals as to show capitalists very slight differences in their estimates [4]'. In competition, then, building entrepreneurs found a strange kind of community—ungoverned and perhaps ungovernable—in which the activities of some affected the interests of all. Reflecting on the estimating debate that had spanned several years in *Carpentry and Building*, one correspondent in 1879 expressed satisfaction that, if nothing else, the universality of the bidding problem had stirred a sense of 'unity of interests financially' among carpenters and builders across the country [5].

But what were the causes of the discrepancies in estimates, and how were they to be resolved? While some bemoaned the recklessness and even the dishonesty of some contractors, many instead argued that the root of the problem was not in fact moral but rather technical—not competition's corruption of traditional ethical codes but 'a lamentable degree of ignorance among the whole class of builders' regarding sound estimating technique [6]. The inclination among a new generation of contractors to forgo formal craft apprenticeships meant that many were left to educate themselves. 'For lack of a competent master to examine and criticise the first efforts of the novice at estimating', wrote one commentator, these 'builders are compelled to gain their experience in the most expensive school, and the errors of judgment incident to all first efforts are paid out of capital [7]'. Some continued to insist that the only sure way to arrive at accurate estimates was by trained judgment and the kind of tacit knowledge that could be gained only from years' spent actually working in the building trades. The predicament was, however, that if a young contractor had 'no definite judgment until he obtains it by experience', then in the meantime he would 'carry on his business in a haphazard way, guessing out his estimates, the very evil we are crying against [8]'. But incompetence in estimating was not unique to newcomers to the building trades; it could also be found among those who may have long ago mastered the technics of their trade but were less expert in the clerical niceties and financial complexities of industrial business. Indeed, by the turn of the twentieth century 'the ability to estimate' was seen as nothing less than 'the dividing line between the journeyman and the master builder [9]'. Given this, it was acknowledged that American 'building interests' generally would be served by systematising methods of estimating and making advice readily available to anyone who was inclined to enter their ranks by way of the competitive tender.

Rule Books and Estimators

At the beginning of the 1870s, however, it was not only that there were no formal modes of training. There were not even any widely circulated books to which American builders could turn for guidance on estimating. The idea of such a book remained novel enough to Americans by 1880 that, when the editor of *Carpentry and Building*, Anson O. Kittredge (whom we will meet again), received a copy that January of a new edition of the *Builder's Price Book and Guide for Estimates*, compiled by one Henry C. Bevis and published in London, he remarked that the book, giving prices of current building materials and machinery, 'differs from anything published upon this side of the Atlantic [10]'. Lamenting that the book itself was 'of small practical value to American builders, because the prices are made for the English market', Kittredge observed that it nevertheless could serve 'to indicate to what system the matter of estimates may be reduced [11]'.

Indeed, the state of estimating at this time was strikingly different in Britain, where building price books and estimators had been readily available to all since at least the early seventeenth century and by the nineteenth century had become a fiercely competitive market in themselves. Annually updated editions were issued by at least three competing publishers—each book known by the names of its original compiler, Robert Laxton, Benjamin Crosby, and Z. Skyring, respectively—in a race to keep up with volatile London prices, prompting some authors to also offer 'perpetual' price books that explained the general principles of estimating and provided formulas for reconciling these with fluctuating prices and local customs [12]. At the same time, the work of building quantification in Britain was being professionalized as a dedicated service by independent surveyors who prepared bills of quantities, 'taken off' from plans and specifications, to serve as the basis for contractors' price estimates [13].

There is no unambiguous explanation for the belated appearance of published building price books in the United States [14]. Several attempts had been made—the first perhaps in 1833 by the young Irish builder and architect James Gallier, then newly arrived in New York from London—to compile a comprehensive set of estimating rules representing all trades into a single book, but none appears to have been successful [15]. It is possible that most antebellum building craftsmen, whose operations remained highly localised even in coastal cities until after the Civil War, would have found a general-purpose price book irrelevant. As scholars have argued, standards of value and measurement are anything but neutral conventions; they either grow from local practices and social relations—varying geographically, situationally, and historically—or they are imposed as instruments of statecraft and infrastructures of commercial expansion [16]. In the tight-knit artisanal communities of agrarian America, conversely, the illegibility of local measurement and valuation practices to would-be interlopers no doubt had its advantages. Well-placed locals, meanwhile, would have had ready access to reliable—if often heavily controlled—price information through their own networks, customs, and institutions. Indeed, another possibility is that the public dissemination of building price information not only would have made no sense in preindustrial America but also could have been actively suppressed.

As it happens, one type of price book could be found within the libraries of American guild halls from the mid-eighteenth through the nineteenth century. These were not, in the strict sense, publications, however. They were instead a proprietary kind of document, jealously guarded by elite companies of master craftsmen in order to maintain a system of 'old price' [17]. Privately printed in small runs or written in manuscript, these books contained schedules of prices for every category of work in the company's trade, as well as elliptical explanations of the rules for measuring and converting dimensional quantities—typically in lineal and cubic feet—into pecuniary quantities, in dollars and cents [18]. The most prominent example of these was the rule book of the Carpenters' Company of the City and County of Philadelphia. When none other than Thomas Jefferson sought a copy in 1817—wishing to consult an authoritative source as he negotiated with builders for the construction of what would become the University of Virginia—he was rebuffed on account of 'an express rule of the Carpenter's Company that the book is not to be seen out of the pale of their Church [19]'. Allowing a non–company member, even a former US president, to peruse the prices was grounds for expulsion according to the company's strictly enforced by-laws, and careful records were kept of members who removed the book from the carpenters' hall. Early editions were printed without prices, the figures added by hand only to the copy that was never to leave the hall; later editions were kept only in manuscript [20]. Not all craft companies were so secretive about their methods of valuation—Jefferson settled for the Pittsburgh carpenters' rule book—but it is notable that the Philadelphia carpenters' price controls seem to have held a special authority in and beyond their own local jurisdiction [21].

The published books on estimating that began to appear in the late nineteenth century, still called 'price books' but more often 'estimators', were very different from the craft companies' rule books, though vestiges of the old order can be seen in them. They reflected not only changing relationships within and among the building trades but also technical, epistemological, and institutional shifts in the reckoning and dissemination of price itself. Unlike the secret books of prices and rules used as regulating instruments of guild power, estimators offered their public readership a compilation of techniques and tools for quantifying the work of not just any one trade but all of them, from brick laying to paper hanging. The once-obscured particulars of each trade, and more, were thus made available to a national market of book-buying mechanics.

The first book that appears to have met with any success was Frank W. Vogdes's *The Architect's and Builder's Pocket Companion and Price Book,* first published in 1871 [22]. An architect practicing in Louisville, Kentucky, who claimed twenty-five years of experience, Vogdes meant for his book 'to afford to the Building Fraternity those facilities and advantages derived by Civil and Mechanical Engineers [23]'. Noting his own need for such a book in his many years of practice as an architect, Vogdes presents the book to 'the profession', hoping that 'it will save the labor of many calculations, of almost hourly occurrence [24]'. From engineering treatises he selected tables to aid in a variety of calculations that he believed would be useful to architects and builders, supplementing them with his own original contributions. As the title of the book promises, Vogdes also included what he called a 'Bill of Prices for Carpenters' Work', compiled from 'the standard of value for such work for over forty years in one of the most flourishing cities in the Union [25]'. While the majority of the items listed in this bill do clearly fall under the carpenter's jurisdiction, they also encompass brick work, excavating, well digging, masonry, slating, painting, glazing, plastering, and tinwork [26]. This peculiar conflation reflects the managerial purview of the American carpenter's position: in a land of plentiful forests carpenters had long been the most powerful among the building craftsmen and were often to be found performing the role of lead contractor, directly overseeing carpentry work while subcontracting with other trades for the rest [27]. Vogdes does not list the categories and items of work in the order of the building process, the convention adopted by most later estimators, but instead alphabetically, which was more common in craft companies' rule books. The language of his price explanations also recalls these books, insofar as a basic rule is given for measuring and valuing a particular building element—usually in terms of lineal or cubic feet—followed by a series of exceptions (most lines beginning with 'for' or 'if') for which percentage adjustments or multipliers are provided. In a clear departure, however, Vogdes explicitly notes that prices are 'presented to those interested in estimating the value of such work, in the full belief that it will prove a valuable assistance both for the purpose of basing a formal "Proposal" upon, and in ascertaining the value of, work after it is completed [28]'.

Filled predominantly with tables of precalculated values—from US weights and measures to standard sizes of drawing paper to properties and units of materials like wood and different metal alloys—Vogdes's handbook more resembles the ready reckoners used by merchants and engineers than it does the earlier craft rule books or the later estimators [29]. The book provides no instructions as to how the task of estimating itself is to be done, conceding that the book is intended as a labour-saving reference for experienced builders rather than as a guidebook for young contractors seeking to learn the technique of estimating. It would have been useful only insofar as readers brought to it their own knowledge of the building and estimating processes. Nonetheless, Vogdes's *Pocket Companion and Price Book* appears to have remained popular among contractors in many parts of the country for as long as two decades, reissued in at least four updated and expanded editions. The last, published in 1895, is almost a hundred pages longer than the first edition—with additional tables quantitatively describing newer materials like concrete—but intriguingly the bill of prices remains constant across all extent editions from 1871 to 1895, with text, numbers, and even typesetting unchanged.

Paper Technologies

A more instrumental response to the estimating question was presented to builders in 1885 by Jasper D. Sibley, an architect, and Anson Kittredge, the editor of *Carpentry and Building*, among other trade journals. This was not a single handbook but rather what I would like to call, borrowing a term from historians of capitalism, a complement of 'paper technologies' that comprised a booklet of 28 *Handy Estimate Blanks*—sold in single copies or by the dozen—and a pocket-sized user's manual of sorts titled *The Practical Estimator* [30]. The latter provided 'full descriptions for [the blank forms'] use, as well as a list of all the items ordinarily entering into a building, so arranged as to be a convenient and systematic reminder' [31]. If Vogdes's project was more about compilation and calculation—collecting various dimensional, mechanical, and pecuniary values together for the experienced builder's labour-saving reference—then Kittredge and Sibley's was one of methodology and discipline, designed above all but not exclusively with the neophyte contractor in mind. Most significantly, neither *The Practical Estimator* nor the *Handy Estimate Blanks*, as the latter name suggests, included any price information whatsoever. Where Vogdes had provided values in dollars and cents, Kittredge and Sibley inserted the opposite: blank spaces.

In addition to introducing a degree of 'system' into the practices of inexperienced contractors, Kittredge and Sibley also saw their book as a kind of machine whose use would benefit even the most seasoned estimators. Estimating itself is a kind of 'machine work', they note, and 'in the absence of adequate machinery for performing it, it is done in an expensive manner, and frequently in a very bungling way [32]'. The problem for any contractor was not just the tedious, rote, and mentally taxing nature of estimating—'the drudgery of the work and the constant tension of mind necessary to recollect little things and place these items in proper place [33]'—but also the conditions under which it was typically performed. Unlike the large contracting firms that had dedicated estimating departments, the small-time contractor found himself estimating at odd hours, between other demands, and sometimes in a hurry when hurry was demanded. Interruptions were unavoidable, with the result that the most common error in estimating was not miscalculation or misjudgement but simple omission due to lapses of memory or attention [34].

The most effective trade technology to alleviate difficulties of this type was nothing more than a list of all the kinds of building work, elements, and materials that might factor into the estimate. *The Practical Estimator* offered just such a list, 'arranged for use as a reminder or "tickler" in preparing estimates [35]'. It divided items by trade—masonry (including excavation); carpentry; painting; tinning, slating, and galvanised metal work; and plumbing and gas fitting—placed them in 'the same order that would be pursued in the erection of the building', and subdivided them further into constituent tasks and items, with additional blank lines on which the user could add his own items. As the media historian Lisa Gitelman has shown, preprinted 'blanks', or blank forms, proliferated in the nineteenth century, particularly in administrative lines of work. Filling in forms helped nineteenth-century Americans 'locate goods, map transactions, and transfer value', she writes, 'while it also helped them to locate themselves or others within or against the sites, practices, and institutions that helped to structure daily life [36]'. Catering to 'the repetition of certain kinds of writing', blanks worked 'to direct and delimit expression', often in order to reform practices that had ossified into inefficient habits [37]. As Kittredge and Sibley themselves point out, blanks were already a common feature in the businesses of 'many of the most prominent and most successful contracting firms in the country'. Representing 'the outgrowth of their experience', a building firm's blanks were (not unlike the craft guild's rule books) guarded as trade secrets, 'for fear some competitor may have the opportunity of copying features which in practice have been found to afford advantages [38]'.

Kittredge and Sibley thus sought to make systematic methods available to the small contractor who built only four or five modest buildings in a year and thus lacked both the experience and the 'bulk of trade' to profit from the institution of any such carefully designed system of information management. What they offered, then, was not so much new information as a machine for methodically organising information the builder presumably already had. While *The Practical Estimator* provided explicit instructions about proper estimating technique, the blanks did a more implicit kind of work—prompting the user for specific details and thereby teaching him what information needed to be gathered, as well as how to structure the knowledge he already possessed [39]. Before the pages pertaining to the estimate proper, for example, the cover of the *Handy Estimate Blanks* booklet offered structured space for contextual details that the average builder might not be in the habit of gathering in a systematic way: blanks for enumerating the drawings and other documents on which the estimate was based, blanks for detailing the project schedule and terms of payment (for these ought to influence the builder's price, the authors argued), blanks for making site-visit notes, and blanks for recording any specific terms on which the proposal was made. Having made a record of all this, the contractor who won the contract could keep track of any changed or additional expectations introduced when it came time to execute the work.

The most important feature of the *Handy Estimate Blanks*, however, were the six ruled columns that appeared to the right of the list of building tasks [40]. The first three were for the estimated quantities, prices, and costs; the second three were for actual quantities, price, and cost, to be recorded as the work progressed if the contract was awarded. This schema, it was hoped, would instil in the mind of the contractor a clear distinction between the concepts of quantity take-offs, market price, and actual cost. But the columns were also meant to encourage habits of systematic record keeping and comparative analysis of costs both estimated and actual. The idea was 'to link together as closely as possible the estimated cost of a piece of work with the actual cost of performing the same [41]'. In *The Practical Estimator*, Kittredge and Sibley discuss the importance of 'systematic comparison' in estimating: 'While the work of taking off quantities from drawings can be reduced to a system and a high degree of accuracy attained, there is scarcely anything but judgement to govern the estimator in the matter of the prices put upon the different items [42]'. The only way to know whether one's estimate had been accurate was to compare it with the actual cost of building. Admitting that filling in every actual figure next to every estimated figure for every item in every project was not likely to be practicable for the ordinary builder, Kittredge and Sibley nevertheless argued that regular 'experiments of this kind' would help 'to keep a wholesome check on estimating' [43].

Conclusion: Of Prices and Costs

In their insistence on the importance of record keeping and analysis, Kittredge and Sibley's *Handy Estimate Blanks* and *Practical Estimator* signal a conceptual shift that would reach full expression in the building industry only in the twentieth century: the shift from the idea of price as given (by custom or by the market) to one based on exacting methods of cost keeping, analysis, and manipulation. This was mirrored in other industries, as well, especially steel production. Upon leaving the railway business to enter steelmaking in the 1870s, Andrew Carnegie was surprised to find that cost keeping was not practiced in the industry. 'Show me your costs sheets,' he would lecture his foremen. 'It is more interesting to know how well and how cheaply you have done this thing than how much money you have made, because the one is a temporary result, due possibly to special conditions of trade, but the other means a permanency [44]'. Kittredge himself, a graduate of the Miami Commercial College in Dayton, Ohio, would play no small part in cultivating a comparable sense of accountability among American builders. Better known today to historians of finance than to historians of construction or architecture, he spent the last decades of the nineteenth century simultaneously editing multiple trade journals for both the building industry and the accounting profession. In *Carpentry and Building* he sustained a continuous discourse on business techniques, taking every opportunity to encourage builders to systematise their estimating, cost-accounting, and timekeeping methods. For these were the techniques that would distinguish the expertise of the successful general contractor from the know-how of the master builder. Building-cost estimating handbooks to come would look less like craft rule books and more like business manuals as their authors turned their attention from compiling prices—listed alongside weights and measures and the mechanical properties of materials, as so many facts arbitrarily given by custom or nature—to instructing contractors on how to keep and analyse their own costs.

References

[1] On American general contractors, see James F. O'Gorman, 'O. W. Norcross, Richardson's "Master Builder": A Preliminary Report', *Journal of the Society of Architectural Historians*, vol. 32, no. 2, May 1973, pp. 104–113; Sara E. Wermiel, 'The Rise of the General Contractor in 19th Century America', *FMI Quarterly*, no. 3, 2008, pp. 116–129; Brian Bowen, 'General Contractors and Architects in Nineteenth-Century America', pp. 383–389 in Ine Wouters et al., (Eds), *Proceedings of the Sixth International Congress on Construction History*, Brussels 2018, vol. 1, Brussels: CRC Press/Balkema, 2018.
[2] 'Necessity of Uniform Prices in the Building Trades', *Carpentry and Building*, vol. 1, no. 6, June 1879, p. 116.
[3] Bryan E. Norwood, 'The Measurer: Quantifying Labor in the Early American Republic', unpublished conference paper presented at the Society of Architectural Historians 73rd Annual International Conference, Seattle/Virtual 2020; Donna J. Rilling, *Making Houses, Crafting Capitalism: Builders in Philadelphia, 1790–1850*, Philadelphia: University of Pennsylvania Press, 2001; Lisa Beth Lubow, 'Artisans in Transition: Early Capitalist Development and the Carpenters of Boston, 1787–1837' (Ph.D. thesis, University of California, Los Angeles, 1987); and Catherine W. Bishir et al., *Architects and Builders in North Carolina: A History of the Practice of Building*, Chapel Hill: University of North Carolina Press, 1990.
[4] 'Methods and rules for Estimating', *Carpentry and Building*, vol. 1, no. 4, April 1879, pp. 77.
[5] 'Discrepancies in Bids: A Standard of Valuation Needed', *Carpentry and Building*, vol. 3, no. 7, July 1879, pp. 137.
[6] Mart, 'Necessity of Uniform Prices in the Building Trades', *Carpentry and Building*, vol. 1, no. 6, June 1879, p. 116.
[7] Anson O. Kittredge and Jasper D. Sibley, *The Practical Estimator*, New York: David Williams, 1885, pp. 1.
[8] Mart (note 6), p. 116.
[9] Edward Nichols and S. R. Noe, *Estimating*, Chicago: American Technical Society, 1924, p. 1.
[10] 'New Publications', *Carpentry and Building*, vol. 2, no. 1, January 1880, p. 9.
[11] Ibid.
[12] See, for example, William Thorne, *The Perpetual Guide*, London: Simpkin & Marshall, 1824; and Richard Elsam, *The Practical Builder's Perpetual Price-Book*, London: Printed for Thomas Kelly, 1837.

[13] Still today the practice of quantity surveying is almost unheard of in the United States, while remaining established custom in the British construction industry. See Brian Bowen, 'The Quantity Surveyor: MIA in the USA', pp. 227–234 in Karl-Eugen Kurrer, Werner Lorenz, and Volker Wetzk (Eds), *Proceedings of the Third International Congress on Construction History*, Cottbus 2009, Cottbus: Brandenburg University of Technology, 2009; and F. M. L. Thompson, *Chartered Surveyors: The Growth of a Profession*, London: Routledge & Kegan Paul, 1968.

[14] American business publishing more generally began only after independence was won from Great Britain. The first American commodity price current was published in Philadelphia in 1783, the year the Treaty of Paris was signed. John J. McCusker, 'The Demise of Distance: The Business Press and the Origins of the Information Revolution in the Early Modern Atlantic World', *American Historical Review*, vol. 110, no. 2, April 2005, pp. 295–321.

[15] James Gallier, *The American Builder's General Price Book and Estimator*, New York: Stanley & Co., 1833.

[16] Witold Kula, *Measures and Men*, trans. R. Szreter. Princeton: Princeton University Press, 1986; and James C. Scott, *Seeing Like a State: How Certain Schemes to Improve the Human Condition Have Failed*, New Haven: Yale University Press, 1998, pp. 9–84.

[17] Originally borrowed from British craft traditions, old price was practiced by company-approved measurers who literally measured a building after the work was finished and used the company's formulas and prices to determine the total building cost. The fee for this service in America was customarily 3 per cent, split between the client and the builder who completed the work. It was also common for the client and builder to each hire their own measurer.

[18] For a near-comprehensive list of American carpenters' price books, see Elizabeth H. Temkin, 'Annotated Bibliography of Builders' Rule Books Published in America', Washington, DC: National Park Service, 1976.

[19] Letter from William Thackara to Benjamin Henry Latrobe, 22 December 1817, enclosed with letter from Latrobe to Thomas Jefferson, ca. 26 December 1817, p. 278 in *The Papers of Thomas Jefferson*, Retirement Series, ed. J. Jefferson Looney, vol. 12, 1 September 1817 to 21 April 1818. Princeton, NJ: Princeton University Press, 2014.

[20] See also Norwood, 'The Measurer' (note 3); and Rilling, *Making Houses* (note 3), pp. 69–90.

[21] Even after the company's power had waned in the late nineteenth century, old editions of the price book were sometimes used by third parties to settle disputes in court. It is also interesting to note that two pirated editions of the book appeared, in 1801 and 1819, under the same title, *House Carpenters' Book of Prices and Rules*.

[22] Vogdes's handbook was also frequently recommended by *Carpentry and Building* correspondents. In the 1883 edition Vogdes thanks the '7,000 purchasers' of earlier editions. This edition of the book was also reviewed favourably among new publications in *Carpentry and Building*, vol. 5, no. 12, December 1883, pp. 245. The notice predicts that the new, expanded edition 'is likely to be even more popular in the future than it has been in the past'.

[23] Vogdes cites four authors as his sources in the preface: Haswell, Nystrom, Byrne, and Scribner. To date I have only been able to locate one of these: John W. Nystrom, *A New Calculating Machine*, Philadelphia: R. W. Barnard & Sons, 1852. Frank W. Vogdes, preface to *The Architect's and Builder's Pocket Companion and Price Book*, Philadelphia: Henry Carey Baird, 1871, p. 9.

[24] Ibid.

[25] Ibid., p. 154. The city is presumably either Louisville, Kentucky, where Vogdes worked and lived, or perhaps St. Louis, Missouri, which had fairer claim to being among the reunited nation's 'most flourishing cities'. Chicago, also relatively nearby, was still a very young city, having a population of only a few hundred white settlers forty years before Vogdes's writing.

[26] Ibid., pp. 14–15.

[27] Mary N. Woods, *From Craft to Profession: The Practice of Architecture in Nineteenth-Century America*, Berkeley: University of California Press, 1999, pp. 10–14.

[28] Vogdes, *Pocket Companion and Price Book* (note 23), p. 154.

[29] Historians of computing have shown that ready reckoners—cheaper and more reliable than mechanical devices—were among the dominant tools used as aids to calculation, particularly multiplication, from the seventeenth through the mid-twentieth century, when digital calculators were introduced. See Bruce O. B. Williams and Roger G. Johnson, 'Ready Reckoners', *IEEE Annals of the History of Computing*, vol. 27, no. 4, October 2005, pp. 64–80. See also William

Deringer, 'Pricing the Future in the Seventeenth Century: Calculating Technologies in Competition', *Technology and Culture*, vol. 58, no. 2, 2017, pp. 506–528.

[30] Seth Rockman has proposed the term paper technologies to describe the 'written means of storing and conveying information [that] functioned as the material infrastructure of the rapidly expanding Atlantic economy' starting in the eighteenth century. Seth Rockman, 'Paper Technologies of Capitalism', *Technology and Culture*, vol. 58, no. 2, 2017, pp. 487–505.

[31] Advertisement for *Handy Estimate Blanks* and *The Practical Estimator*, both published by David Williams, in *Carpentry and Building*, vol. 9, no. 10, October 1887, p. xvii.

[32] Kittredge and Sibley, *Practical Estimator* (note 7), pp. 4–5.

[33] Ibid., p. 4.

[34] Ibid., p. 5.

[35] Ibid., p. 27.

[36] Lisa Gitelman, *Paper Knowledge: Toward a Media History of Documents*, Durham: Duke University Press, 2014, pp. 21–22. See also JoAnne Yates, *Control through Communication: The Rise of System in American Management*, Baltimore: Johns Hopkins University Press, 1989.

[37] Gitelman, *Paper Knowledge* (note 36), p. 22.

[38] Kittredge and Sibley, *Practical Estimator* (note 7), p. 6.

[39] On the disciplinary function of handbooks, see Angela N. H. Creager, Mathias Grote, and Elaine Leong, 'Learning by the Book: Manuals and Handbooks in the History of Science', BJHS Themes, vol. 5, 2020, pp. 10.

[40] Unfortunately I am not aware of an extant copies of the *Handy Estimate Blanks*. This account is based on Kittredge and Sibley's description of them in *The Practical Estimator*.

[41] Kittredge and Sibley, *Practical Estimator* (note 7), p. 21.

[42] Ibid., p. 13.

[43] Ibid., pp. 13–14.

[44] Harold C. Livesay, *Andrew Carnegie and the Rise of Big Business*, New York: Pearson Longman, 2007, p. 112. See also Jonathan Levy, *Ages of American Capitalism: A History of the United States*, New York: Random House, 2021, pp. 229–259.

The Influence of Standards and Regulations for Steel and Reinforced Concrete on the Development of Modern Architecture in Pre-WW1 Paris and Brussels

Nick von Behr
University of Kent, UK

Introduction

How did technical standards and associated building regulations for steel and reinforced concrete influence the development of modern architecture in preWW1 Paris and Brussels? This is the core research question of my PhD project at the Universities of Kent and Lille begun in September 2020. The paper sets out some initial markers on the topic, results of a scoping exercise I have undertaken since September and from which I hope to elicit wider contributions from peers.

Our state of existing technical and practical knowledge about the specifications and use of building materials in the past is founded on a plethora of published literature by academics and professionals studying in a broad range of fields, which can be usefully brought together under the collective umbrella of construction history. There is considerable research evidence available on the use of metals and concrete in monumental, industrial and other buildings in Britain, France and then the USA during the eighteenth and nineteenth centuries.

Research context

The PhD project began by examining the current state of knowledge about materials, standards and regulations in construction history for the period and region to be researched. Because physical archival research in year two of the project will aim to establish valid connections between the emergence of technical standards and regulations for specifically steel and reinforced concrete and the development of modern architecture, a theoretical basis for such an approach will need to be fully ascertained with sufficient conviction to allow useful progress towards completion by the end of year three.

Standards and regulations for new building materials existed in the same space as developing late nineteenth-century and early twentieth-century architecture. The architects, engineers and contractors involved in construction during the period of the Belle Epoque in Paris and Brussels devised new technological approaches, increasingly driven by enabling factors such as speed of construction, economy of resource usage and overall lightness of structure, all for the newer materials when compared to traditional ones such as masonry, brick and iron. Standards were enabling mechanisms for the transfer of new knowledge, which had already been set down within patents or similar technical specifications. My research will investigate how building material standards were drawn up and by whom. It will seek to establish if there was a clear mechanism for dialogue between innovators and exploiters of new, sometimes untested materials, and state-led regulators who were tasked to minimise the risk of any wider harm these materials might cause through, for example, potential structural failure. This regulation process sat within a broader social and political framework within which appeared a growing concern for public health and safety.

The PhD is taking a methodological approach to identifying the historical evidence, starting with a scatter gun shot across all available sources informed by background reading, and then becoming gradually more focused as distinct themes

The Influence of Standards and Regulations for Steel and Reinforced Concrete on the Development of Modern Architecture in Pre-WW1 Paris and Brussels

begin to emerge around the new materials being studies. By looking at evidence from examples of the systematic use of these materials, we can begin to piece together a more granular picture of the key construction (and hopefully architectural) developments at this time and in this geography. However, such an approach acknowledges caution in choosing the most applicable historical resources and case studies; it requires justifying such choices explicitly and objectively, and ensuring that a significant element of intra- and inter-geography comparison emerges from findings so as to maximise relevant analysis and discussion.

Architectural history in nineteenth-century France and Belgium

The intellectual background for the building interests of French and Belgian architects, engineers and contractors of the pre-WW1 period is an equally important context to the PhD, which will study the relationship between technical/tectonic change and aesthetic/decorative continuity through one specific lens linked to new materials.

The dominant nineteenth-century school of architecture in the region was the Ecole des Beaux-Arts in Paris, through which innumerable architects from France and abroad passed on their way to professional practice. The Ecole's heritage had emerged from preceding centuries of professional development, as the French autocratic state moved to control all facets of the built environment through a dedicated body of practitioners. These were at first approved architects and military engineers serving the monarch's monumental and war projects, but over time *civil* engineers developed as distinctive construction professionals. The Ecole des Ponts et Chaussées provided a corpus for these men and the French Revolution solidified their key role in a radical new society which now valued personal merit over the old privileged hierarchy [1].

In parallel, a more scientific approach was being applied to architectural thinking during the later eighteenth century, as it began to question the status of classical orders and styles derived from ancient Graeco-Romano traditions. Iron emerged as a reinforcing material for masonry and brick, and then in its own right as a key structural feature which could better adapt to fireproofing requirements in urban settings as well as the desire for physically and visibly lighter spaces. Paris had many examples of its use in the early nineteenth century, well before London's Crystal Palace. The sub-discipline of architectural technology, concerning the physical nature of buildings as opposed to their purely aesthetic features, acquired an increasingly theoretical basis pushing iron towards potential new uses. In 1872 the French architect and conservator Eugène-Emmanuel Viollet-le-Duc published the second volume of his popular lectures 'Entretiens sur l'architecture' – he was called by Summerson the first theorist of modern architecture, though he walked in the footsteps of others and was at heart a proponent of historicist styles. In the same year, the initial modernisation of the 'Bon Marché' department store was finished in Paris, a 'polite' iron-framed structure naturally lit by glass panes, co-designed by father and son architects Louis-Auguste and Louis-Charles Boileau with civil engineer Armand Moissant. The latter had simultaneously been working on the Menier Chocolate Factory in Noisel, a unique iron-skeleton industrial building on the outskirts of the French capital [2].

Twenty years later during the 1890s, innovative technical and craft approaches to the design of townhouses emerged in Brussels and Paris, having already influenced Anton Gaudi in Barcelona the decade before. The 'Art Nouveau' architectural genre as it came to be known, spread quickly through derived forms to other European cities, sweeping away the more traditional Beaux-Arts approaches before it disappeared just as rapidly, with some distinctive exceptions, before the outbreak of the Great War [3].

The new building materials

Britain had been the world's first industrialising nation, with its textile mills employing iron columns for fireproofing from the end of the eighteenth century, and it had created some unique and much-imitated structures with cast iron frames and plate glass, including the world-renowned Crystal Palace and subsequent railway termini such as those at Paddington and St Pancras, all in nineteenth century London. Similarly, France had become a global leader in the novel use of iron in public structures through key architects such as Henri Labrouste, Henri Baltard, Louis-Auguste and Charles Boileau and Ferdinand Dutert as well as renowned civil engineers such Armand Moisant and Gustave Eiffel. The last-named had completed the eponymous iron tower in Paris despite considerable aesthetic criticism from French peers, many of whom later retracted their initial condemnation [4].

By contrast, international research on the first use of *steel* in polite buildings from the 1880s on has focused on early skyscrapers in the United States, as well as a selection of well-known British structures, mainly in London, including office buildings, hotels and department stores [5]. French and Belgian polite steel-framed buildings have received less academic attention by comparison, with some notable exceptions. One of these is the steel-framed La Samaritaine Magasin 2 department store in central Paris, completed in 1910 by the French architect Frantz Jourdain who employed distinct Art Nouveau features. The American scholar Professor Meredith Clausen first researched Jourdain in the 1980s, and more recently there has been considerable focus on the La Samaritaine department store complex, which has been extensively renovated and is due to reopen in 2021 [6].

Considerably more research in France and Belgium has focused on the early use of reinforced concrete at the turn of the twentieth century; in particular the use of a novel framing system patented by the Belgium-born inventor François Hennebique and adapted superbly by the Perret Brothers in Paris and others elsewhere. While there will be leads in this well-covered area, my own archival research will concentrate more on the activities of the French civil engineer Armand Considère, who invented his own reinforced concrete system in competition with Hennebique [7].

Technical standards for building materials

The crux of this PhD's research is its initial focus on new voluntary technical standards for steel and (components of) reinforced concrete which were first published in 1903 and 1904 by the Engineering Standards Committee, the precursor to the British Standards Institute (BSI) which had been established in 1901 and served the vast British Empire. Over time these were integrated into a worldwide set of standards currently overseen by the International Standards Organisation (ISO) and its other affiliates; these include the Association Française de Normalisation (AFNOR) established in 1926, and the precursor to the current Bureau de Normalisation (NBN) in Belgium, established the following year. All these standards bodies have worked and continue to collaborate closely with parallel governmental laboratories, originally set up in the nineteenth century to standardise scientific and engineering physical measurements [8].

According to Sir John Wolfe Barry, the 'father' of British Standards, in a 1917 lecture, the famous lexicographer Dr. Johnson defined a Standard as "that which is of undoubted authority; that which is the test of other things of the same kind". Agreed technical standards and specifications for the manufacture and use of steel and reinforced concrete became increasingly important as these new materials started to replace timber, bricks, masonry and iron as a more flexible option for building construction, but importantly at increasingly affordable prices. David Yeomans in particular has examined in considerable detail the first British Standards relevant to the construction industry from 1900 [9].

Wolfe Barry reinforced in his 1917 speech the merits of early voluntary standardisation, highlighting the campaign by Sir Joseph Whitworth begun around 1841 for the use of his famous screw thread as a norm for all other similar products. Responding favourably to the eminent civil engineer's speech was the British wartime Minister for Labour, John Hodge MP, who singled out his own pre-war experience working in a rolling-mill, producing a plethora of non-standardised iron and steel sections and parts for demanding engineers and 'faddish' architects [10].

Professors JoAnne Yates and Craig Murphy have examined the history of international engineering standards in a comprehensive 2019 book. They place the historical role of these standards significantly within the mainstream of the world's developing economies over time:

The Influence of Standards and Regulations for Steel and Reinforced Concrete on the Development of Modern Architecture in Pre-WW1 Paris and Brussels

These standards have shaped the course of industrial development by fixing the technological platforms on which further innovation occurs ... Without such standards, most of what we buy would be more difficult to produce, and conflicts between merchants and customers would likely be more intense ... this kind of private standardization has come to provide a critical infrastructure for the global economy [11].

But applying standards to the real world takes time; Yates and Murphy have observed that France had to wait until 1840 to fully adopt the metric system introduced in 1799 by Napoléon Bonaparte. Hence they single out a consensus-based approach, involving voluntary industrial participation, as being essential to the long-term adoption of engineering standards. This proved feasible early on in the new realm of electricity, a novel form of both industrial and domestic power. In 1883, the Société International des Electriciens was established by French electrical engineers, and in the following year a Belgian analogue appeared [12].

Building regulations

Building regulations or codes have been developed globally by local and central government authorities to set and monitor accepted norms in construction – they are legally-tested benchmarks for compliance by individuals and companies. Urban construction codes have pushed architectural styles down more limited routes, and the outcomes of this have not always been welcomed by designer-builders, their clients and even the wider public. The biggest fear for occupants of large buildings still remains uncontrolled fire, evidenced in recent years by raging tower block infernos in global cities. Other concerns about the health and welfare of the general population started to emerge in late nineteenth-century France and Belgium as enlightened liberalism came to the fore, often in response to the threat of radical social upheaval [13].

A seminal paper presented to the 2017 Construction History Society Annual Conference in Cambridge, compared the first building regulations for reinforced concrete in a number of European Countries at the start of the 20th Century. The paper covers the emergence of these regulations in Prussian Germany (1904), France and Belgium (1906), Switzerland (1909), The Netherlands (1912), and the United Kingdom (1915). Of interest to my PhD are the regulations in France and Belgium, though the comparisons between all the systems in place is highly informative. It was the collapse of those new structures using the material which spurred official action. In France this happened with a pedestrian bridge disaster at the 1900 Universal Exposition and so gave reinforced concrete immediate media attention. The published regulations for reinforced concrete, based as they were on the latest scientific and technical standards, came into force in 1906 in France (adopted at the same time by Belgium), though only for public sector civil engineering projects. The Germans and Swiss by contrast were more thorough and extensive in their application of reinforced concrete regulations. A strand of the PhD research will seek to make comparisons between their relative influence on the development of modern architecture in the respective regions [14].

Other examples of published research on building regulations include the 1997 book by Yeomans on British construction materials since 1900, which examines the role of specifications and codes of practice in a range of contemporaneous materials; and a paper by Dr Inge Bertels and Krista de Jonge presented to the 2009 International Congress on Construction History, which studied the evolution of specifications for public building in 19th-century Belgium at various governmental levels [15].

While covering a slightly later period than my PhD and not focusing on the role of standards or regulations, Jonathan Clarke in his recent PhD research on interwar speculative office buildings in London notes that, despite being adopted almost throughout the country as the standard for reinforced concrete construction, the 1915 London County Council regulations for the new material quickly proved restrictive. Concrete frames became more expensive for many types of buildings [16]. Clarke compares this with the London steel regulations of six years earlier, where the allowable stresses and loads were also extremely conservative. But many engineers and reinforced concrete contractors learned quickly how to use the new material and became frustrated with the restrictions. Even well into the 1920s concrete-frame construction remained relatively rare in London. The same cannot be said of Paris and Belgium, which operated under different regulatory regimes.

Potential illustrating examples

My scoping exercise has included the task of identifying potential examples to illustrate the relationship between technical standards and building regulations for the new materials within the region, with possible leads towards key architectural change. This has required undertaking a trawl of original archival and other contemporary materials that make strong enough connections between the use of steel and reinforced concrete and the new opportunities for, or resulting limitations on, the architectural design processes. Suggestions for examples from colleagues with expert knowledge of this area are always very welcome, but below are a few possibilities to begin with.

La Samaritaine Department Store in Paris

The selection of the La Samaritaine department store in Paris as a potential example is related to both the availability of original archival sources and the nature of the key materials covered by the research. La Samaritaine was built as an expanding shopping complex in the Les Halles district of Paris. The site had followed in the footsteps of other well-known nineteenth-century Parisian department stores such as Le Bon Marché and Le Printemps, which had been built with iron framing and plate glass [17].

The respected Art Nouveau advocate Frantz Jourdain was recruited by the owners of La Samaritaine to extend the floor area and improve the attractiveness of the offer to everyday Parisian shoppers. Jourdain had previously advised the French writer Emile Zola on a fictional avant-garde department store for his novel *Au Bonheur des Dames*, and many of its futuristic features appeared in his later designs. The flamboyantly decorated 'Magasin 2' was completed in stages between 1905-10 using steel framing in the core structure and steel and reinforced concrete in an under-road passageway connecting the parts of the complex (Figs. 1-3).

Figure 1. Magasin 2 La Samaritaine, Paris. Architect, Frantz Jourdain. View of completed façade on right, c. 1910. Unknown photographer, La Samaritaine Archives.

The Influence of Standards and Regulations for Steel and Reinforced Concrete on the Development of Modern Architecture in Pre-WW1 Paris and Brussels

Jourdain went on the build a separate Samaritaine de Luxe (1914-17) near the Opera Garnier aimed at a wealthier clientele and then, after the war, began designing an extension to Magasin 2 towards the historic north embankment of the Seine – this work was eventually taken over by Jourdain's protégé Henri Sauvage, who was more diplomatic in adjusting his creative impulses to the needs of others. He designed a plainer, quasi-monumental exterior to the extended steel framing, which was clad in more respectable stone; this was seen by many contemporaries as a natural 'Art Deco' successor to Sauvage's embryonic personalised style, typified by his combined store and office block Immeuble Majorelle in pre-WW1 Paris (1913).

Figure 2. Magasin 2 La Samaritaine, Paris. Architect, Frantz Jourdain. Construction of main atrium using steel framing, c. 1905-10. Unknown photographer, La Samaritaine Archives.

Figure 3. La Samaritaine, Paris. Architect, Frantz Jourdain. Construction of subterranean passageway showing use of steel beams, c. 1905-10. Unknown photographer, La Samaritaine Archives.

Apartment blocks in Brussels and Paris

Another example for the archival research stage would be the development of apartment blocks in Brussels and Paris at the end of the nineteenth century. The emerging French Art Nouveau architect Hector Guimard completed his highly original apartment block Castel Beranger in Paris in 1898 using traditional materials – it remains with us as testimony to his creativity. A group of younger architects with social consciences started to design affordable blocks of flats serving the urban masses called Habitations à Bon Marchés (HBMs). In Brussels the extant HBM at 32 Rue Marconi built by Belgian architect Leon Govaerts in 1901 was the first to use reinforced concrete, though the exact type employed is still to be determined – Govaerts had employed the Hennebique system for some of his other buildings. Four years later, the French architect Henri Provensal completed an HBM at 8 rue de Prague in Paris using reinforced concrete and steel; it was referred to at the time as the 'Louvre of HBMs' [18].

Armand Considère

A final example would centre on a key civil engineer and his consulting business during the period. Armand Considère was a highly-regarded French civil engineer during the late nineteenth and early twentieth centuries, who developed a patent for a new method of constructing reinforced concrete columns he called beton fretté. Considère set up in competition with Hennebique immediately after both had contributed actively to the findings of the French National Commission on reinforced concrete [19]. There is some existing research on the wider technical impact of this rivalry in both France and Britain, much less for Belgium, hence this would need addressing – some potential examples exist in the industrial city of Roubaix which lies between Paris and Brussels and is where the Considère business archives are to be found [20].

Conclusions

As emphasised throughout this paper, it is still early in the PhD project which has operated under the cloud of the COVID-19 lockdowns. However, I have tried to prepare the main research groundwork as thoroughly as possible through a scoping exercise using remotely accessible materials. At the time of writing, I have not yet been able to physically visit any of the examples mentioned, which I very much hope will happen as soon as travel restrictions ease.

It seems clear that any examples chosen must cover both built structures *and* systems/organisations that were a sufficient part of the development of modern architecture during the period and in the region being examined. Through multiple triangulations of research evidence it is expected that a clear, thematic picture will emerge, illustrating the extent to which the key relationships and changes depended on the role of technical standards and associated regulations for steel and reinforced concrete.

One emerging theme is likely to be the fire protection facets of the new materials, which were often promoted exactly for their improved resistance to degradation and structural weaknesses caused by extreme temperatures. Another would be international comparisons between what happened in Paris and Brussels and other relevant localities during the period – new German and Swiss reinforced concrete regulations have already been mentioned, but the USA and Britain would also be good contrasts for their use of early steel framing in multi-storey buildings.

Acknowledgements

I would like to thank my supervisors at Kent School of Architecture and Planning, Professor Gerry Adler and Dr Alan Powers, for their comments on a early draft of this paper, as well as their continual input into my PhD, funded by a Cotutelle Award from Kent-Lille; others who have contributed to my research planning along the way include Dr Tim Brittain-Catlin, Professor Eric Monin, Dr Gilles Maury, Jonathan Clarke, Mike Chrimes, Professor Thomas Leslie,

The Influence of Standards and Regulations for Steel and Reinforced Concrete on the Development of Modern Architecture in Pre-WW1 Paris and Brussels

Professor Stephanie van de Voorde, Dr Sabine Kuban, Professor Jean-Baptiste Minnaert, Laurens Bulckaen and Valentin Gillet.

References

[1] A. Saint, *Architect and Engineer: A Study in Sibling Rivalry*, Yale: Yale University Press, 2008.
[2] P. Collins, *Changing Ideals in Modern Architecture 1750-1950*, London: Faber & Faber, 1965; M. Bressani, *Architecture and the Historical Imagination: Eugène-Emmanuel Viollet-Le-Duc,* Abingdon: Routledge, 2014.
[3] F. Dierkens-Aubry and J. Vandenbreeden, *Art Nouveau in Belgium: Architecture and Interior Design, Duculot/Iannoo*, 1991; P. Greenhalgh, *Art Nouveau 1890-1914*, London: V&A Publications, 2000.
[4] G. Eiffel, Travaux Scientifiques Exécutés à La Tour de 300 Mètres de 1889 à 1900, Paris: L. Maretheux, 1900; S. Gideon, Building in France. Building in Iron. Building in Ferro-Concrete, Los Angeles: Getty Center for the History of Art and the Humanities, 1995; C. C. Mead, *Making Modern Paris: Victor Baltard's Central Markets and the Urban Practice of Architecture*, Pennsylvania State University, 2012.
[5] F. M. Locker, 'The Evolution of Victorian and Early Twentieth Century Office Buildings in Britain' (Ph.D. thesis, University of Edinburgh, 1984); J. Bonshek, 'The Skyscraper: A Catalyst of Change in the Chicago Construction Industries, 1882-1892', *Construction History*, Vol. 4, 1988, pp. 53-74; J. C. Lawrence, 'Steel Frame Architecture versus the London Building Regulations: Selfridges, the Ritz, and American Technology', *Construction History*, Vol. 6, 1990, pp. 23-46; T. Leslie, 'Built like Bridges: Iron, Steel, and Rivets in the Nineteenth-Century Skyscraper.' *Journal of the Society of Architectural Historians*, Vol. 6, 2010, pp. 235-61; J. Clarke, *Early Structural Steel in London Buildings: A Discreet Revolution*, Swindon: English Heritage, 2014.
[6] M. Clausen, *Frantz Jourdain and the Samaritaine: Art Nouveau Theory and Criticism*, Leiden: Brill, 1987.
[7] P. Cusack, 'Reinforced Concrete in Britain: 1897-1908' (Ph.D. thesis, Edinburgh, 1981); J. Abram, 'An Unusual Organisation of Production: The Building Firm of the Perret Brothers, 1897-1954', *Construction History*, Vol. 3, 1987, pp. 75–93; G. Delhumeau, L'invention Du Béton Armé: Hennebique 1890-1914, Paris: Norma, 1999 ; P. Collins, Concrete: The Vision of a New Architecture, Montreal: McGill-Queen's University Press, 2004; S. van de Voorde, 'Hennebique's Journal Le Beton Arme. A Close Reading of the Genesis of Concrete Construction in Belgium', pp. 1453–62 in K.-E. Kurrer, W. Lorenz & V. Wetzk, (Eds), Proceedings of the Third International Congress on Construction History, Cottbus, Berlin: NeunPlus1, 2009.
[8] R. C. McWilliam, 'The Evolution of British Standards' (Ph.D. thesis, University of Reading, 2002); R.C. McWilliam. 'The First British Standards: Specifications and Tests Published by the Engineering Standards Committee, 1903-18', *Transactions of the Newcomen Society,* Vol. 75, 2005, pp. 261–87; J. Yates and C. N. Murphy, Engineering Rules: Global Standard Setting since 1880, Baltimore: John Hopkins University Press, 2019.
[9] J. Wolfe Barry, *The Standardization of Engineering Materials, and Its Influence on the Prosperity of the Country: The James Forrest Lecture*, London: ICE, 1917; D. Yeomans, *Construction Since 1900: Materials,* London: BT Batsford Ltd, 1997.
[10] Wolfe Barry, The James Forrest Lecture, (Note 9).
[11] Yates and Murphy, Engineering Rules, (Note 8), p.2.
[12] ibid.
[13] C. Ford, 'The Paris Housing Crisis and a Social Revolution in Domestic Architecture on the Eve of the First World War', *Journal of Modern History*, Vol. 90, 2018, pp. 580–620.
[14] S. van de Voorde, S. Kuban, and D. Yeomans, 'Early Regulations and Guidelines on Reinforced Concrete in Europe (1900-1950): Towards an International Comparison,' pp. 345-56 in J. Campbell et al, (Eds), *Building Histories, Proceedings of the Fourth Annual Conference of the Construction History Society*, Cambridge: Construction History Society, 2017.
[15] Yeomans, Construction Since 1900, (Note 9); I. Bertels and K. de Jonge, 'Building Specifications and the Growing Standardizing of Public Regulation in Nineteenth-Century Belgium', pp. 197-204 in K.-E. Kurrer, W. Lorenz & V.

Wetzk, (Eds), *Proceedings of the Third International Congress on Construction History*, Cottbus, Berlin: NeunPlus1, 2009.

[16] J. Clarke, 'The Development of the Speculative Office in Inter-War England' (Ph.D. thesis, University of Cambridge, 2021).

[17] Clausen, Frantz Jourdain, (Note 6); H. Lempereur and J.-F. Cabestan, La Samaritaine, Paris, Paris: Picard, 2015.

[18] S. van de Voorde, 'Bouwen in Beton in België (1890-1975): Samenspel van Kennis, Experiment En Innovatie' (Ph.D. thesis, University of Ghent, 2010); Ford, The Paris Housing Crisis, (Note 13).

[19] Delhumeau, L'invention Du Béton Armé, (Note 7).

[20] P. Cusack, 'Agents of Change: Hennebique, Mouchel and Ferro-Concrete in Britain, 1897-1908', *Construction History*, Vol, 3, 1987, pp. 61–74; Van de Voorde, thesis, (Note 18).

Architecture and building traditions in the territory of Cosenza: the 1910 Colonia Silana

Alessandro Campolongo and Valentina Guagliardi
Università della Calabria, Rende (Cosenza),

Historical and environmental background and the Colonia Silana

Sir Ronald Ross, the British medical doctor who received the Nobel Prize for Medicine in 1902, discovered the malarial parasite in the anopheles mosquito and considered malaria as one of the most important diseases affecting humans, "probably the most important of human diseases" [1]. The histories of Southern Italy and malaria have been strongly interrelated, particularly in Calabria, whose peculiarities and contradictions, as well as the genesis of its population and the transformations of its territory, can be more easily understood only if the relationships with this tremendous plague are considered.

It can be said that today's Calabria originated in the eighteenth century, when the agrarian landscape greatly changed, and not at all for the better. It was during the second half of the century that the agrarian crisis led to the progressive deforestation in favour of arable land [2].

Hence the action of man went together with frequent natural catastrophes, like the many earthquakes that changed local orography, causing for example the progressive sinking of the Ionian coast and the consequent slowing down of flow at river mouths that, as in the Paestum plain and Pontine marshes – wrote Norman Douglas – favour the typical environmental conditions for malaria transmission [3]. Moreover, the recurring seismic events in 1783 created in the region more than two hundred lakes that, by drying up, caused a malaria epidemic that killed 18,000 people [4].

The studies of Francesco Genovese, a medical doctor who fought malaria in the early twentieth century and wrote an important essay on this disease in Calabria [5], report that already at the end of the seventeenth century, the entire coastal area was malarial and abandoned, and the environmental conditions got worse because of deforestation carried out in previous years [6]. As a matter of fact, farmlands cultivated with cereals in the few plain and hilly areas were no longer sufficient, so mountain areas had to be used, and deforestation first occurred along fringe areas. Later, forests were systematically and indiscriminately cut down. Hence, every time it rained, tilled soils, no longer held in place by plant roots, tended to slide down bare mountain slopes, carried by wild rivers and streams that inundated cultivated areas and blocked water flowing to the sea, thus creating wide marshlands, the ideal habitat for mosquitoes.

Hydrogeological instability was thus one of the main vehicles of malaria infection between the eighteenth and nineteenth centuries [7]. Paradoxically, as the mountain areas were no longer so isolated, the day labourers who moved towards valley and seaside areas for the harvest season in summer were the cause of malaria diffusion inland where a single diseased person, coming back home after the harvest, could infect a whole village as soon as environmental conditions were favourable to infection.

A decisive trend reversal occurred at the end of the nineteenth century when reforestation interventions were carried out. However, they were not sufficient to improve the environmental conditions. In fact, during the first decades of the twentieth century, large peninsular areas and islands in Italy, "for more than 6,000,000 hectares, with more than 200

Architecture and building traditions in the territory of Cosenza: the 1910 Colonia Silana

settlements and a total population of 8,000,000 inhabitants, are hit by malaria" [8]. Only in the 1920-30s was the anti-malaria fight at least seen as the main goal of agrarian reclamation activities, and lawmakers' attention was focused on drafting pertinent laws. In the 1922 Report the Rome Committee of the Lega Nazionale Contro la Malaria (the Italian Association Against Malaria) – founded in 1909 by Camillo Golgi and Guido Baccelli – reported that "on the one hand, Government action has been only concerned with the allocation of an insufficient amount of money ..., on the other, private enterprises, after being very involved, have now turned into negligence" [9].

While waiting for reclamation actions to be implemented, several medical doctors admirably worked hard to stop new family outbreaks and avoid impaired development and health consequences in children. Particular mention is owed to Bartolomeo Gosio, a renowned medical doctor who actively fought malaria. He promoted the construction of special areas where malaria children could be hosted during summer, thus distancing them from family outbreaks and healing them in environmentally natural conditions that would favour their physical recovery.

After the establishment of the Italian Association Against Malaria many provincial committees were founded in the concerned areas, whose action had also to focus on camp construction: "anti-malaria camps" were thus created. One of these camps, the Colonia Silana, was realized under the guidance of Bartolomeo Gosio and was opened on July 28th, 1910 by the Cosenza Committee, headed by Senator Francesco Mele. The settlement was created by Domenico Migliori, a Cosenza medical doctor, together with Angelo Cosco and Adolfo Tafuri, both from Cosenza [10].

The Cosenza Committee decided to place the camp in the Sila Plateau. A three-hectare area was donated by Cosenza municipality, located in the Federici district near Camigliatello, about 1300 m high, along the road connecting Cosenza to San Giovanni in Fiore, an important administrative centre of the Sila area. A beautiful natural landscape, a cool, non-humid climate, the balmy air of pine woods, a crystal-clear and generous water spring were the camp background. These fundamental characteristics made the place a very good choice and determined the success of the project that lasted about 70 years despite the many difficulties. The settlement developed around the first wooden frame house or pavilion, donated by the Ministry of Domestic Affairs and already employed to shelter the refugees of the 1908 earthquake that had devastated Reggio Calabria and Messina territories two years earlier. Giuseppina Le Maire, from Piedmont, was the tireless woman who, after meeting Gosio and Migliori, devoted all her life to the activities of the Colonia Silana. Remembered as "the friend of the lowly" [11], her undisputed organizational skills and humanitarian commitment were at the basis of the development and good management of the camp. She constantly promoted volunteering and important financial initiatives able to guarantee the survival of the Colonia, particularly at its difficult early stages.

The Colonia was the first new facility that was realized in Calabria after the earthquake and it soon became the first significant cultural centre of the Sila area thanks to the "presence and work of many people of outstanding cultural and humanitarian qualities" [12], capable of attracting the attention of prestigious people and benefactors that allowed the Colonia to develop constantly. In 1911, a year after the camp's opening, the Berlingieri pavilion, after the name of its benefactor, was built of wood, and in 1912 the Ginestra pavilion was erected after the project of engineer Barrese who also sponsored its construction. The building was made of wood, had two floors and the peculiar architectural characters of the Swiss building type called chalet. The pavilion became unstable and was demolished in 1948. The following year (1913) the first "emergency room", was built and opened to the local population. (Fig. 1)

Until 1930s, when the new central pavilion was built, the architectural features of the camp were strongly characterized by wood and very economic constructive techniques, due to limited funds and simple building programs deriving from donations and charity. Thus, very simple building procedures were employed by local workers with skills and equipment characteristic of the local building tradition. The firm run by Antonio Merando, and Pietro Serra and Antonio Arnone, the carpenters who, "under Merando's direction, worked with a kind of religious fervour (...)" [13] deserves to be mentioned.

During the First World War, between 1915 and 1918, the American pavilion was built with the contribution of the USA Red Cross, to be used as the new dormitory and refectory. The 84 m2 wooden one-floor construction had a good building quality, being still to this day a part of the camp's built heritage, though in need of restoration and functional adaptation. Close to the American building, there is the Veranda pavilion, also in need of restoration, that was originally used as a reception hall and later renovated to host the camp management. The 64 m2 building, that was originally made of wood and had one floor, has a mixed wood and masonry load-bearing structure.

1920 was an important year for the Colonia after the very difficult period following the war. In time, the camp had acquired importance, but, to give it an additional impulse, Le Maire involved in the enterprise the Industrialist's Foundation for War Orphans, the Opera Carnegie and the Association for Southern Italy interests [14], that granted the Colonia a regular annual allowance. The construction of the Veranda, together with the realization of an infirmary, a great hall for recreational and amusement purposes and the restoration of the central pavilion with newly panelled outer walls were among the results of the new management that would last for years. (Fig. 2)

Figure 1: The Ginestra Pavilion (1912) and the Americano Pavilion (1915-18)

Figure 2: The Veranda Pavilion (1920) and other pavilions (later years)

Architecture and building traditions in the territory of Cosenza:
the 1910 Colonia Silana

In 1921 new works included two small bridges built on the streams that crossed the settlement, retaining walls, toilets (made of masonry) and the so-called Bath pavilion, a quite small wooden building equipped with bathrooms and showers. In the same year Cosenza Provincial Authority funded the realization of a new emergency pavilion that replaced the old 1913 construction. During this very satisfying development period, a wooden chapel was built in 1926, and its architectural and building characters still makes it the symbol of the first important period of the Colonia Silana. The chapel was enlarged at the end of 1930s and completed with a bell tower that still keeps the bell donated by Giuseppina Le Maire. Its construction marks the passage to a new managerial period in 1927, when the camp administration was entrusted by the Cosenza Prefect to Tommaso Arnoni, the active and competent podestà of the town, who was appointed Commissioner for the special management of the Colonia Silana. However, Giuseppina Le Maire continued to be "the leading figure of the Institution management – writes Peppino Via – thanks to her charisma and personality, till 1933 …"

The buildings of the Colonia Silana

Following the first important action of the government-appointed management, the Colonia became a charitable institution (R. D. 19 May 1930, n. 789): Government granted an extra-ordinary allowance together with the ordinary one, and appointed Arnoni as Government Commissioner. The new government management, having bigger funds, soon built the new large central building that replaced the old original pavilion and the related constructions that were no longer complying with hygiene and structural security requirements. The new building was realized by the construction company Parrini-Landini & C. that completed the work in 1930. The two company partners were also involved in the project as donors, as they donated a substantial sum and renounced to the final accrued credits, as required by the Commissioner. Their contribution allowed the accomplishment of the building program, including the realization of a new medical clinic with an isolation room on the site where the old emergency pavilion stood.

These are the years when Tommaso Arnoni's commitment made Cosenza, in whose province the Colonia is located, one of the most interesting towns in the national cultural landscape, for its modern urban structure and the quality of its architectural heritage that included both public and private residential construction [16]. This was the cultural context in which the Colonia Silana was enriched with new buildings and developed considerably. In 1931, in addition to the new buildings, the aqueduct project for the Colonia, designed by Tommaso Gualano, the head engineer of Cosenza municipality and the author of several public works in the town, was approved and realized for collecting the spring waters of Mount Curcio.

The L-shaped central building rises in the most elevated open space of the settlement. The building has a large semi-circular flight of steps, and its dominant position is highlighted by the slender turret that is the central avant-corps at the top of the access stairs that narrow towards the end to fit to the geometry of the main entrance. It stands between two neoclassical columns supporting a balustrade where there is an opening in line with the entrance. The entrance is an arched portal, an element that is harmoniously repeated in the window series at the ground floor. The turret elevation is one-floor higher than the building's wings and has a balustraded open gallery on top with slender arched openings. (Figs 3-4)

The building façade is thus divided into three parts, each with an overhanging roof on top that covers the decorated upper wall band. The façade has large windows on axis with those at the ground floor, formally connected by a moulding that stops at the sides of the turret where the avant-corps corners, the central rose window and the Colonia sign decorate the façade. The building is completed by a block orthogonally located on the north front where a steel fire escape stands. During the early setting-up stage, a crane was mounted in this area to lift up the heavy boilers for the kitchen. The morphological configuration of the building structure at the end of the Southern section is architectonically interesting: here the one-floor building plan view shows rounded edges that generates uninterrupted curved walls on the side façade where the solids and voids effect created by the windows, perfectly in line with the architectural features of the period, is very effective. This formal appearace is enhanced by the contrast with the traditional elements of mountain houses, strongly characterized by the technological and functional role of some building features that inevitably become elements that morphologically connote the buildings, such as sloping roofs with dormers and overhanging pitches. A culturally interesting design concept characterizes also the medical clinic building that, besides the vernacular typology due to the specific environmental context, goes beyond classicistic architecture, as it occurred during 1930s.

Figure 3: The main building, façade and a detail (photo by Alfonso Morelli - Team Mistery Hunters)

Figure 4: The main building façade (survey by Studio Eng. G. Scarnati)

Architecture and building traditions in the territory of Cosenza:
the 1910 Colonia Silana

With reference to the main central building, the analysis of the masonry structures confirms the use of stone masonry that is a typical construction element of the area in that period. The stones employed came from the quarries present in the regional territory. Quality stones include pink and white-yellow limestones from Mendicino; quarz-diorites from Palmi, Seminara and Bagnara; granites from Serra San Bruno and San Giovanni in Fiore. Stones are both employed as building and finishing materials, in the form of polished, raw or semi-finished blocks. Some elevated parts of the building structure are composite masonry with double courses of stones and solid bricks (every 50 cm) to level uneven rubbles and obtain a better masonry load distribution.

Bricks are employed in cornices and opening casings completed with a thick wooden plank as a lintel. Wooden lintels were used to place window frames that were fixed to the plank or inserted between two ad hoc planks forming a suitable space. Casement windows, generally made of chestnut or pine wood, have shutters directly fastened to the wall, flush with the external wall, with opening framings acting as rabbets. Exterior render finish with a low cement content simulates a large ashlar socle on the façade and a solid brick pattern on the remaining wall.

The originally wooden floor boards were replaced in time, so that different and alternative techniques coexist in the same building. Wooden floors, mainly of pine wood, consist of plain wooden beams with a circular cross-section and an irregular planking covered with a screed of aggregate materials, sometimes with the addition of a gypsum-based mixture to be used as a floor, or finished with cotto or cement tiles. In larger floor slabs, the beams, placed across the shorter span, are supported by inserting one or two thicker cross beams at the intrados. Replacement works mainly consisted in the use of mixed iron bars and hollow bricks, and hollow clay blocks in more recent interventions.

In masonry buildings, the roof has a supporting structure with cross partition walls and ridge beams spanning from gable to gable that do not thrust on the outer walls. Roof coating consists of boards nailed to the beams covered with corrugated iron. The dormers are framed structures connected to the cover boarding with wooden pitches and walls, and a fixed framed window that completes the front structure.

No new wooden constructions were built, so, apart from the load-bearing masonry buildings of the 1930s and minor constructions realized after the Second World War, the settlement's built heritage today consists of the original pavilions that need restoration and functional adaptation. They attest the important building production in the settlement and the technical skills employed by local workers in wood construction. (Figs 5-8)

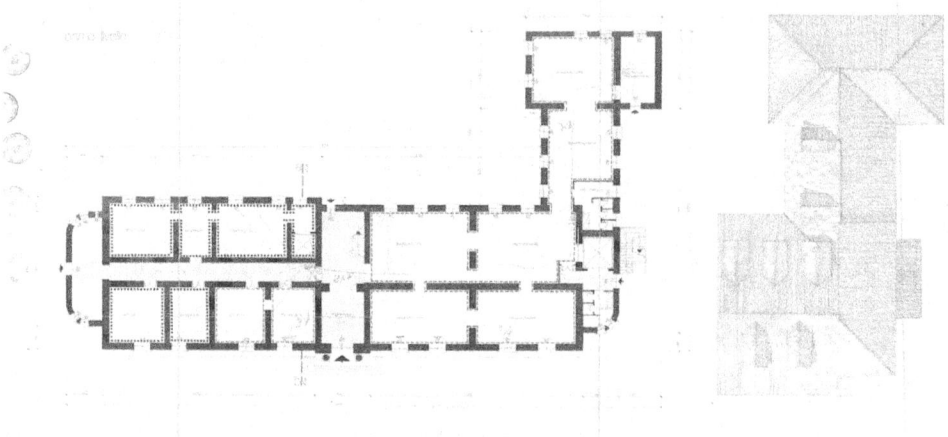

Figure 5: The main building, ground floor plan and roof plan details (survey by Studio Eng. G. Scarnati)

Figure 6: The main building, southern façade and window details (photo by Alfonso Morelli - Team Mistery Hunters)

Figure 7: The main building, overhanging roof details (photo by Alfonso Morelli - Team Mistery Hunters)

Architecture and building traditions in the territory of Cosenza: the 1910 Colonia Silana

Figure 8: The medical clinic, ground floor plan and main façade (survey by Studio Eng. G. Scarnati)

Wooden pavilions are load-bearing wall buildings consisting of simple framed structures also called cavity walls, with a linear framework and wooden infill walls. The wall is made of 8 cm thick vertical posts connected at the upper and lower ends by horizontal stringers that complete the framework.

The rectangular posts double near the truss supports with the longer side placed orthogonally to the wall. At window and door openings, located between two posts, the framework is completed by intermediate horizontal stringers and lintels. A 2-cm thick planking coats the framework structure on both sides; the planking is horizontally mounted on posts and forms a 12-cm cavity wall. The wall is completed with external coating planks vertically arranged side by side and finished by profiles. Internal coating planks have vertical slots and are tongued and grooved.

The walls are not directly placed on the stone masonry foundation walls, but on wooden beam bearings fixed on them. Beam bearings are connected to the lower stringer through post portions laid at a constant distance.

Beam bearings also support the base floor consisting of pine wooden beams on which the planking (2-cm thick fir wooden planks joined together) is nailed. The floor is separated from the soil by a large air chamber so that the direct contact between wood and soil, that would trigger degradation phenomena due to raising damp, is avoided.

Wall openings and windows are generally flush with the internal wall, they have wooden plank casing nailed to wall posts; window sills consist of a board having the same thickness as the planks, 5-6 cm protruding from the wall, and a board nailed beneath as a drip. Windows are completed by an exterior trim around head and jambs and panel shutters opening outward.

The roof load-bearing structure consists in simple trusses formed by two jack rafters with no king post, connected below by beams acting as tie bars that support the attic plank floor. No purlin connects the trusses, so the roof is covered by nailing planks directly to the extrados of truss rafters and covering them with corrugated iron. In the hip-roofed pavilions, cross beams originating from end trusses are laid on the corners and give the roof its typical shape.

Church construction is based on the same system as pavilions, except for its bell tower, whose bearing structure consists of four solid pillars at the corners, connected together by horizontal beams that form a sort of stringcourse at different levels. The outer walls are made of 2-cm thick planks, mounted only on the outer wall. In the middle of the inner bell-tower room, a fifth wooden pillar is the newel of a wooden spiral staircase. The church was restored and interventions involved both masonry foundations and the wooden structure. (Figs 9-10)

Figure 9: Church, main façade and side view (survey by Studio Eng. G. Scarnati; photo by Alfonso Morelli - Team Mistery Hunters)

Figure 10: Existing pavilions, façades and sections (survey by Studio Eng. G. Scarnati)

Architecture and building traditions in the territory of Cosenza:
the 1910 Colonia Silana

During 1930s, the Colonia developed and became more efficient: apart from the new functional buildings that were erected, the camp was provided with an aqueduct, a central radiator heating plant, the only example in the Sila plateau, and an independent electric power plant. These elements aroused national attention on the Colonia's activities. In 1936, a radio broadcast was dedicated to the Colonia Silana, as reported by the newspaper Cronaca di Calabria, while a group of reporters visited it in 1938, triggering media interest in the place. Consequently, the Colonia became a "permanent camp" (not only a summer facility), and in that same year the management was entrusted to Cosenza GIL (Gioventù italiana del littorio), the Italian fascist youth association [17].

During the reconstruction years following the Second World War, the Colonia activities were reorganized and pavilions refurbished, new small buildings were constructed, facilities, including sanitary ones, were upgraded, the external staircase and the park were restored.

In 1950-60s, new interventions were focused on the functional adaptation of old and new building interiors that had to meet new housing, administrative and didactic needs. Different commissioners and the National Association for Southern Italy Interests, headed by Ivanoe Bonomi, that had already been involved in the institution, were in charge of the Colonia management. During the last decades of the twentieth century, the settlement was directly run by Spezzano-della-Sila municipality, then Calabria region, until it was finally abandoned.

Conclusions

This study is part of a research project aimed at gaining a deeper knowledge of the architectural and construction features of the Italian building heritage in the twentieth century. In that period, materials, building techniques, and detail solutions played a very important role and defined building quality and their architectural identity. The study of significant settlements, such as the Colonia Silana, can contribute to acknowledge their value, revive their cultural role and supply the guidelines for their correct restoration and redevelopment.

In particular, the Colonia Silana bears witness to an important experience that involved both public health and technical and building aspects, and developed in the course of 70 years in very difficult economic and environmental conditions characterising the area. It is evidence of an interesting built heritage evolution in the area, today abandoned and in need for urgent interventions and functional adaptation, mainly because it represents the emblematic and significant expression of a condition which is unfortunately very common in Southern Italy.

References

[1] N. Douglas, Vecchia Calabria, Giunti-Martello, Firenze 1967, p. 430.
[2] A. Placanica, 'I caratteri originali', in Augusto Placanica, Piero Bevilacqua (Ed.), Storia d'Italia. Le regioni dall'Unità a oggi. La Calabria, pp. 16-18.
[3] Douglas, (Note 1), pp. 425-427.
[4] *Ibid.*
[5] F. Genovese, La malaria in provincia di Reggio Calabria, riedito a cura di Umberto Zanotti-Bianco, Vallecchi Editore, Firenze 1924.
[6] Douglas, (Note 1), pp.428-429.
[7] *Ibid.*
[8] Comitato promotore del Consorzio di bonifica (Ed.), 'La bonifica nel Mezzogiorno d'Italia', Roma 1925, in Rosario Villari (Ed.), Il Sud nella storia d'Italia. Antologia della questione meridionale, Editori Laterza, Roma-Bari 1981, p. 514.
[9] Lega Nazionale contro la malaria – Comitato Romano (Ed.), Relazione 1922, edito a cura della ditta E. Armani, Roma 1922, pp. 6-8.
[10] G. Le Maire, La Colonia antimalarica della Magna Sila, Tipografia B. Damiani, Roma 1927, p. 6.

[11] Peppino Via, La Colonia Silana di Federici (dalle origini ai giorni nostri), edito a cura dell'Amministrazione Comunale di Spezzano della Sila, Casole Bruzio (Cosenza) 1999, pp. 5-6.
[12] *Ibid.*
[13] Le Maire, (Note 10), pp. 10-12.
[14] *Ibid.*
[15] Via, (Note 11), p. 15.
[16] Alessandro Campolongo, Architettura e metodiche costruttive a Cosenza Nuova. Un'indagine per il recupero dell'edilizia del Novecento, Gangemi Editore, Roma 2009.
[17] Via, (Note 11), pp. 24-25.

The Twentieth Century (1900-2000)

Development of the UK Government's support for Construction-related Research in the 20th Century: the role of the Department of Scientific and Industrial Research

Nina Baker
Independent Engineering Historian

Introduction

The study of the history of construction of the UK in the 20th century has many contexts and viewpoints but one aspect, now almost out of living memory, is that of a particular model of state support for research in the building-related industries. From the First World War until the privatisation of the Thatcherite era, there was a wide spread of funding for both state-run and industrial associations' laboratories, driven by the government's Department of Scientific and Industrial Research (DSIR) [1].

This support for the construction-related industries was literally foundational for most of what was built in the 20th century. The Building Research Station (BRS), still in action today as the Building Research Establishment (BRE), emerged from the preparations for reconstruction after the First World War and was also a crucial player in reconstruction after the Second World War. Other construction-related government establishments, and the many industry-funded research associations, most of which have faded from view, were, in their time, central to the development of the UK's research infrastructure. The trigger for this plethora of organisations was the realisation that, although the fundamentals of structural and civil engineering were well understood by this time, very little basic science had been done on materials, processes and systems used in any branch of construction. The government officially encouraged the blossoming community of industrial laboratory associations and also put significant funding into its own network of laboratories. The paper will not cover the research work undertaken in universities nor that in the private in-house laboratories which many larger companies maintained, but will summarise the histories of how these government and association laboratories came into being and how they interacted.

The Department of Scientific and Industrial Research (DSIR)

In 1915 the experience of developing and producing the materials and machinery needed to fight the First World War alerted the UK government to the nation's previous dependence upon foreign expertise in both research and manufacturing, as well as raw material sourcing from overseas. Whilst there were already some establishments supporting military research needs, any industrial needs were often just 'bought in' from abroad. It was considered that there were "… startling deficiencies in the set up of private endeavour..." [2]. The Department of Scientific and Industrial Research (DSIR) established for the "….application of science to industry..." [3], was the outcome of the report on this problem by Sir William McCormick. The DSIR, established in 1916, continued in this role, facilitating the links between government, science and industry, until 1965 when its functions were distributed to the UK's sectoral research councils and a variety of other government bodies. It covered all fields of pure and applied sciences and all industries, from the primary and extractive to secondary production, services and manufacturing. In the privatisation of government services and agencies in 1997 all the remaining research establishments were put into the private sector.

In the UK civil service, the numbers and grades of permanent employees agreed with the Treasury as being correct for a particular department or organisation are known as the 'establishment'. Deciding on this for the government research organisations was problematic throughout the whole 80 years that they existed. Naturally, they started small, usually led by a senior civil servant who was from the, then entirely male, administrative (non-scientist) ranks. In the early days there were explicit restrictions on employing women in some of the establishments, with even ordinary clerical work only being officially open to them on a temporary basis, perhaps due to the post-war pressure to provide male jobs. Hutchinson's comparisons of status and pay of the two 'classes' of civil servants, administrative and scientific, show how the former's higher status was a persistent problem, even though the supervising Boards were generally made up of scientists or industrialists and even when the directors of establishments complained at the difficulty of recruiting and retaining suitable staff. Staff were paid well below the 'market rate', i.e. what they might get at a university or in industry and were not uniform with the longer-established National Physical Laboratory (NPL) which was considered to employ a more 'academic' type of person.[4] This would continue to be a problem for all the government funded research establishments.

Government research establishments

Fuel Research Station (FRS)

The Fuel Research Board and its Station were the first of the government-run research organisations to be set up, in 1917 and 1918 respectively. The urgency was driven by the need to identify new UK coal seams and make best use of coal as the UK's principal source of energy. The research station was initially beside a gas works in East Greenwich, which was appropriate given that all heating gas then was made from coal. In due course there would be research laboratories in the 9 major coal areas and the industry itself set up major research establishments of its own. Methods of making oil from coal was an important part of its work, as there was then no expectation that the UK would eventually have access to its own mineral oil resources.

Its relevance to the construction industry arose through its work on domestic fuel economisation (Fig.1) and the reduction of air pollution, initially in conjunction with Dr Margaret Fishenden's work at the University of Manchester, which linked it with the Building Research Station's work on heating and ventilation. Both pollution and heating efficiency continued to be key work for all these research laboratories. An unexpected outcome of fuel-efficient stoves and fires was that their fumes condensed within cooler chimneys resulting in acidic deposits which destroyed the mortars and also made stains on the interior plasterwork, which proved to be a continuing problem for householders, plasterers and painters.

During the Second World War, the FRS was involved in work directly relevant to the war [5] developing incendiary mixtures for defensive 'Flame Fougasses' (a network of 50,000 40-gallon drums full of tar-lime petroleum gel intended to explode burning petrol over attackers), tank-borne flame-throwers and layering oil and coal dust on river and dock waters for camouflage purposes [6]. As with the BRS, the wartime work on domestic fuel use was restricted to planning for post-war reconstruction, e.g. for a new Calorimeter Building (at Greenwich) for testing heat flow through spaces and walls, from new appliances.

When the coal industry was nationalised in 1947, the coal-related component of the FRS's work transferred to the National Coal Board, as similarly the nationalised gas boards took over gas-related research. The Greenwich site closed in 1957 (now the site of the Millennium Dome) and the work moved to the Warren Spring Laboratory, Stevenage, where its initial brief was to work on oil from coal and on reduction of air pollution. In 1994, when the other similar government establishments were privatised, this too was closed with most work ending up within the Atomic Energy Agency.

Figure 1. Fuel Research Station domestic heating appliances laboratory. Photo: Public domain [6]

Building Research Station (later Establishment) (BRS/BRE)

In 1917 a Ministry of Reconstruction was set up in order to plan for the post-war era, with a particular emphasis on housing and the structure of the building industry. The popular slogan of the period, "Homes fit for heroes", carried a public expectation of vast amounts of affordable house building of a high quality [7]. The Tudor Walters Report, which laid the foundations for better publicly-funded housing for the rest of the 20th century, also set ambitions for quality and quantity which the construction industry was ill-equipped to provide. The war-time Building Materials Research Committee recommended a permanent solution in the form of a Building Research Board (BRB), established under Lord Salisbury in early 1920. The BRB moved swiftly and the first Building Research Station was set up in a group of huts and a marquee at East Acton in 1921, under the direction of H.O. Weller who had been running forest products research for the Indian Government.

In 1924 Dr Reginald Stradling took over from Weller and oversaw the move to larger permanent premises at Garston in the following year [8]. The demands on the BRS grew in quantity and breadth, initially general research into the science of building covering the efficiency of buildings, weathering, materials and structural strength. However, it soon expanded into the physics of buildings (heating, ventilation, acoustics, lighting, meteorology), the chemistry of building materials (cementitious materials, clay products, stone, bituminous materials, paints, floorings) and engineering (concretes, piling, bridges, vibration, soil mechanics, fire resistance). In many cases, e.g. the Soil Mechanics laboratory founded in 1933 (by which time BRS was under the directorship of Robert Fitzmaurice), the facilities set up for these investigations were the first of their kind in the country. Later, it widened its field of investigation to include the social sciences of method study, and consumer requirements. [9]

Development of the UK Government's support for Construction-related Research in the 20th Century: the role of the Department of Scientific and Industrial Research

The BRS was also expected to undertake contract research for companies and to answer questions which did not require any significant research, from its developing body of knowledge. Its intelligence and special investigations division provided an information bureau for the industry, examined building failures and produced publications. The latter soon included involvement in the development of British Standards, codes of practice and the vast range of briefings and digests. The annual reports list special reports, technical papers and journal articles by staff, the latter rising from 27 in 1931 to 73 in 1955, but the BRS/BRE Digests came to be the most ubiquitous outputs, libraries of which were to be seen in architects' and contractors' offices.

Lea's official history of the BRS was published in 1971, detailing how and why it was set up and the principal research findings to that date. However, Lea's short chapter covering the period of the Second World War explicitly glosses over most of the war-related work, other than a brief mention of the concrete jigs developed to assist in the bending of plywood to make the Mosquito and Hornet aircraft. This is unfortunate since a fascinating project the Station was asked to assist with, in the greatest secrecy, was Operation Chastise, which was the development of the now-famous 'bouncing bombs' for the Dambuster bombing raids on the Ruhr industrial area. The BRS was also asked to look at the design of air-raid shelters, the effect of fire and explosions on structures, and the development of concrete railway sleepers [10].

Lea's view was that the most important work done during the war was preparation for post-war reconstruction, especially to replace the mass destruction of housing, which culminated in the 1944 Housing Manual. The BRS undertook a lot of work for local authorities to try to find cheaper and quicker materials and methods to build houses, schools and hospitals, urgently needed in the post-War era, but to little avail: no 'magic solution' came to light. Even in 1972, when Lea was writing, many of the systems which seemed promising, such as prefabricated panels, were no quicker in producing the final result, and the Ronan Point disaster of 1968 already exposed some systemic problems.

However, the Post-War history of the BRS/E was one of massive growth in staff, facilities and budgets as it pursued completely new lines of research into social, economic and managerial aspects of the building industries. It also cooperated increasingly with new industrial research groups, universities and international bodies, including many in the Commonwealth countries. A 1964 report for the Ministry of Public Buildings and Works noted that £3million pounds a year was being spent by the government on building research by BRS, universities and the industrial associations [11]. Whilst still noting that construction firms individually remained apathetic about research or changing traditionally practice, the working party nevertheless recommended that the industry as a whole should be taking more financial responsibility for its own research. That at a time when every metric showed that the construction industry's R&D spending was by far the least of any of the UK's industrial sectors, largely due to its systemic fragmentation. After the DSIR's responsibilities were redistributed in 1965, to the Ministry of Technology and Science Research Council, there was a gradual decline, accelerating in the Thatcherite era of privatisation, with the BRE gradually absorbing some of the other laboratories. Atkinson [12], writing at this turning point, summarised the BRE's history and highlighted how its own work, and that of the FRS and FPRL which it had absorbed, under state control had the benefit of being able to take the 'long view', build up significant archives. He was worried that the BRE properties might be sold for housing developments and that the expertise would be split up and lost in the government's explicit wish to optimise return for the tax-payer.

Roger Courtney, Director of the BRE when it was fully privatised in a not-for-profit type of 'management buy-out' in 1997, accurately read the political pressure of the time to move away from government finances and scientific priorities, towards commercial work, even if it was not popular within the industry [13].

Case study of BRS/BRE work: Reinforced concrete

Reinforcement in concrete had, of course, been in use long before the BRB came into being but even 10 years later the London County Council was feeling the need for official guidance on the use of reinforced concrete in building, to sit alongside the recently published Code of Practice on the use of structural steel. Despite the limited terms of reference of the Reinforced Concrete Structures Committee (RCSC) which was set up in 1930, that they would not concern themselves with anything beyond advice on best practice and not get into legislation, standards or specifications, it would not be long before the BRS was doing exactly that. The forerunner of the British Standards Institution, the Engineering Standards Council, had been producing standards since 1903 and their most popular early standard, BS12 on Portland Cement specification was published in 1904 [14]. Despite the evident widespread use of cement in mortars and concretes, scientific knowledge of its chemical behaviour with reinforcement was particularly lacking. Work commenced with surveys of codes of practice in other nations, supported by continuing fundamental work on such matters as temperatures within maturing concrete masses, creep and the development of standard strength tests. As soon as 1933 the RCSC was able to make recommendations for the code of practice. It will be no surprise that reinforced concrete research continued to be a major part of the BRS/BRE's work, with the 1938 BRB Report listing a number of papers on such matters as performance of reinforced concrete piles, columns and beams, but the basic science, e.g. of freeze-thaw cracking of concrete dams, was still causing concern in the 1955 BRB Report [15] (Fig.2), and in the 1964 BRB Report work on reinforced concrete for use in nuclear power station engineering was listed.

Figure 2. Testing slender reinforced concrete beam. Photo: Public domain [15]

Development of the UK Government's support for Construction-related Research in the 20th Century: the role of the Department of Scientific and Industrial Research

In a curious link between the RAF, the BRS and the Fire Research Station, the wartime Ministry of Works requisitioned a 1930s hotel, the Thatched Barn, at Barnet in North London to be used as a Field test Unit for larger scale model research. The FTU's wartime work included preliminary tests for the famous Dambuster 'bouncing bombs', utilising the hotel's outdoor swimming pool, and later building model concrete dams, the remains of one (Mohne Dam) being kept at Garston for many years. At the same time the top-secret Special Operations Executive were also using the hotel to train its agents for their infiltration tasks in occupied Europe. In the 1950s the FTU site was granted £40k to develop its abilities to do concrete tests, and in 1956 it was de-requisitioned when replacement concrete testing (and other) facilities at Watford were funded [16].

Forest Products Research Laboratory (FPRL)

Although the Forest Products Research Board was set up in 1921, it was the 'guest' of the Royal Aircraft Establishment (RAE) at Farnborough until it got its own laboratories at Princes Risborough in Buckinghamshire. The impetus to set up the FPRL was a motion passed at the 1920 British Empire Forestry Conference and the connection between the Empire (later the Commonwealth) as suppliers of timber and customers for data on the treatment and uses of wood continued to be important, with staff moving between the UK and India in particular at various times. An important area of research was the best methods for kiln-seasoning of timber and development of chemical treatments for fungal and insect pests.

Transport and Road Research Laboratory (TRRL)

In 1930 the Ministry of Transport set up a Road Experimental Station at Harmondsworth, Middlesex, which was transferred to the DSIR in 1933, becoming the Road Research Laboratory, overseen by a Road Research Board. Even at this early stage the RRL was working to prepare for the coming war, looking into airstrip construction methods and the penetrative effects of projectiles [17]. The general work was mainly on materials and methods of road construction, although initially materials testing was done at the National Physical or Chemical Laboratories. As with the BRS, the RRL's war time work was mainly on civil defence needs but it also assisted with the test programme for the Dam Buster bombs. However, time was found to develop a test for the resistance to crushing of coarse aggregates, a key element in road surface durability [18]. Following the war, the work expanded to include road safety and a Traffic and Safety Division was set up at Langley Hall to the West of London, undertaking new work such as vehicle safety tests and trials of new road markings, lighting and signage. In 1967 it moved to combined facilities at Crowthorne and 1972 it became the Transport and Road Research Laboratory (TRRL), adding a wide range of other topics, including the study of public transport, environmental effects and driver behaviour. Construction-related topics included skid resistance, road materials, methods of construction, outcomes including roundabout designs and road surfaces that made less noise. As with the other government research establishments it was privatised in 1996.

Fire Testing Station (FTS)

The very first fire testing station was set up by the insurance industry's Fire Officers' Committee in 1909 in Manchester, but a more substantial national FTS was established at Elstree, Hertfordshire in 1935, when the DSIR and the Fire Officers joined forces. During the Second World War this work was done by the Fire Research Division of the Ministry of Home Security, itself taken over by the DSIR after the war. The Joint Fire Research Organisation of the DSIR and all those insurance companies, and mutual societies with fire interests, combined their resources to establish a new Fire Research Station at Borehamwood from 1949 until it was absorbed by the BRE in 1994.

As with other areas of construction-related fields, surprisingly little fundamental knowledge existed on the science of fire and the FRS did important work on the behaviour of fire and smoke, building full size, multi-storey buildings for the purpose. This work established such basics as the effects of toxic fumes from burning household items and building materials, whether sprinkler systems would disperse smoke and the flash-over effect when intense heat suddenly ignites everything in a space [19]. Even more basic data such as flash point temperatures of mixtures of normally non-combustible with combustible liquids had to be established. That fire fatalities are nowadays comparatively rare in the UK can be attributed to this type of work. Experiments in the behaviour of smoke and flames in multi-storey blocks of flats were undertaken and informed the original designs of such blocks.

Industrial research establishments and associations

In 1918 the DSIR set up its Imperial Trust for the Encouragement of Scientific and Industrial Research, more usually referred to as the 'Million Fund' [20], from which industries could apply for money to run collaborative research associations. The money was in the form of 'matched funding' which was proportional to funds raised by the organisation from its members, although grants for special equipment were also possible. This generous budget, with few constraints as to how the associations should run themselves, had run out by 1932 and was topped up (Fig. 3) by the government annually until 1971, latterly also being open to similar organisations throughout the Commonwealth nations.

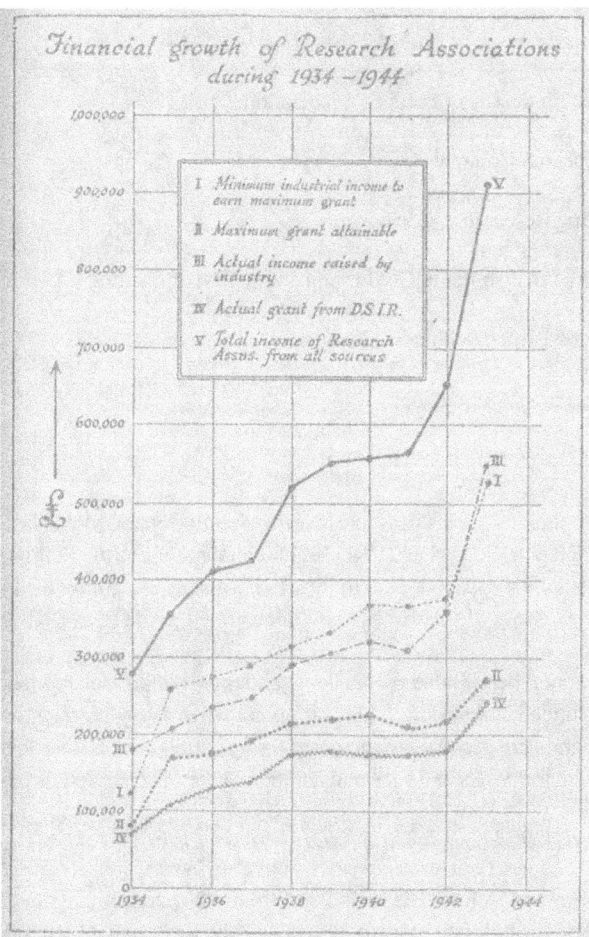

Figure 3. Heath & Heatherington page 347 [2]

Development of the UK Government's support for Construction-related Research in the 20th Century: the role of the Department of Scientific and Industrial Research

In 1945 the government was supporting 25 research associations only 7 of which could be thought of as having a connection to construction [21]. However, by 1962 [22] a total of 52 associations were receiving grants, of which the 1964 Report on the Building Research and Information Service considered the following to be doing work which related to building:

1. British Cast Iron Research Association.
2. British Ceramic Research Association.
3. British Coal Utilisation Research Association.
4. British Electrical and Allied Industries Research Association.
5. British Glass Industry Research Association.
6. British Iron and Steel Research Association.
7. British Non-Ferrous Metals Research Association.
8. British Welding Research Association.
9. Chalk, Lime and Allied Industries Research Association.
10. Civil Engineering Research Council.
11. Heating and Ventilating Research Association.
12. Research Association of British Paint, Colour and Varnish Manufacturers
13. Research Council of the British Whiting Federation.
14. Rubber & Plastics Research Association.
15. Timber Research and Development Association.

Note how few of the above associations' fields of interest seem directly related to construction. This had been an issue from the earliest days of DSIR support, and relates to the fragmented nature of the building industry, both in scale (few large companies but thousands of tiny firms) and in function (materials, component manufacture, transportation, implementation) and is why the majority of such work was concentrated in the BRS/BRE and similar.

The 1964 Report consulted a vast number of other professional and trade bodies, acknowledging that they too did relevant research but were entirely self-funded at that time. This was an era when every product and industry seemed to have its own association and many of them were involved in the price-fixing cartels which were legal until 1957. There were, for instance, 13 such associations just for bricks and tiles and another 24 for other materials used in the building trades [23].

Case Study: Chalk, Lime and Allied Industries Research Association (CLAIRA)

Of the research associations examined in John Bennet's 2012 thesis [24] and in the 1964 Report), the association with seemingly the most obvious link to the building industry was the Chalk, Lime and Allied Industries Research Association.

Its origins were in the whiting industry, whose British Whiting Federation (BWF) was formed in 1943 by amalgamating the regional Whiting Associations. Whiting in this context is calcium carbonate, often chalk. The post-war encouragement for industrial associations led the BWF to set up a Whiting and Industrial Powders Research Council and laboratories at Welwyn Hall in 1947. Its work focussed on establishing the scientific basis for using whiting as a filler in such varying industries as rubber, linoleum, paint and wallpaper. CLAIRA was founded in 1955 and amalgamated with BWF in 1964 to form the Welwyn Hall Research Association (WHRA). The laboratories' work was also linked to other industries, such as papermaking and food, but on the construction side its fundamental research included glazing putties, sand grading [25] and mortar testing [26]. The CLAIRA/BWF amalgamation was short-lived and WHRA folded in 1973, with the BWF becoming the British Calcium Carbonates Federation (BCCF) in 1989 and reverting to its earlier focus on non-construction uses of powdered limestones, marbles and chalks [27].

Hence this multi-named research organisation was, like many others in the post-war period, encouraged into being by the UK government's pro-active support, but its construction-related work later withered.

Discussion

In the century since the DSIR and its various governmental research establishments and supported industrial associations started work, their ways of funding and undertaking the essential research that supports the safety and efficiency of construction have reflected the cycles of political ideologies. The initial years were ones of a socialistic-type government intervention, direction and support, commencing when David Lloyd-George was the UK's Prime Minister (1916-22). Although the spending cuts of the Great Depression in the 1930s were difficult for all organisations relying on state funding, the 'Million Fund' for collaborative industrial research associations was topped up from time to time, demonstrating that the scheme had cross-party parliamentary support for what they achieved, even though some associations closed. Those years did not see a diminishing of outputs from the civil servants in the Research Stations, as the pressure to find cheaper alternatives to traditional materials and quicker construction methods was even more acute. The years of (and before) the Second World War certainly saw some diversion into war preparation and work explicitly supporting the war effort, both on the defensive and offensive sides, but also the lesson, from the First World War: of the need to prepare thoroughly during the war for after the war, had definitely been learnt and implemented. This led to the burgeoning of yet further state direction, funding and intervention even in the difficult years of the 1950s and 60s before the Thatcherite era led to full privatisation of all the organisations in the 1990s. Very few of the former collaborative industrial research associations still exist under their original names or functions and the remaining construction-related government research establishments, other than the Building Research Establishment, either closed or merged. There is scope for further research into the histories of the many construction-related associations of the mid-20th century, both of the research association type and the trades' associations.

What seems not to have changed, despite some state funding for 'knowledge exchange' programmes to link universities and industries, is the fragmented nature of the construction industry and the consequent continuing need for the Building Research Establishment's services, albeit on a paid-for basis.

References

[1] A. Gamble, Privatization, Thatcherism, and the British State, *Journal of Law and Society,* Vol.16, No.1, 1988, pp.1-20.
[2] H.F. Heath & A.L. Heatherington, *Industrial Research and Development in The United Kingdom A Survey*, Faber & Faber Ltd, 1946, p.3
[3] 'RTG' (1930) Obituary of Sir William McCormick, G.B.E., F.R.S. Nature 125, 569–571. Accessed 23 February 2021: https://doi.org/10.1038/125569a0

[4] E. Hutchinson, 'Scientists as an Inferior Class: The Early Years of the DSIR', *Minerva*, July 1970, Vol. 8, No. 3 (July 1970), pp. 396-411.

[5] H. Melville, The Department of Scientific and Industrial Research. The New Whitehall Series No.9. George Allen & Unwin Ltd, 1962, p.41.

[6] HMSO. (1960) Fuel Research 1917-1958. A review of the Fuel Research Organisation of the DSIR.

[7] M. Swenarton, 'Breeze Blocks and Bolshevism: Housing Policy and the Origins of the Building Research Station 1917-21', *Construction History*, Vol. 21, 2005-6

[8] M. Swenarton, 'Houses of paper and brown cardboard: Neville Chamberlain and the establishment of the Building Research Station at Garston in 1925', *Planning Perspectives,* Vol.22, No.3, 2007, pp. 257-281.

[9] F.M. Lea, Science and Building. A history of the Building Research Station, HMSO, 1971.

[10] R. Courtney, 'Building Research Establishment past, present and future', *Building Research & Information*, Vol. 25, No.5, 1997, p.285.

[11] HMSO, Building Research and Information Services Report of a Working Party, Ministry of Public Building and Works, 1964.

[12] G.Atkinson, 'Thoughts during the Building Research Establishment's 75th Anniversary', *Construction History*, Vol. 12, 1996, pp.101-107.

[13] Courtney, (Note 10), p.291.

[14] R. McWilliam, BSI: The first hundred years 1901-2001, 2001, BSI.

[15] HMSO (1956) Building Research 1955, Report of the Building Research Board with the report of the Director of Building Research for the year 1955. DSIR.

[16] Hansard (1956) Ministry of Works. D.S.I.R. (New Buildings). Commons Sitting. HC Deb 17 July 1956 vol 556 cc1009-11 1009. Accessed 30 March 2021: https://api.parliament.uk/historic-hansard/commons/1956/jul/17/dsir-new-buildings

[17] Anon. (1946), 'Obituary. Alfred Herbert Dorlencourt Markwick, 1904-1946', *Journal of the Institution of Civil Engineers*, Vol. 26, No. 7, pp.426-7.

[18] A.H.D. Markwick and F.A. Shergold, 'The Aggregate Crushing Test for Evaluating the Mechanical Strength of Coarse Aggregates', *Journal of the Institution of Civil Engineers,* Vol. 24, No. 6, 1945, pp. 125-133. The test was adopted as the British Standard Test in BS882, 1940.

[19] L.C. Fowler, (1976) Collected Summaries of Fire Research Notes and Current Papers (FRS) 1975. Fire Research Note No1046. BRE Trust (UK). An exemplar document of numerous such reports.

[20] £1million in 1918 would be the equivalent of about £59million in 2021. https://www.in2013dollars.com/uk/inflation/1918?endYear=2021&amount=1000000&future_pct=0.03

[21] Heath & Heatherington, (Note 2), Appendix II.

[22] Melville, (Note 5), Appendix V.

[23] S. Broadberry & N.F.R. Crafts, Competition and Innovation in 1950's Britain, Working Paper No. 57/00. Department of Economic History, London School of Economics, 2000.

[24] J. Bennett, Strategy adopted by research associations for success. PhD thesis The Open University, 2012. Accessed 23 February 2021: http://dx.doi.org/doi:10.21954/ou.ro.0000ee1b

[25] M.J. Purton, 'The effect of sand grading on the calcium silicate brick reaction', *Cement and Concrete Research*, Vol. 4, Issue 1, 1974, pp.13-29,

[26] R. Gillard & H.N. Lee, The Testing of Building Mortars Using the New British Standard Methods. In: The Reaction Parameters of Lime, ASTM STP 472, 1970, pp.82-116.

[27] History of the British Calcium Carbonates Federation. Accessed 28 March 2021: http://www.calcium-carbonate.org.uk/history.asp

David Yeomans

Not just the dirty work: engineers' contributions to architecture

David Yeomans
Independent scholar

Introduction

The sociologist Everett Hughes used the phrase 'the dirty work' to point out that in many areas of work there are those who enjoy prestige in the practice of their profession but who rely upon the work of others to carry out routine tasks – the dirty work [1]. Those who enjoy prestige, and the salaries that go with it, could not practice effectively without those who do the menial work work. An obvious example is the relationship between hospital doctors and the nurses - the latter not expected to make any clinical decisions over the care of patients even if, because of their constant observation, they might be in a position to know as well as the doctor what care was required.

The division we are concerned with here is between architects and structural engineers and the extent to which the latter are simply carrying out the dirty work or might have been able to influence the architectural form. The latter might happen in one of two ways: engineers might collaborate with architects over particular projects perhaps suggesting structures that the architect might not otherwise have considered or engineers might develop forms which architects might then adopt. The latter is easier to observe unlike the former, where individual engineers collaborate closely with individual architects. The questions here are firstly to identify when such collaborations have occurred and secondly to ask what conditions enable collaboration to take place.

When steel and reinforced concrete frames came into use in building it was engineers who were asked to carry out their detailed design because that was beyond the competence of architects. However, the division of responsibility between the architect and the engineers was made clear by an architect writing in 1914 who said that 'It is the architect, and the architect alone, who should determine the position of all main girders, stanchions and supports.'[2] Clearly, no true collaboration between the two professions was expected in the development of the design; engineers were simply to work out the sizes and the detailing of structural members.

However, the position seems to have changed by the 1950s when Furnaux Jordan, writing about the collaboration between Ove Arup and Architects Co-partnership for the design of the Brynmawr factory, said:

> 'Much of the merit of the Brynmawr factory in design and execution- is due to the extraordinary close co-ordination between engineering and architecture ... the engineers understood throughout the aesthetic aims of the architects and themselves made an aesthetic as well as structural contribution.' [3]

The factory was based on a series of shells, novel in Britain at the time, so one might not expect the architects to initiate the idea because they would have had little knowledge of what was possible. How then did this change take place and what effect was it to have?

The inter-war period

Much of the structural design work in the inter-war years was carried out by contractors rather than by consulting engineers. Architects would decide whether a framed building was to be of steel or reinforced concrete and put the work out to tender. Those bidding for the work would then have to carry out at least sufficient design wok to be able to put in a price, which would have to absorb the design costs including those of unsuccessful tenders. These circumstances hardly encouraged contractors' design staff to provide any more than the most basic structures, designed as well as built most cheaply. There were consulting engineers but if the job book of B.L. Hurst is typical they might work for contractors as well as architects carrying out design work that was beyond the capability of those in contractors' offices [4].

Perhaps the first public acknowledgement architecture as a possible collaboration with engineers was by Harry Barnes reviewing the work of Owen Williams and Maxwell Ayrton for the Empire Exhibition buildings.

> Theirs was the marriage of true minds to which there has been no impediment . . . [T]hey have shown the possibility of collaboration and co-operation between architect and engineer each enhancing the work of the other [5].

Sadly however this was a marriage that was not to last. Williams worked as a bridge engineer and worked with Ayrton on bridge designs, particularly those for the A9 road in Scotland which produced some interesting designs. However, when it came to building work with Ayrton things did not go well. They did three buildings together but none made any expression of their concrete structures. Although the warehouse for Pilkingtons designed by Ayrton, with structure by Williams, was described as 'impressive' and a carefully considered work, the elevations proclaimed it to be a brick building in spite of its reinforced concrete frame [6]. Eventually when Ayrton chose to speak at the RIBA on the aesthetics of bridge design there was a rather public break between the two [7].

Williams made an impressive contribution to the Daily Express building, with Ellis & Clarke as architects. There he obtained the commission because he was able to show how to support an existing building above the basement, which housed the presses, increasing the space available by building a concrete structure to carry the existing steel frame above. However, it is clear from his surviving drawings and reports at the time that he did more than that. The building had to cantilever over Shoe Lane to provide a bay for unloading the paper deliveries and the change from the structure of the basement press-room to accommodate the planning of the floors above involved a 2ft reduction in span. Chermayeff's review of the building was fulsome in praise of Owen Williams's contribution to the design [8].

What was more striking about the Daily Express building was the contrast between an early Ellis and Clarke sketch and the final treatment of the building. Their early sketch might be described as 'Fleet Street bombastic' but In the event the building had a modern curtain wall, which is said to have been the idea of Bertram Gallannaugh [9]. While the structure provided by Owen Williams must have had a considerable influence on the overall form of the building we have no idea how much he might have contributed to its external appearance. However, he certainly took an interest in the treatment of the curtain wall because there are sketches for it in the Owen Williams archive that show his engagement with the idea [10].

Owen Williams was then given the commission as both architect and engineer for the paper's Glasgow and Manchester buildings. He seems to have directly copied Ellis and Clarke's details for the cladding for those buildings but at Manchester there was no temptation to have the framing expressed in the cladding because he used flat-slab construction with the columns set back behind the facade. In fact the view from the street to the press hall below required uninterrupted glazing.

Williams adopted flat slabs in other buildings where he acted as architect as well as engineer. His best-known building was the Wets Building for the Boots pharmaceutical company, which used a development of the flat slab, and he used flat slabs in his Pioneer Health Centre. But this device was already making its way into British architecture via another route for commercial buildings. We see this particularly in the Wrigley Factory by Wallis Gilbert and Partners whose structure was designed and built by the Trussed Concrete Steel Company [11]. The client was an American firm requiring this American structural system, slow to be adopted in Britain because it did not fit into the reinforced concrete regulations. Nevertheless, it was being used by contractors in Britain for commercial and industrial buildings as William Arrol's office handbook shows [12].

A contemporary of William was Oscar Faber but his engagement with architects and architecture is a little more enigmatic. He began work with Trollop and Coles with an agreement that he could take on his own consulting work. Then an important client was Herbert Baker with whom he not only provided structural advice but also the designs for the services at the extensions to the Bank of England. Subsequently the design of building services became an important part of his business, which in 1937 provided the service design for the Earls Court Exhibition Centre, designed by the American architect C. Howard Crane [13]. His partner in this was J.R Kell with whom he produced a textbook on heating and air conditioning, which has remained a standard work to this day [14].

As a designer of many industrial buildings Oscar Faber was concerned with their appearance, eventually giving lectures on the subject to the Institution of Civil Engineers [15]. Thus, he might well have felt that he could have made more of a contribution to architecture than he did. When writing on engineering for students of the Architectural Association he advised them to engage an engineer as early as possible in the design process [16]. Nevertheless his only notable work where we see a possible influence on architecture was the structure he provided for the Royal Horticultural Hall in London with architects Easton and Robertson. As Faber subsequently used a similar design for a market hall in Nairobi, one wonders how much influence he might have had on the London building's form.

We have the clearest indication of engineers' engagement with architects in the work of Ove Arup and Felix Samuely. Arup's early work with architects developing novel forms of construction was with Lubetkin and Tecton in the design of flats [17]. Beyond that his articles in *Architectural Design and Construction* may well have influenced other architects [18]. What he proposed for reinforced concrete buildings was a structural arrangement that eliminated the regular grid of beams and columns.

Samuely had made his mark in Britain with the structural design for the De La Warr pavilion, which was the first major building in Britain to be in welded steel. This was doing 'the dirty work' because the form of the building was decided by the competition entry, which the architects had designed on the mistaken assumption that it could be built in reinforced concrete. What they wanted would have been impossible in reinforced concrete but Samuely managed to show how it could be achieved in welded steel.

Samuely had developed a reputation for welded steel design in his practice in Berlin [19]. His later welded structure for Simpson's Store, Piccadilly may well have influenced the design because a deep vierendeel girder was designed to avoid columns within the display windows at street level. Unfortunately the LCC would not approve the design and deep plate girders had to be provided at every floor. This must have been an expensive arrangement and it is possible that a more conventional arrangement with columns in the window space would have been used had the LCC's objections to the original design been known earlier.

His work in reinforced concrete for Wells Coates was equally impressive. Wells Coates made his mark architecturally with the Lawn Road Flats that can reasonably claim to be the first Modern Movement building in Britain. It was a series of single room apartments, each with a small kitchen and bathroom. For that he had used contractors, the Helical Bar Company, to provide the structure, which was a simple frame resulting in columns in the corners of the apartments [20]. However, it is clear from the plan that walls could have been used. Coates then designed a major apartment block, Embassy Court, on the Brighton and Hove seafront with Samuely as structural engineer. For that Samuely intended to use a Hungarian system called Diagrid to avoid downstand beams within the flats but the local authority would not approve it. In the event he used a spine beam layout, where this beam was placed over cupboards built at the back of the living room framed by columns placed next to door openings. Wind loads were transmitted through the floors acting as diaphragms to where there were walls enclosing staircases.

Coats's subsequent Palace Gate Flats would not have been possible without the structural designs by Samuely, which used walls as beams to handle the complex interlocking nature of the apartments. Certainly that could not have been achieved with a simple beam and column structure. Had WWII not intervened this system would have been used in a development of working class flats.

Post-war

The practice of engaging consulting engineers became more common in the immediate pot-war period because of the shortage of materials and the need for post-war reconstruction [21]. Collaboration with engineers would have been encouraged by the appearance of new forms of structure that architects were less comfortable with, such as the shell structures of the Brynmawr factory, and this provided a much greater opportunity for collaboration. Ove Arup was naturally one who was seen to work in that way.

While we have Furnaux Jordan's report of this particular job by Arup there are no reports of his work with other architects that suggest this degree of collaboration. Neither did he try to influence architectural design through publications as he did with his 1935 article. However the formation of what began as the building group within his practice, which then became Arup Associates, is an indication of his commitment to architecture. This was led by Philip Dowson who had originally gone to Cambridge to read mathematics but later studied architecture at the Architectural Association, joining Ove Arup and Partners in 1953. Arup Associates integrated architects, structural and services engineers within a single firm, a pattern that had also developed in the United States.

Interest in architecture within Arup's can also be seen in its seeding of Bureau Happold and the team that won the competition for the Centre Pompidou. While Ted Happold left Arups to found his own firm, Peter Rice, who was the principal figure in the design of the Centre Pompidou remained with Arup's to work closely with a number of major architects on international projects. While André Brown has reproduced a few of Rice's sketches to illustrate his very visual method of working and communicating it is a pity that there are not fuller accounts of the development of his designs illustrated by his sketches [22].

There is much more indication of Samuely's involvement with architects than of Arup's staff. Malcolm Higgs reported that 'It was his practice to sketch a number of alternative structural solutions and to encourage the architect to make the final decision, as to which one was to be pursued.'[23] When he reported on the design for the Skylon at the Festival of Britain, a winning competition entry, he commented on how it was unusual for him to be presented with a completed design, suggesting that engaging in the early design process was more normal for him [24].

He also produced a number of articles promoting such ideas as folded plate structures and star beams. He used folded plates in a number of buildings such as the Thomas Linacre College and a school at Kingston on Thames where he used precast elements as permanent formwork for insitu concrete to form folded plates to span the length of the assembly halls. But it might have been his promotion of this form in publications that had the greatest effect. Of course we have no data that will tell us how many designers were directly influenced by his publications.

A number of significant building were designed by Samuely in precast concrete and while an extensive history of precast concrete has been produced by A.E.J. Morris, his account of post-war Britain largely begins with the period when tower cranes made the handing of precast units relatively simple [25]. He does not deal with the immediate post-war years when the best a contractor could hope for was a Ruston-Bucyrus 22RB with a crane jib mounted on it. It was using such equipment that Hatfield College was built, with Felix Samuely as structural engineer (Fig. 1)[26].

Figure 1: Hatfield College under construction

Samuely also devised a precast wall system in collaboration with Grenfell Baines, used first at Thomas Linacre College, Wigan. But perhaps his most influential collaboration was with Frederick Gibberd for the Dock Labour Board building. Given the detail of the drawings produced for that building we must surely assume a considerable involvement by Samuely in the development of the scheme (Fig. 2). Samuely's more daring use of precast concrete was the frames for the Malago factory at Bedminster, Bristol. Of course, precast concrete was subsequently developed for cladding and load-bearing wall systems, but these early framed structures deserve more recognition than they have received and they rely upon engineers' involvement.

The engineers that then came out of the Samuely stable and were influenced by his method of working were Frank Newby and then in turn Tony Hunt. Newby must have learnt his method of working from Samuely because important collaborations occurred very early in his career when he travelled in America. He spent time in Eero Saarinen's office where he was able to suggest a method for handling the structure of the Milwaukee War Memorial [27]. He also visited Wallace Harrison when he was designing the First Presbyterian Church of Stamford, Connecticut. The sketches for the original design were published in Architectural Forum and bear no relation to the final design [28]. It is clear that Newby must have suggested the folded plate design finally adopted by Harrison because it resulted in Felix Samuely's only job on American soil.

A better picture of Newby's engagement with an architect can be found in a series of sketches sent to Spero Daltas for buildings in Iran. As the two were working at a distance Newby sent sketches with written comment to Daltas to develop the design (Fig. 3). The two buildings built following this exchange were a Coca-Cola bottling plant and a garden building for Princess Fatima, both constructed of brick vaulting on steel armatures. One can readily imagine that the contents of his letters reflected the kind of conversation that Newby would normally have had with architects on a face-to-face basis [29].

Not just the dirty work: engineers contributions to architecture

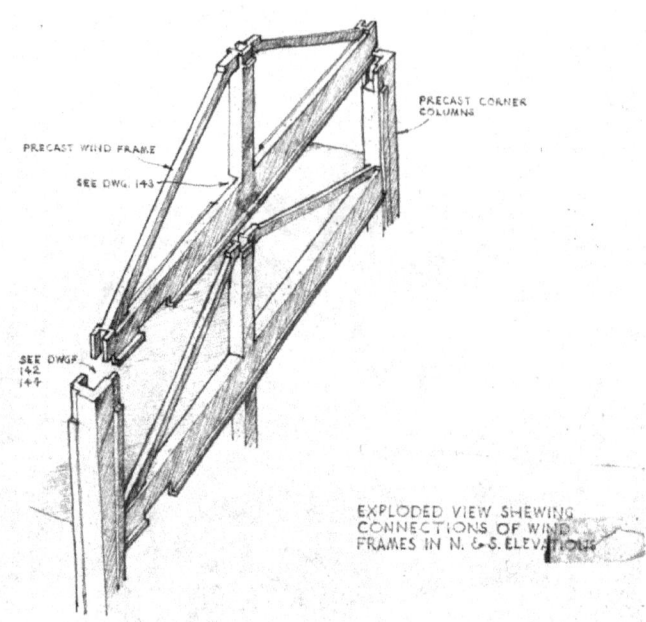

Figure 2: One of a number of assembly drawings for the Dock Labour Board building

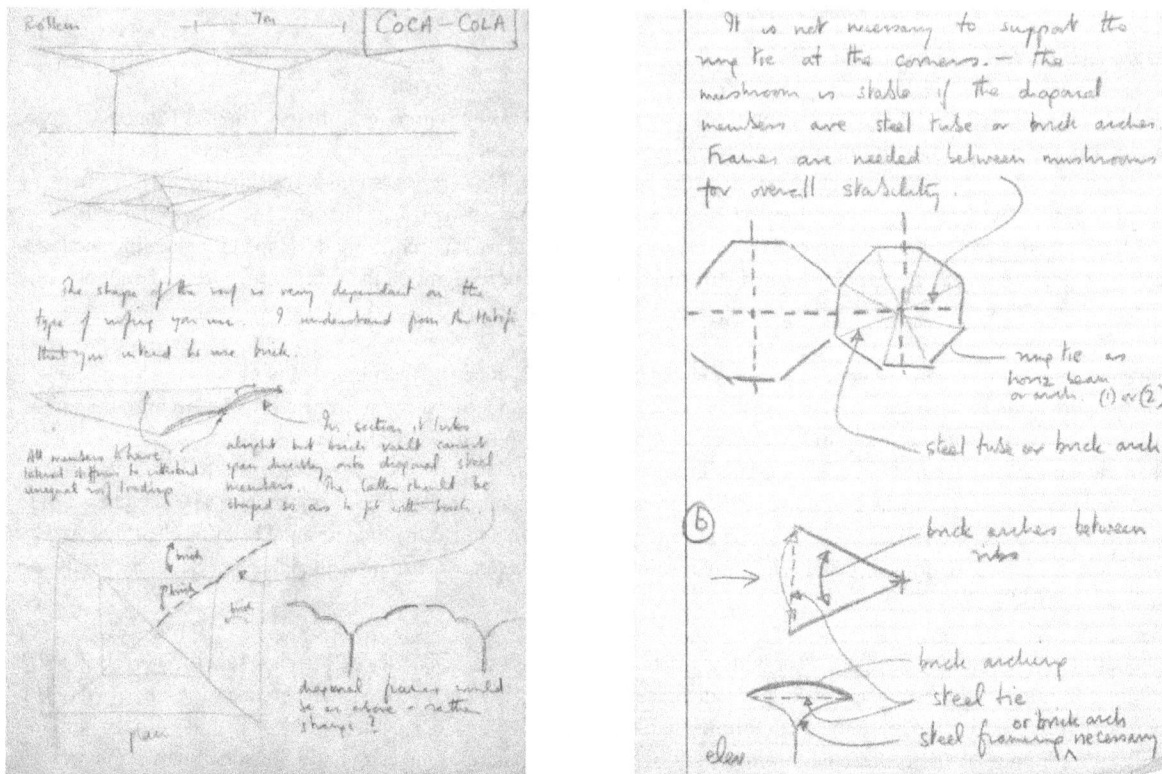

Figure 3: Pages from Newby's letters to Spero Daltas dealing with the design of the Coca-Cola plant and garden building for Princess Fatima

While this correspondence presents a fuller account of collaboration than a simple collection of sketches there are many examples of Newby's approach in sketches that he kept relating to many other jobs. In these we can sometimes see work from the very earliest sketches, which present a picture of the engineer exploring the structural possibilities that would then be presented to and discussed with the architect. For the Luton Airport hangar, for example, he first considered hangars at other airports and then sketched a range of options. For the dining hall at Marlborough College he presented the architect with a number of possibilities from which the architect opted for a reinforced concrete folded plate roof (Fig. 4). A scheme using that was presented to the college but in the event construction considerations must have prevented that from being adopted and the roof as built is a timber structure.

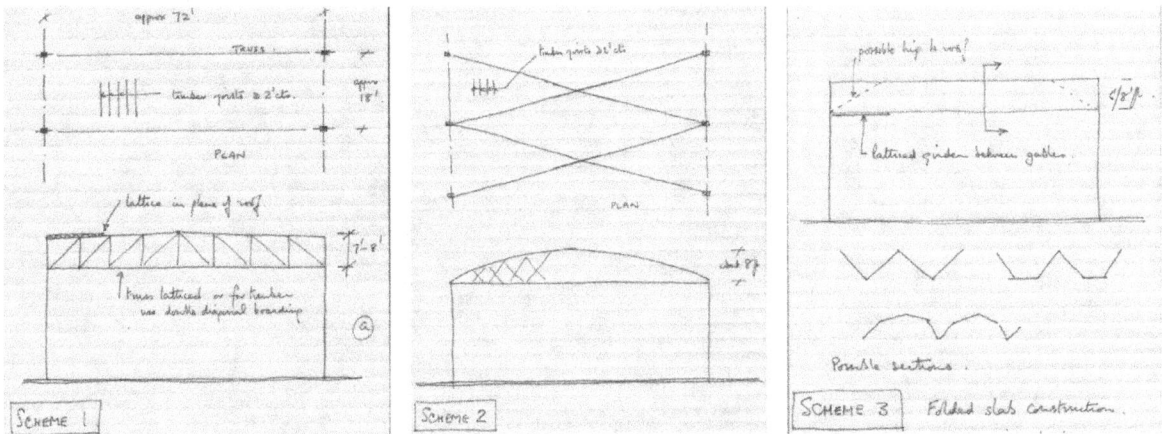

Figure 4: Three contrasting schemes for Marlborough College dining hall

Newby's papers show that an exploration of alternatives was a consistent feature throughout his design process, even when the overall form of the building was decided. He would, for example, consider alternative spanning arrangements for floors and roofs to determine the most advantageous layout. He seems to have considered the exploration of alternatives to be an essential part of the service that he provided for his clients.

The difficulty is that there are few accounts of such collaborative exchanges provided by architects. Bill Howell gave an unusual account of a design carried out with Newby, publishing the sketches that they produced between them [30]. Unfortunately the original sketches have not survived and it is difficult to tell who did which of them so that the sequence, and hence the progress of the design, cannot be followed. In this particular case Howell was after a clear expression of the structure so that it was only natural that he wanted to work closely with his engineer and also be prepared to acknowledge the latter's contribution.

While it is possible to recognize structural ingenuity in completed projects it is not possible to see whether such structural ingenuity has been required by the nature of the architect's design or because the engineer has suggested forms that the architect was unaware of. Only occasionally does this become apparent. There were two clear examples of this in Frank Newby's collaboration with Stirling and Gowan for the design of the engineering laboratory at Leicester University. The architects originally assumed that the large projecting lecture theatre would need to be supported by a pair of columns but Newby demonstrated that it could be cantilevered (Fig. 5). Also the top floor laboratory had columns in the access road that was objected to by the client [31]. There, Newby showed that the columns could slope back to the main structure. Sloping columns were again used to enable the step-back in the floors of the Cambridge history library and to form the main structure of the Florey Building at Oxford. Newby subsequently commented on how Stirling learnt to use this technique [32].

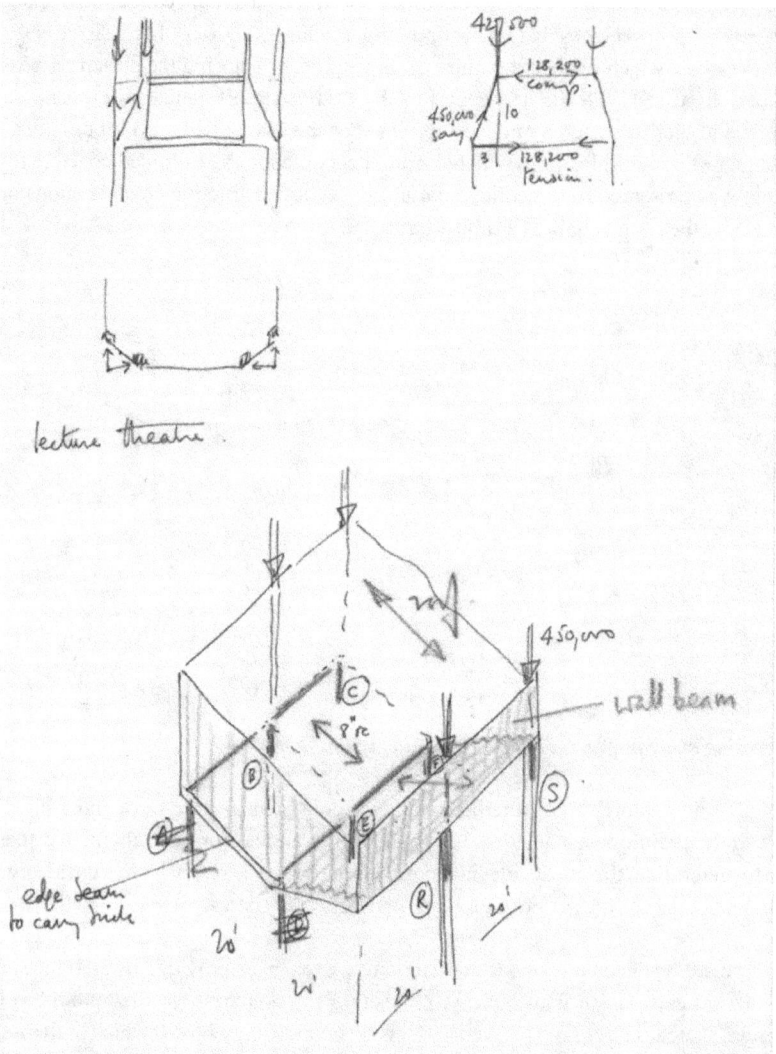

Figure 5: Newby's working sketch for the Leicester Engineering Laboratory lecture hall

Although Anthony Hunt has published a book of his Sketches, illustrating a range of possible structures for different projects, these were hardy produced as part of the conversation with architects [33]. They are just too neat and hardly reflect his description of designing the Don Valley Stadium:

> 'Flood the project with ideas bounced back and forth between the designers and the result will be a concept. Often it is unclear as to who actually designed what because the iterative proves developed between the whole team [34].'

Or for work with Foster Associates:

> '...a process in which everyone draws and scribbles away, people make suggestions, others take them up and develop them ... Gradually the design evolves [35]'

Theses romantic accounts of the collaborative design process cannot apply to all situations, perhaps only for work on competitions. Of his more usual collaborations we know little and it is a pity that his *Sketchbook* does not have some commentary on the process and the choices made.

The process

For there to be effective collaboration between architect and engineer the latter should ideally be engaged at an early stage as advocated by Oscar Faber. However he said nothing about the nature of the relationship.

Engineers rarely write about the design process still less about the process of collaboration but a unique example of an engineer commenting on his collaboration with a particular architect is that by Komendant on his work with Louis Kahn [36]. While his account suggests that Kahn respected his ability to comment on architecture it also suggests that Kahn was unwilling to concede his engineer's ability to be creative. What does seem clear is a rather impractical approach by Kahn when it came to construction, which produced problems at the Kimbell Art Museum. Andrew Saint has drawn attention to the very different recollections that Kahn and Komendant have of the resolution of these problems [37]. But the explanation lies in Komendant's explanation for such divergent views as Kahn's reluctance to credit his associates, something he thought common to almost all architects, a view that Saint also quotes [38].

Experimental work has shown that even when reputations are not at stake designers do not necessarily have good recall about the design process [39]. The experiment simply concerned architects and perhaps recall is poorer when it comes to the contribution of others. Whether or not there is close collaboration between architects and engineers allowing the latter to do more than just the dirty work depends upon the personalities of both. There are clearly architects willing to engage with their engineers while others would prefer to keep them at arms-length until the design is developed. Equally there will be engineers who are happy doing just the dirty work, possibly unwilling to advise on possible options available, perhaps because engineers receive little or no training in design.

Conclusions

We might reasonably ask whether there is any common pattern connecting those engineers who can be identified as working closely with architects. Newby and Hunt both came from the Samuely stable although Newby had a greater contact with architects as a young man throught living at Lawn Road Flats, which was a Mecca for architects. In 1951 he would have met the former members of the Bauhaus returning to London for the Festival of Britain.

Samuely had worked for contractors in Vienna and Berlin before setting up as a consulting engineer. We know of collaborations with Eric Medelsohn and Arthur Korn for whom he designed steel frames. Ove Arup, working for Christiani and Nielsen appears to have had no working contact with architecture until he himself designed the Labworth Café and then worked with Lubetkin and Tecton on buildings for various zoos. He made the important contribution to the Highpoint I flats based on his experience with the structure of concrete silos. His move to J.L. Kier & Co. was to enable him to work more on architectural projects and his later work with Lubetkin and Tecton has been discussed elsewhere [40]. In contrast to Samuely who worked with all structural materials, welded steel, reinforced concrete and timber, Arup remained essentially a reinforced and prestressed concrete engineer.

Oscar Faber initially made his name with research into the strength of reinforced concrete beams. His contemporary, Owen Williams, after graduating as an engineer worked briefly for the Indented Bar and Concrete Engineering Company before going to The Trussed Concrete Steel Company, both contractors with patented reinforcing systems. His career was then largely in bridge engineering with a few but prominent buildings to his name as an architect.

If we compare these different careers the only one with close contact with architects seems to have been Frank Newby. The principal common factor seems to be simply that all of them took an interest in architecture. It is also Newby's personal papers that provide the best insight into working practices when there is collaboration between an engineer and his architect clients. They provide a far from a complete record of the various jobs but they do provide a picture that we are unlikely to find anywhere else.

References

[1] E. C. Hughes, *Men and Their Work*, Glencoe: Free Press, 1958.
[2] W.E.A. Brown, 'The architect and structural engineering', *Concrete and Constructional Engineering*, 1914. Vol.9, pp. 482-4.
[3] R. Furneaux Jordan, 'Brynmawr', *Architectural Review*, Vol.111, Feb. 1952, p. 148.
[4] I am grateful to the late Lawrance Hurst for showing me his father's job book.
[5] H. Barnes, 'The British Empire Exhibition, Wembley', *Architectural Review*, Vol.55, 1924, pp. 2041-17
[6] H.A.N. Brockman, *The British Architect in Industry 1841-1940*, London: George Allen & Unwin, 1974, pp. 150-51.
[7] This was in a response to Ayrton, Maxwell, "Modern Bridges." *Journal of the Royal Institute of British Architects*, Vol.38, 1931, p. 483.
[8] S. Chermayeff, "The New Building for the Daily Express." *Architectural Review*, Vol.72 (n.d.): 3–12. *The* "The Daily Express Building, Fleet Street." *Architect and Building News*, Vol.131, 1932: 3–21 has a better description of the structure.
[9] S. Barston and A. Saint, *A Farewell to Fleet Street*, London: English Heritage, 1988, p. 49.
[10] One of Williams sketches is reproduced in Yeomans, David, and David Cottam. *Owen Williams*. The Engineer's Contribution to Contemporary Architecture. London: Thomas Telford, 2001, p.67.
[11] J. S. Skinner, *Form and Fancy, Factories and Factory Buildings by Walllis, Gilbert & Partners, 1916-1939*, Liverpool: Liverpool U. Press, 1997, pp. 95-99.
[12] E. A. Scott, *Arrol's Reinforced Concrete Reference Book*, London: E & F.N. Spon, 1930, pp. 167-73.
[13] O. Faber and J. R. Kell, 'Mechanical equipment in the Earls Court exhibition building', *Institution of Heating & Ventilating Engineers Journal*, March 1938.
[14] First published in 1936, Faber and Kell's *Heating and Air Conditioning of Buildings* is now in its 11th edition.
[15] O. Faber, *The Aesthetic Aspect of Civil Engineering Design: A Record of Six Lectures*, London: 1945.
[16] *A Book of Design by Senior Students of the Architectural Association School*, London: Earnest Benn, 1924.
[17] D. Yeomans and D. Cottam. 'An Architect, Engineer Collaboration: The Tecton Arup Flats'. *The Structural Engineer*, Vol.67, no.10, 1989, pp. 183–88.
[18] O. Arup, 'Planning in Reinforced Concrete', *Architectural Design and Construction*, Vol.5, 1935, pp. 297–307 & 340–43.
[19] M. Higgs, 'Felix James Samuely'. *Architectural Association Journal*, Vol.76, No.843, June 1960, pp. 1–32.
[20] Application for approval of the design – Minutes of the Town Planning and Building Regulations Committee, Volume for 1931-2, p.341.
[21] D. Yeomans, 'Collaborating with Consulting Engineers', *Twentieth-Century Architecture and Its Histories*, 125–51. London: Society of Architectural Historians of Great Britain, 2000.
[22] A. Brown, *Peter Rice*, The Engineer's Contribution to Contemporary Architecture, London: Thomas Telford, 2001.
[23] Higgs, (Note 19), p. 27.
[24] F. Samuely and P.J.A. Ward, 'The Skylon'. *Proc. Instn. Civil Engrs*, July 1952, p. 448
[25] A.E.J. Morris, *Precast Concrete in Architecture*, London: George Goodwin Ltd, 1978.
[26] See for example 'Hatfield Technical College; Architects: Easton & Robertson', *Architectural Review*, February 1953, pp. 78–87 & 125–26.
[27] R. Landay, 'Engineers and Architects: Newby + Price', *AA Files*, no. 27, Summer 1994, pp. 25–32.
[28] 'A Piranesi for today', *Architectural Forum*, Dec 1953, pp. 93-95.

[29] Copies of the letters sent to Spero Daltas are in the collection of Newby's papers lodged with the Institution of Civil Engineers.
[30] W. Howell, 'Vertebrate Buildings, the Architecture of Structural Space', *Journal of the Royal Institute of British Architects*, Vol.77, 1970, pp. 100–108.
[31] M. Crinson, *Stirling and Gowan, Architecture from Austerity to Affluence*, New Haven & London: Yale University Press, 2012, p.232.
[32] F. Newby, 'Hi Tec or Mystec', *RIBA Transactions* 3, 1984, pp. 18–27.
[33] T. Hunt, *Tony Hunt's Sketchbook*, London: Architectural Press, 1999.
[34] Quoted by A. Macdonald, *Anthony Hunt*, London: Thomas Telford, 2000, p. 38.
[35] *ibid*, p. 65.
[36] A. Komendant, *18 Years with Architect Louis I. Kahn*, Englewood, N.J.: Aloray, 1975.
[37] A. Saint, *Architect and Engineer, A Study in Sibling Rivalry*, New Haven & London: Yale University Press, 2007, pp. 406-08.
[38] *Ibid*. p. 409
[39] D. Yeomans, 'Monitoring Design Processes', *Changing Design*, Chichester: Wiley, 1982, pp.109–124.
[40] Yeomans and Cottam, (Note 17).

The History of the Construction of the Cuban National Capitol

María Mestre-Martí, Pedro M. Jiménez-Vicario and Manuel A. Ródenas-López

Universidad Politécnica de Cartagena, Spain

Introduction

In 2019, the Office of the Historian of the City of Havana (OHCH) completed the restoration of the National Capitol of Cuba. It had begun in 2010. The architectural intervention on this monument is, so far, the largest restoration project the country has ever faced, due to its size, importance and large scale. This article describes its history and construction methods, emphasising the construction and technical innovation that made it possible to complete the work in a very short time for the conditions and techniques of the time: only three years (1926 to 1929) for a building that had 13,483 m2 of construction and 26,391 m2 of parks and gardens, covering a total area of approximately 43,600 m2 [1].

The research goal is to provide information on the construction solutions and materials used to build the monument, based on the extensive graphic and photographic documentation located in the different archives in Havana, consulted by staff from the University of Alicante and the Polytechnic University of Cartagena, throughout 2010 and 2011. This made it possible to carry out a subsequent detailed study of this information. It took approximately two years to deeply understand the innovative construction of a neoclassical style building, made of reinforced concrete and iron but covered in stone, and to be able to redraw, by means of technical axonometries, the load-bearing structure of the central body. The study focuses primarily on the central body of the building, which supports the large dome, and unmasks its highly complicated internal structure.

Materials examined included:

- The original hand-drawn plans, which had never been published
- Historical photographs of the building and surroundings belonging to the Ministry of Public Works
- Photographs of the on-site visits made at the beginning of its restoration.
- Published texts and photographs from The Capitol Book, of which only two physical copies exist in Cuba and five in North American universities.

In addition, several site visits were made, which facilitated the understanding of the internal dome structure and allowed the assessment of the state of conservation of the building, in a prior phase to its architectural rehabilitation.

Historical Context

In the first 20 years of the 20th century, Cuba's population grew, the number of immigrants increased, and the city's urban development began. The economy had grown very rapidly, but growth was based almost exclusively on sugar cane production and trade relations with the United States. However, this independence did not bring any benefits to the population, which led to numerous protests in the country.

The History of the Construction of the Cuban National Capitol

In 1925, General Gerardo Machado y Morales became President, to reconcile the interests of the different sectors of the bourgeoisie and American capital with his economic programme, offering stability to the middle classes and new jobs to the working classes. President Machado conceived, with an almost delirious grandeur, the execution of an ambitious project whose main objective was to carry out a series of remodelling works. These aimed to creating an impressive monumental setting for the Pan-American Conference in Havana in 1928 and the possible inauguration of his second term of office, which was to take place in 1929.

The period between 1920 and the Wall Street Crash of 1929 marked an important time of economic growth for the Cuban ruling class, which promoted American investments that coincided with the creation of the large sugar mills. In addition to the public works that had already been undertaken at the end of the War of Independence (paving, public lighting networks, urban sanitation services, tram systems, etc.), this period was characterised by major public projects, reflecting the megalomania of President Machado, who wanted to turn Havana into a "tropical Paris". The works also had a social objective: to alleviate the pressure exerted by the workers and peasants' unemployment during the so-called "dead time", that is, during the greater part of the year when the sugar harvest did not take place. However, the social purpose was not the President's primary aim, but rather initiatives aimed at constructing perishable symbols representative of his power

Figure 1: Aerial view of the front of the Capitol. Source: Archivo Secretaría de Obras Públicas. Negociado de Construcciones Civiles y Militares (Archive of Public Works Secretariat. Bureau of Civil and Military Constructions). 1938

Among the public works that Machado set in motion as a reflection of the local oligarchy were the Master Plan for Havana. This was a reflection of the desire to adapt the urban framework to his grandiloquent aspirations in the symbolic works of the State, the National Capitol (Fig. 1), similar to the architectural model installed in Washington, and the Model

Prison of Isla de los Pinos. This prison would be the largest and most modern penitentiary establishment of its time in all of Latin America, with a capacity for 5,000 inmates. The financial investment for these constructions obviously came from American banks, "the Chase National Bank made a loan of one hundred million dollars to the Government while the concession of the Central Highway was assigned to the Warren Brothers Company of New York, a company in which Machado and the Minister of Public Works, Carlos Miguel de Céspedes, were shareholders [2]".

In this context, the National Capitol of Cuba, whose dome axis would become the starting point or 'kilometre zero' on which the country's road network was established, fulfilled the dictatorial expectations of having constructed a representative building of President Machado's political achievements, the urban apotheosis of his delusions of grandeur.

The Capitol monumentalised a mirage of benevolent authority. This false munificence soon evaporated during the next few years as, in parallel, a generalised crisis took shape, augmented by the Great Depression between 1929 and 1933. In Cuba this aggravated the existing situation by collapsing the Cuban sugar-based economy and generated a revolutionary situation, whose effects encompassed almost all factions of Cuban society. People organised to confront Machado. Students and trade union organisers staged massive public protests. Civil unrest provoked police brutality. The Capitol and public spaces built by the Machado regime changed from a stage for political theatre to one of revolution.

On 20 March 1930 a general strike was held. Two hundred thousand workers took part under the slogan "Down with Machado". This strike is considered the beginning of the anti-Machado revolution, together with the student *Tángana* (instant student protests) of September 1933, which culminated in August 1933 with another general strike. As a result of these pressures, on 12 August 1933 Machado fled the country. After his flight people destroyed his face engraved on the bas-reliefs of the Capitol gates.

From the inauguration of the building, in 1929, until 1959, year of the Cuban revolution triumph, the Capitol was the Cuban Congress. Since 1959, the building has been used for various purposes. It has been home to the Museum of Natural Sciences, the Cuban Academy of Sciences from 1962 and the Ministry of Science, Technology and Environment, adapting its facilities with each new use. In 2009 it closed its doors to the public and began to move all its workers. The building was vacated in order to begin its rehabilitation and the current unicameral parliament was moved to the building that housed the Senate and House of Representatives, as the Cuban ruler Raúl Castro stated in front of the National Assembly deputies in February 2011.

Historical-construction context

The construction methods of the National Capitol of Cuba were a direct consequence of the success of the North American construction methods and means brought to Cuba at the beginning of the 20th century. After the Spanish-American War, Purdy & Henderson was one of the most pioneering New York firms in the execution of steel-frame and reinforced concrete structures in Cuba and New York, whose first branch was established in Manhattan in 1893. In Cuba, Purdy & Henderson also built the *Lonja del Comercio* building (1909), the *Hotel Plaza* (1909), the *Centro Gallego* (1915), the Royal Bank of Canada building (1919), the *Centro Asturiano* (1927), the *Hotel Nacional* (1930) and the *Radio Centro CMQ* building (1947).

In that sense, the structure of the building was largely tied to American construction standards. The detailed drawings show compliance with the specifications of the American Institute of Steel Construction (AISC), the first edition of which was published in 1923. The material used to construct the steel structure must also conform to the standard specifications of the American Society for Testing Materials for Structural Steel for Buildings (series designation A 9-21) and to the Standard Construction Rules for the Use of Reinforced Concrete, published in 1917 in the United States of America [3].

Figure 2: Bas-relief of one of the main gates of the Capitol depicting its construction. Author's image.

It is also significant to consider the importance of the first prefabricated concrete parts workshops in Havana, whose application to architectural work in the form of mouldings, column drums and decorative elements formed a language of the island's pre-industrial construction time, which left its mark on many works from the beginning of the century. Cuba was the first country to produce cement in Latin America. Workshops such as *El Arte Moderno*, founded in 1911, gave rise to the birth of the cement and plaster foundry Duque y Cia., later called *Compañía Cubana de Piedra Artificial S.A.*, where all the decorative elements of the Bacardí building, completed in 1930, were made, in which the American company Purdy & Henderson also intervened. In many of these prefabricated element workshops, a variety of artificial stone elements, plaster pieces and decorative elements were built. It made it possible to construct works at high speed. In the Capitol, prefabricated elements can be found in the Corinthian capitals of the columns (Fig. 2), in its drums, some mouldings and decorative elements (Fig. 3).

Figure 3: Concrete casting workshop for the 4th floor courtyards, on site. Source: Archivo Secretaría de Obras Públicas. Negociado de Construcciones Civiles y Militares (Archive of Public Works Secretariat. Bureau of Civil and Military Constructions), 1928

The construction of the National Capitol of Cuba

The original building was the result of an international competition, held in July 1910, whose winning project, with the slogan *La República*, was developed by the Cuban architects Eugenio Rayneri Sorrentino and Eugenio Rayneri y Piedra. Construction began in 1911. Work was suspended when General Mario García Menocal assumed the presidency of the Republic in 1913. Menocal decided to build the Presidential Palace on the *Quinta de los Molinos* and to take advantage of the land and the work already begun on the former site of the Villanueva Railway Station for the future building that would house the Congress and Senate. Cuban architects Mario Romañach and Félix Cabarrocas were commissioned to modify the plans and adapt the already built part to the new capitol. Cabarrocas completely changed the original project, as well as the shape and height of the previous dome, which, although construction had already begun, seemed erroneously low.

The construction of the Capitol of the Republic was resumed in 1925 under Machado's mandate on the site of the now-disappeared Villanueva railway station, which served as a hinge between the Old Havana historic city the Centro Habana neighbourhood, as well as forming part of the axis of the Paseo del Prado. The Secretary of Public Works, Carlos Miguel de Céspedes, commissioned the architects Evelio Govantes and Félix Cabarrocas to study a new capitol project based on the one that was being executed to award the contract for the works by auction in January 1926. After several sketches, the final project was made by the architect Eugenio Rayneri Piedra with the help of Ricardo E. Franklyn, an architect from Purdy and Henderson Co. of New York, the company that was awarded the contract for the purchase.

The construction of the Capitol employed 8,000 skilled workers (Fig. 4). This great coordination was carried out by the Purdy and Henderson Co., which was responsible for thousands of workers simultaneously and more than 40 subcontractors with numerous personnel, most of whom were Cubans.

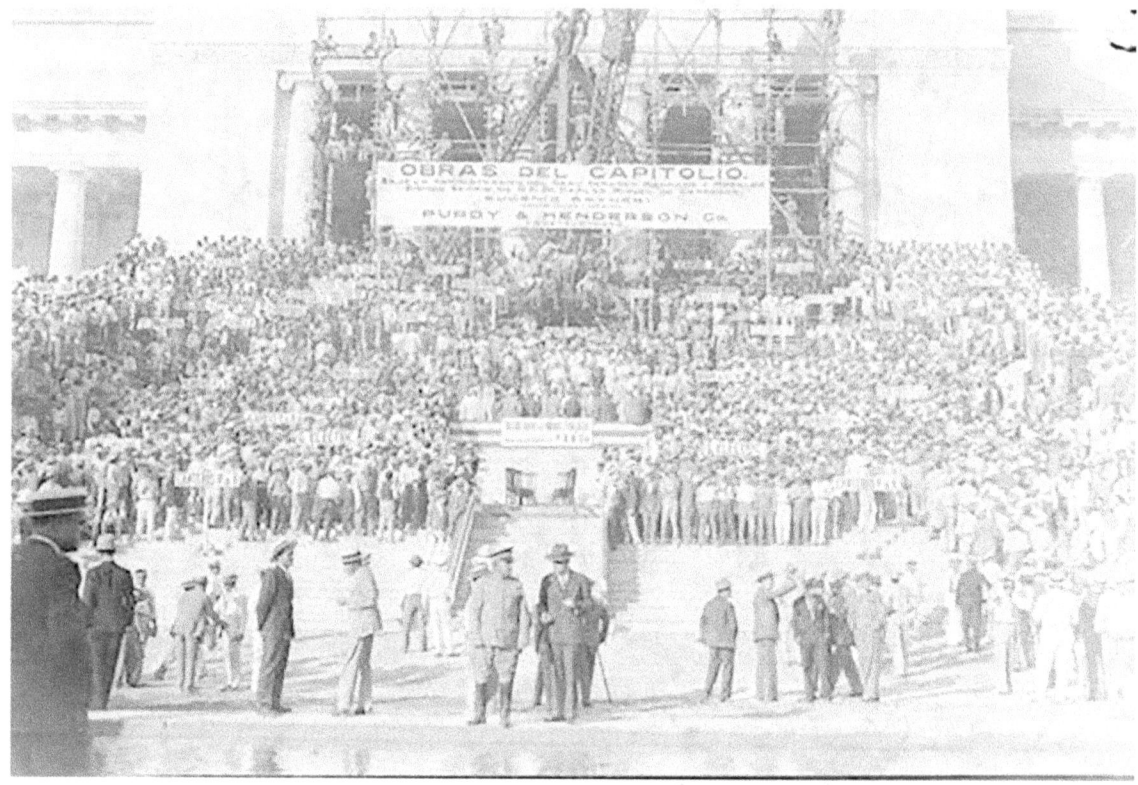

Figure 4: General Gerardo Machado with the Capitol workers, 1929. Source: Archivo Secretaría de Obras Públicas. Negociado de Construcciones Civiles y Militares (Archive of Public Works Secretariat. Bureau of Civil and Military Constructions), 1929

Due to the large scale of the building, many plans had to be drawn up (around 5,000), which meant that there was a large design team, mostly made up of young Cubans and headed by Luis V. Betancourt. The decoration work (woodwork, joinery, painting, etc.) was carried out by Waring and Gillow Ltd. of London, which, with more than 2,000 workers at the same time, completed the work in eight months. The design and calculation of the dome's foundations was carried out by N. A. Richards and H. V. Spurr, engineers of the construction company, in the record time of one week for the foundations and one month for the structure. French and Italian artists led by Mr. Droueker, and Cubans such as Sicre and Betancourt also participated in the design and manufacture of the metopes of the end bodies and the loggias. The marble decoration was done by two companies, Fratelli Remuzzi of Italy, which was in charge of the main floor, the main staircase at the back, the Staircases of Honour and the sides of the porticoes, and Casa Grasyma of Germany for the rest.

The building

The neoclassical building is 207.44 m long and 91.73 m high. It is completely symmetrical with respect to the axis passing through the dome. It has a regular geometry of simple figures: the central body on which the dome rises, two semicircular pieces on the edges corresponding to the Senate and House of Representatives hemicycles and two intermediate volumes that connect the previous ones, where the Salon des Pas Perdus (Hall of the Lost Steps) is located [4]. The central body houses the 'rotunda', the library and the main entrance or central portico, composed of 12 Doric columns and a grand granite entrance staircase with 55 steps.

On the central axis is the dome, which begins to rise above the building above the attic of the portico and consists of a square base. Below this is a cylindrical body or drum with windows that forms the base of the peristyle topped by a balustrade. Above this is the parapet, whose moulding lines coincide with the double pilasters to form wide pillars from which the ribs of the dome start, and finally the lantern.

The dome does not occupy the central place of the building: it is displaced with respect to the transversal axis of symmetry of the building. This is not the case with the longitudinal axis, which was made to coincide with the axis of the Salon des Pas Perdus, instead of rising on the longitudinal axis of the interior courtyards, which coincide with the radii of the hemicycles (Fig. 5). In other words, in a French neoclassical compositional scheme, the dome is brought forward towards the main façade, where the monumental staircase is located, ignoring the gravitational centre of the building.

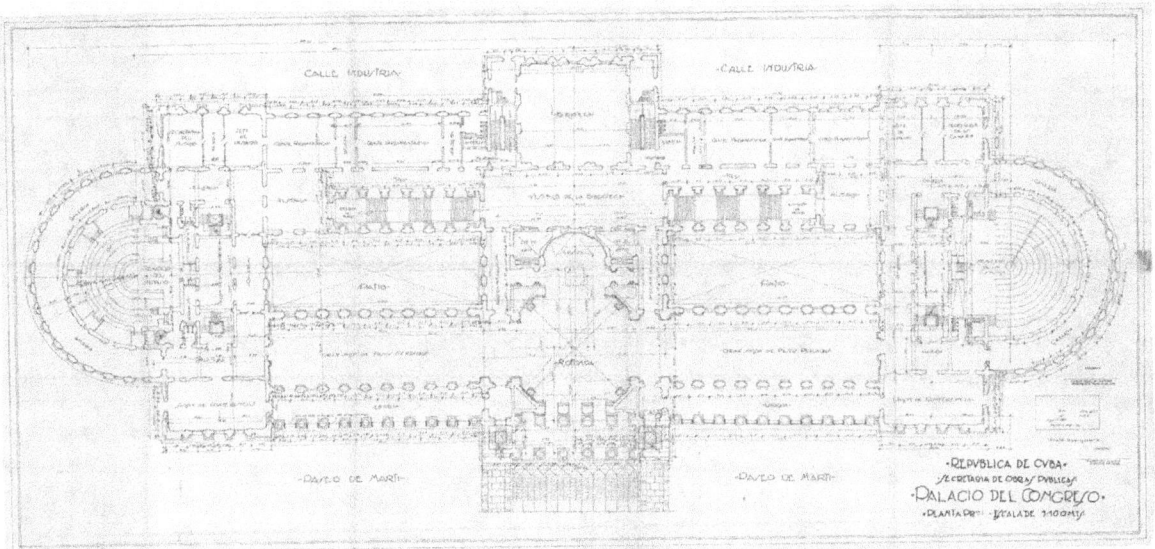

Figure 5: Second (Main) Floor Plan. Source: Hand-drawn plans of the Capitol building.

The construction of the Capitol was mainly reinforced concrete, steel and stone. Almost all this supporting structure consists of mixed structural elements such as columns, beams and slabs, properly braced to withstand tropical winds, clad in concrete. Only pure steel sections are used for the dome trusses and for the bracing and bracing elements, such as the cross-bracing systems (X-shaped) and the tie beams at the base of the drum.

The Internal Supporting Structure of the Dome

Under the dome, on the symmetrical axis of the building and after passing through the doors of the central portico, on the main floor (first floor) is the Central Rotunda, an octagonal space, formed by the dome's supports made up of four triangular-shaped concrete bases. Each base has three steel columns, which support most of the dome's weight and contribute to its rigidity.

If we look up and around, the octagon transitions through pendentives to form a circle, where there is a decorative frieze with the coats of arms of the Republic and its six provinces. This circle is a metal ring that supports the entablature above the pendentives. From here, inside the dome void, 16 mixed steel and concrete interior columns emerge, outlining its circular shape and concealed by a stone cladding. Between these interior columns are large windows that illuminate the interior "rotunda" which houses the statue of the Republic of Cuba.

In addition, the drum has an outer ring of thirty-two Corinthian columns that form the outer peristyle of the drum of the double colonnade, which has a neoclassical appearance. The columns of the peristyle do not assume a structural role. They are made of pieces of artificial stone later assembled by steel rods.

A transverse bracing system is used in the second level of the lower drum. This system connects each inner column to two outer columns and acts as tie rods to limit the loads in the flaring pressure plane and thus to prevent deformations. They contribute to stiffening the perimeter ring with pairs of steel beams so that each inner column is connected to two outer columns (Fig. 6).

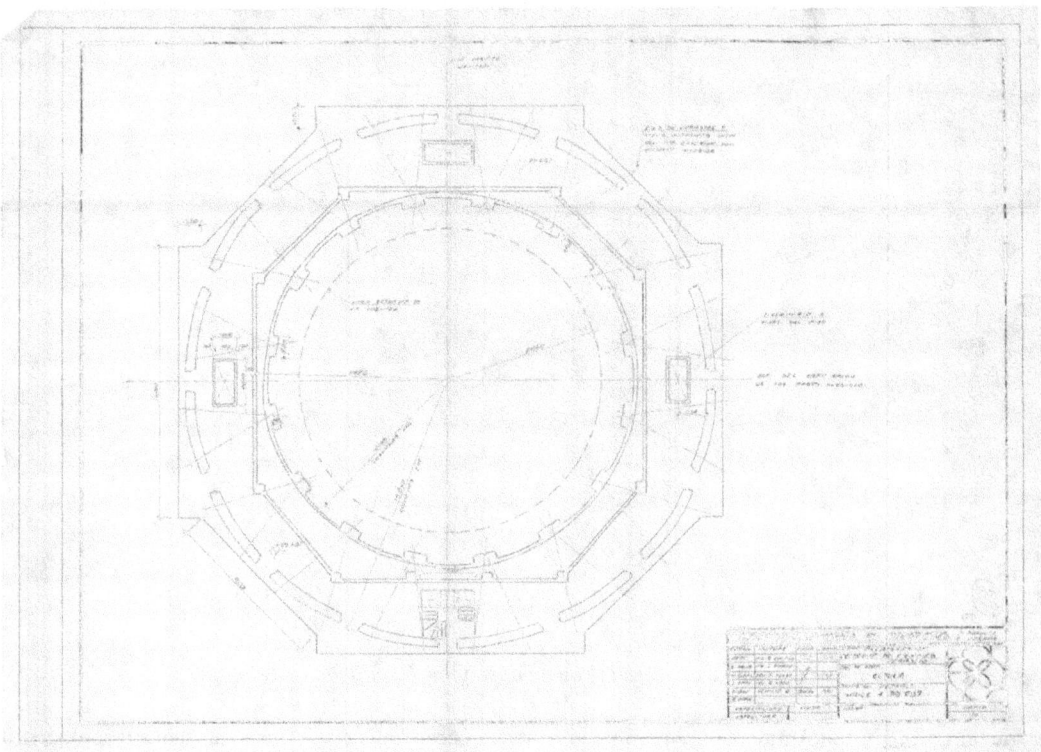

Figure 6: Groundfloor at level +33,28m. Source: Hand-drawn plans of the Capitol building.

The dome was the last part to be built, based on the drawing by the Cuban architect Eugenio Rayneri Piedra. The engineers of the New York firm modified and gave the final design to its load-bearing structure, respecting the proportions and shapes of the original drawings. The dome does not follow the classical load transmission scheme, whereby forces are transmitted through the outer membrane. When examining the cross-section of the dome from the point of view of structural behaviour, the ratio between the thickness of the dome and its span is very small, and the volume of the lantern is too large to be supported by this thin shell. Therefore, it is unquestionably the case that Rayneri's plan (Fig. 7) only shows formal and dimensional intentions but does not contain any information on the construction detail, nor does it include a coherent structural design, delegating the design and structural calculation to the American company.

Figure 7: Dome final drawing, by the Arch. Eugenio Rayneri Piedra. As it can be seen, only the desirable shape of the dome is specified. Internal structure does not appear, as it will be later designed by Purdy & Henderson. Source: Hand-drawn plans of the Capitol Building.

Due to this shape limitation and the excessive slenderness of the outer membrane, the dome would have collapsed as it would not have withstood the horizontal thrusts. According to Foraboschi this would be an incoherent case of structural design that does not bring together knowledge of the material, its use and the structural solution [5]. Therefore, the choice of an internal steel bearing substructure that decreases the lateral thrusts and converts the loads of the dome into vertical point forces transmitted to the supports is understandable (Fig. 8).

The detailed drawing of the dome (Fig. 9) shows that there is a change in the cross-section and consequently also in the structural behaviour of the dome. The lower part is entirely made of in-situ reinforced concrete (reinforced concrete ribs and shell), while in the upper half, although the shell is also of reinforced concrete, the ribs become metal elements from that point onwards and are connected to the rest of the metal substructure. Geometric verifications revealed that this section change occurs near an angle of 30°. This indicates that the steel structure is used from the point of view of the possible hinge formation of a kinematic mechanism, in the case of exceeding the limit of the lower horizontal thrust. This construction decision coincides with the later analysis of Blasi and Foraboschi on the structural behaviour of pointed domes, who stated that this value of the angle of impact (30°-35°) is independent of the thickness of the shell, the span of the dome or the specific weight and that it was already known experimentally in dome construction [6].

The internal structure of the Cuban National Capitol consists of four braced trusses (TD1, TD2 in Fig. 10 and transversally TD3, TD4) that transfer their forces to 8 of the 16 columns that make up the drum. In addition to supporting its own weight and that of the dome frame, this internal structural system must support the weight of the lantern, the access stairs to the dome, as well as the weight of the inner dome and the false ceiling. The geometry of the dome is defined by these trusses, as a total of 16 metal profiles define its curvature and act as ribs of the dome.

According to the Capitol Book, the structure of the lantern was left undefined by the engineers who drew up the project. The final solution was finally adopted as a result of decisions taken on site to reinforce it against the prevailing winds. The structure of the lantern is also made of metal and is supported by the beams of the collar.

Figure 8: Axonometry of the Capitol dome and detail of the inner structure of the cupola. Left: Metallic inner framework of the cupola. Right: exterior image of the dome. Authors' images

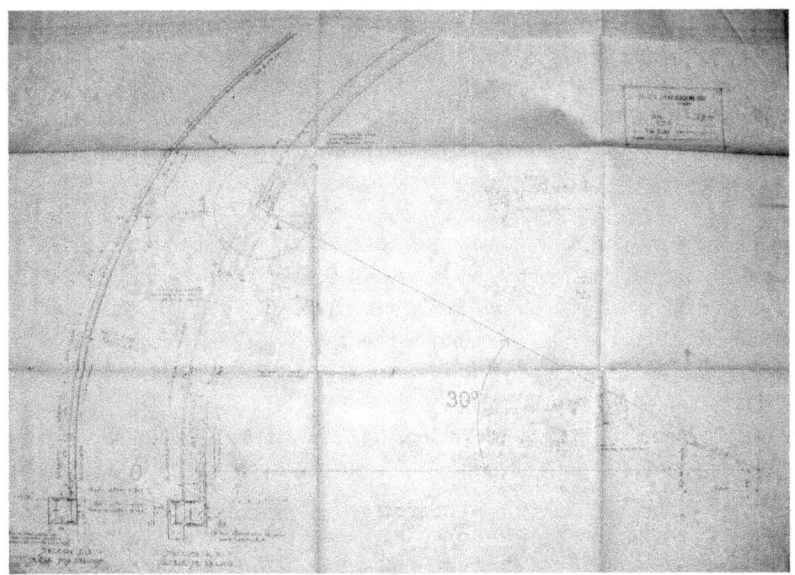

Figure 9: Detail of the dome section, where the angle of the material transition can be distinguished. Points 0 and 1 are respectively the starting and ending points of the reinforced concrete ribs. At point 1 the steel rib (which is part of the steel truss) starts. The overlap length of bars for the connection of the ribs can be seen (Point 1). Authors' analysis based on the hand-drawn plans of the Capitol Building.

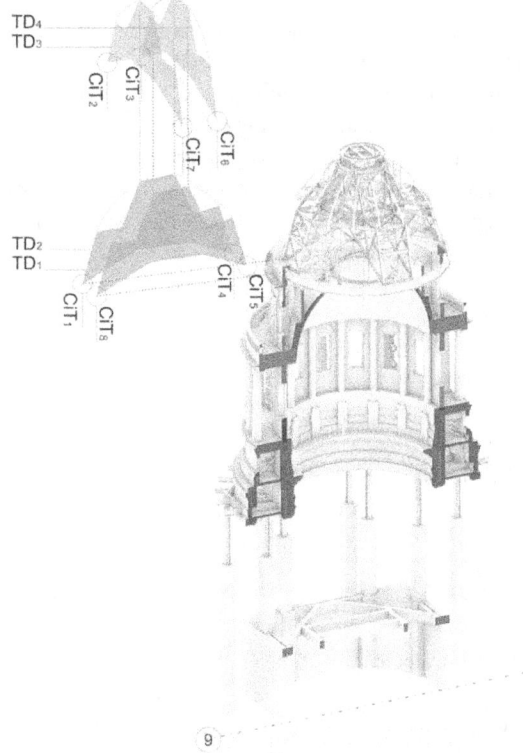

Figure 10: Metallic inner framework of the cupola (reinforced concrete nerves and shell are not shown to visualize the internal dome's structure). Authors' image.

Conclusions

One of the premises that the American company and the Havana Construction Supervision had to face was the necessary adaptation of the new design of the structural system to an already partially-begun work and to a pre-designed neoclassical formal system. In addition, due to the rush to finish the building for the Pan-American Conference in 1928, the structural solutions had to be designed while the work was being carried out.

The mixed nature of the construction of the National Capitol of Cuba can be seen in three aspects. Firstly, it responds in some way to its historical and cultural moment: it is a work designed with a classical 19th century construction methodology (through the structural use of stone and brick walls, vaults, stone columns, etc.) in which some technological improvements of the time are introduced (such as reinforced concrete walls and slabs, pillars, beams and steel trusses), which gives the complex a mixed character.

Secondly, it alternates local materials from Cuba (stone from the island's quarries and jiquí wood for piles) with advanced technology and solutions imported from the United States (compressed air for stone working and carving).

Finally, the structural system itself, is composed of mixed steel and reinforced concrete solutions, because of a later structural adaptation that lacked a previous bar modelling study.

The dome was conceived as a non-self-supporting composite dome, braced and working in collaboration with a very complex internal steel structure consisting basically of four steel trusses. The steel structure functioned as a concealed support for a stone skin that served as both cladding and colossal structure.

This construction euphemism can also be seen in the structural behavior of the dome itself: the lower part differs from the upper part, as they are built differently. The upper part is an upper surface of revolution formed by metal profiles whose contour is a circular arch and a reinforced concrete cap. It transmits the loads from the lantern and the dome envelope to the trusses, which in turn transmit them to the lower supports and the lower reinforced concrete cap. The lower part is a surface of revolution formed by reinforced concrete ribs whose contour is an arch of the same circumference and a reinforced concrete shell. This part of the dome functions structurally as such, being a self-supporting shell that receives the loads from the upper part. At its base, the reinforced concrete ribs and the concrete shell are joined to the column crowning beams, transmitting uniform loads.

The absence of sturdy abutments at the base of the dome is compensated for by various bracing systems to resist the possible hurricane wind thrusts that the dome may receive, due to the climatic conditions of the Caribbean.

The desire to erect an emblematic building representative of Machado's political achievements forced the construction of a more monumental dome. To satisfy his intentions, the idea of a self-supporting dome, as it was the first design by E. Rayneri Sorrentino and his son E. Rayneri Piedra in 1911, had to be discarded in the course of the construction work. This necessitated a complex internal support system to bear the intended loads, with properly braced steel pillars, beams and trusses, and an outer dome consisting of a coated concrete shell.

Acknowledgments

This initiative was possible thanks to the strategic plan of the University of Alicante, Sub-Directorate of Cooperation for Development and Internationalization, who committed to carry out and finance several institutional lines of action (research projects, documentation, dissemination, etc.), among them, the Havana Project, managed since 2008 by the Research Group AEDIFICATIO (Construction, technology, research and development) of the University of Alicante, allowed to carry out this research in Cuba between 2009 and 2011.

References

[1] J. De Las Cuevas Toraya, *500 años de construcciones en Cuba*, La Habana: Chavín. Servicios Gráficos y Editoriales, 2001, S.L.
[2] R. Segre, El sistema monumental en La Ciudad de La Habana: 1900-1930. Revista Ciudad y Territorio. Enero- junio 1985. Pág. pp.17-26.
[3] J.W. Cody, *Exporting American Architecture, 1870- 2000*, London: Routledge (Taylor & Francis Group), 2003. doi:10.4324/9780203986585.
[4] M. Mestre Martí, P.M. Jiménez Vicario, M.A. Ródenas López, El Capitolio de La Habana, geometría y proporción a través de sus planos originales. EGA Expresión Gráfica Arquitectónica, [S.l.], Vol.23, No.33, pp.40-51, jul. 2018. ISSN 2254-6103. https://doi.org/10.4995/ega.2018.8859.
[5] P. Foraboschi, The central role played by structural design in enabling the construction of buildings that advanced and revolutionized architecture. Construction and Building Material, Vol. 114, July 2016, pp. 956-976.
[6] C. Blasi and P. Foraboschi, Analytical approach to collapse mechanisms of circular masonry arch, *Journal of Structural Engineering– ASCE* (United States), Vol. 120, No. 8, 1994, pp.2288–309. doi: 10.1061/(ASCE)0733-9445 (1994)120:8(2288).

Women engineers in UK construction research establishments in the mid-20th century. A preliminary survey.

Nina Baker
Independent Engineering Historian

Introduction

From the advent of the Industrial Revolution in the late 19th century to the start of the First World War in 1914 engineering had made astonishing advances. Steam-driven equipment of many sorts was ubiquitous, the automobile becoming more widely seen and aeroplanes just taking to the skies. However, the UK construction industry had, to a great extent, been left behind in comparison and was mostly still relying on the crafts of many centuries, even when asked to use innovations such as reinforced concrete. What relevant research had been done, into the theories of structures and thermodynamics for instance, in the great universities, did not generally reach the ordinary building contractors, and there were no published standards or specifications. Some of these problems emerged during the war itself and in 1915 the UK government set up a committee to provide for scientific and industrial research. At the end of the war there was a desire to demolish old slums and provide 'homes fit for heroes', at a time when both materials and skilled men had been swallowed up by the war, although many entrepreneurs did try to promote untested innovations. In 1920 the Building Research Board (BRB) was set up and H.O. Weller appointed to run it, establishing its first facility, at East Acton, near London in 1921 [1]. Through a variety of names, structures, locations and funding models this research service for the building world continues to this day [2].

Construction history remains loosely defined but is generally taken to cover the people, methods, materials and systems which have allowed buildings and other structures to be built. Addis' analysis of papers in the Journal of Construction History found that about 9% of articles were biographical and a total of 11% related to the histories of organisations, trades and professions. [3] For most of the period since 1800 (78% of articles) it was difficult or, at best, unusual for women to have access to the sort of training that would enable them to take significant roles in construction and many of the biographical papers relate to the well-known men of various eras. However, it is millennia since construction of most sorts was the outcome of a single individual's work and the emerging stories of the essential work of people other than "The great man" are starting to attract more interest in all historical fields, e.g. the "Hidden Figures" women at NASA [4].

Although many women had worked successfully at all levels of engineering work during the First World War and some were starting to get relevant university degrees [5] the post-war period was overtly hostile to them remaining in or entering engineering at the professional level [6]. However, the inter-war era saw many women enter the defence-related scientific civil service and have successful careers and the 1940s seems to have been when this also happened in the construction-related government research organisations.

Government And Industry Research Organisations

The first half of the 20th century saw many government research establishments and committees established for numerous industrial sectors. Where the government did not provide one, many industries set up their own co-operative research associations under a 1916 scheme which gave them some state support until about 1932. Many continued in various forms and from time to time the government was able to provide some financial aid. In 1965 there were some 48 such associations [7] but most had no direct connection with construction, apart from the Research Association of British Paint, Colour and Varnish Manufacturers, the Timber Research and Development Association and the Heating and Ventilating Research Association. Presumably the remaining specialisms in construction found their needs adequately served by the government's Building (BRS), Fire (FRS), Forest Products (FPRS) and Fuel Research Stations (FuRS) and the Transport and Road Research Laboratory (TRRL).

The Fuel Research Station (Monkhouse 1959) was the first to be set up, at East Greenwich in 1919, and was to work on the usage and uses of various fuels, including the development of smokeless fuels and the production of oil from coal. As coal was the principal fuel until after the Second World War, there were soon a plethora of other coal-related laboratories, both government and industry-funded.

The BRS (later Building Research Establishment BRE) was asked to do general research into the physical and chemical sciences of buildings, their materials, structures and behaviour.

The BRS was also expected to undertake contract research for companies and to answer quicker questions from its developing body of knowledge. It was funded by a varying mixture of state and commercial funding, until full privatisation in the late 20th century.

Women in the Civil Service

Some of the very first women to be regularly employed in public service in the UK were Post Office telegraphists in the 1860s, but it would be a long time before women were able to join the civil service establishment (permanent staff cohort) on an equal basis with men (1929) and yet longer before they were on equal pay and grading systems (1970s). For most of that period women were either required by law, or expected by social convention, to 'retire' on marriage or at least on the birth of a first child. Exemptions from the so-called 'marriage bar' were possible for women of exceptional calibre, where the (male) director of their service was willing to make a case for them to remain. In the period 1930-38, eight such outstanding women were able to remain after marriage [9]. Such male 'allies' would have made a big difference for women entering and progressing in the male-majority technical grades.

Entry by some women into scientific research within the UK civil service was possible and several who entered in the 1920s and 1930s had full careers in, for example, the Royal Aircraft Establishment [10]. It may have been that the structured environment of government service, following the 1929 Tomlin Commission, [11] was a slightly more welcoming one than industry, although few such women rose to the senior grades of the scientific civil service. It would however take until the Second World War before women joined the Building Research Station.

Sources for identifying women who worked at, or were on advisory committees for, the BRS and its sister organisations have been limited to those available directly online or loaned items from helpful colleagues, since most of this research was done after the advent of Covid19 and resultant closures of physical archives. Since the majority of the women do not even have Wikipedia pages, let alone entries in the Oxford Dictionary of National Biography, much of the research has had to be from scratch. Starting points included BRB annual reports to find names, which were then followed through using biographical, genealogical and bibliographical sources.

Fire Safety

It is not surprising that the bombing raids of the Second World War focused minds on the fire safety of various sorts of buildings and the fire resistance of materials. Some of the most influential research into the behaviour of fire and smoke in buildings was by Margaret Law MBE BSc CEng FIFireE FSFPE (1928-2017), who was considered by her contemporaries to be a pioneer in the, then new, field of fire engineering [12]. Law's first job after university was at the government's Fire Research Station in Borehamwood, in 1952 - only 3 years after it was established. Her experimental work featured on the FRS's research report cover in 1952 (Fig.1) [13]. During her 20 year association with the FRS (which later became part of the Building Research Establishment) she contributed to 34 Fire Research Notes [14]. The topics ranged from the small, domestic issues of cooker fires in caravans and prefabs, to the cold war concerns of the potential for nuclear radiation to start fires: "On The Possibility of Ignition of Materials by Radiation from Nuclear Explosions". Her interests were in the effects of materials and structures on fires and how they spread, such as how fire moves through high rise flats with balconies, or the optimum protective coating for structural steelwork. The recent Grenfell Tower fire disaster not long after her death shows how that aspect of Law's work remains relevant [15].

Figure 1. Fire Research Station 1952 Report [14]

In 1974 Law moved to the Ove Arup Partnership to work on the fire engineering for their major projects, and was part of the specialist team that investigated the Bradford City Stadium fire which killed 56 people in 1985, which led to the end of wooden grandstands. Her extensive theoretical and practical research [16] led to changes in Building Regulations, Codes of Practice, and design guides, such that she became one of the world's leading fire scientists.

Law's near-contemporary, Monica M. Raftery BSc (1929-2009) worked first at the British Coal Utilisation Research Association and then spent the rest of her career at the FRS, working on explosivity of industrial dusts and the behaviour of fire in domestic settings. Her work considered the safety or otherwise of modern bedding and soft furnishings [17] as well as the general behaviour of fires in ventilated rooms. As timber framed housing became more prevalent, in 1987 the FRS was asked to investigate if a serious fire could result from membrane ignition particularly where cavity barriers were ineffective of absent. Of the three membranes approved for use at that time, Raftery's work [18] showed that thermoplastic film membranes would be the least likely to support a fire.

Women engineers in UK construction research establishments in the mid-20th century. A preliminary survey

Concerns about fire fatalities in homes in multiple occupation (HMOs) led the Ministry of Housing and Local Government to commission the Fire Research Station in Borehamwood to look into the fire risks in particular. Winifred Nora Daxon (nee Hammond) (1922-2007) undertook the research on this, publishing her results in 1971. She found that portable oil-fuelled heaters (paraffin) were the main cause of fires in HMOs and that:

> "The occupant of a multi-occupancy dwelling is more likely to die in a fire than in a single occupancy, is about 4 times as likely to become a non-fatal casualty and is about 14 times as likely to be placed in a dangerous situation [19]."

HMOs continue to be higher risk from fire than single occupancies and, although paraffin heaters are largely a thing of the past, the risks they (and portable gas heaters) pose continue to be highlighted in HMO regulation and advice [20].

Building Materials

The development and testing of novel building materials was a large part of the work of the BRS between the wars. Reinforcement in concrete was still considered a new technique and many ideas came onto the market to replace traditional masonry work with simulated 'stone' blocks. The masonry industry had been significantly hit by the loss of time-served masons due to the war and that there were not many young men were entering apprenticeships due to the very demanding nature of the work and its associated health risks (silicosis of the lungs). Since the major component of the costs of including traditional stonework in new buildings was the wages for the skilled masons, many building materials suppliers decided that there would be a market for a reconstituted or artificial stone, which could be made in any shape or size required by the client. Mrs. Anne Greaves, a successful Yorkshirewoman who ran her own Weeland Quarries company, devised her own 'Betna cast stone' which she believed would resist attack by acid rain better than real stone.

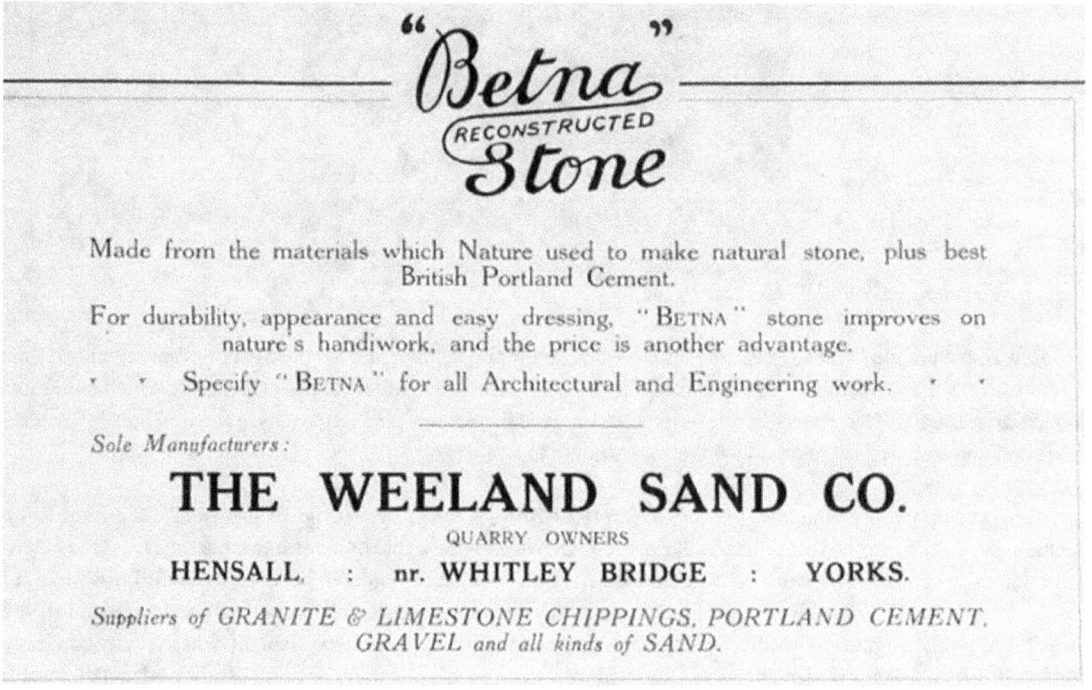

Figure 2. Betna Advertisement [23]

In her 1929 article for The Woman Engineer she commented that

> "Mr. Brady and his assistants at the Government Research Station at Watford have been making very extensive tests on this point... ..... The Director told me they had been doing a very great deal of experimental work on reconstructed stone..." [21]

Greaves was also very well informed on the science of cements, fully appreciating the benefits of not using too much water in a mix, probably because she was an active (and first female) member of the Institute of Quarrying. Her Betna stone was used in several major contracts, for a hospital and some housing.

A generation later, innovative reinforcing materials were being sought for concretes and Valerie Laws, BSc, MSc, having started out doing strength and structures of nylon and wool fibres for fabrics, for Australia's Commonwealth Scientific and Industrial Research Organization, moved to the UK in the early 1960s to work on the properties of coconut fibres, for the Tropical Products Research Institute. She became a Senior Scientific Officer at the BRS, sometimes also at the National Physical laboratory, working on the use of various fibres for reinforcing concretes [22].

Method study

Given the low level of basic scientific understanding of materials and techniques, it is perhaps not surprising that the first 20 years of the BRS were fully engaged looking into those and the need to address efficiency and optimisation was not considered until the war years, when new bricklaying methods and the labour times for housebuilding were examined for the first time. In 1946 a Method Study department was set up, to look at "industrial psychology and physiology, the efficiency of mechanical equipment in terms of economy in labour, and the comparison in labour yield of different forms of construction [23]."

Lemessany and Clapp were the duo that led in this field. Margaret Alison Clapp BSc (1925-1994) was at the BRS from 1959 (maybe earlier) as a Senior Scientific Officer, initially publishing reports on costs and productivity on building sites, as sole or lead author, from 1963-73 [24]. Her work must have involved extended visits to the then exclusively-male environment of building sites, her achievements are all the more remarkable considering she was described by a colleague as "... very quiet and unassuming lady, diligent and effective but not particularly out-going [25]." From the early 1970s Clapp worked with Lemessany. Dr Julia Lemessany (c.1928-? Lemeššanyiova) was originally from the former Czechoslovakia. Although nothing is known of her earlier life, it is thought she came to the UK after the Soviet invasion in the late 1960s, and was naturalised as a UK citizen in 1974 [26]. In contrast to Clapp, Lemessany was recalled as a forceful, determined character and from 1973-87 she was lead author on papers with E.E. Amos and later with Clapp, all on building economics, and labour/materials requirements for local authority construction. Lemessany and Clapp's works continue to be widely cited but many in the industry today do not realise they were both women.

Heating and ventilation

When the Building Research Board started work, by far the majority of British homes were heated by coal, many areas did not have electricity at all and even gas supplies were not ubiquitous, there not being national grids for either gas or electricity at that time [27].

The only woman to be mentioned in Lea's history of the Building Research Station [28], despite never working there and despite some women in her field who were working there at the time but not mentioned, Dr Margaret Fishenden DSc, FIoP (nee White) (1889-1977), was an academic and industrial researcher renowned for her work on air pollution and domestic heating in an almost entirely coal-fired era.

Women engineers in UK construction research establishments in the mid-20th century. A preliminary survey

She joined the Manchester corporation air pollution advisory board in 1916, and began her work on the efficiency or otherwise of coal fires and domestic grates, publishing several books and important reports for the Fuel Research Board. Having gained a DSc in 1919, in 1922 she moved to the Department of Scientific and Industrial Research, joining Dr C. H. Lander and O. A. Saunders, who would be her co-authors for many years. The trio moved to the Department of Engineering, Mechanical and Motive Power at Imperial College in 1932, where she rose to senior lecturer and, in 1947, assistant professor and reader in applied heat, a remarkable achievement for a woman at that time. Her work at Imperial College was largely on heat transfer, on which topic she authored many papers and reports, including for the shipbuilding industry. Her work with the BRB was as an advisor on its heating and ventilation advisory committee, from (or before) 1934 until her retirement in 1957 [29]. This committee (chaired by Sir Alfred Egerton) ensured research was done to ascertain such basics as what standards for home insulation or home heating levels should be set [30]. The standard for home heating was set very low: the background temperature throughout a home should be maintained at 10ºC with additional heating in occupied rooms such as living rooms. More or less no homes were being built with insulation, except the incidental effect of any wall cavities.

Work to clarify what was needed to ensure homes were comfortably warm at an affordable price was undertaken by the duo of Black & Milroy, who published extensively on heating and ventilation for high density social housing and for office blocks. Flora Black BSc (nee Weir, 1919-1998) gained a degree in Natural Philosophy from the University of Aberdeen in 1940, did 2 years research there and then joined the Ministry of Works to do housing design. In 1950 she moved to the Department of Science and Industry's Building Research Establishment at Garston and also published her first sole-author paper, based on her experimental work at the Ministry of Works Field Test Unit at the Thatched Barn Hotel, Barnet. She remained with the BRS, progressing from Senior Scientific Officer to Principal Scientific Officer and retired in 1978. Over the course of her productive and influential career she published numerous BRS Reports and Notes, as well as journal papers. The junior half of the partnership was Elisabeth Anne Milroy (1921-2006), who had a social work diploma and the Chartered Surveyor's Institute's Women Housing Manager's certificate, for which she was awarded the 1945 Octavia Hill Prize for getting the highest marks. Her first professional work was on requisitioning houses and arranging for new homes for bombed-out families. By 1952 she was working at the Building Research Establishment (BRE) and had co-authored her first paper, 'House Heating and the Tenant: Experiments at Abbots Langley'. She remained at the BRE until at least 1969, mostly working as Flora W. Black's assistant and occasional co-author, despite her lack of an engineering education.

Building standards

The slum clearances and the urgency of the housing shortage, following the First World War, led to pioneering housing surveys, mainly in London boroughs but also in Birmingham, Manchester, and Edinburgh. These surveys were commissioned by public authorities and also by private charitable groups hoping to establish social housing associations in their areas. These surveys were done by Irene Turberville Barclay (nee Martin) OBE, FRICS (1894-1989) [31], the first woman to qualify as a chartered surveyor with the Surveyors' Institution (now the Royal Institution of Chartered Surveyors), followed by Evelyn Perry who then joined Barclay in partnership as surveyors and housing managers. Barclay's unique contribution was to involve the local residents in the surveys. She went on to campaign and find funding for (principally, but amongst others) St Pancras Housing Association, for which she also did some design work, as well as managing the properties on a contract basis. Her work significantly raised the standards of space, services (including bathrooms) and building design quality of the homes as well as the provision of gardens, play spaces and social provision for the estates. This at a time when (apocryphally perhaps) it was often openly said of poor people that "if you give these people baths, they will only keep coal in them", to which her riposte was "Why should anyone who has a coal bunker put coal in the bath [32]."

Although not qualified in engineering specifically, Barclay's expertise in heating and ventilation for mass housing was widely recognised and she was actively involved in the Building Research Board's Post-War Studies reconstruction committee on Heating and Ventilation, where she was joined by one other woman, Helen Brown, an Oxford city councillor [33]. Barclay was also active with the Women's Advisory Council on Solid Fuel (unkindly nicknamed The Solid Women) [34]. The WACSF advised women on the selection, use and workings of solid fuel domestic appliances, and advised the industry and government on potential British Standards and design. In this, it did similar work to its better-known sister organisations – the Electrical Association for Women, and the Women's Gas Council.

Picking up from Barclay's pioneering work on housing standards was Evelyn Judith Cibula BSc (nee Elbogen, 1927-2013), who came to the UK as a pre-war Jewish refugee from Poland, and gained her degree from London University. Unusually for the era, Cibula continued her work with the BRS after her marriage, and published a dozen reports on international building standards between 1970-80. Winifred Vere Hole, MA, PhD (c.1913-1992), was of a generation of young adventurous Australians who travelled to the UK in search of opportunities not available at home. Arriving in the early 1950s she had a 30-year career as a social anthropologist at the BRS, gained a PhD from London University, on working class housing. Between 1965-83 she published some 15 reports and is particularly remembered for her work on how post-war social changes were changing the ways in which residents ('users') actually used the indoor and outdoor spaces in local authority housing estates. Her 1966 report on play facilities found that there was no substitute for small playgrounds on each estate and that inactive as well as active play had both to be catered for [35]. An explicitly feminist woman who had little patience with her home country's then misogynist culture, Hole was able to see past her own privilege to discern the needs and preferences of others [36].

Discussion

This necessarily brief survey of some of the work of some of the women scientific civil servants at the BRS/BRE up to about the 1980s, demonstrates the wide range of scientific, technical and sociological contributions they made, especially in the period after the Second World War. It demonstrates that, even when their work is still recalled and cited, the fact that they were women has often been forgotten. Some might argue that this demonstrates that their work was the more important thing about them and that their sex or gender was and is not relevant to the history of the BRS. Whilst we know that some were explicitly feminist, during the 'Second Wave of Feminism', others were either pragmatic or were too immersed in their work to show any opinions on that issue. The construction and extraction industries remain amongst the least diverse in the UK, especially at site level, so one benefit of bringing the work of women to a wider audience is to demonstrate girls and young women that women have been doing important work in those industries for a long time.

The other reason this search for the work of women scientific civil servants is worthwhile, would be equally applicable to their male contemporaries: to remind us that our knowledge today is not just the world-changing discoveries of a handful of famous men much praised in their own lifetimes. It is also dependent upon the contributions of the men and women who never rose to such fame: brick by brick their discoveries set the foundations for each improvement we take for granted in the built environment today.

Acknowledgements

I would like to acknowledge the invaluable help of fellow construction historian, Fiona Smyth, who spared time from her busy life to scan material from her private archive of Building Research Station documents, which would otherwise have been impossible for me to access during the Covid19 restrictions. Also, a retired member of Building Research Establishment staff who shared recollections of some of the women who worked there.

References

[1] F.M. Lea, *Science and building: a history of the Building Research Station*, London: HMSO, 1971.
[2] BRE Group, Our History. Accessed 14 September 2020: https://www.bregroup.com/about-us/our-history/

[3] B. Addis, The contribution made by the Journal of Construction History towards establishing the history of construction as an academic discipline, *Proceedings of the 1st Conference of the Construction History Society,* Cambridge: The Construction History Society, 2014.

[4] M.L. Shetterly, *Hidden Figures: The Untold Story of the African American Women Who Helped Win the Space Race,* William Collins, 2017

[5] N. Baker, 'Early Women Engineering Graduates from Scottish Universities', *Women's History Magazine,* Vol. 60, Summer 2009, pp. 21-30.

[6] HMSO, *Restoration of Pre-War Practices Act 1919,* London: HMSO, 1919.

[7] Hansard. 1965. Parliamentary answer, 15 June 1965. Accessed 1 October 2020: https://hansard.parliament.uk/Commons/1965-06-15/debates/9dc99587-a71a-41a1-a44f-33211ff4b61e/Co-OperativeIndustrialResearchAssociations

[8] DSIR, *Building Research Station Annual Report for the DSIR,* London: HMSO, 1926.

[9] H. Martindale, *Women Servants of The State 1870-1938,* George Allen & Unwin Ltd, 1938.

[10] M. Freudenberg, *Negative Gravity: A Life of Beatrice Shilling*, Charlton Publications, 2013; M. Freudenberg, *Clear Air Turbulence: A Life of Anne Burns*, Charlton Publications, 2009.

[11] B. Morgan, A History of Women in the UK Civil Service, 2015. Accessed 14 September 2020: http://civilservant.org.uk/library/2015_history_of_women_in_the_civil_service.pdf

[12] K. Almand, The fire engineering community loses one of its early leaders, 2017, NPFA blog. Accessed 22 February 2021: https://nfpa.jiveon.com/community/nfpa-today/blog/2017/09/18/the-fire-engineering-community-loses-one-of-its-early-leaders; Lane, B. 2017. Obituary: Professor Margaret Law MBE BSc CEng FIFireE FSFPE. International Fire Professional. Accessed 19 October 2020: http://pavilion-live.co.uk/ifp-news/2017/09/20/professor-margaret-law-mbe-bsc-ceng-fifiree-fsfpe/

[13] DSIR, Fire research 1952, DSIR and Fire Offices' Committee, London: HMSO, 1952. Image is out of copyright and deemed to be in the public domain.

[14] IAFSS. Fire Safety Science Digital Archive. Accessed 22 February 2021: https://www.iafss.org/publications/frn/author/1602

[15] Grenfell Tower Enquiry. Accessed 19 February 2021: https://www.grenfelltowerinquiry.org.uk/

[16] N. Law, Some selected papers by Margaret Law: engineering fire safety. London: Arup, 2002. Accessed 19 October 2020: https://www.arup.com/perspectives/publications/books/section/engineering-fire-safety-some-selected-papers-from-margaret-law

[17] M.M. Raftery, Ignition response and fire test behaviour of modern upholstered furniture, Building Research Establishment, Information paper 17/82, 1982.

[18] M.M. Raftery, Fire behaviour of breather membranes, Building Research Establishment, Information paper 87,6, 1987.

[19] W.N. Daxon, Fire risk in dwellings in multiple occupation, Borehamwood: Fire Research Station, 1971. Fire Research Notes 817; also published in Fire Safety Science, 1971.

[20] Essex Chief Officers Specialist Housing Group. 1985. Housing Act 1985 - Section 352. Houses in Multiple Occupation: Adequate Means of Escape from Fire and Other Fire Precautions. Accessed 3 October 2020: https://www.southend.gov.uk/downloads/file/2313/fire-precautions-for-hmos-code-of-practicepdf .

[21] A. Greaves, 'Cast Stone – The Stone Industry up-to-date', *The Woman Engineer,* Vol. 2, No.19, 1929, Women's Engineering Society. Accessed 22 February 2021: http://www2.theiet.org/resources/library/archives/research/wes/WES_Vol_2a.html; DSIR. 1935. Report of the Building Research Board for the year 1934. London: HMSO. Page 164: Her reference to Mr. Brady is presumed to be F.L. Brady, MSc, AIC, who published numerous reports and journal articles on the properties and performance of cementitious materials.

[22] A.J. Majumdar & V. Laws, Fibre cement composites: research at BRE, Composites, Vol. 10, Issue 1, January 1979, pp. 17-27.

[23] DSIR, *Report of The Building Research Board with The Report of The Director of Building Research for The Year 1946*, London: HMSO, 1949, p.19.

[24] M.A. Clapp, 'Weather conditions and productivity - Detailed study of five building sites', *Building Research Station: Reports Construction Series,* 1966. This is just one example of the papers she wrote in this period.

[25] Private communication from former BRE archivist, by email.

[26] TNA. 1974. Index entry of Naturalisation Certificate 016402 issued 16 December 1974. Home Office file number: L121809. The National Archives: HO 409/27/16402 Page 78.

[27] A. Clendinning, Demons and domesticity: a history of women and the London gas industry 1889-1939. McMaster University PhD thesis, 1999. Accessed 1 October 2020: http://hdl.handle.net/11375/6580 . In 1918 only 6% of all UK homes had an electrical supply of any kind.

[28] Lea, (Note 1).

[29] Private communication from former BRE archivist, (Note 25).

[30] WACSF. 1951. Heating, Cooking, and Hot Water Supplies for the Small House. A Policy Paper for the Women's Advisory Council on Solid Fuel. London: WACSF.

[31] de Silva, C. 2019. Barclay [née Martin], Irene Turberville. Oxford Dictionary of National Biography. 2019. Accessed 28 September 2020: https://www.oxforddnb.com/view/10.1093/ref:odnb/9780198614128.001.0001/odnb-9780198614128-e-111219; Barclay, I. 1976. People Need Roots. London: Bedford Square Press for the National Council of Social Service; RICS. 2017. Irene Barclay FRICS: Social housing pioneer. Accessed 28 September 2020: https://www.rics.org/uk/news-insight/latest-news/rics-150th-anniversary/pride-in-the-profession/irene-barclay-frics-social-housing-pioneer/

[32] Barclay, (Note 31), p. 23.

[33] DSIR, *Building Research Station Report for the DSIR,* London: HMSO, 1945. This report covers the whole war period.

[34] Barclay, (Note 31), p. 92.

[35] W.V. Hole, *Children's Play on Housing Estates*, BRS, London: HMSO, 1966.

[36] J. Beaumont, Dr Winifred Vere Hole, MA Hon. PhD. 1941 – 1944, 'Sociologist and Author. Extracts from article by Jeanette Beaumont', *Women's College Journal,* 1993, Accessed 12 October 2020: https://www.thewomenscollege.com.au/story/dr-winifred-vere-hole-ma-hon-phd-london-1941-44/

Construction Standardisation in Italian Service Stations (1930s-1950s) Projects by Luigi Piccinato and Mario Bacciocchi

Laura Greco
Department of Civil Engineering, University of Calabria, Cosenza, Italy

Introduction

In Italy in the 1960s, after the succession of modernist advancements and conservation actions, which distinguished the evolution of both techniques and the national building manufacturing sector, building industrialisation spread. These developments began in the 1930s, when – in the wake of European experiments – theoretical studies and design research, which engaged intellectuals, designers and industries, advanced. In this decade between the two world wars, metal construction and production of components for walls aimed at spreading assembly production methods, based on the principles and techniques of building industrialisation. The cultural promotion campaign conducted on Casabella by Giuseppe Pagano, the prototypes presented at the V Triennale of Milan in 1933, the development of samples of prefabricated and demountable houses and offices destined for the market of the Italian colonies in East Africa, and the handbooks published in those years, determined a favourable mood for the advancement of the Italian construction framework [1]. These events and circumstances paved the way for the development of an approach to the standardisation of architectural and construction elements, and for the dissemination of knowledge useful for construction process industrialisation. The Second World War (WWII) imposed a pause. New advancements in the long path of industrialisation marked the years of post-war reconstruction and the subsequent economic boom, due to the demand for buildings and spaces for offices, industry and services connected to the motorway network and the increase of the manufacturing sector. At the same time, the long dominance of masonry construction and the spread of reinforced concrete cast on site restrained the development of prefabrication and building industrialisation in the country. The low progress of mechanisation of the sector was a predominant feature of the national framework in the 1950s, as evidenced by the Ina-Casa public housing program, developed throughout the country.

From 1930-1960, the progression of building industrialisation was supported by research conducted by designers and companies and applied to some building types that proved to be suitable for the confirmation of experiments. These were buildings with original typological characteristics and essential functions, but – at the same time – they played a symbolic value in the definition of modern iconography representing the social transformations of the country. Motorway assistance buildings, such as kiosks and service stations, were a privileged field of this experimentation. The repertoires of standardised service stations designed by Luigi Piccinato in 1938-39 for Petrolea-Fiat and by Mario Bacciocchi in 1952 for Agip, are two examples of research in two key decades (1930s and 1950s). They highlight both similarities and divergences between the two periods and contribute to knowledge on relationships between the experimentation of the 1930s and the developments of the 1950s in the field of building industrialisation.

Service Stations and Construction Standardisation in Italy. Design Aspirations and Building Practice

The design and construction of service stations in Italy took shape starting from the first urban constructions, to extend in the mid-1920s to extra-urban roads, with the development of motorway segments in northern Italy (Lombardia and Veneto in particular). In the 1930s, service stations matured to have more specific characters and functional layout, distinguishing themselves for aesthetical and construction innovation of the buildings.

Construction Standardisation in Italian Service Stations (1930s-1950s)
Projects by Luigi Piccinato and Mario Bacciocchi

Inspired by the features of modern architecture, they used reinforced concrete canopies with aerodynamic shapes and glazing panels with thin metal frames [2].

They stood out as unique projects, despite the small size of the buildings, which were highly visible especially in urban areas, as testified by the projects for the service stations on the Venice-Padua motorway (1933), the buildings of Mario Cereghini in Lecco (1937), the Barnabone garage by Giovanni Muzio in Lodi (1933), and the station in Turin by Carlo Agular (1938).

The standardised kiosks for the sale of fuel represented a second and more essential topic of this typological sector. They were built using proto-industrialisation techniques. The kiosks were small boxes for the seller and the storage of products for vehicle assistance, equipped with systems for fuel distribution. They were mainly intended for urban streets and were integrated in the street landscape with increasingly visible and recognisable advertising elements. The kiosks, more than the service stations, participated in 1930s Italian experiments on metal constructions that affected mainly residences and facilities building, thanks to the work of the leading brands of Agip, Siap, Nafta, Aquila, Petrolea, Apir [3].

The repertoire of Luigi Piccinato (1899-1983) was part of this experience, including standard solutions for fuel distribution columns, kiosks, and service stations [4]. The techniques selected by Piccinato for metal construction applied to aesthetical configurations in some cases related to traditional and neoclassical languages. More frequently, this technique adopted innovative options, with modular and expandable layouts.

The Società Anonima Petrolea was founded in Milan on 23 September 1927 by the Russian Nepthesyndacat to trade its products in Italy [5]. In 1935 the S.A. Petrolea was purchased by Fiat (*Fabbrica Italiana Automobili Torino*), the factory founded in Turin in 1899 and leading brand in the Italian automotive industry. By means of the *Servizio Costruzioni e Impianti* (the company's technical department), Fiat promoted the construction of kiosks for the sale of its own oil products and the repair of motor vehicles [6]. Petrolea-Fiat engaged Luigi Piccinato to develop a fuel distribution network able to compete with the leading brands in Italy (Agip and NAFTA in particular). Piccinato's repertoire was based on the combination of four elements: the kiosk, the canopy, the advertising shaft, and the fuel pump. In the international context, these represented the characters of the increasing iconography of service stations. This process of standardisation of functional and architectural elements corresponded to the preference for construction standardisation, based on the use of profiles and metal sheets. The client, designer and builder participated in the definition of Piccinato's typological repertoire and in the production and assembly of components for kiosks and stations. The implementation of this standardisation effort was favoured by Piccinato's collaboration with Fiat and its technical department and, with the company Cos.Met., specialised in metal carpentry and was entrusted with the production of kiosks. The pioneering nature of the Italian manufacturing sector and the resistance of Agip in the 1930s to the spread of the new brand, restrained the construction program of Petrolea-Fiat. In any case, Piccinato's project constituted an important reference for Mario Bacciocchi's work in the 1950s.

In the post-war years, Agip faced a phase of economic difficulty, overcome thanks to the general improvement in the country's conditions. With the appointment of Enrico Mattei in 1946 as vice president of the *Azienda Generale Italiana Petroli* (Agip), the upgrading of the company's building assets began. Mattei created a favourable context. In fact, the development of mass motoring, and the upcoming national infrastructure plan – culminating in the construction of the Autostrada del Sole – stimulated a building program to rationalise the construction costs of kiosks and service stations, to ensure the widespread distribution of assistance points throughout the country and, finally, to define an image of the company in the increasing market of road assistance services.

In 1952, Mattei appointed Mario Bacciocchi (1902-1974) for the development of a catalogue of kiosks and service stations to be spread throughout the country's urban and extra-urban network [7].

In his projects, Bacciocchi expressed modernity through the characters of the three fundamental architectural elements of the service station: the kiosk, the canopy, the advertising shaft [8]. However, he re-elaborated their construction characteristics, making them compatible with the national context of the time, whose technological delay restrained the transfer of the foreign principles of industrialisation to the Italian situation. In fact, Bacciocchi, by selecting masonry structures combined with in situ cast reinforced concrete elements and external cladding in lithoceramics, preferred construction on site, limiting the use of industrialised components.

Evident analogies and decisive divergences, also determined by the different socio-economic contexts of reference, distinguished the two experiences, the analysis of which supports the investigation of these similarities and differences within the Italian construction framework between the 1930s and 1950s.

The Petrolea Repertoire by Luigi Piccinato

As anticipated, Luigi Piccinato's Petrolea-Fiat catalogue contained three basic types of kiosk (small, medium and large) and was marked by the characters of the glazed box, the canopy and of the advertising shaft. The architect produced some variants of each type, to provide dimensional and geometric alternatives. The small kiosk had a rectangular plan (2.15x1.60), with an overhanging canopy that protected the glazed box (Fig. 1). A first variant of this configuration involved the insertion of an advertising shaft for the Petrolea signs and a service space at the side of the box, where the fuel pumps were located. A third option was presented in two drawings dated 6 December 1938, which illustrated the project of the small kiosk with a long side canopy. The scheme (2.15x7.00m) had the glazed box on one end, and the advertising shaft on the opposite side. The entire system was connected by the canopy, below which there were four fuel pumps.

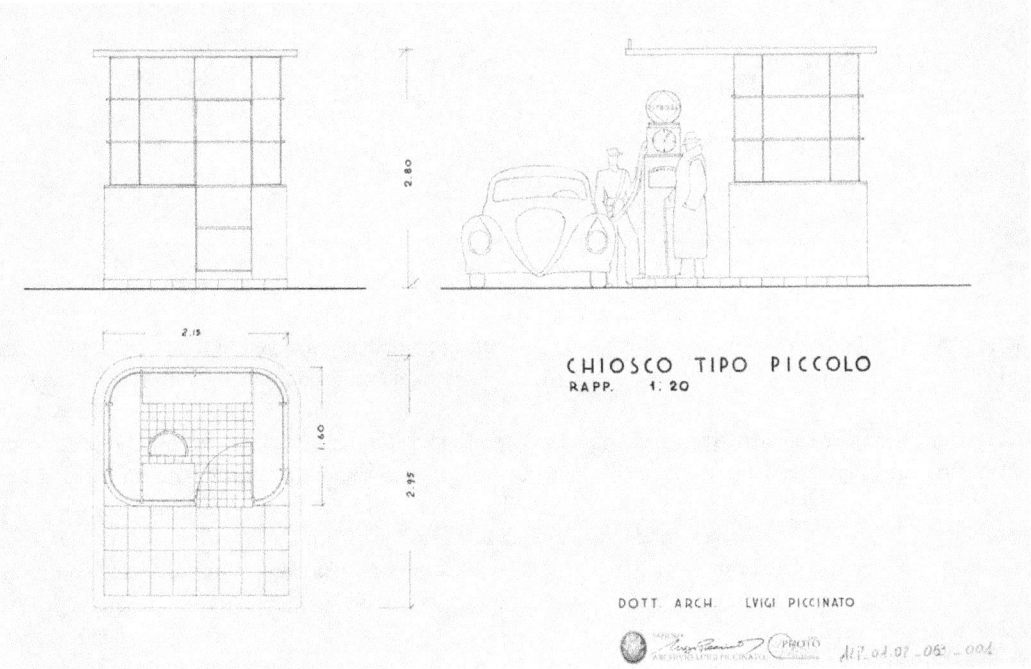

Fig. 1 Petrolea-Fiat small kiosk. Project: Luigi Piccinato, 1938. Source: Archivio Luigi Piccinato, Università di Roma "La Sapienza", Dipartimento di Pianificazione, Design, Tecnologia dell'Architettura (ALP)

The medium kiosk had a similar layout. A first configuration had a short canopy, while some variants had a long lateral roof to protect the fuel pumps (Fig. 2). Also, in this case, the kiosk was located at one end of the layout and, on the other, was the advertising shaft. The medium kiosk with long side canopy was presented at the Milan exhibition in 1939 (Fig. 3). The construction was developed by the company Cos.Met., as documented by the project dated 3 April 1939. The detailed study developed by the company did not modify the functional layout and the architectural features of Piccinato's proposal.

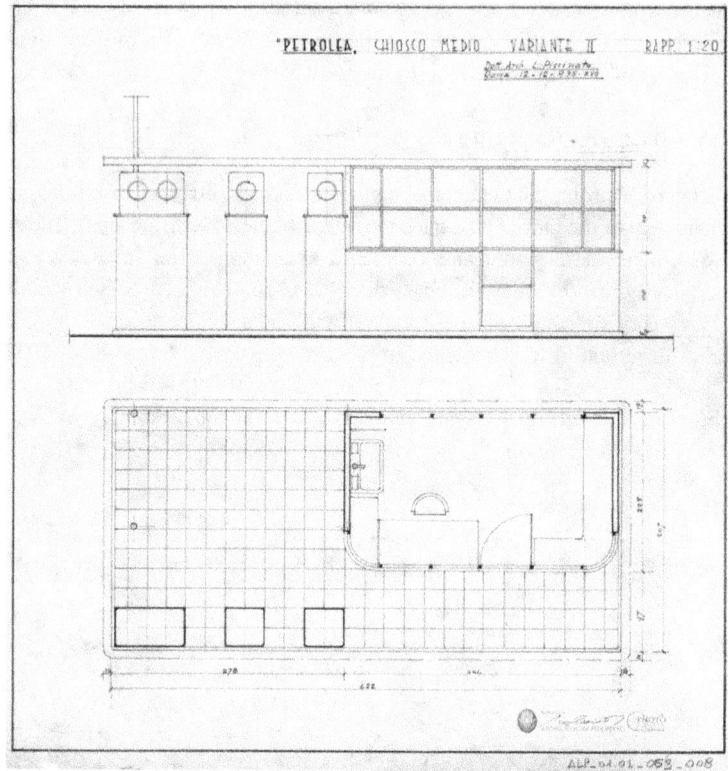

Fig. 2 Petrolea-Fiat medium kiosk with lateral canopy. Project: Luigi Piccinato, 1938. Source: ALP

In general, the design process moved from Piccinato's project, examined and updated by Fiat, and then was developed for production by the company Cos.Met. F. Cassinelli & C. Guercini, specialised in the manufacture of metal carpentry.

Some drawings, executed between April and May 1939, presented the updates advanced by Cos.Met. starting from Piccinato's first drawings and concerning a few dimensional adjustments and some details into the materials and components used. The metal structure consisted of L profiles (60x60 mm) for the uprights; the roof was solved with a framework of NP 50 profiles, metal plates and insulating panels. There was a linoleum floor inside the glazed box, while outside, the area protected by the canopy was paved with stoneware tiles. The innovation of Piccinato's proposal was therefore confirmed by the construction choices that considered the debate on mass construction. In fact, metal construction was promoted in Italy in the cultural and manufacturing debate as a useful option for the implementation of the principles of industrialised construction. On the other hand, materials such as linoleum were analysed and promoted in modern buildings as examples of durability, hygiene and aesthetic versatility.

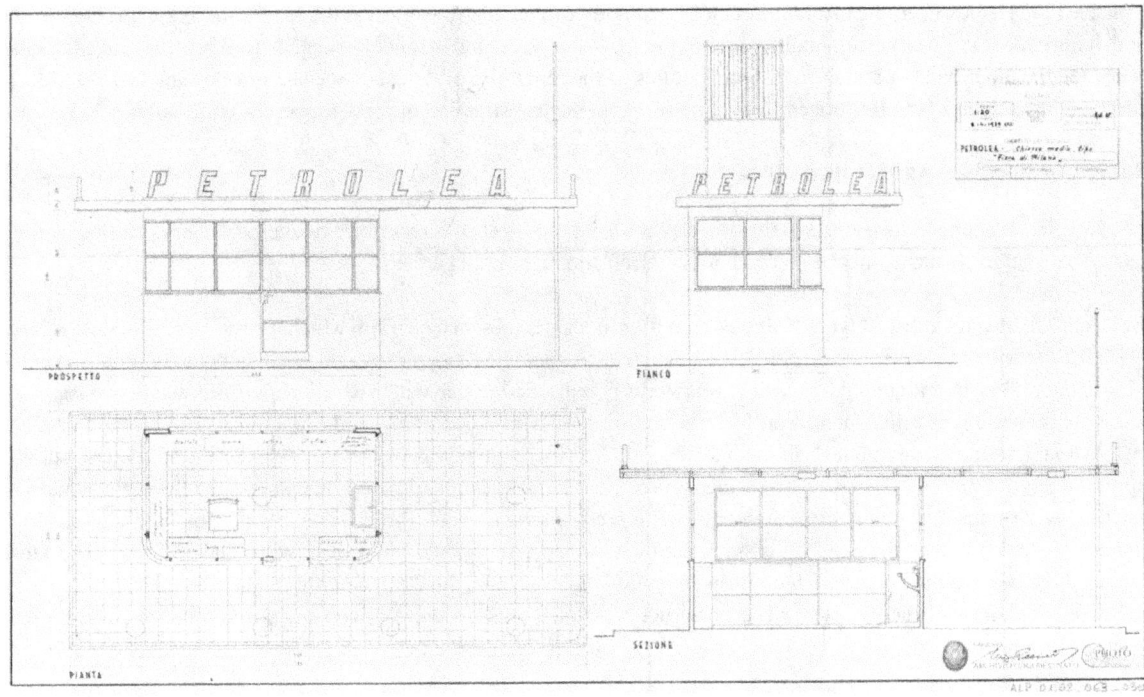

Fig. 3 Petrolea-Fiat medium kiosk at Milan Exhibition, 1937. Source: ALP

From a typological point of view, Piccinato's proposals were influenced by the international context which in the 1930s developed an evident interest in the industrialised production of kiosks and service stations, based on prototypes of the major companies of fuel distribution. In the European context, a reference for Piccinato's work was the Robert Mallet-Stevens station presented at the 1927 Salon d'Automne. Equally decisive for the evolution of the design theme, and useful for the analysis of Piccinato's repertoire, was the experience of the United States, with the types that Norman Bel Geddes developed in 1934 for Socony (later transformed into Mobil), Raymond Loewy's studies for Esso, and those conducted by Walter Dorflin Teague for Texaco [9]. In addition, we consider, the prototypes promoted by companies such as Michel & Pfeffer Iron Works (1926) concerning essential kiosks for urban areas. The echo of this overseas experience affected the Olex production in Germany and, in Italy, the repertoire of Petrolea [10]. A further series of drawings by Piccinato (probably from the early 1940s) concerned the design of a service station (unbuilt) with a reinforced concrete structure, the presence of which was emphasised by the design of the ribs that marked the profile and the intrados of the canopy. Piccinato's approach in these sketches appears more spectacular, with more fluid and aerodynamic shapes, as highlighted by the design of the station and by the profile of the roof slab, whose inclination was studied to define its silhouette. In this case, Piccinato developed a different approach. He studied different station layouts, considering the architectural dimension of the theme. The result was not a prototype of a series, but the definition of more designs of stations; each of them was a unique project. Also, with reference to functional aspects, the buildings were larger and more advanced than the first essential kiosks of 1938-39 and met the needs of a more articulated type of provision to motorists. Referring to the medium-large station, it is noted that the plan was divided into three parts: two service and storage areas were arranged at the ends of the layout; in the centre, a passage protected by the roof slab connected the two supply lanes. The roof, which unified the three functional modules, had a symmetrical profile, with two wings extended over the two supply lanes. In these drawings we can read the influence of European service stations such as the station designed in Madrid by Casto Fernandez-Shaw (1927), the Shell station in Alesund in Norway (1931) and the Aral station by J. Krahn in

Frankfurt, the singular Arne Jacobsen's project in Klamperborg (Denmark) in 1938 and, finally, the BP station in Villejuif in France (1934). However, the most important contribution of Piccinato's work was the repertoire of kiosks. On the one hand, it introduced Agip urban minimal stations of the 1950s based on the use of cold-shaped metal profiles and enamelled sheets. On the other hand, it anticipated some features of the repertoire of Agip service stations designed by Bacciocchi in 1952. The analysis of the Bacciocchi catalogue supports the investigation of these aspects of continuity.

Mario Bacciocchi's Agip Repertoire

In 1952 Erico Mattei commissioned Mario Bacciocchi for the project of a repertoire of shelters, kiosks, filling stations and service stations, which could be placed both in urban and extra-urban areas.

The repertoire, that included 13 types, was based on four fundamental schemes, from which the remaining models derived [11]. The first and most essential was 'Project I', which concerned the canopy provided as either an autonomous element or in support of kiosks and stations (Fig. 4). It was a reinforced concrete slab with a rectilinear profile, set on two supports, its section increasing near the connection with the station roof. The canopy had an asymmetrical geometry: on one side it was set at 3.10 meters high and 1.30 meters long; on the other side it was placed at a height of 2.55 meters and was approximately 1.50 meters deep. The two wings protected the underlying fuel pumps and supported the Agip signs. The system was surmounted by the advertising shaft. The second scheme was 'Project III - Small kiosk without canopy', intended to accommodate the seller in a small cabin equipped with a sink and a desk with chair (Fig. 5). The kiosk combined the box with the canopy which raised about one meter above the 2.50 meter high glass box. Here the echo of the small kiosk of Piccinato is clear. The construction choice was different, given the predominance of reinforced concrete.

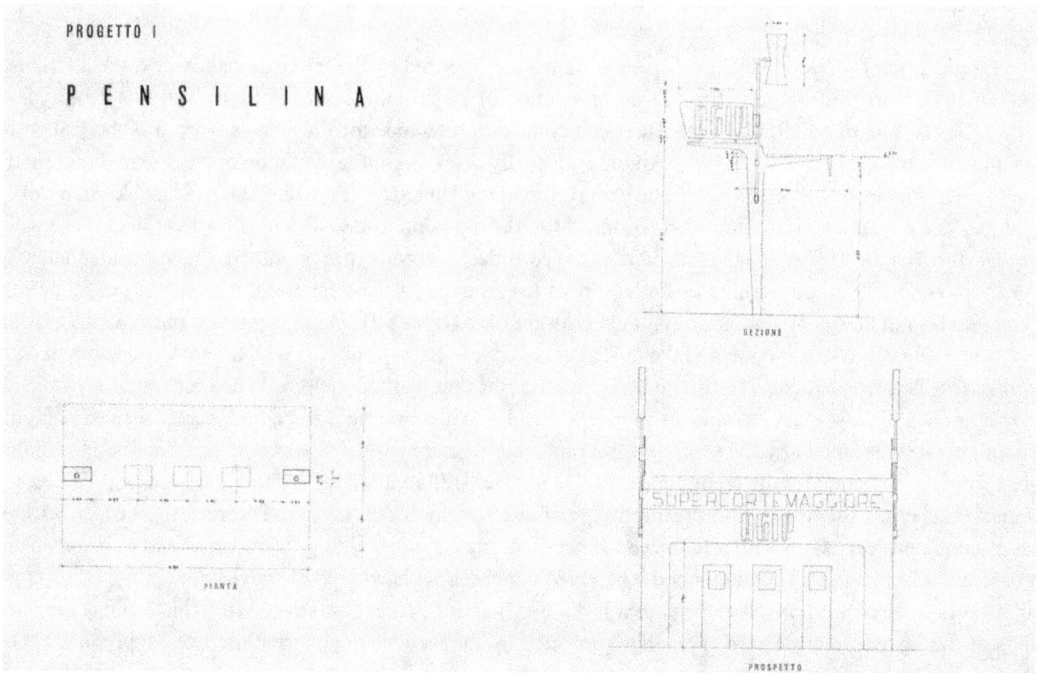

Fig. 4 Canopy of the Agip repertoire (Project I). Project: Mario Bacciocchi, 1952. Source Historical Achive Ente Nazionale Idrocarburi (ENI), Rome (ASE)

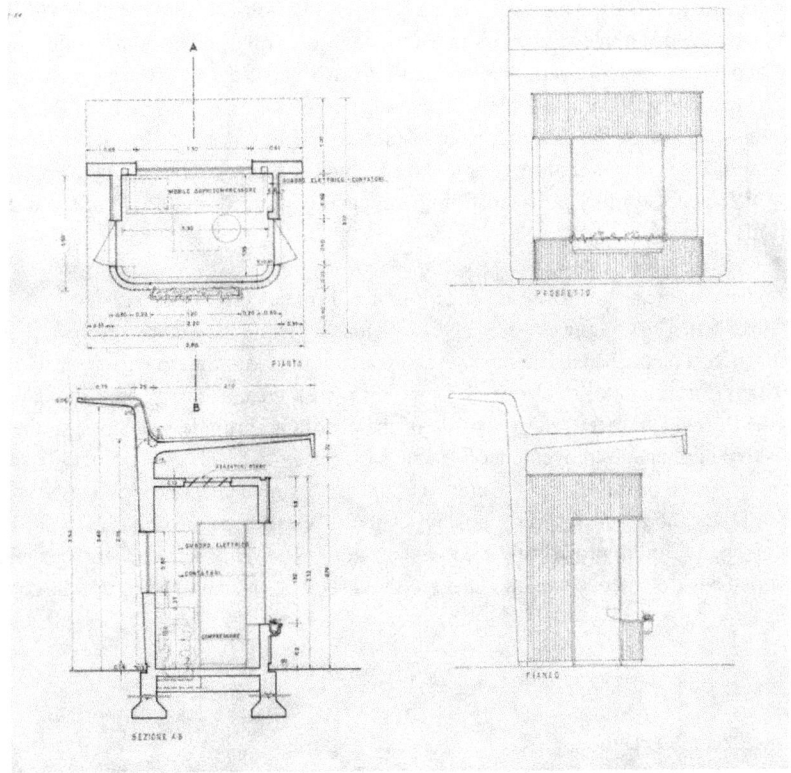

Fig. 5 Small kiosk without canopy of Agip repertoire. Project: Mario Bacciocchi, 1952 Source: ASE

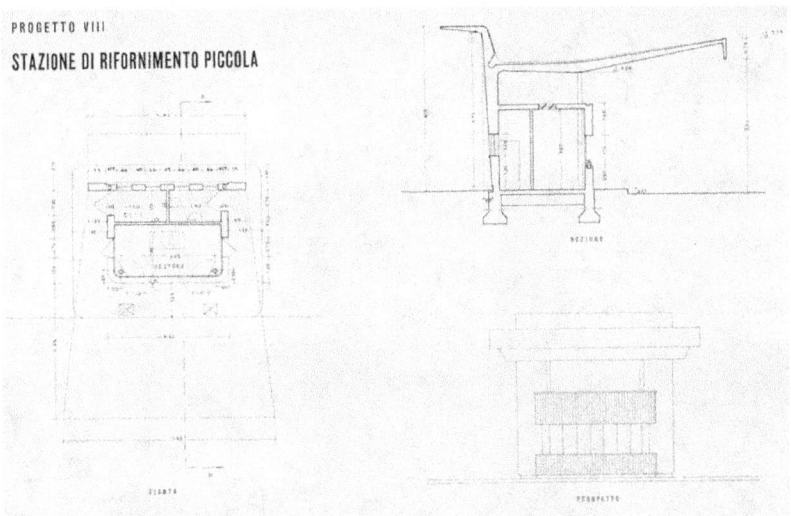

Fig. 6 Small filling station of the Agip repertoire (Project VIII). Project: Mario Bacciocchi, 1952 Source: ASE

The third fundamental scheme of the 1952 repertoire is the 'Project VIII - Small filling station' (Fig. 6). The functional system of the filling station included a sales area, a room for the storage of oils, and customer toilets with access from the outside. The building, about 3.50 meters deep, was divided into two parts, the front one which was more public and reserved for sales and the rear one to accommodate the remaining functions. As in the kiosks of Piccinato, the public part was visible from the outside through the generous windows. Also in this case, as in the kiosk, the aesthetical and construction system of the station consisted of two parts: the box and the canopy. The canopy reached 5 meters in height at the front to allow vehicle access to the protected filling area, and continued up to 6.10 at the back, to complete the usual asymmetrical profile.

The fourth and last fundamental scheme of the repertoire is the 'Project XI - Small service station', organised on a rectangular layout (14.20x6.50). The volume elevated up to 4.95 meters, while the canopy reached a height of 6.20 meters on the front and almost 7 meters on the back. The functional layout, divided into four macro-areas with different surfaces, included a sale zone with rest area and toilet for the manager, a carwash area, a storage area, and an exhibition zone for oils (Fig. 7). In this type, Bacciocchi extended the profile of the canopy to provide protection to the greater number of fuel pumps and to allow the simultaneous movement of several cars. Six cylindrical columns, also arranged symmetrically and with a constant step along the front, marked the construction and aesthetical connection between the canopy and the station box. The profile of the canopy suggested the analogy with the reinforced concrete station presented in Piccinato's sketches of the 1940s, given the similar profile of the concrete canopy. The other schemes of the catalogue derived from the different combination of basic elements (station with or without shelter) and from the size of the configurations (small, medium, large).

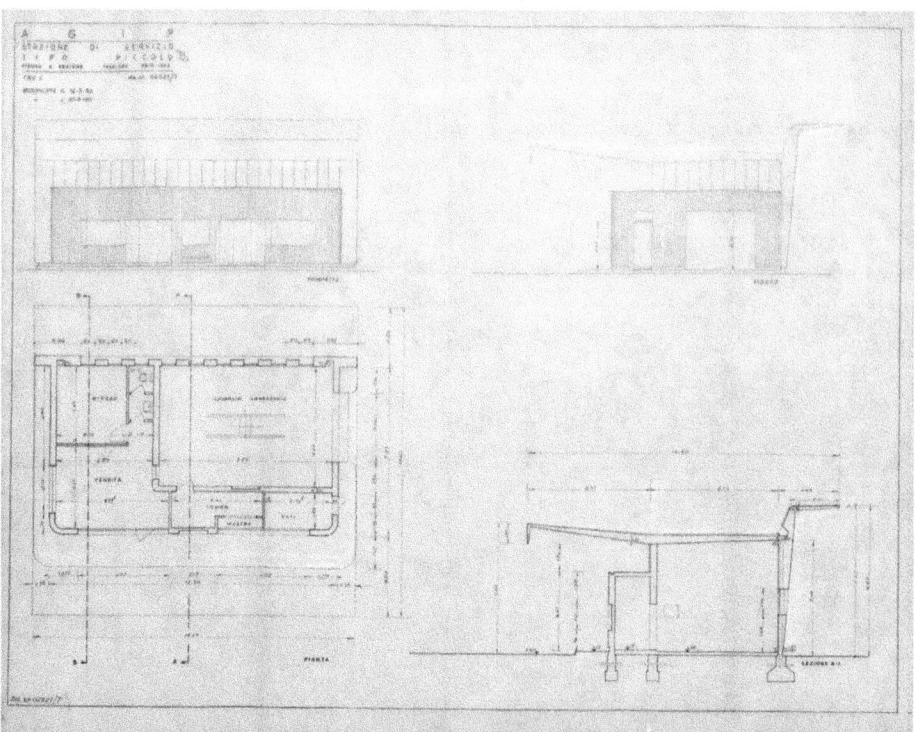

Fig. 7 Small service station of the Agip repertoire (Project XI). Project: Mario Bacciocchi, 1952. Source: ASE

Fig. 8 Service station derived from the Bacciocchi's repertoire built in Barletta (South Italy). Source: ASE

Fig. 9 Small kiosk without canopy of Agip repertoire built in Marostica (Veneto). Source: ASE

Construction Standardisation in Italian Service Stations (1930s-1950s) Projects by Luigi Piccinato and Mario Bacciocchi

Fig. 10 Service station inspired by the Bacciocchi's repertoire and built in Alpine areas. Source: ASE

The selection allowed Bacciocchi to modulate the solutions in relation to as many possible conditions of use and context (Figs. 8-10). It was a paradigm in which the variations of the four matrix projects were defined starting from an original pattern of vehicle assistance functions and the corresponding spatial and construction elements. However, the combination schemes among the parts were pre-established and, in fact, the adjustments over time had transformed the original layout of the Bacciocchi stations, affecting the original features. The functional obsolescence of the earliest schemes was among the factors that, in the mid-1960s, determined the crisis of the 1952 catalogue.

Conclusions

The analysis presented in this study allows us to highlight similarities and divergences between the two repertoires of kiosks and stations. From a methodological point of view, the two experiences show a similar approach of the designers who, aiming at the standardisation of spatial and construction characters of buildings, organised the catalogues starting from few essential patterns from which the further schemes derived. Modular layouts corresponded to this general approach, defined through the combination of spatial elements reserved for specific functions. So, Piccinato and Bacciocchi could vary the functional complexity of the buildings while preserving the basic architectural and construction rules, replicating the layouts in different contexts, defining a recognisable aesthetical and construction system of the kiosks and stations of Petrolea-Fiat and Agip networks.

On the other hand, there is a diversity in the socio-economic and manufacturing context that affected the characterisation of the two repertoires. Piccinato's experience belongs to the events of the 1930s, marked by pioneering experiments and a framework in which the fundamental typological themes of kiosks and service stations took shape. In this period an essential approach prevailed, aimed at ensuring few functions through a basic architectural and construction system, sometimes even using temporary buildings. Bacciocchi's repertoire formed in a period of maturity of motorway architecture, coincided with the formation of the national motorway network and the spread of mass motoring. These assumptions suggested enriching the functions and adopting less essential construction choices. At this stage, the definition of the architectural and construction language was aimed at supporting motorway propaganda towards the Italian middle class with an architectural image able to represent the modernisation of the customs and lifestyles.

Similarly, different construction choices corresponded to this diversity of context. Piccinato's repertoire offered an example, albeit a pioneering one, of real industrialisation of the design and production process of kiosks, with metal construction and prefabrication of the elements. Bacciocchi's repertoire was influenced by the slow evolution of the Italian construction mainstream which, despite the theoretical debate on prefabrication and industrialisation, characterised the period of reconstruction and the 1950s. The preservation of the traditional construction system with few elements of modernity, the preference for construction on site, were choices shared by Bacciocchi's repertoire with the main reconstruction programs developed in Italy in the 1950s.

From these peculiarities derived the different relationships established by the two experiences with the construction framework and with the evolution of the theme of industrialisation in Italy in those years. In Piccinato's repertoire, architectural and construction standardisation was a prerequisite for the industrialisation of the production of kiosks, in compliance with an approach also favoured by the Fiat client, accustomed to mass production and therefore to the development of management models and production processes inspired by criteria of rationalisation of time and resources. In fact, in the 1930s the Servizio Costruzioni e Impianti was a technical structure organised with scientific management standards that pursued the rationalisation of design and construction processes and therefore this spirit affected Piccinato's work.

In Bacciocchi's repertoire, the spatial and construction standardisation of kiosks and stations was aimed at communicative intentions, and therefore at the definition of a recognisable image of Agip throughout the country. Bacciocchi was an architect who worked in his studio with a traditional approach. The Bacciocchi catalogue was the premise on which the technicians of Servizio Costruzioni e Manutenzione di Agip (the company's technical department) developed technical choices, defined the building details, indicated the characteristics of the spaces and of the construction elements in the technical documents. The catalogue was the result of two distinct steps in the design process: first the intuition of the architectural design, then the engineering design developed in terms of rationalisation of techniques and costs [12]. However, the work of Bacciocchi and Agip technicians was aimed at the system of small Italian construction companies, to which it provided a 'manual for construction', useful for ensuring recognisable Agip stations, suitable for the Italian mainstream construction, effective in guaranteeing quality and homogeneous construction standards of stations on the national territory.

Piccinato's repertoire was part of the laboratory on building industrialisation of the 1930s, mainly focused on the use of metal constructions and the relationship between designers and production companies, which was a prelude to the debate on post-war industrialisation. Bacciocchi's repertoire, while not applying real building industrialisation, participated in the debate developed in the post-WWII period on the rationalisation of construction elements to merge construction tradition with the widespread quality requirements of the housing reconstruction programs, of which Agip service stations offered an extensive application in an emerging typological sector both in terms of number and territorial diffusion of achievements.

Ultimately, we can consider the two repertoires as the expressions of the two prevalent approaches to the industrialisation in the Italian framework after WWII: the real industrialisation of the design and construction process through the evolution of all building sector; the standardisation of the architectural and construction elements as premise of a design approach aimed to a more progressive evolution of the construction sector towards the industrialisation.

References

[1] L. Greco, F. Spada, 'The Invulnerabile's prefabricated construction system for Italian temporary buildings in the 1930s' pp.535-548 in J. Campbell (Eds), *Proceedings of the Sixth Conference of the Construction History Society, Cambridge 2019*, Cambridge: Construction History Society, 2019.
[2] A. Sompairac, *Stations-Service*, Paris : Centre Pompidou, 1993.

[3] D. Deschermeier, *Impero Eni. L'architettura aziendale e l'urbanistica di Enrico Mattei*, Bologna: Damiani, 2008, pp. 10-14; S. Caccia, *Tutela e restauro delle stazioni di servizio*, Milan: Franco Angeli, 2012, pp. 37-43.

[4] C. De Sessa, Luigi Piccinato Architetto, Rome: Dedalo, 1993

[5] D. Pozzi, *Dai gatti selvatici al cane a sei zampe. Tecnologia, conoscenza e organizzazione nell'Agip e nell'Eni di Enrico Mattei*, Venice: Marsilio, 2009.

[6] Caccia, Tutela, (Note 3) p. 41.

[7] L. Greco, *Architetture autostradali in Italia. Progetto e costruzione negli edifici per l'assistenza ai viaggiatori*, Rome: Gangemi, 2010; L. Greco, 'Le stazioni di servizio Agip di Mario Bacciocchi: un'esperienza di tipizzazione costruttiva' pp. 939-948 in S. D'Agostino (Ed.) History of engineering. International Conference on history of engineering, Naples: Cuzzolin editore, 2016.

[8] Greco, *Architetture*, (Note 7) pp. 145-149.

[9] Somparaic, *Stations*, (Note 2], pp. 36-37; H. C. Liebs, Main street to miracle mile. American roadside architecture, Boston: Little Browne, 1985, pp. 104-107.

[10] Caccia, *Tutela*, (Note 3) pp. 37-41.

[11] Greco, *Stazioni*, (Note 7).

[12] L. Greco, S. Mornati, *Architetture Eni in Italia (1953-1962)*, Rome: Gangemi, 2018, pp. 36-40.

A Century of Professionalism in Construction in North Macedonia (1920-2020)

Vladimir B. Ladinski
University American College Skopje, North Macedonia

Introduction

On 21st March 1920 the first annual meeting of engineers and architects took place within the territory of the Skopje Construction Direction (*Скопска грађевинска дирекција*). This meeting led to the foundation of the Skopje Section of the Association of Yugoslavian Engineers and Architects (*Удружење југословенских инжењера и архитекта – Секција Скопје*). The minutes from the above meeting dated 29th March 1920 and signed by the Secretary Engineer Dim. S Jevtović (*Дим. С. Јевтовић*) and the Vice-President Engineer Nikola Đurić (*Никола Ђурић*) confirmed the decisions taken at the meeting and enclosed a copy of the association new statute [1, 2]. (Fig. 1) The foundation of the Skopje Section was made possible as more than 50 engineers and architects who were members of the Association of Yugoslavian Engineers and Architects were working on the territory of the Skopje Construction District. This allowed them to form a local Section of the Association, offering Full, Associate, Honorary, Correspondent and Voluntary Membership. The Associate Membership was open to technicians in practice undergoing university education, those in practice awaiting for their final technician exam, and business managers showing exceptional ability in the field. The newly formed Skopje Section undertook to collaborate and contribute to the journal of the Association of Yugoslavian Engineers and Technicians 'Tehnički List' (*Технички Лист*) [3].

The origins of the Association of the Yugoslavian Engineers and Technicians, established in 1919, go back to the foundation of the Technicians Society (*Техничарска дружина*) in Serbia in 1868 and followed by the Association of Serbian Engineers (*Удружење српских инжењера*) in 1890. The first President of the Association of the Yugoslavian Engineers and Architects in 1919 was Professor Kosta Glavinić (*Коста Главинић*). The records show that, within the Kingdom of Serbs, Croats and Slovens (then Kingdom of Yugoslavia from 1929), the Association had a total membership of 1,435 regular members in 1922 and 2,600 in 1934 [4].

The foundation of the Skopje Section of the Association of Yugoslavian Engineers and Architects is considered to be the starting point of the Western professionalism on the contemporary territory of North Macedonia. The centenary of this founding event was celebrated on 20th March 2020 by the Engineering Institution of Macedonia (Инженерска институција на Македонија), the successor organisation of the original Skopje Section of the Association of Yugoslavian Engineers and Architects [5]. The Engineering Institution of Macedonia became a member of the European Federation of National Engineering Associations (FEANI) in 2010 [6].

In 2020, a century after the foundation of the Skopje Section of the Association of Yugoslavian Engineers and Architects, it was estimated that over 10,000 students had graduated from the five-years full time degrees in civil engineering and architecture from the oldest course, founded in 1949, Ss. Cyril and Methodius University (Универзитет Св. Кирил и Методиј) in Skopje alone. At present, in a country of about two million population there are 25 accredited state (n=7) and private (n=18) universities or tertiary education institutions of which 10 of them (five state and five private) offer accredited programmes in civil engineering and/or architecture [7]. Since the 1970s construction companies from North Macedonia have been delivering construction projects in other parts of former Yugoslavia, Eastern and Central Europe,

Mediterranean and Middle Eastern Countries. Engineers and architects from North Macedonia have taken part in number of technical assistance missions following major disasters in former Yugoslavia and in other parts of the world.

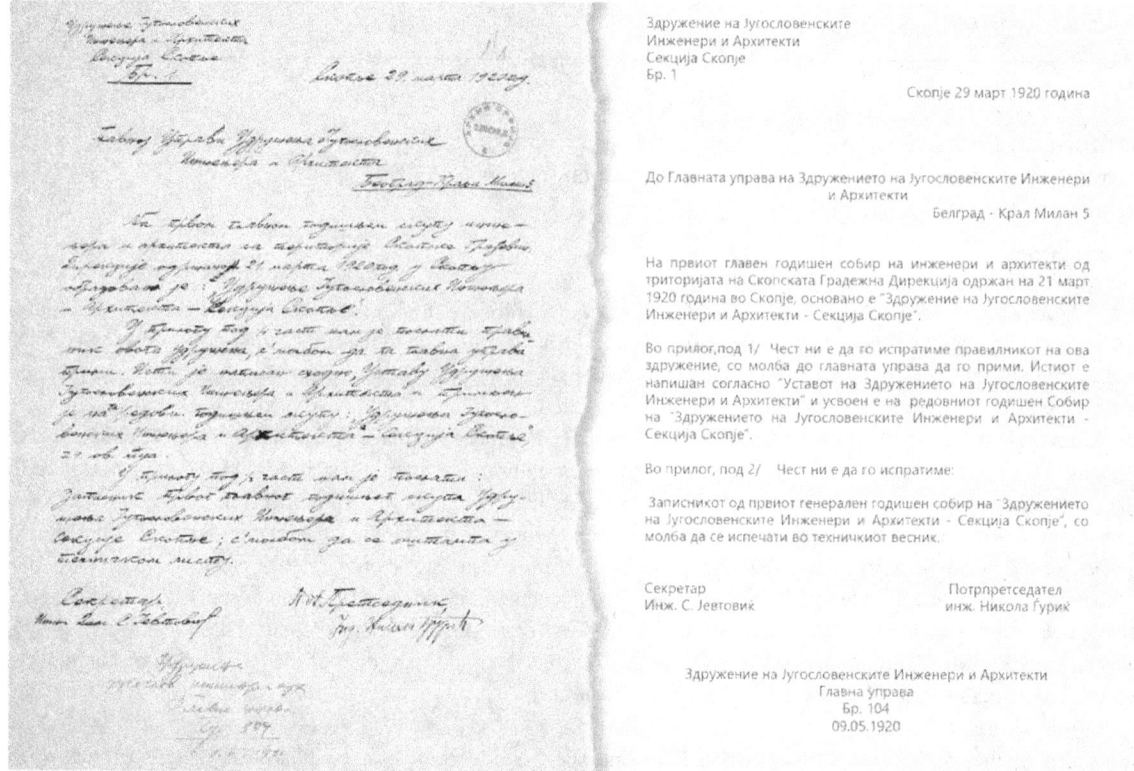

Fig. 1 The letter from the first meeting of the Association of Yugoslav Engineers and Architects - Skopje Section: left, 1920 original in Serbian and right, 2020 Macedonian translation (Engineering, Journal of Engineering Creation and Technology, In Macedonian, 2020, p. 8. - Used with permission by the Engineering Institution of Macedonia)

The turbulent history of the Balkan peninsula during the first half of the 20th Century marked by the decline of the Ottoman Empire, the First and Second Balkan Wars as well as the First and the Second World War, generated a significant level of instability and with only a brief period of about two decades of relative peace and stability between the two World Wars to support the development of professions and professionalism within any field. During that period, the territory of the present North Macedonia was part of the Kingdom of the Serbs, Croats and Slovenes that in 1929 became the Kingdom of Yugoslavia.

This paper focuses on the establishment of the foundation of professionalism within the construction industry in North Macedonia with a particular focus on the period between 1945-63 which coincides with the establishment of the Federal Unit Macedonia within Democratic and Federal Yugoslavia, which then became People's Republic of Macedonia within the People's Federal Republic of Yugoslavia. This study provides a further contribution to the increasing interest in the history of architecture and construction in North Macedonia.

Because of the Covid-19 pandemic associated restriction the research has been limited to an analysis of primary and secondary source materials available in printed form or accessible via digital archives. The key part of this research is based on a the review of 640 available of the 649 originally published Official Gazettes in North Macedonia in the period between January 1945 and March 1963 covering the periods of the Federal Unit Macedonia and the People's Republic of Macedonia [8]. The results of this research, focusing on the state legislation, cover three aspects associated with professionalism: formal education, professional registration and professional organisation.

Formal Professional Construction Related Education

The opportunities for formal professional education in the construction-related disciplines were very limited during the first half of the 20th Century in North Macedonia, both at secondary and tertiary level. As a result, the construction-related professions had to rely on construction education obtained elsewhere within the Kingdom of Yugoslavia, former Yugoslavia or abroad.

Secondary Professional Construction Related Education

It is obvious that the Government of the Federal Unit of Macedonia realised very early on the need to introduce opportunities for construction-related formal education to support the post Second World War reconstruction efforts. Therefore, only few weeks after the liberation of the capital Skopje (13th November 1944), on 7th December 1944 the decision was made to establish the first Secondary Technical (Engineering) School in Skopje, now SGGU Zdravko Cvetkovski (*СГГУ Здравко Цветковски*), in North Macedonia [9].

This was followed by a further decision on 10th June 1946 to introduce Temporary Regulations for the Final Exam at the technical school for 1946 which included three possible engineering pathways: Construction, Electro-Technical and Mechanical [10]. The final exam for those studying Construction consisted of six written and 10 oral exams. The completion of the programme was dependent on three months of compulsory practical experience, organised by the Ministry of Construction, that could be waived by the Ministry on individual basis [11]. It appears that these Temporary Regulations were introduced in order to facilitate completion of the secondary technical education for those whose education was interrupted by the Second World War, including those who have completed a specified number of years within the former Bulgarian Technical School in Bitola [12]. This suggests that there was a Bulgarian Technical School in Bitola established during the Second World War, when most of North Macedonia was occupied by the Axis Powers, and the town of Bitola administered by the Kingdom of Bulgaria. However, it has not been possible to obtain further details on this school.

The development of the professional secondary education in construction related disciplines continued in the following years with the introduction of four-year long secondary school programmes on 16th December 1950 to include secondary-technical schools, as from academic year 1950/1951 [13]. Further changes have followed on 14th March 1956 by the introduction of a Diploma Exam in Secondary Technical Schools with compulsory professional practice and a maximum of three attempts allowed. The Diploma Exam for Construction consisted of four written and two oral exams. A representative from the Educational Council (*Совет за просвета*) had to be in attendance for the oral exams [14]. The amendments of 13th July 1957 waived the restriction on the number of attempts for the Diploma Exam and made the attendance of the representative from the Education Council optional [15].

Further changes in the legislation followed from 20th May 1960 when the Final Exam for the Secondary Technical School allowed for two pathways within the Construction-related discipline, one focusing on Construction (Civil Engineering) and the other on Geodesy (Land Surveying) [16]. Later in the year, on 26th November 1960, the existing Final Exams system was replaced with a new one to commence in the academic year 1960/1961. Under the new system, the existing approach with a number of written and oral exams, was replaced by a project prepared by the candidate during the final year at the school in combination with a written assignment in front of the exam board, culminating in a project related *Voice Viva* examination [17].

Tertiary Professional Construction Related Education

In general, the opportunities for tertiary education in the territory of North Macedonia were very limited in the first half of the 20th Century. The first opportunity for tertiary education came on 16th February 1920 when 33 students enrolled at the Faculty of Philosophy in Skopje, which had been established as an autonomous unit of the University of Belgrade by Royal Decree of 2nd February1920 within the Kingdom of Serbs, Croats and Slovenes. It offered courses in literature, linguistics, history, philosophy and pedagogy. Initially, it was housed within the well-known Ottoman Teachers School Idadija on the outskirts of Skopje, before moving into a purpose-built building the following academic year. However, this faculty ceased to exist at the outbreak of the Second World War in 1941 [18]. (Fig. 2)

Fig. 2 The Old University Library, Skopje (lost in the 1963 Skopje Earthquake) by Unknown (By Unknown – the State Archives of the Republic of Macedonia (DARM), Skopje Department, Public Domain, https://commons.wikimedia.org/wiki/File:Univerzitetska_biblioteka,_Skopje,_pred_zemjotresot.jpg)

According to R. J. Crampton, a King Boris III University was established in Skopje during the Second World War in the Axis Powers occupied part of the country, administered by the Kingdom of Bulgaria, and appears to have been active between 1941 and 1944. However, there is very little information about the institution and the courses offered [19].

After the Second World War, the Faculty of Philosophy (Факултет за филозофија) was the first tertiary education institution to commence working in North Macedonia, offering courses in the academic year 1946/1947 [20]. On 25th November 1949 the University of Skopje Act was passed, leading to the foundation of the University of Skopje (Универзитет во Скопје), now University Ss. Cyril and Methodius (Универзитет Св. Кирил и Методиј), with three faculties: Philosophy, Medicine, and Agriculture and Forestry [21]. This was followed by the establishment of the Institute for Scientific Research in the Industry (Институт за научни истражувања во индустријата) on 31st August

1949 with a focus on applicative research aimed towards improvement and rationalisation of the production processes, discovery of new materials, as well as quality control and improvements that later became part of the Technical Faculty [22].

For construction related disciplines the most important date is the 28th December 1950 when the Technical Faculty in Skopje (Технички факултет во Скопје) was established with two departments, construction (civil engineering) and architecture offering 5 years (10 semesters) full time studies leading to the title Graduate Engineer (дипломиран инженер) in the selected field [23]. It should be noted that the faculty, that became part of the University of Skopje, actually commenced work in 1949, but the formal Government decisions followed later on.

In 1955 a number of improvements were instigated with the aim of improving the quality of tertiary education system. It was directed that, from 23rd May, elections and appointments to the posts of Assistant or Associate Professor could only be made to candidates without *Habilitation* or a Doctorate before 15th July 1958 and appointees who did not have these qualifications at appointment were required to gain a Doctorate or submit their Habilitation within four years of their appointment date [24]. This requirement was further reinforced by the new University of Skopje Act (Закон за Универзитетот во Скопје) published on 31st May 1956 and came into force 15 days later, which laid down a mandatory requirement for all appointments to Assistant, Associate or Full Professors to hold a Doctorate or Habilation. Furthermore, promotion into Associate and Full Professor was available only to those with a significant publication record. The Act allowed for those in professorial teaching positions to remain employed until the end of the academic year in which they reached the age of 70. More importantly, the Act allowed for the introduction of Postgraduate Studies leading to Specialist qualifications or Doctorates [25].

As of 14th March1961 the number of available places in the academic year 1961/1962 was limited to 160 full-time (Construction) and to 100 full-time (Architecture) students. In addition, there were 60 places available for part-time students across all four departments of the Technical Faculty: Construction, Architecture, Technology (Chemical Engineering) and Electro-Mechanical (Engineering) [26]. The number of available places was reduced to 100 full-time and 40 part-time students, and 80 full-time and 40 part-time students for the Department of Construction and Architecture respectively in the academic year 1962/1963 [27].

It is worth noting that it was possible to exit the Technical Faculty with an intermediate qualification leading to the title of Engineer (инженер) in the selected field for those who had successfully completed two and a half years (5 semesters) of full-time studies or part-time equivalent. If desired, they were able to continue their studies, leading to the Graduate Engineer (дипломиран инженер) title later on, by enrolling into the third year of the 5 year full-time programme or the longer part-time equivalent.

Construction-Related Professional Registration

After the end of hostilities, an early decision of the Government of the Federal Unit Macedonia allowed for the design and construction of building and civil works to continue before the official end of the Second World War: on 3rd May 1945, the members of the Association of Engineers and Technicians in Macedonia were officially permitted to engage in the design and building of construction-related works [28].

On 21st January1949 Regulations for Probation (Practical) Experience, Professional Exam and Courses in the Construction Profession (Правилник за приправничкиот стаж, стручните испити и курсеви во градежната струка) were introduced. The Regulations identified five fields in construction discipline: architecture, urbanism, construction (civil engineering), transport (highways and railways) and hydro engineering. For example, in order for a people to qualify as a junior technicians or a junior engineers, upon completion of his/her education, they were expected to complete a minimum of 24 months and maximum of 30 months practical experience, of which at least 12 months had to be in a design role and at least 12 months in a site construction role. The candidates were expected to keep a detailed diary for their practical experience. The Professional Exam for a Junior Technician consisted of a written and an oral exam. The written exam lasted up to five days with no more eight hours a day under constant supervision. Within this period the candidates were expected to prepare: (i) an initial and detailed design for a smaller residential or commercial building based on a given site plan and design brief, (ii) structural calculations for the key load bearing elements of the building, (iii) a cost analysis and (iv) a written justification of the proposal. In addition, they had to sit a minimum two hours oral exam covering the prescribed six areas of competence. Only three attempts were permitted for the exam. The Professional Exam for Junior Engineers was similar with the main difference being that they had a 15 day period to prepare a design for a larger residential, public, industrial or commercial building at home on their own. On successful completion of the written exam, they could proceed to the oral exam covering the prescribed six areas of competence. Similar Professional Exams were prescribed for Assistant Construction Draftsmen, Construction Supervisors Construction Managers and Senior Construction Technicians [29].

Fig. 3 The Main Square, Skopje (number of buildings lost in the 1963 Skopje Earthquake) (By Unknown – the State Archives of the Republic of Macedonia (DARM), Skopje Department, Public Domain, https://commons.wikimedia.org/wiki/Category:Officers%27_Hall,_Skopje#/media/File:Panorama_so_Oficerski_dom.jpg)

Construction Related Professional Bodies

The status of the Association of Engineers and Technicians in Macedonia was reaffirmed in May 1949 and this in part facilitated the creation of more specialised construction-related societies in the years to come. The civil engineers and technicians led the way by gaining permission to establish the Society of Civil Engineers and Technicians of Peoples' Republic of Macedonia (*Друштво на градежни инженери и техници на НРМ*) in Skopje on 9th June 1951 [30], followed by the Society of Architects in People's Republic of Macedonia (*Друштво на архитектите на Народна Република Македонија*) in Skopje on 26th June 1952 [31] and the Society of Electro-Mechanical Engineers and Technicians in Peoples' Republic of Macedonia (*Друштво на електромашинските инженери и техници во Народна Република Македонија*) in Skopje (granted permission on 22nd October1952) [32]. The Society for Urbanism of PR Macedonia (*Урбанистичко друштво на НР Македонија*) was granted permission on 3rd September 1956. A majority of these societies continue to this day [33].

Fig. 4 The National Theatre, Skopje (lost in the 1963 Skopje Earthquake), Skopje by J. Bukovac, E. Bronštajn et al., (By Unknown – the State Archives of the Republic of Macedonia (DARM), Skopje Department, Public Domain, https://commons.wikimedia.org/wiki/File:Skopje,_razglednica_so_teatarot.jpg)

Conclusions

Based on the available information, key milestones associated with the development of construction related professionalism in North Macedonia have been identified, from the modest beginning when some 50 members were able to establish the Skopje Section of the Association of Yugoslavian Architect and Engineers in early 1920, to the current Engineering Institution of Macedonia. Considering the turbulent history of the first half of the 20th Century, the research focused on the early endeavours in the post Second World period when the Federal Unit Macedonia was established within the Democratic and Federal Yugoslavia.

The findings indicate the intense efforts made in the 1945-50 period to establish the foundations of the construction industry and construction-related professionalism in the State. In the context of this research, the development of construction professionalism was investigated through the aspects of formal education, professional registration and professional organisation. The decisions were taken in a realistic and pragmatic manner, with consideration for the limited resources available and appreciation for the need for a post war reconstruction, with an evidence of actual actions taking place even before the decisions were formally made and announced. The early decision in 1945 allowed for the state Association of Engineers and Architect to carry on with the design and construction-related activities whilst new arrangements were put in place in 1949, through the introduction of construction-related professional exams. The initial focus was on establishing a professional constriction related Secondary Technical School in 1944 whilst allowing, through the temporary regulations of 1946, those with incomplete secondary technical education due to the war to complete it. This allowed for the training of much-needed construction-related professionals at a technician level, but also provided a recruitment base for future students and enough time for the establishment of the Technical Faculty at the University of Skopje in 1949. Equally, in 1949 the Institute for Scientific Research for the Industry was formed, stimulating applied research activities.

Fig. 5 Skopje Airport in the Interwar Period, Skopje, by Unknown, (By Unknown – the State Archives of the Republic of Macedonia (DARM), Skopje Department, Public Domain, https://commons.wikimedia.org/wiki/File:Aerodromot_vo_Skopje,_20_vek.jpg)

The following six-year period (1950-56) appears to have been focused on the improvements within the secondary and tertiary education, through the requirements for *Habilitation* or Doctorate for the university teaching posts and the introduction of the possibility of postgraduate studies at the Technical Faculty leading to Specialist qualifications and Doctorates. Within the same period the key construction-related societies were established: Construction Engineers and Technicians (in 1951), Architects (in 1952), Electro-Mechanical Engineers and Technicians (in 1952) and the Urbanism (in 1956).

Thus, this paper has provided an outline of the early efforts aimed at developing construction related professionalism in North Macedonia and illustrated some of their professional achievements between 1920-63. (Fig. 3-10)

Fig. 6 The Main Railway Station, Skopje (lost in part in the 1963 Skopje Earthquake) by V. Gavrilović, (By Unknown – the State Archives of the Republic of Macedonia (DARM), Skopje Department, Public Domain, https://commons.wikimedia.org/wiki/File:Zeleznicka_stanica_pred_zemjotresot.jpg)

Fig. 7 The Grand Hotel Macedonia, Skopje (lost in the 1963 Skopje Earthquake) by Unknown, (By Unknown – the State Archives of the Republic of Macedonia (DARM), Skopje Department, Public Domain, https://commons.wikimedia.org/wiki/File:Hotel_Makedonija_pred_zemjotresot.jpg)

A Century of Professionalism in Construction in North Macedonia (1920-2020)

Fig. 8 Office Block (left) and Educational Building (right), Skopje (both lost in the 1963 Skopje Earthquake) (By Unknown – the State Archives of the Republic of Macedonia (DARM), Skopje Department, Public Domain, https://commons.wikimedia.org/wiki/File:Pogled_od_vlezot_vo_Narodno_sobranie,_pred_zemjotresot.jpg)

Fig. 9 Settlement Karpoš, Skopje, prior to the 1963 Skopje Earthquake (By Unknown – the State Archives of the Republic of Macedonia (DARM), Skopje Department, Public Domain, https://commons.wikimedia.org/wiki/File:Karpos_pred_zemjotresot.jpg)

Fig. 10 Hall One under Construction, Skopje Fare, Skopje (lost in part in the 1963 Skopje Earthquake), by Unknown (By Unknown – the State Archives of the Republic of Macedonia (DARM), Skopje Department, Public Domain, https://commons.wikimedia.org/wiki/File:Hala_1_od_Skopsko_sajmiste,_pred_zemjotresot.jpg)

Acknowledgements

The author would like to express his thanks to the Engineering Institution of Macedonia for the kind permission to use illustration from their journal, the Official Gazette of the Republic of North Macedonia for the availability of their publications as well as to the State Archive of the Republic of North Macedonia for making available historic images of North Macedonia.

References

[1] Инженерство (Engineering), In Macedonian, Списание за инженерско творештво и технологија / Journal of Engineering Creation and Technology, 2020, p. 8.

[2] И. Марић, (I. Marić) (Ed), 'Савез инжењера и техничара Србије: Јубилеј 150 година' (Union of Engineers and Technicians of Serbia: 150 Years Jubilee), In Serbian, Београд: Савез инжењера и техничара Србије, p. 58, 336.

[3] Т. Манџуковски, (T. Mandžukovski) и Х. Спасевска, (H. Spasevska), 'Инженерска институција на Македонија: Еден век партнерство за одржлив развој: 1920 – 2020' (Engineering Institution of Macedonia: A Century of Partnership for Sustainable Development, 1920 – 2020), In Macedonian, Скопје: Асоцијација на здруженија на инженери – Инженерска институција на Македонија, 2020, pp. 8-20.

[4] Марић, (Note 2), p. 52.

[5] Манџуковски, Спасевска, (Note 3), p. 37.

[6] Манџуковски, Спасевска, (Note 3), p. 20.

[7] Република Северна Македонија – Министерство за образование и наука (Republic of North Macedonia – Ministry of Education and Science), Акредитирани универзитети и факултети (Accredited Universities and Faculties), https://mon.gov.mk/page/?id=2047 (Consulted on 31.03.2021).

[8] ЈП Службен Весник на Република Северна Македонија (PE Official Gazette of the Republic of North Macedonia) (2021): Бесплатен пристап до изданија (Free Access to Publications), In Macedonian, https://www.slvesnik.com.mk/besplaten-pristap-do-izdanija.nspx (Consulted between 01.09.2020 and 31.03.2021).

[9] Решение за отварање на средно-техничко училиште во гр. Скопје (Decision to Open a Secondary Technical School in Skopje), In Macedonian, Службен Весник на Феделана Единица Македонија (Official Gazette of Federal Unit Macedonia), Vol. 1, No. 1, 1945, p. 24.

[10] Времен правилник за полагање на матурски испит при државното средно техническо училиште „Здравко Цветковски" во Скопје во учебната 1946 година (Temporary Regulations for the Final Exam at the State Secondary Technical School 'Zdravko Cvetkovski' in Skopje in the Academic Year 1946), In Macedonian, Службен Весник на Народна Република Македонија (Official Gazette of People's Republic of Macedonia), Vol. 2, No. 18, 1946, pp. 167-168.

[11] Ibid, pp. 167-168.

[12] Ibid, p. 167.

[13] Решение за преминување на четиригодишното школување во средните стручни училишта (Decision for Transition into Four Years Education within the Secondary Professional Schools), In Macedonian, Службен Весник на Народна Република Македонија (Official Gazette People's Republic of Macedonia), Vol. 2, No. 18, 1946, pp. 289-290.

[14] Правилник за дипломски испит во средните стручни школи (Regulations for Diploma Exam within the Secondary Professional Schools), In Macedonian, Службен Весник на Народна Република Македонија (Official Gazette People's Republic of Macedonia), Vol. 12, No. 6, 1956, pp. 289-99.

[15] Правилник за изменување и дополнување на правилникот за дипломски испит во средните стручни школи (Amendments to the Regulations for Diploma Exam within the Secondary Professional Schools), In Macedonian, Службен Весник на Народна Република Македонија (Official Gazette People's Republic of Macedonia), Vol. 13, No. 19, 1957, pp. 338-339.

[16] Правилник за изменување и дополнување на правилникот за завршниот испит во техничките и другите средни училишта за стопанството и јавните служби (Amendments to the Regulations for Final Exam within the Technical and Other Professional Schools for the Economy and the Public Services), In Macedonian, Службен Весник на Народна Република Македонија (Official Gazette People's Republic of Macedonia), Vol. 16, No. 16, 1960, pp. 339-341.

[17] Правилник за полагањето на завршниот испит во техничките и другите средни училишта за стопанството и јавните служби (Regulations for Final Exam within the Technical and Other Professional Schools for the Economy and the Public Services), In Macedonian, Службен Весник на Народна Република Македонија (Official Gazette People's Republic of Macedonia), Vol. 17, No. 1, 1961, pp. 14-20.

[18] С. Ѓорѓијевска, (S. Gjorgjijevska), Дали знаете: Кој е најстариот факултет во Македонија? (Do you know: What is the oldest faculty in Macedonia?), https://www.fakulteti.mk/news/01052020/dali-znaete-koj-e-najstariot-fakultet-vo-makedonija (Consulted on 25.03.2021).

[19] R.J. Crampton, 'A Concise History of Bulgaria', Cambridge: Cambridge University Press, 2005, p. 168.

[20] Ѓорѓијевска, (Note 18).

[21] Закон за универзитетот во Скопје (University of Skopje Act), In Macedonian, Службен Весник на Народна Република Македонија (Official Gazette People's Republic of Macedonia), Vol. 5, No. 4, 1949, pp. 41-42.

[22] Уредба за основање и орагнизација на институтот за научни истражувања во индустријата (Decision to Establish the Institute for Scientific Research in the Industry), In Macedonian, Службен Весник на Народна Република Македонија (Official Gazette People's Republic of Macedonia), Vol. 5, No. 19, 1949, p. 157.

[23] Уредба за оснивање на технички факултет во Скопје (Decision to Establish the Technical Faculty in Skopje), In Macedonian, Службен Весник на Народна Република Македонија (Official Gazette People's Republic of Macedonia), Vol. 6, No. 34, 1950, pp. 257-258.

[24] Одлука за примена на одредибите на општиот закон за универзитетоте за хабилитационен труд на факултетите од Универзитетот во Скопје (the University Act for Habilitations at the University of Skopje Faculties), In Macedonian, Службен Весник на Народна Република Македонија (Official Gazette People's Republic of Macedonia), Vol. 11, No. 16, 1955, p. 194.

[25] Указ за прогласување на законот за Универзитетот во Скопје (University of Skopje Act), In Macedonian, Службен весник на Народна Република Македонија (Official Gazette People's Republic of Macedonia), Vol. 12, No. 15, 1956, pp. 249-268.

[26] Одлука за одредување бројот на студентите кои ќе се запишат на одделни факултети на Универзитетот во Скопје (Decision on the Student Intake at the Faculties of the University of Skopje), In Macedonian, Службен весник на Народна Република Македонија (Official Gazette People's Republic of Macedonia), Vol. 17, No. 7, 1961, pp. 106-107.

[27] Одлука за бројот на студентите кои можат да се запишат на одделни факултети на Универзитетот во Скопје (Decision on the Student Intake at the Faculties of the University of Skopje), In Macedonian, Службен весник на Народна Република Македонија (Official Gazette People's Republic of Macedonia), Vol. 18, No. 20, 1961, p. 253.

[28] Повелба за давање право на Удружението на инжинерите и техничарите во Македонија да можи со своите членови да врши проектирање и изведуење на сите часни технички работи (Permission to the Association of Engineers and Technicians in Macedonia with its members to undertake design and construction works), In Macedonian, Службен весник на Федералната Единица Македонија во Демократска и Федеративна Југославија (Official Gazette of the Federal Unit Macedonia within Democratic and Federal Yugoslavia), Vol. 1, No. 5, 1945, p. 1.

[29] Правилник за приправничкиот стаж, стручните испити и курсеви во градежната струка (Regulations for Probation (Practical Experience), Professional Exam and Courses in the Construction Profession), In Macedonian, Службен весник на Народна Република Македонија (Official Gazette People's Republic of Macedonia), Vol. 5, No. 1, 1949, pp. 1-8.

[30] Решение за одобрување оснивањето и работата на Друштвото на градежните инжинери и техници на НРМ со седиште во град Скопје (Granted Permission to Establish the Society of Civil Engineers and Technicians in PRM based in Skopje), In Macedonian, Службен весник на Народна Република Македонија (Official Gazette People's Republic of Macedonia), Vol. 7, No. 25, 1951, p. 167.

[31] Решение за одобрување оснивањето и работата на Друштвото на архитектите на Народна Република Македонија - Скопје (Granted Permission to Establish the Society of Architects of People's Republic Macedonia - Skopje), In Macedonian, Службен весник на Народна Република Македонија (Official Gazette People's Republic of Macedonia), Vol. 8, No. 31, 1952, p. 285.

[32] Решение за одобрување оснивањето и работата на Друштвото на електро-машинските инижинери и техници во Народна Република Македонија (Granted Permission to Establish the Society of Electro-Mechanical Engineers and Technicians in People's Republic Macedonia), In Macedonian, Службен весник на Народна Република Македонија (Official Gazette People's Republic of Macedonia), Vol. 9, No. 13, 1953, p. 101.

[33] Решение за одобрување оснивањето и работата на Урбанистичкото друштвото на НР Македонија (Granted Permission to Establish the Society for Urbanism of the PR Macedonia), In Macedonian, Службен весник на Народна Република Македонија (Official Gazette People's Republic of Macedonia), Vol. 12, No. 35, 1956, p. 553.

From 'Workers' to 'Operators': Labour of Moelven Brug

Maryia Rusak
PhD candidate at the Oslo School of Architecture and Design, Norway

Introduction

Actual construction work introduces a certain element of precarity to any building project: availability of workforce, workers' levels of skills and mastery of craft directly affect projects' budgets and planning. In the post-WWII period that witnessed an extensive reconstruction effort across Europe one of the ways to mitigate these uncertainties and obtain a greater control of the 'human factor' was a turn to prefabrication. Prefabrication transformed a process of construction from building to assembly, gathering different types of construction specialists under one roof and driving professionalization, specialization and process planning. This turn to prefabrication, however, had an ambiguous effect on labour: although a more technologically-driven process required better technical knowledge, it simultaneously diminished the role of craft, deskilling the workers. However, as more recent inquiries focusing on issues of labour in construction show, this was not a zero-sum development and questions of craft, skill and technical knowledge continued to complicate production of prefabricated structures [1].

This paper investigates this duality between professionalisation and deskilling through a study of a Norwegian construction company Moelven Brug. A former sawmill, in the post-WWII period Moelven turned to prefabrication, building housing, schools, sports halls and representative buildings from a system of flat-packaged prefabricated timber panels and housing sections. In just two decades between 1950-70 the company evolved from a small local business largely reliant on hand-craft into a large industrial enterprise with high levels of mechanisation, profoundly transforming ways work was performed. As Moelven incorporated international management models, adapted new technology and process planning, construction work became increasingly fragmented, specialised and professionalised. While this transformation made away with a tradition of local craft, replacing it with a more technological process, it also allowed for a broader pool of workers to be hired, driving local development. As Moelven employees evolved from 'workers' into 'operators', the study of the company's continuous negotiation between craft, technology and scientific expertise at the time of rapid industrial expansion offers new insights into professionalisation of labour within the prefabrication industry.

In Search of Lost Time

Founded in 1899 some 100 kilometres north of Oslo, by the mid-1940s Moelven Brug—literally a 'sawmill of Moelv'—faced a significant crisis. Its products for agriculture—mostly timber wheels, a regional speciality—were growing increasingly obsolete in the post-war era of rapid industrialisation and new sophisticated machines. At the same time, rationalisation, productivity and modernisation were high on the national agenda in all spheres of life. An array of experts and institutions—from a Norwegian Productivity Institute to private rationalisation consultancies—were ready to implement the most recent international managerial models and bring Norwegian businesses up-to-date [2]. Thus, to revamp its production, Moelven turned to IRAS—an Industrial Union's Bureau of Rationalisation—that throughout the 1950s evaluated the company's processes several times and suggested new accounting and managerial systems [3]. At last, another significant aspect awaited modernisation—Moelven workforce. By 1949, the company employed around 50 people—mostly carpenters and professional wood-workers, and it held no records of 'productivity' studies [4]. However, as Moelven started to produce prefabricated buildings that were of higher complexity and required an industrial scale of output, the company's workforce had to be modernised to meet the demands of mass-production. (Fig.1)

Figure 1: Moelven workers in 1959. From M. Antonsen, 75 år med Moelven-klubben i medgang og motgang: 1913-1988, Moelv: Bedriftsklubben Moelven, 1988.

Between December 5-14 1956 and January 10-19 1957 Moelven held two sets of productivity studies in its mechanical workshops following what seemed a nearly-unanimous decision of the production committee [5]. IRAS engineer R. Westby-Eriksen conducted the studies, assisted by Moelven foreman Torbjørn Kårhus. Each study was comprised of ten participants from the mechanical workshop and volunteers from other departments, compensated with 4,25 NOK per hour [6]. Essentially implementing one of the main techniques of scientific management, time-motion studies, IRAS engineers observed and recorded five major work operations from start to finish and several smaller tasks, with an overall observation time tallying to 80 hours. Among major operations observed were, 'assembly welding in a team of two men,' 'welding by one person', 'reinforcement of beams', 'assembly of elements with two men' and studies in a painting workshop [7]. The studies focused on different factors that influenced productivity, accounting for 'lost' and productive time, workers' movements and work methods, quality of tools and workplace arrangement.

Spatial relations between workers' bodies and machines were closely investigated and evaluated with regards to efficiency, distance travelled and time required to perform a certain action. For example, report no.1 detailed 'lost time' in an assembly welding carried out by two men. There, IRAS specialists identified a range of actions that contributed to 'lost time': from 'a conversation with a colleague,' 'getting materials,' 'getting tools' and 'clearing the work place' to 'waiting for a colleague,' 'going around the work station' and 'correcting mistakes.' Put together, they corresponded to 45,60% of overall production time, effectively rationalizing away one worker [8]. In other operations, for example, welding by a single person, 'lost time' accounted for only 11 or 15% and could hardly be reduced further. Besides lost time, IRAS engineers also suggested new arrangements of workshop furniture and tools that would condition more efficient movement of workers' bodies and thus higher productivity—for example, following a study of assembly of two timber elements "Bukk" and "Geit." [9].

Observing these operations, IRAS engineers decomposed work processes into series of discrete actions and movements, codified and recorded them in standardised process schemes and diagrams [10]. These standardised forms left little space for nuance: each action was classified according to predefined categories and fell either under 'operation', 'transport', 'control', 'stay' and 'storage,' traced together in a process flow. (Fig. 2) Time to perform each action was recorded in cmin—decimal fractions of time, as well as distance travelled and precise amount of materials used measured in cubic centimetres. According to technology historian James Beniger, such recording of work processes through standardised forms brought "destruction or ignoring of information in order to facilitate its processing" [11]. Standardised forms, a means of information pre-processing, facilitated governance of socio-technological systems and ushered what Saint-Simon described as a shift from "the government of men to the administration of things" [12]. However, this seemingly impartial government through standardised forms based on the principles of scientific management erased the value of tacit knowledge. Instead of a complex craft with a variety of nuances, work at the factory was now comprised of series of discrete steps, each action measured, rationalized and standardised. However, these forms also recorded and rationalised areas previously uncontrolled: in the words of IRAS engineer Hellern, "to stabilise the human factor" [13]. IRAS engineers were conductors of a new culture of expertise, that, when applied to Moelven production, profoundly transformed ways in which work was performed.

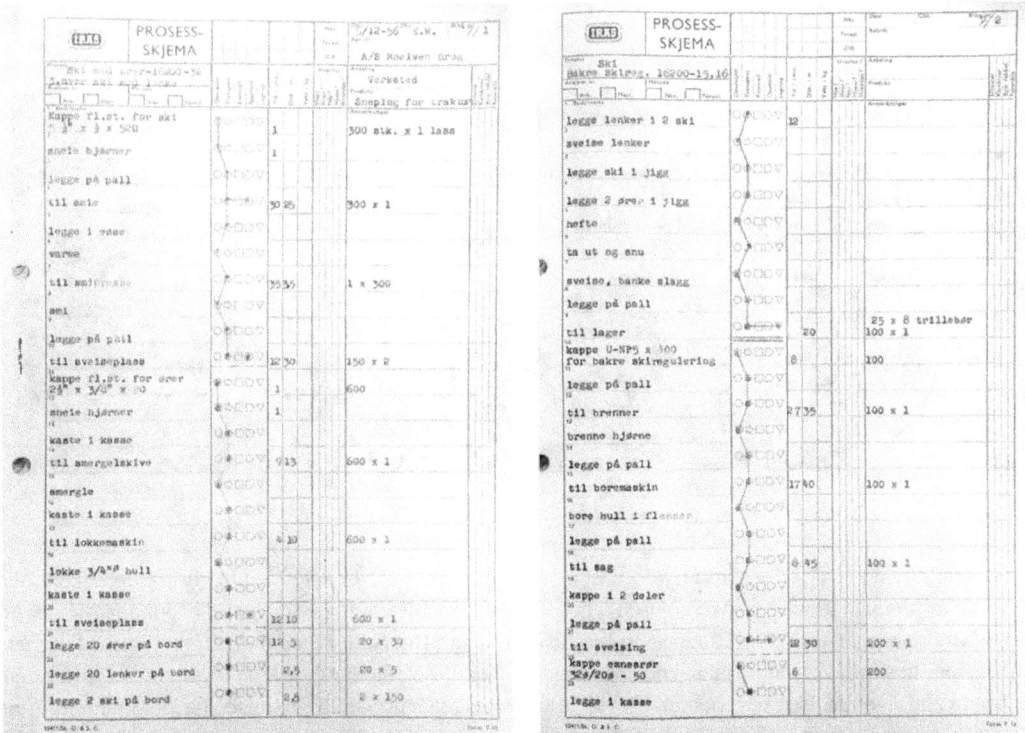

Figure 2: IRAS process diagrams. ARK-287-01/N, State archive in Hamar, Oslo, Norway.

From Craft to Machines

IRAS rationalisation of Moelven Brug in the late 1950s is important, as it can be considered what technology historian Andrew Feenberg calls an 'anti-program' to the former craft-based tradition of Moelven Brug, which allowed the whole system to be re-codified and opened a range of previously impossible potentialities [14]. The decade following IRAS work-studies was a time of rapid expansion: in 1958 Moelven started to produce prefabricated schools, averaging to 12.000 m² of educational space per year; a factory for glued-laminated timber was inaugurated in 1959 and from the early

1960s two new factories delivered prefabricated housing based on two different structural systems. Many Moelven long-term workers experienced this rapid expansion first-hand: when Johannes Karlsen started at Moelven in 1936, there were 80 people and by the 1970s there were nearly 2000 [15]. As the company moved to scaled serial production, the nature of work had also significantly changed. New machinery, in particular, conveyor belt assembly introduced in 1963, simplified work, making it more mechanical and repetitive. (Fig. 3)

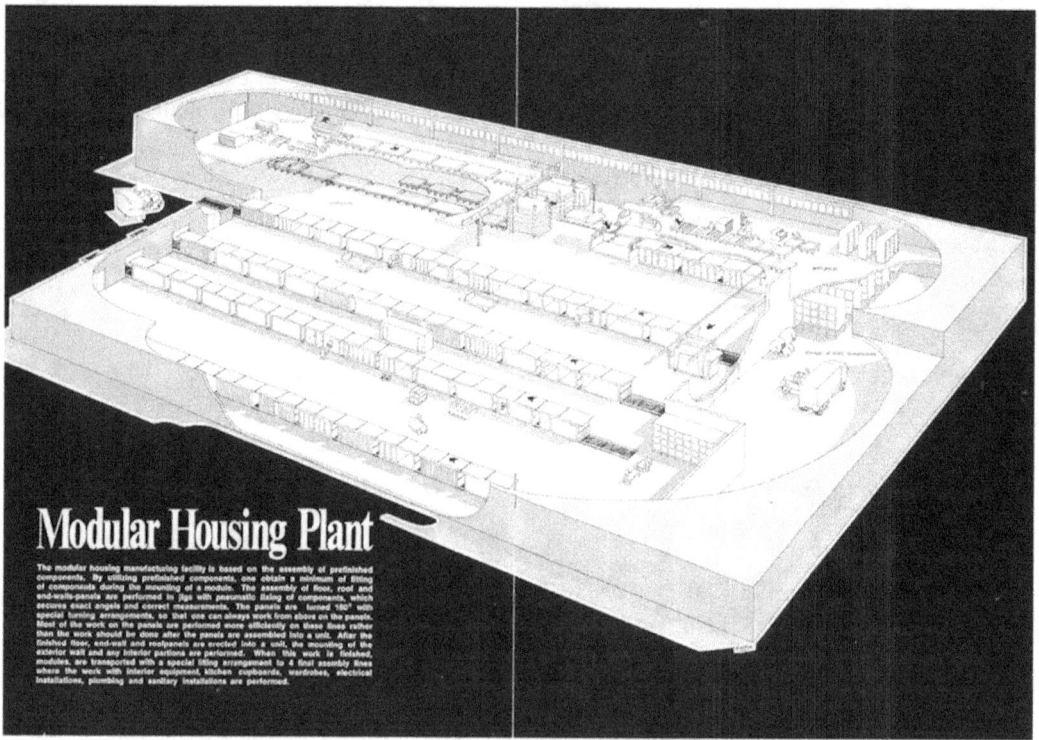

Figure 3: Moelven conveyor belt assembly. Moelven Industrier A/S, 1973.

Syver Smikkerud, a carpenter who started working for Moelven in 1925, in a 1975 interview emphasized, that with increased scale of production workers were put in a position where little could be improved about a particular assigned action and where one had nearly no influence on the final product [16]. Smikkerud thought that in the long term, this parcelling of work that brought industrial alienation would neither do service for the workers nor the company. Similarly, Kåre Kirkevold and Sverre Olsen who had both worked for Moelven since 1925 reminisced about the time, "one had a feeling for making things themselves" [17]. With the new organisation of work, this was hardly possible, work became too monotonous and there was little job satisfaction based on what one produced [18]. Kristian Johannessen, Moelven employee since 1925, also complained about the increased monotony. He noted, that compared to the previous generation of workers, the new one was not interested in learning a specific craft, and instead was happy just fulfilling mechanical tasks required of them [19]. These stories testify to an inescapable social transformation that happened with increased mechanisation: work became simplified, specialised and more monotonous. Instead of being proud of something one produced this sense shifted to a pride of belonging to a large enterprise that delivered complex mechanical products and collective effort put into this process.

As Moelven turned to prefabrication, the company strove to transfer as much construction work from site to factory as possible. However, unlike the British post-war construction industry that saw prefabrication as an opportunity to mitigate a shortage of skilled workers, Moelven was far less concerned with the absence of skilled labour. On the contrary, new production process that relied on conveyor-belt assembly simplified work and thus largely benefited from surplus of unskilled workers as forestry and agriculture industries were modernised. Prior to rapid industrialisation of the 1960s, most of Moelven workers were professionally educated fagarbeidere, who went through a traditional system of apprenticeship. With transition towards prefabrication and work that did not require command of a specific craft, the majority of new Moelven hires specifically in the housing factories were non-professionals. A part of the post-war Norwegian 'solidarity politics' aiming to even out social differences between different classes, the pay gap between professional and non-professional workers' salaries was also significantly reduced, diminishing the importance of specific craft-based education.

New employees went through a couple of weeks of learning through practice and supervision; in a course of just over eight weeks one was thought to have enough knowledge and skills to take nearly any production job [20]. While the 'old crew' lamented diminished autonomy and the fact that new generation did not want to learn a craft, by the end of the 1960s, long-term employees were outnumbered on a scale of 1 to 10. New Moelven hires first and foremost wanted secure work places and the majority of them actually learned new skills [21].

Figure 4: New Moelven workers. Newspaper clipping, Hamar Arbeiderblad, 1965.

New Workers, New Skills

IRAS method studies provided the backbone for this transition to a different labour pool. Prior to 1957, Moelven workers got paid per item of work produced within a set time, a piece-work system, essentially trading their skills [22]. With IRAS method studies that established a benchmark for productivity within a set time interval, Moelven shifted to payment per hour during which a certain amount of work had to be completed: now, Moelven employees traded their time, instead of skill [23]. Architecture and labour historian Christine Wall drawing from Richard Biernacki argues, that these different payment systems, the former characteristic of British industries and the latter of German, when transposed onto construction industry influenced both the perception of labour and the final built product. The German system based on productivity during a fixed period of time essentially appropriated labour power through time, and thus, according to Wall, was more conducive to the success of building process rationalisation [24]. As employer benefits were directly proportional to employees' skills and command of craft, this model encouraged better vocational training and technical education provided by the employer [25]. Since Moelven adapted this time-based payment system, the company was directly interested in improving workers' skills to increase productivity. Thus, it offered ample educational opportunities for its employees.

The first Moelven educational fund was established in 1942 but was significantly updated in 1960, just two years after IRAS studies, and in 1964 with a yearly budget of 35000 NOK [26]. The fund provided interest-free loans that were supposed to be paid over the course of five years, covering expenses for pursuing either professional, *yrkesopplæring*, or higher education programs in "the areas of importance for the company" [27]. In order to qualify, one had to work for Moelven for at least two years and commit to another three after completing the studies. Many have pursued this opportunity: in 1965, for example, Magne Olav Skullerud applied for a loan to support his studies at the Norwegian Technical University (NTH) for three years. He was offered funding on a condition that upon return he would "undertake an appropriate position at Moelven Brug for at least two years" and work at the company throughout summer vacations [28]. In addition to higher education, scholarships were also granted for pursuing a mid-level technical education. For example, in 1967, Jan Pedersen received a loan for his studies at Oslo Elementærtekniske Skole, and Ole Gunnar Larsen for study at the Göteborg's Technical Institute [29]. Another applicant, Kåre Karlsen, pursued a 2 year study course at the professional school in Dovre [30]. For more specialised work, for example element assembly, Moelven employees followed specific courses arranged by the company and external specialists. These efforts, in fact, positively contributed to workers' professionalisation: although starting out with a largely unprofessional workforce, by the late 1970s most Moelven employees at both housing factories had one to three years of professional schooling [31].

For Moelven, workers' education was crucial to meet the specific demands of prefabrication industry, 'a child of its time' and to match the pace of accelerated technological development [32]. Industrial production required workers to have stronger technical knowledge and skills and that were previously not necessary [33]. To fill these gaps, in addition to more formal external educational courses, from the 1960s Moelven started to arrange a number of internal short-term professional courses: for example, TWI an American-style 'training within industry' program, a course on reading technical drawings, lectures on company's organisation and work safety [34]. In 1971, series of courses were held by Hartmark-IRAS, a successor to Moelven's 1950s rationalization agency, on process management and product development, as well as a course on network planning [35]. As these offers were quickly booked out and shortage of places complained about, it is possible to conclude that Moelven employees were actively interested in improving their professional skills [36]. In practice, better education indeed advanced one towards higher engineering and managerial positions—which was the case, for example, with Magne Skullerud [37]. As Moelven employees gained new technical skills, the complexity of technological process increased, and they were requalified from 'workers' to 'operators' [38]. (Fig. 5)

Specialists of the New Machine Age

Moelven products were highly prefabricated, up to 95%, and most construction work usually carried out on site was moved to the factory, heralding a transformation from building to assembly. Serial production and conveyor-belt assembly demanded more managerial work: well-oiled supply and procurement systems, efficient management of contractors and materials, planned transport and storage. While before 1950 Moelven did not have a single engineer on staff, by the 1960s a new class of professionals emerged: constructors, engineers, economists, process planers, product and technical development managers, salesmen, rationalisation specialists, accountants and data managers numbered as many as blacksmiths and carpenters in the inter-war years [39]. Their numbers increased faster than workers on the shop-floor, and the two groups often did not share the same professional identity [40].

Specially educated 'calculators', for example, quantified work, material and product expenses sourced from a multitude of subcontractors and performed complex calculations on work pricing [41]. In turn, constructors, technical engineers, managers and work-studies specialists deconstructed each product into composite parts and work tasks, divided across different teams of workers along a conveyor line [42]. The planning office comprised production technologists implementing new network systems, where cyclical production followed the most detailed time scheduling schemes [43].

Figure 5: Moelven operators. Moelven Industrier A/S, 1973.

Pert-chart and network diagrams visualised flows of materials and exact order of work operations, where all intermediate-stage elements had then to fit together into one final product [44]. Moelven engineers and managers travelled to study similar enterprises abroad, particularly in the United States, simultaneously advancing their own expertise and bringing back technological and organisational know-how.

With the advent of new computers used for accounting and process management, new specialists made their way into the construction industry: programmers, data managers, and computer engineers. In 1969, Moelven hired a civil engineer and data specialist Ove Atle Hagestande who would develop the Moelven data management sector [45]. For more effective calculations, Moelven engineers had to design and run their own programs based on specific aspects of Moelven prefabrication process, leading to a subsequent merger between data and accounting departments by the mid-1970s [46].

Thus, increasing complexity of production had to be matched by a continuous access to high-class specialists, brought up either within the company or hired externally. As Moelven production was comprised of a wide range of products and departments, segmented and specialised construction work had to be streamlined and tightly managed by a new class of process planners and logisticians. Unlike conventional construction firms, these specialists, from production planners, engineers and assembly workers to managers, architects, sales and advertisement professionals, all inhabited the same factory space. (Fig. 6)

Figure 6: White-collar specialists, representation of Moelven process from advertisement booklet. Moelven Industrier A/S, 1974.

Conflicting Representation

Increasing specialisation and professionalisation of the workforce within what essentially was an assembly rather than a building industry, however, posed significant problems within the specific Norwegian system of union representation. In 1968, for example, Moelven prefabricated housing factory employed more than 100 men that worked as carpenters, wallpaperers, painters, plumbers and electricians, mechanics and storage workers. As all Moelven workers were unionised, any conflict situation with a group of workers up or down the assembly line would paralyze the entire production, a similar problem faced by the ship-building industry in Britain [47]. As workers' professional identification increased with time, particularly for electricians, plumbers and sanitary installation specialists, Moelven management constantly referred to the cautionary tale of Danish and British ship-building industries, that with increased specialisation quite literally drowned in union struggles [48]. A conveyor belt assembly of prefabricated products that joined several professionals along the line thus proved to be at odds with a Norwegian tradition of collective pay bargaining and professional representation.

Although Moelven worked generally with timber, most of its employees were a part of Jern og Metallarbeiderforbund, a union for the metal and iron industry, that had a strong local and national representation and powerful weight in professional negotiations [49]. As prefabrication industry was new for Norway and Moelven production had few analogues, it was hard to define which work fell under the jurisdiction of which union and what guidelines were to be followed for professional representation [50]. For example, while union affiliation was easier to define for workers engaged solely with assembly of ready-made houses, the situation was more complex for employees that produced, for example, metal components that later went into ready-made products [51].

Negotiations on union membership, and reluctance of both the company and its workers to join the Bygningsindustriarbeiderforbund, the Construction Industry Workers Union, can be traced through a heated tri-partite exchange between the company and two unions in question [52]. The Construction Industry union righteously wanted to claim more members due to direct nature of their work, while those potential members were reluctant to leave one of the most powerful organisations in the country in favour of a much smaller union with fewer benefits. Eventually, it was suggested that workers that only deal with prefabricated products would join the construction industry, while those that work in other departments, even if their products end up in prefabricated houses, should remain with Jern- og Metall. However, by the 1970s under continuous pressure from the industry only 130 Moelven workers remained a part of the Iron and Metal union, while the rest, around 900 people, were a part of Construction Industry union [53].

Conclusion

Moelven transformation from a small local business reliant on hand-craft to a large building conglomerate with "the most advanced prefabrication technology in Europe" serves as an appropriate case study of professionalisation within a construction industry. Moelven's turn to prefabrication had a profound effect on the company workforce: on the one hand, a highly technological process required new technical knowledge and skills, driving professionalisation and specialisation. A new class of managerial and technical professionals who planned, streamlined and supervised all aspects of serial production and assembly emerged. On the other hand, new 'scientific' methods of work and conveyor-belt assembly simplified labour and diminished the role of craft. This, however, allowed Moelven to hire a broader pool of workers, driving regional development. In fact, new 'unprofessional' Moelven employees had gained professional education through ample educational opportunities offered by the company, evolving from 'workers' to 'operators'. The turn to prefabrication thus brought specialisation of both managerial and assembly work, which with time proved problematic within specific Norwegian context of strong union representation. The case of Moelven Brug thus has to be seen within a context of broader social transformation that happened under rapid Norwegian industrialisation of the 1960-70s that relied on imported and assimilated foreign models of management and work.

References

[1] See for example, William Tatton Brown's speech to a 1956 meeting of 50 modular society members quoted at length in C. Wall, An Architecture of Parts: Architects, Building Workers and Industrialization in Britain 1940-1970. London: Routledge, 2013. p. 111. Also in B. Russell, Building Systems, Industrialization, and Architecture. London: Wiley, 1981. p.318.
[2] R. Amdam, G.Yttri, "The European Productivity Agency, the Norwegian Productivity Institute and Management Education," *Arbeidsnotat*, no.96, Oslo: TMV-senteret, Universitetet i Oslo, 1996. Bernard Hellern, *Rasjonaliseringen som ledd i gjenoppbyggingen*, Oslo: Aschehoug, 1945.
[3] IRAS stands for 'Industriforbundets Rasjonaliseringskontor A/S.' For other IRAS reports for Moelven see 1946 "Rapport til styret i A/S Moelven Brug," 1954 report "Instilling vedrørende avdelingsregnskap organisering i 1950-åra," 1955 "Instansplan IRAS-LN-april 1955," all in Folder 0001 "Lover/vedtekter, organisasjonsplaner," Folder L0001, ARK-287-01/N. State archive in Hamar, Norway (SAH).
[4] "Produksjonsverdi og lönnings forhold i 7-årsperioden 1940-1946," Folder L0002 – Lønnsoverenskomster, in SAH/ARK-287-01/P/Pf.

[5] Production committees—*produksjonsutvalg*—were modelled largely after the British war-time industrial committees that brought together representatives of labour, management, and technical experts. See meeting notes from December 23, 1955; October 2, 1956; all in Folder 0002 "Møtereferat" in "Produksjonsutvalget i Moelven Brug" SAH/ARK-287-01/A/Ac/L0000A.

[6] "Forhandlingsprotokoll," Folder 0001 in "Produksjonsutvalget i Moelven Brug" SAH/ARK-287-01/A/Ac/L0000A.

[7] Industriforbundets Rationaliseringskontor A/S, "Rapport vedrørende rasjonaliseringsundersøkelser i mekanisk verksted", Oslo 9.4.1957, Folder 0009 in SAH/ARK-287-01/N/L0001.

[8] "Bilag no.1", "Samleplan for tapstider; Motasjesveising i gigg;" or "Rapport vedrørende rasjonaliseringsundersøkelser i mekanisk verksted", p.3. All in Folder 0009 in SAH/ARK-287-01/N/L0001.

[9] "Bilag no. 5 & 6" with alternative arrangement of assembly process for two timber elements "Bukk" and "Geit." In "Rapport vedrørende rasjonaliseringsundersøkelser i mekanisk verksted", Folder 0009 in SAH/ARK-287-01/N/L0001.

[10] "Bliag no.7/3","Prosess-skjema." In "Rapport vedrørende rasjonaliseringsundersøkelser i mekanisk verksted", Folder 0009 in SAH/ARK-287-01/N/L0001.

[11] J. R. Beniger, *The Control Revolution: Technological and Economic Origins of the Information Society*, Cambridge, Mass: Harvard University Press, 1986. pp.15–16.

[12] H. Saint-Simon, *Henri Saint-Simon (1760-1825): Selected Writings on Science, Industry, and Social Organisation*, London: Croom Helm, 1975. p.3.

[13] B. Hellern, *Rasjonell bedriftsledelse, Norbok*, Oslo: Norges industriforbund, 1943. p.36.

[14] A. Feenberg, *Questioning Technology*, Psychology Press, 1999. p.117.

[15] M. Antonsen, *75 år med Moelven-klubben i medgang og motgang: 1913-1988*, Moelv: Bedriftsklubben Moelven, 1988. pp.70–71.

[16] *Moelven: bedriftavis for A/S Laminator, A/S Moelven Brug of A/S Ringsakerhus*, no. 17, 1975, p.11.

[17] Antonsen, *75 år*, (Note 15) p.64.

[18] ibid., p.64.

[19] ibid., p.65.

[20] A. Karlsen, *Fra håndverk til masseproduksjon: en studie av omstillinger ved Moelven Brug*, Oslo: Nordlandsforskning, 1994. p. 67. Also see "Kort referat fra møte vedr. Kvinnelig Arbeidskraft 29/8 1974" in Folder 0003, "Ansettelser, instrukser" SAH/ARK-287-01/P/Pc/L0001.

[21] Karlsen, *Fra håndverk*, (Note 20) p.68.

[22] F. Madsen, *Lønnssystemer*, Oslo: Universitetsforlag, 1969. pp.20–22.

[23] In fact, before making a transition to time-based payments, in 1955 Moelven management suggested a mixed tariff system, which a local union representation advised strongly against. Mixed system was more beneficial to the company and less so to the workers. See a letter to Magne Antonsen from J. Larsson and Håkon Thesen, November 25 1955. Folder 0006 "Moelven–Moelven Brug A/S" in AAB/ARK-1659/E/L0249, Arbeiderbevegelsens arkiv og bibliotek, Norsk Jern- og Metallarbeiderforbund Archive.

[24] Wall, *An Architecture of Parts*, (Note 1) pp. 12–13. Original argument in R. Biernacki, *The Fabrication of Labor: Germany and Britain, 1640-1914*, Berkeley: University of California Press, 1995. p.141.

[25] Wall, *An Architecture of Parts*, (Note 1) p.12.

[26] "Vedtekter for A/S Moelven Brug's utdannelsesfond". Item 303 in Folder 0003 "Styreprotokoll Moelven Brug 1944-1969" in SAH/ARK-287-01/A/Aa/L0001.

[27] Board-meeting discussion on September 23 1960, p. 246, item 303 in Folder 0003 "Styreprotokoll Moelven Brug 1944-1969" in SAH/ARK-287-01/A/Aa/L0001. *Hamar Arbeiderblad* (28 September 1964), p.4. Folder L0000A "Forhandlingsprotokoll" in SAH/ARK-287-01/P/Pe/L0000A.

[28] See a letter from Moelven to Herr Magne Olav Skullerud, 13 August 1965. See Folder L0007 "Handelskontrakter, priser mm" in SAH/ARK-287-01/K/Kc/L0007.

[29] *Bedriftavis* (Note 16) no.1, 1967, p.13.

[30] A contract between Kåre Karlsen and Moelven Brug, August 11 1964. See Folder L0007 "Handelskontrakter, priser mm" in SAH/ARK-287-01/K/Kc/L0007.

[31] H. Buflod, *Teknologisk endring av småhusbyggingen: en analyse av drivkrefter og samfunnsmessige konsekvenser*, Oslo: Norsk institutt for by- og regionforskning, 1985. p. 82.
[32] *Bedriftavis* (Note 16) no.2, 1968, p.1.
[33] Årsberetning 1950/1951 in Folder L0001 "Årsberetninger" SAH/ARK-287-01/I/L0001.
[34] *Bedriftavis* (Note 16) no.2, 1968, p.15; *Bedriftavis* no.9, 1970, p.2 and *Bedriftavis* no.10, 1971, p.6.
[35] *Bedriftavis* (Note 16) no.9, 1970, p.2; *Bedriftavis* no.10, 1971, p.6.
[36] *Bedriftavis* (Note 16) no.9, 1971, p.2.; *Bedriftavis* no.10, 1971, p.6; *Bedriftavis* no.14, 1973, p.3.
[37] See a progression of Skullerud studies from a technical track to engineering degrees. Folder L0007 "Handelskontrakter, priser mm" in SAH/ARK-287-01/K/Kc/L0007.
[38] *Bedriftavis* (Note 16) no.14 1973, p.3; *Bedriftavis* no. 17, 1975, p.11.
[39] See Årsberetning 1950/1951 "Vedr. Arbeidseffektiviteten" in Folder L0001 "Årsberetninger" SAH/ARK-287-01/I/L0001. Also in Antonsen, *75 år*, (Note 15) p.76.
[40] Karlsen, *Fra håndverk*, (Note 20) p.98.
[41] *Aftenposten* (7 April 1972), p.36.
[42] J. Mageli, *A/S Moelven brug: karakteristika og synspunkter*, Bergen: Norges handelshøyskole, 1977. p.4.
[43] *Bedriftavis* (Note 16) no.10, 1971, p.6; *Bedriftavis* no.18, 1975, p.6.
[44] *Bedriftavis* (Note 16) no.9, 1971, p.16.
[45] *Bergens Tidende* (26 March 1969), p.27; also *Stavanger Aftenblad, Aftenposten, Drammens Tidende og Buskeruds Blad.*
[46] See "Personaladministrativ håndbok", 1983. In Folder 0001 in SAH/ARK-287-01/P/Pg.
[47] *Bedriftavis* (Note 16) no. 4, 1968, pp.15-16. E. W. Cooney, 'Productivity, Conflict and Order in the British Construction Industry: A Historical View,' *Construction History*, vol. 9, 1993, pp.71-84.
[48] *Bedriftavis* (Note 16) no.4, 1968, pp.14-15.
[49] T. Bergh, *Storhetstid (1945-1965)*, Oslo: Tiden, 1987. pp.107–9. Also *Fra håndverk*, (Note 20) p.101.
[50] See a letter from Moelv Jern- og Metall to Norsk Jern of Metall, on the problems of representation for house-building workers, December 9, 1959. Folder 0006 "Moelven–Moelven Brug A/S" in AAB/ARK-1659/E/L0249, Arbeiderbevegelsens arkiv og bibliotek, Oslo, Norway (AAB).
[51] A letter from Moelv Jern og Metall to Norsk Jern- og Metall, December 9, 1959.
[52] See, for example a letter from Moelven to Mekaniske Verksteders Lansforening, May 8 1959; or a letter from Landsorganisasjonen in Norge (LO) to Norsk Arbeidsgiverforening on the transfer of workers; February 10 1959; or a letter from Norsk Bygningsindustriarbeiderforbund to Moelven Brug on May 18, 1961. All in "Teknologibedriftenes Landsforening TB" archive, RA/PA-1700/M/L0101/0001. A protocol on the workers transfer between unions on September 18 1961; also a letter from Moelv Jern- og Metall to Norsk Jern- og Metall on November 23 1961. All in Folder 0006 in AAB/ARK-1659/E/L0249.
[53] Antonsen, *75 år,* (Note 15) p.22.

David Yeomans

Frank Newby's Star Beams

David Yeomans
Independent scholar

Introduction

Frank Newby graduated from Cambridge, came to London in 1950 and joined Felix Samuely and Partners, eventually becoming the firm's senior partner when Samuely died of a heart attack in 1959. In the intervening years he clearly benefited from learning Samuely's approach to design. In the 1950s Britain was recovering from WWII and had much rebuilding work to do while also having a shortage of building materials. In that climate Felix Samuely was to propose a number of innovative ideas one of which was the use of star beams [1]. The simplest form of star beam is a Y shaped beam on three supports (Fig. 1a). However, other arrangements are also possible as in Figure 1b and 1c. The first record we have of this device was in reinforced concrete and used in the assembly hall of Woodberry Down School. This seems to have been one of the first jobs for which Frank Newby carried out calculations but he was subsequently to use the device in a number of major structures.

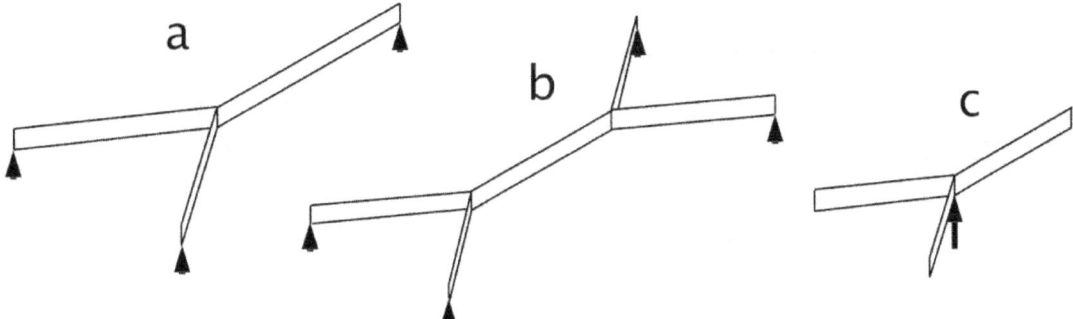

Figure 1: Three possible star beam arrangements

Woodberry Down School

The assembly hall at Woodberry Down School was hexagonal in plan with a gallery across the back and down the two sides. The normal way of supporting a sloping auditorium gallery floor is to have a primary beam halfway down the slope with secondary supports cantilevered forward to support the lower seating. In this case this beam had to be cranked to follow the plan shape and so the cranked beam was picked up at mid-span by a short beam forming the stem of the Y shape. Figure 2 shows the resulting star beam in an isometric drawing produced by the office at the time.

Much easier to understand is the sketch made by Newby as part of the calculations for this (Fig. 3). These, clearly in his hand, survive in the office archive and show both his take off of the loads and a section through the gallery. The star beam is clearly marked in the sketch.

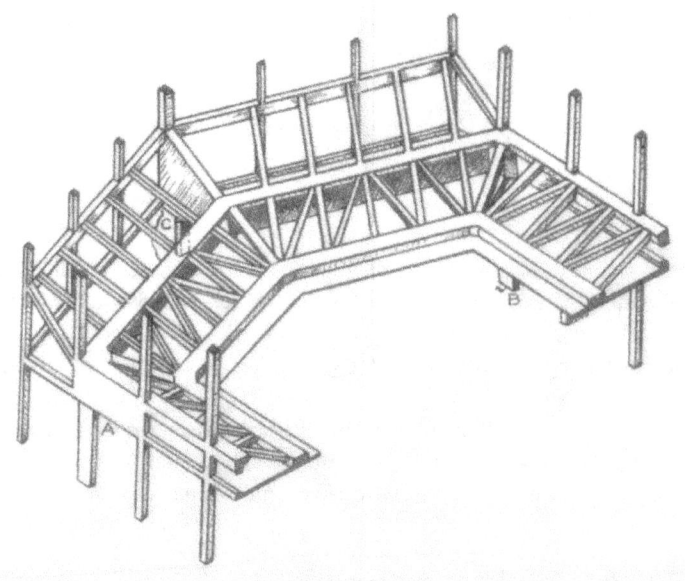

Figure 2: Isometric of the Woodberry Down assembly hall gallery.

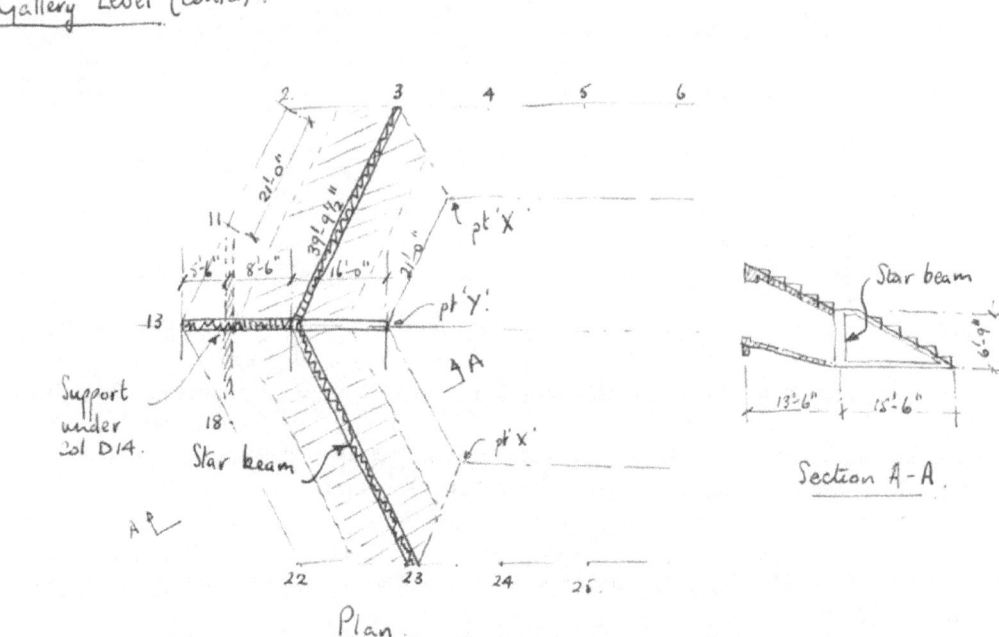

Figure 3: A page from Newby's calculations for the Woodberry Down star beam

London and Leicester

The first star beam designed by Newby himself was for the first floor structure of the US Chancellery, necessary to cope with a 'dragon beam' picking up transverse floor beams at the corner that could not be brought to a corner support. This was formed of two precast units prestressed together (Fig. 4)

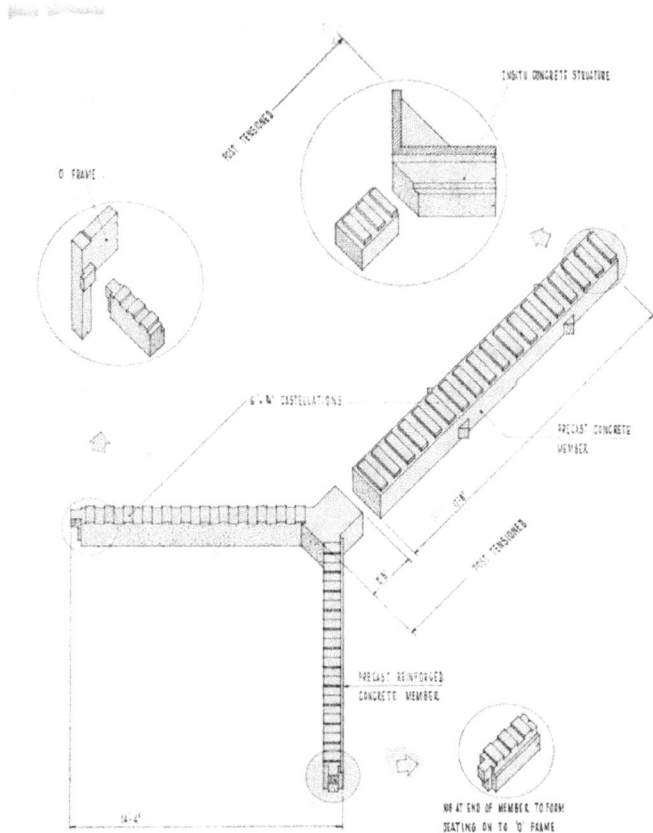

Figure 4 Corner star beam at US Chancellery

At Leicester University Newby used the kind of star beam structure shown in Figure 1b to carry the lowest floor of the office tower. The floors above had been carried by upstand beams round the perimeter of the floors on eight columns. With a change to four corner supports the use of a star beam under the floor allowed the glazing to be brought down to floor level. Newby said of the office tower:

> Construction at the fifth floor level is an eight-inch insitu concrete slab supported by a central spine beam, which has splayed ends as a Y to join the four columns at the corners [2].

Octagonal plans

A number of other architects have used octagonal plans, essentially squares or rectangles with the corners cut off and Newby dealt with a number of those: Gilbert Murray Hall, student accommodation for Leicester University, Fisher House,

Frank Newby's Star Beams

Cambridge University, which is its Catholic Chaplaincy and the University Graduate Centre, also in Cambridge. Each of these involved a search for the best structure although star beams were clearly the best option in each case.

Gilbert Murray Hall

The dining room at Gilbert Murray hall was a square with the corners removed to accommodate doors, the roof a ziggurat to provide for two stages of clerestory lighting. Schemes 1 and 2 (Figs 5 & 6) use paired principal rafters to avoid simple hip rafters requiring support over the doors. The difference in the schemes is that scheme 1 brings the rafters to a central point while scheme 2 uses a compression ring at the top. Note that Newby is exploring different layouts for the common rafters in his sketch of scheme 1. Note also the possibility of cranking the rafters should the height of the windows require it.

Schemes 4 and 5 (Figs 7 & 8) explore similar sections but with star beams instead of paired principal rafters. This was clearly the preferred solution because Newby went on to work out the steel sizes (Fig. 9). In fact that was done for more than one steel layout with workings for this probably done by an assistant. Newby made a hand written table of steel weights and thus approximate costs, presumably to present to the architect.

This was typical of Newby's method of working. He would commonly present more than one possible scheme from which an architect could select or price more than one arrangement so that the architect could see the relative costs.

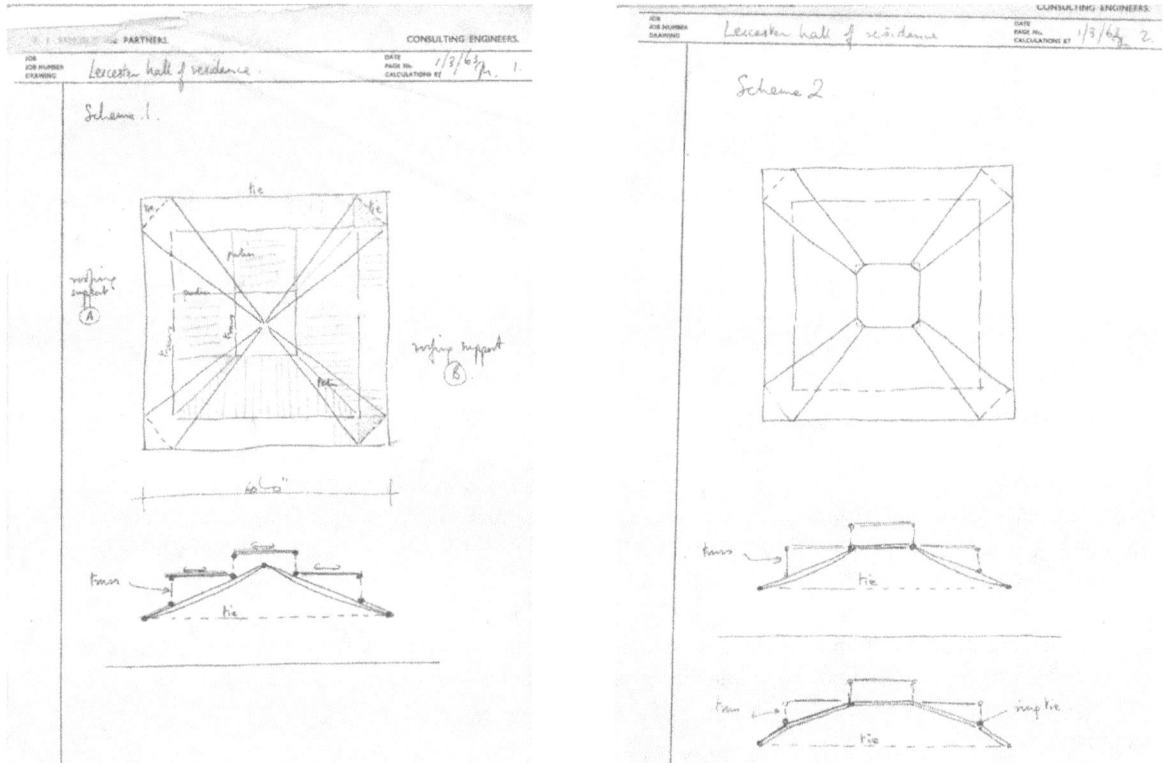

Figures 5: (left) Gilbert Murray Hall - dining room with paired principal rafters
Figure 6: (right) Gilbert Murray Hall - dining room with paired principal rafters and central compression ring.

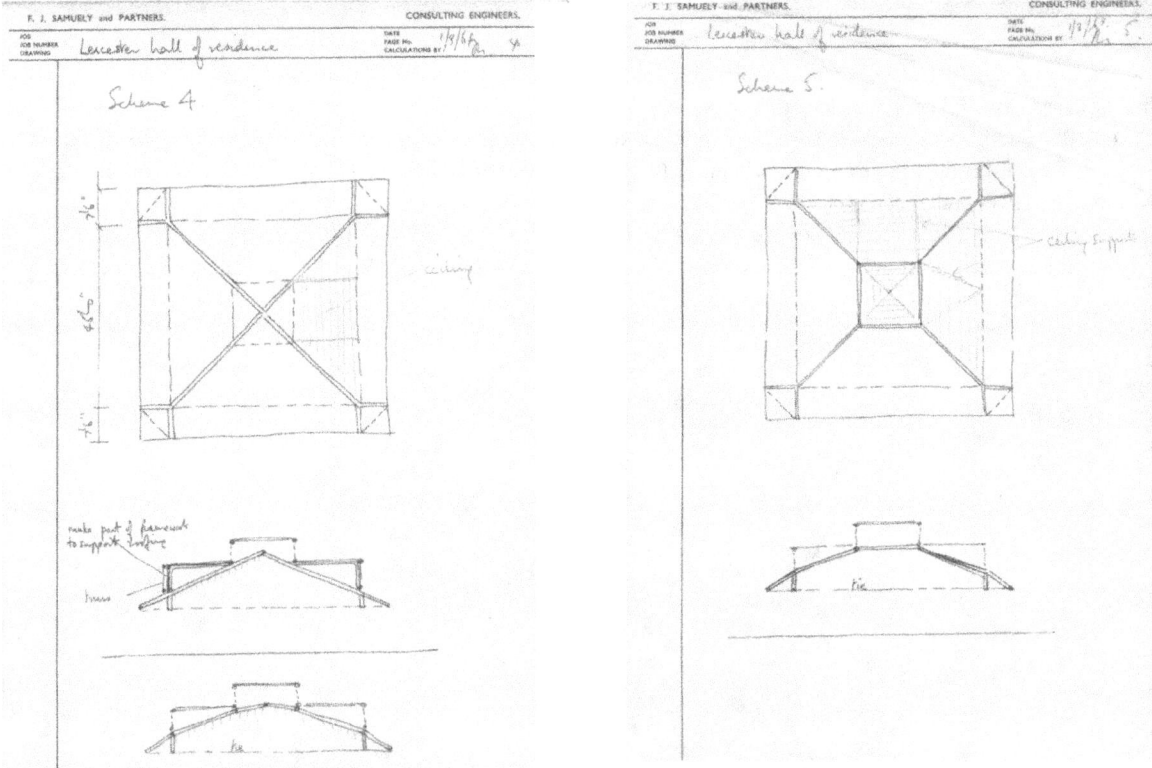

Figures 7: (left) Scheme 4 with star beam
Figure 8: (right) Scheme 5 with star beam and central compression ring

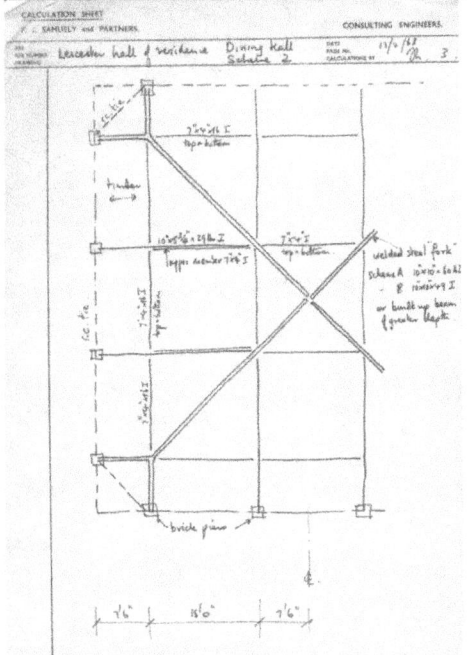

Figure 9: Gilbert Murray Hall – Proposed Steel sizes

Fisher House

The chapel of Fisher House, the Catholic Chaplaincy at Cambridge had a similar plan to the Leicester dining hall but was smaller in span and did not have the corner doors. Newby must have felt that he'd been there before because his scheme A (Fig. 10) explores both the paired principal rafters and the star beam arrangement in a single sketch. He then quickly settles on the star beam arrangement for scheme B (Fig.11). Note again how he considers two different possibilities for the common rafters both with and without purlin support.

The timber structure shown in Figure 12 is formed of paired timbers clasping and bolted to welded steel connectors.

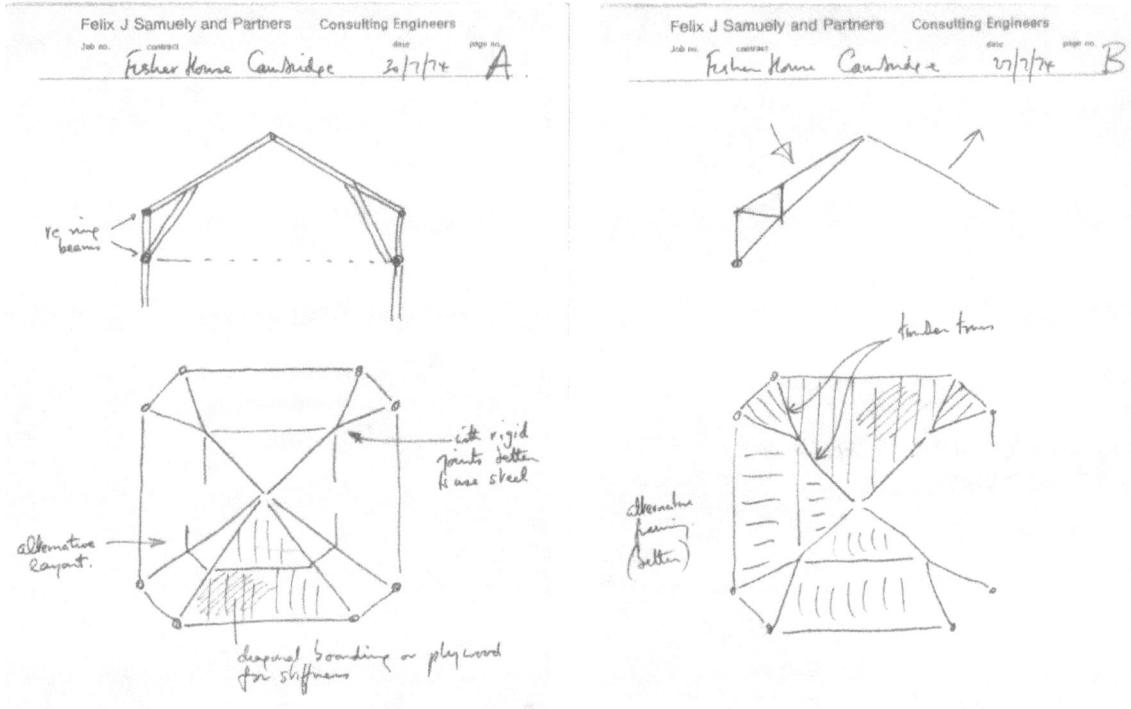

Figure 10: (left) Fisher House with paired rafters and star beam alternatives.
Figure 11: (right) Schemes with star beams

Figure 12: Fisher House chapel roof as built

Graduate Centre, Cambridge

This was a close collaboration between Newby and the architect William Howell. Howell liked the expression of structure in architecture and in an article entitled 'Vertebrate Buildings' he described the design process for Graduate Centre, Cambridge in which he and Frank Newby worked together making sketches of possible structural arrangements. Sadly the originals of these sketches have been lost but they were reproduced in Howell's article [3]. What resulted for the dining room and common rooms were again octagonal spaces but in this case rectangles with the corners removed, three such rooms ran down two sides of the building and over three floors (Fig. 13) Columns are set in from the corners support star beams like those of Figure 1C so that the structure is very visible in these dining and common rooms.

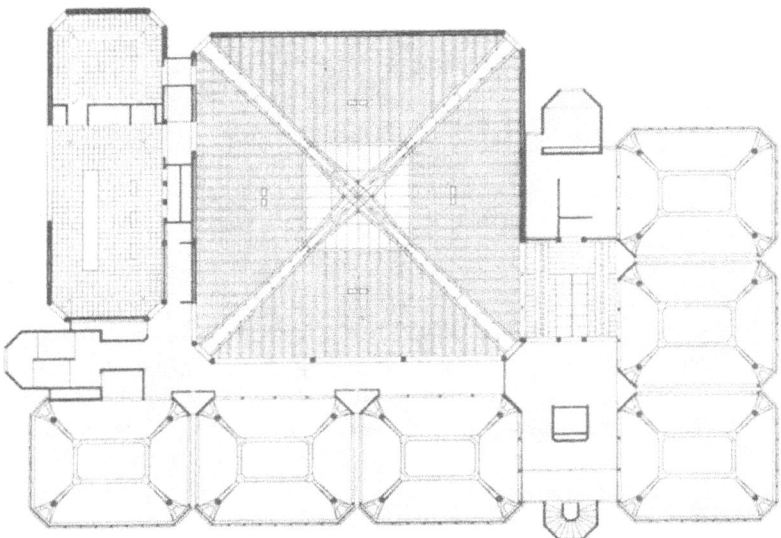

Figure 13: Plan of the Graduate Centre, Cambridge University

Clifton Roman Catholic Cathedral

Clifton Cathedral went through a long design process but Ronald Weeks's plan that eventually emerged was focused on a hexagonal sanctuary (Fig. 14). The congregation was placed on three sides of this, rather like a theatre auditorium round an apron stage. The trapezoidal area at the bottom of Figure 14 is the entrance and baptistery.

The structure provided by Newby is clear from his sketch (Fig. 15) that shows a cranked beam round the front of the sanctuary picked up by the two beams across the 'auditorium' space. Note the small sketch showing a basic star beam arrangement at the bottom of this sheet that must have been drawn to explain the nature of star beams for the benefit of the architect. The dramatic effect can be seen in Figure 16 where the cranked elements of the star beam, pierced by hexagonal openings, form a deep skirt that hides the source of the light flooding down onto the sanctuary.

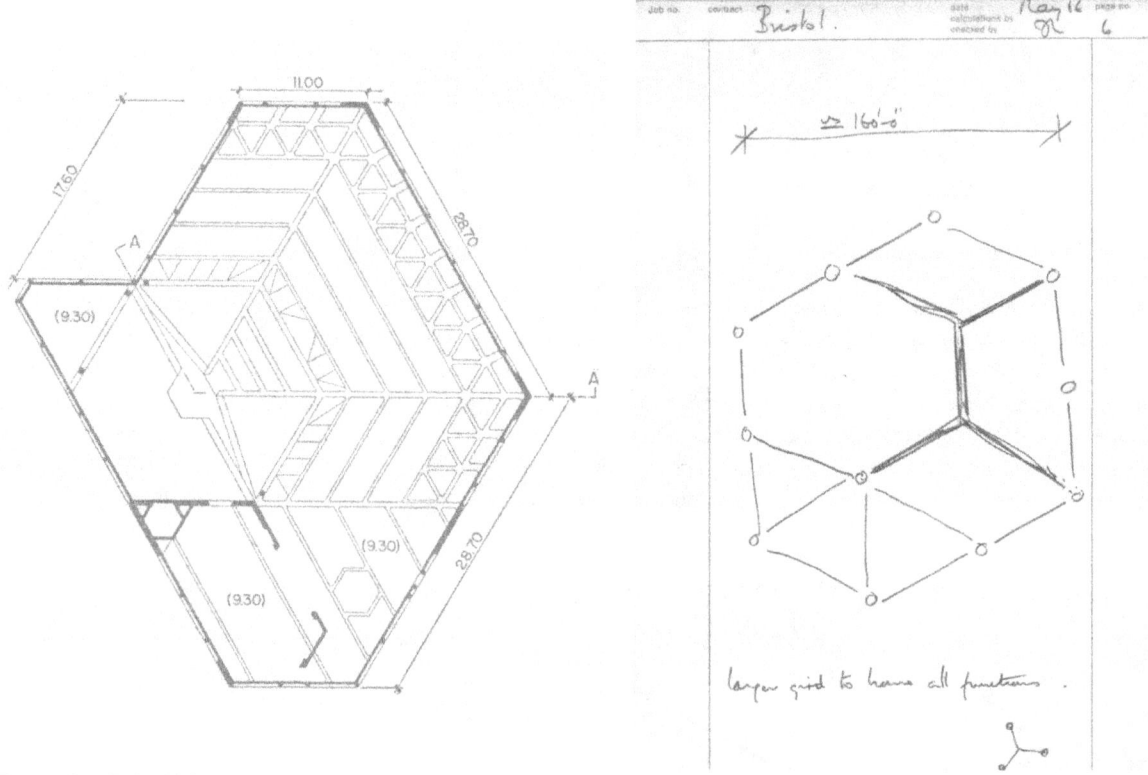

Figure 14: (left) Clifton Cathedral plan
Figure 15: (right) Newby's sketch of the star beam structure

The original design had a hexagonal bell-tower like structure above the sanctuary and Newby produced drawings showing supports for that structure. However, following criticism of that design it was replaced by three spire-like elements supported by continuing the arms of the star beam that spanned over the auditorium beyond the cranked beam to cantilever over the sanctuary (Fig. 17). The three beams between the cantilevers (seen on the plan) frame the rooflights that direct light down into the sanctuary.

Figure 16: Interior of Clifton Cathedral

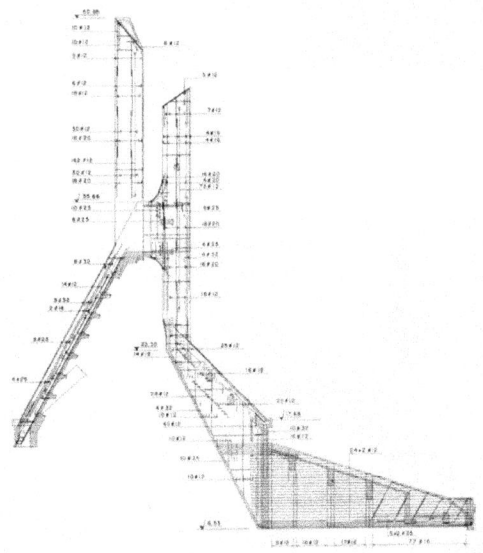

Figure 17: reinforcing drawing of star beam and cantilevered 'spire' support.

Conclusions

Newby worked closely with his architect clients to understand their intentions and provide structures to help them achieve what they wanted. The star beam was one of the tools that he had available to him, a form of structure that was probably unknown to most architects, and perhaps some engineers. Hence his need to explain the device with little sketches showing the basic arrangement that he could then elaborate to suit the architects' intentions.

Acknowledgements

I am grateful to Frank Newby's children for giving me access to their father's personal papers and to Felix Samuely and Partners for access to their records and to both for permission to use them in publications. The Frank Newby papers are now in the Institution of Civil Engineers.

References

[1] F. Samuely, 'Space Frames and Stressed Skin Construction'. *Journal of the Royal Institute of British Architects* 3rd Series, Vol. 59, 1952, pp. 166–178.
[2] F. Newby, 'Engineering Building for Leicester University', *Architectural Review*, April 1964, pp. 252–260.
[3] W. Howell, 'Vertebrate buildings, the architecture of structural space', *Journal of the Royal Institute of British Architects*, Vol. 77, 1970, pp. 100-108.

Società Generale Immobiliare (SGI) Prefabrication Methods for Italian School Buildings in 1960s

Francesco Spada
Department of Civil Engineering, University of Calabria, Rende, Italy

Introduction: Notes on Italian School Buildings in the 1960s

In Italy, at the end of the 1950s, a new approach to construction was needed, in line with other European countries. The Italian post-war reconstruction had pursued a traditional approach, favoring unskilled worker employment. Except for some iconic buildings, construction methods had undergone little evolution compared to the 1930s; the introduction of machines able to speed up traditional techniques had been the most important innovation in on site construction.

In the early 1960s, the strong demographic growth due to improved economic conditions and the increase of national industrialization ignited the debate on prefabrication.

In 1958 the AIP (Associazione italiana per lo studio e lo sviluppo di materiali e sistemi di prefabbricazione) called the first Congress on prefabrication in Naples, in conjunction with Fiera della Casa at the Mostra d'Oltremare. This event highlighted the potential of prefabrication also for school buildings, therefore it confirmed dealings between the AIP and the Ministero della Pubblica Istruzione. This resulted, in 1959, in a ten-year school program enacted by the national government and the first competition for prefabricated buildings was announced.

The renovation of school buildings was an important issue: in 1960 the XII Milan Triennale focused on house and school which were the main sectors affected by population growth. Therefore, they were good occasions for experimentation in prefabrication. The renewal of school buildings was necessary not only for construction aspects but also for pedagogical issues: prefabrication was also interpreted as a tool to pursue innovative teaching models for which traditional buildings were no longer considered suitable. In fact, interdisciplinary collaboration in design was one of the themes of the International Congress of School Building during the XII Triennale.

Regarding the regulatory framework, the state budget for prefabricated school buildings was strengthened by law n. 17 of 01/26/1962: the budget increased from 1.4 billion lire allocated with law n. 53 of 02/15/1961 to 20 billion lire in order to "provide for the deficiency of school classrooms". In 1962 a two-stage national competition was announced, aimed at the construction of 339 school buildings in 35 Italian provinces. 108 companies were invited; 24 passed the first phase and 21 of these were entrusted for the execution, under the Istituto di Sviluppo dell'Edilizia Sociale (ISES) construction management [1].

The first phase of the competition was useful to qualify the construction systems with modular elements proposed by the companies, as well as to express an opinion on their technical and economic capacity to execute the works [2]. It was clear that this was an experimental competition, just as the buildings to be built were experimental, so a preliminary assessment was needed to highlight any design deficiencies. Despite the strong promotion of prefabrication in school buildings, it should be noted that the exhibition of prefabricated schools organized in Rome by the Ministero della Pubblica Istruzione in 1962 showed poor results and was mainly of normal prefabricated houses adapted for schools [3]. Therefore, the national competition included a phase of comparison with the companies, as well as supporting them

Società Generale Immobiliare (SGI) Prefabrication Methods for Italian School Buildings in 1960s

regarding construction choices as to the best way to pursue the construction of innovative buildings technologically suited to new pedagogical needs. The first round in the national competition for school buildings ended in the autumn of 1965 (18 months after construction began in the spring of 1963): 339 buildings (2767 classrooms total) were completed at a cost of approximately 18.6 billion lire [4].

There were other initiatives, which more generally highlight how fundamental the role of the Public Client is for the development of industrialization processes; school buildings were probably the main test bed for prefabrication in Italy. In 1965 a new law was enacted (Regulation n. 5112 of 05/06/1965) that dictated provisions for the construction of school buildings with prefabricated modular elements (comparing them to traditional ones). It increased government funding for experimental school building programs (already allocated by laws n. 47/1963 and 1358/1964), increasing it up to 4.6 billion lire. This was another sign of the stimuli given by the public administration to the construction industry [5].

In1965 the Ministero dei Lavori Pubblici announced a new competition for the construction of 26 buildings in 11 Italian regions: 14 primary and 12 middle schools. 100 Italian construction companies were invited: 19 of these were chosen for their construction systems, including Sogene, the subsidiary construction company of the Società Generale Immobiliare (SGI)[6].

It also operated in prefabrication fields and in the 1950s it built some iconic towers in Milan, referred to as the so-called traditional evolved construction methods [7]. In 1963 it became the exclusive licensee of the French Acier-béton Estiot patent, [8] through which it responded to the market requests for the large volumes of economic housing commissioned by the Istituti Autonomi Case Popolari (IACP) in the early 1960s [9]. Construction companies that had already started experimenting with prefabrication systems in public housing, had (even if minimal) experience which allowed them to respond to calls for school buildings.

Sogene was one of these: after the construction of the towers in Milan and experimenting with heavy prefabrication techniques for low-cost housing, the company expanded the application of industrialized techniques also for school buildings. Interest in schools followed the national trend, so that many Italian companies experimented with prefabrication for this type of construction, encouraged by the Ministero della Pubblica Istruzione calls.

This paper refers to some of SGI's enterprises in school buildings. In particular, it deals with the "S3M" prefabrication system developed by Sogene for the construction of an elementary school in the province of Padua in 1965; Sogene re-proposed this system for participation in other ministerial tenders (also in its "S4" variant) up to the late 1960s. The development of other projects documents Sogene's interest in the topic; some experiences are analyzed below, relating them to the Italian constructive framework of the time.

SOGENE's Construction System for School Buildings

In the 1960s, SGI followed national trends: for the construction of cheap housing it obtained a French patent for a heavy prefabrication system and two years later (1965) developed its own prefabrication method with modular elements to participate in the competitions announced by the Ministero della Pubblica Istruzione.

The "S3M" construction system which gained Sogene the contracts, is described below. Under the Istituto di Sviluppo dell'Edilizia Sociale (ISES) construction management it built the elementary school in Casale di Scodosia in the province of Padua, one of the 26 sites identified by the tender launched by Ministero della Pubblica Istruzione in 1965. The description is taken from an official SGI document dated around 1970 [10]. It is a sort of catalogue, developed after the construction of the school in Casale di Scodosia; it illustrates the "S3M" system and its "S4" variant.

In the 1960s, the Italian government was not particularly "demanding" for economic social housing, accepting mere re-proposals of foreign heavy prefabrication systems with no remarkable results. However, it was more demanding for school constructions, at least for those referred to experimental models: it essentially indicated an idea to complete them with the construction companies' proposals. The competition included a first phase in which construction companies had to present and qualify their construction system; it could be accepted, modified or rejected. After approval it was possible to proceed to the second construction phase.

The Sogene "S3M" system was presented as a tool that allowed the construction of buildings "with any planimetric and altimetric layout[11]". It contemplated the use of U-inverted precast reinforced concrete beams that were packaged in multiple module sizes of 2.10 metres: 4.20 metres long, 6.30 metres long, or 8.40 metres long. They allowed the creation of grids of beams with a distance between centres of 2.10 metres and slabs of 6.30x6.30 metres or 8.40x4.20. Beam cores were prepared for the plant passages; therefore, they were packaged with transversal holes with a diameter of 25 centimetres. The reinforcements were made of electro-welded mesh and ribbed steel with a high elastic limit.

For the "S4" variant, beams were packaged in multiple module sizes of 4.20 metres that allowed the realization of modular slabs with supports 12.60 or 16.80 metres apart (useful for gyms and meeting rooms) or grids of 16.80x16.80 metres. This type of grid was realized by 8 pillars along the perimeter and a 2.10 metres' cantilever along it. In the rectangular section of the beams there were holes with a diameter of 45 centimetres. Floors arranged between the beams of the "S3M" system were made up of prefabricated lightweight concrete slabs with dimensions of 2.10x2.10 metres or 2.10x4.20 metres. Lightening was obtained by sheets of material called "Leca 600" interposed between the upper and lower thin insoles, connected by ribs. The slabs thickness (8 centimetres) was given by two sheets (1.5 centimetres thick) reinforced by high elastic limit electro-welded steel mesh and by "Leca 600" sheet (5 centimetres thick). For the "S4M" system, the slabs were 12 centimetres thick, owing to two concrete slabs (upper and lower) of 2 centimetres (reinforced by electro-welded meshes) and one slab in "Leca 600" (8 centimetres thick).

The pillars were also prefabricated with concrete reinforced by high elastic limit steel (ALE). At the bottom they are prepared with a slub for interlocking in the plinth; at the top with a hole for inserting the armor connection to the horizontal structures and for anchoring the pillar of the upper floor.

The building shell was made up of sandwich panels with a total thickness of 17.5 centimetres: external concrete slab of 5 centimetres (which remains exposed), insulation consisting of 3 centimetres of expanded polystyrene and 8 centimetres of "Leca 600", 1.5 cm internal concrete slab. The joints between the façade panels were sealed with high elasticity mastic. The sandwich was useful for obtaining good levels of performance for thermal insulation: the panels were characterized by a transmittance of 0.53 W/m2K, or 0.68 W/m2K taking into account heat bridges [12]. Prefabricated concrete panels were exposed and could be externally characterized by textures prepared in the formworks; they could be different depending on the building. This reflected a typically Italian approach to prefabrication methods: Italian designers were often worried about not being able to customize the building shell [13]. The Sogene catalogue for prefabricated schools contemplated this possibility, so as to have a wider offer.

Windows had frames in natural anodized aluminium with simple, double, printed or wired glasses, equipped with wooden or PVC roll-up shutters.

Internal walls were also made by 10 cms thick sandwich panels; they were formed from two 2.4 cms thick concrete slabs in the middle of which it was placed a soundproofing panel made by Eraclit [14] and tar paper (5 cms thick). The joints between the panels were closed with Eraclit and smoothing on site based on high resistance sealants. In the Sogene catalogue, this stratigraphy is reported as a "update" of the one used for internal walls of the Casale di Scodosia school as it had better performance from the soundproofing point of view, being characterized by a curve always higher than the limit imposed by the ISES; it corresponds to an evaluation index of 43 at a frequency of 500 Hz. The attention to the performance of technical elements pursued by Sogene was clear; as a result of the construction of Casale di Scodosia school, the company included its system "in the catalogue", with some improvements.

The use of special formwork for the packaging of the panels (both for internal walls and shell) provided perfectly smooth visible surfaces, to the advantage of finishing operations. Then the paint was applied directly, after localized smoothing on small imperfections. The walls, depending on the environments, could alternatively be finished with the application of plastic sheets or coatings, improving hygiene requirements.

Acoustic insulation was also required for the floors, so false ceilings were implemented in the rooms and in the gyms: they were made by sandwich panels consisting of a 2 cm thick Eracoustic [15] panel and a 1 cm thick Eraclit panel, with tar paper interposed. The roof is of the flat type: above the structural slab a cellular concrete screed was made with overlying layers of crossed asphalt for waterproofing and a tile floor. The thermal insulation requirement was satisfied by "Leca 600" layer arranged in the slab [16] and by the false ceiling and its air chamber; ultimately, the roof was characterized by a thermal transmittance of 0.60 W/m2K.

The ground floor slab was prefabricated, resting on concrete walls that were pierced for systems passage and designed to form a 120-cm-high ventilated cavity.

The stairs were cast in place, with walls of the cage that had a bracing function.

The ground floor covering was in vinyl resins. On the upper floor, classrooms and corridors had fine or medium marble floor-tile glued onto cement screed. The gym had an industrial rubber floor. Staircase (tread and rise) and meeting room floor were coated with marble. Grès tiles used for services: WCs, showers, changing rooms, kitchen and dining room. Depending on the flooring material, plastic or marble skirting boards were available.

The water system was made with galvanized iron pipes for supply and lead for the drainage, equipped with a water reserve to ensure the daily supply provided for by the ministerial regulations. The fire-extinguishing system (independent from the potable water one) was made with black steel pipes, fed by the city water network and equipped with storage tanks. The heating system was designed to guarantee a perceived temperature equal to 19 °C (18 °C real) by means of steel radiators in the classrooms and others rooms, exception for the gym where unit heaters were only used when necessary, resulting in energy savings. All thermal units were powered by a diesel central heating plant supplied by underground metal tanks. The lighting system was designed to ensure a good lux degree depending on the environments: in study rooms, classrooms and corridors there was semi-direct lighting using fluorescent lamps (resulting in energy savings) and incandescent lamps in service rooms and outdoor spaces.

The Sogene catalogue also reports a cost parameter per square metre (referred to January 1970) for the construction of school buildings using "S3M" and/or "S4" system: 80,000 lire/sqm. This parameter was obtained was obtained by dividing the construction's parts. The structure cost about 40,000 lire/m2 (50% of the total): 33,000 lire/m2 (41% of the total) it refers to the prefabricated ones and consequent labour for mounting, the remaining part (41% of the total) for traditional reinforced concrete works. Systems cost about 16,500 lire/m2 (20% of the total), the last part (30% of the total) refers to finishes (floors, paintings, coverings, false ceilings), fixtures and waterproofing.

Casale di Scodosia Elementary School

Casale di Scodosia (province of Padua) elementary school was built by Sogene with "S3M" construction system in 1966; it has 5 classrooms. The plan layout is very regular, arranged around an outdoor half-courtyard. It is a single-storey building with large full-height windows that define wide lighting surfaces. Roof beams are very distinctive: they have considerable height, defining an overhang over the entire perimeter of the building.

The building layout is set on a grid with a module equal to 70 cms (sub-module of 2.10 metres featuring the beams), clearly evident studying the plan. According to the system description or possible dimensional configurations, each classroom expands within a structural bay with dimensions of 6.30x6.30 metres or 9x9 modules. Close to classrooms, corridors expand within a structural bay with dimensions of 6.30x4.20 metres or 9x6 modules. There is also a wide meeting room of size equal to 8.40x12.60 metres or 12x18 modules without columns in the central part, supported by 10 perimetric pillars. Also spaces for services, infirmary, hall and central heating plant observe the layout grid. The roof and its overhang (that has size of 2.10 metres or 3 modules) relate all rooms and spaces, including the outer one (covered patio and half-courtyard) (Figs. 1-2).

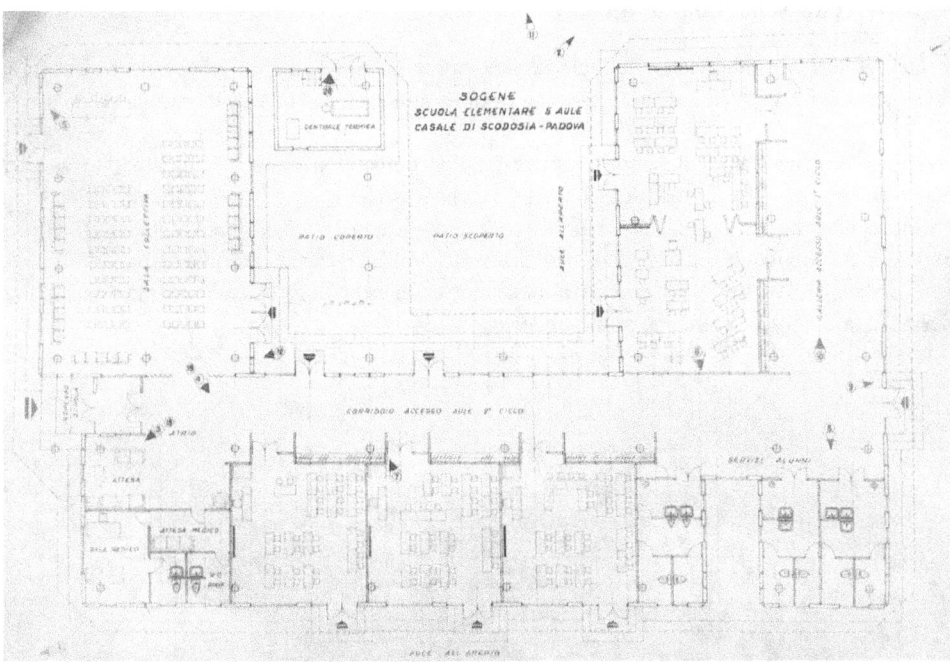

Figure 1: Casale di Scodosia school layout. Courtesy of "Ministero per i Beni e le Attività Culturali", Archivio Centrale dello Stato (Rome), SGI collection (subsequent citations ACS-SGI), folder 4091-261, Scuole prefabricate

Figure 2: Casale di Scodosia school: photos of the building. Source: ACS-SGI, folder 4091-261, Scuole prefabbricate

Società Generale Immobiliare (SGI) Prefabrication Methods for Italian School Buildings in 1960s

Even panels of the shell follow the modular logic, having dimensions equal to 70 or 140 cms (width) and full height; fixtures are inserted alternately with the matt panels (possibly including opaque parts) avoiding interference between the two types of closure.

Vertical partition panels between first and second grade classrooms are movable, allowing to shape a single wide space mixing the two classrooms. This ploy took into account innovative pedagogical guidelines that the Ministero della Pubblica Istruzione had released in the 1960s, as mentioned in the introduction.

Other Sogene projects for school buildings

Sogene implemented projects for other school buildings, although not realized: a high school in Frascati (province of Rome), a secondary school in Montale (Tuscany), a school complex in Rome and two prefabricated schools in Milan.

The Frascati school was designed for 25 classrooms, as a result of a competition announced in 1968; it was a project for an industrial technical institute. Also in this case, building layout was characterized by a modular grid within which classrooms, workshops, laboratories, gymnasium, offices, meeting room, and caretaker's accommodation were organized. In addition, the outdoor area was equipped with basketball and volleyball courts, an auditorium and a parking area. Design perspectives were very suggestive: they gave an idea of the construction technology and at the same time highlighted the space, clearly designed to encourage gathering of the students (Fig. 3).

Figure 3: High School in Frascati: project perspective. Source: ACS-SGI, folder 4091-261, Scuole prefabbricate

The project of the elementary school in Segrate (province of Milan) contemplated 15 classrooms; it should have consisted of two buildings (the school and the gym). The elevations were marked by modular façade panels and the high roof beam, overhanging the entire perimeter (Fig. 4). Still with "S3M" and "S4" systems, Sogene designed another secondary school of 12 classrooms in Montale (province of Pistoia) (Fig. 5) and a school complex titled Sampierdarena II in Rome which consisted of nursery school with 3 classrooms, elementary school with 24 classrooms and a secondary school with 18 classrooms (Fig. 6).

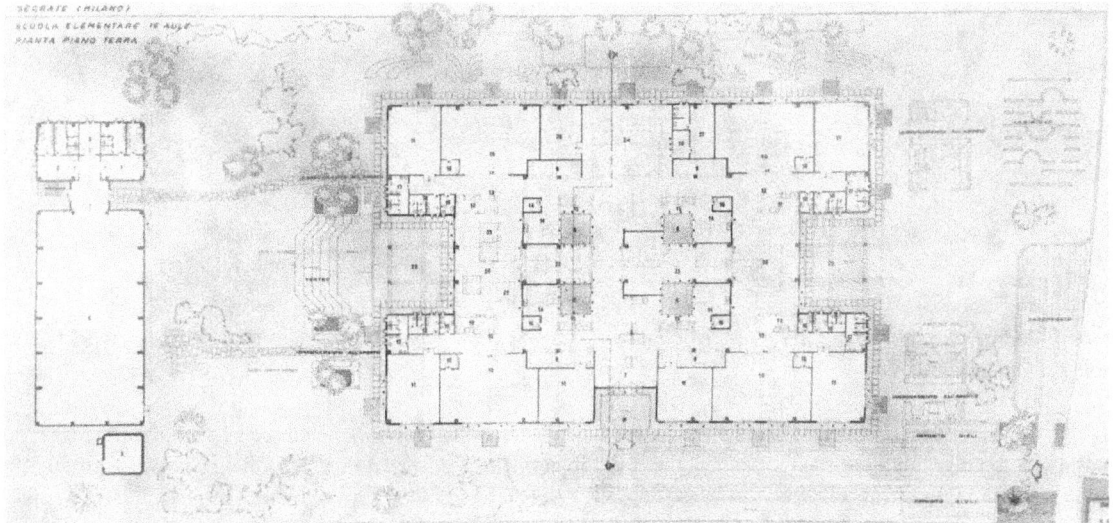

Figure 4: Elementary school in Segrate: layout. Source: ACS-SGI, folder 4091-261, Scuole prefabbricate

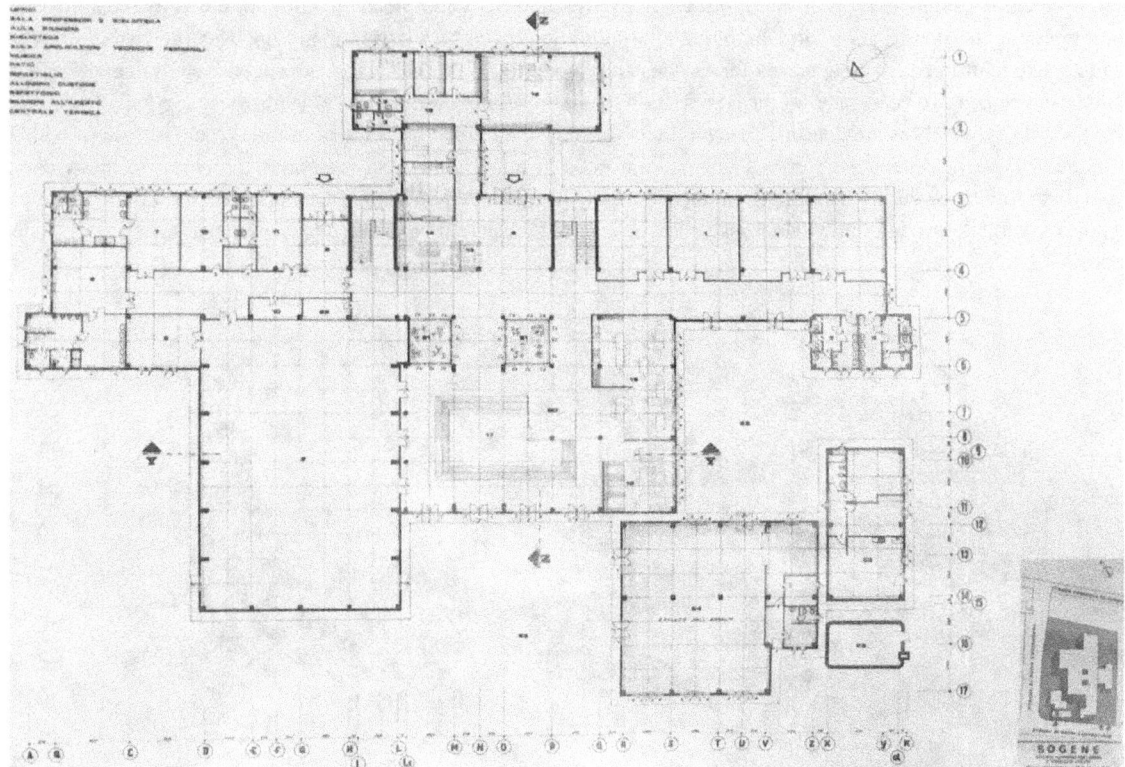

Figure 5: Secondary school in Montale: layout. Source: ACS-SGI, folder 4091-261, Scuole prefabbricate

Società Generale Immobiliare (SGI) Prefabrication Methods for Italian School Buildings in 1960s

Figure 6: "Serpentera II" school in Rome: axonometric drawing of the complex. Source: ACS-SGI, folder 4091-261, Scuole prefabricate

Although Sogene used its construction system only for Casale di Scodosia school, the projects listed highlight company's commitment to contributing to the experiments on the subject, which occurred in Italy in the second half of the 1960s through tender-competition.

Studying SGI's archive, there are documents about the construction of two identical prefabricated schools in Milan, dated between 1964 and 1965: the high school in Uruguay street and the primary and secondary schools in Faenza street [17]. They were built using heavy prefabrication systems, which were widespread in northern Italy in the mid-1960s. Photographs of the construction sites highlight the buildings' assembly: it was made up by large two-dimensional elements, like reinforced concrete panels for facades and floors (Fig. 7). It was a less advanced system than the one that would be developed two years later for the competition for Casale di Scodosia school in 1965: these two Milanese schools were made up by panels as large as one structural bay (or more), mounted by crane or mobile crane, instead of with 70-cm modular elements. Slabs were armed plates, reinforced in longitudinal and transverse directions to allow correct stability and resistance during handling. The façade panels had a cladding in small elements prepared in the formwork and holes suitable for traditional window assembly, instead of transparent panels to replace the matt ones as in Casale di Scodosia school.

Figure 7: Schools built using heavy prefabrication systems in Milan. Source: ACS-SGI, folder 4091-265, Edilizia civile 2

Compared to this, the two Milanese schools were very different technologically, certainly dependent to dissimilar recommendations from the public client. Probably the two Milanese buildings were the result of the great general demand for school buildings that occurred in the early 1960s, due to the significant population increase and the extension of compulsory schooling up to 14 years. They were not experimental constructions, but were ordinary production systems, subject to execution speed constraints to which SGI responded by means of a heavy prefabrication construction system [18]. In fact, Sogene had been the Italian dealership of the French *Acier-béton Estiot* patent since 1963, when the company had participated in the construction of cheap housing for workers following the great requests made by IACP of northern Italy, in the early 1960s.

Conclusions

This study contributes to the reconstruction of part of the SGI's work, a construction company engaged in all fields of construction and civil engineering, which in its third and most prosperous period (from the post World War II period to the early 1970s) provided a contribution to various national trends [19]. Although the company was mainly involved in the construction of large residential complexes, office, executive buildings and some industrial constructions, its strong business organization allowed the company to take part in experimentations promoted by the Ministero della Pubblica Istruzione in the 1960s. Although SGI did not have a portfolio of school buildings comparable to its residential one, the technological effort made by the Company to respond to the 1965 national competition was certainly valuable. So much so that it developed a dedicated system that was subsequently reused to participate in other state competitions, even though the SGI buildings were not built.

In general, Public Client was the main vehicle for the development of industrialization processes and methods in the Italian construction history. This had been known for some time: at the 1965 "*Convegno nazionale sui problemi dell'industrializzazione edilizia*" (National Conference on building industrialization issues) experts agreed that the Government should be the main client for industrialized constructions and also that experiments in school buildings would implement new prefabricated methods. Indeed, in the early 1960s, prefabrication in Italy had developed through the importation of foreign systems, in case the Client's requests changed for the school [20]. It no longer required a quick and large "housing supply" like the IACP in northern Italy, it demanded systems specifically defined "*ex novo*" by companies to respond to the Ministero della Pubblica Istruzione requests, following wider systematic changes linked to new pedagogical models. Therefore, SGI focused on a prefabricated system specifically designed for school buildings, and Sogene used for that of Casale di Scodosia for its participation in various national competitions. Although the SGI was in its period of maximum construction production, especially in the residential field, it also undertook new experiments. This circumstance confirms, also through the specific SGI's experience, that the great "bet" on prefabrication happened in Italy in the early 1960s, initially with economic residential construction, then also with schools. Experiments lasted for the whole decade and continued until the first half of the following one, defining a precise period, not continuing to today.

Therefore, there is a built heritage that is the memory of a national historic construction phase, which is concretely manifested in the presence of technologically unique buildings, often the result of "tailor-made" [21] industrialization experiences, which are worthy of study in order to preserve the building and its technological uniqueness because it represents a built testimony. This is very important because the management of school buildings passed from the State to the Regions starting from the mid-1970s; this interrupted experiments and caused the loss of control over single buildings at a centralized level, especially for maintenance.

The many school prototype buildings present in Italy today, most of which are still in use, correspond to as many construction stories: case studies can help to define guidelines for their maintenance and, more generally, to the strengthening of knowledge concerning the relationships between the construction company system and the evolution of construction techniques.

Società Generale Immobiliare (SGI) Prefabrication Methods for Italian School Buildings in 1960s

References

[1] R. Gulli, 'L'edilizia scolastica prefabbricata in Italia. La sperimentazione degli anni '60' in S. D'Agostino S. (Ed.), *Atti del II Convegno Nazionale di Storia dell'Ingegneria*, Napoli: Cuzzolin, 2008, pp. 681-690
[2] Ibidem.
[3] A. M. Talanti, *L'industrializzazione edilizia in Italia 1: 1955-1974*, Milano: A.I.P., 1981, p. 109.
[4] *Quaderni del Centro Studi per l'Edilizia Scolastica*, n. 4-5/1965.
[5] Talanti, (Note 3), pp. 137-145.
[6] ibid., pp. 145-155.
[7] F. Spada, 'Aspects of constructive innovation in the activity of the Società Generale Immobiliare (SGI) in Italy (1950s-1970s)' in J. Campbell (Eds), *Proceedings of the Seventh International Congress on Construction History*, Cambridge 2020. Cambridge: University Press, 2020, pp. 185-196.
[8] E. Garda, M. Mangosio, 'Edilizia sociale industrializzata a Torino tra 1963 e 1980: brevetti e cantieri' in S. D'Agostino S. (Ed.), *Atti del VI Convegno Nazionale di Storia dell'Ingegneria*, Napoli: Cuzzolin, 2016, pp. 453-462.
[9] S. Poretti, 'La costruzione' in F. Dal Co (Ed.), *Storia dell'architettura italiana – Il secondo Novecento*, Milano: Electa, 1997, pp. 268-293.
[10] Archivio Centrale dello Stato (Rome), SGI collection, folder 4091-261, *Scuole prefabbricate*
[11] ibid.
[12] The document refers to tests commissioned by the company to the Galileo Ferraris Institute laboratory in Turin, carried out taking into account the thermal bridges given by the concrete joints.
[13] I. Giannetti I., 'Reinforced concrete, industry and design: Balency prefabricated panels between France and Italy' in J. Campbell (Eds), *Proceedings of the Seventh International Congress on Construction History*, Cambridge 2020. Cambridge: University Press, 2020, pp. 625-638.
[14] Eraclit "consists of vegetable wool (poplar fraying) treated to be incombustible, antiseptic and rot-proof with impregnations (magnesite) and plastered with a special cement mixture". Source: E. A. Griffini, *Dizionario nuovi materiali per edilizia*, Milano: Hoepli, 1935, p. 25.
[15] This material probably was obtained from glued and compressed wood fibres, with sound-absorbing features.
[16] The stratigraphy of the roof slab is the same as that already described for the inter-floor slab: two 1.5 cm concrete panels with a 5 cm thick "Leca 600" panel interposed.
[17] Archivio Centrale dello Stato (Rome), SGI collection, folder 4091-265, *Edilizia civile 2*
[18] From the dates reported on the archival documents, construction sites started in mid-1964 and the buildings were completed before the start of the new school year (September 1965).
[19] Spada, (Note 7).
[20] Poretti, (Note 9).
[21] I. Giannetti, 'Industrializzazione "su misura": le scuole-pilota di Luigi Pellegrin (1967-1975)' in S. M. Cascone, G. Margani, V. Sapienza (Eds.) Nuovi orizzonti per l'architettura sostenibile, Atti Colloqui.AT.e 2020. Monfalcone (Gorizia): EdicomEdizioni, 2020, pp. 35-47.

High Tech Attitude as a Corrective of Japanese Industrialised Housing: The Work and Discourses of Kohko Takahashi

Shuntaro Nozawa[1] **and Yosuke Komiyama**[2]
1: University of Tokyo, Japan
2: Kyoto University, Japan

Introduction

Japanese architect Kohko Takahashi's housing design became associated with High Tech in the 1980s, when this relatively new term became commonly accepted as part of architectural vocabulary as referring to a certain emergent trend of the era. High Tech, as a term, was first circulated in journalism without clear definition, but according to Reyner Banham's posthumous text: *High Tech and Advanced Engineering* written around 1987, it "often seems to partake of the sense of Advanced Engineering as well as that of visual style and therefore can mean anything from 'slickly mechanistic presentation' to 'at the cutting edge of environmental technology [1]'". Takahashi's works dovetailed with this definition. They were marked by mechanistic idioms: the dry, inorganic textures of exposed steel frames, envelopes of fibre-reinforced plastic (FRP), autoclaved light-weight concrete (ALC), and other advanced materials. Nevertheless, she herself never considered her works as High Tech [2]. Her role as a notable agent of High Tech was, therefore, unintentional, since the trends her works followed emerged prior to their classification as High Tech.

Despite her personal dissociation from the label, prefabrication technology and the industrialisation of building elements were key concepts in both High Tech Architecture and Takahashi's works. She devoted her entire career to developing a personal design strategy which integrated adaptive design, construction method, manufactured or prefabricated materials, and equipment. This article explores Kohko Takahashi's discourses as well as works in the context of the industrialisation of Japanese housing and High Tech. Her commitment to this unique construction-design integrated approach was ascribed not only to her professional training in low-cost housing, but also to the epoch in Japanese housing during which she began her career. During the 1960s, the quantity of industrialised and prefabricated housing increased rapidly due to the influx work by newly established prefab home companies as well as the Japan Housing Corporation—a public institution mainly responsible for building blocks of flats. This exerted pressure on architects to reconsider their roles in housing design, influencing Takahashi's stance and ideologies as well. By drawing lessons from both her professional work on housing projects and her academic research, she attempted to find architectonic remedies for mounting issues recognised in industrialised housing, namely the low quality of structure and dull uniformity of design.

Takahashi dedicated her professional career to housing. After becoming an independent architect in 1962, she was involved in 17 housing projects, including her own home, *Kuda no ie*, 1983. Her career overlapped with the industrialisation of building equipment as well as the rise of prefab home businesses that established their own closed production systems on the basis of variable modules [3]. Her avidity for a modular coordination between the design of the entire house and the building elements that were rapidly becoming standardised and mass-produced led her to engage in the development of unitised fittings, such as prefabricated kitchen equipment and bathrooms through collaboration with manufacturers. Beyond her professional work on housing projects, she taught housing architecture and design at her alma mater—Japan Women's University—for 25 years until 1997, when she died of cancer at age 65. Her achievements have been revealed and catalogued by her students; however, the underlying logic behind her ideology and design strategy and the architectonic features of her works, which encapsulated her tenets of home industrialisation, have rarely been examined in the context of Japanese housing production as a whole [4].

We focus particularly on Takahashi's view of the relationship between industrialised building elements, space, and humans. Her awareness of the interplay between these three components stemmed from her involvement in low-cost house prototyping in her mentor Kiyoshi Ikebe's laboratory in the University of Tokyo, which she joined in 1955, and where she remained for seven years. This article thus begins by defining Takahashi's basic design thinking and principles as constructed early in her career. This allows us to reveal how her construction-design integrated approach was shaped in tandem with, and in response to, the prefab home manufacturers' housing production practices as well as Ikebe's design principles. We will further shed light on the characteristics of her construction and architectural expression, and rediscover her High Tech characteristics.

Unitising Human Life

"I see no other architectural context in which my architecture can be positioned than Ikebe Laboratory's work" [5]. This remark on Takahashi's own architectural stance indicates that her design thinking was greatly influenced by how she absorbed and modified Kiyoshi Ikebe's methodology for housing. Ikebe's architectural production lab was established in 1949 and started with the design of minimal dwellings and the construction of case-study houses, reaching a total number of 95 before its 1979 closure upon his death [6]. He espoused technological determinism, assuming that home affordability and the rationality of domestic life could be achieved by reconciling the design and construction planning processes. His enthusiasm for creating ordinary people's houses stemmed from his desire to materialise and demonstrate his vision of democratised domestic life for the post-war era.

Ikebe's lab embarked on the invention of standardised, segmentalised building components and equipment in the late 1950s, when Takahashi began to engage in case-study housing projects. His attempt to promote the industrialisation of building elements was intertwined with his creation of the unique anthropometric scale of proportions, namely the General Module, to which Takahashi adhered throughout her career [7]. The General Module is a system that enables calculation and choice of modules suited to various design conditions. Assuming n = integral number and $P_1P_2P_3 = 0$ or 1, a module in centimetres (X_n) can be calculated with a formula below:

$$X_n = 2^n + 2^{n-1}P_1 + 2^{n-2}P_2 + 2^{n-3}P_3$$

It is further characterised by allowing multiple scales to be calculated in line with the size of a human body. For example, they are 64 cm (n = 6, $P_1 = 0$, $P_2 = 0$, $P_3 = 0$) and 96 cm (n = 6, $P_1 = 1$, $P_2 = 0$, $P_3 = 0$), which Takahashi frequently used in her housing projects [8]. In addition to Ikebe's attitudes towards the creation of new domestic life, this modular calculation system and its respect for human scale created a conceptual link between construction-focused design and everyday living which continued to influence Takahashi's works.

The rise of mass-produced housing also affected Takahashi's design thinking. From the late 1950s to the early 1960s, the emerging prefab home industry was propelled by post-war social circumstances, where calls for home industrialisation arose in response to severe housing shortages. This was compounded by the promotion of new materials such as light-weight steel, a government homeownership policy that expanded the residence fund loan system, and rapid economic growth. The initial reputation of brand-new prefab homes was dubious and unsavoury due to structural and practical problems, such as leakage during rain. These were attributed to deficiencies in technical know-how for implementing drywall and panel construction, which differed from the conventional post-and-beam construction characterised by earthen walls and mortise and tenon joints [9]. Nonetheless, the refinement of their prefabrication techniques as well as an increasing demand for housing steadily enhanced prefab home companies' desirability and ubiquity.

The name of Takahashi's design studio, Building Unit Design Office, founded in 1965, was the encapsulation of her design principles, moulded amid the ongoing industrialisation of building materials, components, and houses and echoing her critical insight into prefab homes. While she found something peculiarly appealing in these relatively new architectural entities, produced as if they were machines, she questioned the assumption behind the design of the prefab homes. She perceived that they were designed, prefabricated, and assembled by defining the whole house as a box encompassing a cluster of rooms. This cluster therefore became a conceptual unit for segmentalising and industrialising a building [10]. The underlying modelling concept, labelled the Building Element theory, which regarded any type of building surface as a basic constituent for the evaluation of structural features and the conditions of enclosed spaces of a building, prevailed from the late 1950s [11]. It was conceptualised by Yoshichika Uchida, based originally on British architects Richard Llewelyn-Davies's and D. J. Petty's discussion on the assessment of the performance of a building. They associated the complexity of building performance assessment with the rapid advancement of materials and methods, suggesting that it could be achieved by analytically examining the conditions of the components, mainly surface structural elements such as wall, roof, and ceiling [12]. This way of assessment implicitly presumed walled Western architecture, which differed from the wall-less space characterising the orthodox Japanese building, whose composition was determined by the relationship between the position of columns and arrangement of *tatami*-mat flooring. It can be considered that the Building Element theory facilitated the conceptual transformation of a design object from the wall-less to walled house.

In Takahashi's view, what ought to be segmentalised was not the wall, roof, or ceiling, but the connection between patterns of behaviour and spheres of action in domestic spaces [13]. To her, this connection was a basic 'unit' for design. She was explicitly aware that an object-oriented notion behind the design of the prefab homes, based conceptually in the Building Element theory, had the effect of making builders more cognizant of rationality of production and assembly of wall components, rather than practical usability of the resulting space [14].

Furthermore, Takahashi averred that poor module design deprived the prefab homes of the flexible use of domestic spaces. Her conviction was rooted in an analysis conducted in 1969, in which she compared spatial properties between the floor plans of 80 residences designed by architects and 84 industrialised houses and flats, including those of the Japan Housing Association [15]. One conclusion of this "spatial study" was that larger industrialised housing merely mean a larger version, with little variety in design, arrangement, and composition of rooms. She attributed the cause of this tendency to simplistic module optimisation where the relationship between the floor spaces of each room and the whole house was defined by an integral multiple of around 90 cm, a basic dimension widely used for industrialised housing [16]. To her, this finding was evidence of the superiority of the General Module, which allowed architects to calculate and flexibly choose narrower or wider modules suited to their projects.

While being influenced by the modernist Ikebe, Takahashi's attitudes towards segmentalised, standardised, and manufactured building elements elucidated her personal reaction to modernism in architecture. The thought that a house and its fixtures and fittings surrounding a human body were tools to aid people in the production of their daily lives; from meals to cloth to furniture, was shared by both Ikebe and Takahashi, evoking William Morris's conceptualisation of craftmanship and the socialistic creed that underlaid the Arts and Craft movement [17]. In Takahashi's eyes, dwellers of the prefab homes were passively crammed into and domesticated by these boxes for consumption [18]. Her ideal of home industrialisation denied a loss of individuality, and built upon the respect of diversity in design, and the use of space. To Takahashi, prefabricated building materials, components and amenities were also tools to empower architects, engineers, prefab home companies, and other related manufacturers. She believed that the free use of prefabrication techniques was a means to enable the standardisation of industrialised housing in performance which did not result in homogenisation in design and planning; often seen as the main ramification of modernism [19].

High Tech Attitude as a Corrective of Japanese Industrialised Housing:
The Work and Discourses of Kohko Takahashi

Standard Humans

Takahashi's search for diversity in industrialised housing was not unrelated to a growing social demand on dwelling in the late 1960s, when her Building Unit Design Office rose to prominence. By this time, the advancing prefab home businesses and Japan Housing Association had ostensibly relieved housing shortages and population pressure in the metropolises. The uniformity of the indoor as well as urban built environments offered by monotonously standardised prefab homes and flats, however, raised the issue of how diversified needs for the quality of housing could be appropriately answered. Whether discussing industrialised or purpose-built housing, this was not a challenge for her mentor, Ikebe, who started his career just after WWII. He viewed the house as an arena; a sort of public display where architects expressed and incarnated their own visions of democratised family life and the daily life of the future. This strong sense of purpose in designing for the future positioned him as a vanguard of modern housing design, often leading him to reject clients' more conservative requests [20].

While clearly influenced by Ikebe's didactic attitude, the social and architectural ethos of the 1960s steered Takahashi in a different direction. She tried to determine 'units' in clients' daily lives through communication with them, believing that such a process embedded in her construction-design integrated approach led to the diversification of housing design, and ultimately the development of the solution for the betterment of industrialised housing [21]. However, this logic brought a new challenge for her: how to process the diversity of realities and personalised 'units' in order to be able to define consistent basal conditions for proposing a widely applicable model of industrialised housing?

Such methodological uncertainties led Takahashi to take a psychological and structuralist perspective to the issue. She presumed that the nature of "standard humans" in her terms, or the intrinsic characteristics of people (implicitly Japanese in her assumption) in the appropriation of space could be a point of reference for designing industrialised housing [22]. One of her research objects was the personal space created by a person's comfortable distance with others. Her psycho-engineering study made her realise that a more distinctive and psychological barrier between boarded and *tatami* spaces existed in a typical Japanese house. Through experimentation to determine the measurable extent of this intangible barrier surrounding the body, she revealed that proximate distancing was more tolerant in a conventional seating posture—sitting down on *tatami*—than in contemporary one—sitting on a chair [23]. The ways that people habitually occupied certain spaces in the house were also of academic interest to her. The dynamic material relations between "standard humans" and designed spaces were disclosed by investigating time-space patterns of occupancy according to differences in age, sex, and family structure [24].

Takahashi's construction-design integrated approach was not structurally dependent on the compartmentalisation or clear record of the personalised locale where the "standard human" felt comfortable residing. Rather, her approach was attuned to the creation of a wall-less interior with roughly separated rooms entirely covered with a large roof, or orchestrated by corridors that ensured unity and spaciousness. Whoever the clients were, she unvaryingly adopted this one-room system, which harkened back to Ikebe's ideology. His way of materialising equality and democratisation in family life was the minimisation of the number of interior walls—particularly one separating the dining room from the kitchen. In his eyes, the segregation of kitchen and dining in the conventional Japanese house symbolised a historical, feudal hierarchy that distinguished between males and females, and older and younger members of a family. His ideal of a post-war, democratised family was manifested in the design of a centred kitchen-dining space surrounded by adjacent, roughly-partitioned rooms. This formed the basis for one of his unique interior architectural signatures [25].

Takahashi added new meaning to this one-room system. Its open-plan interior was agreeable to her presupposition that as well as individual person's preference, the nature of "standard humans" in the use of domestic spaces would change over time [26]. In her view, a house should be designed to avoid any friction between built spaces and changes in the ways that dwellers appropriated and personalised them. In other words, the one-room system was the solution to the omnipresent contradiction caused by a conflict between the immutability of a designed space, and the constant transformation of peoples' ways of life and thinking. It had much to do with her design philosophy of not over-designing the interior arrangement and finishing. She believed that a designed house ought to be somewhat imperfect and unplanned leaving less elaborately designed margins for flexibility in the use of domestic spaces [27].

Handcrafted Prefab

In her early projects, the expression of spatial flexibility exemplified Takahashi's quest for the ideal design of the one-room system. One of her works in the 1960s, I House, was designed for a particular client, but embodied her societal design purpose. It was assumed that the same house could be mass-produced, and were suited to any dwellers, or "standard humans" [28]. This narrow single-storey house was built on the concrete foundations, running from west to east, and clearly manifesting her enthusiasm for the use of her favourite materials: H beams framing its entire, container-like geometry, and ALC panels that created uniformity for its outer surfaces (Fig. 1). The house featured five segments (four on the north façade, and one on the south) protruding from the exterior geometry of the house, creating interior alcoves which contained storage, closets, and the built-in kitchen sink (Fig. 2). Theoretically, the use of these alcoves was interchangeable in accordance with dwellers' needs. The south-facing kitchen protrusion was not composed of a prefabricated, integrated kitchen system due to a lack of common availability, but was rather meticulously designed by Takahashi with standardised kitchen fittings, such as a stainless sink and tap (Fig. 3). The interior of this house comprised the nursery, a Japanese-style room without *tatami*, the suite of the kitchen-dining room and living room, and the more orthodox *tatami* space, arranged in a row and partitioned not with structural walls, but with wall-like shelves. These movable interior surface elements were, in theory, both removable and changeable. In her view, the long-span H beams allowed the domestic spaces to be freed from any structural wall by which the dwellers' use of space might be restricted.

Fig. 1. Exterior of I House. Photo by Tomio Ohashi from Architectural Culture, December 1968, p. 71.

Fig. 2. North-facing storage and closet segments of I House. Photo by Tomio Ohashi from Architectural Culture, December 1968, p. 73.

Fig. 3. Kitchen alcove of I House. Photo by Tomio Ohashi from Architectural Culture, December 1968, p. 76.

A decade later, I house experienced major improvements proposed by Takahashi, albeit in an unprogrammed way. An arch-shaped roof was added to create attic rooms in this originally flat-roofed, one-storeyed house (Fig. 4), and the ground floor was newly equipped with a larger, integrated kitchen system, instead of the previous kitchen segment that was completely removed [29]. Concurrently, she revisited other work of hers for extension and reconstruction, which made her realise the necessity of a new design approach, whereby the difference in life spans between the fabric of a house and equipment was provisioned for in design, and therefore easily manageable [30].

Fig. 4. Arch-shaped roof of reconstructed I House. Photo by Tomio Ohashi from Architectural Culture, August 1979, p. 52.

From the 1970s onward, the literal sense of the one-room system became the common spatial idiom characterising Takahashi's works. The vaulted ceiling of her house, *Kuda no ie* embraced the daily life of her two-generation household and was framed by the array of steel pipes, from which the inner walls of lauan plywood were structurally divided (Figs 5-6). The birdcage-like structure of this house, complete in 1983, was the result of the application of timber balloon framing, and the tube pillars—with a diameter of 60.5 mm—were erected at 96 cm intervals, according to the General Module [31]. The unadorned atmosphere of the interior, characterised by exposed steel pipes and unpainted plywood, mirrored her ideology that the quality of unfinished and unvarnished building materials was an undesigned element with which dwellers were intended to envision themselves as the catalysts of future change, rather than subjects of the perpetuity of materiality. In fact, the transformation of the physical properties of zinc plates that covered the entire roof and exterior walls of the first floor were anticipated as part of the design (Fig. 7). She looked forward to seeing the process of chemical reaction caused by exposure to rain and wind, which was expected to bring the change of its colour from metallic silver to sober, charcoal grey [32].

High Tech Attitude as a Corrective of Japanese Industrialised Housing:
The Work and Discourses of Kohko Takahashi

Fig. 5. Vaulted ceiling of Kuda no ie. Photo by Tomio Ohashi from Architectural Culture, July 1983, p. 63.

Fig. 6. Kitchen-dining area of Kuda no ie. Photo by Tomio Ohashi from Architectural Culture, July 1983, p. 66.

Fig. 7. Exterior of Kuda no ie. Photo by Tomio Ohashi from Architectural Culture, July 1983, p. 61.

A narrow passage to the site conditioned Takahashi's construction-design integrated approach, requiring a building method without the use of any heavy machinery. This constraint in the construction of *Kuda no ie* led her to utilise manufactured concrete blocks, that were both multifunctional and portable, to create the structural walls of some parts of its ground floor [33]. These exposed concrete block surfaces were the amalgam of her holistic consideration of a range of different factors; the design and structural characteristics of the building, material availability, construction procedures, and masonry work to build them. Her description of *Kuda no ie* as "handcrafted prefab" grasped the essence of her construction-design integrated approach, positioned as the antithesis to the prefab home industry's housing production [34]. On the one hand, the prefab homes were the assemblages of building elements exclusively designed and manufactured as part of a catalogue of the companies' closed systems, while on the other hand, Takahashi rarely took such an object-oriented attitude, but rather enjoyed the process of designing and crafting in a DIY fashion, which created the freedom of choice through the use of prefabricated materials and equipment [35].

Presumably, Takahashi's masonry approach derived from the S House project, 1981 (Fig. 8). This house presumed that the parents' and son's families lived separately on the same parcel of land, thus the building consisted of two isolated wings roughly connected by substantial steel frames shaping their geometries, and a connecting corridor that functioned as the shared library [36]. The structural walls of this library corridor were built with exposed concrete blocks, whose inorganic quality served to accentuate the warm and affectionate relationship between the two households. The fact that the client, fascinated by Ikebe's design philosophy, had previously lived in his work for about two decades, led naturally to the adoption of the one-room system in both structural and ideological terms. Contrary to the steel pipes of *Kuda no ie*, no structural columns of S House were exposed in the interior. This house was rather marked by the exposed truss structure bearing the large roofs as—at least, in Ikebe's and Takahashi's views—the symbol of democratised family life under which all members of the family would congregate (Figs 9-10).

High Tech Attitude as a Corrective of Japanese Industrialised Housing:
The Work and Discourses of Kohko Takahashi

Fig. 8. Exterior of S House. Photo by Tomio Ohashi from Architectural Culture, August 1982, p. 56.

Fig. 9. Kitchen-dining area of S House. Photo by Tomio Ohashi from Architectural Culture, August 1982, p. 61.

Fig. 10. Exposed roof truss of S House. Photo by Tomio Ohashi from Architectural Culture, August 1982, p. 58.

The large windows to let daylight into these open ceiling spaces echoed an inner conflict Takahashi began to experience in pursuing her design policies: the use of manufactured building materials and equipment, and the application of Ikebe's General Module. She believed that the industrialisation of building products assured a greater variety of choice, and thus increased the degree of freedom in architectural design. However, the proliferation of these factory-made items, particularly aluminium frames that became popular during the 1960s, made her realise the gap between the ideal and the real. As with other standardised fittings, the sizes of aluminium frames were generally defined by the conventional system of measurement, whose basic unit was 30.3 cm. In the case of S House, the design module set according to the General Module was 32 cm; this dimension was not necessarily advantageous for coordinating the fabric of the whole house with manufactured building materials, fixtures, and fittings [37]. In addition to the limitations prescribed by available prefabricated units, both colour and texture were increasingly limited in manufactured building products, thus dictating many aspects of housing design. [38]. In S House, or the "handcrafted prefab", she relied—perhaps, reluctantly—upon expensive, custom-made aluminium frames suited to the General Module [39].

Conclusion

While she rarely linked her own works with it, Reyner Banham's assertive, albeit incomplete, theorisation of High Tech was well aligned with the main features of Kohko Takahashi's housing design. In his *High Tech and Advanced Engineering*, Banham described it "as an attitude and as a body of design practices" that espouses advanced engineering, and does not see "buildings simply as passive shelters against the elements, but rather as complete and active environmental systems" [40]. Takahashi works, characterised by her construction-design integrated approach, had the same architectonic features. To optimise this approach that presumed the unity of the exterior and interior of a house, she took a phenomenological and structuralist perspective on 'units', or behavioural connections of spaces-segmentalised elements of a building with both clients and the "standard humans" in mind. These two parties of inhabitants were seen as the invisible cast in dwellings tailored to individuals' needs. While she believed that such a methodology was a means to bring diversity to the design of prefab homes, and better usability in their domestic spaces, her commitment to Ikebe's General Module precluded her from fully capitalising on the value of home industrialisation: affordability in housing. The incompatibility between the General Module and the conventional units of measurement that defined the sizes of most standardised, manufactured materials created inconvenient remnants and dysfunctional modules [41].

As Banham regards High Tech as "an alternative Modernism", both Western High Tech architects and Takahashi embraced a functionalist rationale underlying Modernism, and challenged its consequences [42]. To Takahashi, her High Tech attitude was a corrective of the malady of architectural mass production as well as standardisation: the homogenisation of industrialised housing that prevented dwellers from being unfettered in the appropriation and production of spaces. Likely because her dedication to post-war Japanese housing revolved around the design of detached houses for single families, she hoped more for 'interactions' taking place around the body—harmony between building components, fixtures and fittings, and humans. As the free use of less-elaborately designed spaces was thought of as a path to a life of creativity and subjectivity, in her view, the plain, unornamented quality of exposed steel frames, FRP, and ALC boards comprising her houses were a sort of 'designed' canvas which dwellers were intended to personalise and familiarise themselves with in the course of inhabiting the spaces [43]. In short, these visual properties were the manifestation of her functionalist reliance on ergonomic analysis of personal space and spatial occupation as well as new factory-made materials, prefabricated building elements, and equipment. Her construction-design integrated approach encapsulated her unintentionally High Tech attitude toward the relationship between ever-evolving industrialised building materials, modern amenities, and humans in Japanese housing.

Acknowledgements

This work was supported by a grant from the Housing Research Foundation: Jusoken [grant number 2006]. We are grateful to Jusoken for their support. We would like to thank Mika Kaibara Portugaise for proofreading our manuscript.

References

[1] R. Banham, 'High Tech and Advanced Engineering' in Todd Gannon, (Ed.) *Reyner Banham and the Paradoxes of High Tech*, Los Angeles: The Getty Research Institute, 2017. p. 234.
[2] K. Takahashi, 'Ima haitekku to iwaretemo' [Now Called High Tech], *Space Design*, January 1985, p. 137.
[3] S. Matsumura, K. Sato, Y. Morita, T. Eguchi and T. Gondo, *Hako no sangyo: Purehabu jūtaku gijutsusha tachi no shōgen* [The Industry of the Boxes: The Voices of Prefab Home Engineers], Tokyo: Shokokusha, 2013. p. 15-6.
[4] Japan Women's University, *Jikan no naka no sumai: Takahashi Kohko to itsutsu no sumai no genzai* [Dwelling in Time: Kohko Takahashi's Works Past and Present], Tokyo: Shokokusha, 2003.
[5] Takahashi, (Note 2) p. 137.
[6] K. Namba, *Sengo modanizumu kenchiku no kyokuhoku: Ikebe Kiyoshi shiron* [The Acme of Post-war Modernism in Architecture: Essays on Kiyoshi Ikebe], Tokyo: Shokokusha, 1999.
[7] ibid., pp. 102-35.
[8] Japan Women's University, (Note 4) pp. 46-67.
[9] S. Matsumura et al., (Note 3) pp. 74-8, 229-31.
[10] K. Takahashi, 'Paneru yunitto shisutemu ni yoru jūtaku nidai' [Two Houses Built with Unitised Panels], *Architectural Culture*, June 1966, pp. 97-103.
[11] T. Yoshida, 'BE ron no konnichiteki igi: BE ron toha nandatta noka' [Contemporary Significance of the BE Theory: What was the BE Theory?] in Architectural Institute of Japan, (Ed.) *iBE ron: Birudhingu eremento to kōhō no kako, genzai, mirai* [iBE Theory: The Past, Present and Future of Building Elements, and Construction], Tokyo: Architectural Institute of Japan, 2015, pp. 7-12.

[12] R. Llewelyn-Davies and D. J. Petty, *Building Elements*, London: Architectural Press, 1960.
[13] Takahashi, (Note 10) p. 98.
[14] K. Takahashi, 'Tekkotsu paneru ni yoru ryōsan no tameno moderu hausu: Ki tei' [Model Industrialised House with Steel Panels: Ki House], *Architectural Culture*, August 1969, pp. 125-8.
[15] Building Unit Design Office, 'Supēsu bunseki kara mita jūtaku ryōsanka heno shihyō' [Spatial Analysis on the Criteria for Home Industrialisation], *Architectural Culture*, August 1969, pp. 129-34.
[16] Building Unit Design Office, (Note 15) p. 130.
[17] K. Takahashi, 'Nihon no sumai ni okeru wa to yō' [Japan and the West in Japanese Housing], *ESP: Economy, Society, Policy*, May 1987, pp. 30-3.
[18] K. Takahashi, 'Kansei yutaka ni sōzōteki seikatsu wo itonameru ba to shiteno jūkūkan wo' [Dwelling for Emotional Richness and Creative Life], *Technology and Economy*, January 1984, pp. 60-3.
[19] Building Unit Design Office, (Note 15) p. 129.
[20] Namba, (Note 6) pp. 73-101.
[21] K. Takahashi, 'Seshu no kosei wo toraeru: Ya tei' [Understanding the Personality of the Client: Ya House], *Architectural Culture*, May 1969, pp. 113-9.
[22] 'Dokuritsu jūtaku no sekkei ha nawo imi wo mochiuruka' [Is Architects' Involvement in the Design of a Detached House Still Meaningful?], *Architectural Culture*, February 1971, pp. 95-106.
[23] K. Takahashi, 'Yutaka na kurashi: Ningen kūkan dōgu' [Good Life: Humans, Space and Tools], *Sumai to machi*, November 1990, pp. 55-7.
[24] S.Yamazaki and K. Takahashi, 'Jikanryō ni yoru seikatsu no ruikeika: Seikatsu jikan kara mita kōdō to tairyū kūkan no taiō kankei ni kansuru kenkyū' [Categorisation of the Time-Space Patterns of Lives: The Relationship between Behaviours and Spaces], *Journal of Architecture, Planning and Environmental Engineering*, No. 491, January 1997, pp. 67-74.
[25] Namba, (Note 6) pp. 73-101.
[26] 'Dokuritsu jūtaku no sekkei ha nawo imi wo mochiuruka', (Note 22) p. 106.
[27] Takahashi, (Note 2) p. 137.
[28] K. Takahashi, 'Ryōsanka wo mezashita sekkei purosesu: Is tei' [Design Process toward Mass Production: Is House], *Architectural Culture*, December 1968, pp. 71-6.
[29] K. Takahashi, 'Jūnenme no zōkaichiku: I tei to Y tei' [Extension and Reconstruction after Ten Years: I House and Y House], *Architectural Culture*, August 1979, pp. 50-63.
[30] Takahashi, (Note 29) p. 59.
[31] 'Kuda no ie', *Architectural Culture*, July 1983, pp. 61-8.
[32] ibid., p. 65.
[33] ibid.
[34] ibid.
[35] Matsumura et al., (Note 3) pp. 15-6.
[36] K.Takahashi, 'Nijūnenme no sekkei' [Design after Twenty Years], *Architectural Culture*, August 1982, pp. 55-62.
[37] ibid., p. 60.
[38] K.Takahashi, T. Koizumi and S. Kitada, 'Jūtakuyō buhin wo tsukatte omou koto' [Our Opinions on the Use of Manufactured Building Products], *Architectural World*, vol. 25, no. 8, 1976, pp. 67-72.
[39] Takahashi, (Note 36) p. 60.
[40] Banham, (Note 1) pp. 235, 244.
[41] Japan Women's University, (Note 4) pp. 54-7.
[42] Banham, (Note 1) p. 245.
[43] Takahashi, (Note 2) p. 137.

Experimental structures and reinforced concrete in church building in Italy: design and construction of three hyperbolic paraboloids (1961-68)

Ilaria Giannetti
Università degli Studi di Roma "Tor Vergata"

Introduction

In the second half of the twentieth century, the experimental reinforced concrete structure was the protagonist of the international architectural research of the late modern movement. In this context, the church building, with the inner need to cover spaces with medium and large spans, became a project theme that was particularly suited to the development of new 'structural figures'. Of these, the form-resistant structural elements – folded slabs, thin vaults, hyperbolic paraboloids – became the subject of fervent experimentation.

In Italy, between 1952 and 1962, two special national laws were dedicated to public funding for the construction of church buildings, contributing to the construction of a large number of new works. In the national economic and productive horizon of reinforced concrete construction, the contemporary international rise of Italian engineering [1] and the liturgical renewal introduced by the Second Vatican Council (1962-65) [2], supported a timely structural experimentation extended to the construction of new churches throughout the country.

Investigating this phenomenon in the construction history field, starting from the recent monographic contributions [3], allows to integrate the studies already conducted in the history of Italian architecture [4], with the aim of recognising and disseminating the construction and technical characteristics of a fragile patrimony of experimental reinforced concrete structures, while also making a contribution to the study of Italian structural architecture in the wider international debate. The methodological approach consists of the reconstruction of the procedural and normative framework concerning ecclesiastical buildings (1952-1985) and the construction and technical characteristics of the single works (case studies), by analysis of the literature of the time and the archive sources. In particular, for the reconstruction of the regulatory and procedural framework, the study is based on the documentation of the Archives of the Pontificia Commissione Centrale per l'Arte Sacra in Italia (Pontifical Central Commission for Sacred Art in Italy - PCCASI), stored in the Vatican Apostolic Archives [5], accompanied by the magazine Fede e Arte (Faith and Art), its media outlet. The analysis of the single works is based on the primary sources of the archives of the architects, engineers and local dioceses, supplemented by on-site investigations.

This essay presents the case study of three churches designed by architect Vito Sonzogni (1924-2017) in collaboration with engineer Enzo Lauletta (1927-71) for the diocese of Bergamo and characterised by hypar roofs made of reinforced concrete. Based on the documentation stored in the private archive of Sonzogni, supplemented by the literature of the time, it was possible to reconstruct the design and construction process of the three works.

A state plan for churches of "public utility"

On 18 December 1952, Law "State contribution to the construction of new churches" no. 2522 was published [6]: according to the provision, a loan granted by the Ministry of Public Works covered the purchase of land and the construction of new churches and buildings used for pastoral ministries. Considered works of public utility, the buildings were supported with the financing of 8 billion lire for the 1952-53 financial years. The law also ratified the role of an

Experimental structures and reinforced concrete in church building in Italy: design and construction of three hyperbolic paraboloids (1961-68)

advisory and executive body of the Vatican, the Pontifical Central Commission for Sacred Art in Italy (PCCASI), for the verification and approval, on a technical and aesthetic level, of the projects covered by the funding in accordance with liturgical and sacred art precepts [7]. After the enactment of the law, requests were not long in coming: the projects for the construction of new churches, already financed by the fundraising from the communities of the faithful, spilled over into the applications for funding; between 1952 and 1961, the PCCASI received from all the dioceses throughout the country more than 3,400 case files for the preliminary approval of the projects, drawn up by engineers and architects directly appointed by the diocesan ordinaries and already approved by the Commissions for Art Sacred of the local dioceses.

On 18 April 1962, following the first ten years of work, new law no. 168 – "New regulations relating to the construction and reconstruction of religious buildings" [8]- integrated the first provision, consolidating and ordering the programme of works for the following decade: the list of works to be admitted to the contribution was drawn up annually by the Ministry of Public Works on the proposal of the PCCASI, while the share of expenditure was established by the Ministry, in relation to the number of parishioners. To obtain the loans, the procedure followed the one already established by law no. 2522 of 1952 [9], with the addition of the supervision of the Civil Engineers on the execution of the structural works and the assumption, by the State, of the testing costs. Finally, for the financial coverage of the grant, which would be disbursed according to a new framework that provided for constant lots, for 35 years to the extent of 4% of the eligible expenditure, the ten-year plan (1961-71) was approved, committing 350 million lire for the first year. Between 1962 and 1985, the year in which Law 168/1962 was repealed with the ratification of the new agreements between Church and State, the PCCASI received over 4,300 case files [10]. For the entire period of activity of the PCCASI, the projects of the remaining works, which had been excluded from financing or funded with funds from the congregation or local dioceses, were, however, examined by the territorial Commissions for verification of compliance with the liturgical and sacred art precepts, in constant dialogue with PCCASI [11].

The regulatory requirements excluded all finishing works and the decorative additions from financing so the designers concentrated on the definition of structures that interpreted, in the rustic style, the precepts of liturgical spatiality and sacred art. The PCCASI or the Commissions of the local dioceses, commented on and directed the principles of construction towards "noble and monumental solutions", using a "lively structural concept" [12]. Ideas certainly influenced by the contemporary international recognition of the rise of Italian engineering.

While, in 1956, the architect Saverio Muratori wrote, starting the debate in the magazine *Fede e Arte* [13], "the church is the architectural organism most interested in the current development of technologies, the theme that can impersonate it and express it" [14], the projects that were examined by the PCCASI in 1950s and 1960s were an objective testimony of this.

Three hypars for the diocese of Bergamo (1961-1968)

In the inspiring context of this "lively structural concept" [15], the design collaboration between architect Vito Sonzogni (1924-2017) and engineer Enzo Lauletta (1927-71) developed between 1961-68. The professional partnership led to the construction of three churches - the Sanctuary of Maria SS. Regina in Zogno (1962-66), San Giacomo in Castro (1965-69), and S. Gregorio Barbarigo in Monterosso (1967-71) - characterised by challenging reinforced concrete structures.

Sanctuary of Maria SS. Regina in Zogno (1962-66)

In 1958, the parish priest of Zogno started raising funds from the parishioners for the construction of a new church for the small town, the Sanctuary of Maria SS. Regina. Architect Sonzogni was involved in the project design and in 1960, after the fundraising effort, 50 million lire were allocated: Sonzogni had meanwhile drawn up various proposals for the construction of the church based on an entirely reinforced concrete building characterised by expressive load-bearing structures.

The executive project was developed between 1961 and 1962: based on Sonzogni's preliminary project. Engineer Lauletta [16], then employed at the ISMES *Istituto Sperimentale Modelli e Strutture* (Experimental Institute for Models and Structures) in Bergamo [17], took charge of the calculation of the structure. The collaboration between the two designers was fundamental for the design of the definitive solution: the church, in the executive design phase, passed from a volume characterised by curvilinear partitions and a free-form curved roof, to a rhomboid volume covered by a hyperbolic paraboloids thin shell (Fig.1). The structural drawings, developed by Lauletta between 1961 and 1962, testified to the introduction of the hypar in the geometry of the project: it featured a rhomboid-shaped plan (whose diagonals measured respectively 35 and 26 metres) and projected beyond the perimeter of the building. The shell was only 6 cm thick, with sturdy edge beams; its horizontal thrust on the transverse diagonal, was absorbed by the bell tower, on the left hand side, and the curvilinear walls, on the right.

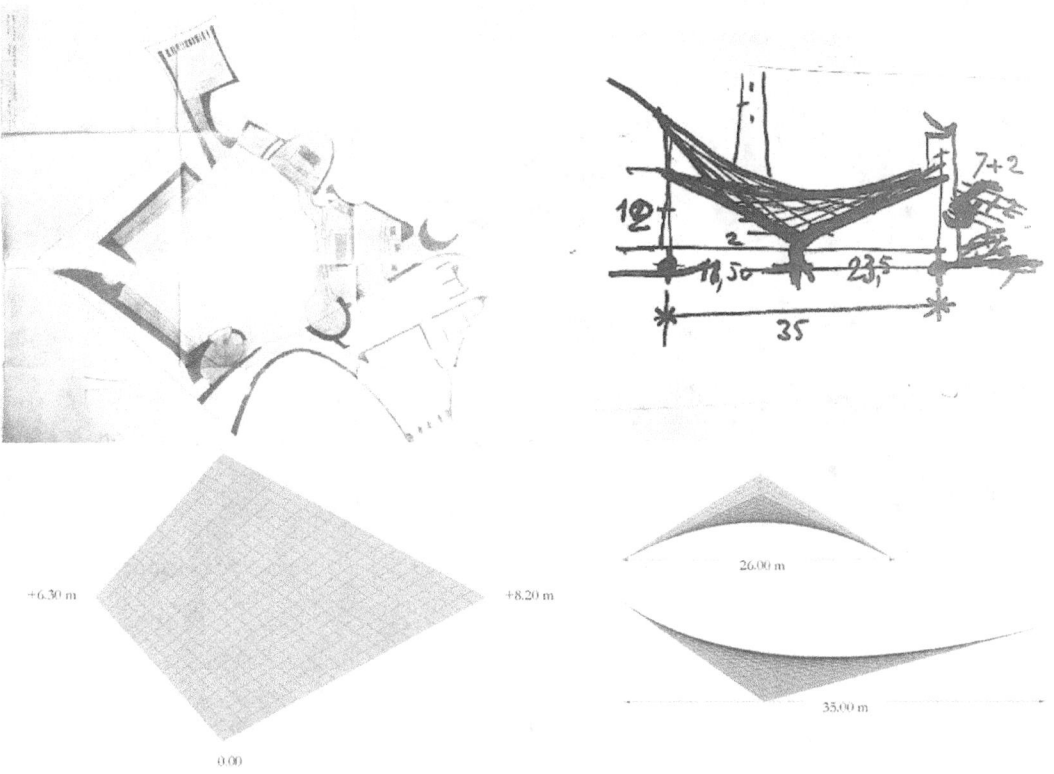

Figure 1: Plan and sketch of the Zogno church, 1961 (courtesy of Laura Sonzogni) and 3D sketch of the hypar geometry

If, as Lauletta affirmed, the hyperbolic paraboloid was easy to construct for small spans and did not even present any calculation difficulties, in the case of roofs with more demanding spans, such as those of the church of Zogno, "new phenomena came to the fore and sometimes dramatically with extensive cracks and even with collapses" [18]: in these cases, in fact, the edge beams could not be considered just simple struts, since they were subject to bending and torsion,

Experimental structures and reinforced concrete in church building in Italy: design and construction of three hyperbolic paraboloids (1961-68)

and the shell itself had to be checked for the danger of buckling. The recourse to the physical model in the calculation of the structure, given Lauletta's professional position at ISMES, was the next step in the design process: as anticipated in the technical report – "fortunately the use of physical models allowed us to study these phenomena and deal with their dangers" [19] - experimentation on the physical model gave the opportunity to closely examine the calculation of thin shells, a research topic to which Lauletta had been dedicating himself since 1961 [20], in the context of the broader international debate [21].

A scale model, reproducing the geometry of the Zogno shell in 1:25 scale, was built in the ISMES laboratories in September 1963 and Lauletta himself carried out the tests.

As shown in Figure 2, the load equipment consisted of rubber dynamometric rings bound at one end to the structure and anchored, on the opposite side, to a rigid floor that, once lowered with the aid of hydraulic jacks, created the tension and, therefore, the application of the load [22]. During the tests, carried out on 25 September, the measurements were carried out with mechanical strain gauges and flexometers. The extensive tests were carried out by supporting the vault at five points, detecting the sags obtained when applying the various loads, up to the collapse of the structure with a load of 1480 kg/m^2 [23].

Figure 2: Structural model of the Zogno hypar, tested by Lauletta at ISMES in Bergamo, 1963 (courtesy Laura Sonzogni)

The checks on the model were then used to redefine the size and layout of the armature, shell and edge beams.

Work started at the construction site of the Sanctuary on 30 June 1962. The contractor for the work was the company belonging to Pietro Sonzogni, Vito's father, whose premises were located on the land adjacent to the land where the sanctuary was to be built: Pietro's company was an established local entrepreneurial business specialising in the installation of electrification poles but had no experience in reinforced concrete construction. Yet, in May 1966, when the Sanctuary had just been finished, the successful execution of the ecclesiastical structure also made the news in the local newspapers, which praised master builder Sonzogni for his "incredible skills in the use of this material" [24].

The construction of the Sanctuary was achieved by using ingenious construction site techniques : the use of the Innocenti tube and coupler [25] scaffolding made it possible to construct the hyperbolic paraboloid as a ruled surface, for which the structure received international recognition. Instead of the traditional wooden scaffolding usually used for the construction of the formwork of the ruled surfaces a structure of tube and coupler was used to support the casting of the hypar (Fig. 3). As evidenced by the evocative photographs of the construction site, the tubes, set-up on the ruled surface generatrix, allowed the arrangement of wooden boards to support the casting of the shell. The boards were arranged crosswise in order to obtain, as Sonzogni intended, an intrados surface "decorated by the traces of the thin and flexible boards" [26]. The shell was then coated in copper with an artisanal cladding where the gutter channels were integrated (Fig. 4).

Figure 3: Zogno church under construction: the set-up of the Innocenti tubes on the ruled surface of the hypar and the arrangement of the wooden boards to support the cast of the shell, 1962 (courtesy Laura Sonzogni)

Figure 4: Interior view of the Zogno church in 1963 (courtesy of Laura Sonzogni) and the Zogno church in July 2020 (pictures by Ilaria Giannetti)

Experimental structures and reinforced concrete in church building in Italy: design and construction of three hyperbolic paraboloids (1961-68)

San Giacomo in Castro (1965-69)

Sonzogni started the design of the Church of San Giacomo in Castro in 1965, during the construction of the Sanctuary in Zogno. The State contribution was required for the construction: the project dossier, initially sent for inspection to the New Churches Committee of Bergamo, on 30 October, was then forwarded to the PCCASI, which issued its favourable opinion approving the financing of 30 million for the construction of the building. In a note dated 2 April 1965, the Ministry of Public Works approved expenditure for the construction of the rustic "building of worship to be erected in the municipality of Castro in the area already owned by the parish" [27].

The building has an elliptical layout, on whose minor axis there is a parabolic curve that included the altar, the cathedra and the tabernacle, while access to the church is on the opposite side, from a large covered atrium, on the sides of which are two chapels, with an independent access. The building is made entirely of exposed reinforced concrete. The roof consists of a double-curved shell that, profiled on a hyperbolic paraboloids ruled surface, covers the space of the hall, the altar and part of the atrium, with challenging spans of 36.75 and 38 metres, on the two diagonals (Fig. 5). The shell, only 6 cm thick, is lined with copper plates.

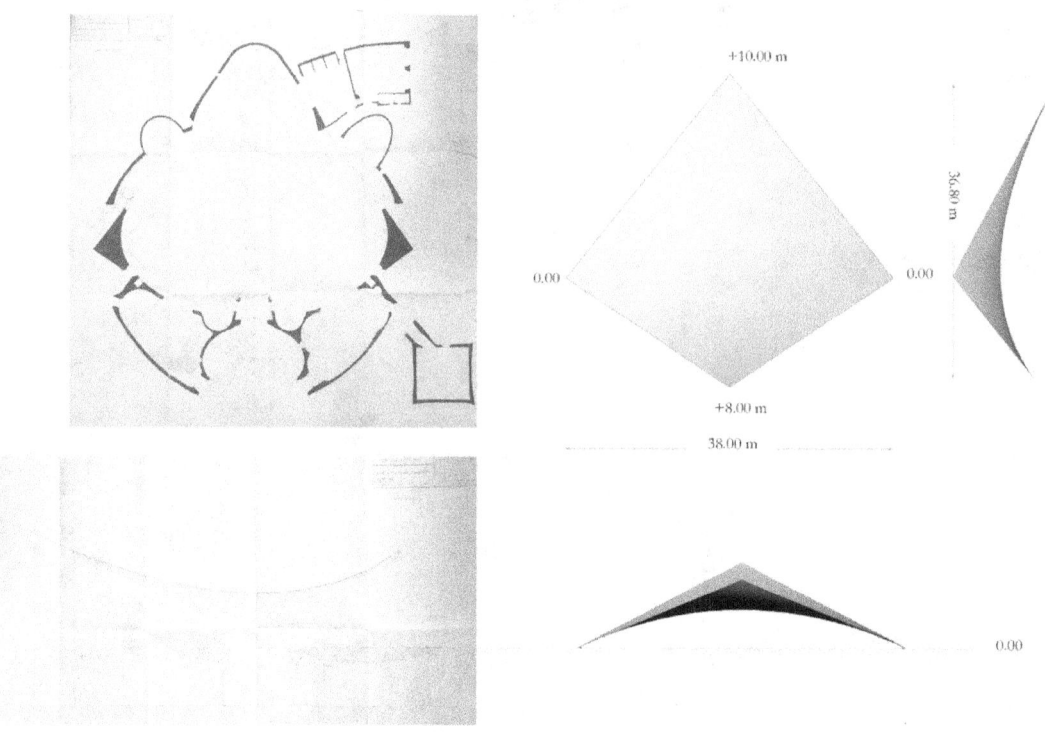

Figure 5: Sonzogni's drawing of the Castro church, 1966 (courtesy Laura Sonzogni), 3D sketches of the hypar geometry

Lauletta signed the structural design on 1 July 1966, sending a copy to Sonzogni on the 18th of the same month. The report contained the criteria for calculating the shell: the procedure adopted was based on the 'membrane theory of shells', disseminated by the literature of the time and studied by Lauletta himself [28], applying it to a hypar model characterised by a geometry that was simpler than that of Castro. The results were integrated with those of the tests carried out on the model of the roof of Zogno.

The hypar presented in the calculation report was, contrary to Castro's, a symmetrical 'warped parallelogram' (described by the equation z=xy/c [29]) with 25 m diagonals and, in the model, the edge beams were considered as four simple struts loaded axially. The external load (P) was divided between "arches and cables" (Fig. 6).

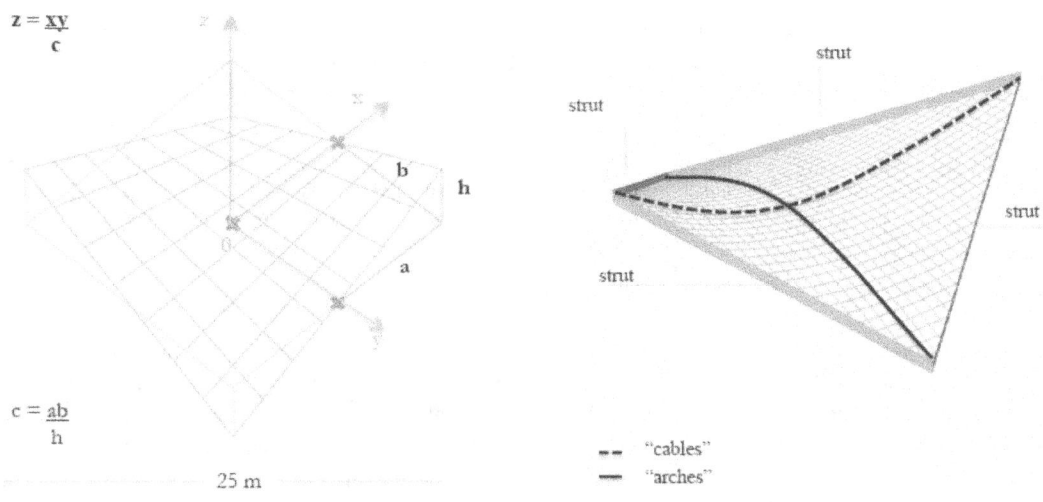

Figure 6: Sketches of the hypar geometry adopted by Lauletta in the calculation for the Castro's shell, 1966

Figure 7: Execution drawing of the Castro shell, 1966 (courtesy Laura Sonzogni), sketches of the warped surface with points coordinates adopted for the shell scaffolding and formworks set up

Experimental structures and reinforced concrete in church building in Italy: design and construction of three hyperbolic paraboloids (1961-68)

Therefore, considering the maximum stresses of the materials, the vault is reinforced with Φ 8 irons placed every 60 cm, on the long side of the warped parallelogram, every 30 cm on the short side and every 20 cm following the warping of the "cables", while to counteract the horizontal forces of the hypar a chain was inserted, in the foundation, at the location of the minor diagonal (Fig. 7) [30].

As at Zogno, the edge beams were subjected not only to axial actions but also to bending, shearing and torsion. The results of the tests on the model were used for analysis and verification of the edge beams which have a tapered section of a constant height of 50 cm and a variable width, from 60 cm to 1 metre at the corner pillars, on the smaller diagonal.

To generate the execution hypar geometry, the ruled line is drawn by dividing the two opposite sides of a skewed quadrilateral, whose vertices on the longitudinal diagonal, were respectively 8 and 10 metres high, in 21 points and drawing the segments that joined them (Fig. 7); the operation was repeated starting from the opposite sides of the same quadrilateral, building a quadrangular grid and thereby identifying the heights of 484 points that would guide the construction of the scaffolding and the support planking for the casting.

The F.lli Pasinetti company, entrusted with the construction of the work following the tender-competition awarded on 12 November 1966, reported the characteristics of the reinforced concrete structure of the church to the Prefecture of Bergamo on 2 February. The construction site opened immediately after. The shell was cast on 29 April 1968 (Fig. 8): the scaffolding, similar to that of Zogno, was made of Innocenti tubes arranged along the short side of the warped parallelogram. The ribs were removed on 8 and 9 May. The church was consecrated on 14 June 1969, following the waterproofing of the roof with the installation of the copper mantle.

Figure 8: The Castro churchs hypar under construction and inner view of the church hall, 1968 (courtesy of Laura Sonzogni)

S. Gregorio Barbarigo in the Monterosso district in Bergamo (1967-71)

Sonzogni and Lauletta's project for the new suburban parish in the Monterosso district of Bergamo started in 1967: the proposal was approved by the Bergamo Sacred Art Commission on 18 January. The church, again with a central system and made entirely in exposed reinforced concrete, has a triangular layout that is covered by juxtaposing three rhomboid-shaped hypars.

The three hypars, 12 cm thick, rest on two sides on the curvilinear perimeter walls, remaining independent (Fig. 9): between the three canopies, evocative interstitial skylights allow the passage of the zenithal light. At the transversal diagonals of the three shells, sturdy vertical supports counteract the forces, functioning as real buttresses, assisted by a system of chains placed in the foundation (Fig. 9).

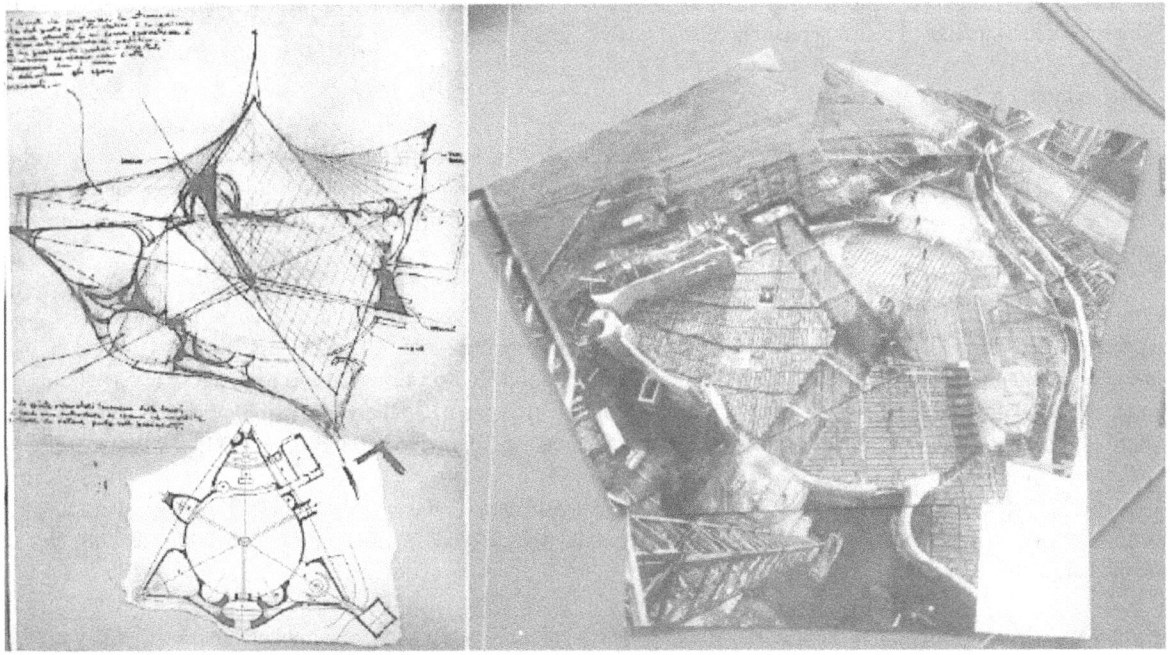

Figure 9: Sonzogni's sketch of the San Gregorio's and the church under construction, 1967 (courtesy Laura Sonzogni)

Figure 10: San Gregorio's and the church under construction, 1967 (courtesy Laura Sonzogni)

Experimental structures and reinforced concrete in church building in Italy: design and construction of three hyperbolic paraboloids (1961-68)

The construction site opened on 18 June 1967. The works were awarded, following a tender competition, to the Augusto Adobati company. In 1970, after the completion of the wall structure, the company left the site: the shell had not yet been built. To save the new structure from ruin, the company of Pietro Sonzogni accepted the contract for the completion of the works on 6 August 1970. As in Zogno, the three hypars were then cast "tracing in negative the geometry of the shell through the fitting of the Innocenti tubes along the ruled surface" (Fig. 10), while a more costly arrangement was agreed, "for the use of flexible and planed boards" [31] to support the castings, in order to decorate the shell with their imprint. The construction site closed on 18 September 1971.

Conclusions

After the Second World War in Italy, the construction, supported by state aid, of the new "mantle of churches in the country" [32] involved engineers and architects in a design and construction experiments throughout the country. There were numerous projects for new churches that focused on plastic-figurative structural inventions, arising from the plasticity of reinforced concrete.

In the 1950s and 1960s, the relationship between the design theme of the intermediate span covering and the renewed expressive needs of the place of worship, suggested and governed by the control of the ecclesiastical bodies, and taking into consideration the precepts of the renewed liturgy of the Second Vatican Council, was resolved in the invention of some structural icons, which spread throughout the country making a capillary (and still relatively unexplored) contribution to the 'structuralist' trends that developed in the maturity of the modern movement [33].

As part of this extensive collective experimentation, this study focuses on the churches built by Sonzogni and Lauletta for the diocese of Bergamo as an original contribution to the design and construction of the hyperbolic parabolic in the second half of the 20th century.

In this sense, the study highlights the characteristics of the experiments of Sonzogni and Lauletta, in comparison with the international experiences on this successful structural element [34], through the most affirmed trends of the Italian School of Engineering [35]: physical modelling, ingenious constructive solutions within the artisan construction site and artistic reflection on structural forms, through a close collaboration between the architect and the engineer.

In this sense, the collaboration between the two was crucial to the success of the project ("I needed Science and I went to get it from Lauletta", wrote Sonzogni [36]). The joint reflection of the two designers deeply involved the principles of the tectonic conception, from the ability to make room for structural forms to the ornamental qualities of the resistant material. The hypar embodied, in the three churches, both the spatial device of the renewed demands of worship expressed by the Second Vatican Council ("beauty is to be sought in the balance between the sense of daring and that of monumentality, a formula offered more by science than by art" [37]) and an ornamental expression through an appreciation of the aesthetic qualities of reinforced concrete ("the shell decorated inside by the imprint of the wooden boards" [38]).

Acknowledgements

The author would like to express her gratitude to the architect Laura Sonzogni for the generous sharing of the original design drawigs and reports preserved at the private archive of Vito Sonzogni in Bergamo.

References

[1] T. Iori, S. Poretti. 'The Rise and Decline of the Italian School of Engineering', Construction History, vol. 33, no. 2, 2018, pp. 85–108. JSTOR, www.jstor.org/stable/26562567. Accessed 31 Mar. 2021.

[2] F. Colombo, S. Pirola, 'Orientamenti dell'architettura sacra tra la fine della seconda guerra mondiale e l'apertura del Concilio Vaticano secondo', *Arte cristiana*, nos. 4-5, 1968.

[3] A. Pugnale, 'The church of Longuelo by Pino Pizzigoni: Design and construction of an experimental structure', *Construction History*, Vol. 25, 2010, pp. 115-140.

[4] A. Longhi, Storie di chiese, storie di comunità. Progetti, cantieri, architetture, Rome, Gangemi, 2018 (in Italian); S. Benedetti, L'architettura delle Chiese contemporanee. Il caso italiano, Milan, Jacabook, 2000 (in Italian).

[5] D. De Marchis (ed), L' Archivio della Commissione Centrale per l'arte sacra in Italia. Archivio Segreto Vaticano. Vatican City, 2013 (in Italian).

[6] F. Marchisano 'Il ruolo della Pontificia Commissione Centrale per l'Arte Sacra in Italia per la costruzione delle chiese nei decenni successivi alla Guerra' in Profezia della Bellezza. Arte sacra tra memoria e progetto. Rome, CISRA edizioni, 1996, pp. 7-19 (in Italian).

[7] 'State contribution to the construction of new churches', *Italian low*, no. 2522, 18 December 1952.

[8] "New regulations relating to the construction and reconstruction of religious buildings", *Italian low,* no. 168, 18 April 1962.

[9] Marchisano, (Note 6).

[10] ibid.; De Marchis (ed), (Note 5).

[11] ibid.

[12] S. Muratori, 'Le tecnica e l'architettura religiosa', *Fede e Arte*, no. 1, 1956, pp. 3-7 (in Italian).

[13] ibid; S. Muratori, 'Tradizione e novità dell'architettura sacra', *Fede e Arte*, no.7, 1956, pp. 267-274 (in Italian); P.L. Nervi, 'Problemi di architettura sacra', *Fede e Arte,* no. 5, 1965, pp. 444-451 (in Italian).

[14] Muratori, (Note 12).

[15] ibid.

[16] C. M. Kovsca, Enzo Lauletta. Un ingegnere all'Istituto Sperimentale modelli e strutture (Ismes), Bergamo, Fondazione per la storia economica e sociale di Bergamo, Istitito di Studi e Ricerche, 2008 (in Italian).

[17] C. Tarisciotti, 'Calcolare con i modelli: il laboratorio dell'Ismes', *Rassegna di Architettura e Urbanistica*, no. 148, 2016, pp. 80-99 (in Italian with English abstract); G. Neri, Capolavori in miniatura. Pier Luigi Nervi e la modellazione strutturale, Mendrisio, Mendrisio Accademy Press, 2014 (in Italian).

[18] E. Lauletta, 'Technical report of the Zogno Sanctuary', unpublished, 1961 (Sonzogni Private Archive)

[19] ibid.

[20] E. Lauletta, Statics of hyperbolical shells. Amsterdam, NHPC, 1961; E. Lauletta, Osservazioni sulla statica delle volte sottili e paraboloide iperbolico, Venezia, ANDIL, 1965.

[21] F. Aimond, 'Les voiles minces en forme de paraboloide hyperbolique', Le Génie Civil, n. 102, 1933, pp. 179-181 (in French); F. Aimond, 'Etude statique des voiles minces en form de paraboloide travaillant sans flexion', Publications International Association of Bridge and Structural Engineering, n. 4, 1936, pp. 1–122 (in French); A. Flügge, Statik und Dynamik der Shalen. Berlin, Springer-Verlag, 1957 (in German); J. Joedicke, Shell Architecture. New York, Reinhold Publishing Corporation, 1963.

[22] E. Lauletta, 'Calculation criteria of the Castro church', unpublished, 1966 (Sonzogni Private Archive).

[23] E. Lauletta, 'Technical report of the Zogno Sanctuary physical model test conducted at ISMES, Bergamo', unpublished, 1963 (Sonzogni Private Archive).

[24] M. Pelliccioli, 'Una bravura quasi incredibile nell'impiego del cemento armato, L'eco di Bergamo, 1966.

[25] I. Giannetti, 'The Italian story of Ferdinando Innocenti's tubolar scaffolding (1934-64)' in B. Bowen, D. Friedman, T. Leslie, J. Ochsendorf (eds.) *Proceedings of the Fifth International Congress on Construction History*, Chicago, Construction History Society of America, 2015.

[26] V. Sonzogni, Santuario a Maria SS. Regina in Zogno, Litorgrafia Icis, Bergamo, 1967.

[27] V. Sonzogni, 'Technical report of the church Giacomo Apostolo a Castro design', unpublished, PCASSI Archive, I, 1965, n. 1-2-3.

[28] Neri, (Note 17); Lauletta, (Note 23).

[29] Aimond, (Note 21).

[30] Lauletta, (Note 22).

[31] E. Lauletta, 'Technical report of the church S. Gregorio Barbarigo', unpublished, 1967 (Sonzogni Private Archive).

[32] Marchisano, (Note 6).

[33] K. Siegel, Structure and Form in Modern Architecture, Rainhold Publishing Corporation, New York, 1961.

[34] D.P. Billington, Thin shell concrete structures, McGraw-Hill Book Company, New York, 1982; T.S. Sprague, 'Beauty, Versatility, Practicality': the Rise of Hyperbolic Paraboloids in Post-War America (1950-1962)', Construction History, n. 28, 2013, pp. 165–184; M. Garlock, D.P. Billington, Felix Candela: Engineer, Builder, Structural Artist, Yale University Press, New Haven, New Haven, 2008.

[35] Iori, Poretti, (Note 1).

[36] Sonzogni, (Note 26).

[37] ibid.

[38] ibid.

www.ingramcontent.com/pod-product-compliance
Lightning Source LLC
Chambersburg PA
CBHW080922020526
44114CB00043B/2438